Democracy

in a World of Tensions

Democracy
in a World of Tensions

A Symposium prepared by UNESCO

Edited by

RICHARD McKEON

with the assistance of

STEIN ROKKAN

GREENWOOD PRESS, PUBLISHERS
NEW YORK

FOREWORD

THE purpose of UNESCO, as set forth in Article I of its Constitution, "is to contribute to peace and security by promoting collaboration among the nations through education, science, and culture in order to further universal respect for justice, for the rule of law, and for the human rights and fundamental freedoms which are affirmed for the peoples of the world, without distinction of race, sex, language, or religion, by the Charter of the United Nations." Debates during the First Session of the General Conference of UNESCO in Paris in 1946 made abundantly clear the differences which are possible in the interpretation of ends accepted as common. The problem of establishing a program of common action based on the different philosophic views, religious beliefs, and political systems represented in the member-states was a practical exercise in exploring the consequences of different conceptions of human rights, democracy, freedom, law, and justice on the co-operation and antagonism of nations. A project to study such differences in the philosophic and historical foundations of the Rights of Man was included in the first program of UNESCO, and work was undertaken on the project in co-operation with the Commission of Human Rights, which had recently been established by the Economic and Social Council of the United Nations. The first stage of the inquiry was completed in July, 1947. The differences which might influence debate concerning a universal declaration of human rights were explored in two dimensions: the historical differences between the grounds of human rights in their classical expressions in the eighteenth century and the grounds available for their statement and defense today, and the philosophic differences underlying different contemporary conceptions and enumerations of human rights.

During the course of the first year of UNESCO's work the close relation of the program of UNESCO to the promotion of human rights, the respect for justice, and the rule of law became increasingly apparent. A Committee of Experts assembled in September, 1947, to frame suggestions concerning the program in philosophy and humanistic studies recommended that UNESCO undertake projects "which, while bearing a close relation to the scholarly and scientific work which UNESCO will assist and stimulate other organizations to undertake, will have as their proper object to apply the resources of philosophy and humanistic studies to the present moral, intellectual, and practical crisis of the world, to improve international understanding, and to raise the level of values sought." UNESCO was urged to undertake these projects itself, rather than assign them to international scholarly organizations, because of their immediate bearing on problems faced by the United Nations and by individual nations. The importance of making the results of such inquiries as widely available to the peoples of the world as possible was stressed.

The committee recommended specifically that the inquiry into human rights be extended and completed and that plans for like inquiries into related ideas be prepared. "The Committee of Experts recommends that the project formulated by the Committee on the Philosophic Bases of Human Rights—to investigate the philosophic grounds of the present conflict of ideologies by examining its manifestations in certain crucial concepts—be undertaken, and that the 'philosophers' consulted in its pursuit should include not only philosophers in the technical sense, but also humanists, social scientists, natural scientists, and, in general, men in all walks of life who take a broad view of their work and of the problems in which the world is involved. It is recommended that in its initial form, the enterprise be concerned with the important differences which separate peoples in their views of right, liberty, democracy, and similar moral and political concepts. If the project succeeds, it may later be extended to value concepts more peculiar to humanistic studies or to basic ideas which have recently been influenced by the progress of science." The studies prepared in the inquiry concerning human rights treated, first, the general problems of human rights reflected in their increase in number by the addition of social, economic, and intellectual rights to the traditional list of civil and political rights, and their increase in scope of application by extension to all men without discrimination; second, particular problems, such as the bearing of rights on problems of cultural diversity, on the progress of science and its social consequences, on the value of objective information and of education, and in the special applications of human rights to primitive peoples, dependent peoples, and law-breakers. These studies were published in 1949 in the UNESCO symposium *Human Rights: Comments and Interpretations.*

The project to investigate conflicts concerning fundamental concepts was made part of the program of UNESCO adopted at the Second Session of the General Conference in Mexico City in 1947, and the study of the idea of democracy was started in 1948. The inquiry was not conceived either as a "scientific" investigation of the nature of democracy or as an "opinion" poll concerning differences in conceptions of democracy; it was an effort, rather, to uncover the traditions of thought and the basic assumptions of theory which influence discussions and negotiations in which "democracy" is involved. Since democracy can operate only insofar as the people understand and are committed to its institutions, the subjective element of disagreements about the nature and the operations of democracy was treated as a vital factor in isolating the ideas and traditions which lend significance, attraction, and force to the opposed conceptions; and the inquiry was directed to exploring the relations and opposition of ideas, preconceptions, and preferences as part of the objective practical situation. The experience gained in the study of human rights suggested the need to develop techniques for this investigation of the practical operations and uses of ideas with respect both to the truth of the ideas and to their influence on attitudes and actions. Basic ideas affect what is accepted as true; and groups which depart from different convictions will come to different conclusions about the objective nature of human rights, democracy, law and like institutions. Basic ideas affect emotions and motivations; and attitudes and opinions, even when they are subconscious and emotional in their origin, can be expressed and communicated only by statements in which basic concepts play a part.

As a first step in the preparation of the inquiry a list was compiled of fundamental texts in which the idea of democracy has been treated in ancient as well as modern theoretic systems and practical contexts. Part at least of the ambiguity in the discussion of concepts like democracy arises from the fact that fundamental and familiar ideas are·thought to be clear and univocal, and the precaution is seldom taken to provide a common body of analysis, context, and association as a basis for the discussion of the meanings of terms and of the uses to which they are put. A selection from this list of texts appears as the bibliography published in Appendix IV of this volume. On the basis of this review of the literature concerning democracy and after consultation with experts in the various member-states who had contributed suggestions for inclusion in the basic texts, a questionnaire was prepared, which is reproduced in Appendix I. This questionnaire was sent to more than five hundred experts in the related fields of philosophy, law, history, political science, sociology, economics, communications analysis, and logic. Approximately twenty-five per cent of those consulted returned replies to the whole questionnaire or to some portions of it; a larger proportion engaged in correspondence about the project. The results of the inquiry were examined in May, 1949, by a Committee of Experts consisting of Professor Edward H. Carr, Chairman; Professor Chaim Perelman, Vice-Chairman; Professor Richard McKeon, *Rapporteur;* and Professors Sergio Buarque de Hollanda, Pierre Ricoeur, and Alf Ross. The Committee prepared a statement concerning the problems presented by ambiguities and confusions about democracy; this statement is reproduced in Appendix II. The report and recommendations of the Committee concerning the material assembled in the inquiry are reproduced in Appendix III. Finally, Professor Arne Naess, who drew up the questionnaire and conducted the inquiry for UNESCO, prepared an analysis of the coincidences and divergences of doctrine in the replies; this analysis is published at the end of the essays.

The questionnaire begins with the problem of the ambiguity of the concept of "democracy" and ends with the problem of fundamental values; the Committee of Experts signalizes for special comment the fact that, for all the differences of interpretation, none of the replies to the questionnaire defend anti-democratic doctrines. The ambiguity is old, but the Committee points out that the unanimity in favoring and professing democracy is new. This agreement, which may seem verbal, hedged by differences, which involve verbal ambiguities, is the framework within which real problems must be formulated and faced in terms which are adequate to treat real changes in the economic, social, and political situation during the period since the eighteenth century and adapted to analyze real differences in democratic institutions and actions, in attitudes toward tolerance and treason, and in fundamental scales of values as they influence thought and action. Agreement on common courses of action depend on verbal agreements, but statements and professions may be instruments of deception and propaganda as well as simple indications of adherence to the doctrines and intentions expressed. The estimation of the significance and of the practical import of statements is not an easy calculation based on self-evident and universal rules, particularly since commitment to one doctrinal position frequently casts doubt on the effectiveness of opposed programs for achieving professed ends and on the seriousness or reliability of the professions of those who express opposed views.

In such a situation agreement on the ideals of democracy, however vaguely or even inconsistently formulated, is a positive advance and possibly even a first step to the resolution of fundamental differences which might easily harden into oppositions irresoluble by other means than violence. For the agreement signifies at least the recognition that technological advances have made the complete restriction of communication difficult and that governments must secure or profess to have secured some sign of the approval of the people and some indication that they are governments of the people. In the degree that such minimum agreements are also indications of a shared conviction that rule by the people is the means—and the good of the people the end—of government the discussion of the nature of the end and the availability of means is the one alternative to blank opposition and asseveration of inconsistent conceptions and policies. In whatever degree the elements are mixed in the world situation today—however much of the difficulties of negotiation are due to deception and bad faith, however much to mutually inconsistent conceptions of means to incompatible ends, and however much to lack of understanding and differences concerning the order of treatment of commonly recognized problems—the one hope for the peaceful resolution of differences is in the faith that the community of all men can be directed to a common good and that agreement concerning the means to the common good can be produced by knowledge and good will. Other expedients may be found for securing agreement than knowledge and understanding, but they depend on force or deception; and knowledge and understanding provide the one test of the suspicion of subterfuge and chicanery and the one defense against them when the suspicion that they are being practiced is verified.

The essays published in this volume are a selection from the materials collected in response to the questionnaire on democracy. Several criteria governed the selection: an effort was made to present clear statements of the problems of democracy and to include all significant shades of doctrinal differences as well as to represent as many nations, cultures, and regions of the world as possible. The thirty-three essays selected according to these criteria are written by authors from fourteen different nations. Since any attempt to label their positions and doctrinal attitudes would require a subtle vocabulary and distinctions that might appear verbal when they were not invidious, the essays are arranged in alphabetical order and are numbered in that order without titles. Some of the essays are addressed to all the questions set forth in the questionnaire, others to some few problems; wherever possible, therefore, the essays are separated into parts and numbered headings are inserted referring to the numbered questions of the questionnaire. The reader will be well advised to read the questionnaire and the statement of the Committee of Experts before the individual essays. Whenever he wishes to have the fuller context of the problems discussed by an author under one of the numbered headings, he will find it by referring to the same numbered heading in the questionnaire. The interrelations of the positions taken on the various problems are set forth in the *Analytical Survey of Agreements and Disagreements* prepared by Professor Arne Naess and in the Report of the Committee of Experts. The topical index is arranged according to the thirty questions of the questionnaire and provides easy reference to the positions taken by the authors on the various questions.

The vast labor of giving the inquiry form and content—drawing up the questionnaire, conducting a world-wide correspondence with scholars and experts, and assembling and analyzing the replies—was carried out by Professor Arne Naess, on leave from the University of Oslo to direct the project. Mr. Stein Rokkan assisted in these various tasks and also in the editorial work of preparing the results of the inquiry for publication. Dr. Jaime Torres-Bodet, Director-General of UNESCO, has found time among his numerous duties to discuss with the co-operating experts and the members of the UNESCO Secretariat the broad problems in which the inquiry was involved and its bearing on the program of UNESCO; and Dr. Julian Huxley, the first Director-General, entered actively into planning the early stages of the project. Many troublesome problems of policy and content were resolved by M. Jean Thomas, Assistant Director-General, and by M. J. J. Mayoux, Director of Philosophic and Humanistic Projects. The completion of the inquiry depended ultimately, however, on the co-operation of the many scholars in all parts of the world who interrupted their research, their teaching, and their co-operation on other practical problems to bring the results of their own labors and of the studies of other scholars to bear on problems of advancing world democracy and co-operation among democracies and to experiment in the innovation by UNESCO of techniques by which to put the instrumentalities of education, science, and culture to work in promoting collaboration among nations in accordance with justice, the rule of law, and human rights.

RICHARD McKEON

CHICAGO, ILLINOIS

January 1950

CONTRIBUTORS

CHARLES BETTELHEIM, Director of Studies, Section des Sciences Économiques et Sociales, École Pratique des Hautes Études, University of Paris; author of *La planification soviétique* (1939), *Les problèmes théoriques et pratiques de la planification* (1946), *L'économie allemande sous le nazisme* (1946), *Bilan de l'économie française, 1919–1946* (1947), *Esquisse d'un tableau économique de l'Europe* (1948).

M. M. BOBER, Professor of Economics, Lawrence College, Appleton, Wisconsin; author of *Karl Marx's Interpretation of History* (1927; new ed. 1949).

G. A. BORGESE, Professor Emeritus of Italian Literature, University of Chicago; Secretary-General, Committee To Frame a World Constitution; editor, *Common Cause*, Chicago; author of *Goliath: The March of Fascism* (1937), *Common Cause* (1943).

D. VAN DANTZIG, Professor of the Theory of Collective Phenomena, University of Amsterdam; author of *Significhe Bechouwingen over de Begrippen "schuld," "straf," e.a. in Verband met het Annexatievraagstruk* (Report for the Dutch Society of International Law, 1946).

JOHN DEWEY, Professor Emeritus of Philosophy, Columbia University, New York; author of *Democracy and Education* (1916), *Human Nature and Conduct* (1922), *Experience and Nature* (1925), *The Public and Its Problems* (1927), *The Quest for Certainty* (1929), *Art as Experience* (1934), *Problems of Men* (1946).

C. J. DUCASSE, Professor of Philosophy, Brown University, Providence, Rhode Island; author of *Causation and the Types of Necessity* (1924), *The Philosophy of Art* (1930), *Philosophy as a Science* (1941).

G. C. FIELD, Professor of Philosophy, University of Bristol; author of *Guild Socialism* (1920), *Moral Theory* (1921), *Plato and His Contemporaries* (1930), *Prejudice and Impartiality* (1932), *Studies in Philosophy* (1939), *Pacifism and Conscientious Objection* (1945), *The Philosophy of Plato* (1949).

RISIERI FRONDIZI, former Director of the Faculty of Philosophy and Letters, University of Tucumán; Visiting Professor of Philosophy, Yale University; author of *El punto de partida del filosofar* (1945).

BARNA HORVATH, Professor of Philosophy, University of Budapest; author of *Rechtssoziologie* (1934).

JØRGEN JØRGENSEN, Professor of Philosophy, University of Copenhagen; author of *A Treatise of Formal Logic*, Vols. I-III (1931), *Psykologi paa biologisk grundlag* (1941–46).

HUMAYUN KABIR, Professor of Philosophy, University of Calcutta; Educational Adviser, Government of India; author of *Poetry, Monads and Society* (1941), *Mahatma and Other Poems* (1944), *Muslim Politics* (1944), *Men and Rivers* (1945), *Our Heritage* (1946).

HORACE M. KALLEN, Professor of Philosophy, Graduate Faculty of Political and Social Science, New School for Social Research, New York; author of *A Free Society* (1934), *The Decline and Rise of the Consumer* (1936), *Art and Freedom*, Vols. I–II (1942), *The Liberal Spirit* (1948), *The Education of Free Men* (1949).

HENRI LEFEBVRE, Research Fellow, Centre National de la Recherche Scientifique, Paris; author of *Le matérialisme dialectique* (1939), *L'existentialisme* (1946), *Critique de la vie quotidienne* (1947), *Le marxisme* (1948).

C. I. LEWIS, Professor of Philosophy, Harvard University; author of *Survey of Symbolic Logic* (1918), *Mind and the World-Order* (1929), *Symbolic Logic* (1932), *An Analysis of Knowledge and Valuation* (1946).

LORD LINDSAY OF BIRKER, Former Master of Balliol College, Oxford; Principal, University College of North Staffordshire; author of *Karl Marx's Capital* (1925), *The Essentials of Democracy* (1929), *Kant* (1934), *The Modern Democratic State* (1942).

J. H. A. LOGEMANN, Former Dutch Minister of Overseas Territories, Professor of Constitutional Law, University of Leiden; author of *Collegeaantekeningen over het staatsrecht van Nederlands Indie* (1947), *Over de theorie van een stellig staatsrecht* (1948).

RICHARD McKEON, Distinguished Service Professor of Philosophy and Greek, University of Chicago; adviser to the United States delegations to the First, Second, and Third sessions of the General Conference of UNESCO; member of the U.S. National Commission for UNESCO; author of *The Philosophy of Spinoza* (1928), editor of *Selections from Medieval Philosophers*, Vols. I–II (1929–30), *The Basic Works of Aristotle* (1941), *Introduction to Aristotle* (1947).

JAMES MARSHALL, Lawyer, New York; author of *Swords and Symbols* (1939), *The Freedom To Be Free* (1943).

EMMANUEL MOUNIER (†1950), Agrégé de philosophie; editor, *Esprit*, Paris; author of *La pensée de Charles Péguy* (1930), *Révolution personnaliste et communautaire* (1934), *Manifeste au service du personnalisme* (1936), *De la propriété capitaliste à la propriété humaine* (1936), *Liberté sous conditions* (1946), *Qu'est-ce que le personnalisme?* (1946), *Traité du caractère* (1946), *Introduction aux existentialismes* (1947).

ARNE NAESS, Professor of Philosophy, University of Oslo; author of *Erkenntnis als wissenschaftliches Verhalten* (1936), *"Truth" as Conceived by Those Who Are Not Professional Philosophers* (1938), *Filosofiske problemer* (1940), *Interpretation and Preciseness* (1947–50).

STANISLAUS OSSOWSKI, Professor of Sociology, University of Warsaw; author of *Sociology of Art* (1936), *Social Bond and Heritage of Blood* (1939), *Toward New Forms of Social Life* (1947) (all in Polish).

UMBERTO A. PADOVANI, Professor of Philosophy, University of Padua; author of *Arturo Schopenhauer* (1934), *La filosofia della religione e il problema della vita* (1937), *Sommario di Storia della filosofia* (1950).

RICARDO R. PASCUAL, Professor of Philosophy, College of Liberal Arts, University of the Philippines, Quezon City, Philippines; author of *A Brief Course in Logic* (1937).

AIMÉ PATRI, Agrégé de Philosophie; editor, *Paru*, Paris.

CHAIM PERELMAN, Professor of Logic and Metaphysics, University of Brussels; author of *De la justice* (1946).

JOHN PETROV PLAMENATZ, Fellow of All Souls College, Oxford; author of *Consent, Freedom and Political Obligation* (1938), *What Is Communism?* (1947), *Mill's Utilitarianism, with a Study of the English Utilitarians* (1949).

ITHIEL DE SOLA POOL, Associate Professor of Politics, Hobart College, Geneva, New York; currently with the Hoover Institute and Library on War, Revolution, and Peace, Stanford University, California; co-author, with Harold D. Lasswell, Nathan Leites, and Associates, of *Language of Politics* (1949); editor of *The Study of Society* (1949).

LADISLAUS RIEGER, Professor of Philosophy, Charles University, Prague; author of *Knowledge of Reality* (1930), *The Idea of Philosophy*, Vol. I (1939) (all in Czech).

WILHELM RÖPKE, Professor of Economics, Institut Universitaire des Hautes Études Internationales, Geneva; author of *Crises and Cycles* (1936), *Die Gesellschaftskrisis der Gegenwart* (1942), trans. *The Social Crisis of Our Time* (1950), *Civitas humana* (1944), *Die Krise des Kollektivismus* (1948).

ALF ROSS, Professor of Jurisprudence, University of Copenhagen; author of *Theorie der Rechtsquellen* (1929), *Kritik der sogenannten praktischen Erkenntnis* (1933), *Towards a Realistic Jurisprudence* (1946), *Hvorfor Demokrati?* (1946), *A Textbook of International Law* (1947); editor of *Nordisk Demokrati* (1949).

RUDOLF SCHLESINGER, Department for the Study of Economic and Social Institutions of the U.S.S.R., University of Glasgow; author of *Soviet Legal Theory* (1945), *Federalism in Central and Eastern Europe* (1945), *The Spirit of Post-war Russia* (1947), *Changing Attitudes in Soviet Russia: The Family* (1949), *Marx, His Time and Ours* (1950).

PAUL M. SWEEZY, former Instructor in Economics, Harvard University; author of *Monopoly and Competition in the English Coal Trade* (1938), *The Theory of Capitalist Development* (1942), *Socialism* (1949).

ERIC WEIL, Research Fellow, Centre National de la Recherche Scientifique, Paris; author of *Hegel et l'état* (forthcoming).

QUINCY WRIGHT, Professor of International Law, University of Chicago; author of *Mandates under the League of Nations* (1930), *The Causes of War and the Conditions of Peace* (1935), *A Study of War*, Vols. I-II (1942).

CONTENTS

xvii

I

CHARLES BETTELHEIM

1. AMBIGUITY.—In my opinion, it can hardly be denied that the term "democracy" is ambiguous. As I shall show in the following, *democratic systems*, each with a specific historical, social, or political meaning, have existed in the past and still do. For this reason, the use of the term "democracy," without any historical, social or political qualification, is inclined to be ambiguous.

I would add that "democracy" is no more ambiguous than most of the terms describing social institutions, activities, or facts, for these things are constantly evolving and may become either the substructure or the expression of new human relationships, without there being any change in the words denoting them; hence the necessity of qualifying these terms. To take one instance, "private property" covers an entirely different social phenomenon according to whether the owner himself exploits his means of production or whether he pays others to do so; in the latter case, these means of production are converted into capital, and private property (while still remaining such) becomes capitalist property.

The terms describing social phenomena are all the more ambiguous, since economic and political interests are bound up with this terminology, which may become an instrument in social warfare between conflicting interests. The use of a certain vocabulary may actually be a means of bluffing and mystifying the credulous. Consequently, any effort to reduce to a minimum the ambiguity of this terminology is an effort not only to expand our knowledge but also to narrow the range of ideological mystification.

To return to the term "democracy," further ambiguity results from its use for denoting certain principles or institutions of a class-divided society. Such societies are characterized by social oppression, whereas the term "democracy" is frequently used to describe a supposed absence of oppression. But in its social forms democracy is not and cannot be freedom from oppression, but merely a *certain form of oppression*. The ambiguity of the term "democracy" is therefore also due to the frequent tendency to regard "democracy" as the antithesis of "oppression," whereas these two concepts, though they are incompatible in one respect, are also inseparably linked with each other. This is the meaning of Lenin's remark that "democracy is one of the forms of the state—one of its varieties" and "consequently, like every state, it consists in organized, systematic application of force against human beings."[1]

In this sense, democracy implies oppression, and the removal of oppression would mean the disappearance of democracy.

It is thus understandable why the same regime can be *both* a dictatorship *and* a democracy, like Athenian democracy, which was a democracy for free men and a dictatorship for the slaves, or bourgeois democracy, which is a democracy for the middle classes and a dictatorship for the proletariat.

In the most democratic form of bourgeois democracy, this dictatorship is essentially ideological: the concepts and ideals that go to maintain middle-class domination are imposed on the proletariat through the school, church, press, radio, films, etc.; but the weapons of material and violent dictatorship (the police and army, law courts and prisons) always remain within reach, and recourse is had to them whenever the proletariat (as during strikes) strays from the path which the middle classes wish it to follow. They are also used when the ideological dictatorship weakens and the proletariat adheres to an ideology other than that of the middle classes; the latter then attempt to replace the former veiled dictatorship with an open dictatorship, and bourgeois democracy disappears.

Proletarian democracy, in its turn, is a democracy for the proletariat and a dictatorship for the middle classes.

6. COMMON CHARACTERISTICS.—The features common to the various types of democracy are admittedly very vague and there are at least as many differences as points of contact between Athenian slave democracy, French parliamentary democracy, and Soviet democracy.

It may then be inquired what makes these different societies democracies. The reply is probably to be found in a certain historical affinity between the *ideological superstructures* of these different societies.

1. *The State and Revolution* (New York, 1932), chap. v, sec. 4, p. 82.

As an ideology, democracy constitutes a complex ideal. Certain elements in this complex predominate at oné period (for definite social reasons), while other elements predominate at another period. The very meaning of these elements (liberty, equality, etc.) changes in the course of time, so that the successive concepts of democracy differ greatly from one another.

Yet what is it that characterizes the complex ideal of democratic ideology?

The reply to such a question would probably be as follows: the characteristic of democratic ideology is its affirmation of the social importance of the principles of liberty and equality, the participation of the whole population (or a large part of it) in important social decisions, free access of all members of society to social and public offices and the availability to all members of society (or a fairly large proportion of them) of the means necessary to their full physical and intellectual development.

But there is no hierarchical order in these various principles and their very meaning is vague. It is thus understandable that during social struggles, one principle and then another is put forward and their whole meaning is modified in the process. The extension to the Roman plebs of a number of rights formerly reserved for the patricians was a "victory for democracy," because a larger section of the population became thus entitled to a say in important social decisions and to hold certain public offices, etc. In this case, "democracy" appears as an extension of specific rights to new categories of the population formerly deprived of them.

To bring out more clearly the complex and variable character of the concept "democracy," it is probably best to consider the successive meanings that have attached to the various democratic principles.

In this paper, we shall merely analyze the three principles which have had the widest repercussions on modern civilization: liberty, equality, and the people's share in important social decisions.

a) *The concept of "liberty."*—Let us first take the concept of liberty, which, as it emerged with bourgeois democracy, is simply "the power to do anything that does not injure others"[2]—that which injures others being determined by law.

As Marx said, this liberty "is not based on the interrelationship of

2. *Déclaration des Droits de l'Homme* (1791).

human beings, but rather on the separation of man from man. It is the right to such separateness, the right of the single individual."[3]

Referring to this concept of freedom, Marx adds that in practice it means the right of private ownership, which he describes as "the right to enjoy and dispose of one's fortune at will, without taking thought for other men or for society; it is the right of selfishness. It is this individual freedom, with its practical application, which lies at the basis of bourgeois society. It makes each person regard his fellow man not as the realization but as the restriction of his freedom."[4]

Bourgeois democracy is founded on this concept of freedom, a concept which only expresses the conditions under which bourgeois property must develop.

According to such a view of freedom, the essential purpose of the political community is to protect property (assimilated to the practical attainment of freedom): this means that the government is the *instrument* for defending the property system on which society is based. The citizen as a member of the political community is, in this form of democracy, "the servant of the selfish 'man' in civil society."[5]

But hardly had these concepts of political society and freedom been formulated than their incoherence became apparent, for under the Terror, the political community (which was supposed to be the mere instrument of individual freedom) set individual freedom at naught, making political life the end and not the means.

The reasons for this contradiction between theory and practice are of no concern to us in this context[6] and, moreover, it is not the logical inconsistency of a conception that historically and socially condemns it.

What condemned this concept of freedom was the emergence of an ever larger class—the proletariat—possessing no property at all. For the man who is condemned to rely for his living on the sale of his labor, on his wages, property always means the property of others and is therefore not the expression of bourgeois freedom but of bourgeois oppression. For the proletariat as a class, freedom is there-

3. Karl Marx, *Zur Judenfrage*, in *Marx-Engels Gesamtausgabe*, ed. D. Rjazanov (Frankfurt-Moscow, 1927), I, Part I, 594.

4. *Ibid.*, p. 595.

5. *Ibid.*, p. 595.

6. Continuing the line of thought in the text quoted above, Marx analyzes these reasons.

fore not the right to private property but the denial of that right. Proletarian democracy is therefore incompatible with bourgeois democracy.

From this point of view, it may be said that bourgeois democracy implies a certain freedom for man, but not his emancipation; it is the freedom to own property but not liberation from the system of ownership; it is the freedom to work and to run private industry but not the emancipation of labor and the industrial system.

Passing from the bourgeois to the proletarian conception of liberty clearly means passing from one conception to another of democracy: this despite the fact that both claim allegiance to liberty.

There are many other sides to the question. When we place ourselves in the situation of the unpropertied classes, for whom the property of others means oppression and not freedom, we see that private ownership is also oppression on the part of the owner. This is true in both the ideological and the material sense.

In a society based on private ownership, the products of labor are converted into merchandise, the production and distribution of which are not decided consciously by men but depend on economic laws inherent in the system of mercantile production and which have the relentless force of natural laws. Under such a system, men (whether they hold property or not) instead of being the masters of the system of production are merely its servants. Mercantile production and its extreme form capitalist production (where man himself becomes merchandise) "makes of every man an agent, an instrument"[7] crushed by an inhuman machine beyond his control.

In a capitalistic society, economic laws, which are merely the expression of the social forces behind private producers, face these producers as external powers to which they must submit. This is fundamentally an *"alienation"* of human freedom and will persist until men realize the social significance of the forces of production and *use them accordingly*[8] by putting an end to private appropriation.

Until this stage is reached, alienation is a source of mystification:

7. We have purposely borrowed the words of de Tocqueville, quoted in the UNESCO questionnaire (p. 517) and have applied it to capitalism.

8. Cf. Fr. Engels, *Herr Eugen Dühring's Revolution in Science* (New York, 1939), p. 345: "Mere knowledge . . . is not enough to bring social forces under the control of society. What is above all necessary for this is a social act," i.e., the taking possession of the means of production; cf. *ibid.*, pp. 305 f.

social relationships appear to dominate men (domination of money, domination of capital) and the decisions of individuals lead to the opposite of the results desired. Thus most decisions are taken haphazardly and not consciously. Here again, there is no freedom, for as Engels says, "Chance is only one pole of a relation whose other pole is named 'necessity.' "[9]

Bourgeois freedom, the basis of bourgeois democracy, thus means the illusion of freedom for the capitalist and the submission to the capitalist for the worker, while for the unemployed, the inevitable concomitants of capitalist freedom, it is a negation of even the illusion of freedom.

The principle of individual liberty in bourgeois democracy also includes what we may call political freedom (freedom of expression, freedom of association, freedom to choose one's leaders, and so forth). As we have seen, the very essence of bourgeois freedom is the freedom of ownership, to which all other forms of freedom are subordinate. This subordination finds expression in the theory that the system of government is merely an instrument for the defense of private property; it takes practical expression whenever this private property is threatened, or appears to be threatened, in the withdrawal (it little matters whether it is a formal withdrawal or not) of political liberties: the banning of meetings (for the men or the party constituting the "threat" to property), suspension of freedom of the press, censorship, martial law, intimidation trials, police terrorism, etc.

Undoubtedly, political freedoms are by nature subordinate to a higher freedom. Political emancipation is but one factor in social emancipation, and this is true at all stages of the emancipation: French society under the Terror was fundamentally nearer a new form of freedom than under the monarchy. Similarly, in a society just emerged from slavery, political dictatorship, which puts an end to this slavery, brings this society much closer to freedom, just as, in the transition from capitalism to socialism, the temporary curtailment of political freedoms by no means precludes a fundamental progress towards liberty.

All the preceding arguments thus go to show not so much the ambiguity as the relativity of the concept of freedom. This is a *social*

9. Fr. Engels, *The Origin of the Family, Private Property, and the State* (New York, 1942), p. 159.

relativity, implying that the underlying meaning of the word alters according to the class system in question. Freedom may thus remain one of the essential principles of democracy, without there being any one concept of democracy.

What is true of the concept "freedom" is also true of "equality."

b) *The concept of "equality."*—Democracy, even bourgeois democracy, implies equality, but what equality?

In the bourgeois conception of democracy, this equality is one of *form:* "Equality implies that the law is the same for all, in both its protective and its punitive aspects."[10]

Equality here means equal opportunity to hold property, but not equality of ownership. Every man has the right to set up a business, to employ paid workers, to bequeath his fortune, etc., even if he has neither money nor fortune.

But just as freedom takes on a different meaning for classes other than the bourgeoisie, so does equality. As long as the proletariat is not organized as a class, equality is taken by the workers to mean "equality of ownership"—a paradoxical concept, since ownership implies inequality. But the proletariat is the only section of society which can grasp this truth. And so, for the proletariat, equality means the abolition of classes by the abolition of private ownership of the means of production. This equality, which is socialist equality as contrasted with capitalist equality, does not mean the end of inequality in the distribution of incomes (to each according to his work). This inequality, according to Marx, is what will remain of "bourgeois law" in a socialist society, and cannot disappear until humanity has reached a later stage of development; only then can real equality (that of communist society: to each according to his needs) take the place of the purely formal equality which still characterizes socialist society.[11]

Here again, we realize the social relativity of the concept "equality," a concept implied by the term "democracy."

c) *The principle of the participation of the whole population (or a large proportion of it) in important social decisions.*—This principle, even when its application is limited to only one section of the population, distinguishes the various types of democracy from personal tyranny. But democratic progress manifests itself in the ex-

10. Article 5 in the French Constitution of 1790.
11. Cf. Lenin, *The State and Revolution*, V, Part 4, 82.

tension of this participation to ever larger sections of the people, which then have a real instead of a merely nominal share in important social decisions. However, this progress can be achieved only by a struggle for recognition of the rights of those classes of the population which have hitherto been deprived of them.

Bourgeois democracy, at the outset, was avowedly a form of government devised by the ruling classes to maintain the property qualification system. This is true of the 1791 and 1795 Constitutions (the 1793 Constitution recognizing universal suffrage was not put into force) and also of the Restoration; it was not until the 1848 Revolution in France that universal suffrage was not merely proclaimed but applied. Even today, the system of property qualification still exists in certain of the southern states of the United States of America.

We can account for such limitations by the obvious antagonism between "popular sovereignty" and the "sovereignty of money" of mercantile society. In mercantile society, money is the universal power to which all classes must bow.

There are three possible ways of avoiding the conflict between the "sovereignty of the people" and the "sovereignty of money": to limit sovereignty of the people to that section possessing the power of money; to grant a nominal extension of "sovereignty" to the whole people, while leaving money as the supreme power (this is what happens with universal suffrage, which under bourgeois democracy, implies that the masses subscribe to capitalist ideology); or lastly to do away with the sovereignty of money by abolishing private property. Only the last solution is regarded as "democratic" by the unpropertied proletariat.

Nevertheless, the solution provided by universal suffrage under bourgeois democracy is worth our notice. How does it manifest itself and what is its significance?

Like every political change, universal suffrage came as the result of a social struggle between not merely the rulers and the exploited, but also between the various strata of the ruling class, certain members of which hoped to find support among the masses. They were able to find such support to the extent they succeeded in interesting the masses in their own quarrels and in making them take sides in their conflicts of interests, mostly put forward as ideological conflicts. A striking case was the political struggle of the nineteenth century between the landowners who were in favor of maintaining high tariffs on wheat, and the industrial capitalists who wished to abolish it. On the ideological plane, this conflict appeared as a dispute between protectionists and free traders. It was settled on the practical, social, and political plane when the English workers (for reasons other than those prompting the industrial capitalists) supported the free traders.

But, though universal suffrage may be established as the result of social struggles, what is its meaning? Within the framework of bourgeois society, it is no doubt a victory for the workers, but a political, not a social victory, for it leads to political, not to social emancipation. Marx, after stressing the necessary limitations of this political emancipation, wrote:

"Political emancipation constitutes, on the whole, a great step forward. It is not the ultimate form of human emancipation, but it is the last stage of emancipation within the framework of the present social order." And he hastens to add: "Let it be clear that what we have in mind is real emancipation—practical emancipation."[12]

However, the significance of universal suffrage goes farther. The abolition of property qualification implies the elimination of the decisive influence of private property on political life. Marx expounded this idea with remarkable clarity in the following passage: "The State as such puts an end to private ownership and man decrees the political abolition of private ownership as soon as he decides to waive the property qualification for the franchise and the eligibility to stand for election."

However, this political abolition is illusory, for it "not merely does not do away with private ownership but even presupposes it. The State has its own way of levelling out distinctions conferred by birth, social rank, education or occupational status, by proclaiming that these factors do not constitute political differences. When ignoring these distinctions, it declares that every subject has an equal share in the sovereignty of the people, and when it treats all these factors making up the real life of the people from the standpoint of the State. Private ownership, education and occupational status are each allowed to exert their influence unimpeded, and these very real distinctions, far from being abolished, are the very hypothesis on which the State is founded. . . ."[13]

In actual fact, the political state, as contrasted with the state of the

12. Karl Marx, *Zur Judenfrage*, in *Marx-Engels Gesamtausgabe*, I, Part 1, 585.
13. *Ibid.*, pp. 582–83.

landowners, the theocratic state, etc., exists only in so far as it, qua state, abolishes all distinctions of property, religion and so forth. But that only means that the state, as such, *ignores* these differences, which are all the more in a position to exert their influence on real life and thereby indirectly on all political decisions.

Engels goes to the root of this problem when, after remarking that the democratic republic does not, officially, recognize property distinctions, he adds that "wealth here employs its power indirectly but all the more surely."[14]

There are abundant instances of this indirect "but all the surer" influence of wealth. Volumes of sociological and socio-economic studies, such as Seldes's *Lords of the Press* and Lundberg's *America's Sixty Families* would be necessary to show all the means (press, books, radio, films, as well as the corruption of parliamentary representatives and government officials, violence and blackmail, etc.) which can be used, and are used by the wealthy classes to insure that, despite universal suffrage, the great bulk of political decisions are not merely not turned against them but, in the long run, redound to their advantage.

For many, however, the "essence" of democracy is summed up in the ceremony of voting, the true social context of which is forgotten. They do not see how this act is tantamount to the alienation, by each elector, of his nominal "sovereignty" to other men, professional politicians, who pay fabulous sums to enter political life and to maintain their position. In the United States, each presidential election costs the two main parties tens of millions of dollars. Lundberg estimates the sum spent by the Republican Party in 1936 at fifty million dollars,[15] while the Democratic Party must have spent about the same amount.

Thus the illusory character of parliamentary democracy is plain to all who do not close their eyes. The masses of the people take no part in social decisions but, submitted to constant ideological pressure and deprived of any real means of information (through lack of time or the necessary education, etc.) are merely required every four or six years to appoint a "representative," who is usually chosen from among the propertied classes. Moreover, the decisions which these representatives are called upon to take are of little mo-

14. Fr. Engels, *The Origin of the Family*, p. 151.
15. Ferdinand Lundberg, *America's Sixty Families* (New York, 1937), p. 483.

ment in comparison with those taken outside parliament. This is another aspect of the practical application of the principle of participation in "important social decisions" to which we must now turn our attention.

In fact, the "important social decisions" are of two types: political and economic. The most momentous political decisions (war or peace, the conclusion of military alliances, etc.) are not taken by parliament, but by governments and their military and diplomatic representatives. Parliament is merely required to "ratify" them. In view of the nature of these decisions and the fact that they are generally fraught with immediate results, parliament rarely has any alternative but to ratify. The "separation of powers" is another means of assigning to others than the elected representatives the responsibility for taking the most important social decisions. And so, to a large extent, the "work" of parliament is limited to speech-making. As Lenin bluntly remarked, "the actual work of the 'state' is done behind the scenes, and is carried out by the departments, the offices and the staffs. Parliament itself is given up to talk for the special purpose of fooling the 'common people.' "[16] And Lenin contrasts parliamentary assemblies with "non-parliamentary but working assemblies" in which are concentrated the "legislative and executive powers."

But the most important social decisions are economic rather than political. The prosperity of a country, the well-being of its inhabitants and the peaceful or aggressive character of its international relations are determined by decisions taken in the sphere of production: the volume of investments, their direction and nature, the purchasing power of the people, etc. But under capitalism, where the means of production are in the hands of private individuals, none of these socially important decisions belong to the sphere of politics; they rank as economic decisions. Neither the people nor their representatives have any say in this sphere. The decisions are taken by capitalists, by boards of directors and by banks. Even under the most democratic of capitalist systems, socially important decisions finally rest with vested interests, as long as private ownership is maintained. Experience has shown that all the "control measures" employed by capitalist governments have little effect when these measures do not coincide with the interests of the majority of capi-

16. Lenin, *The State and Revolution*, p. 40.

talists or of the most powerful among them.

Here, again, only a radical change in the economic and social system can insure that the most important social decisions are arrived at in a democratic way, in a no longer formal but real sense of this word.

It is thus seen how democracy may be defined by a number of principles, but the meaning of these principles evolves in the course of time and, with them, the meaning of democracy. This implies that the notion of democracy is constantly evolving, but it is not a logical progress of the idea in itself, but a social and historic progress.

If it is admitted that the concept of democracy changes during the course of history, it can be readily understood that, with each advance in this concept, what *was* democratic may cease to be so. Thus, Athenian slave democracy was a democracy (in relation to the ideal of democracy which could conceivably be formulated at that time); similarly, the democratic bourgeois republic was a democracy, but ceased to be so once a new and wider concept of democracy was formulated.

There is obviously a fundamental difference between a capitalist state founded on class domination and committed to the maintenance of this domination, and a state which sets out to do away with class distinctions and all factors which may lead to their re-emergence. Before history postulated the necessity of such a state—and above all before any such state actually existed—a class-divided state could be termed democratic if it applied the formal principles of democracy and enabled society to develop, under the existing historic conditions, by reducing to a minimum the extent and weight of the oppression inherent in every class society. Every possible reduction of oppression meant further progress toward democracy.

From this point of view, there are various degrees—historical and not theoretical—in democracy, and the most democratic class society is one which, at every stage in history, reduces to a minimum the extent and weight of oppression.

However, once the removal of class oppression becomes not merely feasible but also a necessity if society is to progress further, every state based on class oppression ceases to be democratic in the historical sense of the word. Henceforward, the only democratic state is one which aims at the abolition of the class system and the removal of those factors which may lead to the rebirth of a class-divided society.

The democratic character of the state itself will depend on the extent to which the masses are really able to share in solving social problems, with due regard to historic circumstances and the effort made to allow the people a conscious and effective part in such decisions. This effort may take on the most varied aspects: measures to raise the living standard of the masses, to give them a broader education and training for employment, and to encourage them to take an active part in public life, and so forth.

22. TOLERATION OF DISSENTIENT OPINION.—The "toleration of dissentient opinions" can by no means be said to constitute the "essence" of democracy, but one of its secondary aspects and one which can develop only under special conditions.

It is a well-known fact that French bourgeois democracy was established during the Terror and consolidated under the Napoleonic regime, neither of which was characterized by the "toleration of dissentient opinions."

But once it is established, bourgeois democracy tolerates dissentient opinion only so long as it does not threaten capitalist domination. This contention is borne out by the anti-communist drives which the capitalist world has been carrying on with varying severity for more than thirty years.

In point of fact, every democracy tolerates only those opinions that uphold the social order on which the democracy in question is based; bourgeois democracy is therefore far more ready to tolerate fascist propaganda (fascism being a form of capitalist domination) than any propaganda advocating the overthrow of capitalism. However, at certain periods, bourgeois democracy has "tolerated" such propaganda, and for two reasons: first, if the propaganda has borne little fruit, it is thought wise to feign ignorance so as not to attract attention to it (though such "ignorance" does not preclude an indirect form of repression), especially as all repression helps to "demystify" the masses by opening their eyes to the purely nominal character of bourgeois class democracy; second, if the propaganda has on the contrary borne fruit, it appears impossible to come out into open battle against a powerful current of opinion, which it is found preferable to combat by new forms of mystification: whenever the workers' movement is flourishing, even the parties representing bourgeois interests profess to be "anti-capitalist" or "socialist" (as in France immediately after the Liberation).

On the other hand, in any society where national and international conditions are such that the expression of divergent opinions is not likely to stand in the way of progress toward a really democratic order, toleration of these opinions is a democratic necessity.

23. REPRESSION OF PROPAGANDA.—The repression of propaganda advocating a change in the form of government is compatible with democratic government in so far as this repression is directed against anti-democratic propaganda (such as fascist propaganda) or propaganda advocating a return to a purely nominal democracy in a country where real democracy exists. On the other hand, such repression is anti-democratic if it is directed against propaganda advocating a broader type of democracy by replacing bourgeois with socialist democracy.

25. ONE-PARTY SYSTEMS.—The plurality of parties is certainly not a necessary feature of democracy. Ancient democracies did not have parties imbued with a common ideology, but "factions" or groups of more or less avowed interests, which is quite a different matter.

The existence of pluralities of parties is peculiar to bourgeois democracy. Their existence only reflects the social antagonisms inherent in capitalist society. The various parties are actually the defenders—under the cloak of various ideologies—of conflicting social interests: interests of the working class, of the petty bourgeoisie and the higher bourgeoisie. The interests of the various groups of the bourgeoisie may even be reflected through different political parties.

It is thus the diversity of the social interests at stake and their antagonisms which account for the diversity of political parties and the rights granted to oppositions. These interests are not proclaimed at their face value but as divergent ideologies, because the political struggle takes place not in the real world, the civil community, but in the state, which is an abstract, imaginary world. The parties accepting this abstract world as if it were real cannot put themselves forward as the spokesmen of any particular group of interests (which belong to the low and vulgar world of civil society), but must make themselves appear as the representatives of the nation's general interests. Their platform policy is therefore not their real policy but a special interpretation of the steps which must be taken for the "general good."

It must also be added that these ideologies are necessary means of mystification: it is only by catching workers' "votes" that the representatives of given industrial interests can hope to win a "majority" that will enable them to prevail against the representatives of other interests. The party system is thus one aspect of the mystification of the masses.

It is because political parties do not really aim at finding general solutions to problems (otherwise political groups would come and go with the problems of the moment, like the "factions" of the ancient world) but are the disguised spokesmen of the various social interests, that they rise and fall with the social classes they represent.

Moreover, the classes which die out—and which have not been able to achieve political supremacy in the form of an open dictatorship, and also witness the disappearance of the political parties through which they traditionally exerted their supremacy—try to re-establish this supremacy through a host of new political formations (parties, rallies, movements and so forth) which proclaim an ideology ever further removed from that of the class they represent. Hence, in Western Europe, there is a multitude of parties (especially of the "left"), which is not a sign of the "soundness" of bourgeois democracy but of its degeneracy. This is another means of diverting the masses (disgusted by this plethora of parties) from parliamentary democracy and trying to regroup them under a single bourgeois or fascist party (which is of course not put forward as such).

The bourgeoisie, again, is all the more ready to regroup as the development of monopolies greatly weakens the antagonisms once existing between the various capitalist groups.

In a socialist society, from which social antagonisms have disappeared, the many-party system has no point. There is room for only one party, which is the political instrument through which the workers bring about the transformation of society through the state.[17] The ways and means of achieving this transformation may

17. It should be clear that the relations between party and state in a developing socialist society and the problems involved in the survival of more or less separate professional, regional and cultural interests, etc., cannot be considered in the replies to the present questionnaire. These problems are particularly complex and the world still has too little practical experience in solving them for us to be able to give more than general suggestions.

give rise to discussion, but in the absence of groups of conflicting social interests, these discussions cannot lead to the regrouping of social forces in the form of parties, just as an association of experts or scientists which has to take decisions on certain questions has no need to break up into "parties." Even the existence of permanent "trends" in a single party has no point, for once problems have been clearly and scientifically solved, they do not have to be thrashed out again.

Indeed, one of the differences between bourgeois and socialist democracy is that the social problems facing the latter can be solved (within the means available to society at each stage of its development) because a socialist society is master of the social forces: on the other hand, under capitalism, most social problems are insoluble and only apparent solutions can be found. These different "solutions," which have been put forward ever since the organization of bourgeois society, are the permanent themes of the bourgeois parties and form the objective basis of the political skepticism inherent in bourgeois democracy.

26. "SKEPTICISM" AND DEMOCRACY.—Skepticism, interpreted as systematic doubt of the value of social knowledge, is perhaps an "article of faith" for bourgeois democracy, which knows only "opinions." On the other hand, acceptance of a scientific philosophy of society, which will really solve the problems created by history, is one of the subjective conditions of socialist democracy.

This absence of skepticism does not mean the absence of a critical spirit. On the contrary, the scientific mind is distinguished by its careful, all-round consideration of every problem and its capacity to go back and recognize its own mistakes (self-criticism). But this critical spirit has no democratic value unless it effectively contributes toward the solution of social problems. This implies that discussions on ideological mysteries and discussions between men who do not have the necessary practical knowledge for a scientific solution of the problem are void of all democratic meaning. Accordingly, the decisions taken by a workers' party may be more democratic than the votes cast, under universal suffrage, by a people who are kept in ignorance of the essential facts of the problems. But democratic progress means increasing as far as possible the number of people capable of, and actually taking an effective part in, solving social problems.

29. ULTIMATE AIMS.—There is probably no "theoretic" incompatibility between the ultimate political aims described by Lenin and the aims proclaimed by "other ideologists." But their tenets are in practice incompatible in that, for Lenin, only a radical transformation of human relationships and of the economic and social system would allow of the attainment of these aims, whereas other ideologists, representing a different class, do not understand the need for this transformation, since they fail to realize that private ownership of the means of production spells oppression for the workers.

Moreover, this is more than a theoretical need; it is becoming an ever more urgent practical necessity, imposed by the facts and the altered balance of strength between the social classes.

30. NATURE OF THE DISAGREEMENT.—Theoretically, disagreement centers around the facts and their interpretation. The ideologists of bourgeois democracy, so far as they are sincere, do not grasp the nominal nature of this democracy and do not see that the real conditions of capitalist society prevent this democracy from being anything but nominal, as it is one of the political expedients for maintaining the mastery of a minority of capitalists over a majority of workers; but this expedient becomes ever more precarious as the antagonisms in capitalist society deepen.

This disagreement over facts and their interpretation and the extent of the disagreement results from a definite historical situation—the coexistence, not only, as in the nineteenth century, of two concepts of democracy, but of two systems: socialism and capitalism. Furthermore, within capitalism itself, the social forces which are consciously in favor of socialism are gathering ever greater strength. This "disagreement" can therefore end only in the triumph of real democracy over nominal democracy. Meanwhile, it is probably possible to compromise between the two systems (as represented by different states) but these compromises cannot prevent the forces in capitalist society that are working for socialism (the proletariat allied with the other working classes) from extending their power until they can overthrow capitalism and replace it by a socialist society, the only really democratic form of society.

II

M. M. BOBER

AN INVENTORY of Marx's and Engels' use of the word democracy is apt to become a barren enterprise in semantics. Marx and Engels were not in the habit of giving clear meaning to their crucial words and phrases. Their concepts, however, while not masterpieces of lucidity and consistency, emerge, after everything which the two writers say is taken into account, with a degree of clarity. We shall accordingly examine their concepts of democracy as they see it evolving in the historical epochs marked by the celebrated Marxian succession of productive systems, the primitive gens, ancient slavery, medieval feudalism, modern capitalism, and future communism.

The discussion revolves around Marx's basic conception that democracy is a type of political state, and that the state is the unique fruit of a given mode of production with its correlative property relations and class divisions. Far from functioning as the *summmum bonum*, as the compromiser of conflicting group interests, as the foundation of law and order, as the servant of the social good, or as Hegel's Divine Idea on earth—the state is pre-eminently the engine of class domination and the instrument of keeping the exploited class, the mass, in subordination; it is the supreme power, exterior to and above the people. To Marx, the state implies one sort or another of slavery: "The existence of the state and the existence of slavery are inseparable."[1] The state is generically a power category, and democracy is a species of the genus.

1. *The gens.*—To Marx and Engels, primitive societies are invariably characterized by family rule, by communal property, and by what non-Marxians would call democratic processes. The people elect elders to attend to matters of common concern, or else decide on such affairs at general meetings. Our two writers do not refer, however, to such a social structure as a democracy. There is no class division, no rule of man over man in production; therefore there

1. Marx-Engels, *Historisch-kritische Gesamtausgabe*, ed. D. Rjazanov (Berlin, 1927–32), Part I, Vol. III, pp. 15, 298.

is no state and no democracy. Their references to the gens are in terms of a "family organization," a "tribal community," "directly associated labor."[2] Such societies, says Engels, are without the idea of "any state or public power"; only with private property and class cleavage the state becomes "inevitable."[3] The state, he teaches, differs from gentilism in that it divides its members by geography and not by kinship; it stands for coercion; it levies taxes; and its officials are elevated over society.[4]

Here we come upon the well-known difficulty confronting the reader of Marx and Engels: contradictions. Engels records that where the gens persisted it developed "the most barbarous form of state, oriental despotism."[5] We are not told why. Still worse, Engels acknowledges that "there were from the beginning certain common interests," like adjusting disputes, disciplining a person for misbehavior, and attending to religious functions, which were taken care of by elected officials, and he terms this "the beginnings of state power."[6] However, such pronouncements have to be treated as the baffling vagaries of careless writers. The basic thought of our two revolutionaries is that in the absence of private property and classes there is no state, and the gens is the first historical example of such a situation.

Marx appreciates the limitations of this primitive social structure,[7] but Engels is lavish in his admiration. "No soldiers, gendarmes, and policemen," he exclaims, "no nobility . . . or judges, no prisons, no lawsuits, and still affairs run smoothly."[8]

It hardly needs emphasizing that the explorations of scholars in this field fail to justify the simple Marxian generalizations about economics and politics in the gens. These old societies display variations with respect to property and inequality and present a spectrum of governments from despotism to democracy.

2. *Capital*, I (Chicago, 1909), 89; III (Chicago, 1909), 1023; Engels, *Anti-Dühring* (New York, 1939), pp. 164, 179.
3. Engels, *Origin of the Family, Private Property, and the State* (Chicago, 1902), pp. 130, 211.
4. *Ibid.*, pp. 206–8.
5. *Anti-Dühring*, p. 200.
6. *Ibid.*, pp. 198, 165; Engels, Preface to Marx's *The Paris Commune* (New York, 1919), pp. 17–18. The more common title of this later work is *Civil War in France*.
7. *Capital*, I, 91.
8. *Origin of the Family*, pp. 107, 117.

2. *Classical democracy.*—The gens went under because of the appearance of private property, classes, and wickedness. How the idyllic environment of the gens was capable of breeding such monstrosities we do not learn. The system of slavery settles upon the ruins of the tribal organism; the state appears as a matter of course.

Marx and Engels see the emergence of democracy in the fifth century B.C. in Greece, and at about the same time in Rome. There are, at least intermittently, parties, issues, and elections; the people vote for offices and policies; now and then leading personalities agitate for reform, and win or lose. Such political devices, in a setting of private property and classes, Marx and his friend regard as democracy. As far as I know, they do not stop to give precise definition to this particular type of state.

Admirers of the great contributions of classical antiquity, our two friends are not prone to extol democracy as a singular achievement in the art of government or as the first serious step in history to recognize the worth of the individual. They welcome the giant strides in civilization made possible by slavery and they see in slavery a humane advance inasmuch as prisoners of war are no longer slain.[9] But in the realm of human relations in the ancient world generally they are in the habit of stressing, both in the period of democracy and in other periods, the supremacy of the master over the slave, of the rich over the poor, and of the creditor over the debtor. Democracy, then as later, is merely another symbol of the power of man over man. To them, democracy, the rule of the people, is a rhetorical expression.[10]

3. *Bourgeois democracy.*—There is no reference in Marx and Engels to democracy in the Middle Ages. The princes, the nobility, and the church hold sway. The serf in the country and the worker in the city have no vote on the large matters of common concern. Absolute monarchy, mitigated by the power of the nobility, appears where pluralism and particularism wane.

The form of state expressive of capitalism is democracy. Democracy is declared to be the "logical" government for the bourgeoisie.[11] The bourgeois revolution against feudalism is labelled as the "demo-

9. Engels, *Anti-Dühring*, pp. 200–201.
10. *Ibid.*, p. 114; *Origin of the Family*, pp. 139, 141–43, 153–57.
11. Marx and Engels, *Selected Correspondence, 1846–1895* (New York, 1942), p. 435.

cratic revolution."[12] Why "logical," Marx and Engels do not explain. It would seem, rather, that the most fitting political form of capitalism would be an explicit and thoroughgoing oligarchy; the few rich, the masters of the means of production, are also the political rulers—openly and categorically. The explanation customarily offered by Marx and his colleague for the rise of modern democracy stresses that the absolute monarchy inherited by the bourgeoisie from the past is cluttered up with feudal regulations hampering the new entrepreneurs at each turn; and accordingly democracy in one form or another is introduced to protect and further the interests of the new privileged class.[13]

This explanation skates on thin ice. First, absolute monarchy prevailed for centuries under capitalism, and, far from obstructing the development of this economic order, eagerly strove to promote it. Witness the mercantilist era in England, France, and elsewhere. Witness Marx's own account of state aid in the rise of capitalism: the state was then an absolute monarchy.[14] Moreover, to explain a historical sequence does not render the sequence logical. The historical is not necessarily the logical.

It goes without saying that when talking about democracy Marx and Engels do not mean to imply that the state is congruous with the people, that the people rule—and they define the people as consisting of "the proletarians, the small peasants, and the mob."[15] They teach that always in a democracy the few rich, the oligarchy, are supreme.[16] By their definition, the state in any form personifies the supremacy of the wealthy few over the many; the state, that is, is generically another word for oligarchy. But this does not resolve the question of why capitalism must adopt a deceptive democracy with the vote privilege given to the many. Why not an outright oligarchy in which the masses are without the franchise even as they are without the means of production?

Be that as it may, democracy is viewed as the most fitting form of state under capitalism. The expression used most often is "democratic republic."[17] We also come across the "bourgeois republic"[18]

12. *Ibid.*
13. *Anti-Dühring*, pp. 115–17.
14. *Capital*, Vol. I, Part VIII.
15. *Selected Correspondence*, p. 193.
16. *Ibid.*, p. 206.
17. *Origin of the Family*, p. 209; *Selected Correspondence*, p. 435.
18. *Selected Correspondence*, pp. 502, 522.

and the "modern representative state."[19] Here, too, there are inconsistencies. We encounter declarations that absolute monarchy is the child of feudalism, is the child of capitalism, aids capitalism, is against capitalism.[20] And against a background of assertions that democracy and capitalism are inseparable companions we run into the statement that "Bonapartism," "semi-dictatorship is the normal form," the "real religion of the modern bourgeoisie."[21]

Bourgeois democracy is painted on a gloomy canvas. The flaming indictments which scorch the pages of *Capital* are a catalogue of inhumanities within the framework of democracy. Increasing toil in the factory, the rising industrial army of the unemployed, and increasing misery and degradation are alike the staple earmarks of capitalism and its handmaid, democracy. Democracy is not the rule of the people, but at the expense of the people. It is no different in the New World exempt from the atavistic heritage of feudalism and the nobility. Says Engels: "It is just in the United States that we can most clearly see the process through which the State acquires a position of independent power over against the society. . . . There exists here no dynasty, no aristocracy. . . . Nevertheless, we have here two great rings of political speculators that alternately take possession of the power of the State and exploit it with the most corrupt purposes. And the nation is powerless against these men, who nominally are its servants, but in reality are its two overruling and plundering hordes of politicians."[22]

The repressive force of democracy may be in lower key in isolated districts or where classes are as yet of feeble development, "as was once the case in certain regions in the United States."[23] But with the maturity of bourgeois society class differences widen, and the proletariat, more critical of existing institutions, becomes more rebellious; then the state becomes proportionately more repressive.[24] Even under "state capitalism," so called by Engels, when the state assumes the management of certain industries, the plight of the worker does not improve. The state merely extends its sway over a

---

19. *Origin of the Family*, p. 209.
20. M. M. Bober, *Karl Marx's Interpretation of History* (2d ed.; Harvard University Press, 1948), pp. 135–36.
21. *Selected Correspondence*, pp. 205, 206.
22. Preface to Marx's *Paris Commune*, p. 18; *Selected Correspondence*, p. 451.
23. *Origin of the Family*, p. 27.
24. *Paris Commune*, Sec. III, par. 3.

wider area; for the private despoiler of labor is substituted the democratic state-employer.[25]

If labor commands a majority vote, as it does in capitalistic countries generally, why does it tolerate abuse? Why does it not transform society into a paradise for itself regardless of the desires of the capitalists? Marx's answer would be clear enough. In the early stages of capitalism the proletariat is not solidified into a self-conscious class acutely aware of its interests, and as yet the realities of capitalism are not impressive enough to teach the workers where their interests lie. The worker, like others, is the victim of what Marx calls illusionism—the disposition to judge by the appearance of things and the failure to penetrate to the "inner connection" of phenomena.[26] "The ruling ideas of each age have ever been the ideas of its ruling class."[27] At first the proletarian is taken in by the ruling ideas assiduously propagated by the predatory class.

But with the progress of capitalism and the hammering impact of its contradictions, the proletariat gains light. Already in 1848, the *Communist Manifesto* declares the worker is sophisticated enough to understand that law, morality, and religion are "so many bourgeois prejudices." At this stage the proletarian turns communist in orientation and revolutionary in conduct. The state becomes more alert and oppressive; the class struggle, destined to achieve the final social synthesis, assumes vehement dimensions. What the voting ballots of the workers can accomplish now will be indicated after the next paragraph.

In the meantime it is necessary to record that always the two revolutionaries are not unmindful of the gains which labor can secure by sustained agitation for reform. Marx speaks warmly of the ten-hour law and of favorable legislation generally.[28] Of course, faithful to his theory of history, Marx treats such legislation as the reflex of capitalist production. Of the Factory Acts in England Marx says that they are "just as much the necessary product of modern industry as cotton yarn, self-actors, and electric telegraph."[29] Ultimately,

25. Engels, *Socialism, Utopian and Scientific* (New York, 1935), p. 67. Cf. *Capital*, III, 918–19.
26. *Capital*, I, 591–92; III, 198–99, 369, 1016–17.
27. *Deutsche Ideologie*, in *Historisch-kritische Gesamtausgabe*, Part I, Vol. V, pp. 35–36.
28. K. Marx, *Die Inauguraladresse der internationalen Arbeiter-Association*, ed. Karl Kautsky (Berlin, 1922), pp. 26, 28–29; *Capital*, I, 297–330.
29. *Capital*, I, 526.

such laws register the concessions and limits of tolerance which the ruling class thinks it can afford. Beyond a certain point, the upper class stands unyielding. For instance, in "conflicts as to the rate of wages . . . Adam Smith has already shown that . . . taken on the whole, the master is always master."[30]

At times Marx and Engels are so impressed by the power of the ballot that in democratic countries they see the possibility of a peaceful transition to communism, a prospect welcome to them because they did not relish a bloody revolution. There is ample evidence of this attitude, but a reference or two will suffice. At the Hague Congress of the International in 1872 Marx says: "We know that the institutions, the manners and the customs of the various countries must be considered, and we do not deny that there are countries like England and America, and, if I understood your arrangements better, I might even add Holland, where the worker may attain his object (that is, "capture political power") by peaceful means. But not in all countries is this the case."[31]

Shortly before his death in 1895 Engels calls attention to universal suffrage as the new weapon, "and one of the sharpest," in the struggle for a new society. "The irony of world history turns everything upside down. We the 'revolutionaries,' the 'rebels,'—we are thriving far better on legal methods than on illegal methods and revolt."[32]

It is important to add, however, that such pronouncements are not made with a sense of finality. Marx and Engels were not convinced that even in a democracy the stepping stones toward communism can be laid, or a quick transition made, without desperate resistance from the intrenched beneficiaries of things as they are. Their faith in the historical mission of revolution, and in the historical right to it, is never renounced. Alongside of declarations of peaceful possibilities is the invariable affirmation of the claim of revolution as an instrument of social emancipation.

4. *Proletarian democracy.*—As Marx has it, "the bourgeois republic is the only political form in which the struggle between the prole-

---

30. *Ibid.*, p. 678.
31. Quoted by Kautsky in his *Dictatorship of the Proletariat* (London, 1919), p. 10. Cf. *Capital*, I, 14, 32.
32. Introduction to Marx's *Class Struggle in France* (New York, 1934), pp. 20, 27–28.

tariat and bourgeoisie can be resolved."[33] It is the task of the revolution to "shatter" the bourgeois state, and a new state is fashioned by the triumphant proletariat during the ensuing period of social reconstruction. Whether this period is antecedent to the first phase of communism, commonly designated as socialism proper, or is congruent with it, is not clear. Clear it is that after the revolution the proletariat succeeds the bourgeoisie as the star performer in history: the dictatorship of the proletariat takes over.[34]

This dictatorship of the proletariat is nothing but a democratic republic. The *Communist Manifesto* states that the first step after the revolution is to make the proletariat "the ruling class; to win the battle of democracy."[35] In his discussion of the Ehrfurt program, Engels asserts that a "democratic republic" is "the specific form of the dictatorship of the proletariat."[36] Of course the democracy applies only to the proletarians: voting, elected officials, and representative institutions are for them; in its relations with the surviving bourgeoisie, this democracy acts like a dictatorship.

Obviously enough, the dictatorship of the proletariat is still a state, since the earmarks of the state are yet in existence. There is the dominant class of proletarians facing the subdued minority, the bourgeoisie, with the concomitant coercion of the former over the latter. There are as yet vestiges of private property. Power is still at the base of the social structure, and the state is identified with the ruling class, the proletariat.

The proletarian form, however, is a milder state, a fitting prologue to the stateless order of true communism. Already about the Paris Commune Engels says that it is not a state "in the proper sense" and that it is more in the nature of a "Gemeinwesen," a commonwealth.[37] First, the proletarian state is not rooted in production, the matrix of political power. There is no upper class deriving an advantage from its position in the processes of production; the proletariat, that is, does not exist on the surplus-value pumped out of the ex-capitalists toiling in the commonly owned factories. Second, the state is an apparatus of the majority; it is a force rising only above the few

33. *Selected Correspondence*, p. 522.
34. Marx and Engels, Introduction of 1872 to the *Communist Manifesto; Marx, Paris Commune*, p. 80; *Critique of the Gotha Programme* (New York, 1933), p. 44; *Selected Correspondence*, p. 57.
35. At about two pages before the end of Part II.
36. *Neue Zeit*, XX, No. 1, 11.
37. Letter to A. Bebel, in A. Bebel, *Aus meinem Leben, II* (Berlin, 1922), 322.

capitalists or ex-capitalists. A government of most of the people (or all the people, as Marx defines people) and congruous with them, the state does not tower over the masses as the expression of arbitrary power. Third, the paramount, and unique, function of this state is to introduce a propertyless, classless order: it labors for self-extinction and the inauguration of the perfect society.

The precise steps to be taken by the dictatorship of the proletariat on the road to communism are reflected in a three-stage evolution in Marx's mind. First comes the milk and water formula of 1848. The *Communist Manifesto*, advocating "despotic inroads on the rights of private property," proposes the abolition of land property, a heavy progressive income tax, state control of banking and transportation, the obligation of all to work, and the like—with the main purpose of transferring the ownership of capital from private hands to the state.[38] By 1872 such measures are regarded as obsolete, and instead the Paris Commune is advanced as the model,[39] standing for the following measures: universal suffrage; elected municipal councillors; the substitution of "armed people" for the regular army; judges, police and other officials, elected and recalled by the people and paid worker's wages; the confiscation of church property; free education for all; delegates of local communes build up district assemblies which send deputies to the national delegation in Paris—a pyramid of democratic centralism as against democratic federalism, reproduced, in the main, in the Soviet government.[40] Marx always spoke of the Commune as a shining example for the victorious proletariat. However, by 1881 he begins to look at the Commune through dwarfing lenses. In a letter that year he states that the Commune represents "merely the rising of a town under exceptional conditions," with the majority of the rebels of nonsocialist persuasion.[41] Apparently, after a spectacular and definitive triumph over the might of the entire bourgeois class in a country he expects radical changes of dramatic dimensions. But he offers no blueprint.

5. *Stateless communism.*—Marx distinguishes two phases of communism. In the first phase the distribution of income is still ruled by bourgeois conceptions of inequality, and the worker's wage depends

38. At a page or so before the end of Part II.
39. Marx and Engels, Introduction of 1872 to the *Communist Manifesto*.
40. Marx, *Paris Commune*, pp. 9–10, 74–75, 85.
41. *Selected Correspondence*, p. 387.

on his efficiency. The second phase introduces genuine communism which enthrones the higher morality, such as prevails in the family. The guiding principle is "From each according to his capacity, to each according to his need."

When private property is abolished and class divisions disappear there is no further need for the citadel of class power, the state. Says Engels: "Do away with capital . . . [and capital is defined by Marx and Engels as the means of production which enable the owner to exact surplus-value from the propertyless worker] and the state will fall away of itself."[42] He teaches: "The government of persons is replaced by the administration of things, and by conduct of the processes of production. The state is not 'abolished.' *It dies out.*"[43] The bourgeois state has to be broken, but the proletarian state simply dissolves when nothing is left to give it existence. Economic functions remain, but the administration of them is a far cry from the apparatus of class compulsion. "Public functions," says Engels, "will lose their political character and will become simple administrative functions concerned with public interests."[44] As was indicated previously in this essay, in the gens such functions suggest to Engels "the beginnings of state power."

Under capitalism production and the fetishism of the commodity dominate society, but in a communist order production is brought under "common control as a law understood by the social mind," and "socialized man, the associated producers, regulate their interchange with nature rationally, bring it under their common control."[45] Instead of state power, we have "a co-operative commonwealth,"[46] a "free and equal association of producers,"[47] an "association in which the free development of each is the condition for the free development of all.[48]

To Marx, as to Hegel, history exhibits an upward trend, a steady progression in human freedom. With Hegel the trend expresses itself in the Absolute Idea. For the Idea Marx substitutes the material realities of production, and he teaches that with the socialization of

42. *Ibid.*, pp. 319–20.
43. *Socialism, Utopian and Scientific* (New York, 1892), pp. 76–77. Engels' italics.
44. "Über das Autoritätsprinzip," *Neue Zeit*, XXXII, No. 1, 39.
45. *Capital*, III, 301, 307, 954.
46. Marx, *Critique of the Gotha Programme*, p. 29.
47. Engels, *Origin of the Family*, p. 211.
48. *Communist Manifesto*, last sentence in Part II.

production the highest degree of human freedom will at last be attained. Under the spell of his economic interpretation, Marx thought that at the root of man's aggression against man lay private property and that with the dissolution of private property the search for power would cease. He ignored the protean aspects of man's persistent desire to be somebody, of his craving for self assertion and power, which will seek an outlet in any setting, even in a setting devoid of economic stimuli. Marx is in good company. With his unique brand of communism for the rulers, Plato committed the same error; so did many thinkers beyond Plato.

III

G. A. BORGESE

"It is true that we are called a democracy, for the administration is in the hands of the many and not of the few. But while the law secures equal justice to all alike in their private disputes, the claim of excellence is also recognized; and when a citizen is in any way distinguished, he is preferred to the public service, not as a matter of privilege, but as the reward of merit. Neither is poverty a bar, but a man may benefit his country whatever be the obscurity of his condition. There is no exclusiveness in our public life, and in our private intercourse we are not suspicious of one another, nor angry with our neighbor if he does what he likes; we do not put on sour looks at him which, though harmless, are not pleasant. While we are thus unconstrained in our private intercourse, a spirit of reverence pervades our public acts; we are prevented from doing wrong by respect for authority and for the laws, having an especial regard to those which are ordained for the protection of the injured as well as to those unwritten laws which bring upon the transgressor of them the reprobation of the general sentiment."

Perhaps because they are too well known, these sentences—from Pericles' Funeral Oration, 431 B.C.—do not figure among the crucial statements on democracy quoted in the UNESCO document introducing the present inquiry. They are, however, the most basic of all, not only on account of their chronological priority on all other attempts at a definition of the keyword, but because no essential progress was made in the intervening twenty-four centuries either in the description of what a democracy claims to be or in a conclusive solution of the difficulties which its practice implies.

It is less well known that Lincoln's funeral address at Gettysburg, 1863, was directly derived from Pericles' oration, of which it provides a lapidary condensation with no decisive change in concept or emotions.[1] On Lincoln's definition of democracy as "the govern-

1. The medium of transmission was Edward Everett's long Gettysburg speech, the manuscript of which reached Lincoln's desk a fortnight before he delivered the

ment of the people, by the people, and for the people" are pivoted, and rightly so, those which one may consider as the capital questions in the inquiry. They provide an opportunity for a brief reply simplifying under one heading the answers that should be given to several of the other 29 questions.

"The relations between the prepositions *by* and *for*," writes UNESCO, "have furnished the basis for violent discussion."

Those difficulties, monosyllabic in Gettysburg, are the same as emerge from the ampler text of the parent oration.

"Neither is poverty a bar," said Pericles, "but a man may benefit his country whatever be the obscurity of his condition." Whatever? Did he mean that poverty, even to the extreme of destitution and hunger, remains an eligible condition for service and loyalty? The plague which broke out in the following season with the perturbation arising concurrently from the moral collapse of the citizenry and the misery of the war refugees pointed to the impossibility of separating liberty from a certain degree of general well-being, the soul of democracy from its economic body.

"It is true that we are called a democracy, for the administration is in the hands of the many and not of the few." How many? And who are they? In other words: What is the people (the demos) who are the people by whom and for whom rulership is exercised in democracy as defined by Lincoln?

Lenin repeated a truth which had been understood or self-understood by everybody in every age when stating that freedom in the ancient Greek republics was "freedom for the slave-owners." For the most exemplary of those democracies, the Athenian as described by Pericles, the qualification is not enough. Freedom was "freedom for the slave-owners in the imperial city."

What the Athenian democracy meant outside the citizenry of the imperial city, the Melians—including those among them who were slave-owners—learned soon, the Syracusans were asked (and refused) to learn. Yet the best comment to that Periclean sentence on government by the people had been offered in advance by Pericles himself in his war inaugural of the year before when admitting that Athens' "allies" are the source of Athens' strength (particularly of her revenues) while admitting in the same breath that they "will not

---

address. For particulars see my "Lincoln and Pericles: An Excursion to Sources," *Common Cause*, III (November, 1949), 182 f.

remain quiet a day after we become unable to march against them."

The analogy with democracy at home in England, France, Belgium, Holland, and government of the people (perhaps for the people, but certainly not by the people) in their colonial empires, is too obvious to be spelled out.

Less obvious is the analogy between the Periclean laissez-faire ("we are not suspicious of one another, nor angry with our neighbor if he does what he likes") and our present situation especially if those liberties are extended from the citizenry of one community to the interrelations among all; in which case any neighbor or stranger is eligible as a good neighbor. The acme of liberalism in this sense was reached by those statesmen in our time—particularly British: Churchill, Eden, Bevin—who said or say that Nazis and Communists could stay Nazi or Communist at home; in which case we, democrats in our own home, can even abstain from putting "sour looks" at the different neighbor.

In a similar vein of pride and confidence Pericles had stated: "Our form of government does not enter into rivalry with the institutions of others." But that olympic simile was not remembered, after defeat and disaster, by the Thirty Tyrants. It was to be totally absent from the Republic of Plato.

There had been, to be sure, a brief time for ideological isolationism—with some kind of contemplative equanimity and skepticism as a part of faith (UNESCO question No. 26)—at the provisional close of the Persian wars. They had been ideological, too, in that they opposed Greek liberty to oriental despotism. The upshot for the time being had been, tentatively, that there was room enough for both systems. The Persian might stay a subject in Persia; the Greek, a citizen in Greece. Herodotus, and to a certain extent Aeschylus himself, polarized the contrast, which was not inevitably a conflict, on conditions of heredity and surrounding which they deemed practically as ineradicable as they were connatural to the two nations. Thus they anticipated, more sharply than Aristotle did after them, the localized and racialized concept of democracy which Montesquieu and Rousseau were to bequeath to countless thinkers (or half-thinkers) and political schemers in our contemporary West.

The adjustment between Persia and Greece as permanent sources of two disparate principles was precarious. It soon gave way to a *tertium quid* which, however, institutionally speaking, was much more closely related to the Persian type than to the Hellenic. The coexistence of two in mutual isolation or insulation within two peaceably recognized spheres of influence did not work long between Athens and Sparta. It did not work, after brief years of futile efforts on either side, between Nazi-Fascism and the West. It did not work, after briefer efforts, between Sovietism and Naziism. It could not work between Sovietism and Democracy as the West understands democracy, if a cold war is, as it is, a war.

All the foregoing is to the effect: (*a*) that the inquiry on the meaning and correct usage of the keyword, or holy word, Democracy, is—neither did the inquirers intend it otherwise—a sample test in a laboratory of semantics, whose results, if any, affect the whole interpretation of the democratic principle and of its applications through all ages and places; (*b*) and that, in fact, the difficulties and ambiguities in the usage of the word are not the result of the particular circumstances under which we are struggling, but reflect inner antinomies of the concept which have proved refractory to an ultimate synthesis from the earliest (possibly Pericles') definition to the later (e.g., Lincoln's) and latest.

Wherever and whenever the source of sovereignty is laid in the people, there is democracy.

Undemocratic by definition are only such regimes whose source of sovereignty is laid in divine right, or inheritable caste privilege, or sheer **force.**

There are cross-breeds, such as constitutional monarchies where certain remainders of the dynastic and caste principle are preserved while the popular will plays a preponderant role.

A different kind of cross-breed was attempted by Fascism. Fascism stressed the importance, and even the decisiveness, of force. But it did not hold that a government could stably "sit on bayonets." It did not adopt unreservedly the norm: "*Oderint dum metuant.*" The use of force (e.g., in Italy or Spain) or the threat of force (e.g., in Hitler's rise) was construed as either an explosion of the popular will breaking through the crust of the disintegrating old regime or as a short cut to win the consent of the people.

Fascism, moreover, strove for democratic justification in two ways: by borrowing the label of "revolution" and by presenting a variant of the democratic concept of mass (as the class of the underprivileged many, proletariat) in the neo-nationalistic concept of the "proletarian nations," the have-nots, bidding for a fairer distribution of goods against the owner nations. Mussolini did not mean to be entirely ironical when defining Fascism as "a strongly accentuated democracy," though, as was noted, "the accent crushed the word but the word protested."

But there is no way, in strict definitional terms, of contesting the use of the keyword democracy to Sovietism, once admitted, as Sovietism admits, that the source of sovereignty is in the people (government *by*) and that the purpose of government is the welfare of the people (government *for*).

Even in regard to the ultimate aim of democratic government, which is the self-obliteration of government, East and West agree. They jointly oppose Fascism, a pessimistic—hence, in Eastern-Western view, inherently undemocratic—doctrine maintaining that government and the use of force (also war) are eternal.

The Marxist-Leninist vision of the "withering away" of the state coincides with the Jefferson-Thoreau line of thought according to which the government is best that governs least—hence, ultimately, that does not govern at all.

The variances appear when the terms of the theoretical definition are refracted in the prisma of the historically conditioned practices.

Those variances should be summarized under four headings. The headings are necessarily interlocked, more or less closely, with one another.

I. MEMBERSHIP IN THE CONSTITUENCY OF SOVEREIGNTY CALLED "THE PEOPLE"

The democracy of Athens was restricted to the slave-owner citizenry of the imperial city. In England and France, not to speak of more recent democracies, democratic sovereignty was long reserved to the propertied electorate. In some cases, such as the Swiss, democracy is still contained within the male half of the demos.

Children are nowhere, nor could they be, included in the membership of sovereignty; women can. Criminals and demented cannot; the unpropertied and pariahs can. The colored and colonials should. (More exactly, there should be no colonials.)

Early America engraved in the Declaration of Independence the equality of all men, but withheld the application of the principle from the slaves. Its democracy, in this respect, was of the Athenian type.

Lincoln's America emancipated juridically the colored, but was unable to fulfil the promise of political equality. Up-to-date America is still a restricted democracy—though no longer of the rigid Athenian type—with sovereignty residing in a majority of first-classers to the partial exclusion or impediment of nether ranks.

As long as no present danger of disruption or degradation is involved, *that democracy is most democratic whose membership is maximum.*

From this angle Soviet—or "people's"—"democracy" has an edge on the Western democracies.

The Western democracies confess, however regretfully, to the persistence among them of racial discrimination or colonial rulership or both, in varying degrees. They are sorry. They look forward, sincerely, to more faithful days.

The Eastern "democracy" disclaims, or at least proclaims to disclaim, discrimination, racial or colonial, altogether. Its demos is assumed to be whole. Whatever suppressive or exterminating actions that democracy has undertaken against one section of the population or another, they were undertaken from motives allegedly politico-social, never avowedly from an impulse of racial or folkish supremacy.

Those actions, therefore, no matter how ruthless, do not affect the propaganda value of the keyword (people's) "democracy," in Russian usage, among Asiatics, Negroes, and subject peoples.

The Yugoslav schism itself left that value intact, as confirmed by the subsequent events in China, inasmuch as Yugoslavia did not cease to be a "people's democracy" when she defied a particular application, not the principle.

II. DELEGATION OF POWER

Power, even in the smallest community, is always delegated.

In proportion as the basic community expands in space and time, the operation of what has been celebrated—part delusionally, part deservedly—as the "direct democracy" of town-meeting or forum, fails. Indirect democracy takes its place. A growing amount of power is intrusted to delegates.

Genetically the representative, or "deputy," is an ambassador of his own basic community to the king, or to the convention of the ambassadors from the sister communities. He is an exponent or spokesman (an "orator," as ambassadors to foreign potentates were called in the Renaissance), a transmitter of messages, with a specific and imperative mandate.

He then achieves a twofold promotion. On the one hand he becomes a representative of the nation, or collectively of the sister communities, at large. He is urged more and more to stand for the interests of the all-comprehensive entity, above—and if need be against—those of the territorial or syndical constituency from which he drew his mandate. On the other hand, while concurrently, the mandate ceases to be imperative. The representative, formerly an envoy or spokesman, assumes—one might say "usurps" if the word, freed of blemish, might be made etymologically to mean "he takes for use"—a power of self-determination which makes him the arbiter of his speech and vote, regardless of what his electorate may feel or will, on any issue which may be presented in the assembly of his peers.

Survivals of the original relationship are observable, most conspicuously in America, in the mail or wires or petitions or polls or other manifestations by which the elector tries to determine on a particular issue the conduct of *his* congressman. The congressman certainly is aware of the relevance of such pressure in regard to his chances for re-election ("Remember in November"). As a rule he will wish to comply. His mandate nonetheless remains arbitrary (or sovereign). It is not brought back to the stage when it was assumed to be of a conditional (or "imperative" or "ambassadorial") nature. The representative who evades or repels the pressure is not subject to recall.

Other processes convergent in the same direction, such as the concentration of functions in the bureaucratic order or the assignment of discretionary authority to the executive, are no less known. *Under any democratic circumstances the power vested in the majority is exercised by a minority.*

It is possible to conceive a democratic system with component parts borrowed from the dynastic and hereditary caste system (as in England and other countries of northwestern Europe) or with reflexes from elective monarchy only (as in America) or with neither kinship (as in Switzerland). But it is impossible to conceive a democracy without a ruling class—though not caste—operating on the body politic in a way analogous to the leadership of the brain in the individual person.

Renan's "Prayer on the Acropolis," if we believe his date (1865), is practically simultaneous with the Gettysburg address (1863) which he anyway did not know. That Prayer is a strange piece, beginning with an incantation and winding up in a recantation.

The incantation offers one more variation on the theme of the Periclean address. To the other virtues of democracy Renan adds peace, which lay implicit in the intellectual tolerance of Pericles, but was not yet explicitly familiar to the self-inclosed city state and could not be introduced into the universal concept of democracy until a threefold medium was opened by Stoicism, Roman world-citizenship, and Christian universality.

"Peace is thy aim," Renan prayed, "O Pacific one. Legislatrice, source of just constitutions: Democracy, thou whose fundamental dogma is that everything good comes from the people, and that whenever there is not a people to feed and inspire genius, there is nothing left. . . ."

Thus the source of sovereignty is located once more in the people, yet as the feeder of the sovereign "genius." "Democracy, thou whose fundamental dogma is," etc., so went on the prayer, "*teach us to extract the diamond from the foul mob.*" The Athenians knew how; we cannot learn the lesson because the conditions within which the Athenian democracy grew cannot be duplicated at will. Those conditions Renan made clear in the prefatory page he added later, playing safe. The Athenian democracy was a success because the whole people of Athens—so, right or wrong, he thought—was "a people of aristocrats." In other terms, if we trust him rather than Aristophanes, there was there no "foul mob." This introduces the motif of the recantation. Aesthetic skepticism replaces the Periclean fervor.

The whole passage, more admired than admirable, is nevertheless a telling instance of the conflict between the idea of democratic sovereignty and the fact of delegated power—in other words, between majority right and minority might—which was nearly lifelong in Renan's mind and has not yet been mediated in the collective mind.

That there is in historical practice no such thing as a democracy by direct majority rule, in the same way as there is no such thing as a monarchy by single-handed autocratic rule, has been a self-evident truth at least since Machiavelli's *Discorsi,* while not occult to common sense before. Any democracy acts through delegation, any autocracy acts through an articulation of hierarchs and partners. It should seem accordingly that the common denominator of all kinds of government is "oligarchy," government by the few.

"Oligarchy," however, is a term whose connotations are usually derogatory. "Aristocracy" in turn has connotations which etymology and usage have made laudatory, besides pointing in ordinary language to inheritable superiority and privilege. In the wake of Mosca and Pareto a neutral term, "élite," has gained wide acceptance. It points to selectivity alone, and is applicable without judgment or prejudice to any type of delegated power, better or worse, closed or open. It seems that any thinker worthy of this name should agree in describing monarchy as "government of the people by one ruler through a few," aristocracy or oligarchy as "government of the people by the few," democracy as "government of the people by the people through a few." The distinctive features of a democratic élite are only that it is appointive, not self-appointed or king-appointed; and that it is fluctuating, open, and statutorily pro tem, not stable, closed, nor hereditary or otherwise self-perpetuating. There is no distinctive feature in regard to quality. A democratic élite can rise to be an aristocracy, government by the best, or sink to demagogy as "cheiristocracy," or government by the worst.

Yet, in the field of democratic semantics East and West, it is relevant: (a) how the élite, or government through the few, is appointed; (b) how few are the few.

In regard to (a), there certainly is semantic agreement among the contrasting regimes of our age in placing the source of sovereignty in the popular mass. Not only Socialism, Communism, Bolshevism (literally the majority) signify the all-demos. Fascism itself (the bundle) and its derivatives, National Socialism, Phalange, totality or totalitarianism of every kind, emphasize the collectivity. They dissent on the processes through which the delegations are picked.

Ancient and modern democracies of the Mediterranean and Atlantic type have developed the electoral, in due course parliamentary, system. They have carried it to ultimate integration in the equal and secret suffrage of all adults.

One error of these democracies consists apparently in the identification of the universal idea of democracy with its particular embodiment in their electoral machinery. It may be upheld that other processes are optional.

It may even be suggested that appointment by lot is intrinsically more democratic (cf. a number of cases in antiquity; also our own panels of jurors; also a forecast of democratic progress in this direction by H. G. Wells).

The founder of Fascism railed at the Western or liberal elections, called them "paper games." He had nonetheless plenty of "elections"—and so had Naziism—not only on account of tactics but also because lip-service to an idol whose altar is not quite overthrown adds insult to injury.

Bolshevik theorists have disputed in a more serious vein the uniqueness of electoralism as the expression of democracy. Their mockery has been in deeds rather than in words. It is achieved—as for that matter it was achieved in the Axis countries and is now in Iberia and several areas of Hispanidad—by the suppression of all competitive candidacy and campaign and by the near unanimous returns. In Soviet Manchuria they were unanimous.

In this respect, as in several others, Fascism and Sovietism coincide, for they have conditioned each other in a tortuous sequence of mutual influences originating either way in the all-comprehensiveness of one class (dictatorship of the proletariat) or party—which, no longer a part, is now the whole.

In substance—under the superficial travesty of elections as usual—what both totalitarian "democracies" propose and practice is the appointment of the political élite by plebiscitarian acclamation instead of by electoral machinery. It may be argued—borrowing a phrase from the UNESCO inquiry—that, "seen from a planetary point of view," the contrast loses much of its sharpness.

It might even be argued in theory that acclamation is intrinsically more democratic than secret balloting, for secrecy presupposes fear and pressure whereas the openness of acclamation postulates courage and freedom. The argument, of course, is a sophism; for acclamation—or election so devised as to be tantamount to it—creates actually the fear and pressure which the secret ballot aims at preventing.

As for (b) (How few are the few?) of course no answer can be given in numbers and percentages. The issue is empirical not doctrinal. At the beginning of the Peloponnesian war an enormous amount of power was concentrated in the hands of one man, Pericles; yet that man, a prince among peers, could still praise his city as the exemplar of democracy. Near the end of the war the top rulers of Athens were awhile four hundred, exponents of five thousand; but the new regime was *de jure* an oligarchy and *de facto* a tyranny.

It can be stated nevertheless that, *coeteris paribus*, when the few are too few a democracy is more liable to result in an oligarchy of the degenerative type, with the power of the élite, finally of the autocrat, resting upon force and fear. It is along this trend that the people's (or economic) democracy of the East has developed its traits of political resemblance with the monarchies of Byzantium and Persia.

Conclusively it can be stated that, while power is always delegated, and while it is not possible (UNESCO question No. 21) to trace exactly "a line of demarcation between 'democratic' and 'undemocratic' delegation of decision power," *that democracy is most democratic where the delegation of power happens under the maximum conditions of persuasion and freedom, under the minimum conditions of pressure and force*, and *that democracy is best where the ruling élite is most numerous and most open to accession and change.*

Democratic perfection would be in a community which could be described as "a whole people of aristocrats." Such a community never dwelt anywhere, save in the visionary Athens of Renan, nor is such a perfection reliably approximated by the Western democracies of today. Their danger of extinction in totalitarian Fascism is hypothetical, and probably overstated; but their decadence in quality is actual.

Yet there can be no doubt that, if tested on the exercise of power and on the processes of the delegation of power, the preposition *by* (government by the people) applies much more correctly to the Western than to the Eastern type of "democracy." From this point of view the Western use of the keyword may be "recommended" as approximately appropriate; the East should be charged with "misuse."

III. SOCIAL VS. OR PLUS POLITICAL DEMOCRACY

Save in some lunatic fringes of aestheticism and hyper-Nietzscheanism, the final clause of the Gettysburg dogma ("government . . . *for* the people") is indorsed equally by East and West.

The contrast as formulated by Bertrand Russell is more striking than convincing.

"The [Anglo-Saxon] definition of 'democracy,' " thus UNESCO quotes him, "is that it consists in the rule of the majority; the Russian view is that it consists in the interests of the majority [these interests being determined in accordance with Marxist political philosophy]."

I have bracketed one word entailing a racial monopoly which history rejects. It should be replaced. I have also bracketed ten words whose relevance is incidental. They should be omitted.

Even so the dilemma is logically questionable. For it is impossible to conceive a "rule of the majority" in which that rule is or may be deliberately or consciously at variance with the "interests of the majority." Such a democracy should be defined the government of the people by the people against the people.

Something of the kind might obtain only in a fictive society, as sketched in UNESCO question No. 20, where 80 per cent of the "democratic" electorate is held at such a level of intellectual and economic inferiority as to make its blind suffrage available for a minority of oppressors. This, a democracy of dupes, would be democracy by forgery.

If "democracies" of this kind were extant, there would be a point in Gromyko's definition of his own "people's democracy." Our purpose, he said, is the well-being of all the people, "whether they like it or not."

The capital error of capitalist democracy, still unabjured in some tory quarters, is the identification (a logical and historical violence) of political freedom with a freedom of economic enterprise inclusive of the freedom to subjugate the other fellow.

The Lincoln of Gettysburg and after was aware of this and similar distortions in the use of religions and doctrines. In what Carl Sandburg calls "the President's last, shortest, and best speech" he said to a lady from Tennessee pleading for the release of her husband, a prisoner of war: "You say your husband is a religious man; tell him when you meet him that, in my opinion, the religion that sets men to rebel and fight against their government, because, as they think, that government does not sufficiently help *some* men to eat their bread in the sweat of *other* men's faces, is not the sort of religion upon which people can get to heaven." This applies also to the religion of political vs. social democracy.

The same inference in regard to the social and economic structure of a political democracy is contained in the remark of Albert Schweitzer that "Those who have very little that they can call their own are in most danger of becoming purely egoistic. A deep truth lies in the parable of Jesus, which makes the servant who had received least the least faithful of all."

The disassociation of the political from the socio-economic is as unworkable as is, at least on earth, the disassociation of soul from body. Democracy is a body-soul.

The feeling of interdependence between the two aspects of a popular society—one might say, between the two faces of the same coin—is making, however toilsomely, headway in the West. Roosevelt's "freedom from want," British socialism, and a general drive everywhere toward planned economy as a subspecies of socialism, point in one direction. Economic royalism—or orthodox economic liberalism, which means the same—though counting a certain number of powerful devotees in some die-hard stronghold, exerts a dwindling appeal on responsible statesmanship.

It would be delusional to say that the "people's democracy" on its part is undertaking the same effort to meet political democracy halfway. Its accent lies still overwhelmingly on "government *for* the people" rather than *by*.

However, as long as penury and subjugation are so appalling on most of the earth, and as long as the Western proposals for a merger of the political with the social remain irresolute and slow, the strictly social democracy has a case.

It has been said that "bread without liberty *in the long run* is poison." But liberty without bread is immediately derision. "Men who do not have bread call bread liberty and do not care for any other kind." With a bitter jest it has even been said that "liberty begins at breakfast."

At the present stage there is no immanent conflict of doctrines, "from a planetary point of view," between West and East. "Classic capitalism and classic communism are romantic: both bygones." Both East and West proclaim allegiance to the "rule of the majority"—however delegated—and to the "interests of the majority"—however specified—as well.

The difference which stands out is that political democracy still stresses, though not unreservedly, "equality of opportunity," social

democracy "equality of status." The latter too is a deceptive promise, but equality of opportunity is a Fata Morgana.

Right or wrong, men today placed before a choice between equality (were it even equality of privation) and struggle for privilege,
choose equality. To the mass feeling of our time an egg today is more
satisfactory than the chicken tomorrow.

Hence the feeling—deep-seated in enormous masses of colored
and poor whites—that the keyword democracy, in this respect, is
more legitimately used by social than by political democracy.

IV. TOLERANCE (OR POLITICO-INTELLECTUAL LIBERALISM)

As there is no government by the people without a delegation of
power, no democracy without an oligarchy, so there neither is nor
ever was or could be a totally liberal democracy with no censorship
or repression of any sort.

Freedom of worship is limited to "superior" religions. Cruel cults
or ritual prostitution are crimes. Even the pious polygamy of the
Mormons is banned. Freedom of expression is not extended to the
propaganda of murder or to the sale of obscenities. Freedom of
peaceful assembly is not undisputed even to the innocence of a nudist
convention.

The demarcation line between the wrong of the judge who pro-
hibits *Madame Bovary* or *Ulysses* and the right of the judge who
punishes the printer of "art pictures" for adults, is too vague for any
statutory pencil to draw. The distinction between free speech and
"overt act" is utterly empirical. It shifts according to circumstances
and moods. It is practically deleted in cases of real or alleged "emergency."

Tolerance then—or, as more positively it is called, liberalism—in
each and all cases is valid only within the limits frankly or tacitly set
to it by the common beliefs, strictly or broadly religious, on which a
certain society is assumed to rest.

All that can be said is that *that democracy is best within which the
orbit of tolerance is largest.*

In the frame of our time it should be said that *that democracy
would be ideally the best which would feel strong and secure enough
to allow maximal liberty to any kind of propaganda even if aimed at
leftist subversion or fascist usurpation.*

There is no doubt, in the present frame of reference, that the
political democracies of the West, though engaged—particularly the

American—in a process of restriction, are still remote from censorship and intolerance as practiced in the social democracy of Soviet type, where music itself is conducted by the state and political opposition of any kind is outlawed.

The latter point is crucial. For wholesale conformism, exacted permanently, obliterates the self-determination of the mind which is a basic element of whatever may have been called in democratic language "the dignity of the human person."

If bread without liberty in the long run is poison, the run of the Soviet "people's democracy"—thirty-two years—has been long enough. A sacrifice of this magnitude, when demanded beyond the time limits of a passing emergency, exceeds the limits of democracy as an historically justifiable proposition.

Should this aspect of Soviet "democracy" last longer, its dialectic materialism would have to pass into some sort of eschatological mysticism like the Orthodox Church which preceded it; democracy woud be theocracy. If no reward in liberty, which is spiritual happiness, can be reliably promised to the present generation or its visible offspring, then the mutilation and abdication cannot be legitimized anywhere but in Millennium and Heaven.

The burden of all the foregoing is that the usage of the keyword democracy is neither wholly legitimate nor wholly illegitimate either West or East. The credentials for its validity are torn in two—like, one might say, the two coupons of a claim check between holder and claimant—in the same way as the content of the concept which that word expresses and its actuality in contemporary history are cut in halves. It seems incontestable, however, that, whatever the failures and defaults, the Western half is conceptually the larger and tendentially in practice the more susceptible to integration and growth. If that is so, the use of the keyword, though imperfect in both cases, is still less arbitrary in the political than in the social democracies at their present stage.

As for the concept of democracy in its perfection and plenitude, I should like to recall a splendid page by the French critic, Ramon Fernandez, where he makes it clear that full health is the abnormal, imperfect health or disease is the norm, the classical and harmonious is the exception, the defective and jarring is the rule.

The same is true of Democracy, as it is of any other Idea (with capital *i*).

The comparative success and comparatively long duration of "Anglo-Saxon" democracy has altered the perspective to a number of Western observers who have contemplated or are contemplating democracy as a permanent and necessarily victorious factor of history.

As a matter of fact democracy always was an emergence of limited expansion in time as well as in space and depth. Through whole stretches of history, under whole continents, it lay unknown or buried.

This is why so perturbing a veil of melancholy is spread over the democratic panegyric of Pericles. Its pathos is not so much born of the heroic mournful occasion of the address—nor of the ex post facto emotions of the reporter, Thucydides, and ourselves, the readers—as it is intrinsic to the caducity of the very thing he praised. It sounds as if he spoke, almost at a last supper, in awareness of an imminent end.

The same sadness, more evidently, sounds in the Gettysburg address. Lincoln is not unfurling the banner of democracy to ultimate triumph for every time and everywhere. His hope and conditional promise are that democracy "shall not perish from the earth." He speaks as if he felt that that ideal is embattled and battered, with one stronghold only left. If that stronghold falls, the whole thing may perish from the earth.

Imperishable nevertheless democracy is in so far as it sets a regulatory ideal, whose substance is faith. Its actual successes may well be in all cases partial and aleatory or precarious—or, in black ages, none. Its potential validity remains supreme and whole as long as man has faith in man.

Concerning the chances in the years ahead for a democratic emergence apt to merge the political with the social and to lift the disputed keyword to the authority of a holyword, two factors in our world society militate for optimism.

One is technology, whose coresponsibilities encompass all strata of population and all condition of life.

The other is evolution, the religion of our age, inasmuch as evolution makes the individual responsible to the species and the species to the individual.

The optimism, however, must be qualified.

For the industrial revolution resulted in the despotism of the factory. Together with its counterpart, mass conscription, it resulted in total war.

Evolution is the religion of our age. But it falls into two churches. One is the sect of Eris (struggle for life and ascendancy of the fittest), the other is the church of Eros (mutual aid). The latter calls for democracy, the former for autocracy and Fascism.

The oration of Pericles confides ·to the inquiring eye the pitfalls of his democracy (and ours). It discloses openly the way which should be trodden toward improvement and fulfilment.

This happens in the final sentence of the paragraph from which these pages took their cue: that sentence where he speaks in religious fervor of the "spirit of reverence," of "especial regard" to the laws "which are ordained for the protection of the injured," and most intensely of "those unwritten laws which bring upon the transgressor of them the reprobation of the general sentiment."

If Pericles and Athenian democracy had lived up to their faith they would have counted among the "injured" their slaves and their "allies" (i.e., imperial underdogs)—though it might have been too early to behave altogether accordingly.

The injured and humbled in our world are obviously the colored, the colonials, and the destitute. If when we say democracy we mean democracy, we must know this—and behave, before it is too late, accordingly.

Nobody can say what nation or group of nations may have leadership in an eventual advance toward some fuller actuation of democracy (keyword and holyword).

It is stirring anyway to note that England, trained by her age-long initiatory experience in institutional and political liberty, claims once more a vanguard assignment in the convergent efforts toward a new democracy which should join the political with the social and make of liberal socialism (a centaur, a contradiction in terms, as Tories see it) a live thing.

The British experiment might well become exemplary if the peaceable liquidation of the British Empire—which is, ethically and socially, the mandatory corollary abroad of democracy at home—is not thwarted or excessively slowed by greed and fear: in which case all the glories of London would avail no more than those of the Athenian democracy did in the Peloponnesian War.

But anticipations and admonitions are beyond the scope of this excursus in semantics.

IV

D. VAN DANTZIG

An inquiry into the function of words used in ideological conflicts can only be of little moment, if it is restricted to an investigation of their relations with other words, or even their relations with objects, events or situations represented by them. Questions as to whether two definitions of the term "democracy" are in accordance with each other, or even whether this term is "justly" or "unjustly" applied to a specified form of government are in themselves of little importance. As to the latter question this is the more true if the valuations underlying the distinction between "justly" and "unjustly" remain unmentioned. Such an inquiry can be helpful in classifying the nature of the conflicts only if the function of a word is considered as a relation in a *triple* respect: (1) to other words, (2) to objects (or situations or occurrences, actions, etc.) denoted by them, (3) to subjects (persons or groups of persons) using them or influenced by them. Whereas in logic the relations 1 and in empirical sciences the relations 2 are the most important ones, here the relations 3 will be the most relevant.[1]

The most elementary form of the phenomena which we have to investigate can therefore not be a single word with its linguistic or etymological properties. Nor can it be a sentence or a more extensive system of words with its logical or syntactical properties, nor even the semantical relations between words and objects (e.g., "denotation," "designation," etc.), but only an *action consisting in the actual use of words*. Such an action will be called an *act of discourse*. The subjects concerned with such an act of discourse, can, if it is of oral form, be divided into *speakers* and *listeners*. These terms will be used in a metaphorical extension, also if the act of discourse is not of an oral nature. So the term "speaker" will be used, as the case may be, also for a "writer," "singer," "actor," "player," "painter," etc.

1. This trichotomy corresponds to the one introduced by Charles W. Morris: syntactics, semantics, and pragmatics. See his *Foundations of the Theory of Signs* (Chicago, 1938).

46

and the term "listener" for "reader" and other persons observing the act or indirectly influenced by it. Generally we shall call the *speaker's aspects* of an act of discourse all phenomena which can be considered as having influenced the act (i.e., having contributed to it as causes). On the other hand, by the term *"listener's aspects"* are meant all phenomena which can be considered as having *been influenced* by it. If, e.g., the act of discourse under consideration is an interview given by a statesman to a news reporter, not only the latter counts as a listener, but also the readers of the interview when published, or persons who have heard about it, without actually having heard it, etc.

In the same way we count as speakers (or, if the distinction is necessary, as cospeakers), e.g., the civil servant who has drawn up the text of the interview or parts of it, the superiors or colleagues of the statesman, with whom he has discussed the text, the desirability and the expediency of the interview, etc. Among the listener's aspects we must also consider the influence the act of discourse has on the speaker himself, whose further behavior may partially be altered by it. In exactly the same way the speaker's aspects comprehend actions of the listener also, e.g., his actually listening, or his behavior during (or before) the act which often greatly influences, e.g., the choice of words by the speaker.

Although conceptual research should preferably be done in an experimental way by observing actual acts of discourse, the means and methods for such observations often fail. In the majority of cases we therefore have to be content with a semi-empirical investigation, which consists in combining parts of the numerous acts of discourse actually observed into a "fictitious" one. Our general experience is often quite sufficient to imagine, how under given circumstances such an act would develop.

II

It hardly needs saying that the speaker's aspects of an act of discourse often greatly differ from the listener's aspects. E.g., a statesman propagates in a speech—as has been done in both World Wars—the idea that his country should go to war "in order to make the world safe for democracy." The latter term may, and often does, have quite a different meaning for him than for the hearer, who, convinced (or persuaded) by his speech actually enlists. If, the war being won, the soldier who comes back does not find democracy realized—viz., democracy as he understands it—he may feel deceived and call the statesman a demagogue, sometimes rather unjustly, because the latter may not have been very well aware at all of any difference between his views on the nature of "democracy" and his audience's.

Such an act of discourse may be said to have been a failure, at least in a considerable part of its listener's aspects. For the expectations the listener had with regard to the consequences of his behaving according to the speaker's advice were not fulfilled on account of an *unnoticed difference between the interpretations of the speaker's words.* Maybe the listener, if he had understood the speaker's interpretation better, would not have enlisted. Perhaps he would even have actually opposed his country's participation in the war. Maybe the speaker, if he had actually foreseen the listener's subsequent disillusion, would have used other arguments fitting in better with the latter's actual desires. But maybe also, of course, the speaker knew about the discrepancy between the interpretations and deliberately made use of it in order to attain his ends. In such a case the listener may easily come to charge the speaker afterward with "misuse" of the term "democracy." Nevertheless the latter may feel quite justified about his way of using it, as it is, e.g., in accordance with definitions given by several well-known authors.

The question whether such a listener was "justified" or not in stamping such a speaker's use of the term "democracy" as a "misuse" is of no importance. Equally unimportant is the question whether the speaker was "justified" or not in stamping the political, social, and/or economic structure of the country expected by him a "democracy." The listener thinks the speaker "misused" the term "democracy," and the speaker thinks the (former) listener "misused" the term "misuse."

The important thing is the fact that the speaker and the listener both *used* the term "democracy" as designating a structure they approved of, but that the observable characteristics which a structure *should have* to obtain their approval were different.

Conceptual research should for these reasons not be restricted—as it is often done—to the comparison of the different *speakers'* aspects of words in different acts of discourse (e.g., different definitions given in books by political scientists or in speeches by politicians or statesmen, etc.). But it should take into account also, or even in the first place, the different *listeners'* aspects and the differences between speaker's and listener's aspects. Moreover, these aspects should not be restricted to the *objects* designated by the words according to speaker and listener, but should include also their *valuations* of such objects, and their *efforts* to change situations they observe.

A word (or a group of words) used in different acts of discourse shows some variability within the speaker's and within the listener's aspects as well as between the speaker's and the listener's aspects. This variability in its different forms will be called the "dispersion" of the word. Although we do not possess any precise definition, nor a method of measuring or precisely estimating the degrees of dispersion of different terms, we can roughly distinguish terms with "large" from terms with "small" dispersion. This could be done somewhat more precisely, e.g., within the listener's aspects by studying the variability in reactions of test persons when hearing the word in various contexts and circumstances.

III

A word within some context generally has some descriptive function (or content), i.e., its relation to the "constatations" of conformity and disparity by speaker(s) and listener(s). It also has often some *emotive function*[2] (or content), i.e., its relation to the emotions of speaker(s) and listener(s). In so far as it is related to emotions of preference, it will be said metaphorically to have a *"positive"* and in so far as it is related to emotions of aversion a *"negative charge."* It often occurs, in particular in political discussions, that two words have practically the same descriptive function, but contrasting emotive functions. This happens if the two words are being used to describe the same object (under which terms we subsume also a situation or an event, etc.) by persons opposedly affected by it. (Examples: "heroic"—"reckless"; "to sustain authority"—"to oppress"; "fighter for right and liberty"—"rebel," "insurgent"—"mischief-maker," etc.)

It is a general experience in conceptual analysis that a person applying a term with strong emotive function to a situation by which

2. A term suggested for the Dutch *"emotionele betekenis"* introduced by Mannoury in 1925.

he is profoundly affected, will not admit, will not even understand often that its "opposite" has the same or almost the same descriptive function. It is only by applying the term to cases which are very remote from the source of affection that one can sometimes make him see the conformity of the descriptive functions. But even then it happens in the majority of cases that he will transpose the source of affection to the remote case also and apply to it his double valuation.

This difficulty is increased by the fact that *some* difference in descriptive function often remains. To take a rather clear example: not every "fighter for justice and liberty" will be called by his enemies a "mischief-maker" and still less will every "mischief-maker" be called a "fighter for justice and liberty" by his admirers. The relation between such terms is rather of a *correlative* nature: in a large number of acts of discourse where one of the terms is applied to an object by persons positively affected by it, the other (or another analogous) term will be applied to the same object by persons negatively affected by it.

This of course raises the question in how far it is possible to attribute to the distinction between descriptive and emotive functions a scientific character, i.e., in how far it is independent of the emotions of the investigator himself. It would lead us too far, however, to go into this question here.

Closely connected with the emotive function of a word, and originally not clearly distinguished from it, is its *volitive function*,[3] i.e., its relation to the speaker's and listener's volitions, in particular to their momentary expectations of their own future behavior. It comprises in particular the speaker's expectations of the change in the hearer's volitions—and, of course, in the hearer's behavior itself—which will be caused by the act of discourse. This aspect of the volitive function may be called the *"incitive function."*

Clearly *some* volitive and even incitive functions can be found in any act of discourse, e.g., simply by asking: "*Why* does the speaker speak and *why* does the listener listen?" But the difficulties mentioned above with regard to discerning the emotive function exist for the volitive function also.

IV

Let us apply these terms to the example mentioned above concerning the difference between speaker's and listener's aspects of an

3. Mannoury: *"volitionelle bedeutung."*

act of discourse which contained a plea for "making the world safe for democracy." We can state that the speaker's and listener's aspects were sufficiently in accord with regard to the *emotive* content of the term "democracy," to which both, speaker and hearer, attributed a strong positive valuation. But then they are at variance with regard to the *descriptive* content of the term, i.e., the characteristics of a structure to which they attributed the term, and also with regard to its *volitive* content, which for one of them may have been the desire to maintain the structure in their country as it was, and for the other to have it altered in a more or less definite way. We might have considered instead of the word "democracy" a description of the form of government existing in their country, which the speaker's speech might also have contained. In that case accordance with regard to the descriptive content may have been considerably greater (though still probably far from complete), but the same discordance which existed before with regard to the descriptive content would then have existed in the emotive content. In fact, it is not necessarily linked up with the term "democracy," or any other word at all: it is based on different *valuations of the actual structure* of the state or of those parts of the structure which each of them actually experiences as fundamental for his conditions of life. Anyhow this underlying difference is of an emotional nature, even if it appears as a difference concerning the *descriptive* content of a term.

This example shows us that it is not sufficient to investigate, whether or not the descriptive, emotive and volitive contents agree in speaker's and listener's aspects. The main problem is to find out *which* observations, *which* valuations, and *which* efforts are expressed by a term in the speaker's and the listener's aspects. Consequently conceptual research becomes to a considerable degree an inquiry into the political, social and economic characteristics of society as a subject *experiences* them, his *valuations* of them and his efforts to *maintain* or to *change* them. Thereby conceptual research is linked up with sociology, psychology and mass psychology.

An inquiry into "the meaning" of a term like "democracy" thereby automatically becomes an inquiry into the ideas and the ideals about the structure of society which are held either by individual political scientists and politicians (who use the term preponderantly as speakers) or large groups of the population (using the term chiefly as listeners [readers] and only occasionally as speakers). It is only by understanding these that the controversies about terms like "de-

mocracy" can be understood. On the other hand from these controversies something can be learned about them. The chief importance
of a conceptual analysis of terms like "democracy" lies in the opportunity they give to find out the underlying emotions and volitions,
and afterwards to express these in a clearer way than is done by
these terms.

V

The main function of the term "democracy" is, I think, rather of
an emotive and a volitive than of a descriptive nature.

The term is used in most cases with a *positive* valuation; the Nazis
usually did not use a term strictly belonging to the "word-family"
"democracy," but some bastardizations like "demo-liberal." Restricting ourselves to the use with positive valuation, there is a very
large dispersion in the *object* of the valuation, i.e., in the elements of
the structure which cause the positive attitude.

This gives rise to difficulties because most authors consider those
elements by which they themselves are positively affected as (necessary and/or sufficient) criteria for the applicability of the term "democracy." These difficulties are increased by the fact that most of
these authors apply the term to structures in which *they believe* the
elements that affect them to be present, a belief which is often not
shared by other authors.

Generally speaking, it seems to me that the term "democracy"
nowadays is applied in most cases to that type of structure which
the speaker would like to exist (and often believes to exist) in the
country he lives in, and which satisfies some rather variable and unprecise conditions.

VI

The term exerts its greatest influence, however, on the actual
behavior of the people in its *listener's* aspects. This is not only the
case with individuals who only occasionally use the term actively,
but in whom the ideas they associate with the term are preponderantly induced by what they have *read* or *heard* about it. They have
interpreted the term and its context in their own way, bringing it
into accordance with their own experience, expectations, wishes,
and volitions. Therefore, the listener's aspects may be—and, very
often are—greatly different from the speaker's ones, *and are hardly
or not at all expressed* by the "definitions."

Perhaps an individual case may illustrate this. During the interbellum an American professor once visited Moscow. One evening he was invited, together with some other foreign scientists, to some festivity. The American did not want to attend the meeting and excused himself on the last moment by saying that he was not shaven. A Russian official accompanying the group said: "Well, that does not matter at all. We are in a democratic country here." The American answered: "Is democracy a reason not to be clean?"

For us the question is: What did the Russian intend to express by the second sentence? How was it connected with the former one? Of course we cannot know, only guess. But perhaps the following conjectured interpretation may be near to his original intentions.

Evidently the Russian knew, either by personal prerevolution experience or from hearsay, that people belonging to the poorer classes had often felt frustrated when they wished to attend luxurious or official meetings, but did not dare to go there. Perhaps they feared to be laughed at or considered uncivilized, because they had no good dress or were dirty or had work-worn hands, or some other deficiency in their outer appearance. Presumably the Russian used the term "democracy" in order to indicate his belief that this kind of frustration did not occur any more in his country, and that he appreciated this fact. The American, who may very well never have experienced such kind of frustration, answered by a witty bon mot, but could, of course, not grasp the Russian's emotions. He may perhaps have added in his thoughts: "If it is true that we are in a democratic country, no damned official shall prevent me from staying in my room when I desire to do so."

Whether this interpretation is completely or partially correct or false, the important thing for us is the fact that in any case such kinds of interpretations most frequently occur, are perhaps strong inducements to many people in their fight for democracy, but that they find hardly any expression or none at all in the current definitions.

I am inclined to regard the study of such highly fluctuating associations, which seem to be the strongest emotional motors, as the most important task of a conceptual analysis of the term "democracy" and of related political terms.

The main difficulty, of course, is the fact that we have no appropriate methods for accomplishing this task. One might think of the investigation of mass opinion. But this would probably not provide us with any but trivial results. For (1) by asking people something one can only obtain knowledge about what people know themselves, whereas often subconscious or even unconscious associations and expectations may have the greatest motive force. And (2) the great variability, in particular the small but relevant half-shades, are wiped out by the statistical treatment.

VII

Another important difficulty (apart from the fact that it will hardly be possible to obtain sufficient empirical material) lies in the mutual dependence of the descriptive, emotive, and volitive contents.

If two subjects are both accustomed to apply or not to apply a term similarly to situations by which they are affected in the same way, they often *disagree* about the applicability of the term to situations which affect them oppositely. Often each of them believes that this difference is not caused by their different affections, but that the situation "has" or "has not" the attributes required for the application of the term, i.e., if both subjects A and B apply the term to a situation S_1, neither of them to S_2, and A but not B to S_3, then the similar way in which A is *affected* by S_1 and S_3 may lead him to *describe* S_1 and S_3 similarly. Unlike B, his attention in such cases will be fixed on *similarity* between S_1 and S_3 and on *dissimilarity* between S_2 and S_3.

Example: A and B are two anti-Nazi Dutchmen with opposite views on the Dutch military action in Indonesia (S_3). Let the term the applicability of which is considered be, e.g., "attack." Let S_1 and S_2 be the German and Allied military operations on May 5, 1940, and June 6, 1944, respectively.

E.g., A may call S_3 as well as S_1 but not S_2 an "attack," by which choice of words he shows to be opposed to S_3, whereas B (assumed to approve of S_3) will apply the term to S_1, but not to S_3. A Nazi would perhaps apply it to S_2, but not to S_1. It is also easy to see, how A and B will apply or not apply terms like "liberation," "rebels," "fighters for liberty," "collaborators," etc., in the three cases.

Apart from this dependence of descriptive on emotive contents we mention also the dependence of volitive on descriptive contents. This is particularly important if, instead of direct observations, *expectations* of eventual future observations are concerned. Let us consider two subjects A and B, using the same descriptive terms for three eventual future situations S_1, S_2, S_3. Let us suppose that S_1 in itself affects none of them particularly (or both in the same way), that S_2 affects both of them positively, S_3 both of them negatively, but that A expects S_1 to lead inevitably to S_2, whereas B expects it to lead to S_3. If they both believe they have some influence on the occurrence of S_1, their volitions toward it will be of an opposite nature, because of its assumed consequences.

Example: A and B are two "socialist" politicians—I shall not try here to replace the highly emotive and vague terms by more descriptive and precise ones. S_1 is an eventual future large unemployment, S_2 a "weakening," and S_3 a "strengthening" of the "power of capitalism." If A believes S_1 to lead to S_2, and B believes it to lead to S_3, their behavior toward S_1 will be opposite. This difference in volitive contents induced by the different descriptive contents related to their different expectations, will, of course, usually have a further repercussion also on the descriptive contents of the terms they use, as mentioned before.

On the other hand we know, of course, that the expectations in their turn are not independent of the volitions. This generally known relation is often overstressed and even inverted by politicians, in order to try to "deduce" the volitions of their opponents from the expectations these express, leaving out of consideration other behavioristic symptoms ("He does not believe S_2 will occur," hence "he does not want it").

Perhaps the most important feature of this dependence of volitive on descriptive, in particular "expectative" contents is the transfer of emotion by a subject A from an eventual future situation S_2 to another S_1 which he considers a necessary and/or sufficient cause of S_2.

This is of particular importance if A is so strongly convinced of the causal relation between S_1 and S_2 that he is completely unaware of it, and consequently of the emotional transfer. He may use all his forces in striving for realization of S_1 and believes his positive valuation of S_1 to be of a fundamental nature. However, on pressing him to explain *why* he values S_1 so highly, the conceptual analyst may perhaps find out that it is only (or mainly) because he is certain of its leading to S_2. This phenomenon of "expectative wishing," as it might be called in contradistinction to "wishful expectation" has, I believe, not been very well studied, as yet, but is probably of the greatest importance in political science.

The interdependence of descriptive and emotive or volitive content is to a considerable degree effectuated by means of terms like "real," "true," "necessary," "certain," etc. We can disentangle these contents somewhat better by attributing these terms to the emotive and volitive contents, instead of to the descriptive one, as is usually done. This, however, also leads to some difficulties, into which we shall not go here.

VIII

I might remark only that the distinction between "actual" or "real" and "imaginary," "illusion," etc., has a meaning only with reference to a judging subject (or to a formal system representing his judgment). In "first approximation" a subject uses the term "real" for what *he* considers as such, and the term "illusion" for what he does not. (The question under which circumstances an individual considers a perception as a "real observation" must remain unconsidered here. The answer might be related to the perception being or not being accompanied by a complex of other perceptions which usually accompany it, e.g., a visual perception by the usually accompanying sensory or auditive perceptions, i.e., those of hearing other persons tell that they have corresponding visual perceptions.)

In "second approximation" a subject uses the term "real" for what in his expectation other individuals (eventually later generations), or at least those whom he considers as "sane," "sufficiently intelligent," etc., will consider as real (say in first approximation). *In any case the term remains relative to some such estimates by the speaker.*

IX

In a conceptual inquiring into the use of political terms something should be said about its purpose, nature, and possible effects, at least as these appear to the present author and, as he has reason to believe, to several other investigators and as they perhaps will appear to a considerably greater number of people by the time when investigations like the present one will have become better known and more generally understood.

In this sense then, the *purpose* of investigations like the present one is a clarification and a bringing to consciousness of the observations, expectations, emotions, and volitions underlying acts of discourse of a political nature, so that such acts may become more successful, in particular in their *listeners'* aspects. In other words, so that the numerous people who, willingly or unwillingly, let their actions be influenced by political acts of discourse, will find the effects of these actions to a far greater degree in accordance with the expectations raised *in them by* these acts of discourse than is at present the case. This purpose itself is, of course, to some degree of a "political" nature, though of a considerably more general and less specific kind than political purposes used to be.

With regard to the *nature* of such an investigation the author thinks it necessary, in order to reach this purpose, *to refrain as much as possible from taking part in the political controversies under examination*, to remain "philosophically detached," as it is put in the introduction to UNESCO's questionnaire. This is of particular importance as many statements which on first sight seem to be completely "detached," on closer examination appear to imply specific valuations, expectations, and volitions which are shared by one party in the controversy, so that accepting them ultimately amounts to taking part without being aware of it. This requires a most careful phrasing of one's ideas, in order to avoid as much as possible a spurious preciseness or a greater intersubjectivity than is justified. A considerable effort in this direction has been made, at the cost of an unavoidable clumsiness of formulation.

Moreover, the purpose we strive for requires that we should not pay too much attention to such questions as whether the controversial parties express their views "correctly" according to some formal scheme. An eventual conclusion on this point would only provide us with a reason for disapproving of them, but would not help us in finding the underlying emotions, etc., of their adherents. "Correctness" of expression will be relevant for us primarily in our own and far less in other political and social scientists' work.

Concerning the *results* which can be reached by means of conceptual research, it will be good not to expect too much. Some popular expectations regarding the effect of "correct" definitions of political terms are rising, which—according to the author's expectation —can only lead to further disappointments. Political terms are vague because they express fluctuating emotions rather than steady observations, ideals rather than actual situations, and vague (often even subconscious) desires rather than precise volitions. Definitions replacing the vagueness of such terms would in most cases be contrary to the views of at least one of the controversial parties. They would, therefore, amount to taking part in the controversy, and conse-

quently be unacceptable for one party. Moreover they would probably require that the emotions, ideals, and desires find other ways
of expression, hence lead to replacement of the former terms by
others which soon might be used in just as vague a way as the original terms. On the other hand, by finding out the underlying emotions, etc., in whatever form they are expressed, we may obtain a
considerably greater insight into the active causes of the controversies. Thereby, it might be possible either to find methods to neutralize them, or at least to know better than before what we and
other people really are fighting for.

It will, perhaps, be useful to consider the principal possible results
of an investigation like the present one if it is summarized in the definition of some political term, e.g., "democracy." It is necessary for
that matter, according to G. Mannoury, to distinguish "synthetic"
definitions, intended to restrict future usages of the term from "analytic" definitions intended only to describe its past usages.

X

An *analytic* definition of a term is (synthetically!) defined as a description of the way in which this term is actually used in acts of
discourse. It is a communication to the reader, which may be *correct*
or not, and is based on observation. A *synthetic* definition, on the
contrary, is a description of the way in which the author intends
to use the term. It is a *proposal* to the reader to accept this usage,
which may be *efficacious* or not (but not "correct or not") and is
based on volition.

In science and philosophy such a proposal is usually accepted, at
least temporarily and at least in its listener's aspect. In politics, however, this is only the case with respect to the adherents of the
speaker. Here the introduction of a definite way of using words is
usually intended to result in a definite type of political behavior.
Therefore the volitional element which is always present in the
acceptance of a proposal becomes here of the greatest importance:
whether such a proposal will be accepted or not becomes mainly
dependent upon whether the listener's purposes are coherent with
or contrary to those of the speaker. Hence in political science the
distinction between analytic and synthetic definitions in a large
number of cases passes into one between analytic and political definitions. An analogous remark holds for other statements than definitions.

XI

When trying to find an analytic definition of the term "democracy" it might perhaps be possible to find some common descriptive content in several of the current usages of the term "democracy" by considering it as a *relative* concept. There might be some chance of finding a really *analytic* definition of the term "democracy" by comparison with political structures *replaced by them* or existing in *neighbor countries*. Perhaps the following attempt might be tested by historians:

A political (and/or economic, and/or social) structure existing in a country at a certain moment is often called "democratic" in comparison with a structure replaced by it in the same country or existing in neighbor countries, if representatives of comparatively larger groups of the population have comparatively greater or more direct influence on the government. (Here the term "representatives" of a group is intended to denote individuals considered as such *by the group itself*, irrespective of their belonging or not belonging to it.)

This attempted analytic definition seems to account for most usages of the term "democracy" in history, in particular for those mentioned in the questionnaire. Athenian democracy, in comparison with previous "tyrannies," with Spartan "aristocracy" and Persian "autocracy," is so called because of the government by representatives of the citizens; medieval democracy is so called as soon as the government by representatives of a king or an emperor was alleviated by privileges granting some local governmental influence to representatives of the citizens, guilds, etc.; bourgeois democracy is so called in comparison with the government by representatives of the king—the clergy and the nobility were replaced or alleviated by representatives of the *tiers état;* proletarian and Soviet democracy is so called in comparison with "bourgeois" democracy, where the influence on government of the numerically smaller so called "possessing classes" was replaced by representatives of numerically larger group of wage-earning laborers. The formulation seems to account also for the difference often made between "true" or "real" and "existing" democracy in so far as it is applied then to a fictitious structure the author has in mind which, in comparison with the one he lives under or he observes in other countries, shows either an increase in the number of people represented in the government, or in the influence their representatives have.

It remains questionable, however, whether or not this proposed definition will be found to cover all usages of the term "democracy" in history and only such usages. Anyhow I do not think that it covers the most important parts of its *present* usages, at least not in their "listener's aspects," which probably are far more concerned with the results than with the form of government.

XII

With regard to an essentially synthetic definition we consider two possibilities:

1. It is so formulated that it might be acceptable to all parties to a controversy. In order that this be possible the definition presumably would have to be either so vague or so trivial that it would not allow any practical application. Even *if* it were so vague or so trivial, it would not be likely to be accepted by all parties, if at least one of the parties is emotionally too strongly bound to a definite ideology. In that case it might decline to accept any statement which is not in *complete* accordance with this ideology, and perhaps even insist upon a definition which *expressis verbis* denounces all other ideologies in one way or another.

2. It is so formulated that it is openly contrary to the views of at least one of the parties. In that case it may be used by the other parties as a means of propaganda against this one, by denying it the "right" to call itself "democratic." Then the isolated party may either (*a*) not bother about the definition at all and stick to its structure as well as its terminology without this "right" to do so; or (*b*) accept the definition and try to circumvent it so that it can maintain its structure and yet call itself "democratic" without indubitably contradicting the definition or (*c*) accept the definition and choose for itself some other term which by tradition is strongly associated with objects or situations that arouse strong positive emotions in many people.

In none of these cases the result would be very much worth while. Nevertheless such a definition might be used to force it upon an isolated party. Most probably this would *not* amount to leaving this party free to choose between *either* changing its structure *or* resigning the right to call itself democratic, but in forcing it to change its structure.

In that case the struggle would *apparently* be fought on philosophical grounds. Actually, however, it would only be imposing one structure upon another, which could have been done quite independent of any definition.

In any case, I think it is clear, 'that *any effort to give a synthetic definition of "democracy"* is an action of a *political*, not of a *philosophical* nature, and therefore does *not* fulfil the requirements of UNESCO's Philosophical Analysis.

V

JOHN DEWEY

In everyday speech "reaching an understanding" is the same as "arriving at an agreement"; in the words of the dictionary, it is the same as "coming to be of one mind." Moreover, in origin the expressions *agreement* and *disagreement* had the meaning of *agreeable* and *disagreeable*, indicating that being of one mind is a good deal more than a coldly intellectual affair.

I

The foregoing reference to familiar ways of speech is introduced because of its relevancy to the work of UNESCO. Such expressions as *arriving at, coming to, reaching,* imply a previous state of difference and discord. No argument is required to convince an observer that the peoples of the world are now in such a state of division as merits the name "Cold War": a division which is historically unprecedented in both extent and pervasiveness. It is also to the point that many nations have been so stirred by discords now constituting international anarchy, with all the threat to civilized life that anarchy brings with it, that they have joined in a concerted move to discover what organized intellectual attack can do to arrive at a common understanding—as a prelude to reach agreement in practice. For nothing less than this is the meaning of UNESCO. It may even be said that its existence stands as an acknowledgment of the place and office of recourse to the method of intelligence in a matter of utmost human concern. For the entire activity of UNESCO is centered in promotion of inquiry, discussion, and conference.

Breakdown of traditional ways of dealing with conflict between nations is without doubt a large factor in bringing UNESCO into being. For long historic periods recourse to armed conflict was successful in at least keeping the peace for a time, though it did not do away with the division of interests that generate war. Now the price paid even by the victor in war tends to bankrupt civilization; destruction is as total as is the enlistment of all the elements of nature,

land, sea, and air, in the work of destruction. With respect to diplomacy as a means of settlement, others than cynics would now agree
with the saying that diplomacy is the means of maintaining, in the
absence of open warfare, the clash of interests that is overt in war
time. Yet when it was first said, it was taken to be a manifestation of
the harsh spirit of an exceedingly bellicose nation.

To say that the formation and the work of UNESCO are an effort
to substitute the method of intelligence for that of force in arriving
at agreement among national states would be an indulgence in in-
flated optimism. But there is no exaggeration in saying that it offers
the peoples of the world a symbol of what is now desirable, and of
what may become an actuality in the future. That which serves as a
symbol must possess some standing on its own account; mere air
bubbles are evanescent as symbols as well as in fact. UNESCO has
met this condition. Proof is found in the two co-operative intellectual explorations already made. The first of the inquiries dealt with
Human Rights; the second with Democracy. No one would deny
that differences, ideological and overtly practical, with respect to
these matters underlie much of the present discord; they also loom
large as threats of open warfare. Differences disclosed in the discussion of human rights centered about the relation of human beings
as individuals to the society of which they are members. Roughly
speaking, differences were found to turn on the fact that representatives of some states emphasized the *rights* of persons as individuals
as against demands put forward on behalf of the state; representatives of other peoples that are organized into national states emphasized the *duties* that individuals owe to the state, and the supreme
right of the latter to compel all its members as individuals to submit
unquestioningly to its authority. Since the same issue is also found
to be a source of division with respect to democracy, no harm can
result if further discussion of the work of UNESCO is centered on
the latter theme.

One of the most significant findings of the discussion of democracy is its conclusion that every nation now claims to be a democracy.
Such a claim is peculiarly important when it is placed in contrast
with the division that separated nations during the interval between
the two World Wars. For at that time the outstanding feature of
international disagreement was the violent attack of some nations
upon the very idea of democracy and upon all democratic institu-

tions with respect to their actual practices. Some nations went so far at that time as to hold that all serious evils and troubles of mankind, internal and external, have their root in attempting to maintain the institutions that came into being after the revolutions of the eighteenth century had overthrown survivals of the feudal order. This work, according to the critics, was wholly negative. It only substituted economic feudalism for the old feudalism of status. The first World War ended in a victory for the nations that continued to assert the sufficiency of democratic institutions. Subsequent events have proved, however, that the military victory was far from settling the issue. For the U.S.S.R. continued exactly the same kind of violent attack upon the older and traditional type of democracy that had marked the Fascist and Nazi states.

Evidence on this matter is conclusive. The "democracies" of the communist type pour forth a constant stream of assertions that political democracies of the older traditional type are a delusion, snare, and willful fraudulent pretense. The assertion is accompanied by an equally persistent effort to create revolutions which will overthrow the type of democracy found in the states which like Great Britain and the United States claim to represent the democratic principle. In its origin the doctrine that political institutions resulting from the eighteenth-century revolutions have now themselves to be overthrown by another revolution was hardly more than an exercise in dialectics that illustrated the union of opposites. But now that the U.S.S.R. is one of the most powerful national states of the whole world, the doctrine has become the central factor in the present world-wide cleavage.

II

UNESCO may initiate and may give direction to inquiries and discussions which will tend to locate the sources of existing disagreement and conflict. This location may serve in turn to indicate what needs to be done to resolve existing discords. But by its very constitution UNESCO cannot by itself alone carry the work of resolution of differences through to practical conclusion. That work can be done only by the peoples who are involved in the present world-wide division.

We cannot refrain accordingly from asking about the chances that the needed work will be undertaken. In particular, what are the obstacles that stand in the way; and what if any are the resources that are available in carrying out adequate development of intellectual approach to reaching an agreement? With respect to the matter of obstacles, recent events clearly point to the fact that adequate recognition of its responsibility on the part of the people of the United States is badly hindered by attacks made upon this country by the communist nations claiming to be democratic. For these attacks have produced an atmosphere in which the mere suggestion of the need for a critical examination of democracy in reference to the standing of one's own nation is widely taken as proof that those suggesting it are infected with communist virus.

Yet the place occupied in the organic law of the United States by guaranty of Civil Rights: rights of free speech, free press, free assembly, and freedom of belief and worship in religious matters, is fundamental and central. Taken collectively they constitute nothing less than an express recognition in the fundamental law of the land of the indispensable place held in a democracy by freedom of discussion and publicity. Philosophers had previously written about the importance of leaving mind free; but in the absence of explicit legal recognition of the right to free *public communication*, freedom "of mind" hardly amounted to more than a pious wish—of concern doubtless to writers on political philosophy and jurisprudence, but of slight importance in the actual conduct of organized social life.

There is now a disposition on the part of some persons to discount the importance of the Bill of Civil Rights on the ground that it represented a fear of government and a desire to limit its activities which are now outmoded. Historically speaking there can be no doubt that dread of governments as tending to extend their range of power until their power became so oppressive of the activities of the populace as to reduce the latter to the status of subjects rather than of citizens inspired the demand for many rights. With the exception of Great Britain, Holland, and some Scandinavian countries, dread of governmental activity was justified by the record of history. There was every reason why the Founding Fathers should have wished to render the citizens of the new Republic immune from the danger of having their freedom impaired by governmental activities. For the historic record upon the whole is that of governments using their power to subordinate the welfare of the mass of the population to the interests of a privileged class. To prevent its happening in its case was an outstanding aim of those who instituted and presided over the destiny of the new Republic.

That the occasion of the presence of guaranteed freedom of speech and free expression was fear of government loses its importance (save as a comment on despotic states) now that the existence and exercise of democratic rights tend to eliminate the conditions that generated the fear. What is now of account is that the Founding Fathers in accepting the theory of Natural and *Pre-political* Rights selected the specific rights of freedom of discussion and public communication as the rights that are so basic and so intrinsic that *political* activity must not be allowed to infringe upon them. This fact is the more significant because the Constitution in its original state contained no guaranty of the primary *political* right—that of taking part, through the exercise of suffrage, in selection of the officials that constitute the governing body. The originally highly restricted right of suffrage has been progressively extended because of the particular liberties that were guaranteed—those of free public discussion of matters that concern the welfare of the people.

No mistake could be more unfortunate than to look upon the civil rights that were selected as prior and basic to political rights as a limitation of democratic political action. For it was a determination of the conditions under which and of the way in which genuinely democratic activity might best be assured. It would also be a mistake to regard the rights in question as simply a privilege to be enjoyed. It *is* a privilege and in ample measure. But at the present juncture, the outstanding fact is that these rights impose a responsibility. Given the present state of affairs both at home and in connection with other states, the way and degree in which we use or fail to use freedom of inquiry and public communication may well be the criterion by which in the end the genuineness of our democracy will be decided in all issues.

In the degree in which we fail to employ guaranteed freedom in the present critical and free discussion, without fear or favor, of the full meaning of democracy, and the relation to it of customs and institutions which now prevail, in that degree we fail to respond to the opportunity and the challenge presented in UNESCO. We reduce its work in effect to that of a debating club. The danger of failure on the part of political democracies in general and the United

States in particular extends, moreover, beyond UNESCO itself to the cause of which it is a symbolic embodiment.

III

The danger to which we are exposed is not vague and general but specific and concrete. Communist national states have taken the relation between economic conditions in prevailing industrial and financial conditions and the welfare of the mass of the population as the exclusive criterion for passing judgment upon the reality that is behind a profession of democracy. In the abstract, temptation is strong to respond by pointing out the repressive and oppressive activity of the states behind the Iron Curtain with respect to other freedoms, and by pointing out how meager is their actual attainment of economic welfare states. But in the concrete, concentration of energy, intellectual and practical, upon this *tu quoque* method of response is an evasion, whether so intended or not, of our own primary responsibility. Moreover, it plays into the hands of communist states. For their methods of suppression are so highly effective that our critical retorts do not reach their peoples, while our practice of freedom of communication is such that their assaults upon our democracy permeate; they make a positive appeal to those elements in our population that feel that our type of democracy is definitely unfavorable to *their* economic security and wellbeing.

The more important point, however, is that the issue of the relation of economic factors to other factors in the everyday life of a people constitutes a problem which would exist even if communist states had never come into being. The problem weighs, moreover, the more heavily the more a country is industrialized; hence it is most acute and most urgent in the United States as the most thoroughly industrialized of all nations. Free and critical discussion of the problem is of course in accord with the constitutional guaranty of the right of inquiry and of public expression. But the issue extends far beyond that point. Extensive critical examination of our own practices provides the only way in which the adequacy of our claim to be genuinely democratic may be tested in the concrete; it is also the only way in which measures for correction of defects can be discovered and put into effect.

Conditions that give rise to the problem of the relation between democracy in political and economic life are intrinsic. They do not depend upon the existence of communist states that are engaged in attacking our democracy. Life in every country of the globe, even in those least affected by the rise of machine and power industry, is undergoing transformation. Technologies which exist only because of the recent and rapid development of scientific knowledge are here to stay. In the United States, transition from a predominantly agrarian and rural economy to an industrial and urban one has gone on at a rate and with a pervasive thoroughness that would have seemed incredible even two short generations ago. The swiftness, the intensity, and extensity of the change left little time for foresight and next to no time for preparation. The rise of communist states may be an occasion for our giving serious attention to the issue. But the issue is with us anyway. It is in the interest of our own democracy to make it and the difficult problems it brings with it a subject of serious and systematic critical concern with a view to action. Superficially, discussion may seem to have got away from the theme of UNESCO. Not so in fact. The troubles that now plague the world are exhibited on the largest scale in tensions due to the splitting of the peoples of one globe into two *human* worlds. But they are far from being exhausted in the evils and dangers that attend this cleavage. The troubles *come home* to the peoples of every country in their own domestic affairs. As far as the work of UNESCO stands as a symbol of approach by the method of intelligence to the problems of international relationships, it also holds and sets forth the method that each several people needs to deal with problems and issues which are not exclusively its own but which it bears the primary responsibility for meeting. Responsibility for dealing with the sources of internal troubles that are due to rapid industrialization now rests most directly upon democracies of the older political type; they are the peoples with the longest experience of industrialization. Among the political democracies it rests with particular weight upon the people of the United States. For they are not only the most thoroughly industrialized among political democracies, but they are organically committed to a type of democracy in which political activity is determined by freedoms of discussion, conference, and communication in which all citizens have the right and the duty to participate.

VI

C. J. DUCASSE

1. AMBIGUITY.—No word is *in itself* either ambiguous or unambiguous; but only *used* ambiguously (or not) on this or that specific occasion. A word is being used ambiguously if the statement (or broader context) in which it figures leaves uncertain in which one of two or more meanings the word is being employed on the given occasion. The uncertainty may exist in the speaker's mind, or the hearer's, or in both. There can be no doubt that "democracy" is used more or less ambiguously in many cases. And not only *ambiguously*, but also *vaguely*, i.e., not only are there *several* senses which it might have in a given statement, but usually *each* of these senses is conceived only in an unanalytical, unprecise, i.e., *vague* manner.

3. MISUSE.—Misuse of a word is *provable* if either: (*a*) a definition of it is *agreed upon*, but the concrete things to which the word is *then* applied lack some of the characters specified in, or implied by, the agreed definition. This is misuse in the sense of misapplication; or, (*b*) one or more concrete things are *agreed upon* as being ones to which the word shall be applied, but the word is *then* employed to connote one or more characters not in fact possessed by all of the concrete things agreed upon as ones to which the word shall be applied. This is misuse in the sense of *mischaracterization*.

Thus, misuse of a word is provable only on the basis of existing agreement as to something: (*a*) *misapplication*, only on the basis of an *agreed connotation*; (*b*) *mischaracterization*, only on the basis of an *agreed denotation*.

Without such a basis of agreement, misuse can be *charged*, but is *unprovable*. The charge then only means that the use asserted to be *misapplication* or, as the case may be, *mischaracterization* is so on the basis of the connotation (or, as the case may be, denotation) which the word has *for the person making the charge*.

4. NEW USES.—I think there is evidence that the word "democracy" is currently being used in significations that should be considered new, at least in relation to nineteenth-century usage. But I do not believe that the history of the applications of the word furnishes any basis for choosing one rather than another of them as the "proper" one.

6. COMMON CHARACTERISTICS.—I believe there is probably some core of meaning common to all the different kinds of "democracy." It seems to be that *all* the people should, for such purpose as one has in view, be taken into account, rather than only some privileged category of them. This is connected with the idea of "justice" of treatment. But justice cannot plausibly be taken to mean that everyone should be treated alike; but only that everyone *that is alike* should be treated alike. And since it is impracticable to take into consideration *all* respects of likeness and of difference, the question then arises as to *which* respects of likeness between persons shall be made the basis of rules of equal treatment and which respects of difference shall be ignored.

The crucial question seems to be, *Who* shall decide *that* question? Some person or persons *self-appointed* by force or by craft to do so? Or some person or persons, *appointed to do so by vote of the majority* of the people? This question remains crucial irrespective of whether the self-appointees are altruistically or egoistically motivated. For even if they are altruistically motivated and in addition intelligent, the question remains whether it is *better* that the people should be *made* to behave wisely, or that they should have freedom to behave foolishly if they are fools and thus *themselves* to distil wisdom out of their folly.

Altruistic intentions and even intelligence in self-appointed rulers, however, do not automatically answer the question as to which of those two is the better. I believe that which is the better depends on a number of variables, e.g., how catastrophic would be mistakes made by the people, or by the rulers; how wise are the rulers; how foolish are the people. The example of a common-sense relation, in a loving family, between the parents and their children at various ages and in various circumstances, is as valuable and suggestive a guide as I can think of for judging whether it is better that a given people should be free or not to make its own mistakes, and which kinds of mistakes and which not.

7. IDEAL VERSUS FACT.—I think the general tendency to use "democracy" to express at the same time a set of ideals and a set of actual conditions is a *great* source of confusion, which would be minimized if each ideology stated clearly and separately: (*a*) the *state of affairs it regards as ideal* and aims to realize, (*b*) the *values* on account of which it regards it as ideal, (*c*) the *means* it proposes to employ to bring about realization of its ideal, (*d*) the *values* on account of which it judges those means as preferable to possible alternative ones.

It may be plausibly argued that ideals never get realized but only approached more or less; and therefore that the *intrinsic values* of the kind of means employed, and not only their capacity to approach the valued end, is an important, or the most important, consideration. It is also a question whether prima facie obvious but unscrupulous means are really more effective for approaching a valued ideal than are more scrupulous but seemingly less promising ones.

8. THE LINCOLN FORMULA.—All the three prepositions *of*, *by*, and *for* may probably be taken to express necessary criteria for anything to be called "democratic" in the Lincolnian sense. But I believe that the question whether something is to be *called* "democratic" is more or less idle. The important question is always whether it is *good*, or *best*, i.e., is *what we want*, in a given case or in all cases of a given kind. As regards forms of government, for instance, Aristotle was right when he pointed out that which form is best depends both on the kind of person or persons who, in a given case, are to do the governing and on those who are to be governed. Again, here the example of a large and devoted family is instructive. As between parents and infant, common sense says that the governing should be *for* the latter's benefit, but not *by* him. As between parents and their adolescent children, common sense recommends that the latter should participate in the governing.

11. "NARROW" VERSUS "BROAD" SENSE.—It is frequently asked whether "democracy" should primarily be used to cover a "narrow" political concept or a "broad" social one. This is not at all the way to put the problem. There is no "should" about it. Sometimes one wishes to talk about methods of decision-making and sometimes instead about a total state of affairs including results as well as methods. Using the same term for two different things only breeds confusion. The way to clarify the meaning a word has

in a given statement is to say the same thing that statement says, but without using the word. One really understands a word only to the extent one is able to do without it.

The crucial question is anything but a terminological one. In the last analysis it turns upon what the opposing parts assume to be the destiny of the individual and the meaning of his life on earth. Is his life on earth *all*, or does he continue to live after death? Again, is intellectual, moral, aesthetic, and spiritual *growth* the essentially important thing in it? If so, then since it is by striving, trying, blundering, suffering, and learning, that one grows, they are also the price one has to pay for growth. Or is intellectual, moral, aesthetic, and spiritual *contentment* what essentially gives meaning to life? If so, and *if* it can be guaranteed by self-abdication and putting one's self wholly in the hands of an all-wise church or state, then that is the thing for the individual to do. But then that church or state must actually deliver the promised and paid-for contentment; and not just tell him that he *ought* to be contented and that it is his own fault if he is not or that he will be if he waits long enough.

15. DEMOCRACY AND SOCIALISM.—The importance of keeping these distinctions clear is vividly felt by anyone trying to analyze political argumentation about the relative merits of "socialism" and "capitalism."

Of countless arguments attempting to show that "democracy" and "socialism" will not go together the ones set forth by Alexis de Tocqueville during the 1848 upheavals have been standing out as particularly potent ones. But Tocqueville's success in persuasion is not matched by the clarity of his distinctions. He praises "democracy" in the sense of a good life, conceived as one in which individual independence and responsibility are great. But he says nothing about "democracy" in the sense of a form of government. On the other hand, he condemns "socialism" in the sense of a form of government, but says nothing about socialism's conception of a good life. In *any* form of government, the individual's independence and responsibility are limited, more or less. So it is not a case of "either ... or...." The two essential questions here, which are most expediently stated without using the emotion-laden terms "democracy" and "socialism," are: (*a*) What kind of a life is a "good" or "the best" life for man? (*b*) What form of government is best adapted to promote it?

17. DEMOCRACY AND CAPITALISM.—On the other hand, the Communist attempts to prove that "real" democracy is impossible under the economic system prevailing in the Western world have not been less confusing. It may well be that the arguments of Lenin and Stalin, as exemplified in the two quotations given in the UNESCO document, have had applicability at certain places and certain times in history. But as applied to the actual state of affairs today in the United States—with its enormously powerful labor unions, its enormous income and inheritance taxes in the upper brackets, its high standard of living and of leisure, its constitutional freedoms and its widespread literacy—those two statements only sound like fundamentalist dogma, blindly clung to in the teeth of the facts.

The state of affairs in the United States is not perfect, of course; and every attempt to remedy its defects should be made. But it is intellectually dishonest to attend exclusively to its defects, and to disregard or minimize the fact that, notwithstanding them, the American economic and political system has turned out actually capable of providing for the masses in the United States the highest material standard of living the world has ever seen; and, what is more, has been able to do so while preserving freedom of the press, freedom of expression and opinion, and in general, civil liberties to an extent vastly greater than has any totalitarian government. Men can be caused to produce things or services of value either by fear of punishment or by hope of reward. The latter is vastly the more efficient and economical of the two, because it functions more or less automatically and therefore only needs some regulation; whereas the former requires at every moment a watcher and enforcer at each person's back. But further, the kind of reward, hope of which most effectively motivates the average man to produce most and most efficiently, is the individual reward consisting of the yield of individual effort and individual thought. On the other hand the kind of reward which consists in consciousness that one is a benefactor of mankind is a strong motive only for relatively few persons, or only under special circumstances such as (for instance in saving a drowning person) certainty that one is rendering a service and that it is a great one.

19. EXPRESSION OF "REAL INTERESTS."—The "real" interests of the individual are those he actually prefers when (a) he knows what the possible alternatives are among which a choice is possible, and

(*b*) knows both the hidden price and the hidden values of each choice, as well as the surface price and values. A method of political decision-making which makes possible the reaching of decisions by the individual in this manner, and which gives expression to them, is *good*. The question whether it is to be called "democratic" or not is idle. Opinion-influencing is justifiable in so far as it consists in *opinion-informing*, as full and impartial as possible. Opinion-influencing by telling people, or allowing them to know, only what will influence them to decide *as one's self thinks they ought to decide* is unjustifiable unless they are babies or otherwise mentally irresponsible.

21. DEMOCRACY AND PLANNING.—Delegation of decision-power is all right so far as it is really delegation, not capture; so far as the powers delegated and not delegated are clear; and so far as delegation of them is revocable periodically or under stated conditions. Whether delegation satisfying these criteria shall be called "democratic" or not is an idle question.

22. TOLERATION OF DISSENTIENT OPINIONS.—The question of toleration essentially concerns not opinions but actions. A person's opinions, anyway, cannot be done away with by being condemned or prohibited. They are relevant only to the extent they are likely to influence him to act, and that the acts they prompt affect his fellowmen in ways *they* consider important. Hence they would be justified in not allowing a person who holds certain opinions to occupy positions that would give him certain powers over them, yet in allowing him to occupy certain other positions.

23. REPRESSION OF PROPAGANDA.—If "propaganda" means telling people *anything*—irrespective of whether it be true, half-true, or false—that one thinks will cause them to act as one's self desires them to act, then it is an arbitrary imposing of one's own will upon them by craft; which is no more justifiable than doing it by force. Propaganda, on the other hand, is justified in so far as it means *information*, true, full, and impartial. Impartiality, however, is practically achievable only by allowing the various partisans to state their case. What is crucial is that they should do so *honestly*. Deliberate lying and distortion is unjustifiable.

29. ULTIMATE AIMS.—So far as I can see, all the ideologies are sincerely aiming at heaven on earth, and I believe they conceive it not

too differently—somewhat, perhaps, after the analogy I have used before, of the conditions existing in a happy family where each does for all what he can out of sheer love and good will. That's the sales talk, and I believe it sincere. The divergences have to do with views as to the reasons why that happy state does not now exist; as to how alterable is a man's nature in what respects and by what kind of means; whether that utopian aim is really attainable or even measurably approachable; whether any means no matter how themselves evil are justified if only they promote, or seem to promote, approach to utopia.

Any ideology can afford beautiful ideals—they are a dime a dozen. I believe that, actually for most men, the quality of the *means* employed to approach the ideal is vastly more important than the problematic, motivating utopia. That a person or a state should practice sincerity, good faith, good will, considerateness, kindness, and respect for the dignity, the freedom, and the responsibility of the individual seems to me a far more potent and realistic means to a good life for mankind than is any utopian ideal so fanatically pursued that the pursuer has no scruples about the intrinsic quality of the means he uses. The way to hell is paved with good intentions. I believe that even if the utopian state of affairs described as the aim in Lenin's quotation is attainable, it will take many thousands of years to reach it. That it can possibly be even measurably approached in a few generations seems to me naïvely optimistic.

Concluding word.—To those comments I would add that if, in discussions between the Western and the Eastern powers, use of the terms "democracy" and "democratic" were abandoned entirely, occasions for misunderstandings and recriminations would probably be diminished. Agreement on some *statement* phrased in terms of the word "democratic" merely deludes the persons concerned into believing they agree, if that word is used in a different sense by each.

On the other hand, if disagreements are brought into the open and their nature made perfectly clear, then the persons can judge much better how the disagreement can best be dealt with—whether by compromise, or by fighting, or by each going his own way and agreeing not to interfere with the other so long as he keeps within some agreed regions.

On the other hand, if two persons really disagree, but think they agree because each uses the same words to state his program, then eventual charges of deceit, bad faith, and hypocrisy become inevitable.

It seems to me that by this time the words "democracy" and "democratic" have been just about wrecked as regards usefulness in discussions between West and East, and that it would be better to say explicitly what one means, each time one is tempted to employ them.

VII

G. C. FIELD

It is obviously desirable for clarity of discussion that the use of any term should be (*a*) as uniform, (*b*) as stable, as possible. Changes in the meaning will, no doubt, occur, but they should have a recognizable continuity with the previous usage. The presumption is always against anyone who wishes to make deliberately a sharp change in the use of the term, and the burden of proof is on him to show that there are strong and exceptional reasons for making such a change. Further, he must (*a*) make it quite clear in explicit terms what the new meaning that he wishes to introduce is, and (*b*) be consistent in his use of it, and not use it sometimes in the old sense and sometimes in the new.

In examining the previous use of the term, in order to preserve continuity, it is desirable to concentrate on its use in serious discussion. Occasional confusions in the popular use of the term will, no doubt, occur from time to time. But they afford no justification for advocating a deliberate change.

Tried by these tests, it is clear that the traditional use of the term "democracy" from the time of the Greeks to the present day has been to describe a form of government. The evidence for this is overwhelming. There may have been, from time to time, departures from or extensions of this use, conscious or unconscious, in popular speech or by individual writers, but the tendency has always been, the more serious the discussion became, to bring it back to the traditional use. The sporadic departures from this, so far as they were not mere confusions of thought which disappeared as soon as they were pointed out, have arisen from a variety of causes.

In some cases there seem strong grounds for the suspicion that there has been a deliberate attempt to confuse the issue in order to attach the emotional associations of the word "democracy" to something quite different. But this is not always the case. For there are some possibilities of confusion into which it is quite easy to fall un-intentionally unless one is careful to guard against them.

a) The most elementary confusion is that between a form of gov-ernment and the policy it adopts. In general, probably everyone would recognize that the two were clearly distinct. Obviously, two or more governments of the same form can, and often do, pursue very different policies on many.points. It is possible, of course, that in some circumstances or on some points one form of government will be much more likely to adopt one line of policy than another. That is a matter of fact to be discussed on the available evidence, difference of opinion will always be possible about it, and in fact judgments have often been made on such a point which have turned out wrong.

An emotional factor which creates confusion comes in when people desire the establishment of a particular form of government solely, or mainly, because they think that it will follow a certain policy, and then by association they transfer the name of the form of government to the policy that they think it ought to follow. So if a government of that form does not follow this policy they deny its right to the name, and sometimes go so far as to give the name to a government of quite a different form which follows the policy they want. This is entirely illegitimate and merely leads to confusion.

b) A more excusable source of confusion arises when it is main-tained that certain conditions (e.g., economic or educational), other than the legal establishment of a form of government, are necessary to make that form of government work well or work at all. On such a point there may often be sharp differences of opinion which can only be decided by the evidence of actual experience. But, while the differences of opinion continue, it is essential to keep clearly in view what we are talking about and not prejudge the question by an alteration or extension of the use of the term. If, however, it is es-tablished that a particular condition is really necessary to enable a form of government to work, it is natural, and, if it is clear what it is doing, excusable, to *include* the fulfilment of this condition in our idea of the meaning of the term. It is not, however, legitimate to *transfer* the use of the term completely to the fulfilment of the necessary condition and forget altogether its original application to the form of government.

Thus, it might be maintained that a democratic form of government cannot work if the great majority of the population is entirely illiterate. If that were accepted, it would be quite reasonable to say of a country whose population is mainly illiterate that it is not a democracy whatever its legal form of government. But it would be absurd to invert that and to say that any country whose population is mainly literate is a democracy whatever its legal form of government. No one, probably, would argue in that way. But substantially the same fallacy has frequently been committed in recent discussions when it was a question of social and economic conditions.

When we come to a positive definition, it is desirable to avoid vague phrases such as the hackneyed, "Government of the people, by the people, for the people." Every government must necessarily be *of* the people. Almost any form of government can, theoretically at any rate, be *for* the people. The crucial question is what meaning we can attach to the phrase "government *by* the people," which is the distinguishing mark of a democracy.

As a rough provisional definition we may describe "government" as consisting in taking a series of decisions, which are recognized as having legal force and being binding on the community or any section of it that they may concern. And the question to answer, about any form of government, is who makes these decisions. When the question is put in that form, it is clear that in fact most, if not all, decisions are influenced to a greater or lesser degree from a variety of different quarters. So the special question about democracy, or "government by the people," resolves itself into the question how far the great body of citizens can effectively influence those decisions.

It is obvious that in no form of government can *all* governmental decisions be taken by vote of the whole body of citizens. This was true even of an ancient city state and is far more so of a large and complicated modern state. But *some* decisions can be so taken, and this fact may influence to a greater or lesser degree the decisions that are actually taken by some other person or body of persons, e.g., the decisions actually taken by a Cabinet or Parliament will undoubtedly be influenced to some extent by the prospect of a forthcoming general election. There are clearly almost infinite possibilities of variation both in the number of decisions that are actually submitted to the whole body of citizens and in the degree to which that influences the decisions actually taken by some other body.

I would, therefore, venture on a provisional short definition. "A state is democratic," not *"if,"* but *"in so far as* the whole body of citizens, or the great majority of them, exercise an effective influence on the decisions of government." This emphasizes the point that democracy is not something which either is or is not, but something of which there can be more or less. That applies, of course, not only to the condition of a state at a given moment, but also to its apparent tendencies of development. It may be tending to move toward an increase of democratic influences or in the opposite direction.

On the other hand, there is, of course, no reason why we should not continue to speak roughly of one state as democratic if it has a considerable degree of democracy and another as undemocratic if it has very little or hardly any at all, in just the same way as we speak of the weather as warm or cold, though we could not fix an exact point on the thermometer at which one ended and the other began. But we must not fall into the blunder, either with regard to democracy or the weather, of speaking as if a difference of degree was not important. The phrase, "It's *only* a difference of degree," is nearly always a mark of political illiteracy.

It is the same with the conditions which help or hinder the development of democracy. Here also it is a case of more or less. Some may make so much difference that they might be described as practically essential (or fatal) to democracy. Others might make it much easier or more difficult, but not to a degree which could not be counteracted. And others, again, might make only a small degree of difference.

Among the conditions which may be regarded as practically essential, I would suggest the following:

a) The legal establishment of democratic machinery or institutions, particularly the legal right to decide important questions by popular vote. It would also include, of course, the provision of facilities for this, e.g., polling places. One of the chief standards of "importance" in this connection would lie in the degree to which the decision of the whole body of voters on one point influenced the decisions taken by some other body on other points. The obvious illustration of that has already been given above, when it was pointed out that the right to elect the Parliament or governing body at regular intervals, even if it is only actually exercised once in every five years or so, has an important influence on all the decisions taken by that body.

It might be maintained that this should be more correctly described, not as a condition so much as an essential part of democracy. It does not much matter in which way we choose to describe it as long as we make it clear that the establishment of legal democratic institutions is not by itself sufficient to make a state democratic. If the legal right to vote were established but, say, 90 per cent of the population never troubled to exercise this right, such a state could hardly be described as a democracy, though it might be a step toward it. It is also worth noting that there have been occasions on which the opinion of the unenfranchised masses has influenced the decisions of the government even without the power of voting. But such occasions would necessarily be rare and exceptional, and such a small amount of popular influence could certainly not be sufficient to warrant us in speaking of the country in which they occurred as a democracy. They might, however, once again be an influence leading toward democracy.

b) A great amount of freedom of criticism, discussion, and the dissemination of information. This is an obvious necessity. If a government had complete control of all information and the exclusive right of putting forth opinions and arguments in support of them, its decisions would not, save in very exceptional circumstances, be influenced by popular opinion, because it would know that it could make that opinion what it liked, if, indeed, we could call it opinion at all in such circumstances.

To the genuine believer in democracy exceptions to this freedom could only be contemplated in occasional and extreme cases, and just because they are exceptional it is impossible to lay down clear-cut rules beforehand to decide when they arise. Obviously, direct incitement to overthrow a democratic form of government by violence could properly be suppressed, and there would be nothing undemocratic about doing so. On the other hand, reasoned criticism of democracy as a form of government must surely be permitted in spite of the remote possibility that it might eventually persuade the majority of the electorate to vote constitutionally for the abolition of democratic institutions. For the rest, there may be rare occasions when the temporary suppression, at a critical moment, of a particular set of opinions even if they do not advocate violence may preserve a democracy which might otherwise be overthrown. But, in considering the possibility of this in any given case, the genuine democrat will remember (*a*) that democracy cannot be founded in a permanent regime of suppression, and (*b*) that there are all sorts of motives, other than the desire to preserve democracy, which may incline any of us toward suppression of opinions that we dislike. These other motives, often subconsciously, may influence our judgment on the question whether democracy is really in danger or not and must be resolutely guarded against. As ancient Greek experience showed, the cry of "Democracy in danger" may be one of the most potent weapons in the hands of would-be dictators.

The genuine democrat, therefore, while admitting the theoretical possibility that occasional temporary suppression of opinion might be in the interests of democracy, would regard any actual proposals for this with the deepest suspicion. He would demand overwhelming proof of its necessity. He would remember that the habit of suppression, once started, may grow very rapidly, and he would be prepared to run great risks rather than have recourse to it. Further than that it is impossible to go.

c) Other necessary conditions might be suggested. The most obvious one is the necessity for at least a minimum standard of education for the whole population. But it is time to go on to some of the suggested claims on which most controversy has been assumed. These controversies can be settled only, if at all, by careful factual analysis of the situation, actual or possible, with the definite question in mind. Does this state of things in fact tend to increase or diminish the degree to which the decisions of government are influenced by the opinions of the great mass of citizens? Two points, in particular, call for special discussion from this point of view, (1) the effect of the existence of political parties, and (2) the effect of social and economic conditions.

(1) There is, theoretically, no reason why a democratic form of government should not be run without organized political parties at all, and in fact parties, as we know them, have not in the past always been a feature of democratic governments. But they have, for a variety of reasons, developed in all modern respesentative governments, and their effect on the degree of democracy is very complicated and to some extent ambivalent. Thus, on the one side, they do much to arouse interest and stir up people to use their democratic institutions, they stimulate discussion, and insure that opinions are expressed and information given which is not all on one side. On the other, the existence of organized parties means that to some extent

opinion is formed and decisions made within the party, sometimes by a small inner hierarchy, before being presented to the electors, and to that extent the influence of popular opinion is restricted. The degree of this varies greatly in different countries and is affected by the general attitude toward parties, the way in which they are organized, the system of voting, and many other influences.

If only one political party is allowed, that is obviously entirely undemocratic in its effect. It restricts, if it does not rule out altogether, public expression of opinion and dissemination of information that does not suit the one party. And it deprives the body of the electorate of any real choice between possible alternative governments, so that the influence of public opinion on the party in power is reduced to the minimum.

(2) The question of the effect of social and economic conditions is highly complicated and cannot be answered by any simple formula. It seems most probable that some social and economic conditions will be more favorable to democracy, as defined above, than others. But which these are and how great their influence is can only be decided by a careful analysis of the facts in each particular case. The question to ask in each case is: How far does this or that condition make it easier or more difficult for a public opinion to be formed among the mass of the citizens, and, when formed, to have an effective influence on the decision of government? That is a question of fact and can only be answered by an examination of facts.

It is just this precise analysis of facts which is lacking in many of the arguments put forward. For instance, the quotations from Lenin and Stalin included in the UNESCO document consist mostly of extremely dogmatic assertions, which are much too vague to be tested by facts or evidence. We get one relatively precise factual statement in Lenin's assertion that in a capitalist society the mass of the people are too "crushed by want and poverty" to take any interest in politics. And, as a factual statement, this is obviously untrue.

The fact is that, while democracy as a form of government is a relatively clear and precise concept, the use of terms such as "economic" or "social democracy" is extremely vague and confused. They are used to cover a variety of different things, which are never clearly distinguished, though they have in reality no necessary connection with each other, or with democracy as a form of government. I should demur, therefore, to the phrasing of some passages in the questionnaire when it speaks of the distinction between a "narrow" and a "broad" conception of democracy. The real distinction in the present controversy is between a more precise and a more confused conception.

Among the varied notions suggested more or less vaguely by the terms "economic" or "social" democracy, we may distinguish the following: (a) Equality of incomes, which has not so far been established in fact by any existing society. (b) Equality of social prestige, which is an important constituent of what we usually mean by "class." This is a matter of people's feelings, which may vary indefinitely and which are quite incapable of being precisely measured. (c) The application of democracy as a form of government to individual concerns within the state, e.g., particular industries or individual businesses or educational institutions. In any of these there may be great differences in the degree to which decisions taken can be influenced by the whole body of people taking part in the work. That, incidentally, is why I have preferred to speak of "democracy as a form of government" rather than "political democracy." The latter suggests an exclusive reference to the government of the state, while the former brings out the point that exactly the same considerations can be raised with regard to the government of any organized body of people within the state or cutting across the state boundaries.

All these points, and others like them, can be discussed as (a) desirable or undesirable in themselves, or (b) favorable or unfavorable to the development of democracy as a form of government in the state. The essential thing is to be clear which we are discussing and what sort of evidence we are using to answer our questions.

Considerable possibilities of confusion arise when we raise the question of "government for the people," i.e., of decisions being taken in the interests of the whole people or the great majority of them. To discuss this would involve the attempt to give some precision to the vague phrase "interests of the whole people." We should also have to distinguish between the intentions and the results of the decisions, i.e., between the decisions made because it is believed and wished that they would be in the general interest and the decisions which in fact are in this interest. The one would demand a judgment on the motives of all the people concerned in making the decisions, and the other on their wisdom and probability of being right.

It has generally been held that at any rate the intentions of the decisions made will be largely determined by who makes them, that, for instance, the interests of the majority of the people are more likely to be pursued in the decisions taken or influenced by the majority than in those taken by any more limited group. This, however, is not theoretically necessary. It would be possible for a small body or a single man, in whose hands the major influence on decisions lay, to be unselfishly devoted to the interests of the people. That idea has long been familiar and has been often expressed in some such phrase as "benevolent despotism." But to call a despotism democracy because it was benevolent would be an entire reversal of the ordinary use of words. At any rate, the distinction would remain between a state in which the question of what is in the interests of the whole people is decided in the main by a single man or a small body and one in which the great mass of people themselves were called upon to take a considerable part in arriving at the decision. If we called both democracies, we should certainly have to invent a new word for the latter to distinguish it from the former.

It remains only to mention two or three points which have been practically ignored in recent discussions, but which in fact have an important influence on the working of democracy. (*a*) The relation of majority and minority. It is sometimes said that democracy is government by the majority. But this may easily be misleading. The intention of democracy is to bring as many of the citizens as possible into the task of making the decisions of government. And when a number, large or small, of people are concerned, as equals, in making decisions, if general agreement is not reached the final decision has to be taken by the vote of a majority. That is a practical necessity rather than part of the ideal. But the extent to which democracy works in practice will be greatly influenced by the relations between the majority and the minority, the way in which they are formed, and their attitude toward each other. (*b*) The size of the community. This is hardly ever seriously considered now as being a problem at all. But it is worth considering whether the size of the community might not make a great deal of difference to the degree to which democracy could be established within it. (*c*) The range of activity of the state as compared with private individuals or other organizations within it. It may well be that the number of functions that the state assumes will have a great deal of influence on the degree to which it can be governed democratically.

I have not attempted to discuss the question of the grounds on which people could believe or disbelieve in democracy. It is very likely true that in the final analysis one would come down to ultimate value-judgments beyond which argument was impossible. But most people are a long way from that, and discussion if it is carried on reasonably can go a great way in clearing up our ideas about what it is exactly that we believe in and why.

Thus, "I believe in democracy" does not necessarily mean "I believe that all questions (or even all the most important questions) should be decided by a vote of the whole electorate." It means rather that I believe that the element of democracy, i.e., the effective influence of the great body of people on the decisions taken, is a thing of positive value in a community and that a considerable degree of it is desirable. I may believe this simply because I think that the decisions taken under this influence will in fact be the decisions of which I approve. That would properly be described as believing in democracy simply as a means to getting certain things done. If another form of government did those things more effectively than a democracy I should prefer the former. But I may also believe that democracy is of positive value irrespective of the decisions actually taken. Such a belief would in the last resort have to be based on a judgment of the sort of people that this form of government would produce, the character or point of view or attitude of mind that it would develop in them, and the kind of life that it would enable them to lead. This will certainly be affected by the way in which the decisions are reached quite as much as or more than by the nature of the decisions themselves.

I can only indicate briefly the kind of qualities of mind I consider the practice of a democratic form of government apt to develop. There is the interest in public affairs, the readiness to think about them critically and the sense of personal responsibility for the decisions made. This is very different from the blind loyalty and the emotional excitement that the familiar methods of totalitarian states seek to arouse when trying to "mobilize the people for active participation in public affairs." There is independence of mind and the sense of one's right to form opinions for one's self. There is also the recognition of the same right for other people, which is not always found with this. This spirit of tolerance and recognition of the rights of other people to form and express their own opinions is one of the great democratic virtues. It is as far as can be from mere indifference,

but rests on a positive attitude of respect for other people's personalities. And the democrat believes that this is an essential part of a
satisfactory relation between individuals which, in its turn, is the test
of a satisfactory organization of society.

Ought we to say, perhaps, that these, and the other attitudes involved, are the end and political democracy merely a means? I think
that that would be misleading and that the sharp distinction between
ends and means hardly applies here. The democrat would maintain,
in the first place, that such qualities could hardly be developed to
any great extent except in a state with a considerable degree of
political democracy. He would also maintain that in so far as these
qualities develop they will naturally seek to express themselves in
the use of democratic institutions, and that they will be stunted or
frustrated without this. And he would further maintain that the developed habit of using democratic institutions will not continue
for long without developing some degree of these qualities. This is
not mere theory, but can be observed happening in practice. And it
may be added it can be observed in a variety of social systems. The
suggestion, for instance, that these results could not arise from
political democracy under a capitalist system is entirely contrary to
observable facts, though, of course, it is perfectly possible to argue
that they would develop better under a different social system provided that the democratic form of government was retained. I may
add that the habits of mind developed in the working of political
institutions will inevitably permeate to a greater or lesser degree into
the whole pattern of our lives.

In conclusion, I would point out that, though the democrat believes that these things are of positive value in themselves, he need
not necessarily maintain that they are the only things of value. But it
merely leads to confusion if, after admitting that other things have
value, he then proceeds to extend the term "democracy" to them.
It is an elementary logical fallacy to argue on the lines: Democracy
is good, X is good, therefore X is Democracy. Take, in particular,
the question of raising the economic well-being of the whole people.
Economic well-being is undoubtedly a good, and it is not the same
as the good of democracy. But it is not an alternative to them. There
is obviously no essential incompatibility, and there is as yet not the
slightest evidence that in fact any other form of government is more
successful than democracy in raising the economic level. But it is,

of course, theoretically possible that an entirely undemocratic state might have a high material standard of living, and even that in certain circumstances it might be more successful than a democratically governed state would be in securing this. If we were faced with such circumstances it would be a question of deciding which of the alternative goods we should sacrifice. This would probably turn on the question of degree. A genuine democrat would probably say that a moderately prosperous democratic state was preferable to an extremely prosperous undemocratic one. If, on the other hand, it was a choice between affluence and starvation he might choose the other way. But he would do so reluctantly with full recognition of the sacrifice involved, and he would demand very convincing proof that the sacrifice was really necessary. All this, however, is purely theoretical, and there is no reason at all for supposing that we are at all likely to be faced with such a choice in practice.

VIII

RISIERI FRONDIZI

1. AMBIGUITY.[1]—The question opening the UNESCO document asks "to what extent the word 'democracy' is ambiguous." This formulation of the problem is unfortunate because it seems to suggest that the term "democracy" is ambiguous "in itself." In fact, the word "democracy" is neither ambiguous nor unambiguous per se; the ambiguity depends upon its usage. There are people who would hold that this is exactly what is meant by the ambiguity of a word. We do not share this opinion: there are other words the ambiguity of which can be discovered without examining their uses; they have been coined to express concepts of an intrinsically ambiguous nature. But that is not the case with "democracy." Its ambiguous or precise meaning depends on how we use it or the way we define it. We can use or define a word in a strictly univocal way; that does not mean, of course, that the word so defined is a true description of reality.

2. EVIDENCE.—In fact, the word "democracy" has been used and is still used with a great variety of meanings, some of them incompatible with each other. Pages after pages can be filled with quotations giving evidence to the divergent uses of the word. Since the UNESCO document itself contains a few examples already (Tocqueville, Lord Bryce and Lenin) any further illustration seems unnecessary.

3. MISUSE.—Under these circumstances, is it at all possible to charge any one with *misuse* of the word "democracy" as suggested in the UNESCO document? Of course not. If the term is used with different meanings, who would have the right to say which is the proper one? We cannot talk about a commonly accepted meaning because there is no such thing; what we commonly find are divergent uses. Besides, common use has no force on a thinker or a writer. Anyone can use the words in the sense he thinks best; the only thing

1. For lack of space and time we shall discuss only the first set of questions that go under the heading of "Ambiguity and Misuse."

he should do is to define the words in a clear way and use it accordingly. He should not contradict himself but he can contradict the common use as many times as he feels necessary. It should be emphasized that within the ambiguity caused by divergent uses there may be perfect clarity and precision in each one of the divergent meanings.

The questionnaire gives one the wrong impression that the word "democracy" is a unique case of ambiguity. In fact, the diversity of meanings of a word is very frequent in philosophy and does not only affect words of secondary order but the most fundamental of them. Words such as reality, being, truth, knowledge, experience, mind, are frequently used by philosophers with quite different meanings that sometimes are even incompatible. And it is unnecessary to stress the importance of the concepts to which these words refer. The varieties, richness, and changeability of the reality which these philosophical concepts try to describe accounts, in part, for the different uses that these words may have.

4. NEW USES.—To explain the so-called "ambiguity" we should pay attention to the fact that democracy is a historical reality and therefore changing through time. With the development of humanity the word "democracy" has acquired new meanings because the reality it tries to describe has developed new aspects and trends. The latest important change is a consequence of the Marxist doctrine, on the theoretical level, and the Russian Revolution, in the world of practice. From these impacts, there has developed an emphasis on social justice and with it the idea of stressing *in whose interest* the government is acting more than *how* the country is run or the government elected.

The present conflict between the so-called East and West is a conflict between this new meaning of democracy—which we may call "social democracy"—and the traditional liberal idea that may be called "political democracy." If one thinks of democracy in political terms—the way the government is elected, the parliamentary system, the rights of the minorities, etc.—the Russian situation is totally antidemocratic; while it is not so if you consider in whose interest the country is run.

Bertrand Russell's distinction between "rule of the majority" and "interest of the majority" clarifies the issue. In fact, it is Lincoln's distinction between the government *by* the people and *for* the people. These two do not usually go together as Lincoln desired; as a matter of fact they are very frequently in conflict. And when they are not, it is because there is no democracy, either politically or socially, as it is the case of a government imposed by a minority and ruling in the interest of a minority.

Up to now we have ignored the deliberate looseness and vagueness of the word "democracy" due to political reasons. The word has acquired a fighting force in the recent past and has become a slogan, a catchword, to which politicians of all countries stick firmly. That is why the opposing countries in a war claim that they are fighting for democracy, and many a dictator today suppresses all kind of freedom in the name of democracy, while the people—also in the name of democracy—are rebelling against him.

This brief analysis seems to show that the word "democracy" has been used with a variety of meanings, that no one meaning can be declared to be the proper one and that the best practical policy could be to qualify democracy in each case by adding an adjective which could show what is meant or at least what is not meant. The adjectives "ancient," "Bourgeois," "Proletarian," "American," "social," "political," etc., added to "democracy" would make for greatest precision and might eliminate some misunderstandings. We should be careful, though, in choosing the adjectives because some of them even increase the ambiguity and confusion. I have in mind words such as "true" or "false," which when added to the word "democracy" could be good enough to get the applause of an audience but do not help a bit to make the meaning of the word more precise.

5. "GENERAL DEMOCRACY."—An entirely different problem is raised when it is asked whether there is such a thing as "democracy in general" or only a series of historically different "democracies." This problem goes beyond the discussion of the "right" or "wrong" use of words; our attitude in this case depends on our stand regarding the problem of universals. Do universals really exist and are particulars only their manifestations? Or, on the contrary, do particulars exist and are universals only a name to designate the common elements that we find in those particulars?

It is impossible to examine in a brief paper like this the problem of universals with all its implications. The only thing we can do is to call the attention to the fact that the problem of democracy, in this respect, is only a case of the whole issue on universals and particulars, and give a general outline of the way we look at the problem.

There is no doubt that the same issue can be raised on all levels of reality from physical things to values. Do beauty or beautiful things have real existence, truth or true propositions, kindness or kind attitudes? In what sense, if any, is there such a thing as the American University? Or is it true that what really exist are only the different particular universities, such as Harvard, Yale, Princeton, California, etc.? The difficultiy of the problem should not be blamed on the loose language of the politicians in this case. And we should not have the naïve hope that the whole problem can be solved definitely by a committee of experts.

Some of the difficulties of this problem arise from the fact that the false notion—that we must choose between democracy in general or its historical forms—is widely spread. As a matter of fact, the questionnaire itself suggests this attitude, which in my opinion is only a case of what we might call "the fallacy of false opposition."

I am suggesting, of course, the possibility of putting together the universal and the particulars; it may be that what really exist are the particulars embodying the universal. In other words, that the universal cannot exist in its abstractness or pure universality, unless we believe in a meta-empirical world of ideas. But, at the same time, the particular cannot exist in its mere particularity because if such a thing happens each particular would be unique and ineffable.

If we apply this general principle to the case of democracy we shall be inclined to say that what exist are the historical democracies but as democracies, that is, embodying the universal "democracy." It seems to be clear that the so-called "democracy in general" does not exist in or by itself. And if it did exist, what kind of knowledge could we have of it if it were completely divorced from every historical actuality?

On the other hand, if we admit that the historical democracies exist, we may get into difficulties as soon as we try to form a clear notion of what a particular democracy is. We have taken for granted that Greek, Bourgeois, Proletarian, or American democracies are particulars. But are they really so? We should not let language deceive us. The existence of a word does not imply the existence of a reality. Is either Greek or American democracy a particular? Or are they only a conventional cut of an uninterrupted historical process? We feel inclined to the second term of the alternative which will throw the particular democracies into the general historical development. But there is another difficulty. In case we disregard the historical process as a whole and pay attention to the particular segment that we call Greek or American democracy, is there a real particular unity in it? Or is it not by itself a process, a development? If so, which shall we take as the representative of American democracy, for instance, Jefferson's, Lincoln's or Truman's? In each period again we see the process: Truman's administration during the war and after the war differ. And so on and so forth. The so-called concrete, particular democracies squeeze between our hands when we try to get hold of them. The only thing we can see is the whole historical process, with landmarks here and there which direct our attention but which we should not confuse with particular realities. If this is so, we should add to our first statement that historical democracies, as democracies, exist, a new idea which is only the counterpart of the other, namely, that what exists is democracy actualized through its historical development.

The concept of democracy cannot be static because the reality it tries to describe develops through time. The process has its ups and downs but it keeps on moving; its final goal seems to be the extension of the rights, duties, and benefits, enjoyed now only by some, to the whole of mankind, to each human being as a human being and because he is a human being. We should be careful not to identify democracy with one of its stages, whether it is the present or a past stage. If we want to keep democracy alive we have to help it in its push forward.

The evolution of humanity and the becoming of new ways of life, from the political, economical, social, and cultural point of view, have been the result of dramatic conflicts. The struggle and opposition, not in the battlefields, but in the world of ideas, interests, and aims, have been from the very beginning the force that keeps history running. In the political field, the opposition within a country is usually maintained through the existence of different political parties, particularly if those parties go for different ideas and not only for different men. With the present general tendency toward unification of the world, the main struggle seems to have transferred to blocks of nations which hold different ideologies.

Should we wish one ideology to suppress the other? If so, what could the contribution of the other ideology be? I think there is no doubt that every important and sound historical movement has something to contribute to humanity. And if we look to the present conflict we may hope to have a synthesis of the opposing ideologies in the future which could be the coming together of the political and the social democracies.

That is the ideal: a political democracy that is not supported by social injustice; or a social democracy that is not built up at the cost of lack of freedom and human dignity. We really hope that this synthesis, which no country or block of countries can offer now, will be a reality in the near future. The actual conflict between East and West, if it does not turn into a barbarians' war, could be the force that pulls humanity toward that synthesis.

IX

BARNA HORVATH

1. AMBIGUITY.—The term "democracy" is not ambiguous in the same sense as, for example, the term "lion-hearted" is. Its *literal* meaning is not opposed to its *figurative* meaning. The word "ambiguity" is, therefore, not a particularly happy expression to denote the wealth and complexity of the concept "democracy."

"The part played in present-day ideological conflicts by different interpretations of the fundamental concepts of liberty, democracy, law and legality" is thus not due to the ambiguity of the term "democracy," in the ordinary sense of the word "ambiguity."

These conflicts arise not from the ambiguity of a word with two possible meanings, one literal and the other figurative, but from the sometimes contradictory *logical consequences* which are believed to be deducible from the general concept when it is applied to facts, and from the ulterior postulates that are laid down for the achievement of democracy. Consequently the conflict does not derive from opposed opinions of the ultimate goal of democracy, but of the best means of achieving it. It is also based on a confusion of the end with the means that are believed to be indispensable to its achievement. The source of the conflict can be traced to disagreement on the question: *What does democracy require and what does it not require?*

There is no uncertainty or ambiguity about the *general meaning* of the word "democracy." Its general meaning comprises two concepts: that of the *people* (*demos*) and that of the *government* (*kratia*). It cannot be said that these two concepts are insufficiently clear. They are the outcome of long *historical experience*, of *empirical induction and generalization*. Throughout human society, in the course of its long history, we find the masses, the human material—the humble, the people—and we also find some form or other of managing or regulating common matters—the government. It would merely be hypercritical to claim that one cannot attach a precise meaning to these two words.

But does not ambiguity arise the moment these two words are

95

linked? The composite word "democracy" means that *the people governs itself*. Is it possible to give a definite meaning to this composite word? Undoubtedly, because the uncertainties that arise only concern the achievement, the technique, of this form of government. The *meaning* of democracy is not affected by difficulties in its achievement. We can, for example, attach to the word "democracy" the meaning of a *unanimous decision that is proved to be beneficial and advantageous to all:* that meaning is perfectly clear. Its achievement is difficult, it opens the door to concessions and compromises, but it is—like Rousseau's "general will"—the *ideal pattern,* the changeless and perfectly precise meaning of democracy.

The precise meaning of democracy—the general meaning which is in no way ambiguous—is *good self-government.* This terse formula means that the governed govern themselves and that their government benefits each and all. The Lincoln formula says the same thing: a government *by* the people and *for* the people. Government *by* the people is the *form;* government *for* the people is the *content: political* democracy is limited to the form, *economic* democracy extends to the content.

A government by universal consent and beneficial to all is the *ideal* type of democracy. It is the *superlative* that cannot be surpassed. *Actual* types, historical examples of democracy, approach more or less to the ideal pattern. Ideological conflicts, "ambiguity," "misuse," arise from the overstressing of one or other element of the ideal pattern, and more especially from the error of *confusing and identifying* a particular existing type, a historical example of democracy, with its ideal pattern; in acclaiming as an accomplishment what are perhaps only first faltering steps.

2. EVIDENCE.—My reply to the first question releases me from the obligation of proving that the term "democracy" is ambiguous; I think I have proved the contrary.

On the other hand I have to show *how* the general meaning of democracy, which in my opinion is nonambiguous and only indicates the ideal pattern, became ambiguous in the realm of concrete fact, through the elementary mistake of confusing the parts with the whole, the partial and concrete achievements, with the ideal.

In the case of historical examples of democracy, some concessions have to be made; some elements in the ideal pattern have to be disregarded. At the outset these concessions appear innocuous, e.g., the

exclusion of children, lunatics, and minors from universal suffrage
and hence from the number of the people taking part in the government. But the accumulation of concessions, e.g., the substitution of
the principle of the *majority* for the principle of unanimity, or the
principle of *representation* for the principle of direct participation in
the government, leads up to making the meaning of the term "democracy" ambiguous and its application questionable. The historical
examples, the actual types of democracy, are, as the result of these
concessions—made because of the difficulty of achieving democracy
in the *absolute sense*, the ideal pattern—for the most part only democracies in a *relative sense*. They approximate more or less to the
ideal pattern. Ambiguity begins when we confuse or identify a
historical example of democracy (i.e., in its relative sense) with
ideal democracy (its absolute sense).

For example, Athenian democracy was certainly a democracy *in
relation to* the tyranny, oligarchy or aristocracy of the ancient
world; but it was not a democracy in the modern sense, since it excluded slaves, foreigners, and women. Now the crisis of modern democracy has shown that equality before the law, the political representation of the masses, universal suffrage and secret ballot are not
enough to produce a completely democratic government. The most
perfect form of political, parliamentary democracy is quite compatible with the worst kind of economic oppression, with the exploitation of the working masses. Moreover, it shows alarming incompetence and inefficiency when faced with the problems of a
world that changes rapidly with the swift development of science
and technology. When, prior to 1914, the European parliamentary
system was confronted with *technical obstruction*, it was clear that
it was becoming more and more an *empty formalism*. Agreement on
fundamental principles had ceased. The minority no longer submits
to the majority, which means that *unanimous* acceptance of the majority principles no longer exists; consequently, the logical connection between unanimous decision-making and majority decision-
making, that is, between democracy and majority rule, is broken.
In default of universal agreement, the one can no longer be substituted for the other. Agreement on the principle of *representation* is
compromised. The citizen may indeed register his vote on a list of
candidates every three or five years, but he does not succeed in convincing himself that, by his choice, he is taking part in the govern-

ment except in a figurative sense. The logical connection between self-government and representation is broken, and no known form of the latter can be easily substituted for the former. The citizen represented no longer recognizes, in the conduct of his representative, either his thought, his wishes, or his interests.

But the fundamental disagreement centers on the question whether the "people" whose self-government is at issue comprises all social classes or only the workers. Is democracy possible in a society based on classes or only in a classless society? Does democracy require a classless society? An affirmative answer to this question involves the exclusion from the "people" of many strata of the population. It implies the idea that a class society necessarily means class oppression, the exploitation of the workers, the reverse of democracy. Here again a logical connection is broken: for the complete equality of men is substituted the bare "equality before the law," a formal, legal, and political equality that conceals glaring economic inequality. Thus modern representative, parliamentary democracy, an actual type superior to ancient democracy, was itself first *perverted* and later *exposed* as a disguised form of the *dictatorship of the bourgeoisie*. The term "democracy" became *ambiguous* first because a historical example, an actual type of democracy, was confused with the ideal type and identified with "real democracy," and subsequently because it was discovered that this form of democracy—representative parliamentary government, pre-eminently a democracy from the point of view of the ruling classes—was experienced as oppression, exploitation, and dictatorship by the masses.

What, on the other hand, is the actual type of democracy in a classless society, which the peoples that have more or less achieved this social structure have evolved in exchange for bourgeois democracy? It takes the form of the *dictatorship of the proletariat* or *popular democracy*. These peoples have dispensed with the formalism and most of the principles of political democracy. They set little store by the electoral system, the principle of representation, the principle of the majority, the separation of powers, or the rights of man. Although they favor applied science, which can immediately be turned to account for production, they have no very great respect for free scientific research or free art. Their great quality is the organization of collective production, the iron discipline of a single party (in some cases accompanied by "satellite" parties), the continuous occupation of a large part of the population with political, administrative, or judicial work, in a word, direct democracy. The maintenance and defense of the classless society involves the prevention of the formation of new propertied classes: it must be proved by experience that the classless society *is* workable; and it is from this need of proof that the fanaticism of partisans and their political strategy and propaganda draw their inspiration and persuasive powers.

But dictatorship—even that of the proletariat—cannot be the ultimate meaning of democracy. That is why these forms are only regarded as transitory. The classless society will either develop more complete forms of democracy or make concessions to classical democracy. Meanwhile the liberal and the classical democrat can only conclude that the new democracy has paid too high a price for its victories. It has sacrificed too much of the historical heritage of man: his rights and liberties, his culture and art. The security of a monotonous and austere life, but without the "exploitation of man by man," is an inadequate compensation for the "unlimited possibilities" which a free economy offers him. The logical connection between the autonomy of the individual and the autonomy of the people, between liberty and democracy, cannot be broken.

When the partisans of the new democracy identify it with "real democracy," the partisans of classical democracy therefore have the impression that the term "democracy" is ambiguous, because the form of government that their adversaries call "democracy" seems to them to be a parody of it. The term "democracy" has become ambiguous as regards its concrete historical achievement because of the substitution for the ideal pattern, in the case of parliamentary government, of a formalism that has lost its content and, in the case of the dictatorship of the proletariat, of a content that destroys the methods of procedure essential to democracy.

15. DEMOCRACY AND SOCIALISM.—For more than a century the discussion of this debatable term "democracy" has centered on the problem of the relation between *democracy and socialism*. Is a socialist organization of society compatible with democracy? For the socialists, for all ideologists of working-class movements, the answer is in the affirmative: democracy can only be achieved after a thoroughgoing reorganization of economic and social relationships. For liberals and defenders of the capitalist system, the answer is in

the negative: democracy will perish in a society where all economic
and political power is concentrated in the state.

Among the numerous expressions of this liberal and capitalist line
of thought, those that we owe to Alexis de Tocqueville have had a
particular importance. UNESCO has made a happy choice in giving
prominence, in the basic document of our inquiry, to the famous
passage in the speech made by de Tocqueville on September 12,
1848: "...Democracy and socialism are linked only by a single
word, equality; but note the difference: democracy wants equality
in freedom, and socialism wants equality in constraint and enslavement."

Like the vast majority of liberals, de Tocqueville argues in a
vacuum. It is useless for him to say that "democracy and socialism
are not bound up together" and that "they are not only different
things but opposites." For it was a process of inescapable historical
evolution that raised the problem that democracy must and can only
solve through socialism.

On the other hand, de Tocqueville points out very clearly the possible threat of a "people's tyranny"—a government "more vexatious,
more meddlesome, more restrictive than any other, with the sole difference that it would be elected by the people and would act in the
name of the people." He rightly remarks that it would amount to
conferring "on tyranny an air of legitimacy which it did not possess,
and thus to ensuring it the strength and omnipotence that it lacked."
It is indeed a menace, but this menace, though very real, is not inescapable. Democracy is not, by definition, antisocial, and socialism
is not, by definition, antidemocratic.

De Tocqueville also foresaw the dangers of socialism for "individual independence." But in saying that democracy enlarges it
while socialism restricts it, he commits the fallacy of comparing a
"good" democracy with a "bad" socialism. It is not true that "socialism makes every man an agent, an instrument, a cipher" or that "socialism postulates equality in constraint and enslavement." Can we
on the other hand conscientiously say that "democracy gives to
every man his full value" or that "democracy wants equality in freedom," if we understand by "democracy" the "narrow" political concept of democracy? De Tocqueville confuses the illness with the
cure. It is not socialism's *desire* that man should be a "cipher" or that
his condition should be "equality in enslavement." But, finding the
working classes in that deplorable condition, which is caused by the

change in productive processes, it wants to insure for man, even in those conditions, "equality in freedom" to the greatest possible extent.

It may, however, fail in its attempt, and what remains of its vast conception—the final goal of which is admittedly the abolition of all submission and of all domination, and hence an *anarchical* social order—is often merely bureaucracy and regulation in an intolerable form. Here undoubtedly de Tocqueville touches the nerve center of socialism and democracy. "Individual independence," individual *freedom* does not follow from the definition of democracy. It is merely, as we have already seen, the preliminary condition for "good self-government," for a people can only be really self-governing if the individuals composing it are also self-governing, that is to say free. The autonomy of the people presupposes the autonomy of the individual. "Individual independence," therefore, is not a fixed heritage of democracy, as de Tocqueville thinks, but is rather a task of considerable difficulty on the fulfilment of which the very character of democracy depends: it is the sword of Damocles over its head. Now socialism—although the word is often used as a *contrast* to individualism—is *not* the antithesis of individualism, any more than *society* is the antithesis of the individual. Only for socialism there is an imminent danger of its sacrificing more individual independence than the exigencies of production require, not wittingly, but through being carried away by its collectivist spirit. It is exactly here that the touchstone of socialism as well as of democracy lies, viz., that in every unnecessary sacrifice of *liberalism* they are damaged and corrupted, profoundly and rapidly. They pay dearly for any excess, for the truth, based on experience, that Acton formulated so felicitously is a particularly grave warning to them: "Power corrupts, and absolute power corrupts absolutely."

16. METHOD VERSUS CONTENT.—I will concede that the narrow term, comprising only "methods," has the advantage of being *more precise*. It is easier to check whether a government is directed *by* the people than to determine whether it is conducted *for* the people. The "methods of decision-making" are in general, like all procedural formalities, much easier to deal with than the "contents of the decision made," which are concerned with the root of the matter.

This narrow term has the additional advantage of excluding *value judgments* as to whether a decision that has been taken does or does not conduce to the welfare of the people. It thus eliminates that *laudatory* use of the term "democracy" which renders it inexact.

Aristotle even describes government directed by the people for the common good as *"polity,"* while *"democracy,"* according to him, promotes the welfare only of the *poor* and not of all. For Aristotle, then, "democracy" is not a *laudatory* term; for him it means rather the *degeneration of the constitution.* But he too only recognizes *evaluating* meanings—one *laudatory* and the other *condemnatory*—of "government of the people." The *neutral* sense of this term, stripped of evaluation, is undoubtedly that of government *by* the people, "methods of decision-making," i.e., the first half of Lincoln's definition.

But I do not think that we can neglect with impunity the second half of that definition. It is impossible to make a clear-cut distinction between "methods" and "content," which are to a large extent mutually conditioned by each other. Every government aims and works for the benefit or for the detriment of the people. It is, then, very difficult to leave out of account the aims set and the results produced by the government. Form and content are *correlative* concepts which *together* go to make up "democracy." If democratic "methods" are disregarded, the "content" will itself, sooner or later, become antidemocratic, and if the democratic "content" is disregarded, the form, the methods, will themselves become antidemocratic.

17. CRUCIAL DIFFERENCES.—The principal grounds of disagreement between liberals and socialists relate to the economic organization of society. Liberals like de Tocqueville see only the restrictive and tyrannical character of socialism, and claim that socialism makes every man a "cipher" and postulates "equality in slavery"; while socialists claim that it is capitalism that produces these evils for which socialism is the sole remedy. Other liberals like Bryce claim that it is possible to distinguish between the "form" of a government and its "aim," that democracy has nothing to do with economic equality and that political equality can exist either with equality of property or independently of it. These views are refuted by the socialist criticism of capitalism. Lenin is irrefutable when he writes that capitalist democracy is "a democracy reserved for the minority, a privilege of the propertied class, an exclusive attribute of the wealthy." And Stalin expresses the same thought with even more force: "Democracy in capitalist countries ... is ... democracy for the strong, democracy for the propertied minority."

The fundamental difference lies then in the failure of formalists like de Tocqueville and Bryce on the one hand and the anxiety of communists like Lenin and Stalin on the other to examine this question: *For whom* does democracy in the formal sense of the term mean "freedom" and *for whom* does it mean "enslavement"?

21. DEMOCRACY AND PLANNING.—The delegation of the power of decision is always a concession made at the expense of democracy in the interests of political realism, because it amounts to the relinquishment of a really autonomous decision, that is to say one made by the same individuals who will be ruled by the decision.

Nevertheless, delegation is indispensable. The entire people cannot take part in all the tasks of government. The criteria of "democratic" delegation are (1) that it should come from the people or issue from a democratic decision in the formal sense of the term; (2) that it should be in the interests of the people or issue from a democratic decision in the material sense of the term; (3) that the delegates should be held responsible to the people for the exercise of their powers; (4) that the powers delegated should be kept well apart and balanced; (5) that the delegation should be of short duration and the persons holding the powers revocable.

But political necessity may require forms of delegation that do not correspond to these criteria. That was already the reason for ancient dictatorships. Modern dictatorships are characterized by an enormous concentration of power, by the exercise of that power in the name of a new kind of party, by their unlimited duration and by the absence of formal guarantees of responsibility, separation of powers or revocation of offices. Still, they may be justified by acute necessity, by the supporting referendum of the people, by the new character of government with its long-term plans, and above all by the ultimate proof of a positive result conducing to the general welfare and by the tendency of dictatorships to become, once more, democracies in full harmony with the ideal pattern.

22. TOLERATION OF DISSENTIENT OPINIONS.—Individual autonomy is a presupposition of democracy because public autonomy presupposes private autonomy. The toleration of dissentient opinions is, therefore, a characteristic of democracy. Only when opinions *hostile* to democracy, that is to say to public and private autonomy, become *dangerous* to it, does it with good reason defend itself.

23. REPRESSION OF PROPAGANDA.—Democracy assumes autonomy, individual freedom, but not that perversion of freedom which would involve freedom to struggle against freedom, or freedom to subject one's self to slavery. Democracy implies no obligation to commit suicide.

A democratic government is, therefore, justified in repressing propaganda that advocates a change of regime if (1) this propaganda seriously threatens the democratic regime and (2) the repression is no more severe than the defense of the democratic regime warrants.

24. DECISIONS INCOMPATIBLE WITH DEMOCRACY.—The criteria that justify a decision calculated to limit "democratic" toleration are the assumptions that: (1) a serious threat to democracy cannot be tolerated because democracy is under no obligation to commit suicide, and (2) the limitation of toleration must not exceed what is absolutely necessary for the defense of democracy.

In a general way, "democracy" implies the existence of restrictions upon the contents that the decisions in question, whether individual or collective, may have, because democracy presupposes the most unlimited freedom of individual opinion, which is still *compatible* with the defense of democracy itself, that is to say with good self-government and equal freedom for all.

"Democracy" certainly presupposes general agreement on fundamental and indisputable principles. These include the fundamental principle of "good self-government," i.e., government *by* the people and *for* the people. Another fundamental principle determines which individuals and which groups of the population belong to the "people" on a footing of equality. But there are also *secondary* principles, e.g., that of the majority, of representation, of the precise connotation of "the welfare of the people," etc. . . . , on which general agreement is presupposed by the working of a democratic regime.

25. ONE-PARTY SYSTEMS.—The development that has led to the growth of modern parties emphasizing iron discipline and more and more taking the character of political armies has not been propitious to democracy. Modern parties are organized on an authoritarian and not on a democratic principle.

The successful functioning of democracy depends on harmony between the living convictions of the governed and the decisions of the governors. This harmony is destroyed by the modern party system. There are probably better methods than the party system of arriving at a unanimous or almost unanimous decision corresponding to the living convictions of the governed.

The single-party system, the party of the "new type," is probably an effort to reach a better method. The "single party" is not a party in the same sense of the word as "the parties" in the plural. It is an organization that develops special methods of insuring the popularity and the autonomous character of the decisions taken by the entire government. These methods are information, propaganda, the discussion of practical and theoretical questions, and, in general, the constant occupation of the people with political, administrative, and judicial work.

26. "SKEPTICISM" AND DEMOCRACY.—The principle requiring that every autonomous opinion should influence democratic decision is assuredly a logical consequence of the principle of "good self-government."

It is, however, very doubtful whether the individual, by adhering to one of the parties, can give expression to his individual autonomous opinion. He is obliged to choose between the programs of the parties without being able to know to what extent they reflect his own real interests.

The multiplicity of parties does not insure the realization of the principle that "no opinion is infallible" and that "no group has any self-evident right to claim universal allegiance to its political creed," because the *majority principle* means precisely that the majority decision becomes *law for all*.

29. ULTIMATE AIMS.—The ultimate aim described by Lenin is the classless society which, evolving into communism, *provides the possibility* of the disappearance of "any necessity to resort, in general, to violence against men, to the *submission* of one man to another . . . for men will *accustom themselves* to observing the elementary conditions of life in society, *without violence* and *without submission*." Other theorists attribute a fundamental or intrinsic value to the objective of a society so completely self-governing that violence or submission is no longer necessary, and in that they are in agreement with Lenin. But they overlook what is, according to Lenin, the prior condition for their common objective: the classless society. This preliminary condition, negligible for them, becomes for Lenin *the ultimate objective*.

X

JØRGEN JØRGENSEN

3. MISUSE.—A great number of those who have analyzed the role of the keyword "democracy" in current ideological conflicts have come to the conclusion that no rational justification can be found for charges of *misuse* of a term so vague and ambiguous as this one.

I do not share this opinion. It is true that it has always been difficult to reach an agreement on what the criteria of misuse should be. But it is nevertheless possible to point to concrete cases of overwhelming agreement on occurrences of misuse. It may be fruitful to start out from an analysis of such a case.

In his *Mein Kampf*, Adolf Hitler defined "the true Germanic democracy" as "the free election of a Fuehrer" taking all responsibility for the conduct of the state and making all decisions without further consultation of the electorate.[1]

I have no hesitation in calling this a case of misuse of the word "democracy" because it is used in a sense essentially divergent from the ones it has otherwise commonly been used in. The only point at which the Hitlerian use seems to coincide with the common uses is in the stipulation of "free election," but it is doubtful whether this election has anything in common with the majority vote procedures otherwise normally associated with "democracy." On all other points there is no doubt that this "true German democracy" of his deviates from what is otherwise meant by "democracy."

It is, in particular, an essential characteristic of democracy, as it is commonly understood, that the leaders—the representatives of the people—shall be responsible to their electors, and it is also generally assumed that the representatives should be equal, so that no one

1. *Mein Kampf* (Munich, 1933), I, 99: "Against this stands the true German democracy of the free election of a Fuehrer, who is found to undertake all responsibility for action or absence of action. It provides, not for voting by a majority on individual questions, but for the appointment of a single man, who is then responsible with his property and life for the decisions he takes. . . ." Cf. II, 501, where the basic principle of the Germanic State is stated as: "Authority of each Fuehrer downwards and responsibility upwards."

representative can make decisions on behalf of all, but that decisions must be made by voting under the majority principle. It is further assumed that the representatives are not elected for life, but that they should (after such periods as seem practicable) place their seats at the disposal of the electorate through a new election. Moreover, the representatives' mandate to make decisions is generally limited by the Constitution, so that certain problems cannot be settled without a renewed and special mandate, which—and this must be emphasized—cannot comprise the abolition of democracy, if this is to be a lasting organization of society. In short, it is essential to democracy, as commonly conceived, that the people—the electorate—should not only elect the government, but that they should also, to the greatest possible extent, be admitted to permanent control of its exercise of the power. As this forms an essential part of the common concept of the word "democracy," it is a misuse of the word to employ it in any divergent sense. But why is it a *misuse?* `

First because, without explicitly stating the fact, Hitler deviates from the common use of the word, and second, because this very deviation is apt to mislead the reader of *Mein Kampf*. If the reader at the moment of reading is an adherent of democracy in one of its commonly accepted forms, he will very likely believe that Hitler is aiming at introducing some such commonly accepted form of democracy, and he may thus easily be led to support the National Socialist tendency although it is really contrary to what he desires. Hitler's use of the word "democracy" misleads the reader, and because it is Hitler who deviates from the common use which the reader, in the absence of any explicit statement to the contrary, is entitled to assume is being applied, it is Hitler's use that must be characterized as a misuse, and no charge of misunderstanding on the part of the reader can be made. In this case, then, the misuse consists of the fact that Hitler, without issuing any explicit warning against misunderstanding, deviates from the common use of the term and thus misleads the reader. And what makes Hitler's deviation particularly odious is the fact that the misleading of the reader is contrary to the reader's interests—a fact that becomes all the more serious if it is assumed that the misleading was intentional. If, on the other hand, Hitler acted in good faith, himself believing that he was using

the word in its commonly accepted sense, it would hardly be possible to speak of any "misuse" of it by Hitler; one might speak of
"erroneous" use due to ignorance of the term's common use. One
would hardly describe as a "misuse" the erroneous use of one's own
language by foreigners or small children; nor would one call it a
misuse of a word if it was expressly and clearly pointed out that the
word was used in a sense differing from that in which it was commonly used, and if it was quite out of the question that any misleading of the listener or reader had been intended.

The criterion of misuse of the word "democracy" in this particular case is, then, as follows: (1) the word is used in a manner deviating from common usage without any express warning against
misunderstanding *and* (2) the object of the divergence has been to
mislead the listener or reader, who accepts the word in its commonly accepted sense in good faith.

As to this, however, two observations must be made: (*a*) Sometimes one speaks about the misuse (or even systematic misuse) of a
word, if it is merely constantly used "wrongly" by a single person
or a minority group within a certain language community, even if
there is no deceitful purpose involved. Such employment of the
term "misuse" does not accord with the latter part of the above-
mentioned criterion. (*b*) According to the criterion, everything
called a (conscious) lie is a misuse, and yet there seems to be a
slight difference in meaning between "lie" and "misuse." Perhaps
this is because "lie" is often (always?) used to describe the misuse
of (completely or incompletely formed) *sentences* (statements,
propositions), whereas "misuse" is often used in reference to *single
words*, or *phrases* that do not have the character of statements.

As far as I can see, the foregoing criterion is quite compatible
with the definition of "misuse" given by Ducasse in his answer,[2] as
this definition may be regarded as a closer interpretation of the *first*
part of the criterion. But as Ducasse says nothing about the *second*
part of the criterion, I cannot accept his definition as conclusive.
I do believe that the word "misuse" involves a *moral stricture* because misuse is or tends to be misleading to the receiver (listener or
reader), and it is this that distinguishes misuse from mere "mistake"
(wrong use). Accordingly, in my opinion, Ducasse's definition
only states a necessary, though not a sufficient, condition for the

2. This volume, p. 69.

employment of the term "misuse." In this connection it may also be noticed that by "correct usage" I am only thinking of observance of the current *semantic* rules of the language, whereas divergences from the *syntactic* rules of the language (which in common everyday speech are downright bewildering) are hardly regarded as misuse, perhaps because of the very fact that they are easily noticeable and for this reason (among others) do not mislead. It might perhaps be expressed thus: for a statement in words to mislead, it must make sense; and therefore statements that are syntactically wrong cannot mislead and so cannot be described as a "misuse."

When Professor Ducasse, analyzing the term "misuse" in his answers to the UNESCO inquiry, expressly points out that speaker and receiver must be in agreement on definite semantic rules if proof of misuse is to be possible, I would here add (*a*) that with regard to the expression "current" usage I also presuppose such agreement (although it is usually tacitly presupposed by the very use of the language), but (*b*) that, as already stated, I do not believe that a deviation from these presupposed common rules of the language is sufficient for proving or even alleging misuse; to that end a consciously deceitful purpose must be present, and this may possibly be proved in certain cases, e.g., if the speaker sooner or later admits it, or if by his conduct he betrays in some other way that he must have been aware that the receiver did not understand the term at issue in the same way in which the speaker, by his general conduct, indicated that he himself understood it.

The formulation of general rules as to the employment of the word "misuse," or of criteria for the misuse of words, seems to me, in any case, a very difficult matter, and I must therefore limit myself to a few general remarks.

In the simplest of cases, there is a misuse of the word W if in the language used by speaker and receiver and common to both of them there are quite definite and absolute semantic rules as to the use of W, and if the speaker with a deceitful purpose in mind in using the word departs from these rules. The common (mutual) language may be either the current language, tacitly presupposed by the speaker, or a special language agreed upon by both speaker and receiver.

As, however, the words of the current language are often ambiguous, and as the deceitful purpose of the speaker often turns on this very ambiguity, most examples of misuse will often in practice be more complicated than in the above-mentioned simplest of cases. Thus, e.g., the word "democracy" is ambiguous in current language, and may therefore be employed in several senses that do not involve misuse. By "democracy" one may, e.g., understand "narrow democracy" or "broad democracy." If one wants to avoid misunderstanding (and such accusations of misuse as it may involve) it is essential to emphasize which of the current meanings one is aiming at in any given context. If this is done, one cannot justly, in my opinion, be accused of misusing the word, and in that event any accusation that the word "democracy" is being misused will itself amount to misusing the word "misuse." If, on the other hand, with a deceitful purpose in view, one employs the word in a sense other than that in which it must be assumed that the receiver understands it in a given context, then one has been guilty of misuse. Thus it is also misusing the word "democracy" if as a matter of course one pretends that only one of the current meanings of this word is the "correct" one, for the purpose of leading the receiver to believe this. The main point then seems to me, at all events, to be *the deceitful purpose*, and perhaps one should adopt merely this as the criterion of misuse. The deviation from current usage would then only be an *indication* that deceitful purpose was involved, that is, if the speaker himself was perfectly acquainted with the current usage (which he, without explicitly stating so, was deliberately departing from). As regards "current usage" we must not merely take the isolated, lexicographical meaning (or meanings) into account, but also bear in mind what interpretation, according to current usage, must be regarded as "natural," plausible, or obvious in the situation or context in question.

11. "NARROW" VERSUS "BROAD" SENSE.—Two main senses may be distinguished in the common usage of the word "democracy." The two senses have been given widely different labels: for our purposes it will suffice to call the one "narrow democracy," the other "broad democracy." Both uses have their firm foundations in the history of usage and are fully justified by the standards of everyday political language. There is no question of "misuse" in the one or the other case. The duplicity of usage is very clearly seen from the fact that "democracy" is generally taken to have two highly different contraries, dictatorship or aristocracy. Dictatorship is the concept opposed to narrow democracy, aristocracy the concept opposed to

broad democracy. In the light of this opposition narrow democracy is identified with popular government based on general and equal suffrage rights, while broad democracy equals the popular organization of society without class or caste distinctions. For popular government maximal political liberty is the decisive factor; for the popular organization of society political liberty is only one among many rights to be maximized: the essential objective is maximal equalization of all liberties for all citizens.

Violent controversies have arisen from this ambiguity in current usage. The questions have been asked: What is the "correct" definition? In which sense should the word be correctly used?

It has been answered that questions of this kind have no sense; that there is no "should" about it, no "correct" usage other than the traditionally established one, if any.

I do not share this opinion. The question would only be senseless if it asked whether the usage actually current "should" be different from what in fact it is. But this is not the question at issue: the problem is which usage should *I* prefer, which usage should *I* recommend. That is a problem that is most certainly open to rational argument: the *purpose* of the application of the word, the *context* of its use and the *public* to which it is addressed will all count in the consideration of "correct" usage. One paramount consideration is clarity: if a term is used in divergent meanings, this fact should not be slurred over but brought out in the open to avoid misunderstanding and deceit. In any such case it is amply justified to ask *which* of the actual senses should be set down as the one to use the word in in the future. Past usage need not be the supreme standard in such cases. The purposes of communication should count as much as the traditions of communication.

In theoretical analyses and descriptions there is no need to "legislate" against one or the other of the two concepts of "democracy." The narrow one may be just as good as the broad one. The only prerequisite to be stressed is that the contextual meaning be explicitly stated in order that any possible misunderstanding be obviated.

Many attempts have, however, been made to justify the tendency to reserve the word "democracy" for the narrow political concept exclusively, thereby branding as "illegitimate" or "propagandistic" the broader use of the term. There are several reasons why I do not think this tendency justified:

1. The broader use has just as deep and strong roots in the history of usage: the use of the word was never confined to the strict description of political instrumentalities only but always connoted aims and objectives of social organization as well as means of government.

2. If ever there was a common core in the variety of senses in which the word was used it would come close to this: a general process of development toward greater and greater equalization of liberties for larger and larger parts of populations. If this is so, "political," "juridical," "social," "cultural," "educational," "industrial," "economic," etc., democracy can be conceived of as different aspects of one identical process of equalization and liberation. There is no reason whatever why "democracy" should be used to cover only one of these aspects, the political one. The most plausible solution, therefore, would be to make "democracy" a common denominator for all the aspects in which members of society can be made equal and then specify the different aspects by adding the appropriate adjectives.

3. The tendency to reserve the word "democracy" for the political concept exclusively may promote a formalist attitude of isolation from social, economic, and cultural issues and breed the dangerous fiction that the political life of a people can exist indepedently of other aspects of social life and have its intrinsic value independently of the social and economic conditions it brings about.

4. There is no reason why the proponents of the narrow political concept should have a monopoly on the positive emotional charge that for a long time already has made "democracy" a most valuable tool of persuasion. By reserving the word for the narrow concept they exploit for their own purposes the traditional good will it has acquired. Their reproach that the broad use is propagandistic can be countered by the argument that the narrow use is just as propagandistic in its effects.

16. METHOD VERSUS CONTENT.—The distinction between methods of decision-making and contents of decisions made may be justified and fruitful if real alternatives to choose between exist and opportunities to implement choices are at hand.

But the restriction of the word "democracy" merely to signify the *method* can only be justified on the assumption that human beings have no other common interest than that it shall be possible to settle differences of opinion without recourse to violent means. But this seems to me fundamentally wrong. Biology, medicine, and psychology show incontrovertibly that a vast series of needs are common to all human beings, and that their interest lies in the broadest possible satisfaction of those needs. If one cherishes the view that no greater regard shall be paid to the needs and wishes of one than to those of another (which seems to be the basis of the introduction of the democratic *method* mentioned), one must aim at the maximum *equal satisfaction of needs,* and not be content *with equal suffrage rights.* The latter may at best serve to ascertain *what* are the needs of the different individuals (and even in that context the biological-medical-psychological investigation of needs is, I believe, better than voting), but it should not be conclusive as to which of the existing needs shall be satisfied, and which must remain unsatisfied for the time being. When the needs have been ascertained (and perhaps classified according to their "vital" natures) they ought *all* to be satisfied *equally* to the greatest possible extent (possibly so that every "vital" need is satisfied equally, before an attempt is made to satisfy a less "vital" need equally, as in the former case). Only by acting thus can one be said to respect the needs or will of all individuals equally or justly. But this is not achieved by majority voting. I therefore regard the limitation of the word "democracy" to connote the *method* only as unsatisfactory, since the method is not apt to lead to the end which it should be a means of realizing.

24. DECISIONS INCOMPATIBLE WITH DEMOCRACY.—If there is to be any sense in recognizing a democratic organization of society as desirable, that organization must be such that it can be achieved and be likely to last through time and tide. These conditions can, in my opinion, only be fulfilled by "broad" democracy. Accordingly the limits of "democratic" tolerance are defined by the consideration that only such political propaganda will be tolerated as is compatible with "broad" democracy, i.e., with a practicable and stable organization of society. "Democracy" as an expression of an ideal or an object of political endeavor involves a general agreement on the principles of the "broad" democracy, which can be briefly summed up as follows: The members of society shall be equal as regards the enjoyment of all the material and spiritual benefits at the disposal of society, whether provided by Nature or created by

society itself, including the choice between political, economic, and other possibilities compatible with "broad" democracy. *The main objective is social equality;* this includes equality of political as well as other kinds of freedom and excludes, *inter alia,* dictatorship by a single person or by a minority. Measures or propaganda aiming at or tending toward the increase of existing inequalities are always undemocratic.

25. ONE-PARTY SYSTEMS.—Prohibition upon the creation of parties is incompatible with the ideal "broad" democracy in so far as it is not a question of antidemocratic parties. But as the creation of parties always serves to aggravate the differences between the citizens, it is on the whole desirable that there should be no creation of different parties at variance with each other; and in certain vital historic situations it may be essential to the introduction of democracy that the creation of parties be prohibited, or that only one party, the democratic party, be permitted. In so far as the creation of parties is an expression of existing contrasts of interest, it shows that the fundamental equality in society has not been achieved or has not been recognized by all members of society, and the existence of parties is in a way an indication that the ideal democracy has not been arrived at. In the ideal democracy there will probably be *no* parties at all, but the members of society will elect the persons best fitted to govern, and these will, in cases of disagreement upon definite concrete questions, each vote according to their best convictions, independently of each other and without forming parties that vote collectively on each controversial question. This method of government is familiar to every union where the members of the committee are elected by the members of the union without their having grouped themselves into parties, and where each member of the committee independently takes his stand on the question at issue and votes according to his convictions, without laying down hard-and-fast general programs as a basis for the formation of parties. I therefore regard the no-party-system as more democratic than either the one-party or the multi-party systems; and I regard the multi-party system as more democratic than the one-party system. But the one-party system is also compatible with democracy, if its function is to work for the "democratization" of a people and a state, where democracy is not yet rooted in sufficiently established traditions.

26. "SKEPTICISM" AND DEMOCRACY.—The problem to be discussed under this head may be thus formulated: Does the fact that

no political opinion can be proved to be the only right one constitute a necessary or sufficient condition for the democratic form of government? Or what amounts to nearly the same: Does this fact constitute a tenable and relevant argument for the democratic form of government?

This is a question I would answer in the negative; for I believe that disagreement about political problems is neither a necessary nor a sufficient basis for recognizing democracy, either in its narrow or in its broad sense. For it would not prevent the recognition of democracy, in one or more of the senses of this word, if all were agreed that it is to be preferred to any other forms or systems of society. Thus the disagreement is no *necessary* condition for recognizing it. Nor is the disagreement a *sufficient* condition for recognizing it, for even if all citizens were *disagreed* on all political questions, this would not imply that any equal regard should be paid to all these divergent opinions: if that is asserted, the democratic principle *has already been presupposed*. This, by the way, holds good equally, if all were *agreed* about every political question. For mere factual agreement or disagreement cannot form any *theoretical* basis whatever for the recognition of a definite form of governance or a definite measure, unless one has previously accepted the agreement or the disagreement as a *criterion* of the "best" form of governance. But viewed in a *practical* light, one may rather say that great *dis*agreement is an argument more for the dictatorial "firm hand" than for democratic procedure in regard to the disagreement. However, it is not this very involved practical question which we have to discuss here, and I accordingly turn to the theoretical question, which I shall examine in some detail.

Quite briefly, I would put it in this way: Does political "skepticism" argue in favor of political democracy (democratic form of governance)? We here take "political skepticism" to have two meanings: (1) as implying partly the view that all forms of government or all special political measures about which there is disagreement are equally good, and (2) the view that human beings are unable to determine whether the forms of governance or the special measures are equally good although "in reality" they may not be so.

In the first case there is no logical reason for preferring one of the possible forms of governance or measures to the others, and the most rational course would then seem to be to draw lots between them.

And the same is true of the second case: if human beings are unable to decide which form of governance or measure is preferable, the most rational course would be to draw lots between all those that seem equally good, and then leave it to experience to decide whether the result proves satisfactory, or whether after some lapse of time the solution chosen by lot should be discarded and fresh lots drawn as between the possibilities that remain.

In neither of these imaginary cases is there any known moral reason why a majority (or qualified majority) or a unanimous vote be allowed to be decisive. In fact, in given conditions postulated, a vote merely amounts to the drawing of lots by a comparatively highly complicated and costly process, for the single votes are given "haphazardly" (i.e., on no basis of logical reasoning), and the majority accordingly obtains no *logical* merit as compared with the minority. By a simple drawing of lots the opinion of every single voter is in fact taken just as much into consideration, provided *all* opinions are represented in the lots, as is achieved by allowing each voter to give his vote, i.e., to draw *his* lot out of the parcel of lots.

But a vote may have this merit, that *most* of the voters are satisfied by the result (or will have to take the responsibility if it proves unsatisfactory). This is only so, however, if an *absolute majority* is obtained in favor of one of the forms of governance or measures possible; otherwise the majority would not in fact obtain satisfaction; if, e.g., 40 per cent of the electorate vote for form of governance or measure No. 1, whereas forms of governance or measures No. 2, No. 3, and No. 4 each secure 20 per cent of the votes, then only 40 per cent will in fact be satisfied with the result of the voting (or will have to take the ensuing responsibility).

And now I come to an all-important point: the very principle that the decision be made by majority vote implies that one has *beforehand* taken up the attitude of formal democracy, and it can therefore *not* be used as an argument for taking up that attitude. The "skeptical" view that it is impossible to prove that one or more of the forms of governance or measures possible is (or are) better than the rest, and that they therefore must (or ought to) have equal opportunities of prevailing, is really no reason for taking a vote, but would rather seem to support a simple and direct drawing of lots between them.

If one does not at the outset recognize the democratic principle that every opinion shall have the same chance as every other opinion, "skepticism" does not imply any definite mode of decision at all. And even presupposing the democratic principle mentioned, "skepticism" does not imply that the decision should be made by purely formal democratic methods; the drawing of lots would, as stated, be more rational.

But for other reasons as well the "skeptic" argument in favor of formal democracy is untenable; because its assumption—that all forms of governance or measures are or must *be regarded as being* equally good—does not hold water in actual social life.

The disagreement among human beings as to what form of governance or measure is the best is *not* a proof that all forms of governance or measures actually *are* or at the outset must *be regarded as being* equally good; not even an incidental agreement (i.e., one not based on reason) would provide such proof. No voting, but only rational reflection based on an empirical examination of the needs of human beings, can have any force of proof, and the democratic principle itself—that equal regard should be paid to the needs (or "ideas" about the needs) of all the members of society—cannot be *proved*, but will have to be *presupposed*, if the method and the result are to be described as democratic.

In consideration of needs it must also be borne in mind that what satisfies one citizen does not always satisfy the other, and that the disagreement is no proof that the opinion of one is as good as that of the other; not even an "incidental" agreement between the two would prove that what they agreed about would necessarily be best for them. What is best for each person depends on how far it satisfies his needs, how far it furthers his success or well-being, etc. And so far as this is concerned, all biological-medical-psychological experience goes to show that all (normal) human beings have, to a preponderant degree, uniform ("common") needs. If therefore one takes the democratic point of view that the government of society shall pay equal regard to the needs of all citizens, the most important task will be to ascertain (*a*) what needs actually exist, (*b*) the size of the groups that have each of these needs, and (*c*) how important each of the needs are. The most vital needs, common to all or to the great majority of the citizens, will then, according to this point of view, prevail over those of minor groups only. For deciding this, the method of voting by mainly inexpert voters, as to which form of governance or measures they prefer, is neither reasonable nor reliable, especially when the "free press" and other vehicles of propaganda, unrestrained save by economic considerations, are allowed to mislead and sway the voters according to the interests of the rulers. Where private capitalism holds sway over press and propaganda there is no guaranty whatever that governments will be elected that will pay equal regard to the needs of the electors according to the degree of urgency of those needs, even if elections by "free and secret" ballots are organized.

An indispensable basis must be: *rational and comprehensive information without any misleading suggestions* as to relevant current conditions, i.e., as to the effect of the different forms of governance and measures possible on the satisfaction of the needs of each elector—not solemn promises, but clear and rational arguments. It is accordingly necessary, first and foremost, to free political information from the influence of economic and other forces, and then to require that the representatives who are candidates for election pass a specific political "personality test" as well as an examination on such matters as they, if elected, will have to settle. Probably the achievement of a democratic organization of society will also necessarily involve the fulfilment of all those conditions that are inherent in the idea of a "broad democracy"; but this is not the place to examine this further in detail, and I accordingly summarize my view of political skepticism as follows: (1) Political skepticism is an attitude that is not well founded. (2) Even if political skepticism were justified, it would not constitute an argument in favor of "narrow" political democracy, the "justification" or desirability of which can hardly be proved, but will have to be presupposed as a postulate about which one may *fight*, but about which one cannot *reason rationally*.

30. NATURE OF THE DISAGREEMENT.—Current ideological controversies are, in my opinion, essentially based on divergent conceptions of communism as opposed to private capitalism. One group regards communism as the best and only way toward ideal democracy, whereas the other group regards communism as a denial of human rights which are firmly established in the "narrow" democracy. The disagreement is on the whole not one of principle, but arises from a *conflict of opinion as to what communism is*, and it should therefore be possible to solve the controversy by a rational

and impartial examination of the question: What is communism in theory and practice? But in my opinion the irreconcilable contrast in principle lies between private capitalism and communism. It is this contrast that leads to an *exaggerated emphasis* on the contrast between narrow and broad democracy, between which there is really *no difference* at all, as broad democracy comprises narrow democracy and even seems to be the basis of the complete achievement of narrow democracy. It is the interest in private capitalism that creates the opposition not only against communist, but against the achievement of both narrow and broad democracy. But the history of recent years seems to show that private capitalism (monopoly capitalism and imperialism) are contrary to the interests of an overwhelming, majority of humanity, as it prevents or impedes the equal satisfaction of fundamental needs of this majority, e.g., needs for food, health, housing, safety and peace, as well as the possibility of an unlimited increase of this satisfaction.

XI

HUMAYUN KABIR

A. Ambiguity and Misuse

There can be no question that the term "democracy" has been used to mean different things in different ages. To the Greeks it meant the rule of demos or the rabble and was opposed to aristocracy or the rule of the élite. It is a far cry from such a view of democracy to the modern attitude when the voice of the people is regarded as the voice of God. It is inevitable that a term which has differed so much in connotation in different ages should also bear different meanings in the same age. Those who are contemporaries in time are not necessarily contemporaries in thought. Some continue to cling to the beliefs of their predecessors; others anticipate the thoughts of their successors.

Variety and even contrariety in contemporary views of democracy are, therefore, easy to understand. This is mainly a historical heritage, but it would still be necessary to explain why the same term has been used to cover such diversity of attitudes. Prima facie, the use of the same term suggests that there must be a core of meaning which remains identical in spite of variations in the concomitant elements.

Against such a view may be objected, as is suggested in the UNESCO document, that the word "democracy" is only too often "used without any definite meaning at all." Argumentation along this line is not convincing since it ignores the elementary truth that whatever has no meaning can evoke no attitude. Initially, we do not have *words* but only *sounds*. They have neither a connotation nor can they evoke an attitude. Through repetitive use, a sound becomes attached to a meaning and it is only when this happens that we have a word. Students of logic know that even proper names which start as mere pointer words soon acquire a significance. Whatever evokes an attitude can do so only on account of the connotation it acquires.

A slogan is effective because some connotation has become attached to it. This is not to say that the connotation is definite or fixed. In fact, no connotation, even of the most abstract terms, can ever be absolutely precise. Scientists and philosophers know that in spite of all their attempts at definition, different writers use philosophical or scientific terms with variations in meaning that give rise to ambiguity.

In a sense, such ambiguity is inevitable to any process of thought. The function of thought is to generalize experience. Since experience is always growing, the terms must fluctuate in their import. A concept, on the other hand, tries to serve as a fixed focus in the midst of such flux of experience. Not only so, but a concept is hardly ever, if at all, completely intellectual. Conception is linked to perception which carries with it a penumbra of affection or sentience. The conative element cannot also be altogether ruled out. Most concepts are, therefore, part concept, part feeling, and part volition. In the case of scientific and philosophical terms, the elements of conation and sentience are at a minimum. In political concepts these elements are not negligible so that their content is a complex of feeling, thought, and volition combined in different proportions. This helps to explain the ambiguity in a term like democracy. There are different historical associations present in the minds of different individuals. There is in addition room for difference due to the different emphasis on the intellectual, emotional, or volitional content of the concept.

It is thus obvious that the term democracy is, and perhaps must be, used in divergent senses. We would not, therefore, be justified in characterizing any use of the term as illegitimate, unless it can be established that the additional content which differentiates such alleged illegitimate use does in fact destroy the core of meaning which has achieved general acceptance as the connotation of the term. New and divergent uses are permissible only if the divergence does not go beyond a certain point. On similar grounds, the application of the term to a country can be regarded as improper only if the state of affairs there violates or denies some of the characteristics which constitute the essence of democracy as generally accepted in that age.

An analogy may help to clarify the point at issue. White and black may be regarded as opposites, but there is a gradation of colors from white to black through different degrees of grayness. If any one of the shades is taken by itself, we may have no hesitation in placing it in one group or the other, but when they are taken seriatim, there are many points at which classification becomes doubtful.

The confusion is increased by the fact that in a concept like democracy the actual and the normative cannot always be kept distinct. In addition to the inevitable fluidity of content in any concept, we have here an additional element of uncertainty in the natural human tendency to confuse ideals with actual conditions. The difficulty of teleological explanations is nowhere greater than in a political concept. This is without doubt a factor for increasing the violence of controversy. An ideal is a state of affairs which is not existent but which is desired and believed capable of achievement. Thus the ideal is a possibility but not an actuality. One consequence of this is that the greater the gulf between the ideal and the actuality, the more vehemently it is desired. This brings an explosive element in all matters concerning the ideal or the normative. The fact that a concept like democracy represents partly the actual and partly the ideal, therefore, increases its emotional charge. It is not surprising that discussion about its import often ceases to be intellectual appraisement and becomes violent support or vehement condemnation.

There is also the difficulty inherent in the nature of language itself. We have already seen that words cannot be confined to a point of meaning but must inevitably cover a more or less wide area of significance. Through definition, this area is narrowed down but there are limits to the process of definition. We choose a particular meaning out of a set of possible meanings by reference to the context. Outside of its context, an isolated term has a bewildering multiplicity of implications and associations. If, in addition, the context itself should be variable, the demand for identity of signification is bound to become a cause of conflict. Where a term seeks to express a broad field of experience, it is inevitable that different users will have different aspects in mind. To insist on uniformity in such cases would be tantamount to denying all interpretations except one's own. Such narrowness of view is bound to provoke opposition. Such labeling, docketing instinct is due to a desire of economizing intellectual energy, but often proves a potent source of conflict.

The crux of the problem, however, is to find a common characteristic, if any, in virtue of which the term "democracy" may be used to describe a series of situations or attitudes diverging from one another in many particulars. To my mind, this point of identity is supplied by a correlation between duties and rights. The one thing which distinguishes all the different political systems and ideologies which we call democratic is the urge to establish an equivalence if not identity between the two.

Historically, this is comparatively a new development in human thought. It was not always accepted as a self-evident truth that rights must be coincident with duties. For long ages, a vast majority of the people had only duties, but few, if any, rights. There has been no stage in society when duties were not enforced, but there have been many periods in history where rights or, at any rate, the same rights were not guaranteed to all. We may, therefore, say that two essential characteristics are found in all concepts of democracy and differentiate it from any other type of social organization. They are (*a*) the attempt to establish the equality of rights and duties for all members of a community and (*b*) the attempt to make rights and duties coincident.

The attempt at equalization of rights and duties for all is absolutely basic to the concept of democracy. It is precisely the absence of such equality which marks an undemocratic society. Where a group has larger rights or, for that matter, duties, than others, we miss the differentia of a democracy. We must, however, give a more precise meaning to the equality of rights. It involves equality of opportunity but does not necessarily involve equality of enjoyment. Individuals differ from one another in a thousand ways. They have their own likes and dislikes, their preferences and aversions. Equality of rights cannot obviously equalize tastes and distastes, but it can and must imply that each individual has equal opportunity of satisfying his or her legitimate claims.

Similarly, equality of duties does not mean identity of functions. Here again, individuals will differ according to their latent faculties and course of development. It would lead to obvious absurdities if the same services were required from individuals with different abilities. Nor is such a demand necessary. No society can survive without a multiplicity of functions and services requiring different types of aptitude and training. It is, however, necessary that they must all be performed in the manner best conducive to the maintenance and progress of social good. Equality of duties, therefore, would mean that whatever be the function of an individual in a society or state, his degree of obligation must be the same.

B. SOCIAL VERSUS POLITICAL DEMOCRACY

The analysis of democracy attempted above would help to resolve the seeming conflict between social versus political democracy. Lincoln's definition of democracy as government *of* the people, *by* the people, *for* the people is as explicit a statement as anyone could expect. Lincoln's definition takes cognizance of all the elements necessary for a democracy. There is reference to the obedience of the people to the government, to the active participation of the people in the framing of decisions and to the value of such decisions for the general welfare of the people. The element of equal obligation for all implies the equality of duty for all citizens. The opportunity of shaping decisions and enjoying their fruits is a recognition of their equality of rights.

If we remember that the equivalence of duties and rights is the differentia of a democracy, the attempt made, e.g., by Bertrand Russell to differentiate between the Anglo-Saxon and the Russian concepts of democracy must break down. The distinction between the rule of the majority and the interests of the majority can never be absolute. Wherever the majority rules, it is certain that, but for stupidity or ignorance, the interests of the majority will prevail. The minority may at times arrogate to it all the wisdom of the community. It may claim and even believe that it is acting in the interests of the community as a whole. This may also hold for a brief interval, but there is no evidence that consistently or over a long period the minority has ruled in the interests of the community. Its interpretation of the communal interests has often been a rationalization of its own purposes and used to defeat the interests of the majority. It may indeed be said that the precise raison d'être of majority rule is to guarantee majority interests. The whole course of historical experience shows that any class or group permanently dissociated from the exercise of power is also permanently in a position of social and political inferiority.

The definition attempted above looks at democracy as a broad movement in human history. Its essence lies in the tendency to broadening of rights and duties and their equalization for all. If this is accepted, it is obvious that democracy cannot be merely a political concept designating methods of decision-making. It is a sociopolitical concept designating conditions and methods as well as results of decision-making.

The conflict between these two points of view is not a mere terminological problem but goes into the very essence of the concept of democracy. It is doubtful if a mere political democracy could ever exist. The attempt to give equality only in the political sphere would be defeated by the existence of inequalities in wealth, position, status, and, most important of all, intelligence and education. The classical jibe at free competition between an unencumbered athlete and a cripple burdened with a load applies even more to the concept of political democracy devoid of all other elements of human equality. The reason why the futility of mere political democracy has escaped the notice of even political philosophers is to be found in the fact that methods of decision-making cannot but influence the content of the decisions. Wherever the control of policy lies in the hands of individuals or cliques it is inevitable that, however disinterested they may be, the decisions taken will directly or indirectly be to their benefit. If for no other reason, this will happen because of the limitation in the point of view or approach of the participants in such an authority. On the other hand, wherever the decision-making body is large and represents diverse interests, it is natural that consideration of various points of view will lead to some decision which will be, if not most acceptable to all, at least be least unacceptable to the majority.

This is also the reason why it can be plausibly argued that political democracy is the best method of achieving the goal of social democracy. The contrary would not, however, be necessarily true. Even in the improbable contingency of achieving social democracy without political democracy, it could not continue to exist for very long. Here again, history offers interesting evidence on the point. Anthropologists are generally agreed that there was a primitive communism where property was held in common by the community. Such a system may be regarded as a type of social democracy. It could not, however, continue. The absence of political democracy meant the concentration of power in the hands of a few individuals or groups with results disastrous to the existence of social democracy.

In the light of the foregoing remarks, de Tocqueville's attempt to differentiate sharply between democracy and socialism cannot be accepted. Socialists, or even Communists, are right in their insistence that democracy necessarily implies the extension of the equality of right from the political to the social and economic fields, that is, the abolition of privileges, the reduction of class distinctions, and perhaps even the socialization of the means of production. The attempt to deny such an extension in the meaning of democracy by insisting on terminological exactitude is like the attempt to hold the sea back with a broomstick.

Like de Tocqueville, Lord Bryce also sought to restrict the meaning of democracy by identifying it with a form of government. Both of them attempted to differentiate the form of government from the purposes to which government may be turned. They, therefore, claimed that political equality could exist either with or apart from equality in property. We have already seen that the whole course of human experience denies the basis underlying such a contention. It may be true that absolute equality in wealth is not necessary for maintaining political equality. It is, however, equally true that political equality becomes a mockery if inequalities in property range from those who have more wealth than they know how to use to those who do not have even the barest means of subsistence.

Another distinction between democracy and socialism sought to be exaggerated is the role of individual enterprise. In de Tocqueville's words, "Democracy extends the sphere of individual independence, socialism contracts it; democracy gives to every man his full value, socialism makes of every man an agent, an instrument, a cypher. . . . Democracy wants equality in freedom, socialism wants equality in constraint and enslavement."

The distinction on which de Tocqueville builds his case is, however, more verbal than real. In a laissez-faire society, the individual is supposed to have independence. As has been pointed out more than once, this freedom is very often nothing more than a freedom to starve. Deprivation of the means of livelihood places very real limitations upon the supposed freedom of an individual in a free society.

We have to remember another fact. In no society, whether free or otherwise, can a human being be regarded on the analogy of an undifferentiated unit in a complex. Even supposing that an individual is initially free, he is tied down by his own act of choice. Assuming that a man freely chooses to become a laborer in a field or a research worker in Relativity Physics, he cannot, without effort and perhaps disruption of his personality, change over from one vocation to the other. Again, the moment he has chosen a vocation, he performs certain social functions and will prosper only so far as he acts as an agent or instrument of social policy. An individual who is continually fighting against social trends or attempting to reverse decisions which he himself has taken, would be much more of a cipher than one who accepts social obligations and carries them out to the best of his ability.

From the opposite point of view, one could argue with equal validity that the scope of individual independence is not and cannot be ruled out even in a socialist state. In a socialist, no less than in a capitalist state, there must be planners, executives, and executants. Someone must attempt to anticipate the future in the light of past experience. Someone must try to devise concrete measures to carry out policies in the light of such anticipations. Someone must be there to carry out the particular acts which follow from the adoption of the plan.

Again, when an individual accepts fully and freely any role assigned to him, he has no sense of constraint in carrying out the actions which follow from the adoption of that role. Nothing gives a greater sense of freedom and creative activity than acceptance of one's station and its duties. It is division of mind and uncertainty about one's objectives that cause hesitation and a sense of frustration. Where, therefore, the objectives of the socialist state are fully and freely accepted, socialism would act not as a factor of constraint but of liberation and release of energies.

What is interesting to note in this connection is that the protagonists of "democracy" and "socialism" are, in spite of their violent disagreement about the relative values of liberty and equality, at one in their dissociation of means from ends. The "democrat" emphasizes liberty and insists that whatever be the result, the method of taking decisions is what matters. So long as the appearance of a free political decision is there, it is immaterial to him whether the consequences bring social justice or not. In other words, he is concerned only with the means and not with the end. Equally, the "socialist" who insists that equality must be established in every sphere of life, whatever be the method adopted for achieving it, is prepared to flaunt his adherence to the view that the end justifies the means. Thus the two agree in the divorce of means from ends even though to one it is the means that alone matters, and to the other, the end.

Without entering into a metaphysical discussion on this point, it may, however, be stated that all such attempts at divorce of ends and means have resulted in contradictions. Ends and means together constitute a unit. Any attempt to judge one element independently of the other invariably leads to one-sided, if not false, conclusions. Such attempts at divorce between the two are based on the uncritical assumption that all relations are external and that elements remain unaltered whether within or outside a context. Even if this should ultimately be so, no one has a right to assume it without examination. Experience shows that elements are *in fact* determined, at least partially, by the context in which they occur. Hence, dissociation of means from ends or ends from means cannot but lead to erroneous conclusions. To sum up, even if ends are not means, means and ends are so related that each modifies the character of the other. The condemnation of an end must, therefore, necessarily lead to the condemnation of the means to it. Contrarily, if the means are indefensible, this would immediately rouse doubts about the justification of the end itself.

C. Tolerance and Treason

We may sum up the result of our discussion in the three following statements: (1) Democracy means a continual attempt at equalization of rights and duties for all; (2) it is a continual process and we cannot foresee its end in any conceivable future; (3) means and ends cannot be divorced from one another without violence to the meaning of each. It would, therefore, follow that democracy must tolerate the existence of opinions divergent from or contrary to those which are accepted by it. It must tolerate dissentient *opinion* even when it is hostile to democracy, provided that, like any other state, a democratic state also reserves the right of opposing or suppressing *action* hostile to its very existence.

The distinction between opinion and action may at times be difficult to draw. Nevertheless the distinction is real and cannot be denied. A person discussing a political concept with half a dozen friends is clearly operating in the realm of opinion. The same ideas expressed before several hundred persons in a university union is a border-line case, while expressed before an audience of ten or twenty thousand, the discussion or speech might itself become violent political action. A democracy must, however, take the risks attendant on the toleration of such expression and interfere only when the expression merges into action.

To deny the right of expression to opinion only on the ground that it is opposed to the prevailing temper of society is manifestly unjustified. To deny it even on the ground that it might lead to subversive activities would be to deny the nature of democracy. We have seen that the connotation of the term is not immutable or fixed. Its meaning has expanded within the period of recorded history and is still expanding. Nor is the process likely to be completed soon. The vitality in the concept of democracy demands that opinions making for change in the prevailing state of affairs must be tolerated. The democratic state would, therefore, be justified only in suppressing the adoption of undemocratic procedures for changing its decisions. So long as changes are brought about through persuasion and acceptance by the majority, a democracy cannot, without denying its nature, suppress propaganda opposed even to the values for which it stands.

The suggestion that dissentient opinions should be allowed only among those who accept the fundamentals of democracy is to beg the question. There are phases of history when the fundamentals of democracy are themselves in dispute. The controversy as to whether equality of opportunity should be restricted only to the political field or should also be extended to the social and economic spheres is only one instance of the fact. History shows that the connotation of the term "democracy" has itself changed and there is no reason to suppose that there will not be further changes.

If the aim of democracy is the equalization of rights and duties, it would follow that a one-party system can hardly ever, if at all, reflect a democratic society. It could, only if both of the two following conditions were satisfied, viz., (1) the equalization of rights and duties has been achieved, and (2) the party in question reflects not only the will but also the interests of the whole community. In fact, however, neither of the conditions has ever been fulfilled. Equalization of rights and duties is still an ideal and must for ages to come remain so. Nor has any political party ever succeeded in reflecting the will and aspiration of an entire people. On a specific issue, it is perhaps possible to achieve unanimity regarding what is good or desirable for society at any stage. Should this happen, a particular party which stands for that program may for the time being act in the name of the community. Even on specific issues, this is a theoretical possibility which is rarely realized in practice.

Unanimity, even if achieved, is precarious for specific issues. For broad concepts of social welfare it is perhaps impossible of achievement. The facts of difference in history, background, experience, and temperament are bound to influence different individuals in different ways. It is, therefore, inconceivable that there should be unanimity with regard to the general picture of social welfare among all members of a society. The absence of parties other than the party in power would immediately evoke the suspicion that differences of opinion have been directly or indirectly suppressed. Those who claim that skepticism is part of our faith are, therefore, right up to a point. The course of philosophical development proves that no opinion is infallible. No group can, therefore, have the self-evident right to claim universal allegiance to its political creed.

To admit the possibility of diversity in opinion and belief is not a sign of lack of faith in democracy. On the contrary, it may well be evidence of firm conviction about the justice of the democratic principle. In behavior, we find that men are most insistent when there is lack of certainty in their beliefs. Where they are absolutely sure of a position, they feel no need to stress its rightness. People react violently when attacked in their weak spots. Disputants lose their temper only when they are uncertain of their grounds. In logical analysis, "must" has in it an inferential element which makes it weaker than a simple, categorical "is." "It must be so" never has nor can have the same force as "it is."

The conflict between advocates of social and political democracy is due primarily to the intolerance which tends to weaken, if not nullify, the concept of democracy itself. Protagonists of either school tend to identify democracy with their own concept. They not only reject all other interpretations but deny their very possibility. They also tend to deny the element of growth and development in the connotation of the term. Much of their difference is due to the historical conditioning of their thought, but even after all instrumental differences have been allowed for, one fundamental difference in valuation remains. This is the opposition between the demands of liberty and security.

We have seen that there can be no political liberty for the individual without a modicum of economic and social security. We have seen that security is equally dependent upon a minimum of personal freedom and initiative. There is, therefore, a broad field where the two concepts converge and the whole attempt of modern man is to extend the area of this convergence. From the nature of the case, there must, however, remain a borderland where the one operates to the exclusion of the other. Perhaps we should not say exclusion, for what happens is that the one principle is more dominant than the other in a particular field or phase of experience.

We may even agree in principle to the fields where the one or the other should predominate. In practice, however, such agreement has never been achieved. Thus we may say that in the field of thought, there should be no limitation to liberty while in the field of behavior, the needs of security should govern our action. No two men would, however, agree as to where to draw the line between thought and action. In fact, such demarcation depends as often on feeling and temperament as on thought or belief. Some individuals are prepared to risk the present for the future. Liberty will have to them a stronger appeal than security. Others would like to assure the present and let the future wait upon its promise. Such men will respond more readily to the appeal of security.

Liberty and security may, therefore, be regarded as the systole and diastole of the human mind. But there will be certain minds to which one will have a greater appeal than the other. Lesser appeal does not, however, mean absence of appeal, for the two values, though distinct, are interrelated. Each is complementary to the other and cannot exist in isolation. Recognition of this should also be the beginning of a toleration which, finding room for both within the concept of democracy, can make its principle a deciding factor in the resolution of human differences.

XII

HORACE M. KALLEN

A. Ambiguity and Misuse

I sincerely doubt whether any fruitful results can come out of an analysis of the "ambiguities" of the word "democracy." I do not believe that the word is ambiguous to any of its users; nor do honest users regard themselves as guilty of misuse. The divergencies between the senses the word is used in by politically opposed users cannot be traced to any kind of "misuse" unless insincerity or malice is evidenced. These constitute all that can properly be meant by "misuse." Now, I do believe that certain modifications in the meaning of "democracy" have become current which tend to effect a mutation from the original intention of the word. Those are due almost entirely to Russian practice, and honest people in other parts of the world have taken over the usage. While I prefer to continue to mean by "democracy" the program initially defined by Jefferson and implemented more or less successfully since his time, I would prefer to let the processes of usage take care of themselves. If the alternative meaning became current, I would try to find another word for the spiritual and behavioral realities for which "democracy" seems generally to be a name. I regard the semantic question as being only incidentally an independent variable. When ideals are merely professions and not programs, it is possible to talk about them as the Sidney Webbs talked about the Russian Constitution. When ideals are programs, they exist in various stages of actualization and "the fight for the ideal" is obviously a fight for whatever in fact actualizes it and not for a label merely.

B. Social versus Political Democracy

I reject the idea of any out and out opposition between "social democracy and political democracy." I think the difference is one of scope and range, but not of character. In Lincoln's formulation, "government of the people, by the people, for the people," the intention of the word "government" must be taken to cover every mode of organization intended to direct behavior. Whatever be the character of the association—political, economic, religious, cultural, recreational, educational, sexual, and what have you—in which people who are different from each other undertake to live together with each other, the basis of the association is voluntary participation by all concerned in the goals, the methods, and the alterations of the control of the common enterprise. This is not true of Russia, even when you accept Bertrand Russell's interpretation of the Russian view of "democracy." The facts of record certainly do not bear out this interpretation of Russell's, since the Russian association is not voluntary and the interests of the majority are not determined by the majority but by a ruling "élite."

From what I have already said it should be obvious that I decline to make a rule as to how the word "democracy" should be used by others. The fact is that it is sometimes applied to limited areas of behavior and sometimes to very extensive ones, and that there is a disposition always to broaden the field of application. It is a matter of record that where "political democracy" obtains people are disposed to employ their political power in order to extend the democratic relation to other fields. As to priorities, there is no evidence yet of "social democracy" leading to "political democracy" while there is evidence of "political democracy" finding extension to "social democracy." As to which is means or which is an end, the answer would depend on the sequence of events. There is no intrinsic quality which requires either to be one thing or the other. What particular pattern of social organization may follow a political pattern seems to me rather a matter of will and purpose than a matter of logical or dialectical necessity. This is particularly valid, I think, in respect to "the socialization of the means of production." Such a process might be the enemy of political liberty as well as a reinforcement of it. When the liberals and conservatives reacted against the idea that "democracy" had economic and social implications it was because, like Socialists, they were concerned about either the holding or the extension of their own powers and privileges. It is now customary to speak of "democratic socialism" so as to distinguish it from communism. Thus the Soviets validate the distinction quoted from de Tocqueville; the British may invalidate it; our own TVA does invalidate it. That men first proposed socialism as an instrument of freedom and now use it as a rationalization of tyranny indicates that "socialism" is as viable a term as "democracy." If you take Bryce's conception of "democracy" as "merely a form of government" and take it to apply to all governments, religious and economic and educational as well as political, you can accept it as far as it goes. But it is obviously not compatible with the propositions of the American Declaration of Independence.

It should be obvious that I do not believe that you can separate "democracy" from liberty. I regard "democracy" as an organization of liberty, anywhere and everywhere. When controversialists such as de Tocqueville and Lenin separate them, they do so not as disinterested observers, but as debaters making special pleas. The terms they select and how they use them are functions of the interests they are endeavoring to serve. Whether these interests are called "real" or illusory depends on who makes the call. Obviously, to no party at interest who is honest and sincere can his interest be illusory. When a diversity of interests are in play, if discussion is free and full, it either comes to a conclusion in a consensus or in a division into majority and minority. The criterion is created by the terminus reached, and it obtains, in a free society, until free and full discussion changes opinion again.

Such discussion, of course, implies a maximum of knowledge. When you speak of a body of voters 80 per cent of whom "were kept in conditions of minimal intellectual independence, etc." you are not talking about a "democratic" society. If, on the other hand, the 80 per cent *kept themselves* in that condition, making no effort to change it, they could very well be "democratic." The difference would turn on the effort to obtain access to alternatives of thought, opinion, etc. Bona fide presentation of alternatives under rules of free communication would be "democratically justifiable." This becomes a guide to drawing the line between "democratic" and "non-democratic" delegation of power. The "democratism" reaches an optimal level in consensus, down to majority. In this country it can be prevented by a senatorial filibuster, and both are subject to continuous checking by a public opinion which depends on an untrammeled right to speak and to *listen* for the drawing of conclusions.

C. Tolerance and Treason

What I have just said points to what I believe to be involved in the rights of opposition. On this point I know of nothing in the record which makes it necessary or desirable to modify the position taken by John Stuart Mill in his essay "On Liberty." It is clear that without a thorough understanding of alternatives the growth and defense of "democracy" is handicapped. The limit is reached where the intention of the alternative is manifestly the destruction of "democracy." Just as, according to Mill, a free man cannot logically choose slavery since he thus chooses the destruction of his freedom, so a free society is not required by its own logic to facilitate its own destruction. The limits are obviously those of the "clear and present danger" invoked by the late Mr. Justice Holmes. That this process is difficult, no one denies, but, on the whole, the American way has not done badly in the handling of the problem of the limits of freedom; and it is well to remember that perfect, foolproof solutions are possible only to God, who has very carefully chosen his confidants regarding these. So far, "democrats" are not among them. In the United States the objection is rather to the violence of change than to the nature of change; but I should myself prefer to oppose any change which cut off the freedom to continue to make changes. In the United States the lines of change are defined in terms of the Declaration of Independence, the Constitution and its amendments, and now also the United Nations Organization with its Bill of Human Rights, etc. These, with their acquiescence in the plurality and diversity of individuals and societies and the right of each to life, liberty, and the pursuit of happiness, would make it necessary to rule out the imposition of a one-party political system. None such can be compatible with a "democratic" form of government, whatever be the area, religious, economic, etc., no less than political. From this it follows obviously that even if there were infallible opinions they could lose nothing of their power and validity if fallible alternatives had every opportunity to survive or perish on their merits in the open market of political opinion. In fact, a demand for "universal allegiance" is a sign of a lack of faith in the power of a doctrine to win and hold allegiance on its own merits. The infallible should be able to survive the challenge of inquiry and the test of experiment without any other help, and skepticism of it could only serve, when free and competent, to vindicate it. Thus the uses of skepticism are correlative to the uses of faith, and the one faith which I regard as indispensable to "democracy" is a faith in freedom. Generally, intolerance is a sign of insecurity, or a concealed or overt skepticism of one's own doxy.

D. The Value Foundations of the Conflict

I regard all value-judgments as ultimately as irreducible as the individuals who make them. In the course of the daily life they are functions of the judges far more than the judges are functions of them. People like to diminish or destroy some aspects of their experience and preserve or expand others. They start, from where they are, to alter it by transformations of this kind. They speak of these transformations as "ought" and "duty." Sometimes they are in the position of two men trying to marry the same girl. They might create a world in which the girl could be the wife of both of them; or they might stay in a world in which they have to fight each other for her possession; or one might care enough about the girl to give her up to the other; or the girl might reject both. The "oughts" in these alternatives would develop as rationalizations of the passions in play. There have been events in history, especially those known as religious wars, where alternatives have been analogous. They could even be extended to the bitter refusal of some sects to eat meat and to insist on vegetables, or to wear their hair in one way and not another for the glory of God. There is no use talking, in such situations, about "primarily local cravings" as against "basic differences." The Civil War between the Big-Enders and the Little-Enders in Lilliput could be called a matter of "local cravings" rather than "basic differences in values"; but it was a Civil War just the same, and wherever individuals or societies are ready to risk their lives for some mode of thought or behavior the issue is "basic" enough.

So when it comes to suppressing fascists and not communists or communists and not fascists, there is a matter of preference and passion more or less explicit. In terms of the "democratic" process, repression weakens "democracy" by keeping it unready. Its stability is not so much a function of the elimination of the infection as it is development of antibodies which neutralize and check the infection. It is this process which makes immunity in matters of health, and I believe the same thing to be true with respect to "democracy."

I do not believe that "ideological controversies" are ever "assuaged." Like the controversy over evolution, they are dropped because one alternative has been able to do the job in which it

claimed proficiency better than its competitor. There are few direct conversions on the mere logical merits of an issue. Sometimes
a common enemy may lead to co-operative defensive action from
which positive co-operative action may stem. It was certainly hoped
for when Russia and the Allies were "united" against Hitler. A natural catastrophe such as an earthquake might also lead to defensive
and remedial co-operation which could spread out into continuous,
positive, constructive collaboration. But it is also possible that one
of the opponents might point to the event with delight as the judgment of God and, instead of helping, gloat. Sometimes the most
that can be expected is that the rivals shall live together in each
other's presence in a sort of painful toleration, or it may be that the
kind of practice of *live and let live* and even *live and help live* may
develop that is achieved by the Protestant sects through the Federal
Council of Churches and that is intended by the Charter of the
United Nations. Again, doctrine may here be entirely contradictory
to discipline, as the teachings of many Christian sects exemplify
and, of course, the whole Marxist gospel. The facts of record and
the doctrinal pretension are polar opposites to each other. Hence,
whether there be any "incompatibility" between Lenin's *terminus
ad quem* and other people's does not make any difference in the
working relationships. But there is an incompatibility for the very
reason that you cannot separate the way of reaching the goal from
the goal reached. The going creates the goal, whatever be the language in which it is described.

XIII

HENRI LEFEBVRE

Before replying to the main points in the questionnaire, I should like to make a few general remarks on the concept of democracy (and what democracies are in reality) and on the *method* by which the full implications of this concept (and the reality it covers) may be analyzed.

If we accept the classic division of thinkers into *empiricists* and *rationalists*, it is easy to demonstrate that no one can possibly acquire a clear understanding of the problem of democracy!

Empiricists concentrate on describing the evidence before them. Relying on what documentary evidence, insight, and personal experience they have, they give a more or less accurate description of the way a particular democratic system functions; but they are prohibited, by their intellectual temperament and the method they employ, from any extensive reference to *history*. They can hardly *compare* various types of democracy; and lastly, how can they make any critical judgment when they confine themselves strictly to the description of facts? We must not forget that the true empiricist, who does no more than note down facts, cannot even bring out the general tendencies behind those facts, for he would have to distinguish between facts which are more or less fundamental, more or less significant, by distinguishing vital elements from others that are degenerating, and by contrasting factors that hold the seeds of the future and have potentialities of development, with those which are decaying and dying. The convinced empiricist believes that any such judgment is a judgment of "value," distinct from the judgment of reality; and he cannot, unless he renounce his principles, make such assessments. *Critical* thought is therefore impossible for him. In describing reality, he accepts it as it is at the moment of description and in the place of description.

The *traditional* rationalist, on the other hand, will reflect on the concept of democracy. He will formulate it, a priori, as an abstraction or an ideal. He will then condescend to come down to the facts, which he will study and judge in relation to the concept previously evolved. In all probability, he will emphasize the discrepancy between fact and ideal; he will be tempted to condemn all actual political systems because they do not correspond to the ideal notion, because, for instance, they do not secure the absolute justice or the absolute equality between men which, for him, are part of the concept. How can the rationalist understand the complexity of history and the trends of history? He may well lapse into skepticism.

To deal effectively with so wide and profound a problem as democracy, a new method of thought is necessary, going farther than the empiricist's description and the rationalist's abstract reasoning. We must be able to penetrate the complex reality, comparing and contrasting facts, so as to give new meaning to an idea as it becomes increasingly concrete. We must not therefore separate facts and history from the attempt to give a rational statement of future problems. We must manage to draw critical conclusions and practical guidance from a study of the vital course and underlying tendencies to be discerned in the facts.

This question of method, which will later help to untangle the problem with which we are concerned, unfortunately begins by making it more complicated. The traditional schools of empiricists and rationalists, by temperament and training, treating one another with a measureless contempt, will yet unite to combat the new form of thought. They will meet it, as they have already been doing ever since it came to birth, with a refusal which is sometimes sincere, an indignation which is sometimes comical, and a "demurrer" which is sometimes extraordinarily obstinate. For instance, when the new type of thinker, the *dialectician*, happens to speak of *contradictions* in facts and ideas, the indignation of empiricists and rationalists knows no bounds. Contradictions are inconceivable to the rationalist; and to the empiricist, they only indicate a mental attitude; a contradiction cannot be observed, for any actual fact capable of description is fact enough; as a real and specific fact, it is consistent.

We must therefore agree about the use of this term. In the following pages, "contradictory" will not mean "absurd" or "impossible." The term will be used to define any reality or idea which, on analysis, is found to contain aspects which are not only different but contrasting in the strongest sense—real conflicts, forces, and ideas at issue with one another.

Those who may be surprised at such a meaning, or may find it curious, or obscure or abstract, are asked to accept it provisionally, as a hypothesis, and to become more familiar with it before rejecting it. If the method here advocated succeeds in shedding some light on the problem, if our analysis does in fact show that there are "contradictory" aspects of democracy as a fact and as a concept, the opponents of the dialectic method will be asked at least to treat the dialectician politely, and not merely, as sometimes happens, to shrug their shoulders or cast up their eyes in horror.

In fact, when we consider the history of democracy since the concept and the fact made their appearance in political life—about 150 years ago—deep-seated contradictions seem to appear.

I. IN THE PHILOSOPHIC, MORAL AND CULTURAL SPHERE

For a century and a half, wherever democracy has been introduced and has not undergone profound transformation, it has found expression in an increasingly noble, beautiful, and attractive *ideal*, which has been given various names: first of all, charity, then justice, and later, more recently, humanism, care for the individual human being.

Unfortunately (as all will agree), in the same period, facts have been becoming more and more disagreeable, more and more ugly and indeed sordid, more and more harsh.

Who would dare assert that the advance in practice and in real life matches the subtle refinements in the development of the ideal? When we look at life at it is, every honest man knows what he feels and sees, and can define it: poverty, misery, weariness, exhausting labor at narrow confining tasks, cruelty suffered from childhood on, loneliness, pessimism, despair—all sorts of habitual distresses with a few additional blows on occasion, such as economic crises, wars, etc.

For a long time, in the old type of democracy, the (apparent) reconciliation of the ideal with reality took the form of *promises*. But promises lose their power when they are never fulfilled, and the discrepancy between ideal and fact, between theory and practice, now gives rise to an intolerable disquietude, because it has become a *contradiction*.

The (apparent) reconciliation has moved into the sphere of distant, inaccessible, transcendent "values." It matters little to the theoretical exponents of "values" that man in reality is oppressed, hounded, and exploited, since the transcendent *value* of the human person remains intact! This, however, is what Marx wrote, making an ironical play on the double meaning of the word: "There came a time when all that men had previously regarded as inalienable was bought and sold in trade. A time when the very things which hitherto had been communicated.but never exchanged—given but never sold—acquired but never bought—virtue, love, opinion, science, conscience, etc.—all these were brought into trade! It was the time of general corruption and universal venality; to use the terms of political economy, it was the time when everything, spiritual or physical, became purchasable and was taken to market for its value to be assessed. . . ." That is the time of transcendent values! The less free men are in reality, and the more each individual's liberty depends on the money he possesses and his readiness to serve money, the more noble, grandiose, and pure do speeches on liberty become!

This is so true that any philosopher worthy of the name, that is to say, with a clear and critical intelligence, wonders what can be the function and significance of the ideal and values. Are they consolations? Compensations? Philosophic fictions? Intellectual illusions? Fine embroidered veils to hide ugliness? Perhaps they are all those things together.

II. IN THE SOCIAL AND POLITICAL SPHERE

We all know that modern jurists, and the state considered from the legal point of view, have created a curious fictitious character—*homo juridicus*, the man who knows all the laws and who, in theory, is to be found in every individual. "No one is supposed to be ignorant of the law."

Everyone has encountered the contradiction between this entity and the real individual man. Everyone has found himself caught in the network of complicated and unfamiliar laws, everyone has lost his way in the maze of regulations and procedure. Whereas every man is supposed to be familiar with all the laws, in practice certain men have to specialize in the study and interpretation of the laws; no one can have a full knowledge of them, but that does not prevent these specialists from earning a living—and sometimes a very good living—by teaching others what everyone is supposed to know.

This same democratic state has established another and still more extraordinary fictitious character: the *Citizen*. The Citizen has carefully considered opinions. He gives a reasoned judgment, based on a full knowledge of the facts, on all the affairs of state. The Citizen is perfectly informed of everything going on in the state and society (just as he is familiar with all the laws). He is free. The Citizen is neither rich nor poor (and therefore—no one knows how, but that does not matter—he finds circumstances propitious for his full employment and development). He is not a shoemaker or a woodcutter, a metal-worker or a banker; he is neither old nor young, man nor woman. And then, he is so many things at once! Endowed, as a human being, with universal reason, he has thereby universal knowledge; being perfectly free, he obeys only the law of morality. Among the citizens there is fraternity, equality, and democratic order. Every citizen has made a free social contract with the other citizens, the state and society. Lastly, the Citizen is the governor!

To discover the position of the real individual in parliamentary (or presidential) democracy, we have simply to take the opposite of the state of affairs we have described above. The real individual never quite knows what is happening in the higher spheres of politics (manifold intrigues, the private work of parliamentary commissions, secret diplomacy, etc.). The real individual is rich or poor (and more often poor than rich). He is young or old, a peasant, a working man or a banker. He is isolated or linked with other individuals by specific interests. He comes up against the state, which is not at all like a free association or a free social contract, but instead takes extremely unpleasant forms (such as taxes and police) and, on closer acquaintance, proves to be "the coldest of all cold monsters" (Nietzsche). The real individual chooses "freely," from time to time, the person or persons to whom he consigns his freedom—his mandatories, his elected representatives, his deputies. One second's liberty against years of submission to the government which emerges, often in an unexpected form, from these "free" elections! The real individual is concerned with more or less honest political organizations: committees, party bosses, the machine or the caucus, as they say in the United States of America. Through the press, he hears about discussions in assemblies, where, as one humorist has said, all private interests are efficiently represented but not the interests of the people or the nation!

But what is the use of continuing this analysis of the contradiction between the Citizen and the Individual, between the political fiction and the social fact? Volumes could be written on the subject —and have been written! For a long time, uneasiness and disquiet about the trend, the fate and the future of this old form of democracy have been spreading.

We shall simply emphasize one point. The disparity between the political state and the facts of society, between the Citizen and the real Individual—deep and distressing as it is—affects the whole of life and makes itself felt in every field. What is the state? It is the community of men which has been distorted and become fictitious because private interests wield too large an influence in it. The real man exists on two levels; he is "simultaneously a part of slavedom and a part of the community" (Marx). In dealing with the abstract community and the political fiction, liberty becomes abstract, liberty to enter into none but free contracts, liberty to choose one's opinion from a series of possible opinions. In dealing with the realities of economic and social life, freedom is the unbridled course of economic entities divorced from all human considerations: the law of competition, the law of the jungle, the law of money and money's domination. It is freedom to enjoy life as we will, provided that the individual is favored by money and fortune, i.e., by chance and circumstances. It is the freedom of the isolated social atom, the freedom of absolute egoism; it is also a freedom which immediately encounters obstacles that cannot be overcome: occupation, environment, social class, work and the demands of work, the selfishness of others.

By consigning all factors making for community to the sphere of the abstract, political fiction (which, at the same time, is dominated in a very practical way by private interests), the old form of democracy allowed the survival of no real links between human beings except the bonds of selfish interests. Behind the stirring slogans of the political fiction, "Liberty, Equality, Fraternity," "All for the people and by the people," etc., the diametrical opposite in the real affairs of mankind is concealed. The old form of democracy, therefore, does not stand solely for a certain attitude toward private property (although that is an essential aspect of its organization). It stands for an attitude toward man as a whole, whom it is gradually disintegrating and decomposing. For this reason, the ideal of progress and humanism with reference to this type of democracy is today particularly misleading.

III. IN THE HISTORICAL SPHERE

The contradictions briefly analyzed above have been apparent in history. It is hardly necessary to remind readers that democracy began in a burst of enthusiasm, hope, faith, and optimism.

Deeply impressed by the American democracy, a fairly unbiased observer, Alexis de Tocqueville, wrote: "The gradual development of equality is a providential dispensation. It has the main characteristics of such a phenomenon: it is universal, it is enduring, every day sees it more firmly established beyond the control of human power; all that has happened, and all sorts of men have aided its development. . . . Can anyone think that, after destroying feudalism and vanquishing kings, democracy will fall back before the bourgeoisie and the rich? Will it stop now that it has grown so strong?"

What must have been the prestige, the impetus, and the strength of democracy a century ago, for anyone like M. de Tocqueville, in whom feudal and bourgeois instincts were combined under the veneer of liberalism, to describe the future of American democracy, and democracy in general, in such terms!

Was M. de Tocqueville right or wrong? He was both. Democracy will doubtless carry the day, in time, on the whole front against the bourgeoisie; but it will not be exactly the democracy which destroyed feudalism and vanquished kings. It will be—it already is—another type of democracy, with some characteristics radically opposed to those of the earliest form.

Where, in history, did the break occur? When was the differentiation established?

In considering this point, a comparative history of the various democracies would be extremely useful. It would extend far beyond the confines of our survey. In England, for instance, the impetus carried on for a long time, strong enough for Marx and Engels to believe in the possibility of an economic and social revolution within the political framework of bourgeois parliamentary democracy. In other instances, so far as Europe, and more particularly France, was concerned, from the time of the 1848 Revolution, and still more after its failure and the events of 1871 (the Paris Commune), Marx considered a political revolution the prerequisite for economic and social reform. As parliamentary democracy disclosed its capitalist leanings and developed into the dictatorship of the bourgeoisie, it then became necessary to substitute for it the dictatorship of the proletariat, to break down and transform the bourgeois state and state machinery into a new type of state, as a temporary but essential means of rejuvenating democracy and making it a *practical fact* in economic and social life.

In France the break occurred in 1848, that fateful year when events moved so rapidly and ruthlessly. The unanimous enthusiasm, infinite hope, and boundless confidence in the future and potentialities of democracy were destroyed in those June days when the French bourgeoisie turned against their allies of yesterday, the people, the proletariat. The proletariat demanded the fulfilment of the promises made them; they wished to win their place in the nation; they had a fierce and passionate desire that democracy should not become merely a political fiction, a "form," but a living force, an economic and social democracy. They demanded advantages commensurate with the extent of their sacrifices in the joint struggle against the monarchy. The French bourgeoisie managed to drive them to despair and revolt. The middle classes crushed the progressive wing of democracy and thus signed the death warrant of that democracy itself! In France at the present day, therefore, we find no new situation, no new words or concepts.

In England, America, and elsewhere, the course of economic change and of changes in the structure of capitalism (the movement from capitalism with free competition to monopolistic capitalism) was to be the only factor determining the time when the original form of democracy was changed into its opposite, when, under the outward forms of democracy, there existed the more or less hostile and more or less open dictatorship of the upper middle classes.

It must be admitted that in other countries many people probably find the situation less clear than in France, for in France the memories of 1848 and 1871 are still very much alive and are part of political experience. But even if, in any given set of circumstances, people are not clearly aware of the position, the existence of that position is not precluded. The only difference is that in France the problem is more clearly stated. When we talk of "contradiction" in the history of peoples, nations, and social classes, we imply problems, *political* problems, efforts to find a solution and movement toward that solution. When we speak of "conscious contradiction," we imply that the solution is taking shape, can be guessed at, is beginning to appear.

The contradictions of democracy under a capitalist regime have been clearly displayed in the history of England. If we agree with the historians that Magna Carta in 1215 was a first step toward freedom and democracy, the English people took seven hundred years to achieve that democracy. They achieved democracy, however, in the parliamentary form, at a time when that form had already been outstripped by history. Was it an advance, the universal suffrage that the English people won after the sufferings and sacrifices of World War I? Yes, certainly, in a sense; it was even an important advance; but at the same time, and in another sense, it was deception and trickery, an apparent concession in form alone, a political maneuver. The historical philosopher, the dialectician, never tires of pondering such ironies of history; in its golden age, the great British democracy was merely an aristocratic democracy, a constitutional monarchy with a property qualification for the vote. When democracy was formally enlarged to a system of universal suffrage, it was too late; monarchy, trusts and monopolies, imperialism, and an imperialistic foreign policy were already established and found justification and confirmation, for the time being, in universal suffrage, which, fifty years earlier, might have led the English democracy on a different course!

We can very easily understand why many British citizens, and particularly workers, have only a confused idea of the real historical position in which they are placed and of the true structure of their democracy. They are still dazzled by their recently won universal suffrage; and, incidentally, their universal suffrage has not yet, by any means, had its full effect. In this old country, political experience in the contemporary sense of the word is still fresh, new, and inarticulate. What irony!

It seems that, in the spiritual and cultural sphere, the governing classes in a parliamentary (bourgeois) democracy pass through the following phases of development: hope and enthusiasm; disappointment and uneasiness; need for justification; greater uneasiness; cynicism, pessimism, and despair.

A. Ambiguity and Abuse

If what is said above means anything, the concept of democracy contains no ambiguity. Democracy clearly implies justice, liberty, order, progress, reason, fraternity, and a living community of individuals within the nation. On the other hand, the concept of democracy and real democracies have also implied, and still imply, no less clearly, a *contradiction*. The inherent contradiction at the origin of democratic society between the bourgeoisie and the proletariat, which at first was latent, develops into a class struggle and a contradictory concept of democracy. On the one hand, we have bourgeois democracy, involving the economic and political supremacy of the capitalist bourgeoisie; and, on the other, we have proletarian democracy, implying the end of bourgeois democracy, the bourgeoisie, and capitalism.

According to the supporters of proletarian democracy, bourgeois democracy has gradually abandoned the aims of progress, justice, fraternity, and equality which were an integral part of the idea; democracy has thus become no more than a *trade name*.

Therefore, in the opinion of these supporters of proletarian democracy, i.e., of the dictatorship of the proletariat over the bourgeoisie, bourgeois democracy corresponds less and less to the real idea of democracy because the bourgeoisie becomes reactionary.

We must surely agree that they put forward serious arguments, deserving very careful attention, in support of their thesis.

The concept of democracy thus seems quite clear, and the contradictions in it cause difficulty only for those who obstinately refuse to admit that a fact or a concept may prove contradictory.

There is, therefore, no ambiguity in the concept, no obscurity, no confusion, but a dialectical contradiction and a historical conflict.

May it not seem that confusion arises and abuse appears when one form of democracy tries to pass itself off as another; that is to say, most often, when middle-class politicians say that theirs is not a bourgeois democracy but is in harmony with the democratic ideal and human "values," that it is therefore the only genuine and acceptable kind?

If this is so, the whole confusion is based on misconception, resulting either from social prejudices which obscure the issues and cloud judgment, affecting even the general methods of thought, or from a deliberate, cynical determination to bamboozle.

B. Social Democracy versus Political Democracy

The foregoing considerations have already made it possible for us to delimit the problems raised by the second group of questions: the relationships between political democracy and social democracy—between *formal* democracy and *real* democracy.

In the absence of any proof to the contrary, it appears that the two concepts of democracy (or the dialectical nature of the concept) give rise to two radically different attitudes toward the facts of human society and mankind as a whole. We shall consider this point at greater length.

One view takes the human being as a universal, generic term in the abstract—the Citizen, the Man of the Declaration of the Rights of Man—and thus leaves exposed to chance, circumstance, and blind and brutal forces the real individual who, as an individual, can claim no practical universality. What is strange and curious in this philosophy of democracy is that it constantly swings from one pole to another. Based on the abstract generality, which is therefore *formal* and without practical content, it constantly claims to understand and defend the real individual whom, in law and fact, it abandons to his sad fate. When, however, anyone raises objections based on the individual's position, showing the individual human being as he really is, i.e., as a collection of needs, desires, tendencies, aspirations, and social relationships, this philosophy immediately takes refuge in the realm of the ideal, remote "values," abstract morality or metaphysics, and, therefore, in formal deliberations. This is the plane, divorced from reality and dealing with arbitrary standards and abstract judgments of values, on which the political philosophy of bourgeois democracy is at ease.

It is so true that such democratic thought and philosophy are confined to the abstract and *formal* plane, that *formalism* has carried the day in every field: abstract, formal painting; abstract, formal poetry, etc. The conjunction of formalism in culture and formalism in politics is too extraordinary to be attributable to chance; it is due to a certain conception of man and culture.

The proposed topic, "social democracy in contrast to political democracy," might be stated in more comprehensive terms: "content versus formalism in all fields." It is obvious, however, that, so stated, the topic is too wide for the present analysis.

And yet, this idea of the *content* is the crux of the discussion, and we must now make some attempt to elucidate it. Philosophic and political discussions show how incomprehensible this idea is to many sincere seekers after truth. On this point there might be a fruitful discussion which, while not reducing opposing contentions, might be conducive to comprehension.

Most present-day thinkers swing, as we have just said, between the abstract universal ("values," moral obligation, duty, and the categorical imperative, or the world and life in general, etc.) and the individual as a phenomenon, as pure "subjectivity."

The idea of *content* immediately escapes from this fluctuation. Content is concrete, objective, and historical. Content is real life, the daily life of real individuals caught up in their trials and sufferings, their daily work and aspirations. Content is the present historical situation, the present moment in history. And content therefore exists before men's awareness of it; it demands and necessitates such awareness, producing it in the same way as a problem gives rise to and produces "awareness" of the problem and of its solution.

There is no need to emphasize the importance of this statement. Comprehension of the content so defined is at first dim and uncertain and then grows clearer and more profound. It may begin with the reflections of one man or a small group of men. For instance, Balzac, that genius of the novel, realized the real content of bourgeois life—selfishness, unscrupulous ambition, and the pursuit of profit, honors, and power—at a time when the bourgeois of fact, while pursuing their very practical aims, were still lost, in the philosophic sphere, in a maze of sentimental, moral verbiage borrowed from the past.

What a striking instance! The genius who has realized the real content of life *represents* human beings, of whom he has a *truer* and more accurate understanding than they have of themselves.

That is the crucial point, philosophically speaking. That is what the thinkers who oscillate between bald subjectivity and abstract generalities are unable either to understand or admit. Philosophically speaking, this is where the misunderstanding resides.

The major consequence of this is that a man of genius (such as Marx) and, later on, a group of men, may be the first to realize the content of real life and the vital and essential requirements of their era. Even if others do not yet understand them, these men nonetheless present the true appearance of the moment in the life of humanity.

What an ambitious claim to make, some people will say. But where do they find any sign that the human intellect should abandon ambition? Neither Plato nor Descartes nor Hegel taught any such renunciation.

In fact, however, the men in question make no claim to be the sole repositories of truth or to be the only ones aware of the implications of their time. On the contrary, they combine modesty with the demands they make, and say that they are only the path by which the "contemporary" era gradually realizes its true nature; that they are only the means by which the masses and the peoples— the essential *content* of true mankind—gradually emerge from their paralysis, their long passivity, their silence.

In this way, what has to be done *for* the people is not necessarily grasped at once or immediately accomplished *by* the people.

The people need to awaken to their own significance as the content, that is to say, as a body of individuals, needs, endeavors, creative efforts, and aspirations.

It is possible, at a given moment, to paralyze this process of awakening to some extent, to inhibit and repress it (to use terms current in psychology). It is also possible to assist it in its efforts, which affect history and man.

It is not impossible that, at a particular time, one man, standing alone or almost alone, may be the true representative of a people or of all the peoples, and of the whole future of mankind.

In 1789, no one contemplated the removal of the king. The very idea would have seemed impious; the religious and almost metaphysical prestige of the royal person was still enormous. In the course of events, a few bold men, as lucid of intellect as they were courageous in politics, had to grasp the idea of the abolition of the royal power for democracy to be established in France.

Nearer our own days, in 1914, when Lenin was living, almost isolated, as a refugee in Switzerland, he wrote *Against the Stream*, arguing against war and proclaiming the need for a revolution.

May it not seem that Lenin, in 1914 (like the Jacobins in the French Revolution) stood for the true understanding of the historical situation, in spite of his isolation? That he thus became an active factor in that situation, grasped the content, the real significance and the underlying trend of history, and was working *for* the peoples?

"What a dangerous statement!" more than one reader will cry. "Anyone will thus be able to say that he is speaking in the people's name and on their behalf, and that he understands the needs and aspirations of the people better than they do themselves. You are arguing in favor of fascism."

Not at all. Sooner or later, the people recognize themselves in those who have expressed their spirit. The realization, by an individual or a group of individuals (and, in particular, by a political party), of the essential needs of the people and the fundamental trends of history can be only the affair of a *moment*. Nothing great can be achieved *without* the people and still less in opposition to them. An ambitious man, a usurper, or a clouder of issues may turn one section of the people against another and, as fascism did, employ for the oppression of the working class other classes which nevertheless belong to the people (some of the middle classes, small shopkeepers, the unemployed, etc.). Sooner or later, history judges and decides—history, which is not an abstract entity, but the movement of the masses and the peoples who fight on, following the lead of those in whom they recognize themselves, and abandon to destruction those who have misled them.

Thus, we may find a distinction between the terms "for the people" and "by the people," but only for a moment. The combination of these terms defines true democracy, i.e., the *content* of the idea. Lincoln's famous definition, in its entirety, with its full significance and scope, is still a very appropriate description of true democracy: government *of* the people, *by* the people, and *for* the people. It determines the content of democracy and, although it does not specify its form, states implicitly that the form must emerge from the content.

This is not surprising. Does not this definition date from the era of enthusiasm? Is it not an expression of the first strong impetus of democracy, the first surge of the people toward democracy?

This deeper analysis thus brings out the significance of the contradiction we had already discovered. It is a contradiction which appears, in history, between the abstract form and the real content, being transcended and resolved, in history, when the content breaks through the abstract form in which men have tried to inclose it and, as it breaks through, produces a new form.

Bertrand Russell[1] is correct in stating that, for Marxism, democracy is defined by the *interests of the majority*—and not by the body of opinions, more or less transient, more or less variable, and more or less well-founded, of the individuals constituting the majority. He thus makes a very good distinction between content and form. He makes a mistake when he adds maliciously that, for Marxists, those interests are determined "in accordance with" their political philosophy. In fact, Marxist political philosophy consists, first and foremost, in the acquisition of understanding, in the most scientific possible detailed study, of those interests. If those interests have objective existence (as a *content* of political thought), surely they must be studied in this way. How could Marxists "determine" them arbitrarily in relation to a pre-existing philosophy? Moreover, the "political philosophy" of Marxism corrects some of the terms "classically" employed by democrats.

The "people" is not a simple idea or a homogeneous body in reality. Only an early democrat—that is to say, one thinking and acting in the original enthusiastic period of democracy—could consider "the people" as an obvious fact, as a whole, or could identify the people with society as a whole without any more profound analysis. A people is a nation, first of all. In any particular nation, the people are a body of social groups whose essential characteristic lies in the fact that they are productive workers (intellectually or materially). The non-productive are not part of the people. No consistent democrat, in Lincoln's time, would have included an aristocrat or a landed proprietor in the people. Surely it is obvious that the economic and social development of the bourgeoisie has proceeded in such a way that it has become difficult, and even impossible, to include certain sections of the middle classes, and particularly the upper middle classes, among the people. In the eighteenth century, the bourgeoisie was obviously a part of the "Third Estate," of the people. That was still true for part of the nineteenth century; less and less so in the second part of the century; and it is not true at all today. The same development can be seen in the United States of America, England, and France. The

1. As quoted in the UNESCO questionnaire, see this volume, p. 516.

"people" is the whole body of the productive groups: the lower middle classes, artisans, peasants, technicians and intellectuals, industrial workers. Of these groups and classes, one is distinguished by what we might call an originally *negative* privilege: the working class, the proletariat. Marx showed that this negative characteristic (maximum amount of work for the minimum share in the advantages of social life) was turning, just because it was negative, into an essentially positive characteristic. The proletariat is becoming the source of creative movement; the other productive classes and groups may, and must, rally round it to organize a new type of society. The working class is becoming the active, fruitful nucleus of the "people."

The idea of "majority" is likewise becoming more profound and gaining new meaning. The "political philosophy" of Marxism asserts that there is no divergence of interests between the various sections, social levels, groups and classes that constitute the "people." The interests of the privileged classes and castes, the feudal or neofeudal landed or moneyed aristocracy, industrial magnates and financiers are opposed to those of the "people." However, beneath apparent and superficial differences—which are of importance only in the structure of apparent and formal democracy—a scientific (economic and sociological) analysis brings out the similarity of the interests of all the "popular" classes. For instance, by specific studies on peasant ownership, the prices of the products of the soil, fertilizers, and agricultural machinery, Lenin was able to show "the immediate and substantial advantage which the agricultural population of France would derive from a proletarian rule."[2] That is the *content* of the confused, abstract and formal concept of the "majority."

We may add that Marxist "political philosophy" bears no resemblance to the sort of speculation evolved by professional philosophers and intellectuals who have specialized in abstractions. There is, of course, a Marxist philosophy, which Marxists say is *scientific*, being based upon a systematic and scientific analysis of manifold facts, and, in particular, of economic and social facts. In the opinion of Marxists, this philosophy is not deduced by the formal process of logic from a few principles arbitrarily fixed in the abstract by philosophers, with varying degrees of skill, consistency, or intelli-

2. Lenin, *Complete Works* (Russian ed.), XXVI, 105.

gence. This philosophy has a practical, historical basis: the necessary endeavors of the working class to change its circumstances and therefore to transform society. The Marxist philosopher does not stand apart from those endeavors; he does not even pose as an observer or detached witness; he thinks out the line of action; he takes as his principle Marx's famous thesis: "Hitherto philosophers have merely interpreted the world in various ways; the task now is to transform it."

The misunderstandings, the "confusions," the failure of the philosophers of bourgeois democracy to understand the "political philosophy" of Marxism obviously originate in a fundamental difference of attitude. Bourgeois democratic philosophers, adopting an abstract, formal, point of view, do not and cannot set themselves the aim of transforming the world or helping in that transformation. Their attitude, their method, their line of reasoning, all lead them to accept the world as it is, to observe and describe, and to fit it, as it stands, into established categories and concepts which are, therefore, already on a "formal" basis. The Marxist philosophers start from the *content*, stressing not only the intolerable aspect of the world as it is, but the *movement* within the world tending to transform it, which is based on the action of the working class.

The contradictions we have already mentioned may thus be analyzed and more deeply comprehended. The inconsistency between form and content is based on the contradiction and conflict between the classes in bourgeois society. The point of view of the content is the point of view of action and action on the part of the proletariat as a class.

This analysis therefore brings us to a closer grasp of the *content* of the concepts, their practical significance, and their real effect in action.

Here two specific problems arise, of limited scope but of primary importance—the problem of *property* and the problem of the *state*.

In any democracy there must be a practical attitude toward property and a practical solution of the problem of property. Where private ownership holds unbridled sway, there can be no question of democracy. In fact, all democracies have imposed and still impose restrictions on the "sacred" principle of private property. The American and English democracies provide abundant proof of this in the very heavy taxes which, in those countries, are levied on inherited property.

Does this mean that a transition from liberal, bourgeois, capitalist democracy to socialist democracy might be conceivable? A number of democratic, or even self-styled "socialist," thinkers have adopted this point of view. It is still, however, an abstract and formal view. Indeed, it fails to introduce the important distinction between consumer goods and the means of production. But we cannot conceive of a true democrat who is not opposed to that form of property which tends to maintain privileges and to increase class differences—the private ownership of the means of production.

The only genuine democracy is defined by an attitude of conscious opposition to the form of property that tends to preserve the privileges, to increase the division of classes: private property in the means of production.

The content of the idea is therefore in conflict with the abstract form on this particular point. True democracy does not consist in equality of property (where property exists, even if it is acquired by work alone, inequality survives, for the productivity and "value" of the work of individuals differ). Nor does it consist in the abolition of property (which would mean retrogression and the encouragement of mediocrity and primitivism); it consists in a change of the social organization based on property and inequality, a change for which a number of *political* measures and decisions are necessary.

Only two paths are open, only two solutions possible: the path of capitalism, becoming less and less democratic even when the outward form of democracy is preserved; and the path of socialism, putting the concept of democracy—its content and not its form—into practice.

There is no third solution; there is no third force (any more than there is a third direction, in "political philosophy" and general philosophy). As early as 1921, Lenin showed that the hypothesis of a third force, a third direction in every field, was based on the hypothesis of a third economic and social factor, independent of the proletariat and the bourgeoisie, socialism, and capitalism.

The issue is clear to anyone who is not duped by the outward forms of democracy (universal suffrage, etc.), Lenin added. ". . . every attempt on the part of the petty bourgeoisie in general, or of the peasants in particular, to realize their strength, to direct economics and politics, has failed. Either under the leadership of the proletariat, or under the leadership of the capitalists—there is no middle course. All those who dream about this middle course are empty dreamers, fantasts. They are refuted by politics, economics, and history."[3]

This brings us face to face with the problem of the democratic state, its structure, tendencies, functions, and its efficiency in economic and social life.

The process of development of the state as well as of democracy is *dialectical;* this point has been emphasized repeatedly by Stalin. "The supreme development of the power of the state, with the object of preparing the way for the withering away of state power—such is the Marxist formula. Is that 'self-contradictory'? Yes, it is 'self-contradictory.' But this contradiction is a living thing, and is a complete reflection of Marxian dialectics."[4]

Thus, at last, the inner contradiction inherent in the concept of *democracy* finds its solution. Democracy is a political system, a form of state organization. All policy implies constraint and follows a particular direction. Any political state is a restrictive force, which may work in diametrically opposite directions. And yet, when we talk of "constraint," we mean the opposite of liberty and therefore of democracy! When democracy is achieved, when the life of society develops in freedom, the state and politics come to an end; therefore the word "democracy" will no longer have any meaning at that stage of history. Over whom would the people, having become an organized association of free men, exercise power? For whom would there still be a "government"? At that stage, democracy transcends itself and, in so doing, resolves its inherent contradiction. Then man enters on the higher epoch of his history: communism.

That is the last word of Marxist "political philosophy"—no doubt incomprehensible to those who are not dialecticians.

C. Toleration and Treason

Theoretically, the answer to the questions regarding the relationship between opinions, the extent to which tolerance is allowed, and the opposition of opinion within a democracy is extremely simple. All problems can be subjected to scientific study. There is

3. Lenin, Speech to the All-Russian Congress of Transport Workers, March 27, 1921, *Selected Works* (New York, 1937), IX, 141.
4. Stalin, *Marxism and the National and Colonial Question* (New York, n.d.), p. 262.

no concept which cannot be rationally comprehended, no solution which does not depend on free (i.e., unprejudiced) reflection and therefore on free discussion.

In fact, unfortunately, the question is set in quite a different form. "Prejudices" intervene; and these "prejudices" must be understood in the broad sense, not only as traditional ideas inherited from earlier ages and accepted without reflection, but as social prejudices and class attitudes. Thus, the "demurrer," the downright refusal to understand that there are *objective* problems raised by economic, social, and political changes, is itself a class attitude—that of those people who are satisfied with the *status quo* and deliberately oppose all change.

The question had arisen long before the influence of the Soviet democracy was felt in the West. To confine discussion to the impact of Soviet democracy is a narrow way of looking at the problem. In this, as in many other matters, the social and political history of France can teach us a great deal. The inherent contradiction in democracy was brought out very clearly, in France, a hundred and fifty years ago, by the political opposition between the *Right* and the *Left*. Although these ideas are commonly considered outdated, they still mean something—they even display a new significance. There is a very interesting political phenomenon in France; there has been a majority of the Left in France for several decades, in spite of the degree of political stability conferred by the social structure; but French policy has never yet been resolutely directed in accordance with the desires of the majority. This country, in which all the vital, active, and productive elements are Leftist, has always been governed by the Right and tended toward the Right. Because of its economic power, the Right has always carried weight in important decisions and imposed its policy. There lies the whole history and the whole tragedy of France and the French democracy.

On the question of toleration, the attitudes of the Right and the Left were decided long ago.

Louis Veuillot, the publicist, set forth the "reactionary" attitude clearly in his well-known aphorism: claiming from democrats, in the name of their principles, what the reactionary party would refuse them in the name of its principles. Possibly none but a Frenchman—therefore Cartesian of mind, with a passion for clear and distinct ideas—could have formulated this policy in such an obvious and compromising form.

The "reactionary party," in a formal democratic system, demands freedom and toleration the better to destroy freedom and toleration. The Right claims tolerance and liberty so long as it is too weak to overwhelm the Left in politics, adopting the disguise of democratic forms. As soon as the position turns in its favor and it has strength on its side, there is no more question of tolerance or liberty. Saint-Just foresaw this situation, as early as 1793, summing it up in an aphorism no less famous than Louis Veuillot's: No freedom for the enemies of freedom!

The experience of other countries appears to confirm that of France. This situation may surprise those who obstinately refuse to see the inherent contradiction in democracy, leaving out of account the *content* of the abstract notion—the material interests and divergent tendencies opposing one another.

By a natural evolution, the situation places us before an alternative, a dilemma. Either democrats act foolishly and are beaten in advance, becoming, consciously or not, the accomplices of their own adversaries, and degenerating, as democrats, into *skepticism*, that is to say, pessimism and despair. They accept their adversaries' point of view, and indeed put themselves in their position instead of in their own. They allow all opinions except that which is openly and effectively democratic.

Or else, they come down clearly on one side or the other. And, in that case, why should not the "party" of those who really stand for true and effective democracy become the only party of democracy?

One word more on the attitude of Marxists. They have complete confidence that their statements are objective and scientific. They are confronted with opponents who generally deny the objective and scientific nature of economic and political problems and the phenomena of human life.

They have adopted the creed of materialism and dialectics, but their purpose is to change the world, to *transform the material circumstances* of men and, first of all, of those who produce and create, the workers. Their aim is not to impose materialism.

It is true that, in order to transform their material circumstances, men—and, in the first place, the workers—must become aware of their *real* circumstances and of their inherent *potentialities*. If they are to become aware of the reality, they must cease to turn their backs on it and borrow their understanding (their ideas and vocabulary) from the various forms of idealism.

On this point, the materialists are trying to lead the peoples, masses and individuals, to a clearer and more accurate awareness of themselves. They rely principally upon experience and reflection rather than on violence. They believe that progress in this direction, the only possible progress, is inevitable; the mists and clouds will melt away sooner or later, and reality will shine forth in the light of day, in all its richness, with all its potentialities.

Unfortunately, their opponents, with less and less trust in reason and in progress, inclining, in philosophy, to irrationalism, and increasingly ready to admit everything irrational, also tend to decline discussion on a rational plane and appear to rely increasingly on that most irrational weapon—violence.

A Marxist cannot, therefore (since he has a reasoned confidence in his position), fail to indorse UNESCO's efforts to lift problems onto the plane of free and rational discussion. UNESCO is thus making an important contribution to the maintenance of a particularly important and essential supremacy—the supremacy of reason among the "values" and principles of the modern world.

D. THE VALUE FOUNDATIONS OF THE CONFLICT

From the foregoing considerations, it follows that the only primary and irreducible value judgment in the ideological conflict centering on the word "democracy" seems to be that concerning reason and scientific thought.

From this point of view, the differences and disagreements appear to be a conflict between *rationalism* (in the fully developed form that Marxists invoke, asserting that dialectical thought represents the highest form of reason) and *irrationalism*, either admitted or disguised. This involves a very serious controversy and a conflict of fundamental principles.

Here we come back to the view we expressed at the beginning of this essay. The point at issue is not only an ideology, or a system of government, or political methods as a whole, it is the very concept of *man*. It is, indeed, a tremendous drama; but it is moving toward its inevitable conclusion.

A century ago, at the beginning of the *Communist Manifesto*, Marx and Engels conjured up the "specter" which was already disturbing Europe—communism. This image reminds us of one of the greatest masterpieces of dramatic art, *Macbeth*, and of the utterances of a great artist of the theater, Edward Gordon Craig. In *Macbeth*, the whole action is governed by an invisible force, and it is the words we do not hear and the dim figures, which give the drama its mysterious beauty, its depth of meaning, its enormous effect, and its principal element of tragedy.[5]

That is the significance of the drama we are living in our present-day world. The words we do not hear, the invisible forces, the dim shapes are the words, the forces, the shape of things to come.

But more and more men are hearing those words, perceiving those forces, divining and beholding those forms. The "specter" is becoming flesh and living reason.

All roads lead to communism!

5. Edward Gordon Craig, *On the Art of the Theatre* (London, 1911).

XIV

C. I. LEWIS

All language is affected, in some manner and degree, by ambiguity. In larger dictionaries, for example, more than one accepted meaning will be given for many, or even the majority, of words defined. Often there will be a "first," original, or strictest meaning, and various secondary, derivative, or looser meanings. Also, in the case of most words, the actually exemplified variants of meaning are too numerous to be listed in any dictionary.

The *application* of words is also affected by two further difficulties. First, many words are so understood that what they name is strictly an ideality to which actual things can approximate only (e.g., a circle is, by definition, a plane figure every point on the periphery of which is equidistant from a point within called the center; and it is doubtful if any actual figure absolutely satisfies this requirement). Such words are applied in practice to things which sufficiently approximate to the ideal in question; but there is no clear manner of deciding *what degree* of such approximation will justify such application. Second, many words (e.g., "blue") are so understand that, while there are some things to which they indubitably apply and other things to which they indubitably do not apply, there is also a third set of things to which their application can only be questionable. That is, the area of their application has no clearly determined boundaries.

Men who address themselves with care to the study of any field of phenomena must, in order to avoid such semantic difficulties and achieve clear formulations, build up a technical vocabulary of precise terms and eschew words which are subject to these problems of application (*a*) by assigning to words borrowed from common usage a strict and scientific meaning to which they confine the use of these terms, (*b*) by coining new words for the expression of precise and agreed upon meanings.

Where no such technical and precise vocabulary exists—as is the case in politics—and where matters under consideration are of vital importance to the public at large, who do not command any technical vocabulary even if one is available, there can be no fully satisfactory solution of the semantic problems arising from ambiguous language and the other difficulties mentioned. Prime requisites for achieving the largest possible measure of clarity and common understanding will be the obvious ones of good will, honest intentions, and objectivity of mind.

In addition to the above-mentioned occasions for controversy about the meanings of words, there is an additional cause of such disagreements which lies in one purpose for which language may be used. The uses of language are in general three: (1) for the formulation of facts and the determination of further facts by logic; (2) for influencing the attitudes and behavior of men; (3) for entertainment or edification. The third of these we may omit, since we are not here concerned with fiction or poetry.

So long as the purpose in using words is the first mentioned—to formulate facts and determine further facts by rational processes of thought—intelligent men will always seek to obviate controversy about the meaning of words; because the use of any word which has different meanings for different parties can only defeat the purposes of intelligent discussion; and because it does not matter for these rational purposes *what* symbols or sounds are used to convey what meanings, but only that those used shall convey the same meaning to all. Those whose interest is in facts will, thus, avoid the use of controversial expressions and replace these by others in the use of which they agreed.

Men who have, by care and good will, achieved community of meaning in the language they use may still differ, of course, with regard to facts in question; and these matters of fact will then constitute the material issues which their discussion will seek to resolve, if possible. But those who persist in controversy about the meaning of words legitimately arouse suspicion that either some lack of intelligence is involved or they have some undeclared purpose which will not be served by determination of the pertinent facts. There can be only one legitimate excuse for verbal controversies, namely, that some other party to a discussion is attempting to confuse issues by wilful use of words in ways which pervert understood meanings and may mislead the unwary or deceive those who are ignorant.

The normal and universally approved manner of influencing the attitudes and behavior of men is by the disclosure of facts in the light of which the recommended attitude or action comports with the interests of those addressed or with what they deem desirable and right. The use of language to induce men to favor that which, in the light of facts, is irrelevant to, or contrary to, their interests or to what they deem desirable and right, was anciently called sophistry and nowadays is sometimes called propaganda. We shall here use the older word.

The cruder methods of sophistry are resort to falsehood and fallacious argument. These, however, are comparatively ineffective and unreliable means to the sophists' end, since the ways in which falsehood and fallacies may be detected are well understood, and detection of them permanently discredits those who resort to such means. A much more subtle method of sophistry is exploitation of the *value suggestions* of words. In addition to the literal meaning which they convey, many words suggest a value or a disvalue in that to which they are applied. When this suggestion is strong, the word acquires honorific and eulogistic significance or, in the opposite case, that of derogatory epithet. It is also true that for any object, situation, or state of affairs, there will be many different terms which literally and correctly apply to it, and still more which can be applied with the color of correctness, if secondary and looser usages of words are exploited. And among such applicable words, some may be honorific while others are neutral or even derogatory in their value suggestion. Thus a man pre-eminently devoted to his country's good may be called a patriot if one wishes that he be approved, or a chauvinist if one wishes to discredit him. The gains of an entrepreneur may be called wages of management or surplus value. An economic regime based on private ownership of means of production may be called a free-enterprise system or wage-slavery. And one based upon state ownership of the means of production may be called a co-operative commonwealth or totalitarian. For sophistical purposes, such exploitation of value significances, by choice of terms carrying the wished-for suggestion of value or disvalue, may be better than an argument, since the sophist does not clearly *assert* goodness in choosing the honorific term, or badness in choosing one which is derogatory, and need not offer any grounds of *fact* in support of what he thus suggests. Also he may have used no word in a manner which is literally and demonstrably inaccurate; and disproof of his value suggestion conveyed—if it be one unsupported by or contrary to the facts—may be almost impossible, since he may have made no literally false statement or violated any principle of logic.

Resort to this sophistical method is the most frequent explanation of controversy which is directed upon the meaning of words instead of upon questions of fact. The struggle is to establish certain value-suggesting and eulogistic words as applying to what is argued for; or certain disvalue-suggesting and derogatory words as applying to what is opposed. Against such sophistry there will be no fully satisfactory defense until men generally come to understand that the use of value-loaded terms, in argument, in preference to value-neutral ones, is presumptive evidence that the arguer is unable to support his contention on grounds of fact and seeks to bolster up his case by the use of question-begging epithet.

1. AMBIGUITY.—"Democracy" is not more ambiguous than most words—not more ambiguous than, for example, "monarchy" or "anarchy"—with respect to its *first, literal,* or *strict* meaning. All will agree that strictly it applies to any political regime in which the sovereign power is vested in the people at large, and that it applies to no other.

Controversy about its meaning is possible, principally, because different parties wish to require *further* characteristics of anything they will allow to be called a democracy, and because they disagree as to *what* further characteristics are to be so required.

2. EVIDENCE.—Perfect examples are found in the questionnaire. De Tocqueville insists that "democracy extends the sphere of individual independence ... (and) socialism contracts it"; whereas Stalin says, "democracy is democracy for the working people," and then, with complete absence of logic, interprets "democracy *for the working people*" as equivalent to "democracy *for all.*"

Bryce (as quoted) supplies the corrective to both; "Democracy ... is merely a form of government.... Political equality can exist either *along with* or *apart from* equality in property" (italics mine).

3. MISUSE.—An ideological group is properly charged with *misuse* of the word "democracy"—or of any other word—whenever, instead of seeking to restrict it to a common and understood meaning, on which there can be agreement, they seek to exploit it as a value-suggesting term, and to establish, by sophistry, an exclusive claim upon this value suggestion for the cause for which they argue. Frequently, such sophistry achieves its measure of plausibility by using the term in question in some secondary, derivative, or loose meaning, instead of its first, restricted, and literal meaning.

4. NEW USES.—The term "social democracy" is historically newer (though it appears in the nineteenth century) and has no clear and fixed meaning. As Bryce observes, the older and strict usage of "democracy" is to designate a form of government, and has no implication of the (social?) purposes to which a government of this form may be turned, whether purposes of extending the sphere of individual independence and initiative or of achieving economic security and economic equality.

The use of an older term, "democracy," with a qualifying adjective, "social," to designate a *particular type* of democracy is, of course, legitimate and may be useful. For purposes of discussion, however, it will not be useful, but on the contrary obstructive, unless or until the qualification, "social," comes to have a clear, fixed, and agreed-upon significance. And the use of "democracy," with *no* qualifying adjective, in such a newer meaning, is not legitimate because it can only lead to misunderstanding, and because such usage deprives those who wish to speak of democracy in the strict and historical sense of the word, of any manner of expressing what they intend without suggesting what they *do not intend to put in question.*

5. "GENERAL DEMOCRACY."—The opinion that there is no such thing as democracy in general, but only historically and geographically different democracies, represents a manner of thinking which is frequent among those who are innocent of logic. There is no such thing as "general democracy," just as there is no such thing as "general triangle." But the fact that historical democracies have differed from one another in many ways—some of them important—does not imply that there is not or cannot be one single clear meaning of "democracy," any more than the fact that there are big triangles and

little triangles, right triangles, acute-angled triangles, and obtuse-angled triangles, triangles in red and triangles in white, means that the word "triangle" is ambiguous and has no clear and useful meaning. But a sure way to destroy any clear meaning of "triangle" would be for one party to refuse to call anything a triangle unless it was drawn in red, and another party to refuse the name to any figure not drawn in white. The same result, destructive for mathematics, could be brought about by insisting that triangles are relative to the historical period and the culture in which they occur.

6. COMMON CHARACTERISTICS.—In so far as the historically different democracies are truly democracies, they have in common two characteristics: (1) sovereignty is vested in the general will of the people, and of all of them equally; (2) the government is such that it is a rule of laws and not of men.

7. IDEAL VERSUS FACT.—No historical democracy, past or present, completely satisfies the requirements of perfect democracy; just as no figure ever drawn completely satisfies the requirements of perfect circularity. (See introductory remarks.) This being so, there is bound to be disagreement, not only as to what *degree* of failure to achieve the democratic ideal warrants refusal to apply the name, but also disagreement as to *what kinds* of imperfection are incompatible with applying the name "democracy." The one important point here is that no unideal character of a regime is pertinent except one with respect to those features which are essential to its *being a democracy*, and included in *what "democracy" means*.

8. THE LINCOLN FORMULA.—I should interpret Lincoln's Gettysburg address as a tribute to the dead, and not as a political document. If taken in the latter sense, then "*of* the people" could not well mean anything different from "*by* the people," since *any* government is *of* those governed, and this sense of "of," in which it differs from "by" could hardly be intended. And any democracy will be "for" the people if the people (who rule in a democracy) are "for" themselves.

But the Lincoln formula cannot very well furnish any adequate criteria for determining whether anything is democratic or not. In any language, prepositions are among the most ambiguous of all words. For example, Webster's International Dictionary lists twenty distinct meanings of "of," eleven of "by," and eleven of "for," indicating also variants (up to the number of eight) under some of these. To make any issue turn upon the meaning of prepositions is, obviously, to invite complete confusion.

11. "Narrow" versus "broad" sense.—The confusion can never be cleared by asking what sense the word *should* be used in, whether a "narrow" political sense or a "broad" social sense. To say that anything *should* be done implies some criterion of correctness. But the understood meanings of words are themselves the criteria of their correct usage. Unless or until there is a clear, understood, and agreed upon meaning of "democracy" the question whether "democracy" *should* be used in one way rather than another is a question which has no answer. Any answer offered will merely exhibit a preference or prejudice of him who answers.

There is *no* clear, common, and generally accepted "broad" sense of "democracy," designating "conditions and methods as well as results in decision making." Among those who extend the concept of "democracy" in this "broad" manner, each does so in that manner which makes it cover what he favors and exclude what he opposes. So used, the term becomes merely a tool of propaganda, and an obstruction to any determination either of fact or of value. Individualists will give the word a "broad" meaning in some manner such as that of de Tocqueville; socialists, in some manner such as that of Stalin.

It is therefore impossible to enter into any serious discussion of the relationships between "political democracy" and "social democracy." Political democracy does not imply private capitalism, nor does it imply state capitalism. It does not imply economic equalitarianism and it does not imply the opposite. It may be a means to any one of these goals if that goal is set by the general will of the people. If the goal of "social democracy"—whatever that means—is what is wanted by the people at large, then political democracy is the most reliable means to it which is possible, since political democracy is government determined by the general will.

14. Historical development of the two usages.—It is to be observed that the democracies of France, Great Britain, and the United States of America all derive their political theory from sources which include the conception of "natural law," and hence of certain "inalienable rights," and the conception that a valid gov-

ernment can only arise by a "social contract" and hence implies the consent of the governed. These conceptions, and corollaries drawn from them, tended to be imported into the accompanying conception of democracy. But they were also held by some monarchists such as Hobbes, and could be considered compatible with either monarchy, aristocracy, or democracy, as by Kant. It is also historic fact that these democracies were characterized by a prevailing temper of individualism, so vigorously expressed by de Tocqueville.

For clarity, one must thus observe that the main tradition of democracy may (1) contain what is desirable or even essential in *any* valid government but *not peculiar to democracy*; (2) contain as a generally accepted ideal something—e.g., the individualism which would rule out economic socialism—which is *not essential* to democracy.

The democratic tradition mentioned above included *political equality*, which may be defined as the principle that no man can legally be bound to any act or any forbearance from acting except that to which he can reciprocally bind every other man in relation to himself. But "equality" was frequently used as a slogan, without any clear limitation to that meaning in which alone these nineteenth-century democracies either conformed to it or held it desirable. This fact has given rise to many unanswerable questions—whether democracy does or does not require this, that, or the other kind of equality.

With the rise of Marxism, economic categories are put forward as fundamental, and political categories are held to be subordinate and derived from the modes of economic production. Hence for Marxist theory a political equality not derivative from economic equality must be repudiated as invalid and illusory. Democracy as a political category has no real interest for this theory. The announced goal is a "classless society" in which, with the liquidation of every class which could exploit any other economically, the need for formal government will cease, and the state will wither away. And for the interval between the disintegration of bourgeois capitalism and full achievement of this classless society, the announced program is the dictatorship of the proletariat. Since neither the dictatorship of a class nor a beneficent anarchy in which the state has withered away can be a political democracy, the futility of any attempt to interest orthodox Marxists in the political institutions cherished by the tradition of French, British, and American democracy, may as well be taken as a premise.

There remain the "social democracies" such as those projected by "Fabian socialism," "Guild socialism," and by other and less well-defined conceptions of a "planned economy," in which the economic functions of the state are to be enlarged, and the economic initiative of individuals correspondingly regulated and restricted. With respect to these, the important point is that "political democracy" holds no implication either for or against them beyond the dictate that the will of the people shall prevail in government, and their economic institutions shall be determined by this general will.

15. DEMOCRACY AND SOCIALISM.—I consider that de Tocqueville confuses the issue of democracy versus monarchy, oligarchy, etc., with that between economic individualism and economic socialism. Both these issues remain important; no good can come of trying to discuss both at once.

16. METHOD VERSUS CONTENT.—Whether this manner of separating the above-mentioned issues has heuristic value, I have no clear opinion. As a test question, I would ask: In a decision that conditions of employment shall be settled by collective bargaining between employer and employed, is the "content of the decision" itself a method of decision-making; and if so, is the distinction well taken?

17. CRUCIAL DIFFERENCES.—I take exception to the question itself. As indicated above, I do not consider that de Tocqueville and Bryce are in agreement, but that Bryce clearly separates political democracy from any issue concerning the economic order and that de Tocqueville confuses them. Also, as indicated, any interest of Stalin and Lenin in any "democracy" excepting a "classless society," must be taken as oblique.

18. REAL AND TERMINOLOGICAL DIFFERENCES.—They are both terminological and material.

19. EXPRESSION OF "REAL INTEREST."—Freedom of speech, of the press, and of assembly, a secret ballot, a multi-party representation in any list of nominations for elective office, trial by jury and the writ of habeas corpus, and the prohibition of methods by which a party, once dominant, can maintain itself in office by pressure or

patronage. But these are *essential instruments* for instituting and maintaining democracy not implied in what it *means*.

20. OPINION: INFLUENCE VERSUS PRESSURE.—As a secondary meaning, that is "democratic" which *conduces to* a government which reflects the will of the people, and what serves to defeat that accord is "undemocratic." As is well known, the *forms* of political democracy do not necessarily assure the substance.

21. DEMOCRACY AND PLANNING.—Delegation of power is, as above, undemocratic if and only if it leads to a use of the delegated power in a manner which does not accord with the general will.

22. TOLERATION OF DISSENTIENT OPINIONS.—Even a democratic state can survive only if it protects itself from the enemies of democracy. That is a law of nature and cannot be changed by man. The issue presented by those who exploit the privileges of a democracy in order to destroy it is an uncomfortable one in a democratic state. But it must be met firmly.

23. REPRESSION OF PROPAGANDA.—Whenever it can be shown that this propaganda is carried out at the dictate of enemies of the state, or of its institutions.

24. DECISIONS INCOMPATIBLE WITH DEMOCRACY.—If I could answer this question, I should not have money enough to mail the answer. The first ten amendments of the Constitution of the United States of America offer one set of premises from which conclusions concerning the question could be drawn.

25. ONE-PARTY SYSTEMS.—No kind.

26. "SKEPTICISM" AND DEMOCRACY.—To no extent.

27. TOLERATION OF THE ANTI-DEMOCRATIC.—I leave that question to the sociologists.

28. MORALITY OF TOLERATION AND REPRESSION.—The question seems to imply that questions of values are beyond dispute or beyond rational dispute. Where the values in question are social values, I would disagree with that assumption.

I believe that men will always compete, and that social purposes will not be served by the attempt to eliminate competition. I also believe that civilization has progressed, and may continue to progress, by elimination of the more *destructive* forms of competition, such as war, and the turning of competitive urges into socially profitable channels, such as the competition of professional men for professional standing.

For the rest, I must confess that I do not understand the intent of the question.

29. ULTIMATE AIMS.—Yes. Lenin would justify any means by reference to the end; others would not. In the political aspects of social life, the means to be used, and those to be foresworn, represent a part at least of the end.

30. NATURE OF THE DISAGREEMENT.—The question is unanswerable because "social democracy" has no clear meaning.

GENERAL COMMENT.—It would be my conviction that if agreement is to be hoped for, then issues must be restricted, sharpened, and separated from one another, instead of multiplied, broadened, and intertwined with one another.

That presently we find those here in question in the latter state is patent; and I observe with approval the concluding paragraph of the UNESCO document opening our inquiry.

XV

LORD LINDSAY OF BIRKER

I wish to begin this lecture[1] by discussing the contrasted meanings of democracy which are prevalent in the world today. The contrast between them is giving us a great deal of trouble. Professor E. H. Carr has recently published a lecture delivered at Nottingham under the Cust Foundation called Democracy in International Affairs where he calls attention to the fact that democracy means one thing to the Western Democracies—certainly to England and America—and quite another thing to Russia.[2] Professor Carr points out that, it was Stalin who placed "democracy" in the forefront of allied war aims. In his broadcast of July 3, 1941, he spoke of the Soviet war against Hitler being "merged with the struggle of the peoples of Europe and America for independence and democratic liberties." Anyone might have known that there was a catch somewhere. Few people in Europe and America outside the wholehearted adherents of Russia thought of Russia as a democratic country. Russia was known to regard the Western capitalist democracies as really plutocracies. It was a commonplace in Communist circles to hold that a political democracy without a foundation of social or economic democracy is a sham. Yet there are times when it is or seems more important to find a form of words on which different people will agree than to ask whether they mean the same thing by the words. At any rate, once democracy got into the proposals of the allies, it assumed a more and more important place. It began in an agreement between Stalin and Poland: it appeared at Teheran in 1943 and at Yalta in 1945. The three powers there announced their intention of "meeting the political and economic problems of liberated Europe in accordance with democratic principles." They did this regardless of the fact that by "democratic

1. This lecture was originally given at Indiana University and is reproduced with the kind permission of the University.

2. Edward Hallett Carr, *The Soviet Impact on the Western World* (New York, 1947), chap. i.

172

principles" the Western nations meant "not Russian principles" and the Russians meant "not English or American principles." According to Potsdam, democratic principles are to be applied to Germany. The allies are now quarreling because that again means one thing to the West and another to Russia. We are now paying the recrimination, frustration, and charges and countercharges of hypocrisy for those accepted ambiguities, and it is worth while to clear them up. The ambiguity is at least being publicly discovered. M. Molotov on September 14, 1946, proposed "a Soviet system of Democracy for Trieste."

Let me begin by saying that the charges of hypocrisy are unfounded. There has always been this difference between the Russian and the Western conceptions of democracy. It used to be assumed that the difference was about facts. The Webbs, for example, in their book about Russia accept the view that Western or bourgeois democracy—as it is called in these quarters—is a sham because economic inequality makes liberty unreal. They assume, however, that the ideal to which on their showing the Western democracies pretend and which the Russians realize is the same ideal. Such assumptions are, I am sure, mistaken. The Russians' claim that their constitution is more democratic is not based on their reading of the facts being different from ours—though, of course, it is—but on their having a quite different conception of what democracy is.

Let me make this clear by some instances. We think that a totalitarian democracy is a contradiction in terms. The Russians think that a democracy which is not totalitarian is so far an imperfect democracy. We think that in democracy government should be under law; the Russians think the power of the Supreme Court to overrule Congress is profoundly undemocratic. We think that democracy implies a tolerated opposition, the Russians do not. We think that democracy implies freedom of discussion and therefore a free press and therefore the upholding of individual rights; the Russians think that a mark of true democracy is the unlimited right of a supposed democratic government over all individuals. The Russians, in fact, claim that dictatorship and democracy are compatible. Vyshinsky has said "between the dictatorship of the proletariat and proletarian democracy not only is there no contradiction whatever but there is complete unity!" Contrast that with these

words of Professor Ernest Barker's: "the doctrine of political tolerance which is only another name for democracy." In this extraordinary difference in the meaning attached to a familiar word, who
is in the right? We shall see, I think, that the answer is neither
or both. For the ambiguity in the meaning of the word "democracy" is of very long standing. We shall find it in Aristotle. But let
me at once say that the difference of meaning attached by the West
and the East to democracy corresponds to a difference of questions
asked about government. In the West to say that a country is democratic is to say *how* or in what manner it is governed: in the East
it is to say *who* governs in it. The Russians mean by a "democracy"
a form of government in which the demos governs—the demos
being the poor, the common people—what the opponents of democracy called and still call "the mob," as opposed to the rich or
aristocrats or the bourgeoisie. Hence the less power anyone but the
poor has in a state, the more perfect a democracy it is. No doubt
the Russians think that, when the class war is at last transcended,
the contrast between the poor and the rest of the state will disappear and democracy will be ruled by the whole people. But that
consummation of democracy is brought about only by the elimination of all but the proletariat or a determination that the rich, like
Negroes in other countries, are not to count. The West means by
"democracy" a government by discussion, believing that from discussion of the right kind something emerges which may be called
the will of the people as a whole. What matters on this view of
democracy is the quality of the discussion, that all different points
of view should contribute to it, that the discussion should be thorough, that therefore minorities should play and should be encouraged to play their part. Because this process of discussion is supposed to produce agreement, democracy by this view is sometimes
called "government by consent." Professor Carr dismisses this as
nonsensical or as a contradiction in terms. It is not quite so that
government cannot rest on particular consent. There can be no
government without orders which have to be obeyed. But we may
manage sometimes that these orders are only applications of general
rules to which we have consented. Even that is not easy. It would
make unanimity a test for valid law. Or we may say that consent
means consent to the persons who shall make the rules, though not
consent to the rules they make—but that would mean unanimous

election. The only real sense in which our democratic governments are governments by consent is that they depend on consent to a machinery of government, so devised that the commands of its officers are likely to be such that they will win consent from most of those to whom they are addressed. The government as a whole is accepted willingly because its subjects are protected against arbitrary commands. Laws must be passed in prescribed forms; the acts and commands of the executive must be subject to judicial revision; and so on. There is no more striking illustration of the contrasting Western and Eastern conceptions of democracy than that given by Professor Carr when he relates that the repeal of that most objectionable of wartime regulations in Great Britain, 18B, which gave to the executive powers of arbitrary arrest and holding without trial was regarded in Britain, of course, as a belated triumph of democratic principle and in Russia as a defeat of democracy.

The ideals of democracy, what democratic governments are trying to achieve, the criterion by which one government is judged democratic and another not, are clearly different to the Russians from what they are to people in England and America.

But that is by no means the whole of the matter. It is clear that, whether democracy be regarded as the rule of the proletariat or government by consent, no modern democracy can ever be what it pretends to be by reason of its size. Our Western democracy had its origin in the agreement reached in the independent congregation or in the sense of the meeting among the churches. The mass of the people could govern in the public meeting of a small city-state, a Swiss forest canton, or a New England town meeting. What happens in the elaborate electoral processes of a modern Western democracy is a very long way from what happens at a Friends' meeting. It is hard enough for a large public meeting to govern in any real sense. A large population is entirely incapable of it. When the believers in either conception of democracy, therefore, talk of the will or the voice of the people, fiction and myth have made their appearance. There is considerable sense in a tiny community of talking of the "sense of the meeting"; the sense of talking of the will of the people of Britain or the United States is doubtful at the best. The assumption that the resolutions of a majority of Parliament and Congress express even what little sense there may be in the will of the people is still more doubtful. So in the other view.

To hold that the proletariat of Russia—whatever that may mean—
has a will is remote enough from the fact. To justify the dictatorship of the proletariat as equivalent to the will of the people is
worse. To say that the orders of Stalin and of his secret police express the will of the people is still more fantastic. To get from the
democratic dream to the concrete political facts, much has to be
dropped. The assumption has to be made that what has been
dropped does not matter and that what has been retained is the
essence of the dream. The fact that different things are dropped
and different things retained by different people accounts for much
of the confusion in our use of the word "democracy." There is
some relation, if not much, between the Russian and the Western
democratic dream. There is some relation, if not very much, between the Western democratic dream and the Western reality, as
there is some between the Russian democratic dream and the Russian reality, but there is practically no relation between the Western
democratic reality and the Russian. There is so much myth in all
talk about democracy that it might seem better to give it up altogether and discuss the different governments as we find them. To
discuss the governments as we find them is something we must do.
There is no subject on which it is easier to talk nonsense than politics. We can never be too careful to get behind the pretenses and
the fictions and try to reckon up as impartially as we can what
actually happens. Nevertheless, when we do that, we find that one
factor in what actually happens is the conception men form to
themselves of what they are doing and what they want to do and
that in consequence, their ideals, democratic or otherwise, are a
factor in what actually happens. It follows, therefore, that misunderstandings of or ambiguities in these ideals are also a factor
in the actual. After all, this lecture started with calling attention
to the obvious and painful fact that the allies thought they had
come to an agreement about their future conduct and are now pain-
fully finding out that they did nothing of the kind because, though
they used the same words, they meant different things by them.
Something is gained even if we find that the whole thing is a swin-
dle and that there is nothing in common between the Western and
the Russian conceptions of democracy and therefore no common
standard to which we can appeal, no common ideal to unite us. We
shall have gained more if we find that, while the differences be-

tween the Western and Russian conceptions of democracy are profound and very important, there is something they have in common, something which when properly understood may be a bond
of union.

I have said that modern democracies express the desire to fit the
ideal experiences of a small community to a large modern state. We
may understand the differences in modern ideals better if we go
back to Aristotle's account of democracy in the city-state. We shall
find there something very like the ambiguity which we have already
noticed. Aristotle in his classification of constitutions starts with a
general distinction between normal and perverted constitutions. In
the normal the government rules in the interests of the whole city;
in the perverted the government rules only in its own interests.
The perverted constitutions are clearly those in which there is what
we have learned to call a class war. Class war was a familiar fact in
the Greek cities of the fifth and fourth centuries B.C., class war as
bitter and avowed as anything described or imagined by Marx.
Aristotle treats it more historically and empirically than does Marx.
He devotes considerable attention to suggestions for its cure or
assuagement. He sees that it is not something definite and absolute
but exists in various degrees. What are called nowadays "plutocracies" were called by Aristotle "oligarchies," but he notes that oligarchies claimed to be aristocracies and justified their rule not on
the ground that they were the richest but on the ground that they
were the best or noblest members of the community. We are to
think, then, of this division by Aristotle of constitutions into normal and perverted as a distinction between two ideal extremes to
either of which actual historical constitutions approach more or
less. This is clear in his treatment of democracy. Theoretically democracy is defined as a perverted constitution, one where the many
poor rule in the interests of the poor. Given a class war, either the
rich or the poor must rule. If the rich rule, Aristotle calls this perversion an "oligarchy"; if the poor rule he calls it a "democracy."
But there are degrees in democracies. The logical extreme, democracy in essence as it were, is a constitution so contrived that the
many poor rule without restraint. That involved a constitution
where the poorer citizens were paid to attend the public meeting
and to serve on juries; where the council—what we may describe
as the agenda committee—was elected by lot and divided into com-

mittees which acted in rotation; this confined it to routine business and prevented a permanent committee or a powerful chairman of committee running the public meeting. Finally, in Aristotle's eyes worst of all, the public meeting was not restrained by any constitutional rules. What it resolved was, by that mere fact, law.

The likeness between the extreme of Greek democracy and the Russian conception will be obvious. A rule of the poor in the interests of the poor, in perpetual conflict with the rich, and the more democratic as it is less restrained by a constitution, the Russian and the Aristotelian conception are the same. The only difference is that Aristotle thinks such a constitution bad and the Russians think it good. Both agree that such a constitution easily becomes a dictatorship or as Aristotle calls it a "tyranny." Aristotle thinks this an additional argument for the badness of democracy, the Russians do not.

But, though Aristotle regards pure democracy as a perverted constitution, he regards with favor a democratic element in constitutions, if it is balanced with other elements. There is a normal form of government, which he simply calls a constitutional government, which acknowledges the three principles expressed abstractly in aristocracy, oligarchy, and democracy. Where a special place and power is given to ability, where some regard is paid to wealth, but where, finally, the democratic principle is recognized that all men, just because they are members of the state and have to live its life, should have some say in what its laws should be. Aristotle rejects the idea that the public meeting and the mass of the citizens should govern, but he thinks they should have some control over their rulers and some power in the making of laws. Further, he gives some very interesting arguments to show why the many should control the eminent few, holding that some things are better judged by everybody than by the specialist, that there may be such a thing as collective wisdom, and so on.

The general result of this discussion which we may carry away for our purpose is that Aristotle thought that the principle of democracy was a valuable ingredient in a constitution but a bad principle of government if taken by itself. The undiluted democrat tended to think that because men had equally a concern in government, therefore they were, as a matter of fact, equal in everything, in ability and character and wisdom, and that therefore any acknowledgment of standards, any claim that goodness or skill or insight should count, was undemocratic, as was any claim that the will of the majority should be restrained by law. We can surely recognize this abstract element in our own democratic thinking.

There is some resemblance between Aristotle's mixed government and what we in the West call "democracy." Our democracy is constitutional, i.e., insists on the rule of law—whether in the form of a rigid constitution or in an independent judiciary; our democracy acknowledges the importance of statesmanship and expert knowledge and thinks the people cannot govern but only exercise a control over the government. So does Aristotle's constitution. Our democracy is, for all its respect for statesmanship and expert knowledge, still a democracy because it insists that government exists for the sake of the whole people and believes that all members of the community should have some say in its government and should in sóme sense be treated as equal. These democratic principles are acknowledged in Aristotle's Constitutional Government.

In contrast with these resemblances, there is, of course, the outstanding difference of size and what follows from that difference. Aristotle's Constitutional State was governed in the final resort or at least controlled by a public meeting of the whole of the citizens. There are modern democracies which try to achieve something of the same results by a referendum of all the citizens. But most modern democracies rely on representatives, on specially elected persons on whom is laid the task of expressing or discovering that elusive thing—the will of a people who cannot meet for discussion in one meeting. The adoption of this advice of representative government is commonly held to be the characteristic difference between the small democratic states of the ancient world and our modern democracies. There is, however, another important respect in which Western modern democracies differ both from Eastern and from ancient democracies. They insist on a recognized opposition, and that insistence is based upon a profound difference between Western democracies and other democracies—the acceptance of toleration. This was the discovery of the seventeenth-century Puritans. No one before them had thought it possible, not just to accept toleration, but to make the acceptance, even the encouragement, of different opinions the basis of government. This new principle of government is far-reaching. It means that, in a democracy, citizens are treated as equal not because they are the same but because they are different. It implies that men are to be treated not as identical atoms but as unique personalities; it implies that it is a good thing when people disagree but that it is a bad thing when people are unanimous. Its aim for the state is diversity in unity, a diversity as great as is compatible with the harmony of a common life. It implies that most differences between men are capable of reconciliation, that agreement between men is reached by discussion and statement of differences. It implies an attitude of mind which finds expression in the common phrase, "It takes all sorts to make a world" or theological expression that, because God is incomprehensible, it takes all believers to express the mind of Christ.

There are those—Professor Carr is among them—who think that men are tolerant only when they are indifferent and do not really believe in anything. It is significant that he quotes in support of this view Madariaga—a Spaniard—and Berdyaev—a Russian. Toleration implies a mood in which we may hold firmly to our own convictions and yet be conscious that there may be something to be said for the convictions of others, may be aware that what we believe is not the last word on the subject and that we may learn something from other people. This is, after all, the attitude of modern science, to have an assurance which is worth acting on, which still does not pretend to infallibility and welcomes correction.

This general attitude of mind which is characteristic of the English and American way of thinking about politics, which welcomes criticism and discussion and compromise, is largely, I think, the outcome of Protestantism. There is an interesting argument in a discussion between the Anglican divine Chillingworth and a Jesuit who had written a work called *Charity Maintained towards Protestants*. Chillingworth's position was that Protestants and Roman Catholics agreed on essentials and differed only on inessentials. The Jesuit maintained that there was no such distinction and that if in any theological matter whatsoever two men differed, one must infallibly be damned because one must be in fundamental and essential error. It took English Protestants to make one of their articles of religion the statement that general councils may err. This attitude of mind is not in itself necessarily democratic. It was certainly a characteristic of Englishmen long before they could have been called in any sense democratic. It might indeed with some plausibility be maintained that it is really an aristocratic virtue. Only men with that sure belief in themselves which membership of an aristocracy produces in men are easily tolerant. But then Western democracy is both aristocratic and democratic—is almost as much one as the other. It bears the marks of its originators, who were Calvinist believers in a doctrine at once aristocratic and democratic and derived much of its institutional devices from the usage of an aristocratic England which kept its king, as well as its lower orders, in his place. However that be, this spirit of compromise, so admirably practiced by Queen Elizabeth in the Elizabethan settlement of the Anglican Chuch and elaborated into a system of political behavior by the eighteenth-century Whigs, produced this new form of democracy in America under the influence of Roger Williams; and, as the nineteenth century wore to its close, the English descendants of the left-wing Puritans, the Nonconformists, at last made Britain a country where all elements of society took an active part in the government and a democracy. The combination of the practice of compromise, discussion, and toleration with the doing away of class privilege produced the distinctive democracies of the West. Toleration and discussion are their most distinctive notes, and there is very little in common with any constitution, democratic or otherwise, which does not accept the principle of toleration and a recognized opposition.

Note, if it has not been made clear already, that, if the principle of agreement by discussion is recognized as fundamental, so that discussion and not voting is regarded as the essence of the democratic principle, there is less difference in principle between the experience of the small meeting and the large state than can possibly happen on the other conception of democracy. For in the Western conception the problem of government is to discover something—that legislation, administration, and general ordering of society which will, when adopted, best satisfy most of the community. The contribution of the ordinary voter at an election is one, but only one, factor in the process of solving that problem. On the other conception that democracy is the expression of the actual will of the mass of the people, there is obviously an enormous gulf between that and the resolutions of any assembly or executive. No one in their senses would call the present government of Russia a

democracy unless he were defending a thesis, and an absurd, fanatical, ideological thesis at that.

The thesis would have to be something like this: Because of the
economic arrangements under communism there is there a social
and economic democracy such as does not and cannot exist under
capitalism. The whole mechanism of the state is directed toward
the economic well-being and the supremacy of the ordinary man.
His welfare comes first, and the welfare of the others is subordinated to it. A government devoted to preserving this economic
welfare for the ordinary man has an understanding of him such as
no capitalist government can have and therefore may be taken to
represent his will as no capitalist government can, however elaborate the parliamentary or other supposed democratic processes.
That seems to me like saying that because the English member of
the Indian Civil Service cared more for the welfare of the Indian
peasant than did the ordinary member of the Congress party, that
therefore the British government of India was democratic. Which
is nonsense. It may easily be the case that an aristocratic or monarchical government looks after the welfare of the common people
admirably. To think otherwise is democratic superstition. But that
a government is efficient in looking after the interests of the community does not make it democratic.

From this subject we may go on to consider last the distinction
between social and political democracy. This distinction is clearly
a real one. A democratic society is one where, as a matter of fact,
everyone treats everyone else as equally a member of society and
therefore equal as a fellow member, a citizen, or, to use slightly
high-flown language, a comrade. It is a commonplace that there is
more social democracy in the United States than in England, as
there is more in Scotland than in England. In this sense there is
more social democracy in Russia than in England and perhaps more
than in America—there is certainly nothing in Russia quite the same
as the position of Negroes in the United States or of Bantus in
South Africa. It is also true that such social democracy is a good
foundation for political democracy, while snobbery and class distinctions make a bad foundation.

But there is another sense in which a community may be called
democratic, whatever its central political government may be. The
structure of its society may be based on small democratic groups—

in which men and women manage their own affairs in a genuinely democratic manner. The groups are small—anyone can take part in running the common business of the group: they can work inside a framework which need not itself be democratic in our sense. It is a commonplace that the success of democracy in the West depended upon a flourishing structure of local government. The more elaborate and artificial structure of state or national democracy is healthy only so long as it rests upon lively local democracy, whether that be the local government of township or the group democracy of churches and other voluntary associations. Both de Tocqueville and Ortega y Gasset, the one writing a hundred years after the other, hold it is only vigorous local government and the vigorous life of the small religious communities which prevent state- or nation-wide democracy from degenerating into the mass democracy which produces dictatorship. It is to be remembered that Hitler sought to secure his totalitarian regime by disintegrating all small groups which could produce loyalties or foci of criticisms or resistance between the individual and the state.

National democratic government, if it is to have any reality, depends upon a high standard of education among the electorate. If ordinary men and women immersed in their daily occupation are to have any appreciation of the issues of policy which face their government they must have a high standard of education and of public interest. They must have an active concern about foreign policy and, in these days, for what their government stands for all over the world. That is a very great deal to ask of any community, however high its standard of education. It implies a standard which even the public of Britain or the United States reach only imperfectly or fitfully—a standard far beyond the capacities of the vast population of Russia or of China.

Here we can avoid the bias one way or the other which discussion of Russia is apt to involve by considering the example of Chinese communism. The revolution from autocracy to democracy which has occurred in Communist China since 1936 consists essentially in the fact that the village peasants have control of the local police and therefore control of the effective day-to-day power which is needed. But they have neither the knowledge nor ordinarily the concern to have any judgment of the affairs of their province, much less of national issues. But in so far as they enjoy active control over the affairs which immediately concern them and of which they have knowledge and understanding, they acquire enough public and political sense to know whom they can trust. Finding those who wish their support in provincial matters to be faithful in the small things which they know, they trust them to be faithful in the larger things which they do not know.

There is far more of this spontaneous local immediate democracy in England than is often recognized. It made itself felt in the war, and there is a vivid description of its working in the first year of the war in Mrs. Allingham's book, *The Oaken Heart*. It finds its national expression with us partly in churches and chapels, partly in the branches of various forms of industrial democracy, trade unions, co-operative societies, friendly societies, and so on.

All the evidence seems to show that this kind of real, simple democracy is vigorous and flourishing in Russia. The management of the collective farm, of the co-operative, of local housing, is in the active hands of the ordinary people. This seems to me the really profound difference between National Socialism and Russian Communism. Hitler, as I have noticed, did everything he could to break down the vitality and initiative of the small group. With him all authority came from the top and went from the top to the individual. This was true of the *Arbeitsfront* as of any other part of National Socialist organization. If one regards in Russia only the central government with its suspicions and secretiveness, its secret policy and sudden arrests, its neglect or indeed its rejection of the safeguards of the rights and liberties of the individual, one may not see very much difference between Hitler's and Stalin's totalitarianism. Russia is still what the Germans call a *Polizei-staat*. But Russia's insistent encouragement of local and unit democracy is completely different from anything found under Hitler, and, if this local democracy maintains its strength and vigor, in time ordinary democratic practices and liberties may extend to the central government and even be allowed or encouraged to extend to the governments of Russia's satellites.

Let me now summarize the general conclusions we have reached. "Democracy" has always been an ambiguous word. If we follow the original meaning that it is rule by the demos and we regard the demos as the poorest part of the population as contrasted with the rest, then the Russians are right in thinking that the test of democracy is whether the poor rule and the degree of democracy depends on the toughness, almost the ruthlessness, with which the poor rule. It is not a good form of government, but then no government is good in a state dominated by class war or by the fanaticism which war breeds.

But it has long been recognized that a democratic element or principle is of great value if it is balanced by other elements, a recognition of the need for leadership, for insight and expertness of government. Western democracies are constitutions based on the belief in the value of diverse elements in the state; that the differences between different classes in the community can be solved by discussion; on the belief in and the capacity for compromise; on a frank recognition that the people as a whole cannot govern but that the mass of ordinary people can exercise control over a government and in that way efficiency and popular control can be combined and a method discovered by which the action of government is more likely than in any other way to reach positive results of which in the event the great mass of the people will approve. Democracy, then, in the Western sense is a method of government, combining aristocratic and democratic elements. For we noticed that discussion and toleration as a method of government was as much an aristocratic invention as a democratic. Our Western constitutional governments are democratic in so far as they insist that in the method of discussion everyone shall somehow play a part and in so far also as they make as vigorous as is possible the democratic initiative of smaller groups and subdivisions by the community.

It will on consideration be clear that this Western kind of democracy depends on conditions which are not very commonly fulfilled. Tolerance and compromise are fruits of peace, not of war. Mixed governments—and such are Western democracies—depend on a balance, and balances are often hard to preserve. In particular, it is worth remembering that the heyday of parliamentary government in England was at a period when there was still a strong aristocratic element in the English constitution and to ask whether the more complete democratization of recent times is really favorable to what we in the West have called "democratic" government; whether, in approaching what may be called "complete" or "universal" democracy, we may not be bringing into peril that mixed constitution of which we are so proud.

XVI

J. H. A. LOGEMANN

One does not go wrong, I think, in stating that, historically speaking, the primitive meaning of the term "democracy" is coextensive with what logically constitutes its primitive and literal sense: the rule of the people. This raises the subsidiary question of the denotation, different according to times and places, of the word "people"—different, that is, according to the social structure within which historically a "rule of the few" is succeeded by a "rule of the many." Originally, therefore, "democracy" denotes any political mechanism attributing direct or indirect influence—and, on principle, *decisive* influence—to the many considered to be full members of the political community. This concept is a *formal* one indicating a method of organizing authority.

This primitive concept is enriched as soon as the question of the *value* of this method is raised: why is it to be preferred to other possible methods? There could hardly be any other reason for this preference than the opinion that democracy (in this primitive sense) allows certain human values to blossom, better than other methods of organizing authority. The same question arises in assessing the phenomenon that democracy has showed various modalities and, especially, the fact that the rule of the many has never been the rule of all.

This may lead to a curious reversal: having first recognized the human values we hope to further by formal democracy, we may then proceed to call democratic all such methods of organizing authority by which these essential values are promoted, excluding those modalities which do not allow their full development. This new concept of democracy does not center on social mechanisms but on human values. It is no longer formal but substantial, and, likewise, normative.

Taking the matter one step further, however, we should realize that, ultimately, the problem of democracy is not concerned with certain well-defined human values but rather with the individual's place in organized society, i.e., with man as a whole. The question is not how certain human values will be guaranteed in society, but what kind of total evaluation of man will preside over the organization of society.

The distinction between formal and substantial democracy being established according to the preceding paragraphs, it may be said that formal democracy will present various modalities in each country, with each people. It will work out in very different ways as regards the question whether the values it is supposed to represent are being actually realized. Formal democracy in this sense is thus an entirely relative concept, it has to acknowledge limits to its possible actualization, it may work out in a satisfactory or in an entirely unsatisfactory way. Thus, formal democracy being relative both as regards its possibility of existence and its ideological value, it is unjustified to treat it as in any sense an absolute concept.

Evaluation of man in society implies posing and accepting a norm, i.e., a value judgment claiming validity, and this validity is an absolute concept, even if it be admitted that human history has witnessed several divergent evaluations of the human personality, just as today they exist together—a fact which, by the way, will prove to be at the base of the entire problem of democracy. If it is asserted that it follows that ethical precepts are relative, no objection will be raised in this context, for even then one does not escape the necessary admission that the individual, being an actor and not simply a looker-on, has to live according to an evaluation accepted by him as governing his attitude towards life. He is obliged to choose one and reject another evaluation. This choice is motivated on a far more fundamental level than the rational one. Coupled with the fact, elucidated above, that the choice is absolute, this explains the passionate character of the struggle for true democracy.

Any society in which a given personality evaluation prevails will wish that this evaluation shall find expression in the political organization of that particular society. Therefore, it can be sustained that everywhere man is the central factor. This has to be qualified by the fact that in certain historical civilizations not every man is considered a "man" in the full sense of the word, e.g., in the Greek democracy (see above). It is a tribute to the prestige of the term "democracy" that civilizations with a special divergent personality evaluation are wont to express the above relation (of man to political organization) by stating that they cultivate democracy—even "true" democracy. Keeping in view what has been stated above, it is only natural that they should postulate the predicate "true" for their own personality evaluation, but by so doing they strip the term "democracy" of all distinctive value as to the substantial sense of the word (see above) and, consequently, as to the formal sense. In order to reduce confusion to a minimum, it would seem right to restrict the use of the term "democracy" (in the material sense) to the personality evaluation generally adopted in those countries of our contemporary world where formal democracy was first introduced. A good example of the confusion it is hereby hoped to avoid is afforded by national socialism (see below). For national socialism, by adopting the term "democracy" for its own personality evaluation, deliberately fostered this confusion in order to camouflage from the gullible public the fact that they were being deprived of old and still cherished values. Moreover, it should be expressly stated that vindication of the term "democracy" for a particular system of evaluation does not necessarily imply that this system is better than any other.

Now let us look at the various divergent views on man's place in society prevailing in today's world. I can see four: (*a*) the *primitive* view—using the term "primitive" in preference to others that I think more apposite, because it is more widely understood; (*b*) the *Western democratic view* (to which a similar rider applies); (*c*) the *Fascist* or *National Socialist* view; (*d*) the *"people's democracy"* view (*sit venia verbo*).

a) *The primitive view.*—Only some highly simplified—indeed, too much simplified—general remarks can be vouchsafed in this context. In this view, no qualitative difference between man and cosmos is recognized. It sees the world's progress as a constant flux and reflux governed by eternal laws. In this circular movement man has his place in the sense that he is responsible at every moment for keeping his life in tune with this eternal process in order to avoid catastrophic consequences for himself and the group to which he belongs. Religion, morals, and law coincide in the endeavor to safeguard harmony with cosmic law; any other endeavor does not appeal to primitive man.

Modern man, on the other hand, being aware that he lives in a rectilinear time, aims at self-realization, knowing, however, that there are norms he is subjected to and according to which his endeavors will be judged. The common element in the three non-primitive views is this new evaluation of man's place in a changing world. This entails—and that is why it is important to include the primitive view in this survey—that all peoples in which the primitive Weltanschauung is still deeply rooted will offer stubborn resistance to leading groups aiming at a reorganization of political life in the modern sense. Their profound lack of understanding of the very basis of modern political thought necessitates the application of educational methods of great delicacy, so much the more as this modernization of people's attitude toward life is a process covering the whole of their lives both individual and social and not confined to education toward democracy. This implies that the necessary conditions for a satisfactory democracy (in the formal sense) hardly exist in these "primitive" civilizations. Therefore, in view of furthering democracy (in the substantial sense) the question arises as to which modality of formal democracy will serve or even, in the last instance, whether another system will not serve better to further the values of substantial democracy. Furthermore, the above remarks imply that "primitive" peoples will be in a different position from more "advanced" ones as regards the choice between the other systems of democracy—or, rather, of personality evaluation—prevailing in the modern world. They will be less subjected to preconceived ideas as to the necessary connection between divergent systems of formal democracy and the underlying personality evaluations. This should be kept in view in considering, e.g., Asia's attitude toward bolshevism.

b) The Western democratic view.—In my opinion the central feature of the "*Western" democratic view* would appear to be the recognition of human dignity in every individual, even in relation to his being subjected to the discipline of organized human society, i.e., seeing man not only as an object of social service but rather as a subject of self-realization whose dignity comes to its own only in so far as he collaborates, on an equal basis with his fellow-men, toward his own welfare. The ultimate source of his dignity, however, is the fact of being individual and in society, to norms that give sense to his life. This explains the close connection, peculiar to the West, between the concepts of "democracy" and "human rights" and also the rather less definite connection with the *Rechtsstaat* principle.

c) The Fascist or National Socialist view.—In Western democracy the value of the community is always conceived of as a function of that of human personality, the test always being whether a given community allows the free development of human dignity. The object of the various Declarations of Rights is just that: to guarantee respect of human dignity by the organized community. This constitutes a radical difference with the system of personality evaluation, obtaining in *fascism and national socialism* in which the community has a value of its own transcending the value and dignity of the individual. True, this community value has to be conceived and realized by individuals. The latter, however, are chosen charismatically, and never by the methods of Western formal democracy. When a state based on this conception calls itself "democratic," it is because it claims to interpret, in its policy, the historical essence of the people and to fulfil its historical mission.

Furthermore, the charismatic leadership pretended to be confirmed, time and again, by popular acclamation. Finally, democracy used to be claimed for such a state because devotion to the national mission (i.e., to the party) allowed to dispense with old-time social class distinctions. This, however, was rather an incidental consequence than a matter of principle.

The question whether these assertions were based on reality needs to be gone into, except in so far that, owing to the radical difference in personality evaluation, there was no room, in this system, either for Western formal democracy or for any other form of considerable political influence of the individual, nor yet for human rights working as a guarantee. Another essential feature is the fact that the supremacy of the impersonal historical mission claimed for the people in fact reduced the individual to the lowest depths.

Finally, the significant circumstance should be noted that the adoption of a national mission of one particular people as the ruling principle removed, both in theory and in practice, the base of an internationally valid personality evaluation, i.e., international democracy.

d) The "people's democracy" view.—The communist ideal, no less than that of Western democracy, aims at the free development of man's spiritual and moral personality. Its materialistic interpretation of history, however, does not admit man to be bound by perennial norms but, instead, sees norms as the transient product of social relationships, and especially of the forms or conditions of production. Communism, therefore, is *directly* concerned not so much with man as with realizing communist society, which, by producing conditions of production commensurate with human dignity, will necessarily lead to this dignity being achieved. A second feature of communism is its fanatical conviction of the scientific inevitability of the historical process which must necessarily lead to a communist society and which cannot be stopped, only retarded or accelerated. Now communism sees as its task to further this process by eliminating all possible resistance, being convinced that any pain this may cause is far outweighed by that which would be caused by allowing the doomed conditions of production to subsist beyond necessity. Therefore, dogma rules within the Soviet state, and whatever conflicts either with dogma or with party tactics that are its consequence is considered as a crime and combated just as the West combats crime, only with a ruthlessness caused by the unalterable conviction of being in the right as well as by the subjection of individual dignity to historical law.

This defines the limits within which spiritual liberty is tolerated. In bolshevist countries political life knows a measure of democracy which is very real, although vitiated, to the Westerner, by the fact that it is "directed democracy," the "director" being the party, the guardian of dogma. The true communist does not abhor these democratic forms, considering them as part of the people's education toward the final phase of communist society. No more convincing evidence could be adduced for the fact that it is divergence in personality evaluation that lies at the bottom of the struggle centered around democracy (in the substantial, normative sense). For why does the communist have no objections against the "compulsion to go in"? Because he is sure of the right way and also because he feels sure that self-realization of the individual will be the natural result of the final phase of the communist revolution. Why, on the other hand, does the "Western" democrat object? Because he sees in the communist system a muzzling of spiritual liberty, the death of the feeling of responsibility for truth and humanity, and a chance of unbridled power for fanatics or bureaucrats, because, in one word, he feels communism on its way toward the human paradise may have dropped the human being before reaching its goal.

As a final touch to this review of current systems of personality evaluation it may be added that the "primitive" Weltanschauung does not, while the other three do, imply a postulate in the sense of a goal seen as desirable. This has two important consequences. In the first place, the adherents of the three modern systems will be under the constant obligation to retest their postulate in the light of events; in the second place, its realization, too, will have to be critically tested. As to formal democracy, the question has to be put again and again: How does it work in practice, here and now? Substantial democracy, on the other hand, has to formulate the norms according to which the previous questions can be answered; in its turn, it is subjected to the further questions as to whether its formulas are a logical consequence of its underlying personality evaluation.

We may now proceed to apply the foregoing criteria to the four clusters of problems treated in the introduction to the UNESCO document.

A. Ambiguity and Misuse

Confusion must arise inevitably from the necessity of handling the "formal" and the "material" concept side by side, as long as they are not clearly distinguished. This also applies to the divergent aspect of both concepts within each of the four types of personality evaluation associated with the four views of democracy. Terminology lags sorely behind in allowing us to make this eightfold distinction. We shall have to endeavor to adapt our terminology to the new requirement of political science. This adaptation will be hindered, but not necessarily frustrated, by political motives tending to slur over these distinctions (what is called in the questionnaire "the sloganlike character of the word 'democracy' ").

B. Social versus Political Democracy

By "social democracy" may be meant extension of planning from the political to the economic and social fields which did not form an object of planning in the heydays of liberalism. This is essentially an extension of political ("formal") democracy to new objects.

This extension will be the consequence of giving further thought to the substantial concept of democracy endeavoring to formulate man's place in society.

C. Tolerance and Treason

Each system of personality evaluations emerges with a claim to universal validity, rejecting every other system. Therefore, each system including the "Western" one will not be justified in extending tolerance beyond a certain limit which may differ partly according to the character of these various ideologies, partly according to the practical question how much a given community can bear without mortal danger to its underlying ideology.

D. The Value Foundations of the Conflict

As appears from this introduction, I believe that the conflict does involve irreducible value-judgments. In so far as the concept of substantial democracy is a normative one (see above), different concepts are irreconcilable. Still there is a difference in *level* between the conflict Western democracy v. communism, on the one hand, and that between Western democracy and national socialism, on the other. Whereas the first is concerned with the dogmatic essence of communism, the second involves ultimate ethical value-judgments. This has important practical consequences although it does not justify an excessively optimistic view on the possibility of bridging the abyss between the West and communism.

XVII

RICHARD McKEON

A. AMBIGUITY AND MISUSE: PRELIMINARY REMARKS

All practical problems which depend for their resolution on the agreements of groups of men who differ in background and conviction are involved in "ideological conflicts." Terms must be clarified and significances explored in agreement on and in execution of a common course of action. Ideological conflicts appear in differences of meaning which inhibit or prevent the resolution of problems. Antagonistic formulations of purpose and method, based on basic differences in philosophies and beliefs, sometimes entail different and contradictory courses of action, yet they are often found to be compatible in practice or even identical in their broad lines and ultimate objectives. A common course of action may be undertaken and justified for different reasons based on different basic principles. The possibility of co-operation and understanding despite differences of meanings is peculiarly relevant to the interplay of statements and actions attached to different meanings of "democracy." The criticisms of improper uses of the term "democracy," whatever the conception of "democracy" on which they are based, always include the accusation of dogmatic denial or delimitation, in theory and in practice, of the prerogatives and the purposes of the people. The basic problem in the ideological conflict concerning "democracy" is the problem of the nature of the conflict: whether it can be resolved only by agreement on a single definition and by abandonment of other meanings which are currently attached to the term or whether it can be resolved by removal of ambiguities in most or in all definitions of democracy and by discovery of the manner in which they are compatible with each other in the practical sense of permitting cooperative action without violence to "democratic" principles in their different acceptations.

The nature of the problem sets the criteria by which the meanings of the term "democracy" may be judged. Criteria of meanings should be stated explicitly before examining the ambiguity of any term. In the philosophic temper of contemporary discussions, when there is a tendency to avoid metaphysics by treating all problems of basic principles semantically, "semantics" has itself become an ambiguous term. There are systems of semantics annexed to *logical* theories which undertake to remove ambiguity by defining the conditions of truth and of the application of terms to .their subject matters; in such systems it is usually important to distinguish between "pure" semantics and "descriptive" semantics. There are systems of semantics annexed to *rhetorical* theories which undertake to remove ambiguity by clarifying the relation of communication between speaker and listener; in such systems it is usually important to distinguish between the symbolic or scientific and the emotive or persuasive use of terms. Much of the discussion of semantics in its philosophic adaptations is directed to advancing or contesting the claims of rival principles of semantic theories designed to relate symbols to things or to meanings, actual or ideal, and to men or to actions, natural or modified by various influences. The clarification of the meanings of "democracy" will have practical significance only if it can avoid initial commitment to any single semantical, metaphysical, theological, or economic theory. This should be possible if the study of meanings be an examination of *historical* usages and of the means actually employed which justify or exemplify those usages, and if the criteria relevant to usages be sought in the *political* and *social* situation rather than in the intention or the feelings of the speaker or the hearer or in the ontological character of the thing he designates or the culture he reflects. The sources of ambiguity of "democracy" should be sought not only in the competing definitions and emotional overtones of the term but also in the competing semantic systems by which the definitions are supported at different times and in different circumstances.

1. AMBIGUITY.—The word "democracy" is ambiguous not in the sense that many different formulas have been proposed to define its meaning, but in the sense that many different interpretations have been proposed and elaborated for a formula on which there has been remarkable continuity of agreement. Very few discussions of democracy, adverse or favorable, would be distorted by interpreting "democracy" as the "rule of the people in their own interest." The ambiguities of this formula arise from two interrelated sources: (1) the determination of the means by which the people

may "rule in their own interest" and (2) the determination of who the "people" are. The discussion of the first source of ambiguity turns on defining terms like "law," "order," "freedom," and "equality," while the discussion of the second source turns on the relations between pairs of contrary terms such as "the many and the few" and "the poor and the rich."

2. EVIDENCE.—In one of the earliest systematic examinations of democracy in Western civilization, Plato observes that democracy, conceived as "the rule of the many," is a single term, but it has two meanings dependent on whether the rule is according to law or without law.[1] His discussion of democracy elsewhere equates the many with the poor and emphasizes the ambiguity of the terms "freedom" and "equality."[2] Aristotle on the other hand distinguishes the perverted from the true forms of constitutions by their purposes and distinguishes different senses of "justice" and "law" appropriate to different constitutions, and he limits the term "democracy" to that form of rule in which the poor rule for their own interest as contrasted to "polity" where they rule with a view to the common good. His discussion is thereafter concerned with different forms of democracy rather than with ambiguities of terms. Pericles calls the government of Athens "democratic" because it is administered by the many and not the few, but he adds that despite the equality of all before the law, public honors are distributed according to merit rather than class, and poverty is no hindrance to public service.[3]

In these three positions concerning democracy in antiquity, as in later discussions, the ambiguity of the word reflects basic theoretic differences: (1) with respect to how the people shall "rule," between those who seek to safeguard the common good by devices to effect, and by theories to justify, the limitation of "absolute" freedom and those who develop the theory that the judgment of the people is the best indication of the common good and seek devices to assure its effective translation into action, and (2) with respect to who the "people" are, between those who seek to encompass all the "people" and the people as a "whole" by identifying the "whole" with the "many," the "multitude," the "poor," or the

1. *Statesman* 302D–303A.
2. *Republic* x. 557A–558C.
3. Thucydides ii. 37.

"workers" and those who take "whole" literally and provide safeguards for the rights of the few from the action of the many. The
theory of popular sovereignty and the devices of representative
government have been evolved to resolve the ambiguities concerning how the people shall "rule," but both the theory of sovereignty
and the devices of parliamentary government are in turn affected
by those ambiguities. The theories of the brotherhood of man, the
law of nature, and the labor theory of value, and the devices established to protect human rights have been evolved to resolve the
ambiguities concerning who the "people" are, but they likewise
have been affected by ambiguity and interpreted according to opposed theories.

The operation of these ambiguities at later stages of history is
illustrated by the distinction made by the authors of *The Federalist*
between a "democracy" and a "republic":[4] (1) in a republic the
government is delegated to a small number of citizens elected by
the rest and (2) a republic may be extended over a greater number
of citizens and a greater sphere of country, and these conditions are
more favorable to the election of proper guardians of the public
weal. The determination of who the people are and how they will
rule operates differently to resolve the same ambiguities in Lenin's
commentary on Engels' argument that the withering away of the
state also means the withering away of democracy. "At first sight
such a statement seems exceedingly strange and incomprehensible;
indeed, some one may even begin to fear lest we be expecting the
advent of such an order of society in which the principle of the
subordination of the minority to the majority will not be respected—for is not a democracy just the recognition of this principle? No, democracy is not identical with the subordination of the
minority to the majority. Democracy is a *state* recognizing the subordination of the minority to the majority, i.e., an organization for
the systematic use of *violence* by one class against the other, by one
part of the population against another."[5] The basic opposition between rich and poor is made the contrast between capitalistic democracy which rejects the poor and democracy of the people
which becomes unnecessary as soon as it is possible: "Thus in a
capitalist society, we have a democracy that is curtailed, poor, false;

4. *The Federalist*, No. 10.
5. *State and Revolution* (New York, 1932), chap. iv, sec. 6, p. 68 (italics Lenin's).

a democracy only for the rich, for the minority. The dictatorship of the proletariat, the period of transition to Communism, will, for the first time, produce democracy for the people, for the majority, side by side with the necessary suppression of the minority—the exploiters. Communism alone is capable of giving a really complete democracy, and the more complete it is the more quickly will it become unnecessary and wither away of itself."[6]

3. MISUSE.—Any charge of misuse of a term depends on a standard of correct usage. Standards of correct usage cannot be established effectively in the field of practical action by linguistic convention, logistic rule, or traditional principle. The charge that the term "democracy" is misused in any usage is part of the statement of the case for any party to the dispute concerning the meaning and operation of democracy. The charge can be justified objectively, not by questioning the motives and sincerity of the proponents of a doctrine or a program, but by examining both the implications of the meaning attached to the word in the context of the tradition of meanings and practices in which it is applied and in the context of the conflict in which the meaning is defended. Such criteria should be products of an inquiry into the bases of ideological conflicts concerning democracy, not presuppositions on which such inquiry is based.

4. NEW USES.—New significances have been attached to the word "democracy" in the sense that the definition of "people" has been progressively extended until it is recognized to include ideally all mankind without discrimination and all mankind in some relation as a humane or cultural whole, and in the sense that the functions proper to government have been increased and new institutions have been devised for the exercise of these enlarged functions over more extensive scopes of people and territory. The word is not used in new significances in the sense of departing from the age-old traditional but ambiguous formula. The changes in interpretation and application are efforts to resolve the problems presented by the fundamental formula, and the historical basis for approving some usages and rejecting others is inseparable from the judgment of the success of institutions and the effectiveness of formulations concerning them. The basic continuity of the formula suggests that a kind of ambiguity is desirable in practical decisions, inasmuch as it

6. *Ibid.*, chap. v, sec. 2, p. 74.

permits (*a*) agreement on a program of action despite differences of basic reasons for the action and (*b*) the progressive and controlled improvement of interpretation and practice.

5. "GENERAL DEMOCRACY."—The argument that there is no such thing as "democracy" but only a series of historical different "democracies" is based in part on an error concerning logical definition and in part on an error concerning political concepts. No definition, not even in Platonic dialectic, requires the "existence" of a "general" exemplar alongside and apart from its particular instances; in the field of political theory and practice definitions are applied to concepts and practices in conformity with institutions, which unlike natural objects and natural processes, are affected in their historical evolution by formulations of purpose and modifications of process.

6. COMMON CHARACTERISTICS.—All democracies have in common (1) political institutions designed to make effective the will of the people in the regulation of the common life, without discrimination, of all the people, and (2) provisions in the organization of those institutions to protect the people against arbitrary action, by such devices as the protection of human rights and the promulgation of a rule of law.

7. IDEAL VERSUS FACT.—No form of democratic government has succeeded in setting up instrumentalities that have fully realized the formula of democratic government in concrete form. It is therefore easy to list the imperfections of all past and present democracies. The violence of controversies seldom results from the confusion of ideals with actual conditions: within a tradition it results from differences concerning the character of the imperfection and the means by which to remove it, and it frequently leads to the suppression of one of the contrary views; between two opposed traditions, it results from differences in the interpretation of the operation of democracy and the method of achieving it, and it frequently leads to propaganda distortions of fact and theory in the opposed statements of the differences or even to attempts at violent suppression.

B. SOCIAL VERSUS POLITICAL DEMOCRACY

8. THE LINCOLN FORMULA.—The basic formula of "democracy" may be discussed in terms of the three prepositions of Lincoln's

Gettysburg Address: all government is *of* the people in a variety of possible senses (the people are the object of government, and the government is the concern or even the possession or property of the people), the distinguishing mark of democratic government being that the people govern and are governed, but government *by* the people, as has been pointed out repeatedly since it was first re-marked in antiquity, is improperly called government and cannot in fact long endure unless it succeeds to some extent in achieving the common good *for* the people.

9. NECESSARY CRITERIA.—In such an interpretation all three of the prepositions *of, by,* and *for* are essential to the concept "democracy." But prior to interpretation all three prepositions are ambiguous and depend in turn for their meaning on the determination of how the "people" shall be identified and how the people shall govern itself to achieve the ends appropriate to the "people" so conceived.

10. WESTERN VERSUS EASTERN DEMOCRACY.—For these reasons government by the people cannot be separated from government for the people, and Bertrand Russell creates a wholly artificial distinction when he attributes a "majority rule" conception of democracy to the West as opposed to a "majority interest" conception attributed to the East. The difference between the Western and the Soviet conceptions of democracy must be found in differences in the interpretation of both "by" and "for," not merely in relative emphases on one or the other. According to Lenin, the establishment, and therefore the disappearance, of democracy depends on government *by* the people: "From the moment when all members of society, or even only the overwhelming majority, have learned how to govern the state *themselves,* have taken this business into their own hands, have 'established' control over the insignificant minority of capitalists, over the gentry with capitalist leanings, and the workers thoroughly demoralized by capitalism—from this moment the need for any government begins to disappear. The more complete the democracy, the nearer the moment when it begins to be unnecessary."[7] The "government by the people," however, takes the form of managing social production, not of electing representatives and delegates. Conversely, Western democracy, no

7. *Ibid.,* chap. v, sec. 4, p. 84.

less than Soviet democracy, emphasizes the common interest, seeking to achieve it by providing means by which the majority may put their decisions into effect rather than by requiring action in accordance with decisions advanced as scientific consequences of the Marxist political philosophy.

11. "NARROW" VERSUS "BROAD" SENSE.—These considerations are sufficient to make clear the erroneous and tendentious coloring lent to the discussion by contrasting a *narrow* and a *broad* concept of "democracy," the one "a political concept designating methods of decision-making," the other "a socio-political concept designating conditions and methods as well as results of decision-making." This formulation of the opposition is colored by the ideology of one of the opposed positions. The issue can be stated in neutral terms which underlie and bring into relation the Western criticism of communist democracy and the communist criticism of Western democracy. The opposition is between two concepts of democracy, *equally broad* so far as their application to the interrelated problems of political, economic, and social life is concerned, but *opposed in their methods* of achieving cooperative action. The one conception of democracy is based on the confidence that the people are the best judge of their own good and that they can achieve it by government responsible to them and by institutions designed to protect doctrinal differences while facilitating agreement on courses of action: social and economic conditions pertinent to the institution and end of democratic government are subject to those decisions. The other conception of democracy is based on the confidence that the application of the method of dialectical materialism to social life and to the history of society has converted socialism from a dream of a better future for humanity into a science and that "the practical activity of the party of the proletariat must not be based on the good wishes of 'outstanding individuals,' not on the dictates of 'reason,' 'universal morals,' etc., but on the laws of development of society and on the study of those laws."[8] The one would provide for social, economic, and political decisions, and even for the use of science in arriving at those decisions, within a frame that makes possible the resolution of differences, according to the preference of the majority, on the assumption that no one has infallible scientific knowledge in any sphere and that the progress of science

8. J. Stalin, *Dialectical and Historical Materialism* (New York, 1940), p. 19.

no less than the equitable resolution of differences depends on the toleration of diversity. The other would provide for social, economic, and political decisions through the application of the principles of dialectical materialism in resolution of problems in these spheres by the party of the proletariat, on the assumption that the method of dialectical materialism is the true scientific method and that not even all the workers (since they have been demoralized by capitalism), much less the capitalists and those who incline toward capitalism, can contribute to the decision.

12. SOCIAL PROBLEM.—When the contrast is formulated neutrally, the second concept of democracy is seen to involve no more elements and no greater breadth than the first. Thus, to take one problem which has important psychological and sociological ramifications, both concepts of democracy depend on "education." Democracy, conceived in the first way, depends on an education designed to develop the abilities essential to the rational considerations and decisions of self-government; conceived in the second way, democracy depends on an education designed to train workers in the management and advancement of social production according to the accepted principles of dialectical materialism. One group of educators holds that the second is an outmoded theory: that it was never possible nor desirable to control men's minds and expression by the inculcation of a single doctrine, however sound its bases or salubrious its consequences may seem to be, and that the progress of science and the invention of modern means of communication make the effort to educate men to a uniform doctrine less justifiable than ever, since it impedes both the advancement of science and the achievement of the social good. Another group of educators holds that the first is an outmoded theory, and subscribes to Edward Hallett Carr's statement: "The view that the exclusive or primary aim of education is to make the individual think for himself is outmoded; few people any longer contest the thesis that the child should be educated 'in' the official ideology of his country."[9] The proper formulation of the question would recognize that neither side conceives itself as adding or needing to add anything borrowed from the other. The relation is not between the broader and the narrower. Therefore, both sides deny both allegations made in criticism: both theories make the claim that they train men to think

9. *The Soviet Impact on the Western World* (New York, 1947), p. 100.

and indeed to think "scientifically," and both would deny the charge that education in their sense is the inculcation of an ideology. The advocates of "Liberalism" in education, thus, defend it as a means of developing the freedom of thought essential to democracy and to science, and the advocates of "Dialectical Materialism" in education, defend it as means of developing the impartial scientific attitude essential to democracy and freedom. In much the same fashion, to go on to another related problem, both conceptions of democracy are opposed to fascism and each accuses the other of fascistic tendencies, for from the one point of view to tolerate doctrines that may be conceived to be inimical to democracy is fascistic, while to suppress freedom of opinion is from the other point of view the mark of fascism.

13. POLITICAL PROBLEM.—The opposition between "political democracy" and "social democracy" is not the opposition between a "narrow" and a "broad" concept. It is the opposition between two interpretations of "democracy" and between two conceptions of the institutions and processes best calculated to put into concrete operation the means and ends which are ambiguously but inseparably connected in the basic formula of democracy. To relate "political democracy" and "social democracy" as means and ends is a rhetorical device suited to the defense of one or the other concept, not an analytic device suited to clarify the semantic differences or the practical issues that separate them. The argument of de Tocqueville, thus, falls within one of the traditions: even the "socialism" which he considers is one elected by and responsible to the people, and he argues that such a form of government is thought to be democratic only because of the ambiguity of the word "equality."

14. HISTORICAL DEVELOPMENT OF THE TWO USAGES.—Much of the ambiguity attached to the term "democracy" results from the mingling of problems and the confusion of meanings proper to two traditions. De Tocqueville presented one of the extremes of opposition in one tradition of the discussion of government. That tradition was engaged in internal controversies which affected and were affected by an opposed tradition. The broader opposition is between the use of factions or classes as a safeguard of the common good against partisan interest, on the one hand, and the appeal to wisdom or knowledge for the discrimination of the true good as opposed to the common good, on the other. The present criticisms

and defenses of forms of democracy inherit semantic tendencies of an earlier form of the discussion of "mixed forms" of government in which democracy played a part. Plato argued that, since a state should be free and wise and in friendship with itself, the government should be blended of two forms, monarchy and democracy,[10] since in their extreme forms monarchy tends through ignorance to reduce people to slavery and hostility, while democracy tends to an extreme of freedom inconsistent with wisdom and friendliness. Aristotle treated the "polity" as a mixture or fusion of oligarchy and democracy,[11] and the success of such a constitution depends on the numbers and strength of the class intermediate between the rich (who rule in an oligarchy) and the poor (who rule in a democracy).[12] Polybius applied the term "democracy" to a form of constitution similar to Aristotle's "polity," but he described it as a mixture of monarchy, aristocracy, and democracy as represented by the Consuls, the Senate, and the People of the Roman constitution. Cicero argued that the best form of government is a mixture of monarchy, aristocracy, and democracy, such as was achieved in the historical development of the Roman Republic.[13] Medieval theory developed the doctrine of *merum et mixtum imperium;* Montesquieu attributed the virtues of the English form of government to the separation of powers; the writers of the *Federalist* papers were convinced that the advantages of the republic in securing public good and private rights consist in the possibility it presents of increasing the number and diversity of factions. The difference is not between the balance of political powers as opposed to the balance of social and economic classes; such an interpretation would lend color to the opposition of a "narrow" political and a "broad" social concept of democracy, but it would be inadequate to the history of the discussion. It is the opposition between, on the one hand, political devices designed to curb the excessive power of any social or economic class and to prevent any one class from dominating the process of making decisions and, on the other hand, political devices designed to eliminate the excesses of freedom and ignorance and to prevent the erroneous notions of a powerful minority from being substituted for the true common good.

10. *Laws* iii. 693A–D.
11. *Politics* iv. 8. 1293b33–38.
12. *Ibid.* 11. 1295b1–1296a21.
13. *De re publica* i. 25–29.

15. DEMOCRACY AND SOCIALISM.—The central problem of the one tradition, therefore, has been to reconcile the principle of majority rule with the preservation of the rights of minorities. One solution, repeatedly advanced, is the establishment of economic equality; it is usually opposed, as de Tocqueville opposes it, on the grounds that it destroys freedom. The central problem of the second tradition is to effect the transition from a society which is not based on a sound science of society to one which is; according to Plato, More, Campanella, and Marx, the transition depends on some form of common ownership of property. One solution, is that the transition may be effected by political means; it is usually opposed, as Lenin opposes it[14] on the grounds that during the transition the minority must be suppressed. Bryce's statement that "political equality can exist either along with or apart from equality in property" is the historian's generalization of the first tradition. It is compatible with both extremes of the debates which lead to the establishment of democracy in England, the United States of America, and France. Thus, Harrington, Paine, and John Adams argue that political equality depends on equality of property. The writers of the *Federalist* papers, on the other hand, find in the unequal distribution of property the most common and durable sources of faction, and they propose not to remove the causes of faction but to control its effects.[15] De Tocqueville's arguments against socialist egalitarianism in property are couched in the language of *laissez-faire* liberalism: the meanings he gave to his terms and the grounds he advanced for his arguments are found repeated in contemporary discussion and in application to contemporary situations. The question of the validity of his arguments is therefore the question of the validity of extreme *laissez-faire* liberalism.

16. METHOD VERSUS CONTENT.—For the reasons stated above I think the distinction between the "method of decision-making" and the "contents of decision made" is ambiguous or meaningless unless "method of decision-making" is thought to entail plurality of parties and diversity of views and "contents of decision made" is thought to entail criteria for disallowing antagonistic parties and divergent views.

14. *State and Revolution*, chap. v, sec. 2, p. 74.
15. Cf. R. McKeon, "The Development of the Concept of Property in Political Philosophy: A Study of the Background of the Constitution," *Ethics*, XLVIII (1938), 350–66.

17. CRUCIAL DIFFERENCES.—The fundamental assumption on which the argument of Lenin and Stalin depends is that "the conditions of the material life of a society" play the primary role in the development of society and that social ideas, social theories, political views and political institutions depend on the material conditions of society of which they are a reflection.[16] This theory does not mean that social ideas cannot be significant, if they correctly reflect the needs of the development of the material life of society, but it does presuppose that the material transformation of the economic conditions can be known in a fashion distinct from the conscious thoughts which are influenced by philosophic, historical, and economic theories. The fundamental assumption on which the argument of liberals like de Tocqueville and Bryce depends is that a form of government may be established in which men of different basic doctrines and different economic status may co-operate, and in which standards of justice and right are applied to social and economic as well as political questions. This theory does not mean either that ideas are independent of the influence of the circumstances in which they arise, or that all ideas have equal value and validity, but it does presuppose that the value of ideas is tested by examining their operation and consequences in competition with conflicting relevant ideas and that the people govern themselves by passing judgment on the truth, the justice, and the utility of ideas. De Tocqueville and Lenin differ in their conception of "liberty" and "equality," the former conceiving equality as freedom from political interference (conjoined with freedom of political action), the latter conceiving equality as freedom from economic exploitation (conjoined with freedom in managing social production).

18. REAL AND TERMINOLOGICAL DIFFERENCES.—These differences are not of a terminological nature in the sense that they can be removed by arbitrary verbal conventions. They are terminological in the sense that differences of meaning obscure the statement of the issue and in the sense that the verbal refutation of either position is easy when it is interpreted according to the meanings assigned to the terms in the other position.

19. EXPRESSION OF "REAL INTERESTS."—Two sets of criteria applicable to methods of decision-making emerge from the two tradi-

16. Stalin, *Dialectical and Historical Materialism*, pp. 20–21.

tions. In the first, the expression of the "real interests" of each individual is protected by civil and political rights; in the second, the "real interests" of each individual are determined by the adjustment of "relations of production" to the "development of the productive forces." The first criteria are addressed to the protection of the interests of *all* and afford grounds for criticism of any suppression of divergences of view or silencing of minority opinions. The second criteria are addressed to the protection of the *real* interests of the people and afford grounds for criticism of the toleration of fundamental ideological differences or of a capitalist minority. By the first criteria, political questions can be separated from social and economic questions; by the second criteria, political and social concepts are determined by economic conditions.

20. OPINION: INFLUENCE VERSUS PRESSURE.—According to the first criteria, the withholding of any right—including the right to education—is detrimental to democratic processes. It does not follow, however, that ability to judge one's interests is coextensive with literacy or limited to literates. "Democratically unjustifiable" processes of opinion-influencing are processes which preclude an equal opportunity for the expression of opposed views under comparable conditions. According to the second criteria, "democratically unjustifiable" processes of opinion-influencing are processes dominated by capitalists and expressive of bourgeois ideology.

21. DEMOCRACY AND PLANNING.—Economic planning is rendered consistent with the liberal tradition of democracy by such devices as the use of the right of eminent domain and the establishment of the requirement of a larger proportionate vote to change than to initiate a long term plan. Undemocratic delegation of power, in this tradition, is found in any distribution of offices (such as the allocation of representatives), or continuation of personnel in office (through patronage or pressure), or assumption by officers of functions not delegated to him, which interferes with the expression or the execution of the will of the people. Economic planning, in the communist tradition, is the prerogative of the party of the proletariat.

C. TOLERANCE AND TREASON

22, 23, AND 24. TOLERATION OF DISSENTIENT OPINIONS, REPRESSION OF PROPAGANDA, AND DECISIONS INCOMPATIBLE WITH DEMOCRACY.—

The freedoms essential to liberal democracy include freedom of thought and expression: that freedom is an expression of the confidence that truth will be apparent and influential in free discussion and, properly interpreted, it is subject to no limitation. Edward Hallett Carr tackles only half of the problem when he argues: "Outside the English-speaking world the doctrine of toleration for fascists in the name of democracy will become more and more difficult to commend to popular support; and the impact of Soviet opinion will be increasingly felt against it."[17] The other horn of the dilemma is that the suppression of doctrines contrary to democracy moves in easy stages from clearer to more obscure instances until scientists, artists, no less than economists and philosophers are induced to abjure as "reactionary and unscientific" doctrines which seemed acceptable even to the authorities until the authoritative condemnation was promulgated. Unsympathetic critics outside the communist world will think the control of doctrines is fascist in method and compatible with the toleration of fascists in action. Both criticisms are part of the ideological conflict.

The principle underlying the toleration of all opinions is stated excellently by Justice Holmes in his dissenting opinion in *Abrams* vs. *United States:*[18] "Persecution for the expression of opinions seems to me perfectly logical. If you have no doubt of your premises or your power and want a certain result with all your heart you naturally express your wishes in law and sweep away all opposition. To allow opposition by speech seems to indicate that you think the speech impotent, as when a man says that he has squared the circle, or that you do not care wholeheartedly for the result, or that you doubt either your power or your premises. But when men have realized that time has upset many fighting faiths, they may come to believe even more than they believe the very foundations of their own conduct that the ultimate good desired is better reached by free trade in ideas—that the best test of truth is the power of the thought to get itself accepted in the competition of the market, and that truth is the only ground upon which their wishes safely can be carried out. That at any rate is the theory of our Constitution. It is an experiment, as all life is an experiment. Every year if not every day we have to wager our salvation upon some prophecy based

17. *The Soviet Impact on the Western World*, p. 17.
18. 250 U.S. 616, 1919.

upon imperfect knowledge. While that experiment is part of our system I think that we should be eternally vigilant against attempts to check the expression of opinions that we loathe and believe to be fraught with death, unless they so imminently threaten immediate interference with the lawful and pressing purposes of the law that an immediate check is required to save the country." Holmes expressed the criterion of that immediacy in terms of "clear and present danger":[19] "The question in every case is whether the words are used in such circumstances and are of such a nature as to create a clear and present danger that they will bring about the substantive evils that Congress has a right to prevent. It is a question of proximity and degree." Actions can and should be regulated by law; freedom of thought and expression may be permitted without prejudice, and cannot be withheld without danger, to the public peace. The extirpation of fascism depends no less on the ability of men to recognize the falsity of a doctrine when expressed, than on the effectiveness of laws to prevent the recurrence of fascist institutions and modes of activity.

Mr. Carr points out, however, that the effectiveness of toleration of dissent varies with social and political conditions. The principle underlying the suppression or restraint of hostile opinion is that freedom and toleration extended to enemies of democracy may weaken policy and effective action.

〔25. ONE-PARTY SYSTEMS.—A one-party system is compatible with democracy in an extremely simple and homogeneous society. In a complex society the one-party system can be presented as compatible with democracy only on the argument that a transition, unrestricted by law and based on force, is necessary to a homogeneous classless society. It is a paradoxical argument since the state will wither away at the moment at which it can be completely democratic, and the dictatorship of the proletariat cannot be "complete" democracy, democracy for all, for the rich as well as for the poor, but it must be a state that is democratic *in a new way, for* the proletarians and the propertyless in general, and dictatorial *in a new way, against* the bourgeoisie.[20] 〕

26. "SKEPTICISM" AND DEMOCRACY.—The principle, "that no opinion is infallible, that no opinion has any self-evident right to

19. *Schenck* vs. *United States*, 249 U.S. 47, 1919.
20. Stalin, *Foundations of Leninism* (New York, 1939), p. 53.

claim universal allegiance to its political creed," is a negative statement of Holmes's principle that the best test of truth is the power of the thought to get itself accepted in competition with other ideas and that truth is the only ground for long-term successful action. This is the principle of liberal democracy, and that is the sense in which I use the term.

27. TOLERATION OF THE ANTI-DEMOCRATIC.—The tolerance of anti-democratic propaganda is, in that tradition, a sign of firm conviction in the principles of democracy. Fear of ideas and suppression of opinions is a sign of lack of confidence.

D. THE VALUE FOUNDATION OF THE CONFLICT

28. MORALITY OF TOLERATION AND REPRESSION.—I have interpreted the questions under the previous heads as concerned with the determination of the philosophic presuppositions of contemporary ideological conflicts as they bear on "democracy." I have, therefore, been at pains to try to state the opposition neutrally and to try to reconstruct the opposed position when the question seemed to me to be limited arbitrarily to consideration of only one side of the conflict. Apart from indicating my conviction in the soundness of the tradition of liberal democracy in reply to the last two questions I have operated on the assumption that, whenever terms are used widely in a given sense, historical and political reasons can be found to justify the usage. The disagreement of those who advocate tolerance of the expression of all opinions, including Fascist propaganda, and those who advocate repression of opinions judged dangerous to "democracy" is not a disagreement concerning the place of values "within hierarchies of values of disputing groups or nations." It is a disagreement concerning methods of determining values and therefore concerning means as well as ends. The nature of the disagreement is well illustrated by the appeal to science in both conceptions of democracy. According to Holmes, the democratic resolution of problems is, like all of life, an experiment in which ideas are tested against other ideas, particularly against ideas that are dangerous. According to Stalin, the guiding principles of the party of the proletariat are derived from the laws of the development of society, whereas the conflict of ideas merely reflects the conflict of classes.

29. ULTIMATE AIMS.—The ultimate political aim of Lenin and the means by which it was proposed to accomplish it—the establishment of a classless society by the violent suppression of a minority—are not compatible with the rule of the majority and the protection of the rights of minorities as well as majorities. Among other differences between Communism and Liberalism the significance of ideological conflicts and their treatment in the process of attaining the respective ends of the two systems are different. Freedom of thought and expression are essential both to the progress of science and to the solution of political, economic, and social problems according to the tradition of liberal democracy. There is a science of society uninfluenced by ideological differences, according to the Marxist tradition, and "a distinction should always be made between the material transformation of the economic conditions of production which can be determined with the precision of natural science, and the legal, political, religious, aesthetic, or philosophic—in short ideological forms in which men become conscious of this conflict and fight it out."[21]

30. NATURE OF THE DISAGREEMENT.—This basic opposition cannot be stated properly in terms of the priority of "political democracy" to "social democracy" or of "social democracy" to "political democracy," since both the political freedom and the social equality are different in the proposed institutions and revolutions. It cannot be stated properly in terms of the priority of freedom, by which knowledge is possible, or of knowledge, by which equality is possible, since "science" is differently conceived in the two cases. Moreover, ideological conflicts have seldom been resolved directly by adjustment of opposed basic principles. The adjustment has come usually either through the suppression by force of one of the opposed positions, and that has seldom been wholly successful, or through the discovery that the practical consequences of the opposed positions were not incompatible, and that has been slow when it has not been accelerated by analysis. The philosophic bases of the opposed conceptions of "democracy" can be examined and elucidated in the history of traditions of thought and in the social and political circumstances in which the conceptions are respectively promulgated and applied. These bases will be stated and inter-

21. Marx, Preface to *A Contribution to the Critique of Political Economy*, in *Selected Works* (London, 1942), I, 356.

preted differently in the two traditions, and recurrence to the oppositions of the fundamental principles will serve to rigidify the opposition of the two traditions. This is not a problem to be settled by
rules of linguistic usage or conventions of logical manipulation.
There is neither help nor comfort in the assurance that terms are
being misused or that ideas and values are being ignored on one or
the other side of the controversy. The real problem is in the fact
that as the oppositions become more rigid those who advocate the
repression of Fascist opinions come to count among the Fascists
those who tolerate dissentient opinions, and those who advocate the
tolerance of diverse opinions come to make an exception and to
advocate the repression of those who repress the expression of differences.

The one hope of resolution is in the fact that the success of either
side in the ideological conflict depends on values and facts associated, however ambiguously, with the determination and achievement by the people of the common good. The contribution of a
semantic analysis of the philosophic bases of different conceptions
of "freedom" must not be sought, therefore, in recommendations
that depend on belling the cat but in the discovery of common
middle grounds of possible harmonious action. The differences in
specific political, social, and economic forms of action are not as
great as ideological and propaganda statements make them seem.
The recommendations which follow from the analysis of the ideological differences should therefore be based on the confidence in
truth which both extremes of the opposition profess in different
fashions and should be directed to reduce the fear, which both extremes express, of the possible use of force by the other. Such
recommendations might be effective since, so conceived, they
would be based in each case on the tenets of the ideology itself and
not on principles contrary to it. One basic form of the recommendations to liberal democracies would thus be the full use of tolerance even in application to communist ideologies and the constant
recognition that liberal democracy is not a form of class conflict
but is based on the realization of the civil, political, social, economic, and intellectual rights of the people. If the advance of these
freedoms is seriousy impeded by economic interferences, the form
and effectiveness of liberal democracy are affected. One basic form
of the recommendations to communist democracies would con-

versely be the use of vigilance in the application of what is presented as the science of society. If that "science" is made a vehicle simply for the expression of the preferences or the whims of those in political power, the grounds of communist democracy are undermined. Ultimately the chief obstacles to the resolution of ideological conflicts are the economic or political restrictions put on freedom and the repression of dissentient opinions or of reformist and revisionist tendencies.

XVIII

JAMES MARSHALL

The question put by UNESCO is whether the Eastern and Western views concerning democracy can be reconciled. Inquiry is made as to whether there is an inevitable contradiction between the "political" democracy of the West and the "social" democracy of the East. Implicit in the questionnaire is the assumption that the West emphasizes the political forms of democracy such as civil rights and free elections while the East places its emphasis on economic equality, but that this may be no more than a mere matter of emphasis. Is it the unexpressed hope, perhaps, that UNESCO may function not only "as a clearing house of ideas, an international forum"—as it is described in the questionnaire—but as a marriage broker who brings about a contract by which the parties agree that under the family name of "Democrcay" can be merged both political freedom and economic equality?

The difficulties with these questions, assumptions and hopes is that they touch on only certain mechanisms and slur over democracy as an ethical end and a problem of human relations. The backgrounds of Western democracy in the Judeo-Christian and Stoic philosophies of equality are ignored. The rich American literature interpreting democratic aims and methods and pushing forward the frontiers of democratic effort is not cited.

In his *Journals*, Emerson wrote: "The root and seed of democracy is the doctrine, Judge for yourself. Reverence thyself. . . . At the same time it replaces the dead with a living check in a true, delicate reverence for superior, congenial minds. 'How is the King greater than I, if he is not more just?' "[1]

John Dewey, in *The Public and Its Problems*, discussing "the nature of the democratic idea in its generic social sense," writes: "From the standpoint of the individual, it consists in having a responsible share according to capacity in forming and directing the activities of the groups to which one belongs and in participating

---

1. Ralph Waldo Emerson, *Journals* (Boston, 1909–14), III, 369.

according to need in the values which the groups sustain. From the standpoint of the groups, it demands liberation of the potentialities of members of a group in harmony with the interests and goods which are common."[2]

The author has suggested that the democratic principle involves: "(1) Respect for individuals and the variations among individuals, their needs and their aspirations. (2) Making possible equal opportunity for every individual to obtain satisfaction by realizing and exercising his capacities and pursuing his interests. (3) Equality of treatment of each individual by those with power or authority. (4) The concept that equality does not mean identity, but rather recognition of differences, a recognition of differences not in the form of favouritism, but as an expression of respect for individuality. (5) Collaboration, rather than competition, or paternalism as the more likely method for achieving mutual respect, equality and development."[3]

The differences between democratic and autocratic administration have been well stated by Louis H. Blumenthal in *Administration of Group Work* as follows:

The Democratic Administrator	The Autocratic Administrator
Works to release energy in others	Works to watch over others
Looks for "answers" from others	Knows all the "answers"
Gets others to share responsibility	Does it all himself
Wants to build up others	Wants to be looked up to
Welcomes contribution	Is afraid of new ideas from others
Is the partner	Is the boss
Is the leader	Is the driver
Exerts power with people	Exerts power over people[4]

Finally, Jeremy Bentham has pointed out that the difference between free and despotic governments depends "on the manner in which the whole mass of power, which taken together is supreme, is in a free state distributed among the several ranks of persons that are sharers in it; on the source from whence their titles to it are successively derived; on the frequent and easy changes of condition between governors and governed, whereby the interests of one class are more or less indistinguishably blended with those of the other; on the responsibility of the governors; *on the right which*

2. John Dewey, *The Public and Its Problems* (New York, 1927), p. 147.
3. James Marshall, *The Freedom To Be Free* (New York, 1941), p. 84.
4. Louis H. Blumenthal, *Administration of Group Work* (New York, 1948), p. 137.

*the subject has of having the reasons publicly assigned and can-
vassed of every act of power that is exerted over him.*"[5]

These quotations indicate that a definition of democracy is possible in terms of human character and relationships. It need not be in
terms of instrumentalities, whether political or economic, whether
civil rights or the ownership of the means of production. *Democracy can be defined in terms of personality*. In such terms certain
instrumentalities tend to develop personalities which are self-re-
specting, co-operative, capable of moving toward the realization of
their capacities, to a great extent free of anxieties and destructive
drives. Other instrumentalities tend to develop personalities which
are dependent, repressed, apathetic, anxious, antagonistic, destructive.

It is necessary to distinguish between a philosophical concept of
democracy which is rooted in human relationships and directed
toward ethical ends and the forms of democracy, the instrumentalities of society. The latter may in one situation contribute to
what Emerson called "the spirit of life for the general good" and
in another stimulate greed, hatred, and lust for power. The same
institutions may lead to freedom or subservience depending upon
the attitudes which at a given time and place may be acceptable to
society. Thus courts of law may be instruments for judging impartially conflicts between individuals and between individuals and
the state; or they may be instruments to enforce subservience to the
state.

It would seem that *one cannot understand the forms of democracy, or of any other social philosophy, without reducing them into
their elements of power. And one cannot understand power without reducing it to human relationships, to impulses, drives, beliefs,
tensions and the like.* Voting, civil rights, forms of control over
goods and the means of production provide answers to needs. They
afford satisfactions or they cause deprivations. In this they are likewise elements in power struggles.

We continually try to find satisfaction and avoid pain. In these
enterprises of living we seek food, clothing, housing. We use our
minds, our reason, to discover what will bring satisfaction and what
pain, and we form systems of belief which reduce our anxieties concerning the unknown things of the universe and the half-known

5. Italics mine.

things of the world which we find ourselves powerless to control. We have impulses to exercise our capacities, especially those which we discover to be socially acceptable within the pattern of our particular culture. Above all, we want love, and this at once makes social beings of us. It causes us to search for satisfying relationships with others and to modify those relationships where they no longer yield satisfaction.

Unsure of what love is, we seek its symbols too. As symbols of love we seek not only sexual response but also status, a recognition of the worth of our capacities, an acknowledgment of the values we place upon ourselves. These symbols, these rewards may be in terms of many things, such as a pat on the back, a prize, a title, a sum of money, an invitation. How pathetically we seek such symbols is illustrated by Mussolini's statement that he "was never the King's guest at his country estate" and only once in Rome to see a moving picture after dinner. Moreover, he said that "all his life he never had any friends."[6]

In this search we frequently become frustrated. To gain one value or satisfaction we must deny ourselves another. We want love or honor or the opportunity to accumulate or the chance to become a judge or play on a great football team. We may overestimate our own capacities; or the chance may not present itself; or we may not recognize our opportunities. Moreover, someone with power over a means of satisfaction may refuse it to us; or someone on whom we are dependent for food or love or recognition or assurance of future security may reject our advances, repress our attempts to satisfy our impulses.

These frustrations result in pain and may lead to aggressive destructive responses. We may seek to destroy or injure the person who has denied us satisfaction or his possessions or beliefs or the institutions of which he is a symbol.

To the extent that society finds means of diverting or harnessing these aggressions they do not become harmful. When directed against objects rather than persons, they may even be the dynamic power of social development and improvement. "The instinct of destruction, when tempered and harnessed (as it were, inhibited in its aim) and directed towards objects, is compelled to provide the ego with satisfaction of its needs and with power over nature."[7]

6. *The Fall of Mussolini*, ed. Max Ascoli (New York, 1948), pp. 52, 156.
7. Sigmund Freud, *Civilization and Its Discontents* (London, 1930), p. 101.

But to the degree that society provides no such outlets, tensions result and destructive forces may be set free. Thus John Dewey has said: "Just because the cause of democratic freedom is the cause of the fullest possible realization of human potentialities, the latter when they are suppressed and oppressed will in time rebel and demand an opportunity for manifestation."[8]

Such rebellions and demands are a threat to power. Consequently those who have exercised power in such a way as to suppress and oppress the realization of human potentialities become caught in the quagmire of their own power. In their struggle to keep on top they sink deeper and deeper.

Out of the search for satisfactions and the aggressions incident to the frustration of this search, the power struggle arises. Singly or in association, people attempt to escape the pain of frustration by attempting to gain power over the causes of their frustration. The political process is the dialectic of power.[9] "In other words, each action of the ruling group brings about some reaction among other parts of the population which in turn demands further compensating action from the rulers."

Economic forces can no more be isolated from the political process than can they be made the sole or even the principal motivating force of human action. If there is any principal motivating force it is the impulse to find satisfaction and avoid pain. This impulse involves the universal search for love expressed in terms of affection, regard, sex, parenthood, approval, recognition, acceptance, or something else deemed to be rewarding. The absence of such satisfactions gives rise to anxiety and fear. The impulse to destructive aggression bred by deprivation arouses not only anxiety and fear but also guilt, which tends to reinforce the aggressive impulse.

Economic force is a power weapon. That is, it can be used to obtain or retain power over others. When exercised as a weapon of power, bread and gold and the means of production impede democracy; they impede democracy just as much as the use of physical force can impede it. For to exercise power of any nature *over* people is to that extent to deny or relieve them of responsibility. This limits their personalities, their opportunities for growth. It represses them. It binds them to dependency.

8. John Dewey, *Freedom and Culture* (New York, 1939), p. 129.
9. Cf. James Marshall, *Swords and Symbols* (New York, 1939), p. 103.

This is the case whether economic power or physical force be exercised by the state or by untrammeled private enterprise. State capitalism or private enterprise can each impose a sense of dependence upon those over whom the economic power is exercised. This will be less complete where democratic political mechanisms are available, as for example, where those who are subject to power, who are oppressed or persecuted, can meet together in protest, can strike, can present their cause in the public press or by the ballot can throw the oppressive rascals or their agents out of office.

Thus political forms which we call democratic, such as the right to vote and civil liberties, afford people power avenues for the release of their aggressions through political competition. Economic conflicts and free expression and debate give the people involved opportunities for the release of their aggressions in the form of economic and intellectual competition. These releases afford satisfactions. Where they exist they are socially acceptable substitutes for destructive aggression, they are outlets for aggression which may be at once constructive and satisfying.

Where the power which controls the economy also controls the weapons of force, that is, the armed services, the police, the courts —which themselves rely in the last analysis on the police power— there is no way out of submission to economic power on the part of those dependent on it. This has been as true in small isolated communities dominated by one industry or one mining company as it is true in great nations in which political and economic life are controlled by the government. The evil effects of a substantial monopoly of power weapons can be discerned under state capitalism or private capitalism. In the latter case, however, such concentrations have never been as complete.

Such submission to economic power is not true in England or the United States today, although there are danger signals. Can the habits of centuries which have planted the traditional British liberties in the hearts of every Englishman withstand the new combination of power weapons in the hands of the British government? Will the stubborn bulwark of the Britisher's belief that his home is his castle be able to resist the encroaching nature of this reinforced governmental power? Will his growing dependence on increasingly centralized authority rob him of the strength to wield his constitutional rights as he has done ever since Coke hurled his misinterpretations of the nature of Magna Carta at the tyrannies of the Stuart kings?

Some of the same questions can well be asked as to the forms of political democracy in the United States. Almost a century and a quarter ago de Tocqueville warned: "In democratic communities nothing but the central power has any stability in its position or any permanence in its undertakings. All the citizens are in ceaseless stir and transformation. Now, it is in the nature of all governments to seek constantly to enlarge their sphere of action; hence it is almost impossible that such a government should not ultimately succeed, because it acts with a fixed principle and a constant will upon men whose position, ideas, and desires are constantly changing. . . .

"Thus a democratic government increases its power simply by the fact of its permanence. Time is on its side; every incident befriends it; the passions of individuals unconsciously promote it; and it may be asserted that the older a democratic community is, the more centralized will its government become."[10]

We see these tendencies accelerated in the United States today under the social service state. Will the people of the United States become so dependent on their government that they too will forfeit the instrumentalities of political democracy? Are they unwittingly building a new paternalism under the illusion that they are free and democratic so long as they can "shake off their state of dependence just long enough to select their master and then relapse into it again"? There are hopeful signs in the United States in the richness of local institutions and also in the numerous "pressure groups," those private voluntary organizations which enable the individual to express his individuality and his views in a growingly complex world.

The saving point in British socialism may lie in the fact that the men of the Labour Party are also men of the trade unions. Trade unions are more than the holders of economic weapons. They are also associations of individuals who have gained integrity, respect, and fellowship through common effort. Unions have given John Doe, the working man, a name and a face. They therefore afford a strong psychological weapon to protect the historic democratic forms from becoming submerged by the new power weapons mobilized in the state.

10. Alexis de Tocqueville, *Democracy in America* (New York, 1945), II, 294 ff.

In terms of power the danger remains that the state, holding the bulk of the weapons of economic and political force, will control the third weapon of sovereignty, that is, psychological power. To retain control those in power tend to regulate freedom of expression, the press, the schools. Where this exists there can be no effective right of the subject "of having the reasons publicly assigned and canvassed of every act of power that is exercised over him."

As distinguished from the autocratic view, the democratic view of the relationship of government to *censorship* turns censorship upside down. This was expressed by Jefferson in his letter to Washington of September 9, 1792: "No government ought to be without censors; and where the press is free, no one ever will. If virtuous, it need not fear the fair operation of attack and defense. Nature has given to man no other means of sifting out the truth, either in religion, law or politics. I think it as honourable to the government neither to know, nor notice, its sycophants or censors, as it would be undignified and criminal to pamper the former and persecute the latter."[11]

The use of slogans as promises of rewards and stimulants to anxiety is the most common use of psychological power. Thus we find such terms as "communism," "fascism," "nationalization," "Five-Year Plan," "New Deal," "the withering state," "popular sovereignty," and many other symbols of reassurance and fear utilized as weapons in the political process.

Today there is psychological value in affixing the label "democracy" to institutions and "democratic" to men just as a century and a half ago the labels "inalienable rights" and "natural rights" called forth the enthusiastic response of men throughout the Western world.

That the term "democratic" is applied as propaganda is evident from its different uses. The Cominform countries refer to themselves as democratic and civil liberties as incidences of the capitalist, bourgeois states. American Communists demand that they be permitted to carry on their fight for communism in the name of their "democratic rights" of free speech, fair trial, suffrage, and assembly. Capitalism and private enterprise have been associated with democracy by captains of industry and in the fulminations of Hitler as well as by Lenin in his *State and Revolution*.[12]

11. Thomas Jefferson, *Writings* (Washington, D.C., 1903), VIII, 406.
12. *The Essentials of Leninism* (London, 1947), II, 200.

We cannot ignore the implications of the power struggle in the use of the words "democracy" or "democratic." Such usages amount to little more than the emotional load they carry. It is only as the paint of propaganda is removed that we can bring to light the solid substance of the group relationships in a society and the personality structures of the group members. Then we can discover whether the prevailing social pattern is autocratic or whether it more nearly fits the definitions. of democracy in the socially dynamic terms of Emerson, Dewey, and the others already quoted.

Certainly to distinguish between democracy as "the rule of the majority," on the one hand, and "rule in the interests of the majority," on the other, as was done by Bertrand Russell,[13] is a failure to analyze the dynamics of democracy and to fall into the trap of power politics. What is more social democracy than that of Emerson and Dewey? How can there be democracy for the people—that is, in the interests of the majority—without there being also democracy of and by the people? The use of the words *of, by,* and *for* in Lincoln's famous Gettysburg Address were not coincidental. Without benefit of modern psychology he understood the importance of popular participation if government was to be *for* the people.

Moreover, majorities are not the only groups to be considered. Minority opinion today may become the majority opinion tomorrow if left free to express itself. Such freedom is the very essence of personal integrity. It is the kernel of Emerson's "Judge for yourself."

Not only does this interchangeability, this fluidity between majority and minority offer hope to those whose needs are left unsatisfied, it also offers them the means to work for the satisfaction of their needs. Such a relationship between majorities and minorities means that people need not passively await some power to do something "*for* the people." It means that the power is "*of* the people" to do something "*by* the people." In such circumstances there can be no fixity of status as in feudalism or under autocracy. For in feudalism and autocracy, authority cannot risk the use of the powers, *of* the people *by* the people. It must use the power for the people; it must keep them dependent. Unfortunately, when power is used by others *for* the people, it generally entails a strong element of aggression. This tends to turn the power against the people in satisfaction

13. In the pamphlet *What Is Democracy?* (London, 1946), p. 14.

of the power needs of those who exercise it.

Psychological methods are the most potent forces which people have to modify or change power balances. They are the most effective means by which people with power may avoid the wastes incident to the use of economic and physical force. This is so because psychological weapons reach the minds and emotions of people. Therefore, they touch belief systems, cultural values, anxieties, moral needs, guilt feelings, hope, and reason. Character and personality are molded and modified through the approaches to the mind and the emotions. Force and bread, politics and economics, make their deeper and more lasting impacts on reason and feeling, not on bodies. That is why the weight of authority can be so great.

Authority can be varied. It can include many things, from social conscience imposed by ancestral ghosts to the centralized state. In a political sense authority means the authorities, those who have substantial power weapons at their control, whether those weapons be force, economic power or psychological. "In psychological terms authority means control over rewards and punishments."[14] In an autocratic society the authorities distribute rewards and punishments. It is this that tends to create dependence. In democratic societies rewards and punishments are to a great extent in the hands of individuals and their voluntary organizations. This results in greater independence or interdependence.

The measure of a people's democracy is the extent of its freedom from dependence. For a people, as for an individual, this freedom is a sign of maturity. Individuals and nations in times of stress tend to retreat to patterns of dependency which they had seemingly outgrown. They will pay the price of more or less submission to authority. In return for the rewards of relief from stress, or for the mere promise of such rewards, they will surrender power here and there and the ability to act for themselves without asking somebody's permission.

Dependence—with its corollaries of submissiveness and apathy—is not democratic. How can dependent, submissive, or apathetic people—or for that matter antagonistic people—judge for themselves or reverence themselves? Freedom from such dependence is the very basis of democracy. It is necessary if men are to develop and utilize their capacities, if society is to be a balance of their

14. Mark A. May, *A Social Psychology of War and Peace* (New Haven, 1943), p. 175.

individualities and not a structure of status. Freedom from dependence is requisite to maturity. For the satisfaction achieved through dependence is an uneasy peace in the shadow of some power in which one has little share. By paying the price of dependence one places a cheap value on one's self.

Dependence may perhaps purchase a measure of food, housing, clothing, social service, and protection by the armed services. It is in fact a form of prostitution. Guilt and anxiety, apathy and impotence, resentment and bigotry are its undertones. From them arise aggressive and destructive impulses which can be channeled or repressed by authority. If they are not channeled to ends of self-realization and free expression these impulses strain for release in war and revolution.

Whatever may have been the condition of the "happy savage" or of some primitive societies, we must accept the fact that some degree of dependence exists in the cultural pattern of every nation today. As infant mortality decreases and more children are reared, as the demand for increased education postpones the productive period of life, as science has lengthened the span of life and thus increased the ratio of elderly people in the community, the demands upon the family as an economic and cultural unit have grown far beyond its capacity to satisfy them. Increasingly, therefore, men have asked for assistance in meeting their burdens, to give adequate care to their dependents. To shift the responsibility of their dependents, the producing members of society have become in turn dependents of the state. The state has not been the only institution to meet these needs, but it has been the principal one.

This in itself might not be so great a threat to man's integrity and inner strength if at the same time the family as a more or less independent producer had not been abolished. Industrialization gave the world more clothing, more food, better housing, more entertainment, greater spice in a greater variety of life. But it has also tended to diminish the great satisfactions derived from family interdependence and self-reliance. The family no longer depends upon its members to perform the services of weaving, sewing, raising food, building its houses, providing its light. Domestic education and the intimate revelries of family life have also given way to mass entertainment and education. For all these goods men have come to depend more and more not on themselves and the family group but upon industry and the state, the economic and national groups in which their individual wills are limited and their individual voices are whispers. Thus they tend to be frustrated and dependent.

The more the power weapons are concentrated the greater that frustration and dependence tend to become. *Those political, economic, and social forms, those philosophies and ideologies which tend to reduce dependence and thus to minimize its incidences are democratic. Those which tend to increase dependence are autocratic.*

It does not follow that the only alternative to dependence is independence, what in American social thinking has sometimes been called "rugged individualism." For that is a fantasy of the frontier. There is another alternative in the recognition of interdependence, of co-operative effort. Through common endeavor, love satisfactions are alone made possible. Men acting with their peers for common purposes can participate "in deciding, planning, executing, and evaluating all matters." They do not have to weigh their acts or their beliefs, nor need they judge what is good or bad for them and theirs against the shadow of the smile or frown of authority.

Thus in the field of economic power the democratic answer is not necessarily private or state capitalism, private enterprise or socialism. It may lie in the middle ground of the co-operative, the functioning of which involves participation by equals in planning and sharing, in responsibility and rewards. Here power is not centered but diffused.

Voluntary organizations, from local committees to church conferences and international labor organizations serve the same purpose. They are outlets for tensions, and group expressions which relieve frustration and minimize dependence. These organizations also tend to diffuse power.

We can see then that words like "democray" and "autocracy" describe far more than political and economic mechanisms. They are descriptive, among other things, of group relationships. As such they are frequently used as slogans and symbols, that is, as psychological weapons of power or as shorthand expressions of moral and philosophical ends.

The important thing to keep in mind is that the terms "democracy" and "autocracy," being descriptive of group relationships, deal with dynamic, living, changing social interactions. It is to be expected that these dynamic group relationships must affect the personality patterns of the members of the group. Where power is highly concentrated, dependence and submissiveness play a great part in personality structure. Where power is diffused, there is generally a broader opportunity for self-realization and a greater variety of possible interrelationships.

Where people are dependent on authority, they have less opportunity to release the energies impounded in them by repression than have those who possess enough power to cause authority to listen to their claims and account to them for its behavior. Under authority the impulse is to look to others, that is, to those with power, to those in authority, to find satisfactions rather than for people to seek satisfactions for themselves.

Neither the concentration nor the diffusion of power will of itself free people of anxieties. Highly dependent people, it is true, may in apathy withdraw from all concern with anxiety-breeding conflicts. On the other hand, throwing people long habituated to dependence into a situation requiring responsibility may well increase their anxieties. It may well happen that in such circumstances, freed from the impositions of authority, "the aggressiveness of conscience carries on the aggressiveness of authority."[15]

But nothing is truer than the psychological principle that you cannot free people of one form of satisfying experience, however anxiety-laden the satisfactions may be, without substituting other satisfactions. "It does not matter how many tension points are raised in the development of the individual, provided proper outlets are permitted."[16]

Where power is more diffused, people will have a greater opportunity of finding for themselves outlets for their tensions, substitute situations, which will more nearly meet their needs. Find for themselves—this is important—for it implies emergence from dependence, a growth of personality out of childhood and adolescence into maturity. In psychological terms this is just what democracy makes possible and autocracy represses. The autocratic school, the autocratic church, the autocratic labor union, the autocratic employer, and the autocratic state depress subordinates and deny them the chance of growth, the chance to realize their capacities, just as in the autocratic home the parents attempt to hold the children in a state of involuntary dependence.

15. Sigmund Freud, *Civilization and Its Discontents* (London, 1930), p. 113.
16. Abram Kardiner, *Psychological Frontiers of Society* (New York, 1945), p. 420.

As we have already stated, it is our desire to be loved that makes social beings of us. The society that is derived from the hope of love of equals, in weakness and strength, will be a different society than one based on the hope of love of subordinates by their superiors and of superiors by their subordinates. Quite different group relationships must follow; quite different personalities must be developed.

True enough, the archetype of a democratic society has not been realized. This does not justify cynicism or doubt. Pragmatically, democracy works where it tends to develop men and women as mature people, prepared to co-operate as equals, free of a large measure of dependence and aggression. And as democratic principle involves the concept of self-realization and the co-operative improvement of society, the validity of a democratic pattern of society cannot be denied because the ideal has yet to be achieved. *The test is the measure of freedom from dependence on authority.* That is why freedom and democracy, and voluntary effort and democracy have been so closely associated.

Certain group relationships and their incidental personality patterns we call autocratic; others may be called democratic. One of the most important aspects of such relationships is to be found in the distribution of power. Such distribution weighs heavily in determining the relative amounts of dependence and self-realization, of unchanneled destructive aggression and of creativity, of subservience and voluntary co-operation, of animosity and love in group and personality patterns.

Political and economic mechanisms contribute to or limit the facility with which power can be used. They provide the large spoons of authority, or the smaller spoons of voluntary groups and individuals, for ladling out rewards and punishments. But to define democracy—or autocracy—in terms of political or economic mechanisms is to ignore social dynamics.

If one adopts this psycho-social approach, two results follow: first, democracy becomes a comparative rather than a normative cultural relationship; and, secondly, democracy is a way of life, a complex of human relationships and not a selection of politico-economic forms, however much those forms may reflect and deflect ways of life.

XIX

EMMANUEL MOUNIER

Setting out to analyze the problems under inquiry, it would be useful to settle on the terms to be used for the two forms of democracy or at least their extremes. The East-West distinction should be banned in spite of the elements of historical truth it contains: first, because in present-day conditions it introduces at the very outset an emotional element detrimental to all efforts of clarification; second, because it obscures the precise problems at issue through the historical and affective associations of the East-West opposition; and, third, because it petrifies into some kind of geographical essence or inevitability what is almost certainly a contingent and swiftly passing historical phenomenon. To go no further than France itself, the democracy defined by the Constitution of 1793, the Second Republic in its early stages, the Commune, and, in certain of their features, the Caesarean republics of the two Napoleons all resemble more or less the democracies called "Eastern" in our day. The "monarchic republic," consistently denounced by Proudhon and the French anarchists, undoubtedly came close to the same democracies, at least in certain respects.

Popular democracy and *bourgeois democracy* define one aspect of reality, but not all, and are only accepted by the Marxists.

The best terms seem to me to be *mass democracy* and *liberal democracy*, the first primarily expressing the rise of the masses and seeking to organize the power of the masses, the second primarily expressing the urge to freedom and seeking to safeguard civil liberties.

Within mass democracy I should suggest a distinction between *totalitarian democracy*, as achieved by the Fascist states, and *popular democracy*, various types of which are found among the states of eastern Europe. These latter democracies cannot be deemed totalitarian in the strict sense (single party, suppression of all opinions other than those of the state, suspension of representative institutions, etc.), despite the fact that they differ structurally from

228

liberal democracies and externally, at least, call to mind certain features of totalitarian democracy.

Liberal democracy I should subdivide into the *parliamentary democracy* typical of European states before 1922 and the *socialist democracy*, on which certain of those states embarked after the Liberation of 1945 before sinking back into amorphous compromises between the two types. The second type resembles the popular democracies in its ends, but does not overturn representative institutions, class relations or the structure of the state.

I

Modern discussions of democracy present a hopeless jumble of arguments, some expressing a philosophic ideal and others clearly—though not always so in the eyes of their originators—doing no more than state in terms of value a given historical situation. For the purpose of clarification, the philosophical or ethical motivations ascribed by democracy to itself must be carefully isolated. By causing them to "settle," in the chemical sense, we will reveal the historical interplay of forces which they involve, without gain to themselves. These will prove to be a relatively small number of dominant lines of force which can bring a measure of light to the discussion of the problem. Elimination of extraneous elements will bring a more just appreciation of their intrinsic worth and thereafter a truer assessment of their relation to the historical situations with which they normally emerge.

It will then be seen that there is as much confusion in the democratic beliefs of a liberal as in those of an anti liberal. Modern democracy's inability to find for itself a coherent philosophy is not peculiar to political thinking. It is one aspect of modern man's continuing inability to hit on a satisfactory and sufficiently widely accepted account of his own condition, ever since the unity of Christendom was broken. Democracy is commonly spoken of as though, in the West, it meant no more than a group of sentiments, forces and values: those that assert the autonomy and personal liberty of the citizen in front of the authorities. Yet clearly the philosophy of democracy has for two centuries past been oscillating between three poles; one of these does indeed embrace the values—and with them the ideas, sentiments, and forces—expressed in the word "liberalism"; the other two, however, bear little resemblance to it.

230 DEMOCRACY IN A WORLD OF TENSIONS

II

To take liberty first, men in the West are becoming increasingly accustomed to think of it as amounting in the final analysis to an attitude of rejection, of *protest*, an opposition to power, whatever that power may be and whatever shape that opposition may take. The search for the beginning of this attitude can be pushed reasonably far back in time, though not as far as Caesar or Cicero lamenting it in Gaul and Latin respectively, for Tacitus could show us Germans as fiercely independent as their rivals. Undoubtedly, however, an inquiry should be made into the way the constitutions of the eighteenth century came to accord so important a place in their conception of liberty to the idea of defense against *encroachment*. Nor can we overlook the great anarchist tradition that bred the beginnings of the Socialist movement, as Liberalism did the beginnings of democracy. Alain, the philosopher of French Radicalism, defined democracy as the system of "the citizen against the authorities." "Everything," he wrote, "which controls and limits power, is democratic." Control, that is, organized suspicion, was, in his mind, the sole essential note of democracy. Today we have Sartre defining the basic behavior of man as an *uprooting*, a flight before the menace of being, and, politically, committing himself to a classically liberal opposition to all totalitarianisms and to all excesses of power, his positive notion of the social bond emerging less clearly. In France the word "liberty" has in many cases vanished from the language of the Left, of which it was so long a part. Contrariwise it reappears in all the movements opposed to any form of socialization (*Parti républicain de la Liberté:* Right Wing Conservatives; *La liberté de l'esprit:* a Gaullist review; etc.). Whether the bugbear be centralized industry, a topheavy administration, a controlled economy, the state, or restrictions, liberty, as understood by this brand of democrat, is always and everywhere freedom *from* something, freedom *against*.

The negative and sterile nature of this attitude is perhaps less marked in a country like the United States which is still, like nineteenth-century Europe, on the crest of an expanding and victorious economy. Unlike modern Europe, that economy had no clogging weight of feudalism or craft guilds to throw off. Nor was the American citizen faced with ancient states fully formed: the whole movement started off, so to speak, in a kind of vacuum. Moreover,

the Americans do not bear within them the childish revolt com-
plexes which still obsess Europeans. Undoubtedly "liberty" has
taken on an important shade of meaning on the far side of the
Atlantic, but with the passage of time, there has been as great a
change of meaning in Europe itself. In 1789 or 1830 "liberty"
meant achievement and progress. Too often today it means acrimony, retrogression, denial of the future in order to get back to the
good old ways, hands free for the individualist struggle for place and
profit. Behind this kind of anarchic nostalgia, which typifies for a
certain class of men release from their community responsibilities,
there is often the ill-defined feeling that all that has its origin in
society or the community can only trouble the happy concord
attained by individuals; or, as a French jurist has put it, "Law is
always an evil." The positive aspect of this state of mind is seen in
those for whom democracy means mainly the existence of, and
respect for, an *opposition*. However, from that attitude to the worship of opposition for its own sake and a pathological fear of unanimity is no more than a step or rather a leap, as when Alain writes:
"The clearest characteristic of the democratic spirit is perhaps that
it is anti-social."[1] From this type of democratic spirit, which un-
happily is widespread, all that may be expected is disorder, war,
and, in the end, slavery from mere weariness of disorder.

Just as pacifism is distorted by arguments based too exclusively
on the fear of danger and death, so democracy is distorted if the
identification of liberty with rejection is allowed to attain a dangerous growth. The totalitarian regimes confused political terminology
still further by substituting for the assumed automatic harmony of
liberties a postulated automatic harmony of the whole as such.
Nevertheless, they caught the imagination, and that of the young in
particular, to the extent that they replaced the values of protest by
those of *conformity* and demonstrated that liberty consists in *fitting
in*, in *self-surrender* after *finding one's place* and not merely in
opposition. If it is true that there is no civic spirit without *genuine*
democracy (pseudo-democracy secretes and stimulates general
anti-social behavior), it is equally true that there is no democracy
without civic spirit. Liberty is one of the dimensions of democracy.
Democracy disintegrates if liberty is made its sole dimension: democracy also postulates an integrated community and an order of
justice.

1. Alain, *Éléments d'une doctrine radicale* (Paris, 1925), p. 129.

III

It would be a serious error to assume that the notion of democracy historically represents no more than the demand for individual freedom. From the very first the core of the concept has been simultaneous concern for individual rights and for society as a whole. It is hardly necessary to call in Rousseau as evidence: with his theory of the general will he is entitled to be deemed not merely one of the fathers of the modern idea of a community, but, within the limits and dangerous implications of his own theories, the daring explorer of the possible course that may lead from mass to totalitarian democracy. The notion of *equality*, which dominates the republican eighteenth century, inflected by the notions of *fraternity* and *concord* (to use the language of the period), is not, as has sometimes been thought, an anarchic, but essentially a social concept. "Equality" is a relation between two terms and is meaningless in relation to one alone. Moreover, an implication at least as weighty as that of the desire for emulation (or to avoid being outstripped) is that of a oneness between all men, urging the reduction of excessive or overprotected differences between individuals. Because it has a livelier sense of the diversity of individuals than the egalitarians, the anarchist political tradition has by the associations its name evokes, led men to forget that, with the exception of Stirner, it was at bottom an anti-individualist movement. Kropotkin regarded individualism as an "infantile complaint" with which anarchism had been infected by a few young bourgeois revolutionaries, and of which it had been rapidly cured by striking roots into the workers' movement. "The freedom of individuals," wrote Bakunin, "is in no respect the work of individuals; it is a collective work, a collective product."[2] And elsewhere: "I am only truly free when all human beings around me, men and women, are equally free. . . . I become free only through the freedom of others."[3]

At least as much as with human dignity, emancipation, and the spirit of revolt, anarchist thought was concerned with the search for a "harmonious city" as Péguy was to say of it later. To Proudhon "the People" is not merely a fiction of reason or a legal construct, as it is to liberalism, "but a true being having a reality, individuality,

2. M. Bakunin, *Conférence aux ouvriers*, in *Œuvres* (Paris, 1913), V, 318.
3. M. Bakunin, *Dieu et l'état*, p. 281.

nature, life, and mode of reason of its own."[4] It is because anarchists believe in the reality of the People that they deny that of the state. Only they do not look on it as a centralized mechanism—the fault with which they reproach communism—but as decentralized and organic. Their fear is lest the living flexible adjustable society may be led astray by the glamor of power and thereby petrified. They are not concerned with the freedom of the individual but with the freedom of the community as such: "The emancipation of the workers must be the work of the workers themselves." It would be fair to say that in their eyes democracy is the freedom of the community, individual liberty occurring and gaining its meaning only within the framework of a free community. It is a shock, sometimes, to hear men of this tradition, far removed from "rightist" feeling (e.g., in certain socialist or federalist circles of the school of Proudhon) criticize democracy in terms that recall in every particular the criticisms of the most conservative thought. Why is this?

The answer is that the terms "people" and "community" are too imprecise. The representative of a "Western" democracy calls himself a "representative of the people," a Soviet minister, a "people's commissar," a Nazi court, a "people's court." Thus the same word is used to describe things which in fact differ widely. In practice the collectivist current of democracy separates into two branches.

The first is what may be styled *liberal collectivism*. There is the same concern for liberty as among the liberals, but reaching beyond the individual to embrace the mass. Men must constitute and maintain a free, living, and flexible entity, and the latter's creative force is affected by any organization too cut-and-dried, by any excess of power, even the power of the whole. Proudhon was radically opposed to the very notion of the general will or the will of the people, on the grounds that "will" is equivalent to "power" and hence to blindness and oppression. "The democracy of the general will," he wrote, "is blind from birth." None has seen more clearly than such "anti-democratic" democrats, the *possible* progress from the "will of the people" through the exclusive concentration of rights in the majority to collective tyranny, from Jacobinism to modern Fascism and Communism. That was the process of corruption to which they opposed the federalist formula that even today

4. P. J. Proudhon, *Idée générale de la révolution*, in *Œuvres complètes* (Nouvelle éd.; Paris, 1923), II, 216.

is in high favor in the center and on the left wing of the movement for European federation. In more modern terms one might put it that at bottom, although the democratic community is in their eyes an indisputable fact existing independently of the individuals that make it up, it is nonetheless a community of persons who neither can, nor should, ever consent to be converted into a monolithic mass.

Examples of mass democracies in the pure, or the purest feasible, state are provided by the Fascist nations. If democracy is no more than the free choice by the people of some system of government (including servile subjection), Fascist Germany and Italy cannot be denied the title of democratic regimes. It was with a measure of irony that the heads of those states dinned into the ears of the Western democratic parties the far more overwhelming majorities which they could rally behind their own party and which, without doubt, would at their apogee have remained nearly as overwhelming, even with free elections. However, experience of democracy has taught us that, just as men can be democrats at heart while oppressing their neighbor (in the Western semi-democracies), the peoples can use the democratic process to give themselves anti-democratic regimes. What right have we to call them "anti-democratic"? None, if democracy is merely the assertion of the power of the people, the right of numbers, whether by majority or unanimity. Peoples, like individuals, can sell themselves into bondage to others and also to themselves, enslave themselves (as Laun, for instance, has well shown). This demonstrates the ambiguity of such phrases as "government of all by all," or "sovereignty of the people." We have to examine what the term "all" may be meant to signify. To what we have styled liberal collectivism, "all" means "all without exception" and the picture is of an articulated *whole* based on individual assent. In the democracies of totalitarian complexion "all" is intended to mean "all as a single unit," not each one severally but *all as one*. Thus an opponent is not a mere variation, though more than average, from the norm of opinion; he is in the strictest sense a secessionist, a cancer to be excised. The ideal is the abolition of all differentiation between governors and governed, between the state and the nation, everyone becoming a ruler (his neighbor's constable, spy, and monitor), and of all differentiation among the governed by the spread of conformity and solidarity through political terrorism.

We have taken Fascist "democracy" as an extreme type of the petrifaction of the democratic organism. The error of conservative critics consists in believing that democracy inevitably and by its nature rushes to that extreme. In the seventh century a political critic would have said that the rising feudalism would inevitably and by its nature lead to anarchy; but would he have retained that view, had he been shown the kingdom of St. Louis or of Louis XIV? At the very moment when contemporary man was about to learn the new art of the mastery of mass societies, the period of the great World Wars imposed the necessity for such mechanical efficiency in operation as in some instances to dehumanize the new creations. We must raise our eyes beyond the ghastly trials of democracy's beginnings. But we must understand, too, that the present fossilization of democracy discloses a constitutional sluggishness in our societies and a predisposition to recurrent major wars, with periods of incubation and convalescence. Democracies that were spared the worst consequences of those wars would be wrong to think themselves immune: the same causes, if brought to bear on them, will have the same effects.

IV

Democracy, then, has elements both centripetal and centrifugal, and we have seen that it becomes noxious to man when it concentrates exclusively either on the individual or on the community. However, the faults of overweighted individualism show us the value of the community, and those of the blind power of the mass, the value of the individual. In point of fact, every apologia for democracy in either camp appeals to a scale of values which it should be democracy's goal to achieve. Thus the question for democracy ceases to be merely the defense of the individual against society or the substitution of collective order for the jungle of individualism, and becomes rather a matter of conducting individuals and societies toward a *state* deemed better or worthier of man. One party describes democracy as the reign of *happiness*, "the greatest good of the greatest number"; or the reign of *security:* "Liberty," wrote Montesquieu, "consists in the security of each citizen and in his awareness of it." This was translated in France, during the war, as: "Democracy means that, when the doorbell rings at 7 in the morning, it's only the milkman." Others define democracy as the

reign of social and economic *justice* (Marx); or of *reason* as opposed to the emotional impulses of the individual or the community
(Proudhon); or of *right* and *law* as opposed to force and power
(Gurvitch). Whatever point of view be adopted, the important
point, as far as we are concerned, would seem to be that the option
for democracy always implies a choice of values, and hence more
than a union for defense or preference for a particular organization.
Experience indicates that the only adequate counterweight to the
egocentricity of the individual and the dead weight of the community is the movement of humanity toward a realm of values
implying the fulfilment of the individual, the achievement of the
brotherhood of man and that mastery of nature in man and beyond
him that is a condition of the other two tasks.

We thus see that a viable democracy and a balanced humanity
alike are borne on a dialectical tripod. Political and humanistic
philosophy are joined together and mutually supporting. Each of
the three legs, the *person*, the *community*, and *value*, leans on the
two others, and the hypertrophy of any one of them overthrows
the tripod. We have dealt with two of the legs, individualism and
totalitarianism. If value in its turn be made a fetish above compromise, as the individual or the community is elsewhere, it too becomes oppressive. As fascism would have done, had it been an economic success, or as authoritarian technocracy from the Right or
the Left would do tomorrow, Dostoievski's Grand Inquisitor sets
up a society where the possession of natural felicity has stifled the
taste for liberty. The democracies of 1939 were very near sacrificing their honor to their security. Again the passionate pursuit of
ultimate justice may bring with it not merely the suspension but
even contempt for man's rights other than the right to well-being.
Legalism can kill life itself. Here as in general social affairs, we see
that one of the major temptations facing human activity is to swal-
low the drug of objectivity and that, where men are concerned, no
organization can leave out of account the strange kind of beings it
is laid on it to organize and their requirements so irritating to the
technocratic mind.

V

We must not overlook certain concepts more modest than the
foregoing, which may be described as *democratic relativism*. They

are more modest because they arrogate to themselves no sovereign virtue and even oppose all political dogmatism; yet they are a staff for the feet of men who are among the firmest supporters of the forms of liberal democracy, although open-minded toward change, provided that progress is made with moderation. These men define democracy as being per se political relativity (Kelsen, LeFur), the way to the fruitful or merely unavoidable coexistence of opposites, of pluralism, or the middle way (Duhamel), a kindly governance of lonely and disconnected destinies (existentialists). In more literary terms Camus has praised "political modesty," which is another way of saying the same thing. It seems likely that these concepts can be those neither of a proletariat harshly conscious of the class war, nor of an expanding bourgeoisie, which will prefer a philosophy of achievement; but rather, so to speak, the ideological delta of an epoch's end, made up of a middle class, the embodiment of the moderate, sheltered, skeptical equipoise which, between upheavals, creeps back to cover the battlefields of politics and society.

XX

STANISLAUS OSSOWSKI

I. IN SEARCH FOR A CONCRETE MEANING

It is a well-known fact that the same set of slogans may be used for very different purposes in the life of society. But it would perhaps be difficult to find a more striking illustration of this commonplace fact than the fate of the term "democracy" and the ideas connected with it.

It was in the name of democracy that the Ephesians—if we are to believe Heraclitus—drove out Hermodorus, "the best man among them," from their town, saying, "We do not allow one of us to be the best." It was in the name of democracy and the interests of the people that the city tyrants of Greece or the early Middle Ages forced their way to absolute power. Similarly, an ambitious modern autocrat, Napoleon III, appealed to the will of the people to press his claim to the imperial crown. The dictators of our own day sought to justify their despotic tendencies by getting them indorsed in plebiscites of the Italian or German people. In the name of democracy, governments based on the will of the majority have been established, and in the name of democracy, people have revolted against the absolutism of those same governments, asserting that the laws they passed infringed the liberty of the minority which was not prepared to accept them. Arguments invoking democracy were the weapons used in the struggle for a parliament based on universal and equal suffrage, secret ballot, and direct and proportional representation. The governing groups in the Fascist or semi-Fascist countries, before the war, used democratic argumentation when they reduced a parliament so elected to impotence, "in order to deliver the people from the power of political party leaders." In the name of democratic principles, laws on compulsory education were passed in America and Europe. In the name of the same principles, protests have been made against taxing the rich to pay for the education of the people, on the plea that it is not right to compel any individual to act counter to his own interests by raising up his enemies or competitors. In the name of democratic liberalism, Herbert Spencer protested against compulsory school attendance as an interference with the rights of parents to decide on the education to be given to their children.

The bourgeoisie plunged into capitalist industrial expansion with the word "democracy" on their lips, and democratic slogans impelled socialists to combat the system. The word "democracy" rings through Walt Whitman's poems. He drew his inspiration from the principles of democracy when he proclaimed the creed of freedom, brotherhood, and companionship "thick as trees along all the rivers of America."[1]

In the last century, various political parties were known as democrats. Ranging from the Democratic Party in the United States of America before the Civil War to the postwar democratic parties of the present day in Japan, Italy, or Austria, they have had very different programs and inclinations. In Poland, in the late nineteenth century, the word "democracy" appeared in both the title of the national party of the middle classes (*Narodowa Demokracja*, "National Democracy") and in that of the revolutionary socialist group (*Socialdemokracja Krolostwa Polskiego i Litwy*, "Social Democracy of the Kingdom of Poland and Lithuania"), from which the leaders of the Polish Communist Party were later to emerge.

In the course of the last war, the call to defend civilization and democracy united the countries of East and West in the struggle against Fascism. And when, after the fall of Hitlerite Germany, a breach between the victors came to light, both camps took to reproaching their opponents with the violation or deformation of the principles of true democracy, each claiming to be the heir of the democratic tradition. Is it a question, in this instance, of a difference in the meanings attributed to the word, or of divergency in the application of abstract principles to the concrete facts of society?

In 1946, when I was listening to the discussions in the United Nations Social Commission and heard the words "democracy" and "democratic" constantly recurring, whoever the speaker was and to whatever line of thought he belonged, I sometimes felt that the words had entirely lost their meaning and had become simply an expression of approval. It sometimes seemed to me that the word "democratic" meant nothing more than "good," "just," "legiti-

1. *Leaves of Grass*, I, "For you, O Democracy."

mate," and was without any descriptive meaning. My impression was not correct. The use of the word "democracy" and its derivatives has in fact been reduced, in political circles, to the status of a convention meaning as little as the usual formulas of social politeness, but that does not indicate that the terms have lost their content of meaning. Their ambiguity—a result of complicated historical processes—will be the subject of these reflections of ours. The universality of the positive emotional connotations of the words "democracy" and "democratic," without regard to the descriptive contents atributed to them—a universality highly characteristic of our times—is likewise the result of historical developments. The emotional force associated with the word "democracy" during the last war is also important. At that time "democracy" was understood to embrace all the forces struggling against the power symbolized by the smoke rising from the death ovens in the concentration camps.

II. CONCEPTUAL MERGER AS A SOCIAL FACT

When we speak of the multiplicity of meanings or the ambiguity of words or expressions, we have to distinguish between two different cases: the multiplicity of meaning or the ambiguity of homonyms, and the multiple meanings of words or expressions whose sense is not clearly enough defined in ordinary conversational use. In the case of homonyms, such as "*vol*" or "*conte*" (*conte, compte, comte*), in French, or "lime," "race," or "sound" in English, we behave as if the same group of letters or sounds belonged to different systems; when we use the word in any given sense, we leave out of account entirely its other meanings, and when we transfer from one sense to another, the function of the word changes for us. The homonymy disappeares when we use synonymous expressions in the place of such words or when we translate into another language. The multiplicity of the meanings of homonyms is not matched by our ideas of the real things they represent, because their different meanings never constitute a single whole.

Every case of multiple meaning of which we are not consciously aware, however, is a matter of concern to the sociologist rather than the linguist. If, among a group of men whose tastes are practical rather than intellectual, we speak of "proletarian poetry," the ambiguity of meaning (poetry written by members of the proletariat or poetry distinguished by a certain type of ideology, whoever may be the author) acquires social relevance. A strict definition of the term in one or the other sense, a strict delimitation of its meanings would have changed something in our attitudes toward proletarian poetry. The same is true of the many meanings of terms such as "religion," "culture" or "country." The word "country" in certain cases stands for the national territory, in others the nation (as, for instance, in the expression "a traitor to the country," "my country right or wrong," etc.), and this fusion of the two meanings, with their emotional charge, is a very important social phenomenon.

Such cases of ambiguity are not confined to a single language, as is the case with hymonyms. We still find them when we try to translate these terms into other languages, so long as we are concerned with the same group of related cultures. It is not a verbal but a conceptual problem. Freud speaks of composite images in dreams (*Mischbildungen*). This comes close to what we have in our case, but ours is in the field of conceptual thinking and not merely in that of images. Every case of multiple meaning of which we are not clearly aware may be considered to be the expression of certain social attitudes in which different notions which are not clearly perceived interact so as to give rise to a specific associative climate. If it were possible to analyze these conceptual mergers by making the sense of the words more precise, this would not leave unaltered the social attitudes of certain circles.

The notion of democracy in contemporary civilization constitutes a conceptual merger of this kind, in which different cultural heritages, more or less common to the various peoples and various social classes, clash with the antagonistic interests of social groups.

III. ORIGIN OF CONTEMPORARY CONCEPTS OF DEMOCRACY

Before considering the divergencies between contemporary interpretations of the word "democracy," it will be helpful to recall how the constituents of the idea have developed through the centuries.

In the etymological sense "democracy" means "the power of the people." It was accordingly a class slogan: we may take it as the counterpart of the modern slogan of the dictatorship of the proletariat. The struggles between democrats and aristocrats in Greece in the fifth and fourth centuries B.C., like those between Plebeians and Patricians in Rome, were struggles between two social classes for supremacy in the state. The democrats were defending the interests of the people (*demos*), which, incidentally, did not mean defending the interests of the class most exploited under the system then existing. The institution of slavery was not, indeed, attacked and there was no protection for the slaves. A characteristic symptom of the tense antagonisms between the classes in the struggles for democracy in the Greek cities during the fifth century is provided by the words of the oath which Aristotle tells us was sworn by the politically organized aristocrats: "I will be an opponent of the people and do all I can to prejudice their interests in the Council."

In the Greek democracies, the power of the people was conceived as the power of the majority; in the affairs of state, the people indicated their will directly by vote or confirmed or rejected the decisions of their elected representatives. As Pericles said, "Although those who can initiate action in political life are few in number, anyone can express his opinion about them." Another sense of the word now enters into the meaning, however. Pericles himself also defined democracy as a form of government guided by the interests of the people.[2] Pericles did not see the difference between the terms "government by the will of the people" and "government guided by the interests of the people," a difference of which Lincoln was probably unaware twenty-three centuries later. If it is admitted that the people desire what is in their interests, and know how to secure it, no such difference can exist: a government willed by the people, a government which can be dismissed at any time by the people's decision, must be a government guided by the interests of the people; and, conversely, a government which is guided by the interests of the people is sure to have the people with it.

The question whether it is possible to govern in accordance with the interests of the people and, at the same time, against their will, was raised by such antidemocratic thinkers as Plato who, in his heart, despised the people and did not believe they were capable of knowing what was really in their interests. The discrepancy between the people's *will* and the people's *interests* was, for Plato, an argument against democracy. Many centuries later, the problem of the divergency between the people's will and their interests ap-

2. Thucydides *The Peloponnesian War*, Book ii.

pears in another form, as the result of the observation that the will
of the people is more uncertain and variable than their interests, and
that those who control adequate means can direct public opinion
counter to the interests of the people. At a time when neither the
wireless, the Hearst press, nor modern plebiscites had been thought
of, Machiavelli said that "it appears to the peoples that kings desire
what the people wish, whereas in reality the people desire what
kings wish." The possibility of persuading the people to vote against
their own interests introduces into the idea of democracy a compli-
cation which was apparently unknown to Greek democracy.

We said above that the word "democracy" in the etymological
sense involved the idea of class. But since the class concerned was
the largest, and the leader of the compaign against the oligarchy,
combating the privileges of the powerful, it should be noted that
yet another factor enters into the primary idea of democracy as
the system in which the government is carried on in the interests
of the people. Beside the principle that the will of the people, expressed by the vote of the majority, is the final arbiter in the affairs
of state, there appears a second, and very important, postulate: the
postulate of equality. The question how far and by what means
that postulate was put into practice in Athens is of no moment; what
matters is that, from the beginning, the idea of the equality of the
citizens is a part of the complex notion of democracy.

We must also note that, although the term "democracy" in opposition to the term "aristocracy" may have a class significance, and
although the postulates of democracy may be class postulates, they
may be so formulated as to stand above class divisions. In fact, decisions rested with the majority of citizens, but among them were included loyal aristocrats: the equality of rights of the citizens extended to all citizens. Nevertheless, the class character of the Greek
democracies was not affected, since the class representing the democratic way of thought could rally the majority of free citizens and
had adopted procedures insuring not only nominal but true equality
of political rights: I have in mind the Athenian practice of appoint-
ing members of the legislative body and magistrates (with the exception of the strategi) by drawing lots. This way of nominating
democratic authorities—the most radical of all those known to us—
not only served to exclude the exercise of any influence on the results of the vote by the rich, by corruption, intimidation or propa-

ganda; it was also a characteristic indication of the belief in the natural equality of all free Athenians; it demonstrated the conviction that every one of them was capable of fulfilling important legislative, executive, and judicial functions. We may note that this belief seems to have been active at the origin of the European idea of democracy. Lincoln's formula: "government by the people" could nowhere have been more logically applied.

The principles of Athenian democracy, which were not extended to the Metics and slaves, governed relations within the ruling class, reducing to the same level those who had previously formed the privileged class. They may therefore be applied in any society divided into classes in which the governing class is large enough to regard itself as the body of citizens enjoying the advantages of all the laws. If this conception of democracy is accepted, the definition *demokracja szlachecka*, "democracy of the nobles," which was applied to the Polish Republic from the sixteenth to the seventeenth century was not a *contradictio in adjecto*. In the struggle against the Magnates in the fifteen and sixteenth centuries, the Polish nobles copied the models of classical times to some extent. The political system that was set up toward the end of the sixteenth century, with a king elected by all the nobles, so far embodied the principle of equality that the acceptance of family titles which would distinguish the families of Magnates from the families of nobles was forbidden, although such a practice was customary in central and eastern Europe. In theory, there was no aristocracy in Poland. Theoretically, the poorest squireen, plowing his fields himself, was the equal of the most powerful Magnates as *elector regum, destructor tyrannorum*. We have here, therefore, another instance of democracy confined to a single class, a democracy which was, however, the dictatorship of a group representing no more than 10 per cent of the population.

A new factor was introduced into the regenerated republican traditions by the emancipated bourgeoisie in the eighteenth century. The idea of democracy was then given a new meaning and the postulates of democracy new justification.

1. The idea of democracy ceased to be a class concept and was extended to cover the whole of mankind. The equality proclaimed in the democratic ideology was no longer conceived as equality restricted to the class of citizens enjoying full rights, but as the equality

of all men. It found justification in the radical interpretation of Christian principles as well as in the views of human nature developed by the philosophers of the age of enlightenment. "We hold these truths to be self-evident, that all men are created equal, that they are endowed by their Creator with certain inalienable rights," proclaimed the Declaration of Independence of the United States of America, in 1776. "Men are born free and equal in rights," said the Declaration of the Rights of Man and of the Citizen, in 1789, a declaration whose very title indicates that the categories of "man" and "citizen" should be co-extensive. The French bourgeoisie did not go into battle in its own name but in that of all the oppressed classes; it entered the lists to do away with all class privileges. After the elimination of the privileges of the nobles and clergy, the Third Estate was to include all the inhabitants of France. It was to be identified with the nation. This was the view of the future of French society set forth by Siéyès in his famous essay: "What is the Third Estate?"

When we contrast the sovereignty of the people with the divine right of kings, we may say, not that the idea of democracy has changed its connotation by abandoning its etymological meaning, but that the term "people" has acquired a new significance by overcoming class barriers. The word "people" is, in fact, an ambiguous term in different European languages. It denotes either a social class or the population as a whole. The interaction of these two meanings is often exploited in political oratory. Perhaps it was already there in the speeches of Pericles.

2. Since the American Revolution and the Great Revolution in France, the word "democracy" has been associated not only with the idea of equality but also with those of liberty and the rights of the citizen. The traditions of the French Revolution have united by a lasting bond the words inscribed on its banners: "Liberty" and "Equality." Tne representatives of this humanitarian democracy speak in the name of man and not of any social group. They justify their position by the appeal to the rights of human nature and defend not only the rights of the majority but the freedom of the individual. In its original meaning, democracy was opposed only to the domination of the privileged classes or the tyranny of a single man; now a new factor enters into the program of the democratic ideology: the protection of the rights of the individual against oppression

of any sort, even oppression by the majority. The authority of the majority must now be reconciled with the rights of the opposition.

"The slavery of fear had made man afraid to think," wrote Paine in the book with the characteristic title of *The Rights of Man* (1792). Democracy was to free man from that slavery—an idea which was to lead Jefferson to prefer a free press with no government to a government without a free press. The decree condemning Socrates, although an act brought about by "the will of the people," would not be democratic from this point of view.

The fundamental principles of revolutionary bourgeois democracy included one, however, that throws light on the intentions of those who formulated the ideal of general equality, in the belief that they were abolishing all class distinctions: the postulate safeguarding private property. "The object of any political association," we read in the Declaration of the Rights of Man and of the Citizen, "is to preserve the natural and indefeasible rights of man; those rights are liberty, property and resistance to oppression."

In contrast to all the principles of democratic ideology, the defense of private property was not a revolutionary idea opposed to the existing system. The introduction of the right of property into the Declaration of the Rights of Man may, on the contrary, be considered to restrict a too far-reaching interpretation of the postulate of equality. It is not surprising, therefore, that it was not inscribed on the standards that were to attract the masses.

In the nineteenth century new interpretations of the fundamental principles of democracy were to arise to compete with those of the triumphant bourgeoisie. Emerging from the revolutionary movements among the working classes, they were to come in conflict with the bourgeois views. And the question which was to divide democrats into two opposing camps was to be the very problem to which the triumphant advent of capitalism gave rise: the problem of the democratization of property relations.

IV. THE COMMON HERITAGE

In his famous speech on September 12, 1848, a few months after the publication of the Communist Manifesto by Marx and Engels, de Tocqueville tried to demonstrate the fundamental opposition between the socialist and the democratic ideologies in their attitude to the postulate of individual liberty. "Democracy and socialism are linked only by one word—equality; but note the difference: democracy wants equality in freedom, and socialism wants equality in constraint and enslavement." This opinion gained popularity and still survives, although de Tocqueville's authorship has been forgotten. Of the two fundamental tenets of democracy, expressed in the words "equality" and "liberty," socialism was held to foster the most sweeping application of the former to the detriment of the latter.

Let us then turn to the works of Marx and Engels as the essential sources of the ideology of modern socialism. A scrutiny of these works will not leave the slightest doubt as to the ideals the authors of the Communist Manifesto appealed to in embarking on the struggle for the rebuilding of the world.

It is something more than the inclination to put into practice abstract principles of social justice. It is even something more than the fight against exploitation and poverty. The world which is to emerge as the result of the general revolution is, first and foremost, a world of free men. Even the struggle against exploitation and poverty is undertaken in the name of freedom and the dignity of man. The liberation of the toiling masses from their dependence on the power of capital keeping them in a state of slavery under the semblance of freedom, the liberation of human relations from the yoke of fetichism,[3] the humanization of economic life, the restoration of the dignity of man, the opening up of channels for the free expansion of the creative forces of mankind—those were the aims set for socialism by the authors of the Communist Manifesto. To them, true freedom for the individual is possible only in a society in which the distinctions between the social classes have disappeared. In a class society, even the representatives of the ruling classes are led astray and yield to the pressure of their own class interests.[4]

The dictatorship of the proletariat that Marxist socialism introduces into its program is advanced as an argument in favor of Tocqueville's contention. But it is often forgotten, in describing the socialist ideology, that the dictatorship of the proletariat is to be merely a path to the abolition of the state as an institution characterized by its monopoly of legal means of violence.

The principles inscribed on the banners of the French Revolution have a long history behind them. The principle of liberty,

3. Marx, *Capital*, Vol. I, sec. 1.
4. Marx, *Die heilige Familie*, chap. iv, Kritische Randglosse, No. II.

which we may consider as the simplest interpretation of the principle of social justice, is derived from various sources. The ideal of equality, which took form in the Greek democracies, and particularly in the Athenian democracy, came into the European tradition through the works of the writers of antiquity. The Athenian idea of equality (ἰσονομία καὶ ἰσηγορία) covering all free citizens was carried to its logical conclusion but was restricted to political life alone: the Athenian Constitution did not even abolish the official division of the citizens into four classes based on economic criteria, although in Pericles' time that division had lost all political significance.

Religious movements in the European tradition have provided other models of social justice in the relationships between men—far more radical models which have played a very important part in the social history of Europe. Even before Marx, it had been realized that, in a society based on finance, the most serious inequality between men was inequality in economic status, and that, if real equality was to be achieved, it was necessary to do away with the classes of the rich and the poor. And since that was a more difficult task than the winning of political equality, divine sanctions had to be sought. Radical equalitarian tendencies, seeking support in religious beliefs, with the conviction that we are all children of the same Father in heaven, find expression in religious communist ideology.

Without going too deeply into the origins of this ideology, which is probably derived from certain social movements of ancient times and springs not only from the principles of social justice but from old traditions of a strong social bond (*communio*) preceding the individualism dominant in urban civilizations, we may follow the course of communist thought from the Gospel of St. Luke, through the Acts of the Apostles, the Epistle of St. James and the works of the Early Fathers of the Church such as St. Basil or St. John Chrysostom. When the official church elected to serve the interests of the rich, the equalitarian ideas were taken up by the medieval brotherhoods and heretical sects, ranging from the Carpocratians to the radical groups among the Czech Hussites and the Anabaptists. This religious current in the communist tradition is not confined to the field of aspirations and moral obligations; the leaders of the peasant revolts in France, England, and Germany all sought justification and stimulus in the Gospel or other religious traditions. The Gospel became a means of propaganda; and the fourteenth-century couplet which originated in England:

When Adam dug and Eve span
Who was then the gentleman?

was found, in various paraphrases, in many European countries.

The third current originated in the utopian ideas of the Greek philosophers, beginning with Plato's aristocratic communism, on the one hand, and the far-reaching equalitarian tendencies of Antisthencs and Zeno, on the other. Many centuries later, those ideas inspired Campanella and Thomas More; and when the bourgeoisie of the Western countries gained power, and modern capitalism came to birth, the communist traditions were to reappear in the works of Meslier and Mably and to lead on, this time without interruption, through the works of the so-called utopian socialists of England and France, to the Communist Manifesto and the First International.

No doubt the ideal of individual liberty has had a less full and varied history than the principle of equality and the communist ideals. The need for individual freedom appears only after the breakup of the simple communities with a strong corporate sense. As everyone knows, both the reaction against collective responsibility and the first signs of a belief in individual immortality make their appearance only in the later books of the Old Testament, when the development of city life in Palestine was already far advanced.

We are accustomed to associating the liberal way of thought and the principle of individual liberty with specific economic tendencies. This is, to use Marx's term, "the ideological superstructure" and, in Pareto's expression, a "derivation" connected with the requirements of capitalist economy. This opinion is confirmed both by the parallel development of capitalism and liberalism and by the arguments of those who propagated the doctrine of laissez faire, beginning with the bourgeois writers of the eighteenth century and ending with the professor at the London School of Economics who, in 1943, in his defense of liberal capitalism, advanced the argument that without "freedom in economic affairs ... personal and political freedom has never existed in the past."[5]

We cannot, however, pass over one other factor. The creed of individual freedom is related to the development of capitalism, but it is also related to the development of modern science. While a certain degree of individual liberty was necessary for the development of capitalism, freedom of thought, and freedom for the communica-

5. F. A. Hayek, The Road to Serfdom (London, 1944), p. 10.

tion of ideas is an essential condition for intellectual activity and the development of science. The parallel development of modern science and modern capitalism leaves no room for doubt of the interdependence of the two processes. Nevertheless, the struggle for freedom of thought that has been carried on since the Renaissance by such illustrious champions as Erasmus of Rotterdam, Montaigne, Giordano Bruno, Galileo, Descartes, Milton, and Spinoza has been immediately inspired by the needs of intellectual activity. In the later period, some importance must be attributed to the formation of the group of professional intellectuals and professional scientists for whom freedom of thought was to be a vital factor enabling them to play their part in society and to carry out their essential functions, just as the system based on liberal economic principles was to determine the social role of industrialists.

The cult of liberty handed down to us by the classical writers and, above all, by the man we associate with the economic and intellectual golden age of Athens, also belongs to the liberal traditions that led up to the Declaration of the Rights of Man and of the Citizen. Naturally, it matters little to us how far the freedom of which Pericles spoke in Athens was an actual fact. What counts is the Athenian idea in the European tradition.

The liberal traditions associated with the name of Pericles, Montaigne, and Galileo are seen to be merely the exclusive traditions of an élite in comparison with the medieval communist traditions derived from the Sermon on the Mount; but the nineteenth century, with its romantic poetry, its struggles for the liberation of oppressed peoples, and its propaganda for human and civic rights, was to create a very strong bond between the pursuit of social justice and the pursuit of liberty in the traditions which have fashioned the Europe of the present day.

I have given this review of the historical background of European culture in order to show that the ideals professed by communism as well as those invoked by liberalism belong to the lasting heritage of European civilization. Modern nonreligious socialism derives from ancient communist traditions as well as from liberal trends of thought. It is not an accident that the representatives of the modern socialist system of ideas lay such stress on the scientific nature of their doctrine, linking it with the history of the freedom of scientific thought; and it is not by mere chance that they look for the freeing of man from the pressure of capital and the pressure of the state in a classless society of the future. Marx is the heir of St. John Chrysostom, Joachim of Floris, the Anabaptists of Münster, Montaigne, Galileo, and Holbach. And the democrats who oppose communism have not renounced the principles in whose name Condorcet, Paine, and Jefferson waged their struggle. Both parties appeal to a common arsenal of values and a common heritage, although that heritage is exploited for different ends.

In following discussions on the questions of principle between the ideological champions of both camps, we are struck by the fact that they even use the same language. That is not true of their discussions with the supporters of racial discrimination and the followers of the Swastika. In explaining the reasons for their programs, both parties invoke the same ideals, although the emphases are not placed in identical ways. The condemnation of the Western democracies by the champions of the socialization of the means of production does not amount to a denial of the creed of liberty. The struggle against economic and bourgeois liberalism may be undertaken in the name of a different conception of liberalism. In such discussions, the arguments generally tend to show that the opposing party has betrayed or debased ideals of which both adversaries approve. By this, I do not wish to minimize the fundamental differences between the two camps, which affect their scales of values and their reactions to various contemporary facts in social and political life. We shall try to discover how it is possible to come to such sharp ideological differences, having started from the same basic postulates. This will also throw some light on the many meanings of the term "democracy."

V. UNIVERSALIST IDEAS AND CLASS INTERESTS

The representatives of the Third Estate who, in 1789, approved the Declaration of the Rights of Man and of the Citizen in the French National Assembly, did not regard themselves as the representatives of the bourgeoisie, but as the champions of the people. They, the defenders of the oppressed classes, were destroying the structure of the old régime. Like their predecessors in America, they were proclaiming liberty and equality for all. The principles inscribed on the banner of the Revolution were to hold for all mankind. The arguments by which they were upheld and which sometimes appealed even to some members of the nobility and the clergy derived their force from ideals valid for humanity as a whole and from the views of the philosophers on human nature and the rights of man.

Nevertheless, the principal motive which drove the French bourgeoisie to revolution was the same which had forced the English middle classes into action a hundred years earlier. Immediately after the first successes, the victors were faced with the problem of how to reconcile humanitarian ideals with the trends of their own class, how to interpret the watchwords of the Revolution not only in such a way as to avoid conflict with the interests of the bourgeoisie but to make it possible to exploit those ideals for its advantage. The demand for liberty was directed against the politically privileged classes under the old system, but, once freedom had been won, there was a danger that the principle in question might become a threat if it could be exploited for the benefit of the working class.

The solution was in accordance with the traditions of antiquity, to which the speakers of the Convention were so fond of referring. The democratic principles contained in the Declaration of the Rights of Man and of the Citizen were given a purely political interpretation, although the emotional associations of broad humanitarianism were preserved. Later generations further elaborated the principle of the isolation of the political aspect of the life of a society from its economic life. The restriction of the principle of liberty to the domain of political rights was to be, on the one hand, the result of compromise with the demands of human nature, with its ineradicable property instinct, apt to develop most fruitfully in the climate of competition and, on the other, the result of the conviction that equality of civic rights creates equal opportunities for social and economic advancement—opportunities in which success is determined by personal merit, talent, and hard work.

Such an opinion might be held sincerely by the democrats of the eighteenth century who had before their eyes the indefensible system of legal restrictions that hampered individual initiative and, to some extent, marked out the field of each man's future activity from the moment of his birth. But the same contention sounds strange on the lips of democrats of the twentieth century, who ought to have a better understanding of the determining influence in society of the "natural inequality" of which Bryce wrote, and who have at hand a wealth of examples of systems based upon the principle of political equality. From this point of view, the Hayek book referred to is extremely instructive, particularly since one feels that the author really believes what he has written.

The universal rights which democracy as confined to the sphere of politics and law accorded to men opened up the way for the fictions typical of this conception of democracy. The abolition of political privileges conferred by birth gained credence for the fiction of equal opportunity, overlooking the fact that the economic and cultural privileges of birth had not been removed. The habit of attaching importance to the letter of the law—a habit sometimes reminiscent of the old awe of magic formulas—gave a semblance of equality in cases where the practical effect of the laws on particular groups of people is governed by social conditions as a whole. A law allowing an elephant and new-hatched chicks to dance on the same floor—if we may paraphrase Robert Lynd's witty comparison—does not give them the same opportunities; nor are the dangers they incur the same. The application of the principle of "equal laws for all men" should result in complete social justice. But, while the "equal laws" in the revolutionary song meant the achievement of real equality in life and activity, so far as it is determined by the social system, the representatives of bourgeois democracy saw in the phrase no more than equality before the law. That was the way the idea of "equal laws" also turned into a conceptual merger.

The social effect of "equal laws" depends on the way they are formulated. Suppose that, in any given country, the law states that everyone is entitled to free education for his children in all types of school, and that, in another, there is a law stipulating that everyone is entitled to education for his children in all types of school provided that he pays the fees and purchases the necessary school supplies, though the laws may be the same for all in each of those countries, they cannot give the same real equality in both cases.

The achievement of democratic liberties opened the field for further fictions. The laws proclaimed freedom for all, but were not concerned with providing means for all the people to exercise that freedom, so that freedom did not threaten the preponderance of the class that had the necessary economic resources. What practical benefit did the working man derive from the right to found a periodical, which was accorded to him on the same terms as to a millionaire? What benefit did he derive from the freedom of the press if he was working twelve hours a day in a factory and had not had the education which only money could buy? And even if he were able to write an article, what benefit would he derive from the freedom of the press, if the publication of his article depended on the decision of those controlling that free press?[6]

The partisans of general democratic liberty closed their eyes to the existence of economic constraints, more complex in their working but no less hampering than physical constraints. As early as 1793, Jacques Roux realized this fact when he said that freedom is a mere illusion if one class is in a position to condemn another to starvation, if the rich, by their monopoly of wealth, possess the power of life and death over the poor.

Economic constraints may appear to us as impersonal forces, such as crises, markets, overproduction, and unemployment. This accounts for the fact that the liberals regarded the apparent laws governing economic problems in the same way as the political structure was regarded in feudal times, i.e., as phenomena in the natural order of things. And yet, in certain circumstances, it is not easy to distinguish economic restrictions from immediate physical restrictions, since the real force of economic pressures in modern society is insured by the police, who protect those applying such pressures.

The disparity between abstract ideals and the way they are applied in modern states with democratic constitutions has not been due solely to a narrow interpretation of fundamental principles. Actual facts have been in conflict even with such an interpretation of the principles. In America, one of the essential principles of the Declaration of Independence, laying down the equality of all men and the general right to freedom, immediately came into conflict with the existence of slavery, and Jefferson's dream of remedying that discrepancy between the facts and the fundamental principles of the Republic did not become reality until more than eighty years later, after the long war in which the southern democrats, belonging to the Democratic Party, fought heroically for the maintenance of slavery. In the second quarter of the nineteenth century, laws were still being enacted imposing heavy fines and prison sentences for teaching

6. This does not mean that political equality does not matter to the working classes. It has made easier their struggle for a real improvement in living conditions and an extension of real freedom. This struggle has been carried on by people who have interpreted democratic ideals more radically than those who urge that state regulation should not be applied to economic life—a view which is also put forward in the name of democratic freedoms.

Negroes to read and write.[7] Even now, 173 years after the proclamation of the Declaration of Independence, there is legal discrimination, not to mention actual discrimination, against Negroes in some states in the oldest of modern democracies. The same situation can be observed in colonial states, where the white peoples have regarded it as natural to exclude the indigenous colored population from all democratic liberties. In Europe, it was for a long time thought possible to reconcile democratic principles with the prohibition of strikes and workers' unions.

These deviations from accepted tenets were justified by an extremely elastic principle, which is also a factor in the varied connotations of the term "democracy," although it is liable to conflict with other principles proclaimed by democrats—the principle of the public interest. This is the principle which, in Bertrand Russell's view, is supposed to distinguish the Russian definition of democracy from that of the Anglo-Saxons.[8]

We shall have occasion to return to this problem, which may also help to illustrate the many meanings of the word "democracy." For the time being, we may note the main conclusion to be drawn from the foregoing considerations. One reason for the divergencies in conceptions of modern democracy is what we might call the "original sin of modern bourgeois democracy": the subordination of the humanitarian ideals which are a lasting part of European culture to the interests of a single class, since the universalistic arguments, applying not only to political questions, that were used to justify political reforms were to make it easier for that class to exploit the mass of workers. The word "liberty" attracted the oppressed classes, spurred on enthusiasts, and gave the actions of the bourgeoisie sufficient moral prestige in the eyes of generations educated by the eighteenth-century philosophers and revolutionary Romanticism to blind them to certain social fictions. The catchword of "liberty" was used to mask economic restrictions. It served to justify the doctrine of laissez faire which deprived the third principle of the Great Revolution—fraternity—of all significance. Anyone familiar with the position of the workers in the first half of the nineteenth century, anyone who knows the democratic arguments that were used to justify a twelve-hour working day for children in factories, any-

7. Cf. E. Westermarck, *Christianity and Morals* (London, 1939), pp. 299–300.
8. See questionnaire, question 10, p. 516.

one who recalls that it was the Tories who defended the workers against the democrats in England, or remembers Cavaignac's defense of French democracy in 1848, must have a lively appreciation of the possible variations of the meaning of the word "democracy."

VI. TWO SOLUTIONS

We have tried to show that socialism's opposition to the bourgeois democratic ideology is not directed against the principles invoked by democrats. As we have said, socialism rests on the same cultural foundation. In the eyes of socialists, the struggle against the democratic ideology is a struggle against a system of social fictions; it is an attack on the ideological façade behind which, whether consciously or not, class interest is concealed. This is the interpretation we have to give to the words of Jacques Roux quoted above—words spoken barely four years after the Declaration of the Rights of Man. We find the same view expressed, twenty years before the Communist Manifesto, in the works of Philippe Buonarotti, *La Conjuration des égaux*.[9]

For a socialist, liberty is meaningless so long as the masses of the nation live under the threat of unemployment and poverty or so long as powerful trusts are in a position to direct the life of society more arbitrarily than political rulers, since they do so in no official capacity. Socialists are convinced that the humanization of economic life is a necessary deduction from the principles of democracy, unless we wish to hide the real facts behind a screen of words and legal phrases.

Here too, however, we shall find that the opposing parties can agree more easily upon general principles than on the way they are to be applied. When a socialist speaks of the humanization of economic life, he has in mind the abolition of the capitalist system, the inhuman (*unmenschlich*) nature of which has been so vividly portrayed not only by Karl Marx but also by non-Marxist writers such as William Morris; the socialist has in mind the socialization of the means of production and the management of economy in accordance with human needs instead of for profit. In the name of the same "human values," however, democrats in the other camp have defended the existing system, in fear of the leveling effect of centralization, and uneasy lest restrictions on private ownership of the means

9. Brussels, 1828.

of production should impoverish the individual characteristics of man and sap his initiative.

At this point, we come up against some psychological problems which are often inadequately appreciated by modern Marxist thinkers. Such problems as the following arise: How far do the reactions of a man brought up under the capitalist system, and his motives for action, change when subjected to the influence of other circumstances, other models, other suggestions? How are the various forms of economic dependence and the different types of co-operation reflected in the formation of human personality? After a more detailed analysis, we should probably find that the concept of property is also a composite notion. One need not be the owner of a school or a library, a theater or a forest, to work therein as a teacher, librarian, actor, stage-manager, or forester. A climber who loves the mountains is the lord of the heights; their conquest gives him a sense of fuller life although they are not his private property and he does not have to pay heavy taxes on them; it is enough for him that they do not belong to anyone else. We need not own any part of our home town to love it and work for it.

I draw attention to these secondary questions, as I wish to emphasize that such psychological problems are of some importance to those anxious to form an opinion on the contradictory ideas associated with the word "democracy" and the different conceptions of the way the fundamental principles of democracy should be applied. I should like to point out that these are practical problems capable of investigation, and that experimental research on them has not, so far as I am aware, been undertaken on any large scale. I feel that, in an era of great social changes, such as the present, it would be worthwhile to embark on such research, and that an organization like UNESCO should be asked to initiate the work, for the international scope of its activities would enable it to select appropriate fields for comparative study.

Criticism of the ideological façade we have just mentioned, and the political struggle against bourgeois democracy which has been carried on since de Tocqueville's time, have influenced the attitude of socialists towards the word "democracy." While, to a sincere liberal, the concept of democracy is a conceptual merger with a definite constructive connotation, in which the ideals of general humanitarianism color the system of parliamentary democracy, to a radical socialist struggling *for democracy against democracy*, the term has mixed emotional associations. Various phases can be distinguished in the history of the socialist attitude towards the term "democracy." At the beginning of the twentieth century, even Lenin was a social democrat. After the split in the socialist movement, the members of the left wing who took the name of "communists" treated the other social democrats as secret supporters of bourgeois democracy, and this had some influence on the attitude of the radical Left to the word "democracy." When, in the struggle against Fascism, this word regained its constructive connotation even in communist circles, and became more widely popular, the supporters of the Left accentuated the ambiguity of the term by tacking on additional adjectives. The basis of this ambiguity—in the Marxist interpretation —is the opposition between the interests of two social classes; the function of the adjectives in question is, therefore, in this case, not to specify but to modify the meaning of the main word: *bourgeois democracy (or Western democracy)* and *popular democracy* are not two types of democracy; the term "democracy" changes its meaning according to the adjective applied to it. The expression "popular democracy" thus ceases to be pleonastic.

Socialism, treating all practical problems from a class standpoint, maintains the universalist interpretation of the principles of democracy as its ultimate aim. If—we read in the Communist Manifesto— the proletariat becomes the dominant class by revolution and, as the dominant class, forcibly abolishes the previous relationships in the process of production, it will simultaneously abolish the reasons for the existence of class conflicts; it will do away with classes in general and even the preponderance of its own class. In the classless society of the future, the term "people" will no longer apply to a specific social class.

The program of the liberal democrats of the West and the program of revolutionary socialism are two different ways of solving the conflict between general ideals and the facts of society with which we are confronted in a class system. The liberal restricted the application of the principles of equality and liberty to political and legal life, compelled (as he saw it) to compromise with human nature and the necessities of economic life—a compromise which, in the eyes of the socialists, was only a specious system of ideas erected to conceal class interests. The revolutionary socialist, starting from the assumption that democratic principles cannot really be applied unless the whole social and economic system is reformed, advances a dynamic solution as the alternative to the static solution of the liberal democrats: the full achievement of the ideal principles of democracy is postponed until the future, becoming the ultimate aim,[10] while the current program takes account of the practical demands of the struggle for that future achievement. This means that, in the transition period, democratic liberties can be extended only so far as the methods of the campaign allow. Following the principles of his theory, the socialist maintains that general assumptions can be viewed only in the perspective of given social conditions, having regard to the direction of historical development.

There is another circumstance which influences the ideology of revolutionary socialism. Since, according to that ideology, the essential condition for complete individual freedom is the abolition of man's exploitation of man, and the establishment of a classless society, the principle of equality and social justice takes precedence over the principle of liberty—in contrast to the ideology of liberal democracy. This first principle, incidentally, makes a more effective appeal to the exploited masses.

As we see, the attitude toward the contemporary era has a great influence on the ideological conflicts between the representatives of liberal democracy and of revolutionary socialism. For a liberal, the present is the time to apply democratic principles, while the task of the future will simply be to perfect the democratic forms of communal life, to defend the democratic system against hostile forces, and to extend it to countries not yet enjoying its benefits. For a revolutionary socialist, on the other hand, the contemporary period is one of struggle for the achievement of aims in the future. Therefore, if a liberal democrat is aware of certain fictions and compromises in the democratic system, he regards them as no more than inevitable discrepancies between fact and ideal, whereas, for a revolutionary socialist, the divergency between his contemporary program and the state of affairs at which he is ultimately aiming represents a difference between end and means or between successive stages of development.

10. Cf. Lenin, *The State and the Revolution,* as quoted in the UNESCO questionnaire, see p. 521.

VII. THE ANTINOMIES OF DEMOCRACY

The point at issue here is the efficiency of the struggle, for the methods of democracy are not its best guaranties, and respect for the rights of opponents may, in certain circumstances, involve great risk. Military organizations, even when inspired by a democratic spirit and mobilized for democratic ends, have never used democratic methods in action. Every attempt to introduce these methods into the army, such as the efforts to make decisions subject to vote and to settle questions by a majority, has been doomed to failure. The democratic republics of classical times made provision for calling in a dictator in case of enemy attack. In wartime, democracy has always given place to a more flexible autocratic system, less slow in decision. The strengthening of state organization and methods of coercion may therefore be considered a prerequisite for the abolition of the state as an instrument of coercion. The dictatorship of the proletariat may aim at the abolition of all social class distinctions. Control of the press may be a weapon in the struggle for a society in which the press is to be actually, and not merely apparently, free. The refusal of democratic rights to the enemies of democracy may prove necessary if democracy is to be achieved or preserved.

Marxists explain the use of these methods by reference to the principles of materialist dialectics, teaching us that evolution proceeds by the surmounting of contradictions. The question of using antidemocratic means for democratic purposes, however, also confronts ideologists in the bourgeois democracies whenever they are threatened by any serious danger and, in particular, in case of war or internal unrest. When he introduced the Terror, Robespierre in no way renounced the democratic principles contained in the Declaration of the Rights of Man.

The degree of restriction on democratic liberties is generally very closely connected with the seriousness of the threat. In Gladstone's time, England had no need to introduce legal restrictions on freedom of speech. But, in 1934, when life seemed less stable, the Sedition Bill was passed. Bertrand Russell's attitude toward this measure taken by his government shows how much respect for democratic freedom is affected by the sense of security. If I remember rightly, Russell then stated that he had no objection to applying the Sedition Bill to an orator in Trafalgar Square who might urge a crowd to attack the Palace of Westminster, for the proximity of Trafalgar Square and

Whitehall made the danger real. If, however, a speaker made a similar appeal in Edinburgh, he could be left unmolested, as the distance between Edinburgh and London would give the crowd time to come to their senses. The same factor, i.e., the gravity of the threat, probably accounts for the fact that, before the war, an Indian in London would be allowed to speak against the government of Great Britain, while a similar speech in Calcutta would have sent the orator to prison for some years. The seriousness of the danger, in an uncertain situation, explains why the problem of the difference between ends and means is encountered, in such an acute form, among the revolutionaries.

For a liberal democrat who cannot appeal to materialist dialectics, the question of *renouncing democratic methods to save democracy* is paradoxical and may even give rise to tragic conflict. This antinomy appears clearly in the watchword: "No democratic liberties for the enemies of democracy." It might be expressed in the following form: "Which is the democrat—he who renounces the principles of democracy for its salvation, or he who is prepared to lose democracy to remain true to its postulates?" This paradox can be solved in two different ways. The first solution—which no man of action can accept—is expressed in the phrase *Pereat mundus, fiat iustitia.* The second solution invokes the interests of the community as the decisive argument. Those interests are sometimes cited to justify the application of antidemocratic methods to native peoples in colonial policy (this seems to be the case with Bryce, for instance). The conflict between the postulate that we should always employ democratic methods and the postulate that we ought always to consider the welfare of the community or the welfare of the people may serve to illustrate the inconsistency of the ideas contained in the concept of democracy.

It is easy to overlook this antinomy when the time in which antidemocratic methods are applied for democratic purposes is a period of warfare, revolution, or threat from any other transient danger, which everyone regards as exceptional. But the situation is different when the period is longer and begins to seem a normal state of affairs, for then the educational consequences of such a system become apparent; they are pernicious to democratic ideals. It is well known that our habits and scales of values are differently formed in circumstances considered normal and circumstances regarded as exceptional and temporary. Continual fear of unemployment or police terror is not conducive to the training of particularly desirable psychological attitudes from the point of view of the assumptions of democracy. A constant threat is very dangerous to the spirit of democracy, and sincere democrats are continually being put to the test, as they are confronted with conflicts which are extremely difficult to solve. It is therefore impossible, at the present day, to separate the problem of democracy from the problems of international cooperation.

The new circumstances of social life raise new questions. In the present state of technical development and of the evolution of organizing methods, democratic ideology has to solve a very important problem, which appears to be one of the most difficult in modern democracy. It is the problem of a planned society. This problem, in its turn, also seems to involve an antinomy.

In December, 1943, F. A. Hayek, a professor at the London School of Economics, completed a book directed against social planning. This book gives the impression of being a desperate attempt to put back the clock. "Economic liberalism," the author writes, "is opposed to competition being supplanted by inferior [sic!] methods of co-ordinating individual efforts."[11] The same month, Robert Lynd, a professor at Columbia University, made a speech, on the other side of the Atlantic, at a meeting of the 38th Congress of the American Sociological Society on the subject: "Sociology and Planning." In Lynd's opinion, a planned economy is inevitable, and American democracy is at present faced with the alternatives, either that "private industry will take charge and govern the State in the Fascist way," or that "the democratic State will take charge and socialize the economy."[12] Lynd is anxious that American sociology should endeavor to develop social responsibility and co-operation by democratic methods.

The contradiction between these two statements on planned economy is particularly striking as both the authors are representatives of Western democracy. Hayek, staunchly supporting opinions current in the nineteenth century, does not seem aware of the fundamentals of the problem.

For democrats who realize that a planned economy is inevitable

11. F. A. Hayek, *The Road to Serfdom*, p. 27.
12. Robert S. Lynd, "The Implications of Economic Planning for Sociology," *American Sociological Review*, IX (1944), 14-20.

and essential for the humanization of economic life, the problem may be stated as follows: How is it possible to reconcile spontaneous reaction in economic and cultural processes with the existence of the central guiding plan which is essential if social life is to develop rationally, without disturbances due to inadequate co-ordination of various human activities? How can such centralization be reconciled with local autonomy to enable men to live their lives in different ways, making a free choice, and to preserve initiative in individuals and small groups? This problem appears particularly important as it affects more than the economic side of man's life, for it is not only in economics that planning is essential to carry out the principles of democracy. It is equally necessary to secure true democracy in education, to reorganize the large towns and cities, and to bring the greatest treasures of culture within the reach of all.

An economic system which, for lack of any central plan, squanders tremendous sources of power, or a country, like the United States of America, which has enormous resources and in which all cultural questions are governed by the power of the dollar, seems an anachronism today, in spite of its superiority in technical development.

At the same time, however, it is well known that a variety of cultural types enables the individual to choose that most adapted to his needs; that such variety is necessary to protect civilization from the risk of becoming petrified; that attacks on democracy are generally associated with a tendency to standardize, and that even the best example loses much of its social value if it becomes the only example and can therefore no longer be freely chosen.

In spite of appearances, this problem does not necessarily entail a paradox. To demonstrate this, it would be necessary to embark on a detailed analysis, which we cannot do in the space available. We therefore merely draw attention to the fact.

VIII. CONCLUSIONS

1. The term "democracy" has many meanings. The notion of democracy is a conceptual merger resulting from certain historical processes.

2. Different factors are combined in the content of this notion: the etymological sense of the term (power of the people), abstract principles of equality and liberty, contrasting ideas on the appli-

cation of those principles, and concrete models of political systems held democratic.

Two ideas interact with one another: the idea of the power of the people and the idea of government *in the interests of the people.* The expression "power of the people" combines two connotations of the word "people" (*demos*), one connected with class and the other of universal application.

Lastly, the composite notion of democracy contains the absolute sense of the term (the organization of all social life in accordance with the principles of equality and liberty) and the relative sense (the application of democratic methods within a single group, sometimes a small one).

3. Two types of social factors determine social ideologies and political program: (*a*) contemporary social and economic conditions; (*b*) the cultural heritage.

4. Revolutionary socialism and liberal democracy have a common cultural foundation and appeal to the same principles.

5. The ideological controversies between revolutionary socialism and liberal democracy may be summed up as: (*a*) different interpretations of fundamental principles; (*b*) difference of opinion regarding the method of applying them, and the function of the present period in the process of their application; (*c*) difference of opinion concerning the question which of the traditional principles of democracy must be maintained, if, having been specifically interpreted, those principles prove not to form a consistent whole. These ideological disputes are caused by the contemporary conflict of class interests.

6. By the use of a humanitarian ideology identical with that on which socialism is based, and by recourse to arguments which appear to transcend all class barriers, bourgeois democracy restricts the question of equality to political and legal considerations alone, thus managing—with the aid of the principle safeguarding private property—to create a state of affairs favoring bourgeois interests. The ambiguity of the word "democracy" enables the middle classes to take advantage of the emotional content of the term.

7. The question: which is the "right" sense of the word "democracy" has little meaning. The use of each of the opposed senses is justified by history.

8. In the phrases "popular democracy" and "bourgeois democracy" (or "Western democracy"), the function of the adjectives is not to *specify* but to *modify* the meaning of the word "democracy," which varies in each case. "Popular democracy" is therefore not a pleonasm.

9. The temporary restriction of "democratic liberties" in the revolutionary socialist program is due, its adherents are convinced, to the needs of the struggle for the complete realization of the fundamental principles of democracy. These principles are held to lead to a classless society and to the humanization of economic life. If the struggle is too long-drawn-out, such restrictions may have results which the supporters of this program neither foresee nor desire. The necessities of the struggle entangle some of the democratic principles in antinomies.

10. At the present time, the two questions concerning democracy which appear most important are: (*a*) the problem of international co-operation, without which full application of the principles of democracy in every country of the world is impossible; (*b*) the organization of a planned economy. In spite of appearances, this second problem does not, in my opinion, involve any irreducible antinomy.

XXI

UMBERTO A. PADOVANI

In order to arrive at a satisfactory definition of the concept of "democracy," we should first trace to its source the concept of "civil society." Civil society derives from the nature of man as a living and rationally sentient being, whose activity is accordingly organized and inspired by reason; this is the essential feature distinguishing man from other living and sentient beings, the feature from which his other characteristics are derived.

Man, the human individual, the person, cannot achieve his "humanity"—a human existence, or civilization—without society. This is because society necessarily presupposes the division of and specialization in the various forms of activity—which is essential to their improvement and perfection—and organized exchanges between them, which are tantamount to civilized society itself. Civilization, of course, also presupposes another form of society, apart from present, contemporary, space-dimensional society, namely, the society of succeeding generations, which is transitory and historical and results in progress.

Just as an individual cannot of himself do everything required to fulfil in every respect his own "humanity" (his "rationality"), because of the disproportion between the human "ought" and each individual's capacity to achieve it, but draws profit from the activity of others with whom he lives together in society, so the various generations of men draw profit from the contributions made to civilization by previous generations, which in fact come to "progress."

Naturally, progress and civilization, which are achieved by human society, must not be regarded in a purely material or economic light, for then the "humanity" of man himself could not be achieved. Material progress and civilization are an essential requirement, although not the highest of human nature; they are essential to progress and to spiritual, cultural, and moral civilization, to the achievement of spiritual values, to which, accordingly, they must be subordinate. The actual achievement of spiritual values, whereby man's "humanity" is inspired, can only be an individual task, which each man must fulfil of himself, because what constitutes the full achievement of man's "humanity" is his inner essence, his freedom, and his rational independence, and it is by this standard that the true value of man is measured.

Now any society (and therefore civilized society) requires an organization, since it is one unit in a series; and this organization must be hierarchical, since the unit consists of various elements whose qualfications differ in degree. This vertical unit comprises the civil power, the political authority, the government, which must be a government by all for the good of all, adjusted to the human and hierarchical value of each individual.

The essential and basic feature of a government is that it should provide for the *good of all*, so that the "humanity" of each individual may be achieved, because each man is a person; and it must be a concrete achievement, because individuals, too, are concrete. The individual is not made for the state, but the state for the individual, for the human individual is a person, as Kant would say, an end and not a means.

Another essential feature of an ideal state is that it should provide for *government by all*, again because each man is a person, an end in himself, and hence cannot be subjected to other men or become their instrument or chattel (slavery). He ought to be dependent on himself alone, on his own reason; he should be dependent upon others only in so far as this is reasonable, the measure of such dependence being decided by himself and dictated by his own reasoning. Here, too, participation in public affairs must be allotted concretely, according to the capacities of each individual, for the very reason that the various individuals are concrete and differentiated beings.

The ideal political régime, therefore, should be "government by all for the good of all," in other words, democracy. It should involve not only *formal, political* democracy (of the usual liberal type), under which all individuals should be legally guaranteed the same political rights, e.g., equal or universal suffrage. It must also, and in the first place, involve *real, social* democracy (economic, educational, etc., democracy) under which all individuals should legally be able to achieve their own "humanity," and hence enjoy basically those economic resources without which they can neither achieve it nor exercise effectively their political rights, as formal democracy requires.

This formal democracy has shortcomings by way both of excess and of omission. Excess, because while all individuals, as men, should enjoy political rights, they cannot all enjoy the same political rights, owing to the concrete factor, the deep-lying differences between individuals that have already been mentioned. Omission, because freedom and political equality, proclaimed abstractly to be absolute and guaranteed by law, continue, in the last resort, to remain the prerogative of economically privileged minorities, enabling those minorities to secure for themselves, furthermore, adequate political training.

Thus, formal and legal democracy not only does not imply *government by all*, since it is "government by all" only in an abstract sense that cannot be translated into practice for those lacking the necessary economic means of leading a cultural, moral, and hence a political form of existence; it cannot even achieve the *good of all*, because in practice it ends by achieving the good only of those who can effectively exercise political rights by reason of their education, culture, and economic resources, and can therefore secure control of public affairs.

The foregoing definition of democracy deals with the *"ought,"* its ideal substance. Its translation into historical fact seems to involve considerable modifications, as in the case of the illusion of formal democracy, which cloaks a negation of real democracy. For it is a question not only of adjusting the general to the particular and the abstract to the concrete, which should merely mean achieving the former within the latter; but of adjusting the universal, the abstract, to an individual, to a concrete factor, that resists and opposes it, mainly because of active human egoism (which is not synonymous with reasoned interest) and hence because of human wickedness spurred on by egoism. This conflict between *ought* and *is* is an instance of what normally happens on the moral plane, from which politics cannot be excluded.

Even though the function of the state should be not only negative and repressive (the liberal conception) but also positive and organizational (the ethical conception), in actual historical practice states rise and take root, more or less, as a result of human egoism and in order to control that egoism. They are based, that is to say, on the egoism of a few violent and astute men, who impose their will on the egoism of many conflicting individuals (*homo homini lupus, bellum omnium contra omnes*), which need not necessarily prevent this repression of separate individual egoisms redounding to the advantage of the governed. In this respect the views of Machiavelli and Hobbes are unprejudiced but thoroughgoing.

With the coming of the state, the state of nature ceases for the subject, but remains for the prince. In order to defend themselves against the egoism of the prince (one or several, a tyranny or an oligarchy), the subjects generally resort to rebellions and revolutions, and it is thus, usually, that democracies arise, their ideal being government by all for the good of all, as against government by the few for the good of the few.

But in this struggle against egoism, human egoism itself re-emerges: the egoism of the few who, in a democratic environment, are clever rather than violent, *foxes* rather than *lions;* an egoism that by means of propaganda, deception and corruption usually succeeds in controlling the majority, though at the same time making provision for their interests.

It is true that under a democratic régime the constitution should legally guarantee government by all for the good of all; and constitutions are often, in fact, theoretical monuments of political justice. But in concrete terms, when adjusting the general to the particular, we find ourselves always, more or less, face to face with human egoism, the egoism of some who are concerned, more or less, to oppress, exploit, and dehumanize the others and therefore do not hesitate by guile or violence to override the constitution itself, if they are able to. History, past and present, shows this to be true.

Under democratic régimes, the people usually form themselves into political parties. We do not here propose to consider the relationship between party, class, and economic interest, though we may say that the economic factor (or egoism) plays a fundamental part in the forming of parties and classes. Usually, one of the political parties (or a coalition thereof) secures the power, the reins of government, and so succeeds, more or less, in obtaining control of affairs and excluding others from it, i.e., force invests it with right. Such are the modern parliamentary régimes, where the "formal democratic" guaranties (parliamentary questions, and freedom of the press and of expression) end by becoming more or less ineffective in face of the parliamentary majority and the government based upon it, i.e., the apparatus of the dominant parties.

In face of this party egoism, the people (represented in other parties) can always, of course, resort to force, e.g., to that type of modern revolution known as a strike, the usual immediate object of which is an economic one but indirectly has also the political significance of a protest or reaction against the political régime that favors or tolerates unjust social inequalities. When, however, the political rule of one party is succeeded by the political rule of another, all that really happens is that one egoism is replaced by another, as history shows.

But is it then impossible to achieve democracy, in the form of a government by all for the good of all? There is no doubt that it must remain the ideal inspiring the political history of man. As regards its concrete application, the first consideration must be the *good of all*, whereby all men can (in practice) achieve their own "humanity." *Government by all* should be implemented not so much by the exercise of this right, as through a régime that shall in the first place educate the masses of the people morally and politically and transform it into a people than can govern itself, just as boys must be educated to become men, not by being left to their own devices, but through a positive training imparted by their family. Formal democracy does not educate the politically uneducated masses, but (and in this it resembles the ancient sophistry) exploits them through propaganda, for its own economic purposes. Thus, pending the arrival of true democracy, it is better to have "paternal" governments, when they really are such.

In order that a democracy shall be achieved in political practice, it is necessary, not only to have the most reasonable possible constitution, having regard to concrete situations or to *what ought to be* and *what is*, but to bring about that balance between egoisms that prevents some elements dominating others, and that can be achieved by a great politician. This, in the Middle Ages, in the presence of an urge of moral and religious conscience, was effected by natural law and divine law. In more modern times, after the revolutions brought about by Protestantism and the Renaissance, it was effected by "paternal" Christian monarchies. In the contemporary era, since the Kantian and French Revolutions, constitutional monarchies, democratic republics and popular dictatorships, in one way or another, have sought to bring it about.

Constitutional monarchies effect it by concentrating on the balance between the parties and on their political dialectics, which are based on their conflicting egoisms—these monarchies being above the parties hierarchically and above them as regards time by reason of the continuing dynasty. Democratic republics have sought the necessary guaranties in the establishment of constitutional courts that pronounce on the actions of the government. Popular dictatorships, which are more concerned with justice than with liberty, aim at the actual welfare of the masses as an essential condition for political training and democratic education.

In the light of these historical experiments and for the purpose aimed at, it would have to be concluded that the only way of achieving democracy was through absolutism, assuming that peaceful succession in the reigning house and a political control of the prince himself were insured. It should be borne in mind that, while it is essential above all to provide for the material and economic needs of the people, which is essential if the spiritual values are to be achieved, it is these values that must, in the last resort, be aimed at, constituting, as they do, the basic nature of man.

With a view to underlining the foregoing considerations regarding the "*ought*" and the "*is*" of democracy, it may be useful to recall the origins and development of democracy itself in the modern age. Modern European democracy, apart from the English democracy, derives politically from the French Revolution and ideally from the philosophy of the Enlightenment. And it took the shape of a formal, political democracy, as a claim to freedom and political equality, by way of reaction against the old régime of absolutism and caste.

But this formal, political democracy was not flanked by any social and economic democracy; economic equality did not accompany political equality; thus there was no "integral" democracy. Formal, political democracy was demanded by the bourgeoisie, the economic power of which was constantly rising, but which was thwarted by a régime based on political and hence on economic privilege; this gave rise to the French Revolution. Through that was achieved that freedom and political equality, that formal democracy, which was in its turn to serve as the legal instrument of the economic interests of the bourgeoisie, its political freedom being the counterpart of the economic freedom it had desired.

This freedom admittedly represented some progress in relation to privileges that had become inequitable and had produced stagnation. But at the same time it represented the triumph of egoism in another form and led to the freedom of a new ruling class (the bourgeoisie) to exploit the people, by regarding the worker as a means for their own enrichment, a commodity subject to the laws of supply and demand.

This was a classical liberal—an empty and negative—conception of freedom, quite different from the positive, ethical conception. And this "liberal" freedom prescribed a new form of slavery, the slavery imposed by the bourgeois, capitalist régime of the nineteenth century, since liberal "naturalism" disregarded the element of the "person," the "end in himself" that every human being should be considered to be. Economic liberalism—bourgeois capitalism—brought much wealth to some, but at the cost of much misery for others, and a high degree of material civilization, but at the cost of as much human sweat and blood as the monuments of the Pharaohs had caused; those monuments however had the advantage that they were monuments to art and religion, both of which were spiritual values.

It was therefore natural that socialism and communism should arise for the defense of the "humanity" of the working masses, just as the French Revolution had been provoked in the interests of the bourgeoisie. These new movements may be linked, ideally, with the French Revolution itself, if not so much through the concept of freedom, at any rate through the concept of equality, not in a formal and theoretically political but in an integral sense, and hence in a sense implying human fraternity and solidarity.

Communism, admittedly, did advance its cause by seeking its bases in a Hegelian, immanent, historical, and naturalistic metaphysics, which would imply the collapse of all spiritual and moral values and hence of the human individuality itself, in the cause of which heroic battles were being fought. It was in any case impossible to prevent the ultimate collapse of the liberal, bourgeois, economic and utilitarian conception, which was no less immanent and naturalistic than communism, but was less "human" than it in spirit. The bourgeois régime was far inferior to the old aristocracies, which ideologically were based on religious and Christian principles, teaching duty and honor, not utility and pleasure. Communism, however, derived from Hegelian dialectics a strong urge to pass from theory to practice, more precisely through the dialectical concept of struggle toward the revolution which, concretely speaking, is the extreme practical method of subduing inextinguishable human egoism.

Communism postulates a real, integral, social democracy, as against the formal, fictive, political democracy that culminates in a political and economic system favoring the egoism of the rich at the expense of the poor, and thus ultimately led to the effective negation of democracy. As its means of achieving integral democracy, communism selects, in the main, collectivism, a one-class system, and dictatorship.

But collectivism achieves social justice at the cost of human freedom, which is buttressed by private property; material property, however, is a reinforcement of the body, just as the body represents a reinforcement of the spirit. Property, therefore, must be not abolished but universalized, and thus be made to serve the human dignity of all men; the immoral accumulation of private wealth must be limited by law, and misery and poverty must be legally fought by social legislation through an economy planned and controlled in all its workings. Given, and not granted, that this might prejudice economic values and material civilization, it would redound to the advantage of moral values and of spiritual civilization, which are of immeasurably greater importance.

The one-class system is justified as a reaction against the multiclass system, which is based on unjust economic inequalities. It is not justified if regard be had to the fact that society, and therefore the state, is a unit made up of different elements, of persons engaged in various activities, with varying clear-cut qualities, functions, and needs; and therefore that individuals engaged in the same activity naturally tend to ally, organize, and even relate themselves with each other through those corporative institutions that are distinctive of the professional life of society. The aim, therefore, is an assortment, not of economic classes, but of professional corporations.

As for dictatorship as the vehicle of integral democracy (as well as the architect of social democracy), it may be justified by the observation that we have already made, viz., that a people is not educated for democracy democratically, but rather with a freedom that would soon become license, demagogy, and anarchy. Indeed, there must be some permanent form of more or less dictatorial authority, even though it gradually draws nearer to what may prove to be its negation, because the majority of humanity will be always more or less in an infantile state, owing to all the limitations and conflicts, both intellectual and moral, that exist within humanity itself. This is in conflict with the principle that communism seems to have in common with modern immanent, historical, optimistic, Hegelian thought—the principle of infinite progress and of the absoluteness of the world. But such a dictatorial authority—aiming at the good of all, and educating for democracy—must never sacrifice freedom to (economic) justice, if by freedom we understand, as we must do, moral freedom, which is as far from tyrannical slavery as from liberal "free-will."

In conclusion, we would say that it is the *"ought"* of democracy—ideal democracy—that must be the ultimate goal in the political history of humanity. But this ideal democracy must be achieved, more or less, through partial negations of it, given the resistance shown by human egoism (and hence by injustice) that will never be rooted out from man, so congenitally inclined as he is to act like a wolf toward his brother. It may be regarded as a sign of progress toward integral democracy that the Western democracies (which are formalistic, political, and liberal) are obliged to introduce features of real, social democracy, like, for example, labor legislation, the socialization of certain means of production, limitations placed upon private property, planned economy, etc.; the more or less dictatorial function of one party or one man, the president of the state or the head of the government; and tendencies, overt or latent, toward corporative and one-class systems. (Just as the contrary is necessarily taking place in the Eastern democracies.) A typical example is that of England, which in modern political history seems to have the singular privilege of bringing about a dialectical synthesis of opposing values—the old and the new, monarchy and aristocracy, aristocracy and democracy, formal democracy and real democracy; the only exception is in the field of philosophy, where empiricism and pragmatism ought to be placed in the context of classical rationalism and Christian asceticism.

XXII

RICARDO R. PASCUAL

10. WESTERN VERSUS EASTERN DEMOCRACY.—In my political theory, "democracy" is a type of social order established by the relations holding between the elements that make up society. "Democracy" is not primarily political nor primarily economic but a social system determined by economic relations as well as by political ones. If this view is agreed to, there will also be agreement that the current emphasis on an ineradicable opposition between a "Western" liberal conception and an "Eastern" communist conception of democracy is without justification. Bertrand Russell simplifies matters in a dangerous way when he asserts that "The Anglo-Saxon definition of 'democracy' is that it consists in the *rule of the majority*; the Russian view is that it consists in rule in *the interests of the majority*, these interests being determined in accordance with Marxist political philosophy."[1]

Each of these definitions expresses aspects only of the social order made up by "democracy." They are not in opposition to each other but supplement each other, in so far as the "democracies" thus defined fulfil the requirements implied. But in the opinion of Bertrand Russell, one of them, Soviet Russia, does not fulfil these requirements even if judged by the "interests of the majority" definition only; his statement seems to imply the likeliness of a discrepancy between these interests as determined by Marxist philosophy and as determined by the people itself.

11. "NARROW" VERSUS "BROAD" SENSE.—"Democracy" has become a broad social concept and cannot any more be confined to political instrumentalities only. It does not designate methods of decision-making only, but has come to be used to cover a socio-political concept designating conditions and methods as well as results of decision-making on every social matter and not merely on political ones. This is the way the term should be used. Short of this broad usage the word "democracy" must never be used at all because

1. My italics.

275

any other use will make it a mere means of propaganda. Sincerity of analysis precludes the inclusion of the propaganda value of "democracy" in its meaning.

"Democracy" cannot be thought of as political only without losing its fundamental meaning. Social life cannot be split up into exclusive airtight compartments labeled political, economic, or social. Therefore there is no "democracy" unless it is taken in its broad sense.

Political democracy and economic democracy are not two different kinds of democracies such that the one may be related as a means to the other. On the contrary they are both aspects of a single "democracy" and it is a matter of historical accident which one of them comes first in time. A nation need not have been politically democratic before it achieves economic democracy. The historical development of political democracies which have so far failed to achieve economic democracy cannot be cited as evidence for the priority of political democracy over economic. In fact, the "political democracy" developed in some countries has constituted a reactionary force thwarting economic democratization. This only shows the more clearly that the two aspects of "democracy" are not related to each other as means to end. And yet they are as clearly compatible with each other.

15. ECONOMIC DEMOCRACY.[2]—*Economic democracy* has an enticing resonance; it is an impressive "song hit" with familiar notes and a revolutionizing tempo. Will those who dance to the tune of *political democracy* be able to lift their feet and sway their heads to the rhythm and tempo of this new piece? The patriarchs of political democracy whose backs of individualism already crack with the rheumatism and lumbago of state paternalism dare not lift a foot to the new tune for fear that they will fall dead before the dance is only half-way; the care-free brats of the *have-not's*, the problem-children in the economic slums of political democracy dance merrily with abandon without even taking time to catch their breath or caring to know whither the piper of Marxian Hamelin will lead them. But the sober ones, the not-too-old and not-too-young, the middle class between the *abundantly-owning-have's* and *wretched-have-not's*, the minor-property-owning ones, whose number is legion, are now re-

2. The following section is an extract from an unpublished work of mine, "Partyless Democracy."

hearsing with the sway of their heads and the tapping of their feet to see how they can enjoy the tune before they make up their mind to lead their business personalities to the middle of the floor and dance to the merry tune. Let us don this attitude of broadmindedness.

What does "economic democracy" mean? *Democracy* in its familiar sense means the government of the people, for the people, and by the people; and in this category it is *political democracy*. Since economics deals with the production, distribution, and consumption of wealth or goods of the nation and individuals, analogical with political democracy, *economic democracy* should mean the production and distribution of wealth or economic goods *by* the people and *for* the people, and which should belong to the people, that is they must be *of* the people. We have strained our language in order to express justly the purpose of the implied analogy, intended by the linguistic simile (*political democracy* and *economic democracy*). But the production, distribution, and consumption of economic goods are *by* and *for* the people only if such products or goods belong to the people, that is, if they are *of* the people. That the products are of the people is primarily a matter of ownership of the products. If this ownership is the people's then the production, distribution, and consumption of the goods will be *by* and *for* the people. In plain words, *economic democracy* means that: ownership, hence consumption and appropriation of economic goods, must be *by* the people, *by* whom they are produced; they who produced the goods should own the goods; the goods are produced *by* the people *for* their welfare, hence, they must be distributed and owned *for* their welfare; economic goods are *of* the people, i.e., the people's goods *of* the people who produced them. The ownership of goods, of course, includes the ownership of the means of production of such goods, for the means of production is but a form of economic goods. We have here in brief what economic democracy should mean if we know what political democracy means. Is there an analogy between political democracy and economic democracy? or, does the meaning of economic democracy give a mere transcendental implication of *democracy* which was not possible in its political form?

In *political democracy*, sovereignty is the subject matter and it is this which is *of*, *for*, and *by* the people. But this sovereignty of the people does not reside in the people as individuals who may exercise them at will; this sovereignty is not in a state of anarchy; it is embodied in the state. The sovereignty of the state is the sovereignty of the people only when the people are the state. What is the counterpart of sovereignty in economic democracy? The power to produce economic goods is human labor power and, for being physiological and psychological, is not analogous to political sovereignty. The power to distribute economic goods is derived from the right of ownership which political sovereignty regulates. We can say then that *ownership* is the economic counterpart of sovereignty. In economic democracy this *ownership* must reside in the people. To stop at this point is only to stop at the gate of a hall of confusing intricacies. Let us keep the phrases rolling at the tip of our tongue: *political sovereignty; economic ownership*. There are two aspects, in political democracy, of the people's sovereignty. The first aspect is negative, namely, that no person within the society or country has a sovereignty over and above any other person within that community. Any exercise of sovereignty by one man, or a group of men, is only a delegated office in a democracy and, for the sake of efficient operation of the people's sovereignty it is delegated for a definite short period. The other aspect is positive, *i.e.*, the people's sovereignty is a unity of several individual sovereignties as expressed by the will of the majority in the usual manner—election. In a negative expression this means that the people's sovereignty does not find cognizance as individual's sovereignty. Whatever right—not sovereignty—an individual might retain is subject to the majority's sovereignty in the form of the state, which regulates the residual right left to each individual.

Let us now inquire: How about the case of economic ownership? Should it mean, first, negatively, that no person shall have ownership over any person (say, in the form of slavery)? It is conceded that no person can own another person and this is taken care of even in political democracy. It is the principle for which the great American champion of democracy, Lincoln, fought and died. On the positive aspect, if we are to analyze economic democracy very closely to political democracy, ownership must be a unity of several individual ownerships as embodied in the social ownership which may be identified as state-ownership. In the same way that politically the individuals are not left to exercise their sovereignty individually so must ownership, economically, not be left to the individuals to be exercised individually. Economic democracy cannot mean that no individual must be denied the individual exercise of ownership in the same manner that political democracy does not mean that no person is denied the individual exercise of his sovereignty. The individual as individual has no sovereignty; any sovereignty resides in the people as a collective whole, not as discrete individuals. Similarly, the individual as individual cannot exercise ownership; in economic democracy, any ownership must reside in the whole people as a whole and not as individuals. This refined distinction is important, for not to deny ownership to any individual would not amount to economic democracy. In individualistic capitalism, where no individual is denied ownership, though individuals own quantitatively different goods, there is no economic democracy. Let us now investigate what at first sight appears to be verbal quibbling. Ownership, even of a million dollar estate, is not different from the ownership of, let us say, a five-cent pencil. Ownership, in this sense, is an abstraction which has only logical and not quantitative status. There is, therefore, no question that in this sense, ownership has not been denied to anybody, for somehow anybody must own any piece of something, a piece of rag, let us say. Now, if this be democracy in economic sense, there is economic democracy even in individualistic capitalism. This is the kind of democratic ownership prevailing in all the capitalistic political democracies today. But *this is not the state of affairs which economic democracy seeks.*

Economic democracy cannot therefore be expressed in the following words: No person shall own any goods more than any other person within the community. This is quantitative equality of goods owned and consequently equality of ownership. But it is not economic democracy. It is now clear that *equality of ownership* does not mean *equality of goods* but *equality of goods owned* is *equality of* ownership, logically and quantitatively. But equality of the goods owned would imply the following set-up. Let us grant that goods are divided equally among the individuals of a nation. Shall we allow each individual to be the custodian of the goods pertaining to each? If we do, that would erroneously require that the rate of consumption of different individuals be the same, which is not the case, for while some may consume fast and/or much, others may consume slowly and/or little. It is bad psychology and maladministration to assume that different people live with the same frugality. Let consumption be scientifically regulated. To do this is to make no individual the custodian of his own goods. Let the state do so. Let it not be impertinently insisted that ownership is now taken from the individual by the state, for while the individual owns the goods the state is merely the custodian of the goods. Shall regulation of ration be according to the rate of consumption or on the basis of equality for all individuals, regardless of physiological build? If in equal rates, it is poor knowledge of physiology, for different individuals have different rates of consumption, depending upon their physiological conditions. If according to individual needs, then equal goods distributed at unequal rates will not last for equal periods of time. Hence, the scheme will create the problem of supplying those who have consumed all their goods before the end of the calculated time. If this goes on from one period to another there will be the old inequality, for there will systematically accumulate the surplus with some individuals and the deficiency with others. All this starts from the assumption that goods are to be divided equally while consumption proceeds at unequal rates.

Why not divide the goods unequally, according to needs or to ability to produce? Then some individuals will consume more than others or will produce more than others, hence they will receive more than others. But this will not be the equality of goods or the equality of ownership. Certainly not; nor is equality of goods or equality of ownership economic democracy. In economic democracy ownership is not to be equally exercised by the individuals, for in political democracy sovereignty is not equally exercised by the individuals. But ownership, like sovereignty, must be exercised collectively, and not individually, by the state. In this way, while the ultimate source of sovereignty is the individual, the state is the active trust of such sovereignty. This would mean that ownership, like sovereignty, is not to be given to the individual and therefore no individual will have ownership which he may use for his advantage over the other individuals. Like sovereignty which is given to the state, or which is of the state, ownership is to be exercised and operated by the state. Nobody then should own the primary essence of economic wealth as nobody is sovereign in its supreme category. Then the means of production which are the primary essence of economic wealth must be owned by the people through the state; no individual should own the means of production, in the same way that the state, in the political sense, is the supreme power, authority, and the only focus of loyalty. This will be the analogous meaning of economic democracy as drawn from the meaning of political democracy.

In political democracy, theoretically, the exercise of sovereignty is *for* the people, *of* whom sovereignty is. Should economic democracy mean that the exercise of ownership of means of production be *for* the people? A government *for* the people means a government whose activities, policies, and expenditures are *for* the people, i.e., *for the welfare* of the people. Similarly, in economic democracy production, distribution, and consumption must be *for the welfare* of the people. There will be no question that whether in present political democracies, or in the projected economic democracy, production of economic goods is *for the people*, for no industrial firm ever produces anything which is not *for human consumption*. But whether what is *for human consumption* is *consumption for the welfare of the people* or not is the question. Whether too, capitalistic distribution of goods is for the welfare of the people or not is another question. Economic democracy, undoubtedly, should mean that the production, distribution, and consumption of goods must be for the welfare of the people.

In political democracy the governance of the people's welfare is exercised by the people. The people govern themselves, so to speak. They pass judgment on the policies, objectives, and plans of the government, on the assumption that nobody but the people know what is good for them. In economic democracy I presume, economic planning, objectives, and policies must be passed on by the people. In the same way that in political democracy the people do not scrutinize the problems of government and decide the governmental affairs by themselves but instead they elect their representatives, who, they take, will decide their problems better than they, themselves, can do, in economic democracy the people are not called upon to do the elaborate thinking for themselves about their economic problems but they are supposed to elect their representatives who shall study the planning, objectives, and policies for them. In this way, there is an almost perfect analogy between political democracy and economic democracy. Let us not be rushed to think that the question is to choose between political democracy and economic democracy. We cannot even say that the two types of democracy are incompatible. Since any body politic is called upon to legislate on economic matter the question is not to accept one and reject the other. The only pertinent problem is whether to preserve or not the beauties or virtues of both types of democracy.

XXIII

AIME PATRI

It is understood that, theoretically, definitions are free to the extent they are mere conventions designed to render more precise the meaning of words in the vocabulary of the user; thus it might be permissible to call a dog a "cat" and a cat a "dog" provided that the listener was warned and provided that he remembered to make the necessary transposition in every case as when passing from one language to another. I suppose, however, that the UNESCO inquiry has been undertaken in order to avoid such an extremity and in the hope of discovering a common terminology.

In these circumstances, it appears necessary to take account of the most common use of the word, thus restricting the theoretical liberty of definition; this must lead us to draw attention to abuses of terminology if occasion arises. Moreover, by all the rules of traditional logic, a definition must, at the same time, cover the whole of what is defined and no more than what is defined. If that is admitted, it is impossible to support the opinion that there is no such thing as "democracy in general" but only different types of historically characterized "democracies"; the use of the same word to designate sets of facts which, *ex hypothesi,* have nothing in common, cannot be justified. The definition of democracy must be wide enough to be compatible with the diversity of historical types but must preserve the idea of a common species; otherwise the word would have no meaning, as the rule of correspondence between the definition and "the whole of what is defined" would not be observed. The word "democracy" would likewise be meaningless unless the conditions of its use were so regulated as to enable a "democratic" régime to be distinguished from another régime which is not democratic. As this latter requirement corresponds to the rule "no more than what is defined," it is the major condition to insure that the word "democracy" shall not be employed in a vague sense, varying at the arbitrary will of every user.

8. THE LINCOLN FORMULA.—Abraham Lincoln's famous phrase: "Government of the people, by the people, for the people" may be taken as a satisfactory basis of discussion for the working out of a definition. In my opinion, the following comments are called for:

1. *Government of the people.*—It should be noted that democracy is here described as a form of government, that is to say, in the wide sense of the word "government," as a political régime. We may therefore note that the first meaning of the word "democracy" is that of "political democracy." This sense should, in all circumstances, be respected in all discussions involving normal usage, since there is no proof that it has become obsolete. Democracy in the political sense alone may not be the highest form of democracy, but the existence of the corresponding institutions, and their effective operation, is the minimum requirement for the correct application of the term to any given régime.

The use of the term "democracy" to describe a form of economic and social organization represents a meaning derived from the preceding one by analogy, making the necessary transpositions. This extended use may be considered legitimate as a supplementary means of designating the maximum conditions of democracy. But this derived meaning cannot be allowed to prevail over the primary meaning of the term: without political democracy, there can be no question of "democracy" at all.

On the other hand, as "democracy" is described as "government of the people," the supposition is that a government does in fact exist, which is capable of functioning normally. "Democracy" cannot, therefore, except by abuse, be assimilated to "anarchy," either in the sense that socialist or libertarian theorists give to the latter term when contemplating the ideal of the final elimination of the function of the "government of men" (Saint-Simon, Proudhon, Marx and Engels, Bakunin, Lenin) or in the popular disparaging sense in which it is taken by pamphleteers denouncing the inconsistency or weakness of the public authorities. It is self-evident that the term "anarchy," in the popular and depreciatory sense, may be employed to criticize the operation of democracy or any other régime, but that does not mean that it can be considered an element in the definition of "democracy." In addition, it should be noted that "anarchy," in the sense it is used in by theorists is a meta-political ideal, the conditions for the realization of which are only to be found "beyond democracy." It is only when interpreted in this way that statements like that quoted from Lenin in the UNESCO document can make sense. The ultimate aim as described by Lenin cannot be taken into account when characterizing a form of government, since the aim in view is the very elimination of that institution. The question whether "democracy" implies, as an ideal, "anarchy" in the nonpejorative sense must be left aside. In any case, there is no reason to introduce it into the definition.

2. *Government by the people.*—The second part of the Lincoln formula may be taken to express the essense of the definition as it stresses the specific difference which separates democratic political régimes from those which cannot lay claim to that title without an abuse of words.

It might be pointed out that a narrow literal interpretation of the expression "government of the people by the people" might seem meaningless; as all distinction between governors and governed seems to be removed, we apparently arrive at the negation of government, thus coming back to the definition of anarchy. This remark was made by the jurist Duguit and, before him by Proudhon, with quite another purpose, in the *Idée générale de la Révolution au XIXe siècle.* In order to remove this difficulty, it is helpful to have recourse to the distinction between the "Prince" and the "Sovereign" as set forth in Rousseau's "Social Contract": the "Sovereign" is responsible for making the laws, and the "Prince" for enforcing them. The function of the "Prince," which is assimilated to that of the "government" in the narrow sense, corresponds to the executive power, while the legislative power is the proper function of the "Sovereign." It therefore seems preferable to define democracy, as is usually done in France, as the form of political organization in which the people is sovereign.[1]

By "people," we understand the whole body of those governed. The distinction between "Prince" and "Sovereign" preserves the difference between governed and governors, and therefore the institution of government itself, by removing in the very words the confusion between democracy and anarchy. The spirit of the defi-

1. It is noteworthy that Rousseau himself does not succeed in giving a literal definition of "democracy," because he relates the definition to the "Prince" and not the "Sovereign"; the assimilation of the "Prince" to the people seems to him to introduce a utopian requirement which could only be realized among a "God-like people."

nition currently accepted is the same as that of the Lincoln formula, although the letter may differ.

The separation of the powers—at least of two powers—thus appears to be a corollary of the definition of democracy, and it was solely on a basis of verbal misunderstanding that Rousseau seemed to be opposed to Montesquieu on this point: the Genevan interpreted the separation of powers to mean complete independence of one another and rightly considered that an impossible condition. The power of legislation is called the power of the "Sovereign," i.e., the principal power, because it is upon its definition that depend the definitions of all the other powers which can be exercised only within the bounds of the laws. Confusion of the powers leads to anarchy or despotism. But it must be understood that, in a democratic régime, the "Prince" cannot be omnipotent. The power of the "Prince" can be exercised only within the limits laid down by the "Sovereign," to whom he has, periodically, to answer for his administration. The democratic system can operate only if the "Prince" is subject to dismissal. A still clearer definition of democracy, capable of removing all ambiguity, would be the following: democracy is the political régime in which the governors agree to regard themselves as responsible to the governed, and therefore to submit to their judgment in matters concerning both the general principles on which their administration is to be based and the assessment of their methods of administration. When the distinction between the "Prince" and the "Sovereign" is once accepted (and it is necessary for the clear understanding of the concept), no form of despotism can be compatible with democracy.

The power of the sovereign people may be exercised either directly or indirectly through elected representatives who are responsible for making the laws and supervising the actions of the government.

No criterion other than the professed intentions of the governors can be admissable.

On the other hand, it seems to me that a distinction might be made between democratic and undemocratic political régimes by recourse to the following consideration: any régime which regards the "people," i.e., the body of those governed, as incompetent to judge of its own interest, is not democratic, however excellent may be the intentions professed or the results obtained by the régime, and however much ground there may be for considering the people incom-

petent (for instance, the poverty and ignorance of the people resulting from a previous régime). Or, in other words, any régime in
which the relationship between governors and governed is held to be
similar to that between men and animals (the metaphor of the "shepherd" and his "flock") or that between minor children and their
parents or guardian (the metaphor of the "father")—any such
régime, I repeat, is not democratic. On the contrary, it is the essence
of democracy that the governed shall be considered free and adult to
the same degree as the governors.

A democratic government may be described as one which does
not admit the possibility of doing what is good for the people whether they want it or not, i.e., without their consent. From this, we see
that we are entitled to ask whether the people are sufficiently "enlightened" for a "democratic" régime to function in a normal way.
It does not follow from the mere definition of democracy that a
political system of this type can be applied everywhere and at all
times.

This last consideration might absolve the scruples of those who
consider it disgraceful that a régime cannot be called "democratic"
and therefore try to find shelter behind an ambiguous terminology
in order to cover up the system they really prefer. In any case, however, it does not seem likely that supporters of the systems in force
on the other side of what is commonly called the "Iron Curtain" in
Europe would be willing to accept the distinction suggested by
Bertrand Russell[2] between the two meanings of the word "democracy": the "Eastern democracies" regard themselves officially as
régimes established not only "for the people" but also "by the
people," and more subject to permanent control by the people than
the capitalist democracies of the West. The question whether or not
such régimes usurp the title of "democracy" and even, with a significant redundancy, of "people's democracy," is not one of words but
of fact: the point at issue is whether, given the one-party system (or
its equivalents in the form of compulsory blocks or "national
fronts"), the popular control of the state proclaimed in the constitutions can be anything other than a legal fiction.

Several varieties of democracy may therefore be considered:
direct, and indirect or parliamentary democracy, the proportions
varying with the institutions. Under a régime of full, direct democ-

2. As quoted in the UNESCO questionnaire, see p. 516.

racy, laws would be directly ratified by popular vote and could be proposed on the initiative of the people in a similar way, while the magistrates responsible for their enforcement, constituting the "Princely" authority, should themselves be elected. In the United States of America, the popular election of the president is a factor of direct democracy which makes the absence of parliamentary government compatible with democracy. In any case, democracy cannot be confused with the parliamentary system; at the beginning, the tendency of the Soviet system was to substitute direct for indirect democracy. The distinction between direct and indirect democracy, combined with consideration of the proportions in which institutions of either type are set up, may provide an exhaustive system of classification for all varieties of "democracy" found in history. It is well known that, as Rousseau saw it in the *Social Contract*, only institutions based on direct democracy could be reconciled with real popular sovereignty; in taking this view, he is going on the principle that sovereignty cannot be alienated to representatives. But there is no reason to identify delegation, provided it is periodically revocable, with alienation in any real sense of that word. It may therefore be admitted that democracy can be reconciled with the parliamentary system, although the adoption of that system is not required by the definition of democracy.

3. *Government for the people.*—It seems to me impossible to admit that the last of the elements in the Lincoln formula, the *"for* the people" element, by itself constitutes a sufficient criterion of "democracy," in the absence of institutions fulfilling the two other parts of the definition, particularly the second. In fact, "government for the people" but not "by the people" has a name familiar in political history—"enlightened despotism"—and whatever opinion one may hold of the benefits conferred by that régime, it cannot, without an abuse of words, be described by a term which is, moreover, not commonly applied to it, and denotes an entirely different political system.

Furthermore, no political régime known to history has ever been prepared to consider its administration directed to securing any interests other than those of the people. According to the fundamental observation made by Plato, who was himself the first theorist of "enlightened despotism," in the dialogue *The Republic*, every government asserts that it is established in the interest of the governed and not of the governors. Even the most violent dictatorships are no exceptions, if the declarations made by their leaders are considered alone. In these circumstances, any régime would be entitled to lay claim to being "democratic." The "government for the people" formula by itself provides no criterion to distinguish democratic from undemocratic régimes. The idea of judging the declared intentions by the actions of the government and their results might be entertained. But who would be the judge? In the case of "enlightened despotism" (government for the people, but not by the people), as the people are presumed incompetent ("unenlightened"), the government itself would be the judge, that is to say, both judge and party in the case.

15. DEMOCRACY AND SOCIALISM.—The questions which may be raised in connection with this particularly difficult problem, which is probably the crux of contemporary controversies, may be classified as follows: (*a*) Is it possible to be a democrat without being a socialist? (*b*) It is possible to be a socialist without being a democrat? (*c*) Is socialism compatible with democracy?

Is it possible to be a democrat without being a socialist? To this first question, I should certainly give an affirmative answer, although I myself profess both socialist and democratic opinions: the definition of democracy in accordance with current usage of the term is that of a political régime, while socialism is an economic system characterized by the socialization of the means of production and exchange, that is, by the abolition of private ownership at least in the main sectors of economic life. The two concepts thus, a priori, have nothing in common and there is no reason why they should not be either combined or separated. There is an abundance of historical grounds for holding that a believer in private ownership may be a democrat in politics, although he is naturally not inevitably so. Even contemporary Communists have admitted this on various occasions.

It is none the less true that, from the socialist point of view, the type of democrat who does not feel compelled to adopt socialist opinions may be considered inferior. If democracy in the purely political sense is considered the minimum compatible with the definition of the term, democracy in the economic and social sense, in which it becomes assimilated with socialism, would be the higher form of democracy.

Is it possible to be a socialist without being a democrat? The answer here must be that it depends on the way the term "socialism"

itself is defined. If we content ourselves with the definition of socialism, still frequently given, which states, as the sole criterion, the
public ownership of the principal means of production and exchange, i.e., the abolition of private property in the corresponding
sectors, we find that, in the course of history, this type of "socialism" has been reconciled with other forms of political régime than
democracy. One may point—as Liberal economists have missed no
opportunity of doing (cf. in particular Yves Guyot in his controversy with Lafargue)—to the régime of the Pharaohs in ancient
Egypt, to that of the Incas in America before the coming of Colum-
bus, and to that established by the Jesuits in Paraguay. In addition,
Plato, who set forth a socialist theory which is very close to fully
developed communism (the abolition of private ownership of consumer goods), is formally opposed to political democracy; the same
is true, in varying degrees, of a number of utopian socialists with
paternalist tendencies.

It may, however, be pointed out that the definition of "socialism"
so conceived is possibly not a full one and that, in any case, it is not
in consonance with the aspirations of modern socialism as developed
since 1848. A full definition of "modern socialism" as understood by
Marx and Engels would introduce three factors: (1) socialization of
the means of production and exchange, i.e., the substitution of public
for private ownership (at least in those sectors in which the individual producer is no longer the owner of the means of production
even in a capitalist system); (2) democratic control by the society
over the management of the socialized means of production and exchange; (3) gradual progress toward the removal of social class distinctions and, in particular, of "the humiliating distinction between
intellectual work and manual work" that Marx considered summed
up those class distinctions: ultimate abolition, therefore, of any
hierarchy between the functions of command and obedience and of
the institution of government itself; substitution of the "administration of things" for the "government of men," to use the phrase of
Saint-Simon which was adopted by Marx and Engels.

"Socialism" prior to modern times could be antidemocratic because neither the second nor the third condition entered into its
aspirations or achievements; in Plato's *Republic*, we can see that the
abolition of private property is reconcilable with a hierarchy between functions of command and functions of obedience, a hier-

archy which is itself based on the ancient division into three orders.

Modern socialism, on the other hand, by reason of the second condition, introduces democracy into the definition of the operation of the economic system. This democracy is in fact the political democracy defined above, i.e., the responsibility of governments toward the governed, but is adapted to new conditions, since the functions of the governors responsible for the management of the public property have become economic as well as political. Political democracy, which is sometimes described as "formal," and economic and social democracy, described as "real," cannot therefore be opposed to one another. "Formal" democracy (in the direct or indirect form) is the only means of insuring that the public property is not withdrawn from the control of the collective owner; it is the guaranty of "real" democracy. If that guaranty is removed, the difference between modern socialism and the ancient régime of the Pharaohs ceases to exist: instead of "socialism," we then find in modern times the "managerial" régime as defined by Burnham.

The third criterion in the definition of "modern socialism" introduces conditions relating to an ideal which is certainly not antidemocratic but which might justifiably be described as "meta-democratic," since its attainment would be equivalent to anarchy, as we have already seen in connection with the comments made on a quotation from Lenin's writings.

Is socialism compatible with democracy? This question may legitimately be asked, since modern democratic socialism is as yet no more than an aspiration, and there is no certain proof that it will be achieved. According to the logicians, no definition implies the existence of the thing defined, which must be proved in some other way. The possibility of a "square circle" is therefore not excluded.

In the opinion of Liberal or neo-Liberal economists (Ludwig von Mises, Hayek, etc.) the first, second, and third terms in the definition of democratic socialism would be incompatible. The quotation from Alexis de Tocqueville in the UNESCO document[3] inclines to the same view. The main argument seems to be as follows: a "socialist" régime satisfying the first criterion, which implies the management of the economy in accordance with a general plan prepared by technical experts who are the only persons competent for the purpose, could only be "dictated" from above and would necessarily exclude

3. See p. 517.

the possibility of democratic control over the execution, as well as the elaboration, of the plan. Secondly, as the conditions for economic freedom which are associated with private property are excluded, any other form of freedom would be abolished; as the citizens would be materially bound by their state of economic dependence on the public authorities, democratic control would, in any case, be abolished, since there would be no effective means available for persons and groups to exercise it in the ordinary way.

This line of argument is strengthened by the examples that can be referred to of régimes satisfying the first criterion of "socialism" but not the other two (the U.S.S.R. at the present day would come into this category). Logically, however, the contention is not conclusive; the clear possibility of condemning the three criteria in a particular case does not imply any necessary incompatibility between them. The functioning of a régime of "democratic socialism" which may at least be designed with the idea of an economic plan, does not lead to the corollary that it can only be inspired and executed dictatorially by all-powerful technical experts. The normal competency of technical experts is naturally restricted; in a normal régime of economic and social democracy, the technical experts propose and the sovereign people dispose. The objection then advanced against the competency of the sovereign people could likewise be used against democracy in general and political democracy itself. There is no real reason to suppose that the sovereign people, either directly, or indirectly through their representatives, and either at the national or the local level, should be less competent in economic matters than in any other respect. While it is normally the business of the technical experts to suggest means of achieving any given purpose, it is not within their province to decide on the end to be pursued in preference to any other, and still less to claim to be the arbiters of how far the way in which they have attained it is satisfactory. As Aristotle had already pointed out in his rebuttal of Plato's antidemocratic line of reasoning based on the principle of the incompetence of the people, from both these points of view, the user, i.e., the ordinary member of the population, is the only competent judge of what he desires and of how far he has received satisfaction. Furthermore, the risk indicated of the actual disappearance of all public freedoms if economic freedom should be abolished is only hypothetical; the conversion of the principal means of production and exchange into public service does not imply that the government can employ them as it likes and at its own discretion, as a private owner would do. It is conceivable that the citizens should have normal access to them, both as individuals and collectively, and that this right should be guaranteed by the Constitution, so that no legal obstacle can, for practical purposes, be put in the way of the operation of democratic institutions.

The neo-Liberal line of argument is, however, of vital interest to the supporters of "democratic socialism"; as it is a warning against the possible, and already certainly observable, degeneration of the institutions they advocate, it should induce them to give a fresh and more precise definition of the conditions necessary to insure that "socialism" works "democratically."

22. TOLERATION OF DISSENTIENT OPINION.—This question may be subdivided as follows: (1) Can a régime be considered "democratic" if the right of opposition in general is not recognized? (2) Can a democratic régime tolerate antidemocratic propaganda, i.e., propaganda directed against the régime itself?

1. *The right of opposition in general.*—Democracy is sometimes described as the régime in which the majority imposes its law on the minority, the latter having no right save that of submission. This oversimplified, ambiguous, and ruthless conception is contrary to both the spirit and the letter of democracy; it was traditionally maintained by the avowed opponents of the democratic régime, who wished to identify that régime with the despotism of the majority, and has today been taken up afresh to justify authoritarian and totalitarian régimes anxious, improperly, to call themselves "democracies." The ambiguity in it can easily be resolved, provided that we agree to make a distinction between active interference with the execution of majority decisions, and the legitimate and normal exercise of the right of criticism that is essential to the very functioning of the system. The rules of democracy require that the minority should submit to the majority, that is to say, that it should not actively oppose the decisions taken; but they also require that, in return, the majority should respect the minority's right of criticism. If this right should be contested, as the party or coalition in power represents, *ex hypothesi*, the expression of the majority opinion at the last plebiscite, no overthrow of the majority could legally be conceived; the fact of once having obtained a majority would be sufficient to

insure indefinite maintenance in power so long as there was no violent eviction or palace revolution; the governors would no longer be subject to the control of the governed and therefore the conditions of democracy would no longer be fulfilled.

It is the essence of a despotic system of government to identify intellectual criticism with active sabotage of decisions. When this confusion (which could easily be removed by pointing out that there is, for instance, a great difference between refusing to pay a tax and carrying on propaganda to secure the constitutional rescindment of the corresponding fiscal measure) is systematically fostered, it does, however, produce its effects; without a recognized right of criticism, opposition can have no other means of expression than sabotage, since every other avenue is closed.

From the foregoing considerations, it follows that a single-party system, or a compulsory coalition of parties which is alone entitled to put forward lists at elections, is incompatible with political democracy. As the single party or its substitute is, *ex hypothesi*, the government party, it ensues that elections become merely an empty formality; the government need expect nothing but the ratification of its actions by plebiscite, which proves the hypothesis.

2. *The case of opposition to the régime.*—The question whether democracy can tolerate opposition to its own régime is extremely difficult and must be carefully distinguished from the previous case, which is concerned with the hypothesis of a legal opposition resolved to take no action for which existing democratic institutions do not provide and determined to maintain those institutions. According to certain adversaries of political democracy, the régime, apart from its own principles, is not entitled to defend itself. That is the sense of the famous phrase attributed to Louis Veuillot: "In the name of your principles, I demand of you the freedom that I refuse you in the name of mine." Should a democracy, in order to remain faithful to its tenets, in certain circumstances, accept what is tantamount to suicide? At least one such case of "suicide" is known, since Hitler appears, generally speaking, to have attained his antidemocratic ends by acceding to power through the normal channels of parliamentary democracy.

On the other side, the famous axiom of Saint-Just may be advanced: "There is no freedom for the enemies of freedom." But the application of this formula might be dangerous. The government may be tempted to present its ordinary opponents as opponents of the régime, instituting a sort of law against suspects of the crime of "antidemocracy," a crime which is intrinsically very vague, owing to the possible fluctuations in the sense of the word (sometimes interpreted in the political, and sometimes in the economic and social sense), and still more vague when the question of suspect intentions is introduced. On the other hand, if the application of the formula is to be restricted to the *avowed* opponents of democracy, dissimulation and political hypocrisy will be encouraged: the adversaries of democracy will say that they are more "democratic" than anybody else, owing to the specialized interpretation they give to the term.

When all is said and done, and the advantages and disadvantages of both attitudes are weighed against one another, it appears that a democratic régime cannot apply to its opponents any other jurisdiction than that of the common law; a democratic system, as such, cannot, without denying its own tenets, institute offenses of opinion. It does not even seem that it would be to its advantage to do so, since such ill-advised action might be turned against its authors. When the opponents of democracy attack it by antidemocratic means (active sabotage, coup d'état), it is as justified in defending itself as any other régime; democratic freedom exercised within the bounds of the laws is not unrestricted freedom. When its adversaries employ democratic methods, abiding by the rules of those methods, it is the business of democracy to defend itself on its own ground and in its own way, i.e., by its own achievements, which should be a sufficient answer to attacks made upon the system. There is a risk involved, but the risk is vital to the survival of the system. Saying this, we should bear in mind what was said above—that the conditions of democracy may not be applicable everywhere and at all times.

XXIV

CHAIM PERELMAN

A. Ambiguity and Misuse

Unquestionably, very different meanings have been and continue to be applied to the word "democracy." If one of these meanings is regarded as the "true sense" of the word, as denoting "real democracy," all the others must be either deliberate or unconscious misuses of the term. The true sense would then be that in which the word *should* be used, for the idea of truth suggests that there can be only one meaning and presupposes some objective link between a term and what it denotes. This objective link implies that there is a certain rigid norm for the correct use of the word "democracy."

It is only logical that those who hold such a view should consider the term "democracy" to be free of any ambiguity and label any but their own application of the word a misuse.

Whatever may be the philosophic justification for the establishment of such a link between a word and the meaning attaching to it, the practical result is obviously to impose a certain definition—a "persuasive definition"—which, it is claimed, has an objective validity and should therefore be accepted by everyone.

Others, taking a less absolute stand, try to fix on a meaning which, though not invariable, may be regarded as the "normal" sense of the word. Historical contingencies are naturally taken into consideration in such a process, for the normal is the most usual sense in the limited field in which investigations are carried out. It will be illuminating to know the normal acceptance of the word "democracy," as any attempt to use this word in an "abnormal" sense may then be put down as a misuse. According to this argument, there is little difference between the "normal" and the "true" meaning.

It should nevertheless be noted that the normal sense may be used without making it a norm, if explicit mention is made of the historic circumstances under which the use of the word "democracy" is normal in any particular sense. According to this view, the "normal

296 DEMOCRACY IN A WORLD OF TENSIONS

sense" of the word "democracy" is relative to a specific cultural environment; but the same word might be regularly used in different senses in a different cultural milieu.

The problem we are now considering, and which might appear to be a purely semantic question, is complicated by the fact that democracy today is regarded as an ideal régime, symbolizing a positive value, for which men will fight. By giving "democracy" a certain definition, this positive value is transferred to the meaning just defined, so that discussion on the meaning of "democracy" centers, not on the question of language, but on the ideal political régime.

It is typical of our twentieth-century ideology that democracy is considered to be an ideal form of government. In the past, it was merely one régime among others and could thus be defined more or less objectively by contrasting it with other systems. However, it should be noted that the definition of democracy will differ according to whether, like the Greeks, we contrast it with tyranny, aristocracy, oligarchy, or demagogy, or, as during the eighteenth century in France, with the monarchical system, or, again, as is the fashion in the twentieth century, with the fascist régimes. Even if we adopt the latter course and regard democracy as an anti-fascist régime—a definition on which it would not be difficult to arrive at a theoretical agreement today—different phenomena may be described as constituting the *essence* of fascism. The opposite of these essential characteristics will then be taken as "the essence of true democracy." The only advantage of such a method is to transfer the discussion from the term "democracy" to the concept of fascism.

In the light of the foregoing considerations, democracy seems to be a *confused* concept and it would probably be mistaken to try to put it forward as a *clear* concept. Moreover, whenever we ask ourselves whether a given political régime is democratic or not, we have to clarify the meaning of the word "democracy," for it is questionable whether certain typical features of a particular régime, left out in the consideration of other systems, are compatible with the idea we form of a democracy. For instance, how far is the granting of different political rights to the citizens of a state, depending on their religion, political views, income, educational level, sex, and age, compatible with our idea of democracy? Must a state which does not extend the franchise to women or to religious nonconformists be regarded as democratic? How far is the granting of hereditary privileges to certain persons reconcilable with a democratic system? We know that the eighteenth century felt the existence of certain privileged classes to be inconsistent with the democratic ideal; how far must the meaning of the word "democracy" now be modified to cover certain monarchies? The application of the term "democracy" to a new political entity raises in every case a problem of interpretation and adaptation, so that a conception of this notion, based entirely on historical contingencies, cannot supply an infallible criterion that would fix the meaning of the term once and for all.

An attempt might be made to determine empirically the elements common to the various known historical uses of the word "democracy." We should then arrive at a formula containing at least one variable (which would take the form of a propositional function fx) and it might be possible to agree on this formula by centering the discussion on the different values to be assigned to the variable. We should thus obtain a quite general definition of democracy as a political régime the purpose of which could be described as the well-being, equality or freedom of its citizens. But it will at once be seen that the discussion would then turn on the meaning to be attributed to the words "well-being," "equality," "freedom," etc.

B. Social Democracy versus Political Democracy

Lincoln's definition of democracy as "government of the people, by the people, for the people" has enjoyed great success among political philosophers, because, when separated from its context, it can always be given an interpretation to fit in with opposed political ideals; we have only to vary slightly the interpretation of the elements in this formula or to emphasize one aspect more than another. I was rather surprised at the interpretation of the expression "government of the people" suggested in the basic document of the UNESCO inquiry: the preposition "of" is there taken to indicate the *obedience* of the people to the government. Personally, I interpret this expression to indicate that the people is the *source* of power in a democracy, for I fail to see how the obedience of the people to the government is more characteristic of democracy than of any other system. It is difficult to say whether the three prepositions in Lincoln's phrase express three necessary criteria of a democratic régime, since this formula is too vague to allow of the establishment of any sufficiently precise criterion; it will always be possible to find an interpretation and adaptation of the formula, ena-

bling it to be applied to systems which many would be loath to regard as democratic.

It is oversimplifying the problem to describe Western democracy
as the rule of the majority and Eastern democracy as government in
the interests of the majority. The mere fact of voting for a given
form of government can by no means be considered democratic unless all the citizens are sufficiently well informed to grasp the significance of their vote and provision is made to insure for the citizens
the choice between several possibilities. We all know that in a Western democracy, the government in power can seldom claim to represent as large a proportion of citizens as voted for the National Socialists in Germany at all elections after 1933. On the other hand, it may
safely be stated that the Western democracies attend to the interests
of the people more than any other form of government, as otherwise they could not again obtain the electors' vote.

In the discussion on the words "rights" and "freedom," where the
points of view of de Tocqueville and Bryce are contrasted with
those of Lenin and Stalin, these words are taken in two different
senses; according to the former, they denote absence of government
interference and the granting of legal protection to certain interests,
while according to the latter, all citizens are guaranteed a certain
minimum degree of power even if they themselves have not had any.
For the former philosophers, rights imply merely legal protection,
while for the latter, they signify effective possession. According to
the liberal view, the term "right to work" would mean that no one
may be prevented from working, whereas according to the opposite
view, it denotes the right to demand work or insurance against unemployment. The liberals take freedom to mean freedom from government interference, but the Marxists define it as the satisfaction of
certain needs regarded as essential for the individual. For the liberals,
the independence and dignity of the individual must be safeguarded
against interference by the public authorities; for the Marxist, this
independence and dignity would be no more than a sham without
the intervention of the authorities. Freedom of expression is very
precious to the person who has something to say, but, as Stirner re-
marked, it is of no use at all to the sheep that can only bleat. An apt
analogy may help to clarify the divergence between these two concepts of freedom. In the United States of America, before 1941, two
different ideas were entertained as to what constituted political
neutrality, an attitude which, theoretically, was not intended to

profit any of the belligerents. According to the first view, no arms could be supplied to any belligerent, while, according to the second, each belligerent could purchase arms from the United States if it conformed to the "cash and carry" clause. In both cases, the same treatment was theoretically extended to all belligerents, but in practice, the first concept of neutrality favored Germany, while the second favored Great Britain, which had sole command of the seas. The same applies to the forms of freedom: if all persons were in exactly the same position, so that the adoption of a certain form of freedom would affect all alike, the choice of one or the other of these forms would not have given rise to such heated controversy. He who is satisfied with the powers he possesses and who would be bound to suffer from state intervention, seeks to avoid it, while he who looks to the state for the benefits he is unable to secure unaided, sees only the advantage of such intervention. There is a dispute over the two views of freedom whenever the achievement of freedom for the adherents of the one conception is opposed to the achievement of freedom for the adherents of the other, for one cannot be achieved but at the expense of the other. Hence, the terminological discrepancy between the two concepts of freedom results from the different material circumstances of the persons who would be affected by the embodiment of these concepts in any given law. It should further be noted that in a utopian society, neither liberals nor Marxists desire the interference of the public authorities; ultimately, both views are reconciled in their support of an anarchical form of society. The present conflict between them is due to the fact that we are not living in utopia and account has to be taken of the real inequalities found to exist between citizens. I therefore do not think that the disagreement between ideologists who claim that either "political" or "social" democracy should take precedence over the other is merely one of terminology.

C. Tolerance and Treason

The problem of tolerance is concerned with the attitude of the majority or at least of the ruling class toward the minority or the opposition group. Tolerance therefore assumes: (1) the existence of a common group to which both the majority and minority belong and which is characterized by the fact that all its members respect certain rules they consider fundamental and (2) that the rules on which the majority and minority are divided are felt to be less important than those that determine their loyalty to the common group.

Tolerance can only extend to the attitude toward these secondary rules; no government has ever tolerated transgression of rules which are deemed to safeguard public order. The field of tolerance is therefore limited by the fundamental rules of society and includes all that is not specified in these rules. Societies may be described as more or less tolerant according to the area of this field. Incidentally, tolerance cannot be regarded a priori as a blessing, at least in relation to behavior that is felt to be "intolerable" and that should be controlled by laws to safeguard public order. It is obvious that what is regarded as tolerable or intolerable varies with circumstances: everyone admits that no government can tolerate in wartime all the actions it permits in time of peace. Instead of describing in exact terms the relationship between tolerance and democracy—which presupposes a very clear-cut idea of democracy—I would prefer to bring the discussion on tolerance down to earth and to deal with specific situations instead of enunciating universally valid rules.

The existence of a one-party system precludes the establishment of another party with a different political platform as incompatible with public order. The maintenance of the single party thus becomes tantamount to the maintenance of public order. Tolerance will be extended only to various trends within the single party. It may even happen that the party's platform gradually becomes so cut-and-dried as to exclude opposition even within the party; the scope of tolerance could thus be further diminished. Reasons could certainly be found for regarding a one-party system as democratic, but any government which history has recognized as fascist might make the same claim without attributing any absurd meaning to the word "democratic."

In so far as certain divergencies of behavior are tolerated, the rules which might govern such behavior are not regarded as binding; in other words, allowance is made for the possibility and validity of conduct other than that required by the rules. Although reluctance to impose on others a rule which one obeys one's self may, in a sense, be regarded as skepticism, because, on the other hand, universal acceptance is demanded of rules which are believed to have an objective validity; such an attitude should not necessarily be considered as a sign of wavering faith in these rules. Actually, feelings of superiority and even social hierarchies may be based on rules that are not universal, and many people would be distressed if no such proofs of "distinction" had existed. However, it is obvious that skepticism in this sense is one of the bases of tolerance.

Toleration of attacks upon the fundamental rules of a political society is a symptom of a tendency to relegate these rules to a secondary place, as may well happen if other rules come to be considered more fundamental.

D. The Value Foundations of the Conflict

Disputes over the meaning of such words as "democracy," "freedom," etc., would certainly be less violent if these words did not denote positive values. Ideologists attempt to exploit the decidedly emotional element in these words to win support for a particular view. Such tactics have as little justification with regard to democracy and freedom as with regard to a definition of true neutrality that would allow of a choice between the two opposite concepts of neutrality entertained in the United States before 1941. It is because the word "democracy" seems on the way to winning unchallenged support, so that no one now dares to advocate any other political régime in preference to democracy, that the discussion must turn only upon the conflict between various forms of democracy. It is only natural that, in so far as the concept of democracy denotes a value held in universal esteem, the meaning attaching to this concept should become all the more confused. This confusion is by no means reduced by the consoling thought that all political philosophers proclaim the same ultimate goal. The ideological differences relate to real societies and not to utopia. Once conditions allow for the attainment of a utopian society, ideological conflicts will lose all interest and meaning.

Conclusion

To enable agreement to be reached on the meaning which should be attributed to a given concept, it is essential to determine the context in which this meaning is sought. A concept like democracy has no clear meaning in itself. Before agreeing on the use of a term, agreement must be reached on the system of thought within which this concept should be used. The absence of such a common reference system is the main reason why conflicts about words like "democracy" are possible and why it is apparently so difficult to agree on the subject.

XXV

JOHN PETROV PLAMENATZ

I. THE WORD "DEMOCRACY"

We are interested, I take it, in "democracy" only in the modern senses of that word, the senses in which it has been used since the birth of radicalism, since the end of the eighteenth century.

Everybody says that in modern times "democracy" has meant different things to different people and to the same persons at different times. I do not wish to deny this fact. It is something that every political theorist must accept. But I do wish to suggest that too much importance is attached to it, and that the difficulties it is supposed to create are a great deal smaller than many people think.

I suggest that as great difficulties have resulted from the attempt to create too precise a political vocabulary as from the variety and vagueness of the senses in which political terms are currently used. People understand each other rather better than they understand each other's definitions.

It is a mistake to suppose, as some people have done, that we can escape the difficulties created by the vagueness of the words we use by elaborating a more precise vocabulary. It is not possible to create a technical, and therefore precise, vocabulary before the science that is to use it comes into existence. The political theorist cannot, like the artisan, go to work with his tools made ready for him. The ambiguous or vague uses to which we put social and political terms reflect our comparative ignorance of the phenomena we seek to describe by means of them. We shall not arrive at a really precise vocabulary before we have greatly extended our knowledge. I do not wish to suggest that we must look after things, and words will look after themselves. It is not as simple as that. We must always be interested in words; we must always look for definitions as precise as the state of our knowledge will allow. But we must not insist upon a greater precision. What we are trying to do is to define the senses in which a word is used; and if these senses are vague, so too must be our definitions.

To ask too much of words, to insist on definitions more precise than our knowledge can sustain, is to be guilty of an error that can be fatal to a study still only on the threshold of science. The medieval schoolmen knew almost nothing about natural phenomena, and yet they offered their students a host of definitions. Not all the subtlety and intelligence they displayed could make those definitions useful. The position with politics (and the social studies in general) is not nearly as bad today. We already have a considerable knowledge, ill assorted and insufficient though it is; and we can certainly be usefully employed in trying to distinguish between the various senses in which we use political terms. But we must never forget the danger of scholasticism, to which our study, precisely because it is not yet properly a science, is peculiarly liable. And we must learn not to take the modern schoolmen, especially the Marxists, too seriously. We must try to understand what they are saying, but we must not attach too much importance to the business of refuting them. Above all, we must not take too much notice of their definitions, of their statements about the science they claim to possess, of what they have to say about the political terms they use. We must be interested rather in what they have to say about the world and about the social and political behavior of mankind.

I think these preliminary remarks are necessary in order that certain misunderstandings should be avoided. I neither propose to give a really precise definition of "democracy" (for such a definition is, I believe, impossible) nor to refute other people's definitions. What I do propose to do is to argue that the word "democracy" has a single primary meaning and several secondary or derivative meanings. The primary meaning can, I think, be roughly defined as government by persons who are freely chosen by and responsible to the governed.[1] This sense is primary not because it is necessarily included in the other secondary senses, nor yet because it is implied by most people's definitions of "democracy." It is primary only because it is implied by most of the statements people make about democratic government. And democracy, as the etymology of the word indicates, is above all a form of government. This sense is primary because, however people may define the words "democratic government," they do not contrive to use it for long without im-

1. Direct democracy is nowadays so rare that I shall deal only with representative democracy.

plying that this is at least part of its meaning. I must repeat that what is important to establish is how people use the word "democracy" and not how they, or those who put themselves forward as their interpreters, define it. No one, I think, would deny that in the West, (i.e., in western Europe and North America) we mean by "democratic government," government by persons freely chosen by and responsible to the governed, whatever our views may be about what constitutes "free choice" and "responsibility." But we have also got into the habit of saying that "democracy" means one thing east of the "iron curtain" and something different to the west of it. As I think this is false and that it is important it should be known to be false, I shall be at some pains to prove that it is so. Now, it is obvious that what exists in the Soviet Union, Poland, and Yugoslavia and is called "democracy" in those countries is something different from what is called by the same name in the United States, France, and Britain. The phenomena spoken of in the two cases are different from each other. But it does not, I think, follow from this that there is nothing in common between the "Eastern" and the "Western" meanings of the word; and that there is no real quarrel about democracy between Easterners and Westerners, but only the appearance of one due to the accident that they both use the same word to refer to very different things. Words are not mere tools, of which men are always the masters and never the slaves. It has not come about that "democracy," an important word with a long history behind it, has got loose from its origins and can be used by Easterners and Westerners just as they please and to suit their own convenience. The political processes that Russians or Americans refer to when they talk of democracy may be different from each other, but what they want to say about them, when they call them "democracy," may be pretty much the same. We must not forget that the politicians and writers of Europe and America, the most important users of a political vocabulary inherited from the Greeks, have not lived in spiritual isolation from one another. They have been reading each other's books and discussing more or less similar problems and theories for nearly two centuries. Out of their discussions have arisen the two prevalent political philosophies, liberalism and Marxism. It would be a most extraordinary thing if the political vocabularies employed by adherents of these two philosophies were very different. They may both be, and indeed are, ambiguous and vague; but it is unlikely that the words common to both, especially the most important and frequently used of them, have acquired meanings so different that arguments conducted by means of them between adherents of the rival creeds have ceased to be genuine. Both Marxism and liberalism are creeds of Western origin, and they have a long doctrinal ancestry in common.

Marxism has prevailed in eastern Europe, where conditions are in many important respects different from those prevailing in the West. The Marxist vocabulary, already two generations old before Marxism ceased to be a creed the vast majority of whose adherents were Westerners, is now used to describe conditions unknown to Marx and Engels. It was born in one world and has been transported to another. But the transportation occurred only a short time ago. The Marxist vocabulary, even in the Soviet Union, has not ceased to mean what it meant to Marx and Engels. It has, no doubt, changed, but it is still very close to its origins. In essentials, Stalin still speaks the language of Marx.

I shall now try to establish my point that, whatever the definitions they offer, what both Easterners and Westerners[2] mean when they talk about democracy is "government by persons freely chosen by and responsible to the governed." That this is so is, I think, made clear by the attitude of each to what the other calls democracy. The Easterner and the Western Marxist speak of what they call "bourgeois democracy" as if it were an inferior or even spurious kind of democracy. And the Westerner and Eastern Liberal speak in the same way of the sort of democracy prevalent east of the "iron curtain." Scholars, anxious to maintain the appearance of impartiality, may talk of both kinds of democracy as if there were no point in calling one better or more genuine than the other. But politicians, journalists, and the general public are not so cautious.

It is also clear, I think, that the Easterner or the Westerner, when he calls the other kind of democracy inferior, does not mean that it is as much democracy as the kind he prefers but is merely inferior in quality. He does not mean that there are two kinds of democracy, each as genuinely democratic as the other, though one of the two is intrinsically superior. He is not saying, as a man might say who preferred an intellectual to a sensual pleasure, that each is as pleasant

2. I shall use the words "Easterner" and "Marxist" and "Westerner" and "Liberal," interchangeably; and whenever necessary, I shall talk of "Western Marxists" and "Eastern Liberals."

as the other, though the former is of a higher order. He is saying that the one is more truly democratic; and that though both may appear to be democratic, there is more of the substance of democracy in the one case than in the other.

It is not difficult to discover what Marx thought about democracy. He nowhere suggests that it is government in the interest of the majority. His attacks on bourgeois parliamentarism and on the plebiscites of Louis Napoleon do, of course, make it clear that he did not believe that the counting of heads is in itself sufficient to establish the will of the people. In his opinion, only a popular government will govern in the interest of the majority. But his assertion that an apparently popular government may act in the interest of the minority does not imply that any government promoting the welfare of the people is for that reason alone democratic. Marx always believed that every social class seeks to promote its own interest. From this it follows that no minority will ever promote the interest of a majority, unless their two interests should happen to coincide; but Marx, of course, did not believe they would coincide, since he taught that class conflicts are inevitable. He believed that only a government truly responsible to the people will govern for their advantage. The notion of an "elite" or "minority," governing independently of the peope's will and yet seeking their good—such a notion would have appeared to Marx purely utopian. If ever he taught anything consistently (and he was not seldom inconsistent), it was that the workers must seek their own salvation and that they cannot attain it until they have become the great majority of the people, democratically organized and fully aware of what they want.

Marx did, of course, believe that a class might be a majority and yet incapable of government. Such a class, in his opinion, were the peasants, destined in the end to disappear but, while they existed, always liable to be used as tools by such reactionaries as Louis Napoleon. The only progressive class were the proletariat. Since they alone could destroy the bourgeois ascendancy, truly popular government could not exist until the proletariat had become the majority.

If we want to know what Marx thought of proletarian democracy, we cannot do better than look at his pamphlet, *The Civil War in France*. The workers first created a government of their own in 1871 in Paris. Now, as Marx probably knew as well as anyone, a proletarian revolution in Paris, while Bismarck was the master of France, was not likely to be successful. And the Paris Commune, whatever its virtues and faults, was certainly disliked by the great majority of Frenchmen. But in Paris in 1871, because so many of the better-to-do had left the capital to avoid the rigors of the siege, the workers were certainly the majority. The Commune was certainly a proletarian government. Indeed, its proletarian character is much less open to doubt than that of any Russian government since 1917. Marx knew it was proletarian, and in *The Civil War in France* he pointed out those of its characteristics that best attested its proletarian character. Let me quote Marx's own words: "The Commune was formed of the municipal councillors chosen by universal suffrage in various wards of the town, responsible and revocable at short terms. The majority of its members were naturally working men or acknowledged representatives of the working class. The Commune was to be a working, not a parliamentary body, executive and legislative at the same time. Instead of continuing to be the agents of the central government, the police were at once stripped of their political attributes, and turned into the responsible and at all times revocable agents of the Commune. So were the officials of all other branches of the administration. From the members of the Commune downwards, the public service had to be done at workmen's wages. . . . Public functions ceased to be the private property of the tools of the central government."[3]

What is the most striking feature of this, Marx's classic description of proletarian democracy? It is surely his insistence on the very close and direct, almost day-to-day, responsibility of the governors to the governed. Now, though Marx was in some respects a severe critic of the Commune, he never criticized it for being the sort of democracy it was. He never suggested that, had it been dominated by a small and highly organized body of determined men who knew the people's interest better than they knew it themselves, it would have been either a better or a more democratic government. He said that the Commune made some fatal mistakes, and he attributed these mistakes largely to the Communards' misplaced respect for bourgeois institutions (e.g., the Bank of France). The Communards, then, if we are to draw the natural conclusion from what Marx said, were not really aware of what was to the greatest advantage of the work-

3. *The Civil War in France*, p. 40.

ers. But Marx did not therefore say, or even suggest, that the Commune was not properly democratic. On the contrary, he said of it that "it supplied the republic with the basis of really democratic institutions"; and also that "it was essentially a working-class government, the product of the struggle of the producing against the appropriating class, the political form at last discovered under which to work out the economic emancipation of Labour."[4] And nothing that Marx ever said (and he said very little) about the "dictatorship of the proletariat" can make a difference. As Engels said in 1891 to those who were frightened by the phrase: "Do you want to know what this dictatorship looks like? Look at the Paris Commune. That was the dictatorship of the proletariat."[5] We have it, then, on the highest possible authority that the dictatorship of the proletariat is incompatible with a political police.

Lenin had his own views, not to be found in Marx and Engels, about the relations of the proletarian political party to the proletariat and also about the peasantry. But none of these views imply a new conception of democracy. It would be absurd to interpret Lenin's writings before the October revolution as if they were apologies for Bolshevik action after that revolution. Lenin certainly believed, as his pamphlet *One Step Forward Two Steps Back* (Geneva, 1904) proves, that the Russian Social-Democratic Party must be organized and disciplined, that it must be distinct from the class (the proletariat) whose interest it promotes. "To forget the distinction between the vanguard and the whole of the masses that gravitate towards it, to forget the constant duty of the vanguard to raise ever wider strata to the most advanced level, means merely to deceive oneself, to shut one's eyes to the immensity of our tasks. . . ." The task of the party is to educate, to lead, to take the initiative; but Lenin nowhere suggests that it is justified in imposing its will on the proletariat, in leading it for its own good where it does not want to go. In this same pamphlet, Lenin quotes with approval Kautsky's assertion that "Democracy is not anarchy; it is the rule of the masses over their delegates, as distinct from other forms of government in which the alleged servants of the people are really the masters of the people." This is the description of democracy that Lenin quotes with approval in precisely that pamphlet in which he insists, with

4. *Ibid.*, p. 43.
5. In a Preface to a reprint to Marx's *The Civil War in France.*

the greatest energy, on the guiding role of what he calls the "vanguard of the proletariat."

Lenin, it is true, believed that the proletariat might make a successful revolution in Russia before it became the majority. He believed this because he thought that the Russian peasants were potentially a revolutionary class, who might be won over to a firm alliance with the urban workers. The proletariat would, of course, play the leading part, both during the revolution and after it; for the urban workers are par excellence the revolutionary class. But the relations of leader to led, as Lenin conceived them before 1917, both between the vanguard and the proletariat and between the proletariat and the peasants, were altogether "democratic," in what I have called the primary meaning of that word, common to Marx and the Western Liberals.

When the Bolsheviks made their revolution in the autumn of 1917, they and their allies, the Left Wing Socialist Revolutionaries, were supported by the great majority of the workers and the peasants. The workers and the peasants knew nothing of the ultimate purposes of their leaders; they were not, in the Marxist sense, "self-conscious" and politically organized classes having full confidence in their chosen leaders, because they shared their beliefs and relied on their wisdom and integrity. The workers and peasants supported the Bolsheviks and their allies, because they were the people who, at that time, promised them most of what they wanted. But later on, when the Bolsheviks were involved in a civil war, they found they could not rely as completely as they must if they were to achieve victory on the understanding and loyalty of the exploited classes on whose behalf they believed they were acting. Victory (and also the survival of the Bolsheviks) depended upon their becoming the masters rather than the servants of the classes for whose welfare they said they were fighting. Lenin did not hesitate to do whatever he thought necessary to achieve victory, for he believed that defeat would put off for a long time both socialism and proletarian democracy. If he did not force the workers and peasants to come to heel, he could not defeat their enemies; and while their enemies were undefeated the emancipation of the exploited classes was impossible. Lenin was probably quite well aware of what he was doing; he was depriving the workers and peasants, in what he believed was their own interest, of the little freedom they had recently acquired; and he was doing it to prevent their falling a prey once again to their former exploiters. He was depriving them of freedom in the present that they might have it more abundantly in the future. These hard decisions were, he thought, forced on him by the circumstances; but it is unlikely that he had illusions about what he was doing. He was not enlarging freedom, he was not establishing democracy. Though he may have sincerely believed that what he was doing was for the ultimate good of the people, he never suggested that that was alone sufficient to make his government democratic. No doubt he believed that what he did was necessary if genuine proletarian democracy were eventually to be possible; but there is no evidence that he was by this time so little a Marxist as to believe that a régime that had created a political police, had forcibly suppressed all rival parties, had assumed full control of the trade unions, and had evolved many other similar expedients during the civil war was democratic for no better reason than that the governors thought these things necessary for the ultimate good of the people. Before the revolution, Lenin had never dreamed that, should he ever become the ruler of Russia, he might be driven to such expedients. Circumstances had forced him on an even harder and more tortuous road than he had expected. It was, he thought, the road leading to socialism and proletarian democracy, but while he drove the workers and peasants along it, it is unlikely that so shrewd a man should have mistaken his own slogans and cries of exhortation for the voice of the people. No man likes to admit that what has happened is very different from what he expected, especially when he has had as large a hand as anyone in bringing it about. Lenin was naturally anxious to make as little fuss as he could about the expedients to which he was driven, to minimize their importance and to insist on their temporary character; but he did not deny them nor call them democratic. He continued to call the régime that had evolved during the civil war "the dictatorship of the proletariat," even though it had become something altogether unlike the proletarian democracy described by Marx in *The Civil War in France*. But we cannot believe that Lenin, who had made a very thorough study of that particular pamphlet, should not have noticed the difference. That he did not insist upon it, that he did not officiously point it out to other people, is no evidence that he had evolved a new conception of democracy, a conception that made it equivalent to government in the interest of the majority and not in accordance with their will.

We know that Lenin had some misgivings toward the end of his life about what was happening in Russia. Stalin has, perhaps, been less liable to suffer in this way. But he, too, seems to have remained loyal to the old Marxist and Liberal conception of democracy. In a speech he made in 1937, when he accepted nomination as a candidate for election to the Supreme Soviet, he said: "The point is not that our elections are universal, equal, secret, and direct, although that fact is itself of great importance. The point is that our universal elections will be carried out as the freest elections and the most democratic of any country in the world. Universal elections exist and are held in some capitalist countries, too, so-called democratic countries. But in what atmosphere are elections held there? In an atmosphere of class conflicts, in an atmosphere of class enmity, in an atmosphere of pressure brought to bear on the electors by the capitalists, landlords, bankers and other capitalist sharks . . . here, in our country, on the contrary elections are held in an entirely different atmosphere. Here there are no capitalists and landlords, and consequently, no pressure is exerted by propertied classes on non-propertied classes." Stalin did not mention any other kind of pressure, and he presumably intended his audience to understand that there was none. It does not matter, in the least, whether Stalin himself believed what he said, for that has nothing to do with the sense in which he was using the word "democratic." It may or may not correctly describe the political elections in the Soviet Union, but its meaning is clear enough. By calling those elections democratic, he was saying that in the U.S.S.R. the people freely choose the persons who are to govern them. The word "democratic" means for him just what Churchill and Roosevelt have usually meant when they have used it.

I hope I have said enough to establish my point. The sort of things that are called democratic by Easterners are certainly not the same as are called democratic in the West. But this does not mean that the word "democracy" is used in different senses on one side and the other of the "iron curtain." It means, rather, that Westerners and Easterners have different opinions about these things. When the bourgeois writer or politician calls Britain a democracy, he means that British governments are responsible to the people. He may be mistaken, but this is what he means. When Stalin calls the Soviet Union a democracy, he also means that the Soviet government is responsible to the people. He, too, may be mistaken, or he may not believe what he says; but it is what he wants to say. The primary meaning of "democracy," which is government by persons freely chosen by and responsible to the governed, is the same in Russia, Poland, and Yugoslavia as it is in France, Britain, and the Americas. The notion that "democracy" means to the Communists, government in the interest of the people, is, I think, an invention of Western journalists. It corresponds in no way whatever with the facts. Because the Communists may have ceased to behave as Marxists (and even Leninists) should, it does not follow that they have also ceased to speak the language of Marx. And Marx, a shrewd but not always clear writer, was seldom less ambiguous than when he spoke of democracy. I don't know who it was, in the West, who invented the "Eastern" conception of democracy. It was invented only a little time ago, and I rather suspect that the culprit is Professor Edward Hallett Carr.

The alleged difference between the "Western" and "Eastern" conceptions of democracy is the only one that has recently attracted much attention; and it is because I thought it important to clear away certain misunderstandings about it that I have devoted so much space to it. But it does not follow, because there is no essential difference between the "Eastern" and "Western" conceptions of democracy, that the word has only one meaning or that that meaning is clear and precise. I have said that the primary meaning of "democracy" is government by persons freely chosen by, and responsible to, the governed. This simple definition is not easily interpreted in terms of actual political phenomena. What constitutes a free choice? At what point does persuasion cease and intimidation begin? In other words, how can we ever know that the people's will is free? Even when there is no intimidation, can we say that an ignorant choice is free? If the elector does not understand the alternatives presented to him, can he be said to make a free choice between them? If conditions are such that the elector, having made his choice, has almost no power to control his deputy's actions, can the latter be truly responsible to him? What sort of relation between electors and their deputies is implied by the notion of responsibility? It may be that the deputy, though he owes his position in the first place to his electors, finds, as soon as he takes his seat in the legislature, that he is subject to influences to which it is easier and more profitable to submit than to the will of his constituents. There are two sorts of problems that the student of democracy can investigate: What is involved in the notions of political freedom and responsibility? and, What conditions must exist before this freedom and responsibility are possible?

Now, however many definitions there may be of "freedom" and "responsibility" and therefore of what I have called the primary meaning of democracy, it may yet be that these words have each only one meaning. No definition of a word is its meaning unless it is a correct definition. It is not definition but usage that gives meaning to a word. We can never argue from a multiplicity of definitions to a multiplicity of meanings. It would be different if people first defined the more important words they intended to use and then used them consistently in the senses defined. But they never do this, especially when they are political theorists. Even when they do offer definitions, they soon abandon them and use the words defined pretty much as other people do. And it is well they do so, for people who use private languages seldom talk sense. I do not want to deny the advantages of a technical and precise vocabulary, for without it science can scarcely make progress; but such a vocabulary is as much the product as it is the condition of the accumulation of knowledge. In spite of the difficulty of precise definition and the great variety of definitions offered, it seems to me that there is, after all, only one primary·meaning of "democracy," a meaning territorially limited only to the extent that the old Greek word has not been adopted by all the languages of the world.

What, then, are the other, secondary, meanings of "democracy"? And why should they be called secondary? A society is often called democratic when its members are free to form associations, to discuss what they please, to criticize their governments, to propagate their opinions, to worship God as they think he ought to be worshipped. These rights are said to be democratic. Most of them, but not all, must exist if democracy, in the primary sense, is to be possible. For if the people are not free to form associations, how can they give effective expression to their will? If they may not discuss what they please, how can they make a real choice between the alternatives put to them? And the rights to criticize government and to propagate opinions are equally necessary for the same reasons. These rights are valued not only because they are the conditions of democratic government; they are also valued—and this is often the main reason for the esteem in which they are held—because they are considered the means to the "good life" or to the "full development of the individual." What these ends are and whether these are the means to them is a matter that does not concern us. What does concern us is that they are called democratic rights because, in the opinion of those who so call them, democracy, i.e., government by the freely chosen and responsible agents of the governed, would be impossible without them. Otherwise, there would be no point in calling them democratic.

There are many other things that can be regarded as the indispensable conditions of democratic government. Equality of property or, at least, no more than moderate inequality; social equality; popular education; the existence of several independent political parties; the absence of all parties (*vide* Rousseau's *Social Contract*); the emancipation of women; the abolition of organized religion—all these things, and many more, have been called conditions of true popular government and, for that reason, democratic. Many devices, believed by some people to be democratic, have been called undemocratic by others, who thought that their function was to maintain the illusion and not the reality of popular government. Thus it was that parliamentarism, as it exists in the West, came to be called undemocratic or only formally democratic. And in a like manner, the freedom of the press, by those who believed it was the privilege of the few and only apparently the right of the many.

Now to call many different things by one name is not, in itself, to extend the meaning of that name. To say that the various conditions of democratic government are "democratic" may be only to say that there is some one quality they all have in common. But, as a matter of fact, the meaning of the adjective "democratic" (and therefore also of the substantive from which it is derived) has been greatly extended. It has often been used as if it meant whatever, on the particular occasion of its use, appeared to the user to be an indispensable condition of democratic government. Those who have so used it have forgotten the reason that first prompted them to do so; and they have therefore used it as if it meant the same thing as, to take only four examples, "equal" or "tolerant" or "free" or "classless." And because they have habitually used the word "democratic" as if it meant any one of these four (and innumerable other) qualities, that quality is one of its meanings.

Of the secondary meanings of "democratic," some are more often used east of the "iron curtain" and others more often west of it. But I dare say that many, if not most of them, are in common use on both sides of it. For instance, of the four meanings chosen at random in the last paragraph, "equal" and "free" are as much used by Easterners as Westerners; while "tolerant" is more peculiar to the West, and "classless" to the East.

II. THE CONDITIONS OF DEMOCRACY

Under what conditions is government by persons freely chosen by and responsible to the governed possible? It is in their answers to this question, and not in their views about the nature of democracy, that Marxists and Liberals have differed most. And it is also in their answers to this question that modern Communists have moved furthest away from Marx. The explanation of this latter fact is not far to seek. Marx had merely to show that parliamentarism is not what its adherents say it is; while modern Communists must also attempt to prove that what exists in the Soviet Union is more or less accurately described by the rulers of that country. Marx had much to attack and nothing to defend, except when he chose to put in a good word for such people as the Communards. But, today, the Communists, especially those who live in the West and are therefore exposed to daily criticism, are in a much more difficult position; for in politics attack is nearly always easier than defense. Besides, these Western apologists of Eastern democracy have to justify behavior they are powerless to control, behavior occurring in countries where many of the inhibitions prevalent in the West are unknown.

On the other hand, defenders of "bourgeois democracy" have a rather easier task than they once had. It is less obvious than it used to be that the workers are exploited. For instance, in Great Britain the workers are better off in many respects than they ever were; and they are so in spite of a considerable impoverishment of the community as a whole. The other classes accept this fact with a good grace that would have been impossible fifty years ago. They accept it because they have been "conditioned" by the political controversies of the last two generations, in which most of the best arguments were produced by the radicals. The right to property, except where the property is for personal use, is, of all rights, perhaps the least respected in modern England, where no one can do what He wants with his "own," if his "own" happens to be a factory or business. This right has already become as "formal" as any of the rights originally called "formal" by the critics of bourgeois democracy. What is more, the workers are better organized and better educated than ever before. All this does not mean that social equality exists in modern England, or that nobody receives an income except for work done, or that the political influence of every class is in proportion to its numerical strength. But it does mean that the "formal" democracy of the West, if it is formal, must be proved to be so by other arguments than those invented forty to eighty years ago. Before the Communists can have anything to say worth listening to about the Western democracies, they must first take a look at what they pretend to describe. Marx himself was always interested in the contemporary world, and he never tried to prove anything about it by quoting from authorities who wrote in the previous century. Until his disciples learn to follow his example, they can never hope to be formidable in controversy. But still, it is no use complaining that they are not worth listening to; they talk so loud, one cannot help but hear them; and it will, after all, be impossible to discuss the conditions of democracy without taking some notice of what they have to say.

a) First of all, we must try to answer the question: When can we know that a man has understood alternatives between which he must choose? As I have already suggested, this question must not be taken literally, for we can never know what it is that other men understand. We must put the question in this form: Under what conditions do we think we are justified in assuming that a man has understood the alternatives put to him well enough to be able to make a genuine choice between them? I think it is possible to give an answer, and that this answer must be vague. I am inclined to say that we ordinarily assume that a man has this understanding if he, being a person not abnormally stupid, has had about as much opportunity as other men, who are not experts, usually have to acquire information that is relevant. This is far, indeed, from being a precise statement, and I am not at all sure it corresponds with the truth. But it is not its lack of precision that gives rise to my doubts, for the words and phrases we use when we discuss human behavior seldom have precise meanings. My doubts arise because, not having seen this matter anywhere thoroughly discussed, I have no better opinions than my own to guide me. I put forward my account of it only tentatively. At the moment, it seems to me rather more plausible than any other I can think of.

It have been said, no doubt truly, that only experts (and they not always) understand the merits of most of the questions that modern electorates are expected to decide. But we do not say for that reason that the electors can never make a genuine decision, that because they choose in comparative ignorance they do not choose at all; or, if we do say it, we must conclude not only that democracy is impossible but also that it is not an illusion maintained for the benefit of any particular social class. Whatever the degree of knowledge required to make a man an expert, it is clear that the rich are no more experts than the poor. Modern society is too complicated for any of us to understand it, and we all (except the expert within the small compass of his competence), when we make up our minds about matters of public importance, choose in comparative ignorance of the alternatives that present themselves to our minds. It is true, and a truth of the greatest importance, that in politics no one knows exactly what he is doing, the real significance in terms of human misery and happiness of any decision he may take; but this melancholy truth is hardly relevant to the inquiry we are making. And in any case, its truth is no more incompatible with democracy than with oligarchy or autocracy. Governments exist, they make decisions and know something of the matters these decisions relate to; and they are influenced by many different people, who also know something of them. These modest facts are enough to make democracy, as well as oligarchy and autocracy, possible.

Under what circumstances does ignorance limit the political influence of a social class? We have seen that, in modern society, everyone, whatever his class, has only a little knowledge of most of the problems that governments are faced with. Even the expert is as ignorant as the next man about all except a few of them. Modern society is like a great building, dimly lit and full of holes and obstacles, in which no man can move except by groping his way; and even those (the experts) who have torches find their light put out as soon as they stray from the corners familiar to them. When comparative ignorance is the general rule, what is the knowledge that gives power? There are, I think, two answers to this question.

However ignorant or knowledgeable people may be about any-thing, they can yet have opinions and evolve a vocabulary in which to discuss it. Whoever does not use this vocabulary is not listened to; he is a man without influence. The working classes, until quite re-cently, did not know how to use the vocabulary of politics; they had almost nothing to say about most of the matters governments are concerned with. They had no political influence because they were inarticulate. Unfamiliar with the language of politics, they could not find the words with which to answer the questions put to them in that language. When they got the vote, they did not know what to do with it. They took the advice of those persons who seemed to them familiar with that language and at the same time well disposed toward themselves. It was rather because they were inarticulate than because they were ignorant that they were politically at a disadvantage. I do not mean to suggest that in politics nothing matters except noise. Knowledge, courage, and patience also have their place, as they do in every important sphere of human activity. I mean only that persons unfamiliar with the language in which business is currently transacted cannot take part in that busi-ness. And this is true, however inadequate and vague that language may be, however little suited to intelligent and perceptive discussion. For though a man who uses it with skill and conviction may have neither knowledge nor probable opinion, he will have what is often in practice much better: he will have authoritative opinion. He will appear to have knowledge and he will be listened to. My first answer, then, to the question: What is the knowledge that gives power? is this: It is the ability to use with conviction and authority the politi-cal vocabulary current in the society to which one belongs.

It seems to me that in the West the workers have become articu-late and that their representatives discuss political questions with almost as much conviction and authority as anyone else. If they lack knowledge, so, too, do other people; and they are no more than anyone else at a loss for words that the masses are inclined to take notice of. I think the workers, when they vote, understand the issues about as much and as little as their employers. That they do not do so, that they are kept in ignorance, that the political vocabulary current among them is one evolved in the interest of the rich—all these statements appear to me to be false. The political vocabulary in current use is much larger than it was two hundred years ago, and most of the words and phrases added to it were invented by radicals and socialists. Indeed, many of them were either coined by Marx or else made popular by him. The language of politics, as it is spoken in western Europe, is as much "proletarian" as it is anything else. The workers did not give birth to it; they found it ready for their use. But it is as well adapted to the discussion of their needs, aspirations, and prejudices as to those of any other social class. Of course, it is best adapted to the needs of politicians and intellectuals, who are not a social class but a professional group recruited from all classes. And it is but natural this should be so, for tools nearly always suit those persons best who most frequently use them.

The rich, someone will perhaps object, are surely better educated than the poor. It may be that they are. But what is it they know better? They know rather more about history, about literature, and about the arts. Their knowledge of history is so superficial as to add nothing to their wisdom in politics; and their other knowledge (such as it is) is irrelevant. Will anyone, who has often read the reports in Hansard of important debates in the House of Commons, venture to say that members of Parliament of working-class origin speak with less knowledge or less persuasively than the others? And the members of Parliament who are called "intellectuals," and who are, perhaps, rather better informed than the others, belong to all parties. The unversities, frequented in large numbers by the sons of workers as well as of capitalists, are almost the only places in which social, economic, and political questions are studied at all seriously. They are the institutions that do most to form the "climate" of intellectual opinion. It was not always so but is so now. And it is precisely from these same universities that, almost everywhere in western Europe except England, the hosts of Communist intellectuals emerge. It may be curious that they should produce so many professed "scientists" in a sphere in which science is perhaps not yet possible, but it does prove that they are not instruments of class domination. So much, then, for the view that in western Europe the workers and their friends, either because they are kept in ignorance or because they are misled by current prejudices, maintained (whether consciously or unconsciously) for the benefit of the propertied classes, have less than their proper share of political influence. Ignorance and prejudice exist in abundance, and we are all the worse off for their existence. But they are not maintained in anyone's interest. They are a special disadvantage to the poor only in this sense, that they make it more difficult to find effective remedies for evils that still weigh more heavily on some classes than on others. We must not deny these evils, nor minimize their importance. One of their causes, though not by any means the only one, is inequality of property. Those who benefit from this inequality do not want it abolished. But it does not follow that the function of the political, social, and economic theories prevalent in the West is to maintain that inequality. If democracy is still an illusion among us, it is certainly not because the poor are "indoctrinated," nor yet because they are so ignorant and so busy that, in Lenin's phrase, they "cannot be bothered with politics." The disadvantages of ignorance and preoccupation they share with the other classes.

The other knowledge that gives power is, of course, what is commonly called expert knowledge. In the political sphere, it is the civil servants and professional politicians who possess it. It is knowledge that must be distinguished from the mere ability to make skilful and eloquent use of the current political vocabulary. It is knowledge about administration, parliamentary procedure, party organization, propaganda. It is knowledge that is essentially technical. That a minority should possess it does not of itself limit democracy, any more than the special knowledge of the architect limits the free choice of his client. On the contrary, it is only because the architect has this knowledge that his client can reasonably expect to get the sort of building he wants. The better an agent knows his job, the more likely that his principal will be satisfied. And this is not the less true because the agent offers advice about ends as well as means. It is only when the agent uses his special knowledge to his own advantage[6] or to that of persons to whom he is not responsible that he uses it to thwart his principal, to limit his power of getting what he wants.

To what extent do politicians and civil servants use their knowledge in this way, not as agents of the people but for purposes of their own? I can only attempt (and that with much hesitation) an answer to this question as it relates to Great Britain. I hope I am not prejudiced, but I believe that Great Britain is as much a democracy and as honest a democracy as any in the world. And yet I believe that

6. I mean, of course, when his advantage is not compatible with that of his client. It does not matter how selfish an agent is so long as he is true to his trust.

this special political knowledge is often used in this country by politicians (but not nearly so much by civil servants) to promote their own and their friends' interests. If this is true of Great Britain, it is probably not less true of the other Western democracies. This is not due to the exceptional dishonesty of politicians but to circumstances peculiar to their profession. When a man employs an architect, he gives him precise instructions. Not only does the architect know what is expected of him; he is also able to consult his client as often as he pleases and, whenever he is in doubt, to ask for new instructions. But the politician receives "instructions" that are always extremely vague; he receives them only at determinate intervals, though the situation may have changed completely between any two of them; and the "instructions" he receives are not first elaborated by his constituents and then modified in consultation with himself, but are chosen from among a few alternatives offered by often highly organized political parties. The politician, even when he is by nature exceptionally honest, soon discovers that he is the agent of people who have only the vaguest notion of what they want, and that he must attempt to give it them with the assistance of persons who, like himself, though they may be skilful parliamentarians well acquainted with the rules of the game, know little enough about the best means of creating the kind of society desired by the electorate. The man who employs an architect knows exactly what he wants and the architect knows how to provide it. The electors who choose a representative, though they prefer him and his sort of talk to whatever else has been offered them, know rather better what they do not than what they do want; while he and his colleagues, though expert politicians, have much less knowledge than is required to bring into existence what they suppose their electors want. One man or a few men, when they make decisions affecting only themselves, find it easy to give precise instructions to their agents; and because these instructions are narrow and precise it is easy for their agents (e.g., engineers, architects, doctors, etc.) to acquire the special knowledge needed to carry them out; and their clients can readily discover whether they have done so. But when large numbers of people try to make decisions affecting the welfare of great communities, they can hardly give such precise instructions; and even if they could, it would be most difficult for anyone to acquire the knowledge of how to achieve such vast objectives, and for the people to decide whether they had been achieved.

The will of the people, such as it is, must be elicited; and it can be elicited only by political parties that soon acquire interests of their own. Though every member of the community should be intelligent and articulate, the people, as a whole, cannot take the initiative, as a man does when he decides to consult his doctor. The people cannot talk; they can only make signs on appropriate occasions. It is the business of political parties to organize these occasions, to put alternatives before the people, so that, when they see what pleases them best, they can make signs on pieces of paper.

Two sorts of political organizations have come into existence in the West: political parties and what the Americans call "pressure groups." The function of pressure groups is to promote the interests of various sections of the community by trying to influence the decisions of legislators, ministers, and civil servants. They can exert pressure either because politicians fear that if they do not do what is asked of them the sections whose interests these groups represent will not support them at the next elections, or else because they have rewards to offer. Among the most powerful pressure groups in all free industrial countries are the trade unions. But it is the businessmen who have formed much the largest number of these groups; and, though they have fewer votes to offer at elections, they are also, in the aggregate, much wealthier. They can offer directorships in large and prosperous companies and many other rewards.

Now, it cannot be denied that political parties, like all large organizations, always tend to become oligarchic. It is not merely that their active members are never more than a minority of the supporters who vote for them at the polls; it is also that, among these members, some few at the top possess more power than all the others put together. And the same is true of pressure groups. Those that represent large sections of the population, precisely because they are large, tend to become oligarchic; while the others, in any case, represent only small numbers of people. Whenever politicians use their special knowledge, their skill at manipulating political machinery, to further party ends or for the benefit of those who control pressure groups, democracy is circumscribed. There can be no denying that they do this very often. It is not merely that party bosses and pressure groups have much to offer to the docile politician; it is also that their requirements are much more precise than the "mandate" received from the electorate, a mandate of which, in any case, the politicians, guided by conventions current among themselves, are the only interpreters.[7] It is always much easier to satisfy the precise demands of individuals and small groups than to give effect to the vague will of the people or to promote their welfare. We must not be surprised if politicians, like other men, take the line of least resistance.

Mankind has never known pure democracy; the tendency toward oligarchy has always been too strong, and no devices yet invented have done more than moderate it. Oligarchy is the normal form of government. Democracy and autocracy are ideals never fully attained, though, by taking thought, men can eliminate more and more of what is foreign to whichever of the two they wish to establish. Even in a classless society,[8] the tendency toward oligarchy would exist; and the larger and more complex that society, the stronger that tendency. Where there are classes, the tendency is, of course, stronger than the mere size and complexity of society could account for; and this is especially true when the poor, though they have the vote, are illiterate and unorganized. But if they do have the vote and are literate and organized, they use (as they are doing in Europe and America) what political power they have to increase their economic security and to reduce the privileges of other classes. The greater their success, the smaller the importance of a multiplicity of classes as a factor reinforcing the tendency natural to all societies toward oligarchy. The rich, not because they are less ignorant but because the pressure groups representing them, though smaller, are the most numerous and have the most to offer, probably still possess, in all the Western democracies, political influence much greater than in proportion to their numbers. But this influence has diminished and is diminishing even more rapidly than their wealth. Whether it will continue to do so is another matter.

b) I have discussed the sort of understanding required to make a free choice at elections possible, and also the ways in which special knowledge can be used by its possessors to thwart or override the will of the people. Now, when agents use their knowledge to

7. They are, however, liable to punishment at the polls should the people convict them of too gross a misinterpretation.

8. The word "class" can be so defined as to make it a tautology that wherever there is oligarchy, there must be more than one class. The politically privileged can be treated as a separate class just because they are privileged. But if classes are defined, as Marxists define them, in terms of the properties they own or do not own, then it is possible for a classless society to be an oligarchy.

thwart their principals, they cease to act as their agents. I have therefore also, though only by implication, given my views about the extent to which, in the Western democracies, the peoples' representatives are truly responsible to them. The next question to be considered is this: When can we reasonably assume that no person or set of persons has prescribed all or most of the alternatives between which the electors are expected to choose? Every human choice is limited by the situation in which it occurs; and when a man has innumerable alternatives to choose from, we rather pity than congratulate him. That the practical alternatives before me are limited in number is not in itself a restriction on my freedom. I must, if I am to understand or believe I understand what I am doing, be familiar with the circumstances in which I act. I must have only a few alternatives, and each must appear to me sufficiently distinct from the others. My freedom is restricted only if some other person has the power to decide what these alternatives shall be, if the area of my choice is confined by someone whose interest it is that certain alternatives should be denied to me.

In the West, the alternatives between which electors must choose are determined beforehand by the political parties; and no party, unless it is fairly well organized and has money to spend, can make its alternative known to the people. But no single person or set of persons acting together determine all the alternatives. Nor are the persons who determine them all members of a single class, who, though they may not act in concert, are unconsciously moved to prescribe for the people only what would benefit their own class. Active politicians in the West no longer all belong to any one class; and the interests they have in common are not class but professional interests. The parties they belong to are independent of one another and are genuine rivals for power. Parties do not make programs in order to restrict the people's choice. They are not interested in either enlarging or restricting that choice. They make their programs to attract votes. Like all competitors for popular favor (and this is so whether they are selfish or unselfish), they promise the people what they think the people want or can be induced to want. Even if we suppose that every party is selfish, that it is much more inclined to make attractive promises than to keep them, it is still true that the others are interested in exposing this fact. The vagueness of the promises may make it easier to insist that they have been kept, or the opposition of other parties may provide an excuse for not keeping them. These are defects not to be avoided in a populous and complex society. But the competition of political parties, when it is real and not merely apparent, does make it the interest of each, not only to make attractive promises, but to try to keep them. Where there is competition for votes, the competitors must try to please as many people as possible; and this is true even when the competitors accept rewards from the rich. A party is not worth bribing unless it delivers the votes; and it cannot, in competition with other parties, deliver them unless it somehow contrives to please the people. A small party with no ambition to become great may be content to serve a minority. But a large party and a real competitor for power, however conservative it may be, must always serve two masters, of which one will be the people. In a democracy, the party of the rich, subject to unceasing criticism from the other parties, soon finds that it can serve its clients only by making ever greater concessions to the poor. The cost of defending privilege continually rises. Meanwhile, the concessions made to the poor strengthen them, and those who speak for them become more effective competitors for power.

Democracy, as Plato understood and regretted, is of its nature more favorable to the poor than the rich; and this is as true of parliamentary democracy as of any other kind. Democracy and social equality are brothers. They are not, for that reason, inseparable, but no society will enjoy the one for long without trying to introduce the other. By social equality, I do not mean absolute equality of riches; I mean only the absence of inequalities great enough to create distinctions of class. If the question is asked: Is social equality prior to political democracy, or is the opposite true? the answer is, I think, that we have no good reason for believing that either is necessarily prior to the other. In modern Europe, the demand for democracy did not arise until the poor had become less poor than they used to be, but in the meantime the rich had also become richer, so that it was an increase in general prosperity rather than greater equality that caused Western societies to move toward democracy. But as soon as something like genuine democracy was established, one reform was introduced after another to increase the security and well-being of the poor at the expense of the tax-paying rich.

It has been said that in a democracy several independent and competing parties are not always necessary. Those who have said it have not had in mind a society so small that there is no need for organized parties to present alternatives to vast numbers of people. On the contrary, they have had in mind the largest country in the world and one of the most populous. Their argument has been something like this: Several parties exist only where there are several rival classes, so that in a society soon to become classless and in which the workers, the great majority of the people, are the masters of the state, there is, no need for more than one party. Or else they have argued that in a "proletarian" democracy, though other classes may survive in large numbers for a time, only one party is needed because the workers, who are the ruling class, though not already, are soon destined to become the great majority. These arguments are not to be found in Marx, and we can only guess what he would have thought of their inventors.

Confronted by such statements one is at first tempted to leave them alone. Who would argue with a man, seated in Trafalgar Square and not apparently blind, who asserted that the Nelson column is ten miles high? But he would be best left alone only because those who heard him would not believe him. A false assertion, however astonishing, is always worth an argument, if there are people innocent enough to take it seriously. How could anyone know that the number of parties must be the same as the number of classes? Can this be known a priori? But we are concerned with politics and not with an abstract science. Is it a truth vouched for by experience? But there have sometimes been four or five times as many parties in France as in Britain. Does it follow that the French have four or five times as many rival classes? And when, as sometimes happens within the space of a few years, the number of parties is halved, and then again, after a little while, is once more what it was, does it mean that half the classes in society have died and been born again? If it is said that, though where there are several rival classes there will be several parties, it does not follow that there will be the same number of each, how then can we infer that where the workers, being the great majority, are the unchallengeable masters of the state, there will be only one party? If classes confront one another as rivals, is it not more likely that each will endeavor to present a united front to the others, than that a class, already predominant and much more numerous than any of the others, will do so? In a proletarian state, where private property in the means of production has been abolished, where the urban workers and collectivized peasants are the immense majority, in a society soon to become classless and in which the ruling class has no serious rival for power, there can be no need for a united front against domestic enemies. But it is inconceivable that people, however much they may have interests in common, should never have differences of opinion about how those interests are best to be promoted. It is often said by the apologists of "one-party proletarian democracy" that, in the West, the bourgeois, despite all appearances to the contrary, are the ruling class. They are admittedly only a minority and yet, according to those people, they somehow contrive to maintain their ascendancy though they do not themselves all belong to one party nor forbid other classes to form parties. Do these people really believe in the immense natural superiority of capitalists over workers, for this is the only assumption that can make sense of their argument? A thousand sheep had better maintain a united front, though there is only one wolf among them; but ten wolves ruling a thousand sheep can afford (though they, too, have interests in common against the sheep) to differ and even to quarrel with one another.

Rousseau disliked parties, and he taught that the will of the people can find expression only where they do not exist. He was opposed to representative government, and he preferred the small state in which alone direct democracy is possible. He was, no doubt, right; it is in the small state, without classes, without parties and with no inequalities of wealth great enough to make some men subservient to others, that democracy is likely to be least imperfect. But such states are no longer possible; or, if they do exist, they cannot be independent. In large states, democracy must be representative and it cannot function, even as imperfectly as it does, without parties. Now, parties, like all other organized bodies, have a natural tendency toward oligarchy; and where there is only one party, those who dominate it are the master of the state. Democracy is impossible in large states unless there are several independent and competing parties, for it is this competition which alone insures that to please the people is at least one of the indispensable conditions of obtaining power. This would be true even if there were such a thing as the "Eastern conception of democracy," for rulers who do not need to please the people will not for long seek to serve their interests. This will be true "until philosophers become kings." But perhaps there are people who believe that, somewhere in the world, this miracle has happened?

XXVI

ITHIEL DE SOLA POOL

AMBIGUITY AND MISUSE

All words in the natural language are ambiguous. In general, the greater their emotional charge the more ambiguous they are. "Democracy" falls under that rule. Furthermore, in a conflict situation, uncopyrighted favorably charged terms originally identified with one of the parties quickly lose their specificity of reference and are reinterpreted by the other party to cover its message too. This principle is a special aspect of the principle of minimum differentiation discovered by the economists in imperfect competition. "The general rule for any new manufacturer coming into an industry is 'make your product as like the existing products as you can without destroying the differences.'"[1] The ideal solution is to copy every distinctive claim of your rival, but to add one or a few uncopyable distinctions of your own. If your competitor puts out his soap in a red and yellow box and calls it "Whistle," put yours out in a red and yellow box and call it "Yodel" but add that it contains a patented ingredient "Lustrium."

In the political sphere this takes the form of taking over the enemy's slogans and promises. This is easily demonstrated by comparing platforms of rival parties. They seldom differ much. In the United States this uniformity is summed up in the popular bromide "We are all Republicans; we are all Democrats." In France one might coin a similar quip about Radicals and Socialists.

This tendency toward minimum differentiation varies in strength inversely as the number of rival parties (all other factors, as always, being constant). In the economic struggles of firms, consciousness of the competitor naturally varies as his role in the total market situation. In politics, in addition to this factor, there is the common rule that one must gain 50 per cent of the vote to govern. In a multiparty system where no party hopes to gain this and govern alone, the party may appeal to a special interest group and try to represent

1. G. Boulding, *Economic Analysis* (New York, 1941), p. 601.

solely its solid vote. In a two-party system, however, no party can hope to govern unless it can gain a majority for itself in the not too distant future. Unless interest groups happen to be so divided as to give very nearly a 50-50 split of the vote—a rare situation—then each party must appeal, at least in part, to the same interest groups as its rival. Neither party can afford to permit its rival the solid favor of the largest groups of the population. When one party does gain such a hold, the other may as well give up and usually does, permitting a realignment by a split in the dominant party. A model illustration is the collapse of the Federalist Party after 1800 when the growth of the agrarian West made its subsequent success improbable. Eventually the Democratic Party split, giving birth to a successor party to the Federalists, the Whigs, who, however, were sufficiently demagogic to be viable. The Whigs, unlike the Federalists, had the wisdom to appropriate the democratic symbolism.

In view of this general pattern of minimum differentiation, "democracy" was bound to undergo confusion of meaning as soon as it became a successfully used symbol of identification. Democracy did not become a positive symbol for any major political movement until the French Revolution. It is only in retrospect that we can apply the term "democratic" to the ideologies of the Puritan revolutionaries, John Locke, or the American revolutionaries. "Democratic" was generally a term of condemnation in their days. "Commonwealth," "free government," "political liberty," or "republic" were the ideals proclaimed by the forerunners of modern democracy. It was only in the last decade of the eighteenth century that self-proclaimed democrats became a major political force. For about forty years their possession of the word was largely unchallenged, their conservative opponents being glad to damn them with their own label. Then as "democracy" became more popular, the inevitable borrowing took place. In the United States the election of 1840 may be taken as the dividing line. In France the writings of de Tocqueville (discussed below) and the debate between the *Reforme* and the *National*[2] on who were the true democrats may be taken as the dividing line. In England the transition was later and slower, perhaps due to the monarchy.[3] After this time democracy

2. Cf. A. Rosenberg, *Democracy and Socialism* (New York, 1939), pp. 44 ff.
3. Cf. the recent poll report that 95 per cent of Swedes, 88 per cent of Americans, 67 per cent of Netherlanders, 65 per cent of Frenchmen, 57 per cent of Canadians, but only 50 per cent of Englishmen thought they had democracy in their homeland (*Public Opinion Quarterly*, XI [1947], 282 ff.).

became a more and more amorphous symbol, until by 1870 it had undergone a marked change of meaning and had become a widely accepted symbol of the status quo rather than the opposite. By World War I democracy had become so diffuse a symbol that it was possible to make it in many countries the goal of comprehensive national unity in the struggle against the enemy.

The period since then, particularly the years since World War II, have been marked by global political polarization between parties both of which have adopted the term democracy. Now, when there is a world-wide two-party struggle going on, it is clearly impossible for either party to yield the highly valued symbol of "democracy" to the other. At the same time, the real issues between these rival political philosophies grow sharper. As the real issues become sharper, naturally the indignation of each side about the appropriation of one of its favorite key symbols by the other also increases. Each side claims that it alone uses the term "democracy" properly and that the other side distorts it.

Which side is "right" in its use of the word democracy is strictly speaking a meaningless question. All definitions are arbitrary. Anyone has a right to define any term in any way he wishes. The only demand that may legitimately be made of any theorist is for explicitness and clarity of definition, and even that requirement cannot be successfully asked of lay publics. When a word is actually used by large groups of people it is mere pedantry to ask if it is used correctly. Whatever meaning or series of related meanings it is given by the public is its meaning.

The scholar faced by such a situation may profitably probe two types of problems. He may conduct a semantic analysis designed to distinguish the variety of meanings confused in the natural language and to formulate precise definitions of each. Also, he may conduct a historical investigation into how and why these usages have changed through time. Growing out of these investigations charges could be levied, although not charges of "misuse." One party or another could be accused of singular ambiguity or contradictions in its use of a term. Similarly, a party could be charged with either deliberately, or unconsciously, confusing the issue by changing a historically accepted usage.

THE CLASSICAL VERSUS THE TWO MODERN USES

a) *The classical use.*—Although the word "democracy" has undergone recent drastic transformations, it had a fairly uniform meaning from when it was coined in ancient Greece until the nineteenth century. This meaning ranged between the related concepts of "government by the many" and "government by the poor." Aristotle, who belongs to the minority of writers using the latter of these definitions, discusses the distinction between them, indicating that this was probably a subject of debate in ancient Greece.[4] But until modern times the definition was always some variant of government by the demos.

In contrast to this conception stand *both* of the outstanding contemporary conceptions of democracy. The usual Western conception is that of representative government with extensive civil liberties. The Eastern conception is that of government by an élite, on behalf of the many, or poor. At first glance it would seem that the Russian conception is closer to the historical meaning than is the Western. In a strictly formal sense this is true. The verbal changes involved in getting from the classic to the Russian definition are smaller than those involved in getting to the Western definition. Aristotle would have understood Vyshinsky, but not Thomas E. Dewey.

In a realistic sense, however, Western "democracy" is far closer to classical "democracy" than is Russian, since the facts referred to in the Western definition are largely correlates of classical "democracy" under modern conditions, while the facts referred to by the Russian definition are incompatible with classical "democracy." Pericles could have operated in London or Paris, but not in Moscow. Let us document some of these assertions.

The narrow Western concept of "democracy" as a way of making decisions through the popular election of representative assemblies is quite new. The older usage would have restricted the term "democracy" to government by direct participation of the masses of the people. The broader term "republic" would have covered the modern Western type of representative government. The *Federalist Papers*, for example, define a republic as "a government which derives all its powers directly or *indirectly* from the great body of

4. Aristotle *Politics* 1279b ff.

the people."[5] Democracy used to mean rule *directly by* a cross-section of the common people.

Election, the distinctive mark of democracy in the current Western sense, results in rule by a selected élite, and is thus anything but a purely democratic measure in the classical sense. Aristotle, for example, considered election of officials to be the characteristic oligarchic procedure in contrast to the democratic lot. In elections, a body of voters will choose persons from among the higher status levels in the group. The result is a governing body representing the views of the élite. That this is so has been implicitly recognized by those who have wished to make republics less democratic by a process of repeated or indirect election. The framers of the United States Constitution (whose oligarchic bias has been demonstrated by Beard) resorted to this device for choosing senators and the president so as to assure their selection from the élite of the élite. De Tocqueville placed great emphasis on this device as a way to mitigate democracy. Granted, election of representatives may be as close to town-meeting democracy as is practicable in a modern nation state, still there has been a change which we should not deny in the meaning of the term.

That the classic conception of democracy was indeed participation in ruling by the masses themselves becomes abundantly clear if we look at the amazingly consistent democratic programs down through the ages.

"For all to rule and be ruled in turn," was, according to Aristotle, a principle of liberty and the basis of democracy.[6] To achieve this democracy in extreme form he suggested among other things:[7] election by lot, short terms of office, rotation of office, a weak bureaucracy, pay for public office, abolition of property qualifications and wide extension of citizenship, popular juries, conversion of private associations into public ones, social welfare and security measures, redistribution of land or graduated taxes, avoidance of standing armies.

Similar programs have marked democratic parties all through history. Skipping to the nineteenth century, we find that the Chartist program included: universal suffrage, the secret ballot, annual par-

5. *The Federalist*, No. 38. My emphasis. This corresponds also to Montesquieu's distinction between democratic and aristocratic republics.
6. Aristotle *Politics* 1317a ff.
7. *Ibid.* 1317b–1320b.

liaments, payment for members of parliament.

The program of the democratic wing of the American Revolution as culminated in Jacksonian democracy included: short terms of office ("Where annual elections end there tyranny begins"), rotation of office (Tenure of Office Act), a weak bureaucracy, pay for public office, abolition of property qualifications and easy extension of citizenship (manhood suffrage), suspicion of corporations, social welfare measures (abolition of imprisonment for debt, cheap loans, etc.), cheap land, avoidance of standing armies, general extension of education.

Popular juries already existed, so of Aristotle's list only the lot had no counterpart. Universal education is a significant modern addition.

One could cite in the same way various programs of 1848, but to avoid repetition let us skip to the outstanding spokesman of modern socialism, Karl Marx. His program was substantially the same. Some might object that Marx was not a democrat, and by either the current Western or Eastern definition perhaps that is so. Here, however, we are looking at "democracy" in historical context, and Marx was certainly a democrat in the classical tradition. First we might note that he considered himself one. The miserable phrase "dictatorship of the proletariat" which has since caused so much confusion was used only three times in his writing.[8] On the other hand he called himself a democrat and talked of democracy all through his lifetime. As Rosenberg has shown, the Communist movement was part and parcel of the democratic movement until after 1848. Marx was vice-president of the "Democratic Union" in Brussels in 1847. In the *Communist Manifesto* he describes the revolution and incidentally defines democracy as follows: "The first step in the revolution by the working class is to raise the proletariat to the position of ruling class, to establish democracy." The immediate measures listed in the Manifesto as steps in the democratic program include: abolition of property in land, a graduated income tax and abolition of inheritance, equal obligation on all to work, free education for all.

Later on the experience of the Paris Commune of 1871 filled out Marx's conception of the program of the revolution and in *The*

8. *Class Struggles in France* (1850); letter to Weydemeyer, 1852; *Critique of the Gotha Program* (1875). Cf. Lucien Laurat, *Le Marxisme en faillite?* (Paris, 1939), pp. 41 f.

Civil War in France he added: universal suffrage, short terms, the recall, abolition of the standing army, abolition of the bureaucracy, elective, recallable judges.

Thus we find the classical democratic program largely unchanged over 2,000 years.

All of these democratic programs have been listed, however, not to show their similarity—striking as that may be—but to demonstrate their uniform emphasis upon popular self-government in the most literal sense: ruling and being ruled in turn, raising the proletariat to the position of ruling class. All of the specific measures are designed either to reduce class distinction (i.e., to increase the number among the influential) or to increase the control of the citizen over the office-holder, or finally to increase the number and representativeness of the citizens holding office. Thus democracy until the middle of the nineteenth century implied nothing so much as a social equality that was not merely equality before the law, but an actual equality of influence.

De Tocqueville's *Democracy in America* is, perhaps, the most famous illustration of the identification of the two concepts, democracy and equality. In this book the words are synonymous. They differ only in emphasis, the one emphasizing the economic and social facet of the complex, the other emphasizing the political. On the first page of the Introduction, de Tocqueville identifies equality and democracy in stating the subject of the book. A little later he summarizes a section called "The Striking Characteristic of the Social Condition of the Anglo-Americans Is Its Essential Democracy," with the sentences: "America then exhibits in her social state an extraordinary phenomenon. Men are there seen on a greater equality in point of fortune and intellect, or in other words, more equal in their strength, than in any other country in the world." In 1835 "democracy" clearly still retained for de Tocqueville its classical meaning.

Because of this fact, civil liberty, which is an essential of the current Western definition of democracy, was then not at all identified by him with democracy. On the contrary the problem of *Democracy in America* was: "How could liberty be preserved in the face of the inevitable growth of democracy?" The tyranny of the majority was his great phobia.

In this he was not alone. A large nineteenth-century literature exists on the conflict of liberalism and democracy. This is not the place to survey it. Suffice it to note that it was only gradually over the last century that the concept "democracy" was adopted by the individualist tradition and reinterpreted to include personal freedom as an essential. Until this redefinition was accomplished, self-styled liberal writers feared democracy as a form of despotism.

b) *Transition to the Western use.*—This redefinition and assimilation of the term "democracy" is apparent in the writings of de Tocqueville himself. The first volume of *Democracy in America* which appeared in 1835 shows no signs of it and sticks to the classical conception. The second volume, which appeared in 1840, seemed to show an even greater expectation of democratic despotism than the first. This, however, may be because in the latter volume his attention was more directed toward French than American conditions. At the same time he began to have doubts about how tyrannical democracy, even in its despotic forms, would be: "I had remarked during my stay in the United States that a democratic state of society, similar to that of the Americans, might offer singular facilities for the establishment of despotism. . . .

"A more accurate examination of the subject and five years of further meditation, have not diminished my fears, but have changed their object. . . .

"It would seem that if despotism were to be established among the democratic nations of our days, it might assume a different character; it would be more extensive and more mild; it would degrade men without tormenting them. . . . This same principle of equality which facilitates despotism tempers its rigor. We have seen how the customs of society become more humane and gentle in proportion as men become more equal and alike."[9]

By 1848 de Tocqueville was using "democracy" in a new sense and identifying it with liberty. The temper of the times required compromise by the more conservative elements. "Democracy" was adopted by them against more radical Communist symbols. Speaking in the Assembly during the great 1848 debate on the right to work, de Tocqueville made the statement, quoted in the UNESCO document, in which he used the term "democracy" in its new sense: "La démocratie et le socialisme ne se tiennent que par un mot, l'égalité; mais remarquer la différence: La démocratie veut l'égalité

9. Alexis de Tocqueville, *Democracy in America* (New York, 1945), II, 316 ff.

dans la liberté, et le socialisme veut l'égalité dans la gêne et dans la servitude."

By now it should be clear that the new (liberal-parliamentary) and old (classical) conceptions of democracy are not the same. We have seen that the term "republic" once covered the modern Western conception of democracy, and referred to oligarchic as well as democratic situations. We have said that "democracy" meant rule by direct participation of the people, and we have seen this illustrated by typical democratic programs. We have seen that classical democracy meant social equality since rule by the many means the diffusion of influence until the rank and file and élite are one. Certainly, periodic popular ratification of the policies of an élite is a very thinned-down version of the idea of popular government conveyed by the classical conception of democracy.

c) Transition to the Eastern use.—In the Eastern development, the conception of "democracy" has also undergone changes. In the Leninist version of Marxism a shift was made from the concept of government *by* the people to government *for* the people.

The root of the Eastern conception of democracy is the organismic fallacy. From Karl Marx to now the failure to adequately analyze the problem of the relation of the individual to the group has gradually led further and further away from the classical conception of democracy. Karl Marx was a democrat in the classical sense. If he differed from other democrats it was only in being consistent to the point of fantasy. Democracy is an ideal that realistic advocates try to achieve to the extent possible. Marx took total realization as on the order of the day. This can be seen if we examine Marx's major philosophical work, *The German Ideology*.

In his later works, especially *Capital*, he "proved" the inevitability of revolution through an economic analysis which showed that society was becoming more and more polarized. The economic proof, however, merely confirmed a conclusion Marx had already come to on other grounds. In *The German Ideology* the conclusion is the same: the condition of the masses gets worse and worse and the chasm between them and their exploiters gets bigger and bigger. But the proof has nothing to do with economics. It turns entirely on the individual's need for freedom.

The division of labor, according to Marx, enslaves. The social role in which an individual finds himself determines his way of life.

Complete freedom becomes possible only when the individual can live a many-sided life, that is can engage in any activity he wishes unrestricted by a predetermined social role. In Marx's own words: "... as soon as labor is distributed, each man has a particular exclusive sphere of activity, which is forced upon him and from which he cannot escape. He is a hunter, a fisherman, a shepherd, or a critical critic, and must remain so if he does not want to lose his means of livelihood; while in communist society ... society regulates the general production and thus makes it possible for me to do one thing today and another tomorrow, to hunt in the morning, fish in the afternoon, rear cattle in the evening, criticize after dinner, just as I have a mind, without ever becoming hunter, fisherman, shepherd, or critic."[10]

It is man's reaction to enslavement by the division of labor which makes the revolution inevitable. Estrangement from control over their conditions of life has rendered the great mass of men powerless over the outcome of their labor, i.e., propertyless. When this happens and when at the same time productive forces exist to produce a high level of wealth and culture, men will revolt.

Thus comes the Communist revolution. It is the instrument by which the heterogeneity of modern life is replaced by a homogeneous community. This is a world community with all national divisions eliminated. It is also a community in which the separation of town and country has been broken down. Most important of all the division between direction (or mental labor) and menial work (or physical labor) is also abolished. The individual in this ideal community which has no hierarchy and no social structure is completely free and controls his own destiny.

Marx, however, fully realized that in a modern industrial society the individual could not gain control of his own destiny by privately appropriating his own individual means of existence. The new society would be communal, the individuals collectively and consciously controlling the means of their existence. Mankind would then freely, consciously, and rationally plan nature rather than being controlled by it. It must be emphasized, however, that free and conscious control is by the community, not by a segment of it that does the mental labor.

10. Karl Marx and Friedrich Engels, *The German Ideology* (New York, 1939), p. 22.

"With the community of revolutionary proletarians . . . it is as individuals that the individuals participate in it. It is just this combination of individuals . . . which puts the conditions of the free development and movement of individuals under their control—conditions which were previously abandoned to chance and had won an independent existence over against the separate individuals just because of their separation as individuals, and because their combination had been determined by the division of labor, and through their separation had become a bond alien to them."[11]

This is just about all that Marx tells us about the future Communist community, but even though he refused to write the kitchen recipes of the future, we have enough here to state categorically that the utopia is one of total democracy. The development of the free personality capable of self-activity, of spontaneity and initiative is indeed the goal of the whole thing. This personality type Marx expected to see realized in the course of class struggles. Marx did not differ from John Stuart Mill and others in thinking that a prerequisite of socialism was the education of the proletariat, but he disagreed with them on the curriculum suited to the purpose. Not school lessons but the experience of aggressiveness and self-reliance in struggle was what he expected to do the job. "We say to the workers: You have got to go through fifteen, twenty, fifty years of civil wars and national wars not merely in order to change your conditions but in order to change yourselves and become qualified for political power."[12] Whatever the merits of this as educational theory, it is clear that Marx was intensely concerned with the development of a democratic self-reliant personality type.

Marx, however, never really faced the problem of the relationship of the individual and the group. The modern sociologist familiar with sociometry or the Western Electric studies takes it for granted that every group, even the smallest, rapidly acquires a hierarchy. Some members will initiate, some will not. Some will be subordinate and some superior. This seems an inevitable characteristic of group activity, and the larger the group the more complex will be its structure. But Marx would not have admitted this inevitability. Although he never faced the problem directly, his works seem to say that hierarchy is a product of a certain type of econ-

11. *Ibid.*, p. 75.
12. Karl Marx and Friedrich Engels, *Correspondence* (New York, 1936), p. 92.

omy, and that modern technology is producing a society where free association of equals will be possible and adequate to cope with the problems.

This optimism regarding the ease of administration rests upon an erroneous projection of a technological trend of his day. The industrial revolution has been the outcome of inventions of different varieties of labor-saving devices, capital-saving devices, and new products; new sources of power, new materials, new combinations of tools, and utilization of hitherto unknown phenomena. The industrial revolution of the eighteenth century had been particularly marked by the development of labor-saving machines which combined tools in new ways making it possible to perform simple manual operations by machine. The spinning jenny and various other devices that revolutionized the textile industry are cases in point. It is to inventions of this kind that Marx almost always alludes when in *Capital* and elsewhere he analyzes the effects of industrialization.[13] Inventions of this kind reduce costs in the way which Marx thought increased the rate of surplus value while decreasing the rate of profit. Inventions of this kind produce unemployment or as Marx called it an industrial reserve army. Inventions of this kind replace the skilled craftsman with the unskilled worker—perhaps a woman or child. If all inventions were of this kind we might well project as the end product of industrialization a society with a material culture not very different from that which exists, but produced by very small amounts of unskilled routine labor. Such a society might have relatively simple administrative routines, and permit persons to engage more or less freely in a wide range of activities. That, however, has not been the actual trend of technology. The industrial revolution of the nineteenth and even more of the twentieth century has been marked by the development of fabulously complex productive processes tapping electro-magnetic energy and other power sources the very existence of which was not previously known, by the invention of new commodities and services such as radio entertainment or out of season foods, and by capital saving devices such as synthetic products which replace metals and wood. Technology today offers no promise of simplify-

13. Marx admits his own lacks as an analyst of technology in a very interesting letter to Engels. "It is the same for me with mechanics as it is with languages. I understand the mathematical laws, but the simplest technical reality demanding perception is harder to me than to the biggest blockheads."

ing productive organization nor of requiring only an undifferentiated race of semi-skilled mechanics. The material basis for Marx's prediction of an end to the division of labor and of a social organization without hierarchy has failed to appear.

Beyond implying that the development of technology will produce a more homogeneous and therefore classless society Marx never deals with the problem of the individual and the group. He simply does not recognize the generic problem of the conflict between the dissident individual and the majority. "Only in community with others," he says, "has each individual the means of cultivating his gifts in all directions; only in the community, therefore, is personal freedom possible."[14] We have here, in revised form, the Hegelian proposition that true freedom at the highest level is the submergence of the individual in the state. Marx the democrat answers, "No, not in the state, but in a true community." Here we have one version of that pervasive doctrine of Hegel's which through Dupont-White, Bosanquet, Mary Follet, and T. H. Green found its way into so much of modern thought. Even in its democratic form it assumes some general will of the people separate and apart from the various petty desires of the individuals who make up the group. This is the organismic fallacy. We find the roots of it in Marx in that he assumes that it will be easy for a classless community to arrive at a common will in which the individuals will join. He states over and over with untiring emphasis that it is individuality he is concerned with, but by identifying that and the community will, he left the way open for his followers to substitute the general will for the will of each. This is what they did and in consequence democracy ceased to mean initiative of each in meeting problems, but only action by the bearers of the general will for all.

This is quite apparent if we compare Lenin's conception of the role of the party and the masses with Marx's. Marx rejected the notion that the party should persuade the masses of their proper desires. The classic statement of his views is in the Communist Manifesto: "The Communists . . . do not set up any sectarian principles of their own, by which to shape and mould the proletarian movement."

And to these views Marx adhered in practice. He attacked utopia

14. *The German Ideology*, p. 74.

building. He always stood for broad, inclusive, loose political organizations in opposition to secret sects or leader-dominated organizations.[15] In short he thought of the Communists merely as agitators stirring up the working class, which once stirred up would go where it pleased. The Communists, at most, could guess the course a little better than the others. This approach which says, I want to teach you to think and act, not *what* to think and act, is found sometimes in educators (and is sometimes used as the definition of education in contrast to propaganda), but is utterly rare in politics. Lenin, much more of a politician than Marx, though he used Marx's formulas could not help but drift back into the usual manipulative approach to politics.

The seminal work in Lenin's revision of Marxism is *What Is To Be Done*. This does not deal with government as such. It deals with party tactics. However, the emphasis it places on philanthropic élite elements who show the masses what is good for them is a complete reversal of previous Marxian doctrine and is the basis for the later theory of *State and Revolution*. In the latter work Lenin applied this élite leadership program to a party in power rather than out, thus arriving at the theory of proletarian dictatorship.

The whole burden of *What Is To Be Done* is a rejection of the Marxian conception of the relationship of the party to the masses. Lenin believed the party must direct the workers:

"We said that *there could not yet be* Social-Democratic consciousness among the workers. This could only be brought to them from without. The history of all countries shows that the working-class, exclusively by its own effort, is able to develop only trade-union consciousness. . . .

"The theory of Socialism, however, grew out of the philosophic, historical and economic theories that were elaborated by the educated representatives of the propertied classes, the intellectuals."[16]

Lenin even talks of "training" the working class.

Stalin carries this emphasis on the role of the party still further: "The 'theory' of spontaneity is the theory of opportunism. It is the theory of deference to the spontaneity of the labor movement, the

15. Cf. his conflict with Weitling over the Committees of Correspondence, his conditions for joining the League of the Just, his opposition to the Communist League in Cologne in 1848, his opposition to Lassalle (Cf. Engels' letter to J. P. Becker, *Correspondence*, p. 381).
16. *Collected Works* (New York, 1929), IV, 114 f.

theory that actually denies to the vanguard of the working-class, to the party of the working-class, its leading role."[17]

If there is such a leading vanguard it clearly limits the access of others to influential roles. This conclusion is drawn explicitly by Stalin in a striking quotation which relegates most of the masses to the role of sympathetic observers. *"The dictatorship of the proletariat is the domination of the proletariat over the bourgeoisie, untrammeled by law and based on violence and enjoying the sympathy and support of the toiling and exploited masses."*[18]

This dictatorship over, rather than of, the proletariat was rationalized as a necessary means to the desired end. Thus Klara Zetkin justified Soviet violations of democracy on the grounds that "Democracy is of a two-fold nature, being simultaneously means and end of historic evolution. As end or goal of historic evolution it may come into conflict with itself as means of historic evolution."[19]

To some extent it is an oversimplification to portray Soviet political theory simply as having deviated from Marxism in restricting the concept of democracy to government *for* and not *by* the people. It is an oversimplification because Soviet writings take both stands without much effort to reconcile them. One might cite practice as conclusive proof of the deviation of Eastern democracy from the classical conceptions, but that might be out of order in this ideological investigation. Let us therefore examine a piece of current Soviet writing on the subject. In Vyshinsky's *Law of the Soviet State*, we discover that classical statements about democracy are still made and then contradicted or explained away to suit the practice. There is a section called "The Soviets of the Deputies of the Toilers—the Highest Type of Democracy." In here a formal definition of democracy is given. "Democracy signifies literally 'the authority of the people.' "[20] This is the classical definition. Furthermore Vyshinsky makes other statements embodying the classical conception of democracy:

"In contrast with the false, hypocritical and anti-scientific declarations of bourgeois states as to the 'authority of the people,' the

17. *Foundations of Leninism* (New York, 1934), p. 29.
18. *Ibid.*, p. 51.
19. *Through Dictatorship to Democracy* (London, n.d.), p. 9. Zetkin in this pamphlet made one of the rare admissions that this represents a revision of Marx (pp. 13 f.).
20. P. 168.

Soviet state made real . . . that authority is actually and totally in the hands of the toilers. . . .

"The working class . . . declared through Stalin in his report at the Third All-Russian Congress of Soviets (January 28, 1918): *'To us, who represent the lowly workers, it is necessary that the people not only vote but rule as well. Those who rule—not those who choose and elect—are the ones in authority.'*

"From the very first days of its existence, the central task of Soviet authority was that of the broadest possible attraction of toiling masses to govern all the affairs of state."[21]

Thus we find at least verbal allegiance to all elements of the classic conception of democracy. Not only is equality stressed, but it is also claimed that there is wide participation of the masses in governing. Finally in statements about the "new Soviet man" we find something approaching a description of the democratic personality. Indeed, verbally the Soviet conception of democracy seems to be close to the classical conception. The reality can be so very different because all these statements are modified by an identification of the will of the working class with that of the party. This organismic myth permits a complete reversal of the classic conception of democracy with little verbal change.

Vyshinsky is explicit that the party is the embodiment of the will of the working class. Note above how that vast heterogeneous mass of persons called the working class declares its will through one man, Stalin. A full discussion of this identification is found in a section entitled "Soviet Authority as Authority Which Embodies the Will of the People." After the above-quoted definition ("Democracy signifies literally 'the authority of the people' ") this section proceeds to explain it in terms of a general will. "Only that state authority which is guided in its activity by the will of the people, and embodies that will in practice is truly democratic."[22] In typical Soviet fashion Vyshinsky projects against the external world those accusations to which he is most liable. He attacks the bourgeois theory of the general will. But he never denies that there is such a thing. He says: "In conditions of bourgeois society, we are concerned with the falsification of this will, the will of the majority of society. In conditions where antagonistic classes exist, a single 'pop-

21. P. 165.
22. P. 168.

ular will' is, in general, impossible."[23] In a classless society, and the Soviet Union is by definition such, there is such a will.

"The most important task of the class struggle of the proletariat is: (1) to unite its own ranks by a single class will, and (2) to convince the non-proletarian masses of toilers that the proletarian will embrace the rooted interests of all toilers. . . . "Having overcome the resistance of the Mensheviks, SR's, Trotskyists, Bukharinists, and other traitors who demonstrated that the majority of the people were supposedly against all the fullness of authority passing to the Soviets—against the dictatorship of the proletariat—the Bolsheviks won over most of the toilers and brought them to the side of the socialist revolution. It is the will of the majority to which the Soviets gave expression.

". . . No there never was, and there never can be, a single measure of the Soviet authority going counter to the interests and will of the majority.

"The victory of socialism—the liquidation of the kulaks as a class—signifies a new phase. . . . If, in conditions of the existence of exploiter classes, the will of the worker class and peasantry, and likewise of toiling Soviet intellectuals, was the will of the *majority of the people*—so in present conditions this is *the will of the entire Soviet people*. Speaking of will in the social or political sense, we have in view neither the mechanical 'sum total of wills' of separate persons, nor the mythical 'national will' (existing only in imagination, or rather as portrayed by every sort of bourgeois liberal or reactionary sociologist and political scientist). Following the Marx-Lenin doctrine, we have in mind the will of the social classes. To the extent that exploiters in Soviet society are liquidated as a class, we have a right to speak of *a single will* of the Soviet people."[24]

Thus we see that by a mystical equation of the will of the party with that of the people we get, without changing any of the words of the classical conception, a definition of democracy that can be described as "government *for* the people."

d) Summary.—We are now in a position to compare in a nutshell what happened as the classical conception of democracy evolved into Eastern and Western conceptions. In the Western world the broad social conception of democracy was watered down to en-

23. *Ibid.*, p. 169.
24. *Ibid.*, pp. 170 ff.

compass the particular political means which were used by modern democrats to achieve their goals, i.e., representative government and civil liberties.

In the Eastern world an extreme theory of total democracy in the classical sense was transformed into a justification of its opposite. In part this happened because the best is the worst enemy of the better. Chiliastic goals, though themselves unrealizable, lead their adherents to reject the nearest possible approaches to them as worthless compromises. This kind of fanatical all-or-none thinking is encouraged by presenting, as Marx does, absolute ideals as in the realm of reality. The role of this aspect of Marxism in explaining the change from Marx's classical conception of democracy to the current Eastern one has often been analyzed. We have therefore skipped over it, concentrating rather on that error, the organismic fallacy, which made the transformation easy.

In the East, building on the tradition of Rousseau and Hegel, the formal classical definition of democracy was kept, but although the words were unchanged, an error was made in interpreting them which logicians call the fallacy of composition. In talking of the rule of "the many," "the many" was interpreted not as a collection of individuals to whom power was to be severally given but as a corporate group with a general will which was embodied in a special organ, the party. In this way a tyranny of that organ was labelled democracy.

THE RELATION OF THE THREE SENSES OF "DEMOCRACY"

Having traced the historical development of the two modern meanings of democracy out of the classical one, let us now consider the relationship of these three meanings.

If we look at the various democratic programs that have been listed we find three main conditions of classical democracy: (1) equality in the distribution of status symbols, (2) ready access by large numbers of persons to influential roles, (3) the development in large numbers of personalities prone to self-confidence and initiative in solving problem.

The democratic ideal as conceived until the nineteenth century consisted of the total realization and diffusion of these three components. Actual political programs, of course, have to demand something less than total realization and have to make selections

346 DEMOCRACY IN A WORLD OF TENSIONS

when these goals themselves come into conflict with each other. That is the problem that faced nineteenth- and twentieth-century democrats and on which they split. Let us, therefore, examine more closely the difficulties of realizing and reconciling these three goals.

1. Equality in the distribution of status symbols is the objective of redistribution of land, graduated taxes, social welfare legislation, etc. The establishment of equalitarian social conditions requires energetic leveling action by the organs of government and was, therefore, an element of democracy that nineteenth-century liberal writers were apt to devalue. Thus authors like James Fenimore Cooper and Dicey deny that democracy implies substantive social equality, limiting it to equality before the law.

The flaw in this argument is that the three elements of democracy, although sometimes in partial conflict, are also mutually reinforcing. A society marked by great economic and social inequality between classes probably cannot remain democratic in its political structure. Those persons who have secured control of the wealth and other prestige symbols will probably also monopolize the influential positions and compel the masses to assume passive attitudes. To that extent the Eastern critics of Western democracy are on sound grounds in so far as Western democracy has shied away from vigorously promoting economic equality. The timidity of Western democracy in this respect, however, has been much exaggerated by critics. With social legislation and graduated income taxes playing the role they do, the most that can be said is that Western conservatives tried, largely unsuccessfully, to take over the term "democracy" while dropping out this element of meaning.

2. Ready access by large numbers of persons to influential roles is the objective of rotation of office, short terms of office, pay for public office, the lot, popular juries, abolition of property qualifications, abolition of standing armies, abolition of bureaucracies, nobilities, etc. The achievement of this objective conflicts head on with the need of large-scale organization for specialization, expertism, and hierarchy. In a bureaucratized society non-élite groups may attempt to acquire influence by organizing to challenge the existing élites. When they do so they are apt to use democratic slogans, and indeed in the short run their objective of promoting access of non-élite persons to the élite is democratic. Such groups,

however, acquire a hierarchy of their own[25] and when successful merely change the composition and structure of the élite. The triumph of a new bureaucracy is not the same thing as democracy. Thus the organization of trade unions, labor parties, etc., is not by itself an adequate democratic program in a complexly organized society. The failure to see that a short-run challenge to the existing élite is not the same as a long-run challenge to élites per se is one of the critical errors responsible for the Eastern conception of democracy.

The classical democratic objective of the diffusion of power cannot be achieved within massive organizations, but only by their disintegration. Only in a society characterized by numerous relatively small units will large numbers of persons find themselves exercising relatively equal power.

If power is bureaucratically concentrated, on the other hand, there is little reason to expect that status symbols will be distributed evenly either. The power wielders will probably appropriate wealth or other status symbols to themselves. This has certainly happened in Soviet Russia where recent studies show a distribution of wages and salaries remarkably like that in the West.[26] The Eastern conception of democracy, which erred in minimizing in practice the second element of democracy, thereby undermined the first too.

3. The development in large numbers of persons of personalities prone to self-confidence and initiative in solving problem is an objective promoted by anything which places large numbers of persons in power-wielding positions and also by popular education. It is almost undoubtedly also a product of certain kinds of infant training, but that has not been realized for long enough to have yet had much influence on democratic political programs. Most societies compel large numbers of persons to develop passive attitudes. They make the successful achievement of personal goals so unlikely that the individual in self-defense must rationalize his frustration and justify his withdrawal from the attempt to achieve the impossible. Noncompetitive societies provide personality structures and moral codes which easily justify such passivity. Societies which admire competition on the other hand rub sand in the wound if they

25. Roberto Michels, *Political Parties: A Sociological Study of the Oligarchical Tendencies of Modern Democracy* (New York, 1915; new ed., Glencoe, Ill., 1949).
26. Abram Bergson, *The Structure of Soviet Wages* (Cambridge, Mass., 1944).

are not democratic. Hopelessness of future success makes more bitter the forced acceptance of a subordinate role. Thus Kardiner suggests in his discussion of the Comanche that competition produces hostility when it is reinforced by passive attitudes that result from the probability of success being small. Among the Comanche, on the contrary, the prestige accompanying success lasts only till the next war party and no vested interests in property or anything else give an advantage in the next try. Competition among the Comanche is therefore compatible with a great degree of solidarity among the competitors, all of whom are sanguine of the future.[27]

The lessons of this for democratic theory are clear. Unless there is fluidity or equality of status symbols, and unless there is easy access to influential roles people will develop passive attitudes. Conversely a society in which a large proportion of the persons do have passive attitudes cannot expect roles of influence to be widely diffused. This element of democracy, too, therefore cannot be simply dropped out without undermining the complex. This has not been fully recognized by some persons who have claimed the title of democrat in the West, but it has been even more disregarded in the East. Obedience, discipline, fulsome adulation of leaders are among the outstanding virtues in the "new democracies." Class differentiation may be rejected in theory, but role distinctions involving such categories as the party, army, etc., are very important. No more conclusive evidence on this exists than recent developments in Soviet education. The rules for school children adopted in 1943 require the student "to obey without question the orders of school directors and teachers," "to sit erect during the lesson period, not leaning on the elbows or slouching in the seat," "to rise as the teacher or director enters or leaves the classroom," "to rise and stand erect while reciting; to sit down only on permission of the teacher." Submission is emphasized further in the definition of a request in a Soviet textbook on pedagogy: "A request is a demand of the teacher couched in a mild form. It refers to something which the pupil is obliged to do. But in certain cases, for one reason or another, he shows inner resentment toward a direct command."[28] With such demands for passivity democracy in its classical conception is impossible.

27. *Psychological Frontiers of Society* (New York, 1945), pp. 99 ff.
28. Boris Petrovich Esipov, *I Want To Be like Stalin,* trans. George S. Counts (New York, 1947), p. 110.

The three elements of classical democracy which we have examined depend upon and reinforce each other. The continued existence of one without the other is difficult. It is no accident that the three of them together came to be designated as a single whole: democracy. Sociologically if not analytically they are a whole. Both in the East and West democracy has been weakened by a tendency to lose sight of certain parts of this whole.

If we ask which of the new meanings Eastern or Western is closer to the complex whole of the classical democratic ideal, the answer must be that verbally the Eastern idea may be closer, but realistically it is not.

The Western conception of democracy, for all its deviations from the classical one, is not unrelated to its forerunner. The complex problems of modern technology and culture have at least for the present reduced in large areas the possibilities of direct popular rule. Andrew Jackson in defense of rotation of office argued that "The duties of all public officers are, or at least admit of being made, so plain and simple that men of intelligence may readily qualify themselves for their performance." Few persons would accept that thesis today. Perhaps the evolution of future technology may produce a push-button world where this will be true. For the moment the trend seems to be contrary. As long as this is the case any uncompromising program of pure democracy in the classical sense is utopian. Popular selection (direct or indirect) of experts and the periodic ratification of their policies is a legitimate compromise solution and one that is capable of being made by degrees more and more democratic to the extent that the technical requirements permit. Thus whatever the verbal relation of the Western conception of representative government and the classic conception of democracy, they are far from irreconcilable in practice if one will accept compromises of degree.

Furthermore, civil liberty, a crucial element in the modern Western conception of democracy, is a *sine qua non* of democracy in the classic sense too: There is thus no contradiction between these two senses, only a historical evolution from a more trenchant and specific idea to one less so.

The Eastern conception on the other hand by discarding individual liberty, this *sine qua non* of democracy, has turned the word "democracy" into a name for its opposite. The third condition of democracy, individualism, is one without which it cannot exist. It is more than a historical accident that the two great periods of individualism, ancient Greece and modern times, are also the two great periods of democracy.

The classical conception of democracy makes no sense except from an individualist point of view. The demand for equality of status symbols, the demand for access to a position of power, the demand for self-confidence and initiative, makes sense only for the individual who, conscious of his own desires, feels a conflict between them and those of other wielders of power. The demand to rule and be ruled in turn is the demand of the jealously self-conscious individual. Where there is some general will which ony an élite knows, then the promotion into the influential jobs of a cross-section of the populace and the encouraging of them to think for themselves makes no sense at all. Democracy in its classic sense and in its Western sense can exist only in an individualistic society with extensive liberties for the citizen.

Eradication of dissident views could be defended as democratic only for a homogeneous society where all but insignificantly few individuals think alike.

A two-party or multi-party system would have been meaningless in Zuñi, or Comanche, or Eskimo society. There were no conflicting ideologies or interest groups. The only political issues that would have existed, if politics in our sense had been introduced, would have centered about persons. The only justification of a one-party system is a lack of issues.

The defenders of the one-party system where it now exists use this justification, but without foundation. They claim to have a classless society and thus one without issues. If the facts were thus the argument would be valid, but the facts are not so. It is utterly inconceivable that any modern industrial society could be thus homogeneous. The occupational division of labor alone is so complex as to make any such claim spurious. Workers, farmers, writers, plumbers, teachers and housewives are bound to see things differently. Totalitarianism is an artificial attempt to impose a fictitious unity on a society that in reality is so divided that it has lost its voluntary consensus. Because in modern society a spontaneous homogeneity is impossible any movement that sets such unification as its goal is bound to be authoritarian.

In a nonhomogeneous society such as exists both in Russia and in the United States the problem of democracy is to encourage the energetic self-expression of all strata of society, particularly the humble and subordinate. Rosa Luxembourg made this point from the Socialist point of view:[29]

"Lenin says: 'The bourgeois state is an instrument of oppression of the working class; the socialist state, of the bourgeoisie. To a certain extent,' he says, 'it is only the capitalist state stood on its head.' This simplified view misses the most essential thing: bourgeois class rule has no need of the political training and education of the entire mass of the people, at least not beyond certain narrow limits. But for the proletarian dictatorship that is the life element, the very air without which it is not able to exist. . . .

". . . Decree, dictatorial force of the factory overseer, draconic penalties, rule by terror,–all these things are but palliatives. The only way to rebirth is the school of public life itself, the most unlimited, the broadest democracy and public opinion."

That is the nub of the contradiction between the classical and Eastern conceptions of democracy. Verbally they are very close: government *by* the many and government *for* the many. But in practice they are poles apart since government *by others* that claims to be *for* the many never is what it claims. There is no more invariable rule of politics than that he who claims to dictate to another for the other's good is deceived or deceiving.

This is true not only because men are corruptible and power corrupts. It is also true because only by individual spontaneity, only by free activity, can the many develop and experience the self-reliance, power, and understanding which is the highest goal of democratic politics. Freedom is thus an essential condition of democracy despite the contrary view of many thinkers, both historic and Eastern.

We saw above that many nineteenth-century antidemocratic writers who used the word "democracy" in the classic sense feared a democratic tyranny of the majority. They erred in two directions. They failed to recognize the more tolerant and humanistic tenor of the masses than of narrow groups in a heterogeneous segmentalized urban society. (This point, it will be recalled, de Tocqueville began to see in his second volume. It should be noted, how-

29. Rosa Luxembourg, *The Russian Revolution* (New York, 1940), pp. 44 ff. This pamphlet was written in 1918.

ever, that his first volume, which purported to give a picture of the democratic government of the United States, failed at any point to mention the Bill of Rights, a slip of such magnitude as to be explicable only in terms of a major observational bias.)

Secondly, those who wrote of democratic despotism failed to recognize that popular rule is impossible unless the people have those liberties of speech, assembly, etc., which permit the crystallization and implementation of the diffused attitudes of the mass.[30]

The Greeks, who had more direct experience with a variety of democracies than did the writers of the nineteenth century, did not make these errors. Even such antidemocratic writers as Aristotle and Plato knew that in a democracy "the city is full of freedom and frankness—a man may say and do what he likes"; also that it is marked by "humanity" and a "forgiving spirit."[31] These writers were quite aware that extreme or revolutionary democracy slipped easily into tyranny, but they did not confuse the two. Both our days and their days have shown how the strong demagogue, who puts the masses in motion behind a democratic program, may make himself a tyrant and enslave those for whom he spoke. But when he has done so, there is no more democracy. Clearly, there is a vast difference between the statement that democracy is compatible with tyranny or dictatorship and the genetic statement that democratic movements often lead to tyrannical results.

It is the failure to make this distinction that has lent much of the apparent strength to the arguments both of nineteenth-century critics of democracy and of the current expositors of the Eastern theory of democracy. Both of these schools of thought were not fully aware of the principle of inadvertence in human action, i.e., that the consequences of what we do are not what we intend. The apologists of Eastern "democracy" are prone to stress the indubitably democratic origins of many of the social impulses that gave strength to their movement (land reform, self-determination, etc.). They either deny or overlook the process by which a movement that was *for* the people ceased being for the people because it was not *by* the people.

30. The best treatment of this aspect of the problem of liberty and democracy is O. Kirchheimer and N. C. Leites, "Bemerkung zu Carl Schmitt's 'Legalität und Legitimität," *Archiv für Sozialwissenschaft und Sozialpolitik*, LXVIII (1933), 457–87.
31. Plato *Republic* 557 f.

Thus, the Eastern conception of democracy—government *for* the people by the party—is in practice in complete antithesis to the classical conception of democracy. It is, in fact, nothing else than the classical conception of tyranny: a dictatorship which grew out of a popular movement, but which has since been turned by the demagogues to their own benefit. The verbal changes necessary to disguise the important historical changes and stress only the historical continuity may be small, but the material changes in the positions of the many and the élite are all-embracing.

XXVII

LADISLAUS RIEGER

I venture to say that the ideological conflicts that are being waged around the word "democracy" are the results, the reflection—and index—of class antagonisms, class interests, and not the cause of these antagonisms, these opposed interests. Class antagonisms cannot be removed by analysis of ideological formulations. But the clarification of the relationship between the current conflict of ideas and its background in class antagonisms is of the greatest significance: by clarifying this relationship we can bring about an understanding of the very essence of history and thus take an active part in the forging of our destinies.

In this era we have arrived at a crossroads in the course of history: for the first time in his evolution man is in a position to give reality to a society free from all implacable class antagonisms based on and caused by the exploitation of one group of men by another. Materially as well as spiritually a higher level of civilization, a widening of human culture, can be brought about. The victory of bourgeois capitalism over the feudal order could once be justified because it led to a general rise and spread of civilization: in exactly the same way the superiority of the socialist order of society over the capitalist is in our day justified by the increase and expansion of culture that can only be realized through the victory of the working class. This is so much more true as this victory does not mean the exchange of one class of exploiters for another but ultimately the total removal of all exploitation and suppression of man by fellow-man.

We are therefore convinced that the future belongs to socialism as the higher form of civilization. Through the instauration of this higher form of civilization the great majority of mankind will be enabled to live a humanly noble life and to enjoy further material and cultural development: thus will be eradicated all traces of the lower forms of civilization based on exploitation and coercion. The capitalist and socialist civilizations are facing each other in a great struggle. The development of history will prove which of the two—

imperialistic capitalism or democratic socialism—is capable of insuring a higher degree of civilization for the people, a better life for all, the progress of the whole of mankind.

The term "democracy" is of Greek origin: it meant the direct participation of the people in the administration of the community. But the "people" did not include immigrants, women, and, particularly, slaves; the Greek "democracy" was a "slave democracy." But, whatever its shortcomings, it was the opposite of oligarchy and tyranny.

Modern democracy is of a different kind: it is representative, not direct as Greek democracy was. From the beginning of the modern era two divergent conceptions have struggled for superiority: the individualist conception of democracy and the collectivist conception. In the individualist conception, "democracy" means the freedom to compete and the freedom to profit: the state is there only to protect these "fundamental rights of the citizens." In this liberal-individualist conception the happiness of a society is identified with the happiness of successful individuals: society is nothing but the sum of selfish individuals. Against this conception thinkers like Jean-Jacques Rousseau opposed the collectivist one: individuals had resigned their individual will in forming the state as an "organ of the general will." Rousseau even went back to the Greek conception in postulating as an ideal democracy the direct participation of the people in the government; to him, representative and parliamentary democracy was only an "elective aristocracy."

The first, individualist, conception had as its factual corollary the domination of the state by the propertied interests. Those who had no property had no share in the powers of the state. The state was, in fact, nothing but the organ of superiority of the bourgeois class of property-owners. The liberal-individualist "democracy" in the end became an oligarchy of a small group of wealthy families.

In the highest phase of the development of bourgeois capitalism, in the epoch of imperialism, of the concentration of economic power in the great international industrial and financial concerns struggling for the world market, the liberalism of the earlier ideology is gradually replaced by more brutal methods to insure the hegemony of these oligarchic groups in the bourgeois "democracies." In its ultimate phase capitalism leads toward fascism as its last argument. Through militarization and police terror the monopolistic groups of reactionary capitalists head toward violent dictatorship as the only means for the continuation of their power. This development does not only find expression in interior policies but also in foreign interventions: imperialistic invasions, economic and military occupations. Public opinion may still exercise some degree of pressure on these governments, and thus the struggle for democracy goes on within these states; but in reality the people have lost all control over the handling of the administration of their state. Decisive actions in foreign politics lie beyond the reach of popular control, even beyond parliamentary control since the representatives are usually faced by *faits accomplis.*

Against this trend of degeneration of bourgeois democracy into an oligarchy of imperialistic monopolists, attempts have been made since the Great October Revolution to build up a new and complete democracy on the basis of thoroughgoing changes in the economic and political organization of society. These attempts lead through the actual sovereignty of the people—of the workers—toward the establishment of a socialist democracy and the instauration of a classless society. These new forms of democracy are characterized by the direct participation of the whole working people in the government of the state and by the permanent control of its administration. This new form of democracy is thus opposed to the bourgeois system of indirect democracy controlled through representation; hence its name: *people's democracy.* In the course of their development these people's democracies will lead toward a socialist democracy and toward a classless society. With the removal of the economic basis of the class struggles the political forms that reflected them will also disappear. There will no longer be any need for the fights between the political parties that represented the interests of the classes opposing each other in their relation to the means of production. The opposition of the old capitalist class to this development is combatted by the overwhelming majority of the people: political parties defending the old order of exploitation are not allowed in people's democracies and socialist democracies. The aim of these democracies is the raising of the level of civilization both in its material and spiritual forms and its spreading to the benefit of all without discrimination of sex, race, or religion. The ultimate aim is the security of total freedom to participate in the fruits of civilization and the complete solidarity and brotherhood of all nations, of all humanity. In its most perfect form this democracy will culminate in the removal of every pressure from the state power in the classless, the Communist society. We in Czechoslovakia are indeed already experiencing some degree of decentralization of the power of the state in our local national committees.

As long as the population of a state is divided by class interests, democracy cannot but be class-biased and therefore incomplete. Capitalism can never remove these class antagonisms as its essence is the necessary exploitation of labor. In its present imperialist phase capitalism also means the sharpening of the class struggle on an international scale, it means exterior and interior wars and therefore a setback in civilization. The only rescue, materially as well as spiritually, lies in the application of scientific socialism: Marxism-Leninism. Everything else is mere mystification and utopism or, what is worse, "solution" through the barbarism of fascism.

Democracy is therefore nothing unchangeable, general, fixed, and definite: no abstract formula, but the concrete expression for the trend of social orders developing through history, higher forms always struggling against and supplanting lower ones. Today this struggle takes its concrete form in the opposition on a world-wide scale between socialist democracy and bourgeois democracy. The struggle is justified by the idea of progress toward a higher form of society, the idea of an ascending and spreading civilization. It is a struggle for a new Man, the ruler of the earth forging his own destinies, liberating himself from the oppression of material exploitation and mutual strife, and breaking loose from all superstitions and idealistic mystifications: it is a struggle for the birth of a new Promethean civilization. Today the rescue of this civilization is at stake, and the only salvation can come from the idea of the democracy of the workers, the idea of Marxism-Leninism, the new way of humanity. To us Czechoslovaks this way of liberation from oppression is the old traditional way since the days of Hussitism, and we would be happy to see other nations solve this problem in the same peaceful way as we have done it.

22. TOLERATION OF DISSENTIENT OPINIONS.—The UNESCO document at the basis of this inquiry lays much stress on the problem of *the right of opposition* as a clue to the analysis of the differences between the two conceptions of democracy confronting each other in current ideological conflicts. However logically put together, the

questions under this head remain on the surface of the matter. In order to discover the core of the matter it is necessary to analyze the concrete setting of the problem at issue and avoid any abstract discussion of generalities. The setting of the problem is highly different in bourgeois-liberal democracies from what it is in people's democracies and in socialist democracies. Why is this? In class societies participation in government is based on the system of political parties representing the major class interests opposing each other within society. Whenever the position of the governing class is threatened or seems to be threatened, all tolerance disappears: prohibition of political assemblies, strikes and demonstrations, limitation of the freedom of the press, martial law, and military terror are readily accepted. All barriers to the spread of fascism disappear. Some democracies had to pay for this. The tolerance of movements of this kind is a threat to democracy and therefore cannot be part of its essence.

The same applies to the problem of tolerance in people's democracies. Parties defending the interests of those who exploit the labor of others cannot be tolerated because they threaten the very foundation of the order which is being established. This is just as natural as anything the bourgeois democracies do to protect themselves against anarchistic tendencies threatening the disintegration of the foundations of the system upheld in their societies; they do not allow anybody to start movements advocating theft of private property and they tend to outlaw Communist parties whenever there is a feeling that the basic institutions of capitalism are endangered.

26. ONE-PARTY SYSTEMS.—The process leading to the removal of the economic bases of class antagonisms also leads to the total disappearance of the problems that gave rise to the party systems, nay even of the problem of the toleration of dissentient opinions. In a society where all exploitation of the labor of others has been made impossible and where the ownership of all means of production has been returned to the whole of society, there cannot be any divergent opinions on this fundamental question. This also answers the question whether one-party or many-party systems are to be preferred. It is all a question of stage of development. Actually there is no reason for posing it at all in a classless society. Discussion and criticism will certainly continue, but there will be full agreement on the common aim and no opposition between groups exploiting and groups

exploited; all basis for an opposition between political parties has disappeared.

In the later stages of bourgeois democracy, the opposition between parties is very often just a sham. Two-party systems generally only serve to cover up the dictatorship of the governing oligarchy of wealth. So far no scholar was able to define clearly the difference between the Democratic and Republican parties in the United States —waiving the promises they give during election campaigns. The political practice of both parties is the same: they both uphold the régime of capitalist-imperialist dominance.

29. ULTIMATE AIMS.—If we agree on the aim of human endeavor, the constant development toward higher possibilities of civilization, it is possible to decide on the way and the suitable means. History has already taught us all that is necessary to that effect. We have learned first of all that if we want to build a house for people to live in we must not build it out of the air but on firm foundations in the soil. This was the mistake that all social reform movements made from the beginning of Christianity to the phase of utopian socialism. The failure of two thousand years of idealistic striving could be overcome only by the scientific approach of Marxism-Leninism. Secondly, we have learned that the way of parliamentary compromise will never lead out of the blind alley of class conflict; at the utmost it can only enveil the realities of class antagonism over short periods of time. Even the policy of gradual reform can only lead to the ripening of a situation that will in the end call for drastic and revolutionary action; the conflicts between the classes will be sharpened to the point where the workers will take over the power of government and nationalize the means of production. Finally, we have learned that there are situations in which a revolution of this kind can take place without leading to the disasters of civil war; this was the case in Czechoslovakia and other people's democracies.

Even if there are no theoretical disagreements on the general aim of raising and spreading civilization there necessarily are and will be conflicts over the fundamental changes in ownership without which this aim cannot be attained. It is of the greatest importance that all illusions on this point be unveiled and that every effort be made to bring to light the fundamental fact that in a world so far advanced in productive power, technological development, and mass consciousness as ours, capitalism has lost all its useful functions and is a completely archaic system which can only lead to anarchy and dis-integration. It is necessary to create a general awareness of the un-reasonable senselessness and inhumanity of imperialism, of the con-spiration of a small minority to preserve their privileges against the general progress toward a higher and wider form of civilization. It is necessary to do this because otherwise there will be a continued repetition of wars, economic and military, destroying the fruits of the labor of generations and thus putting back the clock of history.

The only solution and the only way, therefore, is socialism and its victory. The real history of mankind started only one hundred years ago with the advent of scientific socialism: the new social order it inspired took its concrete form in the great Russian revo-lution and was strengthened by the victory over fascism in World War II and by the triumph of democratic China in the years after.

Culture cannot develop in width and depth among all groups in a society where the working man lives in constant fear of losing his daily bread, where the individual is left to himself without protec-tion against the fatalism of economic laws, the catastrophes of un-employment, and the disasters of wars recurring with almost natu-ral necessity. We have learned that these forces have been brought about by the anarchy of capitalism, and we know that we are strong enough to tame them. We are struggling for the most perfect gov-ernment of, by, and for the people, for a socialist democracy in which our children can live as citizens liberated from all terror and oppression and in which there will be no exploitation, no human degradation in subservience to wealth and capital. In this society the individual, no longer in constant fear of his livelihood but carried to his fulfilment through the common efforts of the whole of society, will rediscover the meaning of his life in the merging of his person-ality into the social whole. These new generations will not even know of the problems that Hegel called those of the isolated "un-happy consciousness," neither will they understand the anxieties that filled Hamlet nor the dilemmas that harassed Faustus. A new Man will arise, the ruler of the earth and, in the atomic age, perhaps even the ruler of other planets—the ruler of a new history the curve of which will continuously rise toward higher degrees of spiritual and material civilization, thus overcoming all lower stages in har-mony with the cosmic dialectics of being.

XXVIII

WILHELM RÖPKE

I believe the term "democracy" a particularly good example for
the way in which unprecise words are misunderstood by the one—
liberal—part of the world and misused with grinning cynicism by
the other—totalitarian or collectivist—part of the world. If it were
only a misunderstanding between both parts we could hope to clear
it up by a discussion. But, unfortunately, it is much more. If we want
to have a real discussion by which we might hope finally to settle
disagreements by appeal to reason and to arrive at what both parties
must admit to be the truth, a minimum of conditions must be fulfilled. There must be a minimum of common ground between both
parties. There must be *unitas in necessariis:* a common belief in absolute ultimate values of a moral character. Otherwise there is no discussion but only a wrangle or a show. If the other partner believes
that the interest of his nation, race, or class is the ultimate moral
measure we might still hope to find some *modus vivendi* for a while,
but it is utterly illusionary to enter with him into a rational—scientific—discussion. That is why I always refused to have a discussion
with a National Socialist, and that is also why I always refuse to
enter into a discussion with a Communist. It is not only a waste of
time, but a duel with highly unequal weapons.

Therefore, if there are ideological differences which refer to the
ultimate values I am extremely pessimistic as to the chances of narrowing the gulf by discussion, unless you shatter the other partner's
belief in his ultimate values, or un-values. As far as this latter point
is concerned I am much less pessimistic. I think there are profound
and elementary anthropological "constants" through time and space.
Man is a "social animal," with all the implications of this term, and
it is by no means impossible to shake the dogmatism of a National
Socialist or a Communist to such an extent as to make him see that
his doctrine is "inhuman," i.e., in conflict with those "constants."
But I am doubtful whether you will shake him by a discussion, and

the types you are most unlikely to shake are the doctrinaire "intellectuals."

To repeat: the epistemological relativism of the "totalitarians," i.e., what, by a very curious terminology, we feel to be the opposite of the "democratic" world—whether the relativism of Marxism, of nationalism or racialism—precludes, by definition, a rational discussion with people belonging to another system of references. If we want to clear up the term "democracy," therefore, we must confine the discussion to those who fulfil the conditions of a rational discussion. That, however, is highly desirable because the term is highly ambiguous and rationally "impure." We must arrive at a list of what we can mean by "democracy," define these meanings very carefully, and, finally, perhaps agree on different terms for these different meanings. According to *one* of these meanings, "democracy" really implies, by necessity, the respect of minorities, but here again it would be suicidal blindness—the tendency toward "intellectual absolutism" which ignores everywhere the conditions and limitations of any concept—to believe that this "democratic" tolerance *must* imply the tolerance of those who are determined to use the democratic tolerance only to make an end of it. It is to think very low of democratic tolerance to imperil it in this way. That is not to deny that "democracy"—in this sense which really means "liberalism"—should be tolerant to the ultimate limits. But that implies, on the other hand, that it might be suicide and betrayal of its own principles for "democracy" *not* to outlaw national socialism or communism.

XXIX

ALF ROSS

The term "democracy"—as well as the corresponding adjective "democratic" and all other derivatives—is ambiguous not only because it is used for widely divergent characterizations of one identical subject matter but also because it is used for characterization of distinctly heterogeneous subject matters.

In its basic signification, the term "democracy" serves to characterize legally sanctioned power relations in any social context. Power relations within the state make up a particularly important species of such relations but are not the only ones; in its basic connotation, the term can also be used to characterize juridically established power relations in associations, foundations, international organizations, etc.

The basic signification of the term is ambiguous because "democracy" may refer sometimes to the legal form of government, the method by which decisions are made and carried out, sometimes to the socio-economic contents of decisions and the goals of government. A distinction should accordingly be made between a constitutional and a socio-economic concept of democracy.

By derivation, the term has come to be used in a largely indiscriminate way to characterize any category of power, command, or influence relationship whether it is established by legal sanctions or not; thus in common usage the term is very often used to characterize relationships like those between husband and wife, parents and children, teacher and pupils, priest and congregation, employer and employees.

The derivative sense suffers from an ambiguity corresponding to that of the basic sense. The conduct of a leader in relation to his followers may well be characterized as "democratic" in a derivative sense if it conforms to the standards and the spirit of democracy in its basic signification, but the characterization is indeterminate in so far as it gives no indication whether emphasis is given to the legal methods of decision-making or to the objectives to be served by the decisions.

2. EVIDENCE.—Examples taken from everyday usage give clear evidence to the ambiguities of the word "democracy" and its derivatives: (*a*) The Danish state is a democracy. (*b*) This law, which deprives widows of their economic support, is undemocratic. (*c*) The army ought to be democratized. (*d*) It is undemocratic not to take one's meals with the servants.

The most significant examples of ambiguities in the term "democracy" can be found in the use that has been made of it in political propaganda and international documents during and after World War II.

3. MISUSE.—Charges of misuse of the word "democracy," i.e., protestations against the meanings the word is used in in given contexts, may be based on considerations of the following kinds:

a) *Theoretical considerations of scientific clarity.*—In the interest of science efforts should be made to increase the preciseness of concepts, to avoid the use of ambiguous terms and to conform as far as possible to the usage established by tradition.

Traditionally at least, the term "democracy" covers a constitutional concept, not a socio-economic concept. Waiving periphrases, there is no other word in common usage that can be used to signify the formal method of government. On the other hand, the socio-economic policy contents associated with "democracy" may very well be signified by other traditionally established words; the most convenient one is the term "socialism." The logic of science as well as considerations of technical expediency accordingly demands that the word "democracy" be exclusively reserved for the formal concept; any other use of the word must, on these criteria, be banned as misuse.

b) *Practical-ideological considerations of fairness in political propaganda.*—It is in the interest of fairness that in political propaganda the word be used as far as possible in the sense it is assumed it will be understood in. Through the traditions of its usage the word "democracy" has come to carry with it all the good will associated with the ideas of liberty and human rights, the ideas of the French Revolution. The tendency to give new significations to the word, different from the original one, has provided possibilities of usurping this good will and misleading the public as to the real issues. If the term "democracy" is applied to a régime denying the ideas of liberty and human rights, the public will be misled into believing, contrary to what is the truth, that the régime pleaded for is basically at one with the traditional Western idea of democracy, deviating only in the ways and means chosen, not in central aspirations.

This is a well-known trick in propaganda: the Nazis excelled in reinterpreting such keywords as "democracy," "liberty," "*Rechtsstaat,*" "socialism," etc., so as to exploit the traditional good will of these words. Such dishonest reinterpretations are regularly recognized by the frequent use of adjectives like "true," "real," "genuine," prefixed to the keywords.[1]

A juridical variation of this kind of misuse occurs when in international treaties and agreements one party uses the word in a sense different from the one in which it must be assumed that the co-contractor will understand it.

6. COMMON CHARACTERISTICS.—Attempts to determine the meaning of "democracy" through Aristotelian definitions *per genus proximum et differentiam specificam* can only lead astray. A more fruitful approach to the determination of concepts of democracy lies in the construction of multidimensional *models* for the analysis of the different elements that have to be taken account of. In this way a concept of democracy can be determined as an *ideal type.*[2] The *ideal type* is a purely cognitive tool and does not imply any value preferences. The *ideal type* democracy does not mirror any existing order but makes up a conceptual model embodying at their maximal values the factors that in actual reality occur in smaller or larger degrees only.

A conceptual model of this kind can be graphically represented by a system of lines all starting out from one point, the zero point. Given possibilities of scale measurements along each line, actually occurring political orders may be characterized in terms of a "topographical scheme" within the model; for each of the relevant factors, a point indicating the actual degree of realization can be determined between the minimum at zero point and the maximum at the end of each line. As a result, each *real type* can be determined by its distance, along each of the lines, from the *ideal type* representing the

1. Such processes of reinterpretation have been thoroughly analyzed by Charles L. Stevenson in the chapter on "persuasive definitions" in his *Ethics and Language* (New Haven, 1944), chap. ix.
2. See Carl G. Hempel and Paul Oppenheim, *Der Typusbegriff im Lichte der modernen Logik* (Leiden, 1936).

maximum, but certainly not the optimum, for each of the factors that are postulated as relevant in the model.

A very simple model[3] of this kind can be made up of three dimensions representing three factors of "democraticity" widely recognized as relevant ones:

I. Intensity, i.e., the percentage of the population that through the instrumentalities of, votes and elections are given opportunities to influence government;

II. Efficacy, i.e., the effect with which the people is able to make its views count in the control of government;

III. Extension, i.e., the scope of public matters subject to regular influence and control by the people.

The relationship between an *ideal type* democracy of maximal intensity, efficacy, and extension, and different *real type* democracies can be illustrated by a simple diagram.

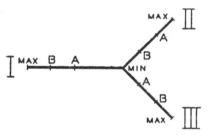

In the figure the numbers *I, II, III* refer to the factors of intensity, efficacy, and extension. The letters *A–A–A* and *B–B–B* refer to two different political orders and the location of the letter points on the lines indicates the degree with which each system fulfils each of the functions.

Given models of this kind, there is little sense in opposing absolutely "democratic" states to absolutely "undemocratic" states. It is all a matter of degree and a question of frame of reference. One state may be said to be "undemocratic" as compared to another with respect to *one* factor, but may well be found to be comparatively "undemocratic" with respect to *other* factors. Thus the Soviet Union as it operates today may be said to be undemocratic in a manner very different from the way early nineteenth-century England was undemocratic.

3. Details of this model are elaborated in my work *Hvorfor Demokrati?* (Copenhagen, 1946), chap. iv.

8. THE LINCOLN FORMULA. The Gettysburg formula cannot very well serve the purpose of furnishing the elements of a plausible and convenient definition of democracy. At the utmost the formula can only be recognized as a vague and sloganized approximation to possible definitions.

The preposition *of* would not seem to indicate anything beyond the bare fact that a government exists: any government is a government of the people. Who else should it govern?

The preposition *by* indicates in the briefest possible way the essence of democracy: the form of government that gives to the whole of the people the ultimate and decisive control of the will of the state and the execution of public authority.

The preposition *for* does not indicate any element of relevance to the concept of democracy as defined the way I think it should be defined. No consideration should be given, in defining the term, to the social conditions that are aimed at by the government or regularly related to it. By this statement I do not by any means want to imply that I am indifferent to what social goals are aimed at or that I deny any natural connections between democratic methods and social goals of certain kinds. But considerations of social goals should not enter into the definition. It is still quite possible to defend the statement that the democratic form of government is the one best suited to further the general welfare of the people—in some plausible interpretation of that phrase. But this is a synthetic statement of matters of fact, not an analytical statement defining the use of the word "democracy." The confusion of fact statements with definitional statements is, however, a very widespread phenomenon; it may explain how Abraham Lincoln came to include the preposition *for* in his formula.

11. "NARROW" VERSUS "BROAD" SENSE.—The distinction between a "narrow" political concept of democracy and a "broad" socioeconomic *and* political concept cannot serve any purposes of analytical clarification. It is much more likely to serve as an ideological device in the propaganda wars that are being waged.

Logically, the "broad" concept is a monstrosity. The political method and the socio-economic content are two different things, which it is impossible to imagine joined in one concept. It would obviously be necessary to have a specific concept of each of the two components to determine the "broad democracy." It is a question of simple addition as in the expression "a sound mind in a sound body." It is sometimes maintained that the factual combination of political form and social content would justify the joining of both elements in the definition. It would be as justified to maintain that "body" and "soul" or "thunder" and "lightning" would have to be joined in one concept. The idea is absurd. The clear conceptual distinction between different components does not prevent, but on the contrary, furthers the assertion of clear empirical propositions about their mutual relations.

Besides, I shall have to declare myself in absolute disagreement with the premise implied in the formulation of the UNESCO question: that the contrast between the "Eastern" and the "Western" conception of democracy can be traced back to the contrast between a "broad" and "narrow" concept of democracy. This vague and metaphorical formula is highly likely to prove misleading: it is likely to suggest that Russian democracy is a concept of wider scope, embracing as one of its components political democracy in its Western sense. Who would not like to eat his cake and have it too: both political democracy and social democracy? It is unfortunate that a terminology of this kind has been accepted in the UNESCO document; it has given a deplorable bias to the posing of the problems at this crucial point.

For even if the Russian conception of democracy implies a socialist economy, it is by no means a fact that it also embraces a political method of the kind advocated as democratic in the West. There cannot be any serious doubt that constitutional democracy in the Western sense does not exist in Soviet Russia. Anybody hesitating in admitting this fact should be referred to Stalin's famous speech on the 1936 Constitution. In this speech he admitted "that the draft of the new Constitution does preserve the régime of the dictatorship of the working class, just as it also preserves unchanged the present leading position of the Communist Party of the U.S.S.R." At the same time the constitution is described as "the only thoroughly democratic Constitution in the world."[4]

It should be obvious that a constitution based on dictatorship and a one-party system has no relation whatever to democracy as it is conceived in western Europe and in America. There is accordingly no "narrow" democracy comprised within the "broad" democracy;

4. Stalin, *Leninism* (London, 1940), pp. 578, 579.

as applied to the East-West contrast these expressions are misleading in favor of the Eastern cause.

12–13. SOCIAL PROBLEM, POLITICAL PROBLEM.—In my opinion the problem of the relation between "political democracy," as a constitutional system, and "social democracy," as socialist economic organization, cannot be primarily analyzed in terms of "ends" and "means." "Ends" refer to subjective ideological valuations; "means" imply objective insight into causal relationships. The problem should accordingly be posed in sociologically objective terms. Ideological considerations may be dealt with afterwards.

The primary sociological problem would probably be most fruitfully clarified if divided into two questions: (1) Under what political conditions is a socialist economy possible? (2) Under what social conditions is political democracy possible?

By way of introduction it should be noted, first, that both questions must be understood as adding "in the long run"; observed during a shorter spell of time the sociological relations of interdependence with which we are dealing could hardly make themselves felt; it takes some time for the social forces to assert themselves.

Secondly, it is my opinion that we do not possess any safe experimental knowledge that would enable us to answer the questions put before us. In both cases we shall at the most attain vague hypothetical estimates. Yet the questions are so fatefully important that it seems imperative not to throw them aside, but, with all due reservations for the insufficiencies of our knowledge, do our best to formulate a coherent and well-founded opinion of their possible solution.

1. *Under what political conditions is a socialist economy possible?*—Marxist economics rest on the assumption that those who control the means of production will always, such is human nature, make use of this control to exploit other people. The solution, therefore, is assumed to consist in the transfer of the control of the means of production to the state. But this gives, inevitably, rise to the question: who controls the state? If the state is controlled by a minority, it must, according to the very assumptions of Marxism, be an enigma why this minority should not exploit its position of power to its own advantage. Experience from Russia has confirmed that the result of the transfer of the ownership of the means of production to the state need by no means be socialism, but rather the introduction of new

privileges, new class divisions, new "exploitation." If the executors of state power are not under the democratic control of the people, there is no guaranty that the command of the state over the means of production will not be utilized for the introduction of new privileges. On the contrary, it would be strange if innate egotism should not lead the new masters to turn their sway to their own advantage. In flat contradiction to the Communist thesis, it would then be safe to assume that lasting socialism cannot be introduced by revolutionary means. Revolution implies dictatorship, and dictatorship will again, sooner or later, inevitably lead to the use of power to the advantage of the ruling political party, even if the latter persists in calling itself the exponent of the will of the masses. According to the laws of human nature this guaranty must sooner or later give way.

The question before us must therefore be answered thus: a socialist economy is, in the long run, only possible if based on political democracy.

2. *Under what social conditions is political democracy possible?* —This is an exceedingly complex cluster of problems. Much would be gained if a distinction between a *static* approach to the problems and a *dynamic* approach be consistently kept in mind. The static approach aims at assessing the compatibility of democracy with, on the one hand, a social organization based on a consistently capitalist economy assumed to be firmly established through majority approval, and, on the other, a social organization based on a consistently socialist economy equally firmly established through majority approval. The dynamic approach aims at assessing the chances of democracy in a society caught in constant evolution from a capitalist to a socialist economy, i.e., in a society where there is no longer, or not yet, any general agreement on the moral and economic principles guiding the organization of the relations of production.

It is not feasible in this context to enter into all these aspects of the problem cluster.[5] Let me confine myself to a few words on a couple of points I consider essential.

Democracy and capitalism.—There is indubitably a kernel of truth in the Communist assertion that capitalist control of the formation of opinion tends to make democracy a fake. But in its

5. I have given a detailed analysis of these problems in chap. vii of my book *Hvorfor Demokrati?*

current formulations the charge is certainly vastly exaggerated. Conditions can certainly be greatly improved by the spread of enlightenment and education, even within the framework of capitalism. And what is more important: the present ills cannot be eradicated but will, on the contrary, be exceedingly aggravated by the transfer of the control of the means of propaganda to a one-party state. As experience goes to show, state control of opinion formation opens up possibilities of systematic *Gleichschaltung*, news distortion, and coercion of opinion that are without any counterpart in democratic-capitalist states.

Democracy and socialism.—It is an extremely important and extremely difficult question whether it is possible to maintain a real democracy and not merely mock democratic forms under the conditions of a fully accomplished socialist economy.

As everybody knows, a series of liberal economists and political scientists, as e.g., the Austrian Friedrich Hayek or the Swedish Herbert Tingsten, have vigorously maintained that democratic freedom and socialist economy are incompatible. My own view, which it would take too long to account for in detail, goes to show (1) that the assertion may be correct if "socialist economy" is taken in the sense of a totalitarian, centralized, state-directed economy on the Russian pattern, (2) that one has to make allowance for the possibility of a number of dangerous factors, but that (3), not forgetting those factors, it might be judged possible to combine genuinely democratic institutions with a socialist economy in the sense of a planned economy which within its framework would give suitable scope for decentralized autonomy.

With these premises in mind the *secondary, ideological* problem might be elucidated as follows:

Democracy as a political form may be valued either as an end in itself or as the only means, or at any rate the best means, of realizing the ideals implied in the concept of socialist economy. Whether one or the other is the case is a question of fact. It may of course occur that political dictatorship is valued as a means of realizing socialist economy. But this valuation rests on an erroneous conception of sociological interrelations according to the premises stated.

It is often asserted that political democracy as a form can never be valued as an end in itself. This is a postulate jarring with facts.

The question is, as already stated, of a factual nature: Do people value democracy not or not only for its real or supposed economic consequences, but only or also for the quality of the human interrelations that are direct consequences of democratic institutions, the right of active self-determination, legal security, freedom of speech, etc.? It is a fact that human interrelations under political democracy differ in a number of ways from what they are under political dictatorship; this may already serve as a basis for a valuation. It is furthermore an ideological fact that it is precisely this democratic liberty and way of life which to many people is a decisive factor in their valuation of democracy; they would prefer this form of government even if for one reason or another they did not value the economic consequences it leads or may be supposed to lead to.

22. TOLERATION OF DISSENTIENT OPINIONS.—To understand the problem of toleration in the setting of institutional democracy it is first of all necessary to delimit the problem. It is obvious that the freedom of expression can never be unlimited. There are a number of restrictions that do not constitute any violation of democratic ideals. The problem does not arise before these limits are transcended.

It is first of all obvious that democratic freedom of expression as an ideal cannot comprise expressions in writing or speech through which crimes may be committed: libel, lascivious utterances, false charges or testimony, disclosure of professional secrets, fraud, blackmail, etc.

In the same way, it also follows from the common principles of criminal law that the state must be entitled to punish the preparation of a crime that is brought about by words: instigation, advice, and planning with regard to the perpetration of a crime.

As a specific, but especially important case, one might mention the preparation or participation in preparation of the crime of forcible subversion of the constitution. It follows hence, that on the basis of the common principles of penal law it is justified to prohibit and punish participation in as well as propaganda for political movements advocating the forcible overthrow of the social order. Whether it is expedient to do so is another question: what is important in this context is only to emphasize that, if democracy will not tolerate the organization and propaganda of a party aiming at the use of violence this does not imply any curtailment of the freedom of expression as a basic democratic privilege. The use of violence has no right of existence in a democratic society, nor, consequently, have words or acts serving as a preparation thereof. There is nothing within the very system of the ideas of democracy to encourage a laissez faire attitude in front of forcible attacks on individuals or on the organization of society. Violence and the preparation of violence may, to the extent it is deemed necessary, be met by violence, by the organized power of the state. This is a more precise formulation of the idea that the democratic state is under no obligation to any individual who does not intend to "play the game," but has a right to give tit for tat. It has nothing to do with a restriction of the freedom of expression as a basic democratic right. The blow is directed not at a particular opinion but only at the means by which it is intended to be realized against violence.

What is more, commonly recognized principles allow that the state need not tolerate political propaganda carried on by dishonest or other unfair means. Just as democracy cannot tolerate the use of violence as a means to obtain changes in social conditions, neither can it tolerate any agitation preventing the free formation of ideas by poisoning public discussion with all the refined means of a ruthless propaganda of lies, slander, and agitation. Nor has this anything to do with restriction of the freedom of expression. No blow is struck at any particular opinion or conception, but only against means used in their propagation.

Discarding in this way the obvious excesses, freedom of expression as a democratic ideal may be defined as the freedom to state any political view, irrespective of its content, and to make propaganda for its realization, provided that the propaganda does not use improper means and does not aim at accomplishment through violence.

Accordingly, there is no restriction upon the freedom of expression until the propagation of political views is forbidden on account of their content.

Those in favor of such a restriction justify their stand by maintaining that it will pay to accept an admittedly regrettable loss—measured by the standard of the absolute ideal—because in return a better chance is gained that the reduced freedom will be safeguarded for the future. The principle is: a curtailed freedom that will last is better than an unrestricted freedom that runs the risk of being lost.

Whether this view is correct will depend on an estimation of the security to be obtained through the restriction, on one hand, and of the loss implied by the actual restriction in itself, on the other.

In my opinion, it is possible from both points of view to urge highly relevant arguments against restriction:

Objection 1: The security for the future that will be obtained through restrictions of the freedom of expression is in the main illusory. It is possible to shut people's mouths, but it is not possible to bind their thoughts. It is possible to forbid public propaganda, but never to prevent underground propaganda. The noxious germs may be thus prevented from spreading but not even this is certain. I think it is much better to let the evil out into broad daylight. It may then serve to immunize the people by creating antitoxins in the form of criticism and counterpropaganda.

If public opinion is carefully protected so that its ears never perceive any dangerous antidemocratic talk, there is an even greater risk that the evil will suddenly burst out and conquer the defenseless body. When last comes to last, the existence of democracy depends on nothing else than the strength with which the love for, and the faith in, the ideas of freedom, justice, and humanity are kept alive in a people. I do not think it possible to protect these ideas by restrictions. If they do not have the inward strength to hold their own in a contest with other ideas, neither are they strong enough to support the state.

When in Germany and elsewhere democracy broke down so easily, it was not because it recognized its opponents' right to speak, but among other things because the ideas of democracy had never really taken root in these newly established régimes.

To wish to perpetuate democracy by making its fundamentals indisputable is, in my opinion, impracticable. As soon as the majority, or even a considerable minority, have lost a living faith in the strength of these principles, democracy has already perished and cannot be saved by rules and regulations. In the long run it is no use stopping people's ears, as was done to Ulysses, in order that they shall not hear the song of the sirens. It is possible to force a people to live in slavery, it is not possible to force it to be free. Freedom grows solely through will power and faith, not through compulsion.

I admit that these views of mine cannot claim to be the expression of scientifically verified truths, but rest solely on a subjective *Weltanschauung* based on general experience of life.

Objection 2: The curtailment allocated in the freedom of expression is in its consequences a far greater infringement of democratic ideas than its adherents have realized. It entails an imminent danger that democracy may perish—not from any abuse of freedom of expression, but from its continuous restriction. If once we abandon the straightforward principle that violence can be met by violence, opinions only by opinions, the intricate problem arises: which opinions are to enjoy the protection of regulations sanctioned by the power of the state? If it is answered that the restrictions serve the protection of the fundamental ideas of democracy against antidemocratic propaganda, it must be remembered that views differ very widely on what constitutes the essence of democracy. After all, it is the majority that has to decide what is to be regarded as democratic and what as antidemocratic. Views on where to draw the line are bound to vary, with the effect that restrictions enforced under one party will differ radically from those enforced if another party were in power. In this way there is serious reason to fear that the power to restrict the freedom of expression will degenerate from an armor serving the protection of basic values into a weapon which can be used in the clashes of party politics and, before we realize it, will have undermined democratic freedom.

These reflections lead me to conclude that it is of vital importance to democracy to cling to the clear principle expressed in the formula: *Violence can be met by violence, opinions can only be fought with opinions.*

XXX

RUDOLF SCHLESINGER

The two basic concepts.—Present-day ideological conflicts are currently said to be waged between proponents of a "Western" and proponents of an "Eastern" conception of democracy. Actually the issue underlying the conceptual opposition is in its origin an exclusively Western one. There is no acceptable justification for the current way of labeling the opposed conceptions beyond the fact that political movements inspired by the economic and political teachings of Karl Marx have gained ultimate power in eastern Europe and large parts of Asia. But Marxism was itself only one of many divergent trends within Western democratic thought. The current conflict over the meaning of democracy reflects an issue of old standing within Western political thinking. The current East-West labeling of the conflicting conceptions ·can only gain some justification from the facts of the prevailing international power constellation.[1]

In a general way, the opposition may be described as one between a *sociological* and an *institutional* conception of democracy. The "sociological" conception is by far the elder one: Aristotle defines (*Politics* iv. 1290b) democracy as a régime based upon the poor freemen, and he expressly points out (*Politics* iii. 1280a) that poverty, not numerical majority, is the decisive criterion, a régime of the rich being termed an "oligarchy" even if the rich should happen to make up a majority, and a régime of the poor being termed a "democracy" even if the poor should be in minority. The transition from the sense "rule of the poor" to the sense "rule of the majority" has largely come about as a reflection of the social fact that there normally are more smallholders and artisans than merchants and usurers, more peasants than landlords, more workers than capitalists and that accordingly institutions based on majority-rule principles are likely to favor the interests of the lower-class

---

1. In certain contexts, therefore, the current terminology may be convenient; cf. my article "Western and Soviet Democracy," *Yearbook of World Affairs* (London, 1947).

376

strata of the population. The institutional conception of democracy actually emerged as a by-product of mass movements inspired by the original, the sociological, conception; in our days it has gradually become impossible to preserve any political order without the support of the majority of the governed. While revolutionary groups have ceaselessly been claiming to defend and promote the interests of the popular majority, ruling groups have not been less persistent in invoking the principle of majority consent in their efforts to preserve the existing social and political order. The institutional conception of democracy has only been able to intrench itself in countries where some scope has existed for gradual reforms in the conditions of the majority of the people, while the sociological conception of democracy as a process of liberation for the former underdog has come to prevail in countries where thoroughgoing revolutions have been found to be the only real solution of the social and economic problems.

But these two aspects of democracy cannot be finally separated: on the one hand, the institutional conception of democracy will furnish nothing but an empty formula unless the majority finds itself confronted with genuine opportunities of improving its conditions through the use of the control ideologically attributed to it; on the other, the sociological conception of democracy will degenerate into a mere phraseology unless concrete and reliable institutions are developed through which majority control and support can find regular and effective expression. In either case the application of "democratic" ideology would ultimately fail to serve its purpose, the strengthening of the régime saved by it.

In consequence, neither the proponents of the sociological nor the proponents of the institutional conceptions should be charged with misuse of the term "democracy"; the two conceptions do nothing but emphasize different aspects of one and the same sociopolitical problem. Misuse can only be charged when any action, any policy, any pattern of organization fitting the needs of the socioeconomic system preferred is indiscriminately praised as "democratic" whatever their relation to the establishment and preservation of majority rule and control.

"Democracy" was regularly misused in this way by laissez faire liberals and bourgeois ideologists. When de Tocqueville argued against socialism by identifying democracy with the preservation of "individual freedom" through free capitalist enterprise, he made an a priori case for bourgeois disobedience of majority decisions introducing socialist measures. He *misused* the term "democracy" by delimiting its possible contents in a way that was apt to go counter to the will and interests of the popular majority.

The identification of democracy with liberalism has been largely characteristic of Anglo-Saxon political thinking. Central European and eastern European thinking has generally taken a diametrically opposite stand; at the universities as well as in practical political life such an identification was definitely rejected. Democracy and liberalism were frequently regarded as not only different but opposite trends; this was so not only in the negative sense that democracy was rejected as contrary to liberal principles, but even in the positive sense that mass movements like the Catholic Center were eagerly proclaiming their allegiance to democracy even though they were outspokenly antiliberal.

It is important to emphasize the difference between the misuse of "democracy" as a synonym for economic liberalism and the definitions and standards of usage arrived at by historical analysts like Lord Bryce. In his *Modern Democracies* Lord Bryce simply makes the case for the institutional conception of democracy, divorcing it entirely from any social or economic contents. He does not misuse the term because his definition sets no limits to the kinds of decisions or policies a popular majority can vote for.

In the Eastern sphere it is even easier to find examples of automatic identification of "democracy" with the socio-economic order that is advocated, but this is a mere by-product of the normal urge for self-assertion characteristic of socialist movements at the stage when they are no longer fighting in opposition but have assumed the burden of leadership in the government of their states. But in all his writings between 1905—the year mass parties became possible in Russia—and 1917—the year of the Revolution—Lenin never fell for the temptation to identify democracy and socialism: he willingly described as democratic all parties opposing the czarist régime and operating upon mass support, including his main rivals, the Mensheviks and the Social Revolutionaries, although he was thoroughly convinced that they were both betraying the principles of socialism and even the cause of the democratic revolution.

The Soviet conception of democracy.—To take the Gettysburg

of, by, for formula as a point of departure for the analysis of the
differences between the Western and the Soviet conception of democracy may be inviting; but it is bound to be misleading: at least
since the defeat of the fascist régimes no government is conceivable
in any of the major countries which would not claim conformity to
all the three criteria laid down in the formula. *Of* indicates nothing
but the derivation of legitimacy: as distinct from paternal or oligarchic power "democratic" power finds its legitimation in its
derivation from the will of the people. *Of* might even, as is indicated in the UNESCO document, be interpreted to express the
mere truism that the people is being governed; in that case the
preposition would be even less suitable as an index of a specific
criterion of democracy. Current attempts to reduce the opposition
between the Western and the Soviet conception to one between
government *by* and government *for* the people may lead disastrous-
ly astray as is seen in the case of a statement made by Bertrand Russell: "The Anglo-Saxon definition of 'democracy' is that it consists
in the rule of the majority; the Russian view is that it consists in rule
in the interests of the majority, these interests being determined in
accordance with Marxist political philosophy."

This statement is misleading not so much for what it actually says
but for what it implies. Certainly the Anglo-Saxon conception of
democracy is of the majority-rule brand. Certainly the Soviet Russians regard their democracy as serving the interests of the people.
What makes the statement misleading is the juxtaposition of these
very crude definitions and the implication that their difference reflects the fundamental ideological opposition. Soviet political thinking has consistently stressed the participation as much as the interests of the masses, the *by* as much as the *for*. On the other side, not
all Western non-Marxists have fallen into the pitfall of out-and-out
emphasis on the formal participation element in democracy to the
total neglect of social and economic bearings. The fundamental opposition cannot be sought in a divergency of emphasis, but in differences in the interpretation and implementation of participation as
well as of interests.

By the people?—Lenin and all the Bolshevist authors along with
him have invariably stressed the participation element. They never
questioned the majority-rule characteristic of democracy. What
Lenin criticized in his *State and Revolution* was the assertion that

this characteristic sufficed to express the meaning of democracy: "We do not expect the advent of an order of society in which the principle of the subordination of the minority to the majority will not be observed."

But mere acceptance of the principle of minority obedience does not yet constitute democracy: "Democracy is a *state* which recognizes the subordination of the minority to the majority, i.e., an organization for the systematic use of *violence* by one class against the other."[2]

In Lenin's conception the Soviet régime is majority rule. In his *Contribution to the History of the Question of Dictatorship* he thus describes "the *fundamental* distinction" between the Soviet power and the former organs of power: "The latter were organs of the minority over the people, over the masses of workers and peasants. The former were organs of power of the people, of the workers and peasants, over the minority. . . . That is the distinction between a dictatorship *over* the people and a dictatorship *of* the revolutionary people. . . . The old power, as a dictatorship of the minority, could maintain itself only by police stratagems, only by preventing and diverting the masses from participation in the government, from controlling the government. The old power persistently distrusted the masses, feared the light, maintained itself by means of deception. The new power, as a dictatorship of the overwhelming majority, could and did maintain itself only by winning the confidence of the great masses, only by drawing, in the freest, broadest, and most energetic manner, all the masses into the work of government."[3]

What opposes Lenin's conception to the "Western" one, therefore, is not the rejection, on his part, of the principle of majority rule. On the contrary, Lenin may be said to have criticized bourgeois democracy primarily because it did not give any scope for consistent and effective majority rule. What Lenin rejected was the institutional forms cherished in the "Western" conception as the infallible expression of the actual political attitudes of the majority. To Lenin, democracy was not merely an institutional term, but a sociological one: democracy being characterized by the opportunity given to the majority of the people to participate in govern-

2. *Selected Works* (Moscow, 1936), VII, 75.
3. *Ibid.*, p. 252.

ment, a social organization, an institution, a policy should only be held "democratic" to the extent that it actually did allow for such opportunities. In this sense, socialism becomes democratic by definition: it makes the administration of economic life, the most essential part of the citizen's environment, a matter of public concern and policy and as a consequence places it within the *possible* range of majority decision-making. This does not imply that the possibility of majority control is necessarily realized with the victory of socialism; criticism of "bureaucracy"—of failure to appeal to the creative co-operation of the citizens—is at least as frequent in the field of economics as it is in other fields of Soviet life.

There is an obvious objection to this line of analysis of the Bolshevist point of view: it covers the experiences—possibly the delusions—of the early revolutionary era when there were yet open opportunities for the awakening masses to participate in the control of government, but it does not take into account the realities of the stabilized state that has since developed to the point where a well-organized bureaucracy has taken over all the main responsibilities, so that only a minority of citizens, as a leisure-time interest, take an active part in those state activities, mass participation in which is invited. After all, we do not base our judgments on Western democracy merely on the opportunities offered to a small but active minority, but primarily on the standards of general majority rule applied in the régimes in question. But in this context we are only concerned with the *standards* of Soviet government. There can be no doubt that Stalin acquired ultimate power over his opponents within the Communist Party precisely by giving constant emphasis to the urgency of basing the Soviet régime on the active participation and collaboration of the large majority of the people, not only of party members but particularly of those who were outside the party. In *On the Problems of Leninism* Stalin accepts the Leninist principle of party leadership in the working-class dictatorship, but with the rider that any such leadership presupposes relations of "mutual confidence" between the party and the masses. But "What if the Party itself begins, in some way or other, to contrast itself to the class, thus disturbing the foundations of its correct mutual relations with the class, thus disturbing the foundations of 'mutual confidence'? Are such cases possible? Yes, they are. They are possible:

"1. *If* the Party begins to build its prestige amongst the masses, not on its work and on the confidence of the masses, but on its 'unrestricted' rights;

"2. *If* the Party's policy is obviously wrong and the Party is unwilling to reconsider and rectify its mistake;

"3. *If* the Party's policy, although in general correct, is one which the masses are not yet ready to adopt, and the Party is either unwilling or unable to bide its time so as to give the masses an opportunity to become convinced by their experience that the Party's policy is correct.

"Can the Party impose its leadership on the class by force? No, it cannot. At all events, *such* a leadership cannot be to any degree a durable one."[4]

And Stalin sharply rejects the use of the term "dictatorship of the proletariat" in ways that would discourage the nonparty masses from contradicting and arguing with the party. In his fight first against Trotsky, later against the Sinovyev-Kamenev opposition he took a firm stand for mass co-operation and participation in government: "The dictatorship of the proletariat is not simply a government by an upper stratum 'skillfully selected' by the careful hand of an 'experienced strategist' and 'judiciously relying' on the support of one section or another of the population. The dictatorship of the proletariat is a class alliance between the proletariat and the labouring masses of the peasantry for the purpose of overthrowing capital, for achieving the final victory of socialism, on the condition that the guiding force of this alliance is the proletariat."[5]

Leadership of the working class and of the masses in general is defined as "the ability to convince the masses of the correctness of the Party's policy; the ability to put forward and to carry out such slogans as bring the masses to the Party position and help them to realize by their own experience the correctness of the Party's policy; the ability to raise the masses to the Party's level of consciousness and thus secure the support of the masses and their readiness for the decisive struggle.

"Therefore, the method of persuasion is the principal method employed by the Party in leading the class. . . .

"This does not mean, of course, that the Party must convince all the workers, down to the last man, and that only when this has been

4. *Leninism* (London, 1940), pp. 143 ff.
5. *Ibid.*, pp. 89-90.

achieved it is possible to proceed to action. . . . It only means that before entering upon decisive political actions the Party must, by means of prolonged revolutionary work, secure for itself the support of the majority of the workers or at least the benevolent neutrality of the majority of the class. . . .

"Well, and what is to be done with the minority, if it does not wish, if it does not agree voluntarily to submit to the will of the majority? Can the Party, should the Party enjoying the confidence of the majority compel the minority to submit to the will of the majority? Yes, it can and it should. Leadership is ensured by the method of persuading the masses. . . . This, however, does not preclude, but presupposes, the use of coercion, if such coercion is based on the confidence and support of the majority of the working class for the Party, if it is applied to the minority after the Party has convinced the majority."[6]

Statements like these give full evidence that the difference between the Soviet conception and the "Western" conception is not based on any disagreement on the principle of popular participation in political decision-making. Both conceptions stress the need for government by the consent of the governed. But the Soviet conception is opposed to the Western one by the unique function it assigns to the party in controlling all the means by which this consent can be brought into being.[7] It is important to keep in mind, however, that the current charges brought against the one-party system almost without exception overlook the crucial point that as distinct from most Westerners the Bolshevist Party does *not* believe in the all-embracing power of propaganda; it holds that only experience can confirm the correctness of any political line and that the masses by exchanging their experiences with those of the party have an opportunity to influence political decisions. As long as this exchange is effective and as long as mutual relations of confidence continue, the one-party system makes up an institutional form in which concrete realization can be given to government *by* the people, just as in a "Western" system the power of a wavering minority to tip the balances between two parties can be regarded as an institutional form in which at least the disagreement of the governed with their governors can be registered. Soviet Communists, how-

6. *Ibid.*, p. 146.
7. Cf. articles 125-26 of the 1936 Constitution.

ever realistic they may be as to the actual scope of the influence of mass reactions on their policy, may have ample reason to retort to any charges against their system by pointing to the limited scope given to electoral influence on established policy even within the Western system. In the Soviet as well as in the Western system agreement on the basic concepts of social and political life is taken for granted; in both, the scope of policy modifications open to the impact of variations in mass reactions has its very definite limits.

In a statement he made in 1918, Lenin saw a main advantage of the Soviet proletarian democracy in the fact "that the best mass organisation of the vanguard of the toilers, i.e., the proletariat engaged in large scale industry, is created, which enables it to lead the vast masses of the exploited, to draw them into independent political life, to educate them politically by their own experience, and that for the first time a start is thus made in teaching the *whole* of the population the art of administration, and in their beginning to administer."[8]

Indeed, when all elements of a slightly utopian flavor are discarded, this statement of Lenin's gives expression to what in my opinion still constitutes the essence of the Soviet conception of democracy. It is a conception that gives primary emphasis to government *by* the people by encouraging mass organization in order to obtain a maximum of popular participation in the functions of the state. And this emphasis on popular participation takes on even more importance when seen on the background of the vast scope of public functions that has developed in the Soviet Union with the increasing need for planning and regulation of the social and economic life of the people.

The emphasis on mass participation can be followed up in all current expositions of the functions of Soviet government. Take the 1946 edition of a university textbook on *Administrative Law*.[9] After a quotation from one of Stalin's speeches on the lessons of the purge, it is stated: "... *one of the fundamental elements* of adminis-

8. *The Immediate Tasks of the Soviet Government*, ed. cit., pp. 345–46.
9. I. I. Evtikhiev and V. A. Vlasov, *Administrativnoye Pravo S.S.S.R.* (Moscow: Jurisdat, 1946). The unfavorable reviews of this book in the Soviet press (some of which went to the length of describing it as dealing with police rather than with administrative law) even strengthen our case for using the quoted passage as a formulation of the *minimum* demands made in Soviet thought on mass participation in government.

trative practice, namely the issue of administrative acts, their execution and the check upon their execution, should be made directly dependent on the experience and the support of the masses.

"The organs of State administration are under an obligation to operate in their activities in close contact with mass organisations established for public purposes, to support their growth by all means, and to offer them ample opportunities for participation in administration.

"The most important aspect of the participation of the broad masses in public administration is their participation in the formation of the activities of the local Soviets. The Soviet system of local government grants the possibility of introducing a large part of the population to active work in reconstruction. Article 24 of the Statute on the Village Soviets (of 1930) states that "the introduction of the broad masses of the toilers of the village to immediate participation in government is a most important task of the Village Soviets," and article 25 prescribes the establishment of various departments at the Village Soviets "in order to attract the broad masses of the toilers to the Soviet's day-to-day work, and also in order to let all members of the Soviet participate in that work." Similarly a considerable body of active workers (*aktiv*[10]) is attracted to the work of the District and Town Soviets in the course of leisure-time social activities (*v poryadke obshchestoenoy raboty*[10]), especially in the fields of cultural and *bytovie*[11] services.

"Soviet State administration is characterized not only by broad participation of the masses of the population in administration, but also by differentiated forms of such participation. One of the basic forms of the participation of the toilers in administration is social (*obshchestvenye*) control. It may be carried out by observation of the work of the administrative machinery and result in suggestions to the administration through broad social meetings (Production Conferences, Trade Union meetings, meetings of the Factory Committee of the Trade Union with its *aktiv* of collaborators, etc.). The

10. *Obshchestvennaya rabota* means voluntary public service by Soviet citizens, as distinct from the officials' paid activities or compulsory civic service (e.g., in defense). *Aktiv* is the group of members of an organization, or employees of some enterprise, who regularly fulfil such "social work" and periodically meet in order to exchange their experience and to make suggestions.

11. Verbally: connected with (everyday) life, e.g., welfare, housing, family conditions, etc.

participation of the toilers in government may also be realised by direct help given to officials (e.g., . . . in carrying out mass observations) or by organized technical help (e.g., by associations of scientists or architects . . .)."

In these instances, and in others, such as parents' associations in the schools, social inspectors of state support and welfare activities for the dependents of soldiers; etc., the active citizens and their organizations merely support the organs of administration but do not relieve them from their ultimate responsibility for the decisions taken. The authors of the textbook, however, mention further examples (mainly relating to trade union activities in the health services, in administering social insurance, factory inspection, etc.) where the mass organizations, without losing their character as such, are granted executive administrative functions through legislative provisions and their decisions given binding force.

In the textbook *Soviet Public Law* the statement that the Soviets are the "most democratic, and, therefore, the most authoritative organization of the masses" is based upon the assertion that "first, they enable the fullest participation of the people in the construction of the State because the popular masses, through their representatives, establish the Constitution, and, secondly, the people takes an immediate share in administration."[12]

In the textbook *Foundations of Soviet State and Law*[13] four political principles are held to characterize Soviet democracy: (1) popular sovereignty, (2) concentration of all power in the hands of the Soviets, (3) "immediate democracy": mass participation in administration, (4) material guaranties for civic rights.

The fourth of these principles is embodied in the articles of the Soviet Constitution which guarantee the right of assembly by granting popular associations meeting-halls, the right of freedom of expression by granting them access to printing presses, and so on. The enactment of this principle gives legal expression to one of the major charges leveled by Marxist ideology against the "formal" democracy of the West: the constitutional rights given to the workers have no real meaning as long as economic and other barriers keep them from making practical use of the freedoms granted them on

---

12. *Sovietskoye Gossudarstvennoye Pravo* (Moscow: Jurisdat., 1947), p. 186.
13. *Osnovy Sovietskovo Gossudarstva i Prava* (Moscow: Jurisdat., 1947), pp. 98–99.

paper. This point, however, is of minor relevance to the analysis of the opposed conceptions of democracy; it is primarily polemical in intent and does not add to the actual contents of Soviet democracy as judged by its own standards.

Argument between the two opposed conceptions of democracy must not start out from questioning the opposite party's allegiance to the "*by* the people" principle, but by discussing the divergent views held in the two camps on the way "the people" can make its voice heard and the actual influence it has in the one system and in the other. In the Soviet conception "the people" makes its voice heard through the medium of public opinion encouraged by education, economic reforms and the extension of state functions to fields of decisive importance to the life of the citizens; in this conception, the people takes a vigorous part in the execution of government policies, a large part of the citizens becoming "active" helpers in state administration and in the management of the nationalized economy, and an even larger part finding it worth while to listen to and discuss reports from administrators, managers, judges, and so on, with a view to setting forth suggestions, criticisms, and counterproposals. In the Anglo-American conception, on the contrary, "the people" can mainly influence the policies of the state by "swinging the pendulum": that part of the people which has the weakest party allegiances may turn against the governing faction and give power to the alternative one, this prospect being regarded as a safeguard against the possibility of measures being carried through without majority consent.

Somewhere in *An American Dilemma* Gunnar Myrdal made the observation that American democracy is essentially characterized by a combination of mass passivity with individual leadership. Using this formula, the present analysis may justify us in characterizing Soviet democracy as a combination of mass activity with organized collective leadership.

For the people?—Every modern régime claims to govern *for* the people. The identification of Soviet democracy with "government *for* the people" gives no sense unless interpreted as a polite expression of the charge that the Soviet régime is *not* governed *by* the people but by leaders who think they know better than the people what is good for it. But so thinks every political leader and no differentiating characteristic of Soviet democracy can be found in that way.

If, on the other hand, the identification of Soviet democracy with government *for* the people is meant to imply that primary emphasis is given to *mass consumption* in the Soviet system, the statement of identification is definitely misleading. It is true that *ultimately* the masses are expected to profit, even as consumers, from the policies of socialist democracy, but as early as in 1936 a leading Soviet economist[14] was forced to withdraw the assertion that mass consumption was the main purpose of the Socialist reproduction process: in fact it was directed toward the creation of a Communist society. In all statements by Stalin on the objectives of economic policy the emphasis is laid on the urgency of increasing the *productive capacities* of socialist society. Soviet democracy is *not* based upon the assumption that it can supply the masses with milk and honey. On the contrary, if it could, it would be just as satisfied with mass passivity as older and wealthier systems have been. *Soviet democracy is based on the conviction that a state cannot expect its citizens to bring serious sacrifices for policies which have been adopted without their participation. All social and economic reforms in the Soviet system should be discussed less in terms of "raising the standard of life of the masses" than of "elevation of the economic and cultural level of the masses" in order to bring about "their active involvement in public affairs."*[15]

This conception of the ultimate aims of political action is clearly manifested in Soviet policies adopted for "backward" nationalities. To quote a statement by Stalin made in 1923:

"Equality of legal status, although in itself a factor of the utmost importance in the history of the development of the Soviet republics, is still a long way from actual equality. Formally, all the backward nationalities and all the tribes enjoy all the rights enjoyed by the other, more advanced nationalities of our federation. But the trouble is that some nationalities have no proletarians of their own, have never passed through the stage of industrial development, or even entered that stage, are frightfully backward culturally and are entirely unable to take advantage of the rights granted them by the

14. Academician Strumilin; cf. my report in *Zeitschrift für Sozialforschung*, 1938.
15. I consciously repeat the formulations used by Dr. Sweezy in his answers published elsewhere in this volume.

revolution. . . . Some of our comrades here think that the knot can be unravelled by stressing the question of schools and language. That is not so, comrades. Schools will not get you very far. The schools are developing, so are the languages; but actual inequality is the basis of all discord and friction. . . . Apart from schools and language, the Russian proletariat must take every necessary measure to establish centers of industry in the border regions in the republics which are culturally backward—and they are backward not through any fault of their own but because they were formerly looked upon as sources of raw materials."[16]

The chain of political purposes runs this way: capital investments for the development of industry, transformation of the social structure of the backward nations through the increase of the working class, better education, enlarged opportunities to develop the national forms of the common socialist culture, broader participation by the people in political life, strengthening of the ties of the Union. Compare with this policy trend the attitude of even very broad-minded Western democracies (after World War I) to the emancipation of colonial peoples: autonomy, even formal independence, may well be granted, but beyond very general stipulations about suffrage and elementary education nothing is done to bring about any advancement in the internal social and economic life of the country thus "set free." The aims of Soviet and Western policy toward dependent peoples are of course the same: the preservation of the actual economic and power-political links with the mother-country. But in the Soviet conception this aim is believed to be best served by a chain of positive measures strengthening local political life and stimulating economic activities in the backward countries, and not, as in the traditional Western conception, merely by granting them formal autonomy and leaving the rest to be settled internally.

Conclusion.—The UNESCO document underlying the present inquiry suggests a cleavage between democracy concepts stressing *methods* of decision-making and democracy concepts stressing *contents* of decision-making. It may well be that this distinction has some historical validity; liberals like de Tocqueville as well as socialists and syndicalists of all kinds gave definitional emphasis to the

16. Stalin, *Marxism and the National and Colonial Question* (English ed.; Moscow, 1940), pp. 137-38.

contents of democratic policy as of greater importance than the mere methods by which policy was determined. But any attempt to limit the use of the word "democracy" to specific policy contents prior to the determination of the actual preferences of the majority will only serve ideological purposes and lead to confusion of the issues at hand.

Soviet theorists would not quarrel on this point. To them democracy is majority rule. Lenin and Lord Bryce actually speak of *one* concept of democracy: a form of government in which public policies are determined by the preferences of the majority of the citizens. When Lenin attacked the Anglo-Saxon democracies he did not attack this definition, but the inconsistencies and imperfections manifested in all bourgeois attempts to implement it.

The real issue between Lenin and Bryce as far as the definition of democracy is concerned lies elsewhere: Should democracy be defined by the *method* alone or should the definition also include the *conditions* in which the methods are to be applied? This is the crucial point: there is agreement that governmental policy should be determined by the preferences of the majority, but there is disagreement on the social and economic conditions that must be realized if the people are to have genuine opportunities of knowing the alternatives and making up their minds about them.

The Lenin-Stalin position is clear: in the democracies of the West the broad masses of the working-class people are not living in conditions that make it possible for them to see the real alternatives and make effective choices between them. The defenders of the Western democracies may retort that whatever the imperfections of the conditions in their systems, the Soviet régime has even narrowed down the actual scope of effective popular preferences. But the fact remains that a purely legal formulation of the concept of democracy can never suffice in practical politics: a great number of non-legal data, of factors affecting "conditions of decision-making" have to be included if the electorate is to be given any real choice. Only in that way can the argument be pushed beyond the strictly ideological use of "democracy" in the propaganda war between the two camps and lead to serious discussion of the concrete social and political conditions of definite countries claiming to be "democratic," and of the effective range of choice actually open to the electorate under such conditions.

XXXI

PAUL M. SWEEZY

4. NEW USES.—It seems to me that the two main meanings of the word "democracy" which are current today are not essentially new but are rather the outgrowth of usages which go back at least as far as the nearly nineteenth century.

The central difference between these two usages concerns their attitude toward property, and to this most of the other differences can be directly or indirectly related. What may be called the "Western" usage takes for granted the inviolability of private property in the means of production; while the "Eastern" usage is basically hostile to private property in the means of production.

It can hardly be denied that both these usages have a long history in the Western countries themselves. Indeed I should say that what is now generally considered to be the Eastern conception of democracy is as much a product of western European history as is the Western conception itself.

That the Western conception of democracy is an outgrowth of a long tradition will probably be generally conceded. The fact, for example, that the Democratic Party in the United States has a more or less continuous history reaching back into the eighteenth century is eloquent testimony to this. The Democratic Party has undergone numerous changes; but throughout this period of more than a century and a half it has consistently associated the name democracy with the assertion (if not always with the practice) of certain principles which would be universally admitted to be central to the present-day Western usage of the term.

I think it is no less clear that the Eastern conception of democracy, with its economic emphasis and its rejection of private property in the means of production, has a long history behind it. Consider, for instance, the international society of Fraternal Democrats, which existed from 1846 to 1853 and which has been described as the true forerunner of the First International. The program of the Fraternal Democrats declared: "We renounce, re-

391

pudiate, and condemn all political hereditary inequalities and distinctions of caste; we declare that the present state of society which permits idlers and schemers to monopolize the fruits of the earth, and the productions of industry, and compels the working class to labour for inadequate rewards, and even condemns them to social slavery, destitution and degradation, is essentially unjust."[1] The Fraternal Democrats were thus outspoken socialists and revolutionaries. The average "Westerner" today might be inclined to assume that by calling themselves "democrats" they hoped to deceive the masses; but it is hardly likely that such an idea would have occurred to their contemporaries.

The fact is, as E. H. Carr has pointed out, that in Europe "before 1848 nobody had doubted that *political democracy* (one man, one vote) carried with it *social democracy* (equality or the levelling of classes), and that the progressive middle class which wanted universal suffrage was therefore fighting the cause of the masses."[2] He goes on to explain that "from 1848 onwards . . . political democracy ('liberal democracy') and social democracy ('socialism' or 'communism') were to be found on opposite sides of the barricades"; but this change did not take place until a half a century later in England where "the word democracy long remained in bad odour with the . . . ruling classes."[3]

Even in the United States, despite the long history of the Democratic Party, there are still those who reject the application of the term democracy to our political system. I recall a letter to the editor (it appeared in either the *New York Times* or the *New York Herald Tribune* within the past year or two) which scolded an editorial writer for calling the United States a democracy rather than a republic and implied, if it did not openly assert, that democracy is synonymous with the lawless rule of the majority which inevitably tramples on the sacred rights of private property.

The use of the term "democracy" in two different senses can be found in Marxian writings almost from the beginning. In the Com-

---

1. Theodore Rothstein, *From Chartism to Labourism* (1929), p. 131.
2. *The Soviet Impact on the Western World*, p. 8.
3. *Ibid.*, p. 9. Even on the Continent the old usage did not disappear overnight. For example, Renan remarks in the Introduction to his *Life of Jesus* (1st ed., 1863) that Luke "was a warm Evionite and democrat, that is to say, much opposed to property, and persuaded that the triumph of the poor is approaching" ("Modern Library" ed., p. 52). A present-day "Westerner" would hardly use the term in this way, but would not an "Eastern" democrat find it perfectly natural?

munist Manifesto (published early in 1848) I believe the only reference to democracy occurs in the following passage: "The first step in the revolution by the working class is to raise the proletariat to the position of ruling class, to establish democracy" (17th par. from end of Part II). Two years later, in the *First Address of the Central Committee of the Communist League to its Members in Germany*, Marx and Engels use the terms "democrat" and "democracy" to designate the petty bourgeois, antiworking-class party or element. But in one paragraph where this usage occurs we find the term "proletarian democracy" deliberately contrasted to it.

From this time until the Russian Revolution, I think it is safe to say that Marxists generally used the unqualified terms "democrat" and "democracy" in the bourgeois sense of the words. During this period they referred to their own brand of democracy as "social democracy" or "proletarian democracy." After the split in the world socialist movement which took place during World War I, the Communists repudiated the name "social democrat" and gradually dropped the qualifying adjective "proletarian" when referring to the Soviet system. Nowadays when the Communists speak of the Western democratic countries they generally use the qualifying adjectives "capitalist" or "bourgeois." Meanwhile the non-Communist wing of the Socialist movement has come to accept "bourgeois democracy" as the only possible form of democracy and has assumed that it can be carried over unchanged to a socialist system.

These few notes on the terminological history of democracy should, I think, be enough to show that there is ample *historical* basis for both the Western and the Eastern usages of the term.

8. THE LINCOLN FORMULA.—I have several fundamental objections to the interpretation of the three Lincolnian prepositions suggested in the UNESCO document: *of* indicating "the obedience of the people to the government"; *by* indicating "the active participation of the people in the formation of the decisions taken by the government"; and *for* indicating "the value of these decisions for the general welfare of the people."

First, and most important, I think that to interpret the preposition "of" as implying "the obedience of the people to the government" is a complete misreading of Lincoln's thought. I think that what he meant by "of the people" is *belonging to* the people; thus government of the people is government which emanates from and forms an inseparable part of the people, the polar opposite of government which is alienated from and stands above and opposed to the people. The point at issue here is crucial. Was Lincoln a quite ordinary admirer of law and order? Or was he voicing what is in its implications a revolutionary view, that the people must staff and run their own government? For my part, I have no doubt that the latter is the correct interpretation.

Second, I think the interpretation put upon "by" in the questionnaire is altogether too narrow. It is not simply a question of "active participation of the people in the *formation of the decisions* taken by the government." It is also, and at least as importantly, a question of the participation of the people in *carrying out the decisions* of the government.

Third, in the case of "for," the crux of the matter is not simply the value of government *decisions* for the general welfare of the people, but the primacy of the people's welfare for all aspects of governmental activity.

Finally, no interpretation of Lincoln's phrase is complete which neglects his use of the term "people." By "the people" Lincoln meant much more than merely the sum total of individuals living in the country. He meant first and foremost working people, the poor, the underprivileged. Lincoln was certainly no socialist, and he had no intention of excluding the wealthy; but I think there is little doubt that he felt that the true concern of government is with the masses and not with the wealthy.

9. NECESSARY CRITERIA.—If Lincoln's statement is interpreted in what seems to me to be the proper way, it establishes goals which democrats can strive to reach, but it hardly sets up criteria by which to judge whether a given government is or is not democratic. If Lincoln's formula is used with care and discrimination, it will help us to say whether one government is *more* or *less* democratic than another, and it will certainly help us to discuss the problem of democracy in relation to a given system of government rationally and intelligently. But I think it most unlikely that criteria can ever be found which will permit us to reach clear-cut conclusions on questions of this sort.

10. WESTERN VERSUS EASTERN DEMOCRACY.—The UNESCO document quotes a statement by Bertrand Russell reducing the

West-East opposition on "democracy" to an opposition between its definition as "the rule of the majority" and its definition as "rule in the interests of the majority"—as determined by the Marxist political philosophy.

In my judgment, this is not only an oversimplification, which, of course, could hardly be avoided in a single sentence, but a highly misleading oversimplification.

Bertrand Russell more specifically states the opposition to be one between an "Anglo-Saxon" and a Russian conception of democracy. I take it that he means to include the United States among the nations pledged to the "Anglo-Saxon" conception. The ensuing comments will focus on the United States. To avoid misunderstanding, however, it should be explained that when I speak of the American conception of democracy I do not mean, let us say, that which is implicit in the Gettysburg Address. I mean what could be called the "official" American conception—the conception which, for example, President Truman has in mind when he declares that the defense of democracy is one of the chief aims of American foreign policy.

In *this sense*, it seems to me that the essence of democracy is not at all the rule of the majority but the inviolability of the rights and privileges of minorities. Moreover, minorities are conceived in a broad sense to include all sorts of groups and classes, not merely ethnic and religious groups. Now social classes, as distinct from ethnic and religious groups, are what they are because of the nature of the underlying property system. Under capitalism, of course, the minority classes are the propertied classes; and not only their rights but their very existence depends upon the protection of the system of private property in the means of production. It follows that the obligation to protect the rights of minorities, as it is construed in the American conception of democracy, includes protection of the system of private property in the means of production; and in fact, if not in theory, it is this which constitutes the heart and core of that conception.

So far as the character of the government is concerned, this conception of democracy has purely formal standards which may or may not insure the rule of the majority. There must be two or more political parties competing for power, elections must be free from overt coercion, and the actions of the government must be okayed by an elected legislature. In countries with a long tradition of representative government, a system of this sort does in normal circumstances (and within the framework of the existing social order) insure majority rule; but in countries without such a tradition it can easily be manipulated by powerful minorities for their own benefit.

Bertrand Russell's assertion that the Russian conception of democracy "consists in the interests of the majority, these interests being determined in accordance with Marxist political philosophy," can hardly be described as wrong; but it is too indefinite to be of much use. It seems to me that the essence of the Russian (i.e., Soviet) conception of democracy is rather the elevation of the economic and cultural level of the masses and their active involvement in public affairs. The Russians, as Marxists, take it for granted that these objectives can be achieved only under socialism, i.e., public ownership of the means of production and comprehensive economic planning. Moreover, in the Soviet view, forms (which are so important to the Western conception of democracy) do not mean very much. People who are ignorant and exploited cannot govern themselves by any devices known to political science. It follows that at least for a considerable period of time democracy can have real meaning only to the extent that it is identified with a *process* of raising the standard of life of the masses.

11–13. POLITICAL DEMOCRACY–SOCIAL DEMOCRACY.—It is often asked whether "democracy" should be used in a "narrow" political sense or in a "broad" social sense. I am inclined to think that questions of this kind pose pseudo-problems. The term "democracy" is, in fact, used in both the narrow and the broad senses, and both usages can claim ample historical justification. Under these circumstances, I do not see how it is possible to say that the term "should" be used in one way and "should not" be used in another. What is important is that there should be general awareness of the fact that "democracy" means different things to different people. When this awareness has been achieved, we shall be able to dispense with accusations of dishonesty and bad faith and can concentrate on the real issues at stake between the proponents of different kinds of democracy. In other words, it seems to me that *clarity* in the use of the term is much more important than *uniformity* (which could, in any case, not be obtained).

In discussing the relationships between what is called "political

democracy" and what is called "social democracy," it is important
first to make explicit what these much battered terms are assumed
to imply. In the ensuing comments, "political democracy" will be
roughly equated with universal suffrage combined with freedom of
expression and organization; while "social democracy" is taken as
roughly synonymous with the process of raising the economic and
cultural level of the masses without discrimination on grounds of
race, sex, or religion.

Another important premise of my conclusions should also be
made explicit: I have assumed, without attempting to prove, that at
any rate for the vast majority of mankind the possibilities of achieving social democracy are extremely limited under capitalism and
that only under socialism can the tremendous potentialities of modern technology be fully realized. (It goes without saying that anyone who rejects this second assumption will also reject most, if not
all, of what follows.)

With so much understood, let us consider the various parts of the
question in order.

First, is "political democracy" the best means to achieve the goal
of "social democracy"? The answer, I think, must be that for
capitalist (or pre-capitalist) countries some gains can be achieved
by the methods of political democracy, but that ultimately the
question has to be transformed into: Is "political democracy" the
best (or even a possible) means to achieve socialism?

This is, of course, a question which socialists have debated for
many decades without arriving at any generally agreed solution.
My own opinion—and I think it was also the opinion of Marx and
Engels—is that there is no universally valid answer. Under certain
historical conditions it is possible for socialism to be achieved by
the methods of political democracy. Thus, for example, Marx,
speaking in 1872 at the Hague Congress of the First International,
specifically named England and the United States as countries
where this might be done. Engels repeated the assertion with regard
to England in his introduction to the English translation of Volume
I of *Capital* (1886): Marx was led by lifelong study, Engels wrote,
to "the conclusion that, at least in Europe, England is the only
country where the inevitable social revolution might be effected
entirely by peaceful and legal means." Writing *State and Revolution* in 1917, Lenin concluded that such possibilities no longer

existed; but already by 1924 Stalin felt justified in asserting once again the possibility of a " 'peaceful' transition," this time in countries which might become subject to a "Socialist encirclement" (*Foundations of Leninism*). If it is correct, as I believe it is, to equate "peaceful" and "legal" in these quotations with the methods of political democracy as the term is here used, then it must be admitted that even the revolutionary school of Marxism has never taken a dogmatic position on this question. On the other hand, it is equally clear that there are historical conditions in which the methods of political democracy either cannot be used at all or could not lead to the achievement of socialism.

To sum up: political democracy cannot lead directly to the goal of social democracy, but under certain historical conditions it is the best means to the achievement of socialism which can and will lead to the goal of social democracy.

Second, is "social democracy" the best means to achieve the goal of "political democracy"? I do not consider political democracy in the present sense to be a goal at all. It is true that freedom of expression must exist in a developed social democracy, since it is essential to the attainment of a high general cultural level. But freedom of expression is conceivable in the absence of a multiplicity of political parties and even in the absence of *any* political parties. It may be that in practice something like what we now call political democracy will turn out to be an effective, perhaps even an essential, method of bringing social democracy to its fullest development. But supposing this to be the case, political democracy remains a means, never an end.

Third, is "political democracy" a means to any single goal at all? Certainly not. Political democracy can lead in quite different directions depending upon specific historical conditions. The example of certain countries today even suggests that political democracy is compatible with a type of aggressive imperialism which threatens the peace of the world. It all depends on *who* uses political democracy *for what*. The belief that political democracy *must* lead in a definite, predetermined direction is irrational and untenable.

Fourth, are the two concepts at all related as means to ends? My answer to this has been given, at least by implication, in the preceding paragraphs: under certain circumstances political democracy can be an indirect means to the end of social democracy. It may be well to add that this is likely to be the case where political democracy has deep historical roots, while it is unlikely to be so in countries where, for a complex of reasons which cannot be discussed here, it is possible to move more or less directly from a predominantly pre-capitalist social system to socialism. In such countries, socialism will eventually bring social democracy as well as those aspects of political democracy which can be regarded as desirable for their own sake. It may also bring political democracy as such, but on this point we cannot yet speak with assurance.

16. METHOD VERSUS CONTENTS.—The UNESCO document repeatedly attempts to clarify the ideological opposition by focusing on the much debated distinction between *methods* of decision-making and *contents* of decision-making. I assume that "decision" can be considered synonymous with "policy" and that accordingly the alleged distinction can be taken to be equivalent to that between the way policies are determined and what the policies are.

When the matter is put in this way, it immediately strikes one that a third aspect of the governmental process is altogether left out in the formulation of the question. I refer, of course, to the carrying out of policies. Thus I would make a threefold rather than a twofold distinction: *determination* of policy, *content* of policy, and *execution* of policy.

Like all distinctions, these can be helpful or misleading, depending upon how they are used. If they are used for the purpose of chopping up what is really a single process into separate parts or stages, the conclusions reached will almost certainly be misleading. On the other hand, if they are used to focus attention on the interconnecting elements of what is recognized to be a single process, they will help us to achieve clarity and understanding.

There is not much to be said, I think, for reserving the term "democracy" for one element of this process. I should rather say that the process as a whole is more or less democratic to the extent that the people (*a*) play a role in policy determination, (*b*) benefit from the policies adopted, and (*c*) participate actively in the execution of policies. Thus I would say that a government with several parties, an honest electoral system, and formal freedom of discussion (in other words, a government which would presumably be perfectly democratic in the view of the "narrow" constructionists) can be less democratic in any sense that has substantial meaning than a government which may be dominated by one party. This would be the case if the one-party government were sufficiently ahead of the multi-party government in working for the people's welfare and in mobilizing the people for active participation in public affairs. I would even say that the multi-party government may be less democratic in the narrow sense of allowing the people to participate in policy determination, for such a government may in reality be completely dominated by the "invisible" forces which control the party machines and mold public opinion.

17. CRUCIAL DIFFERENCES.—It seems to me that when classical liberals like de Tocqueville and Bryce speak of democracy in general and without qualification they mean much the same as Lenin does by "democracy for the minority, only for the possessing classes, only for the rich." The crucial difference between the two lines of argumentation, therefore, consists in this, that de Tocqueville and Bryce implicitly assume that in capitalist society democracy means the same thing to everyone, while Lenin explicitly denies this.

The explanation of this difference is not far to seek. De Tocqueville and Bryce were members of the ruling and possessing classes and were in a position to enjoy all the benefits of democracy. They naturally tended to generalize from their own experience and to assume that democracy, since it applies to everyone, must bring the same advantages to all. From this point of view, furthermore, the organization of social life implied in socialism would necessarily mean a restriction of *their* freedom and hence, by a parity of reasoning, a general limitation of freedom. Lenin, on the other hand, had consciously taken his stand with the exploited and underprivileged classes, and he understood that the great majority lacked the means—economic, intellectual, cultural—to take advantage of the formal rights accorded to them by democracy. Hence to Lenin socialism meant, on the one hand, a restriction of the freedom of a few and, on the other, a vast expansion in the field of choice, which is the basis of all freedom, for the many. It was natural for Lenin to conclude that democracy could have real meaning for the masses only under socialism; and it seems that to be consistent he would have had to add, only *after* socialism had already begun to accomplish its work of elevating the economic and cultural level of the masses.

It should be particularly noted that neither Lenin nor Stalin deny the right of capitalist countries to use the term "democracy." What they claim is that democracy as practiced in capitalist countries is democracy for the few, while democracy for the many can be realized only under socialism. Since the tasks of the state are necessarily very different under socialism from what they are under capitalism, it follows that two very different governmental structures can with good reason be called "democratic." We thus arrive by a different route at a conclusion reached above that the term "democracy" has more than one legitimate meaning and cannot be claimed as the exclusive property of any form of government or social system.

19. EXPRESSION OF "REAL INTERESTS."—Let me rephrase this question as follows: How can you tell whether a given method of decision-making gives a full and equal expression to the real interests of everyone?

The answer, I think, is that *no* method of decision-making can possibly accomplish this end. The method of political decision-making is one small element in a vast and complex socio-economic system. As such, it must operate, within relatively limited margins of tolerance, according to the design of the system as a whole. It follows that if the system runs counter to the interests of a particular group or class, there is no possible way for those interests to receive "full and equal" expression within the framework of that system.

It should be added that this does not mean that the method of political decision-making is unimportant. The margins of tolerance do exist, and some methods will come closer to the goal of giving expression to the interests of all than others.

23. REPRESSION OF PROPAGANDA.—In answering this question, I must revert to an idea expressed previously, namely, that it is not possible to label actual governments or social systems either "democratic" or "not democratic." In practice it is always a question of "more democratic" or "less democratic."

I regard any limitation on freedom of expression as *ipso facto* a move in the "less democratic" direction—let us call it a retreat. But there are obviously occasions on which a retreat is necessary either to prevent a rout or to prepare the way for a subsequent advance.

There are other occasions on which a retreat is either quite unnecessary or the first stage of complete defeat. In judging any given act of suppression, we have to decide what sort of situation we are dealing with. Are we dealing with an infringement of democracy which is designed to help make possible later advances toward greater democracy? Or are we dealing with an infringement of democracy which will pave the way for further infringements in the future?

These, I think, are the crucial questions, and unfortunately there are no ready-made formulas for answering them. Moreover, bourgeois and socialist are likely to come to different conclusions even in the event that they can reach agreement on the facts of the case. Thus, for example, a socialist believes that in the long run the fullest realization of democracy will be possible only under socialism. He could therefore hardly be expected to regard the suppression of socialist propaganda as a strategic retreat in a larger battle for greater democracy. One who believes that capitalism is the best possible system, on the other hand, might come to precisely this conclusion. In the case of an already established socialist system, the roles might be reversed. Here the socialist might consider the suppression of capitalist propaganda necessary in order to make possible the advances to greater democracy which the development of socialism will bring with it; while the advocate of capitalism would of course take an opposite position. We cannot conclude, however, that Bourgeois and Socialist can *never* agree that suppression is in the interest of democracy. When it comes to doctrines like Fascism, which reject democracy in principle, bourgeois democrats and socialists can agree on the necessity for suppression. Indeed, most of the wartime compacts between Roosevelt and Churchill, on the one hand, and Stalin, on the other, were based on just such an agreement.

There are, of course, many more problems which inevitably arise in any careful consideration of the relation between democracy and limitations on the freedom of expression. Perhaps the most important and difficult problem can be illustrated as follows.

Let us concede that in the long-run interests of democracy a Socialist society is justified in suppressing dissent which threatens the stability of the system. How is it to be decided which kinds of dissent fall in this category? No general answer to this question seems possible: every situation in which it arises must be analyzed separately, and it is to be expected that in no two cases will the conclusions be the same. It goes without saying that this problem exists for others besides Socialists; *any* supporter of democracy—unless he believes in absolute tolerance regardless of the consequences—has to face it in times like these.

A vexing aspect of this whole question arises from the way in which dissent tends to get mixed up with treason when competing social systems take the concrete form of co-existing sovereign nations. Under these circumstances, it is obvious that the rivalry between the two systems is always likely to take the form of international war, and those who live under one system and favor the other are bound to be under suspicion of treason. Since everyone takes it for granted that a nation has the right to suppress treason, there is naturally a strong temptation to use the allegation of treason as a pretext for suppressing dissent. That democracy can be gravely impaired in this way goes without saying.

If it is asked whether the *kind* of change advocated is relevant to the question of repression, it must be recognized that one's answer to this question, as in the case of so many others in this questionnaire, depends upon one's basic social philosophy. Whoever believes that the existing social system (whatever it may be) is the only one under which democracy can flourish will say that the kind of change does not matter. Whoever believes that the existing system is inimical to the development of democracy will say that it certainly does matter. One can decide these issues (if at all) only at the most fundamental level of social analysis. I think I have made my own position clear in answers to earlier questions; and, since it would be impossible to present the reasoning behind it in a brief space, there is nothing to be gained from repetition at this point.

26. "SKEPTICISM" AND DEMOCRACY.—First, let me say that, if formulated as in the UNESCO document, the alleged justification of party multiplicity from philosophical "skepticism" seems to me an absurdity. Obviously "no opinion is infallible" and "no group has any self-evident right" to claim anything, let alone universal allegiance to its political creed. The questions which are relevant to the problem under discussion are quite different and may be posed

as follows: (1) Are all opinions equally valid? and (2) Among competing political creeds, is there one which is more likely than the others to be compatible with the long-run maintenance and development of democracy?

The most confirmed skeptic would hardly claim that all opinions are equally valid. For example, even Mr. Brogan would presumably reject voodooism as a basis for diagnosing and curing the ills of society. But why reject voodooism? Surely because a rational analysis, using the ordinary methods of scientific inquiry, shows that it is unreliable. If this much is granted, then we are entitled to ask why it is not possible, *at least in principle,* to apply the same methods to other opinions and find out which are and which are not reliable. Perhaps this has not yet been done for all possible opinions; it may be that we do not yet know how to do it in the case of some. But neither of these facts (assuming that they are facts) provides any justification for raising skepticism to the level of a philosophical principle.

Once we have dethroned skepticism and admitted the possibility of genuine social science, there is no longer any reason to deny that one political creed may be more compatible with democracy than others. It is a question of fact to be settled by rational analysis and not by appeal to philosophical principles.

This argument, it should be noted, provides no justification for either a one-party or a multi-party system. But it does deprive the multi-party system of any special philosophically guaranteed sanctions.

29. ULTIMATE AIMS.—A comparison of the ultimate aims of political action as professed by Lenin and Stalin with those professed, say, by traditional British or American liberals brings into relief the crucial differences of approach. The aims proclaimed by Lenin would be acceptable to liberals with hardly a trace of dissent, and yet this does not mean for a moment that Leninism and liberalism are reconcilable. Once again, we have to do with basic differences of social analysis and interpretation.

The liberal would argue, I think, that the aims set forth in the quotation from Lenin are altogether admirable and praiseworthy but that they are hopelessly utopian. The liberal then establishes what he considers to be practical aims, which are in fact nothing but relatively small reforms within the framework of the existing social system. Thus, despite agreement on ultimate values, the aims of the Leninist and the liberal are widely apart and imply radically different courses of action.

Nor is this all. The liberal is likely to feel that the Leninist who is a genuine idealist and passionately believes in the attainment of his utopia is for these very reasons an extremely dangerous person. The liberal argues that the perfect will drive out the good and leave only the bad. The Leninist, for his part, is likely to feel that the liberal's profession of lofty ideals is sheer hypocrisy since he deliberately refuses to seek to realize them in practice. Thus the very fact that they both accept the same ultimate values turns into a source of contention and bitterness.

I conclude that the common belief that only disputes which involve ultimate values are deep-seated and intractable is entirely fallacious.

30. THE BASIS OF THE CONFLICT.—I think the disagreements with which we are concerned are all these things: terminological and factual as well as normative. But as I have repeatedly suggested, I think it is perhaps first of all a disagreement over the analysis and interpretation of society. Or, to put it otherwise, it is a disagreement over human nature and the meaning of history. If agreement could be reached on *these* issues, I believe that differences of a terminological, factual, and normative character, though they would certainly not disappear overnight, would prove to be relatively easy to deal with.

From my point of view, I should explain, this is an optimistic conclusion. I think that Marxism is a genuine science of society which will ultimately command general assent for the same reason that, e.g., modern physics commands general assent, i.e., because it is true. If this is right, then what I regard as the most intractable disagreements of an ideological character will gradually disappear.

What is holding this process up at the present time? The answer, I think, is that those who have vested interests in the maintenance of capitalism do not want the truth to be taught. This is certainly a formidable obstacle, but there can hardly be any doubt that it will eventually be overcome.

C. J. DUCASSE, COMMENTS ON DR. SWEEZY'S ANSWERS

Dr. Sweezy's answers follow for the most part logically enough from his premises. The disagreements between him and those who oppose Communism are thus ultimately rooted, as he suggests in his last answer, in disagreement with the analysis and interpretation of society which he presupposes.

His basic premise is that "Marxism is a genuine science of society"—genuine and authoritative in the same sense and for the same kind of reasons as physics, namely, because it alone has the truth as to the matters it deals with.

Now, that Marxism in particular, or "social science" in general has the same scientific status as physics is, I submit, a piece of wishful thinking as patent as that which leads the theologians of various religions to claim the status of knowledge for the contents of the particular scriptures they accept.

The fact is that social science, so called, is today in its infancy, whereas physics is the most mature of the sciences.

It is the most mature because it is the easiest; and it is the easiest because: (a) the variables it studies are fewer than in any other science; (b) experimentation in its field is easily possible; (c) the conditions necessary to make an experiment significant, namely, introduction of only one change at a time in the experimental setup, can, in physics, be satisfied relatively easily and rigorously; (d) the things physics observes are relatively uniform: individual differences are much less there than, for instance, in biology or in psychology; (e) until one comes to sub-atomic particles, the behavior of the things physics studies is not altered at the time of observation by the fact that they are being observed; and, (f) their future behavior is not altered by acquisition of knowledge of the laws which their behavior exhibits in the absence of such knowledge.

In social science, on the other hand, what we find is the contrary of each of these features of physics. Because of this, social science today is hardly even as much of a science, properly so called, as was physics in the days of Galileo. Indeed, the last of the differences mentioned between it and physics makes highly dubious whether social science can ever be a science of anything more than the *past;* for human beings have a unique peculiarity, namely, that their becoming aware of the factors that have until then motivated their behavior creates for them the possibility of being thereafter motivated no more, or motivated differently, by those same factors: There is hardly a man who, if he were to witness a movietone of his acts and words of the day, would not thereby be motivated to behave differently to some extent the next day. *Man is the animal that cannot with immunity look into a mirror.*

With regard to physics, one more remark is pertinent, namely, that although it is the most advanced of the sciences, it claims for its theories no such truth and finality as does Dr. Sweezy for the Marxist theory of society. Physics claims for its theories only more or less of probability, the degree of probability claimed being strictly relative to the amount and nature of the evidence possessed at the time, and being always susceptible of alteration down or up by new evidence.

In the light of these facts, I submit that the assertion either that social science in general, or specifically the Marxist analysis and interpretation of society, is a science fairly comparable with physics as regards method or authoritativeness, is seen to be patently false; and that the claim by the adherents of Marxism to speak in the name of scientific method is but the counterpart of the theologian's equally wishful claim to be speaking in the name of God.

It is but a way of investing themselves in the eyes of the credulous, who include themselves, with an authority they lack in fact. The theologies, too, claim to be sciences, but in either instance what one actually finds are only various sets of speculative opinions, more or less internally coherent, and leaning on piously accepted scriptures, but conflicting with other sets, and, like their rivals, empirically supported only by scanty and highly precarious evidence. This, unfortunately, does not deter the adherents of either from fanatical devotism to the particular creed they accept, nor from violent or crafty attack on all others.

Since then the factual situation we have is not demonstrated truth on one side and demonstrated errors on the other, but as yet only several more or less divergent opinions as to the analysis and interpretation of society, it follows that the multi-party system for dealing with practical affairs does have over the one-party system the advantage of giving to the claims of each of the divergent opinions their chance to be presented and presented by those who believe them valid. This insures that the practical decision eventually reached shall proceed, not indeed from assured knowledge, yet not from blind opinion either, but from opinion that will have been enlightened as fully as possible by having listened to the variety of claims presented.

Dr. Sweezy's statement that "social classes . . . are what they are because of the underlying property system" is, of course, an article of the Communist creed. As against this, it may be contended that differences in degree of power and in kinds of powers are what really make social classes, whether it be property or something else that confers the power. For example, even under the Soviet system, there are still those who command and those who obey; those who ride and those who walk; those who enjoy good living quarters and good food and those who have to put up with poor lodgings and poor food. And the *de facto* use and enjoyment of these things, or the lack of it, is what actually counts in the lives of the individuals concerned, and not whether such use and enjoyment derives from "ownership" or from something else. For the individual, ownership that does not confer them is, whether personal or collective, purely technical and concretely worthless; whereas political position that, even without ownership, does confer them is practical and concretely worth having.

Moreover, if it be said that what confers them in Russia is "service to the people," the reply is that this indeed is the theory, but that the "service" rendered is "service" *as defined by those in power* who render it, *not* by those who have to receive it no matter whether they themselves would call it service or perhaps tyranny.

But, further, precisely the same claim is made for the capitalistic system by its protagonists, that under it, service to the people is what brings to those who render it property and such power and enjoyments as it confers. And, in *both* cases, the claim is true to *some* extent. But, in both cases, what originally *brings* power is one thing; and what is *done with* the power once it is attained, by those who have it, can be and often is quite another thing. Arbitrary or selfish use of power is nothing peculiar to the capitalistic system.

Again, any argument phrased in terms of such epithets as "exploited" and "underprivileged" on the one hand, and on the other "exploiter," "propertied," and "privileged"—with their respective connotations of "deserving" and "undeserving"—is question-begging; and is so as patently as it would be to label *ab initio* the same two groups, respectively, "the shiftless, improvident, and lazy," and "the industrious, farsighted and courageous entrepreneurs, who make jobs for the many that haven't the wit or the will to do it for themselves."

The fact is that all four of these labels fit *some* persons. But greedy, unscrupulous, and selfish persons are just as common among the masses as among capitalists. Loafers and irresponsibles are equally so whether they be more particularly "tramps" or "playboys." And many property owners work as hard, as long, and as usefully to society as do many manual laborers, and are as conscientious, as fair dealing, and as mindful of the welfare of their fellow-men.

To classify men into "the good" and "the wicked" is childish, no matter whether one does so nakedly or, on the contrary, deviously by means of such question-begging epithets as "proletarian," "capitalist," "worker," "bourgeois," "revolutionary," "reactionary," "enemy of the people," and the like. Indeed, even "objectivism" is now used by Communists as a term of opprobrium. Comparably arrogant and irresponsible identification of the truth with what they themselves believe is to be found only among the most bigoted devotees of some of the religions.

Paul M. Sweezy, Reply to Professor Ducasse

I never asserted that Marxism "has the same scientific status as physics," nor did I claim for Marxism a degree of truth and finality which goes beyond any of the claims of physics. It just isn't so. I do not know where Professor Ducasse got the idea from. What Professor Ducasse says of physics holds of Marxism without mitigation, namely, that it "claims for its theories only more or less of probability, the degree of probability claimed being strictly relative to the amount and nature of the evidence possessed at the time, and being always susceptible of alteration down or up by new evidence." All of which does not prevent physics from claiming a very high degree of probability for the law of gravity or Marxism from claiming a very high degree of probability for the thesis that capitalism is a self-contradictory system which is being replaced and will continue to be replaced by socialism.

The crucial problem raised by criticism along the line indicated in Professor Ducasse's comments is this:

Are Marxists justified in concluding that because Marxism is a valid social science they would have the right—assuming that they had the power—to suppress all opposing opinions? In my judgment, the answer is "certainly not." Just because an opinion is wrong—and regardless of whether the reason is ignorance, superstition, or learned attachment to a false theory—is no reason why it should be suppressed. It is rather a reason why the person holding the wrong opinion should be patiently shown *why* it is wrong and educated to hold what is, so far as the state of scientific knowledge permits us to know, the right opinion. And, it may be added, it will be possible to show and educate large masses of people holding wrong opinions only when the conditions which foster ignorance, superstition, and false theories have been done away with, that is to say, when society is based on the rational principle of planned production for the general welfare.

That this is the traditional attitude of Marxism can, I think, easily be shown. Take the case of religion in the sense of belief in the existence of a supernatural deity. As is well known Marxism rejects religion in this sense. But does that mean that it is a part of the program of Marxism to suppress religious views and practices? Of course not. Marxists believe, to quote Engels, that: "When society, by taking possession of all means of production and using them on a planned basis, has freed itself and all its members from the bondage in which they are now held by these means of production which they themselves have produced but which now confront them as an irresistible extraneous force; when therefore man no longer merely proposes, but also disposes—only then will the last extraneous force which is still reflected in religion vanish; and with it also will vanish the religious reflection itself, for the simple reason that then there will be nothing left to reflect."[1]

And the Marxist attitude toward any attempt to suppress religion by force is spelled out by Engels in the next paragraph: "Herr Dühring, however, cannot wait until religion dies this natural death. He proceeds in more deep-rooted fashion. He out-Bismarcks Bismarck; he decrees sharper May laws not only against catholicism, but against all religion whatsoever; he incites his gendarmes of the

1. Fr. Engels, *Anti-Dühring*, Part III, chap. v.

future to attack religion, and thereby helps it to martyrdom and a prolonged lease of life."

It is clear, therefore, that Marxism does not claim science as a justification for suppressing opposing opinions. Unfortunately, however, this does not quite dispose of the problem. There are times, particularly revolutionary times, when opinions become so involved in social conflict that they cannot escape being treated as weapons. Now Marxists are revolutionaries (though not conspirators, as their opponents persist in believing), and whenever they succeed (as they are convinced they will succeed everywhere, sooner or later) they claim the revolutionary right to protect the new order against counter-revolution. To a varying extent, depending on specific conditions and historical backgrounds, the defense of a revolution may involve suppressing opinions. This is unfortunate, and I think all Marxists should regret it in exactly the same way that they regret the fact that people lose their lives in revolutions. They should hope and work for revolutions from which both bloodshed and the suppression of opinions are absent, and they should of course not justify suppression by self-righteous appeals to science.

This is one side of the question of the relation between social science and democracy. But there is another side, as I indicated in my original reply to the UNESCO questionnaire. If, as I believe to be the case, Marxism *is* a valid social science, then certainly I, as a Marxist, cannot admit the tenability of the defense of multi-party democracy and free expression on the ground that there is no such thing as a valid social science. To do so would be absurd. Multi-party democracy and freedom of expression can be defended on many different grounds, but in my judgment they emphatically cannot be defended on the ground that we do not have or cannot achieve valid knowledge of society, its real interests, and the possible ways it can develop in the future.

Finally, a word about Professor Ducasse's opinion that the multi-party system "insures that the practical decision eventually reached shall proceed, not indeed from assured knowledge, yet not from blind opinion either; but from opinion that will have been enlightened as fully as possible by having listened to the variety of claims presented." Quite apart from the question as to whether and to what extent assured knowledge is attainable, I find this a somewhat less than adequate description of the way the multi-party system actually operates. It would require us, for example, to regard the press and educational institutions of the United States as the representatives of "divergent opinions as to the analysis and interpretation of society" rather than what they are, namely, to an overwhelming extent the representatives of the highly uniform opinions and ideology of the small class which happens to own the means of production.

C. G. FIELD, COMMENTS ON DR. SWEEZY'S ANSWERS

Dr. Sweezy's answers are of great interest as throwing light, sometimes unconsciously, on the Marxian approach to the problems raised by the UNESCO inquiry. On some points, I feel in considerable agreement with him, but there are several others on which I feel in sharp disagreement. Some of these, I think, are already dealt with by implication in my response to the UNESCO questionnaire, but I think it worth while for the general clarification of the issues to deal more specifically with three or four points which raise further questions, in these comments.

Sweezy on the historical basis of the "Eastern" usage.—I think that Dr. Sweezy entirely fails to make out his case for a historical basis for what is called the "Eastern" usage of the word "democracy."

Of course, a person or group who wanted democracy in the traditional sense might, and often did, *also* advocate greater economic and social equality and the rest. What is true is that most people thought in the first part of the nineteenth century that democracy would in fact lead to equality, i.e., that if the majority of people had the vote they would use it to equalize property or abolish it altogether. But that does not show that they confused or identified democracy with the policy that they thought it would follow. What Dr. Sweezy must find to make his point would be clear statements to the effect that if an absolute dictator or small group of rulers, without allowing the mass of people to vote freely on the subject or to have a share in the decision at all, were to establish equality of property, or carry through other desired reforms to the economic system, then that would be properly called a democracy. And I very much doubt whether he can find any such statement.

Sweezy on the central difference between the two usages.—But I think that the most glaring fallacy, which vitiates a great deal of his argument, is committed in his first answer. He there says that the "central difference between these two usages lies in their attitude toward property," and he goes on to say that "what may be called the 'Western' usage takes for granted the inviolability of private property in the means of production." How he can have come to make a statement so obviously at variance with the facts as that contained in his last sentence passes my understanding. In fact, belief in democracy in the Western sense, i.e., as a system of government, is compatible with almost any view about private property. The Socialist movement in this country, as Dr. Sweezy seems to recognize in one passage, has, in the main, been democratic in its views, but has certainly not "taken for granted the inviolability, etc." It is democratic in so far as it holds that a fundamental change like the abolition of private property in the means of production, desirable though it is, should not be brought about unless and until the majority of the people, after full and free discussion, have declared themselves in favor of it. The Eastern view, stripped of the verbiage in which it is too often wrapped up, is that the abolition of this kind of property is so desirable that, whenever occasion offers, it should be brought about by any means, whether the majority of the people want it or not. Those two views are sharply opposed to each other, and to claim that they can both be called democratic is to make the use of language an absurdity.

Sweezy on decisions versus policies.—A point of detail that puzzles me is Dr. Sweezy's apparent difficulty in attaching a meaning to "making decisions" or similar phrases. He seeks to explain this by equating it with "policy," which to my mind is a much vaguer and less exact term. It seems to me that the clearest way to think of it is in terms of a series of decisions at different levels of generality, e.g., the general decision to extend social services, the decision to establish a national health service, the decision to deal with the hospitals on certain lines, the decision that a particular hospital should be classed as a teaching hospital, and so on. The point of this is that it throws doubt on the value of Dr. Sweezy's sharp distinction between "policy" and "execution." Any one of the above decisions, except perhaps the last, could be described as "policy" in relation to the one below it, and any one, except perhaps the first, as "execution" in relation to the one above it. All these decisions can be influenced in varying degrees by popular opinion, and, of course, the decisions at one level will largely influence the decisions at another.

On the other hand, this must be distinguished from "execution" in the simple sense of individuals obeying the law. In that sense, the people must "participate actively in the execution of policies" under any form of government, if it is to be an effective government at all. There is nothing specially democratic about this; and some of the ways in which obedience can be secured would not, I think, be regarded as democratic in any sense of the word. For instance, Hitler had a very successful technique of "mobilizing the people for active participation in public affairs." So when Dr. Sweezy speaks of this as one of the marks by which democracy can be distinguished, his language seems to me highly ambiguous.

Sweezy on social versus political democracy.—I find further difficulty in Dr. Sweezy's attempt to include among the essential marks of democracy that "the people . . . benefit from the policies adopted." This is equated elsewhere with "the process of raising the economic and cultural level of the masses without discrimination, etc." This is what he calls "social democracy," and he seems to present it as an alternative meaning of the word to "political democracy." But this does not seem to me a legitimate antithesis.

The phrases used are, of course, extremely vague, and there are infinite possibilities of difference of opinion about what they would involve in practice. But, in a general way, most serious people nowadays would agree that this was a proper end for any form of government to pursue. To suggest, however, that anything that is good can therefore be called democracy seems to me merely to lead to confusion. There still remains the question how and by whom it is to be decided what is to the benefit of the people. And we must have some words to express the different views that can be held on this point.

A particular confusion arises because Dr. Sweezy does not make clear whether, in order to be democratic, the policies adopted must be *intended* to benefit the people or whether they must in fact do so. If the former, I should agree, in a general way, that this is the ideal which any democrat, in any sense, would wish to see realized. There is, of course, in fact no way of guaranteeing the motive or intention of the people making the decisions. But one can at least claim that the more the great mass of citizens both have and use the machinery for influencing the decisions the less likelihood there is of the interests of any considerable section being ignored.

If the latter is meant, the case is different. Good intentions, of course, afford no guaranty that the intentions will be realized. That will depend partly on the wisdom and forethought of the people making the decisions and partly on luck, i.e., unforeseeable or uncontrollable factors. The latter is, perhaps, not relevant here, as I should imagine that no one would contend that being lucky is the same thing as being democratic. But the former is very relevant. Everyone, democrat or not, would agree that, in itself, it is a good thing that the decisions made should be as wise as possible. But it has often been argued that the more the great body of people influence the decisions the less likely these decisions are to be wise and farseeing, and idealistic reformers, from Plato onward, have been attracted by the idea of a carefully selected élite of exceptionally wise and unselfish people who would make all the important decisions in the interests of the whole community. In the past, however, this has always been regarded as the absolute antithesis of democracy, and the modern Communist parties who in practice, whatever they may say in theory, work on the basis of this view are clearly simply shifting the meaning of the word round, quite arbitrarily, to what has always hitherto been regarded as its opposite. As an ordinary citizen, I am keenly conscious of the difference between having decisions made for me by people supposedly wiser and better than myself and being summoned to take some share in making these decisions myself. And to use language which obscured this distinction is to make for confusion rather than clarity.

As a postscript I would add that, if I had to select a platform slogan for democracy, I should choose, rather than Lincoln's phrase, the words of William Jennings Bryan, "The people have a right to make their own mistakes." The connection of that with what has just been said should be obvious.

The crux of our disagreement.—I have some difficulty in deciding where the most fundamental differences lie between Dr. Sweezy and myself. I feel sure that they extend beyond differences about the proper use of language, important though these are. But it is not easy to decide just how far they go, and Dr. Sweezy's own statements about the differences between his point of view and the "liberal" or "Western" seem to me to be based very largely on a misunderstanding of the latter. For instance, as I have already pointed out, to equate the difference between the Eastern and Western views of democracy with the difference between socialism and capitalism is a fundamental fallacy. Apart from this there are one or two points which suggest themselves as of special importance.

a) I think that a great deal of Dr. Sweezy's argument is colored by the conviction that the Marxian theory is a scientific theory established in the same way as the theories of modern physics and therefore calling for the same acceptance as these. This leads on to the familiar Marxian corollary that the refusal to accept this theory must either be due to stupidity or ignorance, or else, consciously or unconsciously, to motives of self-interest. This must naturally react on one's attitude to criticism and the toleration of it. Criticism from interested motives of an established scientific fact can naturally not be regarded as of any benefit to anyone, and toleration would be accorded to it, if at all, merely as a matter of convenience.

It would be impossible to discuss this at length here. As far as Marxism goes, I should maintain that it certainly presents us with none of the kind of proofs on which the theories of physics are based, and is accepted, when it is, far more on emotional grounds than on any scientific evidence. To some extent, the same might be said of all political and social theories and generalizations. Though some of them seem to me to have a much higher degree of probability than Marxism, they can none of them claim to be scientifically established in the same sense as some physical theories. That does not mean that one opinion is just as good as another. It is certainly possible to approach these matters more scientifically or less scientifically. But the true scientific approach (which is not by any means necessarily the same as the approach adopted by actual scientists when they enter upon political speculation) is to recognize that conclusions on these matters are never more than a balance of probabilities to be accepted provisionally as the best conclusion from the available evidence, with the realization that a large number of unknown or unnoticed factors are always involved. In fact, if we want a parallel from natural science, the nearest that occurs to me is weather forecasting. Similarly, in the practical application of these theories, the scientific approach would always tend to be tentative and experimental, which is the only approach appropriate to the stage of knowledge that we have actually reached.

From this point of view, criticism and difference of opinion will be regarded, in general, as positively beneficial, something to be welcomed, not grudgingly tolerated. Very likely a great many of the views put forward will be foolish, ill-informed, or prejudiced. But even so we can never tell beforehand that they may not contain something of value or call attention to some factor in a complicated situation that we have overlooked. This may be largely independent of the motives from which the criticisms are put forward, and that is the truth at the back of Dr. Sweezy's assertion that "liberals are accustomed to treating individuals or movements as what they appear to be or what they claim to be." As it stands this statement is quite untrue. Liberals are only too well aware of the divergence between the claims and the realities of many political movements. But it is true that, ideally at any rate, they will try to see if anything of value can be found by examining the arguments as arguments, instead of dismissing them with little or no examination because of the supposedly sinister motives of those who put them forward. It may also be true that they will be more ready to recognize the possibility of honest differences of opinion and less ready than some political movements to dismiss all opinions that they dislike as due to sinister motives.

b) I think that a more fundamental difference about values can be detected in Dr. Sweezy's statement that he does not regard political democracy as a goal or end at all. This may be partly due to the fact that he seems—though I am not quite sure about this—to be inclined to equate "political democracy" with the legal establishment of democratic machinery or institutions. But, of course, no democrat in the traditional or Western sense would regard that by itself as enough to make a state democratic. As I explained in my memorandum, democracy in this sense means not only the establishment of democratic institutions but the will to use them on the part of the great majority of the people, though, of course, the will is of no effect unless the institutions are there to be used.

I do not know how far Dr. Sweezy's view would be modified if he accepted this extension. But in any case it is vital to the democratic position, as I understand it. It is the will to use and the habit of using democratic institutions which is the important thing. For that necessarily tends to bring with it certain states or attitudes of mind which to the believer in democracy appear of value in themselves as part of his conception of the good life. Of course, these states or attitudes will be developed to greatly differing degrees in different people, and hardly anyone will develop them up to the ideal limit. But that applies, of course, to every virtue which we want to develop. A little of them is better than none at all, and more of them is better than less. What these qualities, the democratic virtues, are has been indicated in my original essay.

PAUL M. SWEEZY, REPLY TO PROFESSOR FIELD

Professor Field on the historical background of the Eastern usage.—Professor Field doubts the historical basis for the Eastern usage of the term "democracy." I am not a political scientist and have no intention of entering into any learned debate on this subject. I can only say that his arguments leave me quite unconvinced.

Professor Field's main argument is stated in this way: "... most people in the first half of the nineteenth century [thought] that democracy would in fact lead to equality, i.e., that if the majority of the people had the vote they would use it to equalize property or abolish it altogether. But that does not show that they confused or identified democracy with the policy that they thought it would follow." I think the first part of this quotation is undoubtedly correct. But the second part seems to me to be partly wrong and hence wholly misleading. It is true that some people—possibly a majority—did not "confuse or identify democracy with the policy they thought it would follow." But the point is that many others were "guilty" of precisely this "confusion or identification." And it is in this fact that we can trace the background of the present-day Eastern usage of the term "democracy." When those who had believed that formal democracy would lead to equality found that they were wrong—primarily as a consequence of the experiences of 1848 and the immediately succeeding years—they did not renounce democracy, for the obvious reason that to them the heart of democracy was not political form but economic equality. From now on they paid much less attention to political forms and much more attention to economic reforms.

The issue can be presented in a different way. During the first half of the nineteenth century people tended to confuse two separate problems, the problem of political rights and the problem of political power. It was assumed more or less as a matter of course that if the masses had political rights they would and could use them to attain political power. Democracy was at bottom giving (or being forced to give) political rights to the masses. Conservatives were antidemocratic because they wanted the propertied classes to hold on to political power; radicals were democrats because they wanted the masses to have political power. The revolutions of 1848 showed that the political theory underlying these beliefs was vastly oversimplified. The masses could have political rights while the propertied retained political power. A sharp change in thinking about democracy now became inevitable. Conservatives could now safely be democrats. Democrats, however, did not cease to be democrats; they simply tended to broaden the concept and shift the center of gravity of their thinking away from political form and toward economic content. Thus the two modern usages of the term "democracy" have a common origin in the first half of the nineteenth century; they became differentiated and gradually diverged in the hundred years following 1848.

Professor Field's contention that my interpretation requires me to find statements which apply the term "democracy" to a certain kind of dictatorship or oligarchy seems to me to be quite beside the point. The problem would never have occurred to any one in that form. As I have indicated above, the crux of the matter was *political power to the masses*. In the earlier period it was taken for granted that this would be assured by the formula "one man, one vote." When it was found that this was not necessarily so, it did not follow that thinking should turn to an "absolute dictator or a small group of leaders." For the most part radical thought continued to assume that political power to the masses would involve the usual democratic rights for the great majority of the people. But the important thing is that the emphasis tended to move away from the political forms and to center on real power, which, of course, it was expected would be exercised primarily in the economic field. It seems to me that the modern Eastern usage of democracy is a logical development of this tendency.

I am afraid I have not succeeded in explaining my position on this question as clearly as would be desirable. But in any case, I want to make one final point as unambiguously as possible. I do not maintain that "democracy" was used in western Europe in the first half of the nineteenth century in exactly the same way that it is used in eastern Europe today. What I do maintain is that there is a continuous historical thread connecting the two usages and that in this sense the latter is just as legitimate as any other usage of the term.

Professor Field on the Western usage.—I think that if Professor Field lived in the United States he would find less absurd my statement that the Western conception of democracy takes for granted the inviolability of private property in the means of production. He can believe it or not, but it is true that to the great majority of the American ruling class today democracy means, almost to the exclusion of everything else, the preservation of private property in the means of production. It is neither accident nor altogether hypocritical propaganda that causes the greatest American newspapers like the *New York Times* and the *New York Herald Tribune,* to say nothing of the highest officials of government, to write day after day about "democratic Greece," Kuomintang China as a part of the "world democratic front," etc. Moreover, I believe such views are not unknown in Britain.

Now, of course, Professor Field can maintain that this is an abuse of the word which has nothing to do with the traditional Western usage. I am afraid I must disagree. On the contrary, I believe that it is just as natural an outgrowth of one strand in the Western tradition as the Eastern usage is of the other strand. And in my opinion divergent attitudes toward private property originally produced the division into two strands and conditioned their subsequent development.

The Western social democratic movement—I avoid the term "socialist" in this connection because Communists are socialists too—presents a special problem. No doubt the British Labour Party, for example, sincerely believes that it is possible to abolish private property without in the least deviating from the traditional forms of political democracy. But even so, this is apparently still regarded as a problem for the distant future. All the nationalizations so far have shown a scrupulous regard for the property rights of the owners of the nationalized industries. And in any case only a small percentage of the means of production have either been nationalized or marked for nationalization during the next five-year period. In the meantime, the ease with which the leaders of the Labour Party and the Labour Government identify themselves, politically and ideologically, with the American ruling class speaks volumes about what the Western conception of democracy takes for granted.

Professor Field on decisions versus policies.—I do not want to argue about "decisions" versus "policies." As Professor Field says, this is a point of detail.

The substantial issue raised under this head, I think, can be put in its simplest form as follows. Does democracy imply only that the people go to the polls every so often and elect a government which then makes decisions or policies and carries them out through a professional civil service? Or does democracy imply *also* that as large a proportion of the people as possible are drawn into the process of making and carrying out decisions or policies at every level where it is feasible? I think democracy implies the latter, and I add explicitly that I do not mean to say that everyone who obeys the law is thereby actively participating in public affairs.

One further point in this connection should be emphasized. In comparing systems, one must always keep in mind that not only the degree of public participation but also the scope of governmental action is important in judging the extent of democracy. Under capitalism, the most important decisions, i.e., economic decisions, are made by a handful of private oligarchies. Only where economic affairs are public affairs can democracy have real depth.

Political versus social democracy.—When I suggested as one of the criteria of democracy the extent to which the people "benefit from the policies adopted," I was only trying to make explicit the meaning of Lincoln's "government for the people." I don't see what else Lincoln could have meant, and for my part I think it is a perfectly legitimate criterion.

No one says that "anything that is good" is therefore democratic. But I do say that government that is good *for the people* is to that extent democratic. Professor Field may not like to use the term this way. Others do, and I agree with them. I say again, as I said in my original paper, that there are perfectly legitimate uses of the word which differ among themselves and that the important thing is to achieve clarity, not uniformity.

When I say "good for the people" I mean just that, not "intended to be good for the people." Everyone, except a relatively small number of abnormal individuals, intends to do good for the people, and there is hardly such a thing as a political party which does not imagine that its own rule would benefit the people. There is simply no sense in raising the question of good will or sincerity in politics; it is better to assume at the outset that every one means to do good and is sincere. (For example, Hitler was undoubtedly sincere and passionately believed that Naziism was good for the German people.) There are undoubted exceptions, but they are relatively unimportant.

The question, then, is this: Is a certain system of government more, or less, likely than another to produce policies which are in the real interests of the people? One can give an intelligent answer to this question, in my judgment, only if one understands that under capitalism *no* government can really govern in the interests of the people. The capitalist system itself is diametrically opposed to the interests of the overwhelming majority of the people. How can a government which operates within the framework and limitations of this system govern in the interests of the people?

I do not mean to say that a government under capitalism is wholly undemocratic. I only say that in one very important respect— most people in the world today will probably consider it *the most* important respect—no capitalist government can be judged democratic. On the other hand, the very nature of socialism (abolition of private property and appropriation plus comprehensive economic planning) obliges a government, whatever its other characteristics, to pursue policies which promote the life and growth of the whole community and are in this sense in the interests of the people.

The crux of our disagreement.—For reasons which are probably clear by now (especially in view of the two preceding paragraphs) I persist in what Professor Field regards as the fallacy of equating the difference between the Eastern and the Western views of democracy with the difference between socialism and capitalism. Or rather, I do not so much "equate" the differences as I regard them as intimately related in the sense that the difference between the two conceptions of democracy can be understood only in terms of the difference between capitalism and socialism.

Professor Field is certainly correct that a great deal of my argument is colored by the conviction that Marxism is a genuine social science. I do not want to get into a controversy at this point, however, as to whether Marxian theory is established in the "same" way as physical theories or calls for the "same" acceptance. I will only say that Marxian theory is established by observation, generalization, and testing and hence at the very least has much in common with the natural sciences. Even so, however, I do not think it is a "familiar Marxian corollary that the refusal to accept this theory must either be due to stupidity or ignorance, or else, consciously or unconsciously, to motives of self-interest." (I should like to know, incidentally, whether Professor Field thinks this is a conscious or an unconscious corollary. If the former, he should be able to cite supporting evidence, and I would like to know what it is.) The matter is in reality much more complicated. Refusal to accept Marxian theory is mainly due, I think, to acceptance of attitudes (using the term in the sense of modern psychological theory) which reflect, directly or indirectly, the values and norms of a ruling class whose interests are mortally endangered by the spread of the truth about different forms of social organization. (I wonder, in this connection, whether Professor Field doubts [a] that the interests of the ruling class *can* be in conflict with the interests of society at large; [b] that the values and norms of the ruling class are the generally prevalent ones; and [c] that these values and norms will condition attitudes which are often and to a far-reaching extent in conflict with the real interests of the individuals holding them?)

It does not seem to me that the relation between Marxian theory, on the one hand, and freedom of discussion and the tolerance of differing opinions, on the other, is of the kind postulated by Professor Field. Of course, I speak only for myself, but my own position is that such freedom and tolerance are always desirable in themselves but that there are occasions on which they just are not possible. As the contradictions of capitalism deepen and as the class struggle sharpens, the possibility of solving social problems by discussion and compromise becomes ever slighter. Perhaps some countries can manage it all the same; I certainly hope so. But most of the world obviously cannot. In this great majority of the countries of the world, it seems to me that the real interests of democracy in any meaningful sense of the word, and certainly the attainment of a reasonable level of free discussion and tolerance, can be served only by the earliest possible establishment of a socialist economy.

Once again, I come to the conclusion that we have reached a stage of world history in which it is quite impossible to discuss the problem of democracy realistically except in terms of the antithesis between capitalism and socialism.

Professor Field thinks he detects an inclination on my part to equate "political democracy" with legal establishment of democratic machinery or institutions. This is no doubt correct, though I hasten to add that it does not represent my own view of what does or should constitute political democracy. In my judgment, however, it is precisely the official Western conception of democracy, and for this reason it has a very great importance in the world today. It is the announced policy of the United States, for example, to help spread democracy everywhere. In my judgment, democracy in this context goes no deeper than formally democratic constitutions.

I take it that Professor Field would agree with me that it is absurd to suppose that democracy can be exported or grafted on a country at will. This seems to be the implication of his statement that "it is the will to use and the habit of using democratic institutions which is the important thing." I maintain that such will and habit, as Professor Field understands them, exist only in a very few countries and that they cannot be acquired under conditions of profound economic disturbance, widespread civil conflict, and threatened international war of unprecedented destructiveness. Moreover, if these conditions continue, the will and the habit will weaken and eventually disappear even in the countries which have them.

In the final analysis, I suppose, one's attitude today toward the different types of democracy—and, indeed, toward most social norms and institutions—is determined by how one explains the fact that in the last three or four decades "conditions of profound economic disturbance, widespread civil conflict, and threatened international war of unprecedented destructiveness" have become nearly universal and ever present. Marxism gives a straightforward and rational answer which has relatively clear implications for the subject of this inquiry. I would be very much interested to know what answer is given by Professor Field and those who think like him.

XXXII

ERIC WEIL

I. *The present-day meaning of the word "democracy."*—As a first approximation, democracy may be defined as the system of government which resolves the conflicts between the various groups, existing within every society, by nonviolent means: political decisions are taken with the collaboration and under the direct or indirect control of all or at least of the majority of the citizens who appoint and dismiss the men responsible for the administration of public affairs by virtue of a right guaranteed and regulated by certain forms of procedure which all are pledged to observe (a constitution).

Closer examination, however, immediately shows this definition to be inadequate. The rules of procedure may be drawn up in such a way as to render the rights they are supposed to safeguard illusory. The citizens may be so ignorant of public affairs that they fail to appreciate the importance of the problems involved and may well have no desire to express an opinion on them. Social, and especially economic, pressure, though entirely without constitutional foundation, may be strong enough to prevent the majority, or at any rate a large number, of citizens from openly expressing their convictions and preferences.

The formal democracy of the nineteenth century (incidentally it did not exist all through that century, and we meet it also at other periods) was characterized, in the social sense, by the orthodox doctrine of laissez faire; in the political sense, by the abrogation of all inequalities in the legal status of individuals. It assumed that the free play of forces and interests would lead, by a kind of natural necessity, to the promotion of the greatest good of the greatest number in a nonviolent society. The fallacy of this doctrine was revealed by the uprisings and revolutions of the nineteenth century. It was refuted on the theoretical side by the antiliberal—but not necessarily antidemocratic—doctrines which evolved at the same time.

In other words, modern democracy has always defined itself as a political system making for the material and moral *progress* of the members of the body politic.[1] But whereas the nineteenth century believed that this progress was achieved by freeing all individual and group forces, present political thought seems convinced that progress can be achieved only by conscious and organized action. The state, and the democratic state, perhaps, above all, must consciously seek out the true interest of its citizens, promote material progress by the elimination of violence ("social stresses"), and, through material progress, promote moral progress toward the ideal of nonviolence.

In the light of the above, we can now make a closer examination of the modern concept of "democracy." It retains the characteristics of the classical definition: equality of all citizens before the law; equal political rights for all adult citizens, the acquisition of these rights by all the inhabitants of the territory concerned, or at least all those born and habitually resident there; a government appointed by and subject to the control of all the citizens; eligibility of all citizens for public office; and protection of the citizens against public persecution on grounds of opinion (for extolling decisions at variance with the policy of the government or with the wishes of the majority). At the present day, however, further stipulations are added, the chief of which are:

1. *Social* conditions must be such as to give all citizens not only the right but also the possibility of participating in the political life of the state (education, freedom from economic pressure, access to important information, etc.).

2. In view of the important influence of material conditions of life on the attainment of this end, governments must strive for the constant improvement of the citizens' living conditions.

We are entitled to assume that all who call themselves democrats will subscribe to this definition. Closer examination, however, reveals a fundamental difficulty. The first part of the definition (the "classical" definition) guarantees to everyone the right to work, subject to the law, for the ends he considers desirable, to work for

1. Because Greek philosophy knew nothing of progress (history), its ideal state was *astasiastos* (devoid of revolutionary tension); correspondingly its ideal citizen was *egkrates* (who controls his desires), *autarkes* (sufficient unto himself), etc. Whereas the modern democratic state seeks political stability through the satisfaction of the (reasonable) desires of the majority, the democracy of ancient times sought it through the (reasonable) suppression of desires.

his *satisfaction.* The second part of the definition requires that the body politic as a whole should strive for progress, i.e., for the good of the community, *determined objectively.* But, once we have shed the quasi-naturalist optimism of nineteenth-century liberalism, what guaranty is there that the *desires* of the citizens[2] and the *interests* of the community will coincide? The interests of the community may be determined scientifically, once the value of progress is admitted: in order to raise the standard of living on a long-term basis, for instance, a comparatively large proportion of the output of a society will have to be expended on capital goods, involving, on a short-term basis, lowering or at any rate stabilizing the standard of living; but there is no proof that the majority of citizens will necessarily agree with such a policy.

The problem is further complicated by the fact that in the modern world, consisting as it does of independent states, politically, economically, and militarily competing with one another, priority is given to technical efficiency and material progress; the factors that govern a country's chances of progressive enrichment, and therefore of survival in the event of an international conflict, are the productive capacity of society and the individual, the degree of scientific development, the national wealth, etc. In other words, the interests of the community are increasingly opposed to the individual and traditional desires of its citizens. At the same time, and for the same reason, technical problems are becoming both more important and more complex, with the result that the vast majority, if not all, of the citizens no longer understand either their meaning or their scope. We shall attempt, in the following pages, to show the philosophical significance of this duality of *desire* and *public good,* which is the kernel of all the problems of democracy. But, before doing so, let us draw some preliminary conclusions from what has been said above and thus remove certain common misunderstandings.

2. These desires are not merely the whims of individuals; strictly individual desires are to be found only in madmen or criminals. On the contrary, the desires in question are entirely comprehensible, representing, in fact, the living tradition of a community, with its scale of values, way of life, code of morals, etc. It is precisely this living tradition that may come into conflict with the democratic idea of scientific progress in a nonviolent society; or, more correctly, it is with this tradition that the democratic idea may come into conflict, since this idea arises only when the tradition has ceased to be strong enough to prevent the appearance of social tensions sufficiently serious to endanger the community.

All democrats, both "formal" and "popular," have one thing in common—they are opposed to all "eternalist" theories about man, to all doctrines which assert that man, always and everywhere, is determined by certain nonhistorical factors (race, predestination, etc.). Democracy is seen as a system of progress which is nonviolent in character, is defined *objectively* (absence of violence, standard of living, average length of life, leisure, equal distribution of consumer goods, etc.) and pursued *scientifically*, with the aim of achieving the *good* and *contentment* of all the citizens.

The democratic thesis thus presupposes and asserts that man is a reasonable being, i.e., that the problems facing man in his community life can be formulated and solved in terms of science,[3] and thus with the agreement of all reasonable men.

Or, to state the problem the other way round, without changing the sense: any problem which cannot be formulated (which presents itself only in terms of the individual, of sentiment, of passion, etc.) and which can be shown to be insoluble in terms of science is not a political problem.[4]

Since *no science* ever considers that it has reached the final stage of its development, or admits any absolute truths (apart from formal truths), it follows that the essential democratic method consists of *discussion*.[5] On the other hand, since science moves more slowly than history and history cannot always await the pronouncements of science, the nonviolent solution of conflicts is frequently achieved by *compromise:* though all the opposing theses claim to constitute the truth, their supporters, if they adhere to de-

3. The term "science" is here, of course, not restricted to the exact sciences.
4. This is what appears to be understood by the terms "neutrality of the state" and "rights of the individual." It is clear that, as a political fact, the meaning of these terms depends on (*a*) what is regarded as science, and (*b*) what is regarded as a group problem (as opposed to an individual problem).
5. Democracy is thus not based on skepticism, as is sometimes asserted. Or rather, its skepticism is the skepticism of modern science, which likewise refuses to recognize truths that are both complete and concrete; any truth attained is subject to correction and, in the case of formal (identical) truths, to revaluation. Democracy cannot prove that the values it recognizes are the only "true" values; but it is fully capable of defining its values and stating what is incompatible with them and what steps must be taken, in a given situation, to achieve them. Neither is it true that democracy is opposed to, or skeptical about, "eternal" values; the democrat recognizes all these truths but demands that they be kept out of discussions on the subject of progress. Nothing that cannot be discussed reasonably should be discussed on the political plane. The foundation of democracy is therefore reason and not, as Montesquieu averred, virtue.

mocracy, rule out the use of violence, and so agree to try to find a formula which, without giving complete satisfaction to any party, is acceptable to all.

The asperity which characterizes past and present discussions on the subject of democracy is due partly to the divergence of views concerning what is and what is not scientifically proved or susceptible of scientific proof. The opposing parties hold, in particular, divergent views on the possibilities and results of a scientific interpretation of history: Are there in history several possible meanings and does man decide which course will be taken? Or is there only one possible meaning, and does man's freedom, in the face of this historical evolution, consist merely of the negative freedom to run counter to the course of history, smashing himself against it, without succeeding in deflecting it definitely (the meaning of history being fulfilled in that case at a later stage)? If there does exist such a historical course, is it discernible? Has it been discovered? The difference between the various outlooks—liberal, Catholic, Calvinist, Buddhist, and Communist—arises from the difference in the answers to these questions.

Nevertheless, each of these doctrines may consider itself democratic, in that, *once certain principles are admitted*, reasonable discussion and search for solutions and compromises may be the accepted methods of procedure. The conflict between the different systems arises from the refusal to permit discussion of the primary principles of each community.

Now, democracy can only be achieved if *every* value of *every* group is subject to *universal discussion*. So long as there are values that are both irreconcilable *and* in active opposition, perfect democracy is unattainable. In other words, in order for democracy to be possible, the state *must* be so organized that the irreconcilable and conflicting values (the two conditions are not identical) do not provoke a violent clash; precisely the ultimate values are then regarded as "private affairs."

It is a question of fact whether, in a given situation, this neutralization of ultimate values and this neutrality of the state are possible without destruction of the state's monopoly of the use of violence, and without risk of the state being weakened to the point of becoming a tempting prey for other states.

In principle, however, every democratic system claims to be reasonable, and so to appeal not to man's passions and sentiments, but to his reason. In its very principle, it claims to be universal or (to be exact at the cost of a rather ugly neologism) a "universalizable." It is not democracy when the political system excludes a section of the people from discussion of ends and means *and* when that section is determined by characteristics that are regarded as nonamenable to modification by the reason of the members of that section. The cultural level of certain groups may be such as to render all discussion with them impossible; it may even prevent certain groups from wishing to participate in discussion. Nevertheless, even if the democratic community or the democratic state feels it must restrain such groups, i.e., refuse them equal participation in public affairs for the time being, there still remains an essential difference between their exclusion and the all-time exclusion of certain castes, certain "inferior races," "slaves by birth."[6] Every democracy assumes that every man, unless he be mad, is open to conviction by reason; and it must therefore formulate ultimate principles such that each can subscribe to them without admitting that he is irremediably inferior to his fellows.

It is true that perfect democracy is an ideal which has nowhere been attained, and which no one believes to be immediately attainable.[7] Even the staunchest upholders of democracy admit the existence of culturally "backward" people, who are "not yet ripe" for democracy, who "need education." Nowhere is there absolutely free discussion; and incitement to violence, betrayal of national interests (at least in time of war), appeal to the passions (e.g., pornography), and libel are regarded as crimes by the laws of all countries. Countries which boast most insistently of their democracy, regardless of their particular interpretation of the word, make a distinction between loyal minorities (which accept the principles of

6. Yet another meaning of the *rights of man.*
7. It will be noted that the democratic principle of nonviolence has been best implemented by those countries that have allowed those of their nationals holding views radically opposed to the basic principles of the community to emigrate, while maintaining their cultural and linguistic traditions, i.e., to form colonies—Athens, Great Britain, and the United States of America. Authoritarian and dictatorial forms of government are most likely to be set up in countries where the dissident elements are either unable or forbidden to emigrate or are required to make overgreat sacrifices in case they emigrate.

the community) and disloyal minorities;[8] these latter they treat as enemies, either persecuting them, or excluding them from certain public functions, certain occupations, and certain careers. Democracy is everywhere imperfect and must remain so until the individual becomes a reasonable being, guided in all his actions by logical and universalizable principles, and until violence ceases to represent the last resort of states in their relations with other states.[9]

It will not be out of place to add here a corollary which follows immediately from the foregoing considerations, but which has a certain importance, since it discounts an argument frequently used in discussions about democracy. It is often asserted that democracy is characterized by recognition and defense of the rights of the individual.[10] This is correct in so far as democracy is contrasted with absolutist and Fascist systems, which do not admit the equality of men and grant certain groups or individuals some or all political rights while denying them to others. But taken absolutely, this assertion, though coinciding with the characteristics enumerated, leads to a serious confusion of the issue. For there exists and can exist no state, were it even the world state, which gives the individual total freedom, since such freedom would have to include, in the last resort, the freedom to use violence and to reject reason. This is, however, what we often unconsciously think of (if the word "think" is applicable here) when speaking of the freedom of the individual. The so-called "definitions" which are sometimes added are merely formal and meaningless: the right to free expression of all thoughts does not and cannot exist anywhere; secrecy of correspondence and freedom of association cannot be absolutely guaranteed (conspiracy, fraud, etc.); freedom of movement within the frontiers of a country must necessarily be restricted in many cases (military service, civil service, economic pressure and/or pressure exercised by the government for the purpose of relieving over-

8. I.e., minorities which not only refuse to recognize the principles of the community but are even prepared to overthrow the government or the constitution by violence.

9. When threatened from without, the *interests* of the state conflict, if it is a democratic state, with its *principles*, and this may, in extreme cases, lead to exclusive value being attached to *loyalty* toward the government and to *efficiency* in preparation for, or in the conduct of, war. Democracy is thus transformed into a temporary or permanent dictatorship.

10. We have already pointed out the ambiguity of this expression.

crowding in towns, repopulating districts, etc.); freedom of conscience means nothing unless it is accompanied by the right to speak and act according to one's conscience, which rights cannot but be restricted; defense of economic interests can be permitted only in as far as it does not harm the interests of the community; and even defense of the rights of the family and of religion can be accepted in the modern state only subject to the observance of certain minimum conditions of "decency" and the protection of women and children. Absolute freedom of the individual is possible only in a society composed exclusively of reasonable men[11]—and in such a society there would be no question either of these rights or of their defense.

The question of the rights of man should therefore be brought into line with the question of reasonable discussion and expressed in the following formula: *Democracy may be said to exist if all members of the community have the possibility of participating, on a basis of equality, in the discussion of public affairs,*[12] i.e., in the drawing-up of the community's labor program, in determining the purpose of that labor, and in the distribution of profits. To put it more cautiously, it may be said that *democracy does not exist unless these conditions are fulfilled.*

.II. *Government by the people—government for the people.*— Translated into modern terms, the Platonic criticism of democracy questions the possibility of reconciling reason (government for the people) with contentment (government by the people).

For Lincoln (as also for Wilson) the reconciliation of these two factors presented no problem. Plato, for his part, considered such a reconciliation impossible, and it was for this reason that his ideal state was planned on lines opposed to democracy. His objections contain an analysis of profound difficulties inherent in democracy, though we are not obliged to accept the conclusions which he drew therefrom.

That criticism centers, in fact, on the meaning of the word *"for."*

11. And organized in a world state: the national state, in competition with other national states, will, in case of real or imagined danger, inevitably attach greater importance to technical efficiency than to the *rights of man;* not only in so far as these rights, in practice, militate against technical efficiency, but also inasmuch as they do not appear to make any positive contribution to increased efficiency.

12. We might add: and without being exposed to danger as a result of their participation; but this is implied by the term *equal* participation. This latter condition may be regarded as another definition of the *rights of man.*

According to Plato, democracy is incapable of achieving the *good* of the community; it can strive only for the contentment of the community (or of the greater part of it). In other terms: if the state is to achieve the good of its citizens, democracy is possible and the action of the community can usefully be directed by the majority or all of its citizens only if all (or the majority) of the citizens are reasonable beings; only, that is, if each citizen agrees to forego the arbitrary exercise of his free will, and to judge proposals not according to the immediate advantages he personally may expect from them, but according to their benefit to the community as a whole, basing his assessment on the law of science. Good is achieved, not by compromise between existing desires (which may all be erroneous and run counter to the real interests of the community, hence also to the interests of all the citizens), but by a compromise for *the purpose of achieving good*, for the purpose of insuring the survival of a nonviolent community capable of securing for its members a standard of living sufficiently above the level of want and permitting them to live and enjoy their life as thinking beings.

Those observations are still valid today. What is more, their validity is admitted everywhere, implicitly or explicitly: the existence, in all modern states, of a distinction between *government* and *administration* betrays an awareness that compromise between existing desires is not sufficient and that, taking account of the conditions of political action in general and the technical conditions of progress in particular, the possibilities of compromise have to be restricted. A chief engineer of naval constructions, a chief of the general staff of the army, or a district medical officer are not elected by majority vote; they are not, at any rate, chosen by general election from among all eligible citizens. The civil servant is judged solely by his technical efficiency. In short, the modern state surrounds itself with institutional obstacles calculated to prevent it from pursuing its desires without regard to its objective interests. The government (and hence the people, which, in a democracy, it represents) wants qualified technical experts capable of informing the political leaders of the existing technical possibilities, the means of attaining certain ends, and the consequences of certain acts. The modern state depends on this body of civil servants for the execution of the decisions taken by the government; it turns to them for advice, even before taking decisions.

Modern states have thus remedied some of the weaknesses enumerated by Plato. But while, in the *organization* of the state, technical competence intervenes between the wishes of the people and their execution, the problem recurs at the governmental level. The administration can indicate means and show what is technically desirable or impracticable; but it cannot choose between the various possibilities (the aims technically attainable); and the questions with which it deals remain questions of detail. It is the government which makes the decisions. We are thus back again at the principle of compromise between existing desires, without regard, despite the safeguards introduced, to the *good* of the state.

If this is so, it may appear that there is an irreconcilable incompatibility between government *by* the people and government *for* the people; that good, as far as it can be defined objectively (better living conditions for the citizens, absence of violence) would more easily be achieved by enlightened despotism—even more, that enlightened despotism is the only means of attaining this good.

It is not in the facts, however, that the real issue lies. We are faced by two diametrically opposed conceptions of man. And it is important to stress that this is not the conflict between "formal" democrats and "popular" democrats, who are both on the same side of the fence, in that both admit that man is reasonable or, at any rate, amenable to reason; that he is not by nature evil, but only ignorant; and that he is capable of improvement by his own efforts.

In Plato's view, man is a being determined by nature, either "born good" or "born bad." Against his thesis, the Christian—or post-Christian—adoption of democracy does not seek justification in proof but is based on a postulate as undemonstrable and irrefutable as Plato's. *The democratic doctrine postulates that compromise is possible between the demands of good (for the people) and contentment (by the people), that every man is reasonable and can, as a citizen, be persuaded to act in accordance with reason, following universalizable maxims.*

This is the postulate on which democracy is based, and it is of vital importance that this philosophical basis should be recognized for what it is: an anthropological (or, if we so prefer, a metaphysical) postulate forming the starting point from which experience (in this case historical experience) is organized, and which can, therefore, be neither proved nor disproved by experience. It is not the only possible principle; there are other principles from which experience will be organized differently.[13] But it is a principle upon which it is possible to establish a coherent body of historical experience, free of internal contradictions. We can no more prove democracy than we can prove reason; we can opt for it. This postulate, by systematizing experience, imparts to action a certain direction, so that action is then determined not only by conditions but by aims as well. But it remains a postulate; it is not a statement of fact. In practice, men are not yet reasonable beings; if they were, all political problems, i.e., those problems relating to the nonviolent coexistence of men in a state of contentment, would have ceased to exist. In other words, the postulate does not state that man is absolutely reasonable, but that he is motivated both by desire *and* by reason: the desire of the individual *can* be subordinated to reason (ancient conception of democracy); *or* desire in itself is reasonable and thus automatically achieves a world dominated by the laws of reason (classical liberal conception of democracy); *or*, finally, desire, without being either reasonable or unreasonable, inevitably turns to reason and seeks fulfilment, as reasonable desire, in a conscious attempt to create a world in which every man is, and is conscious of being, both content and reasonable.

It is thus no accident that the idea of progress (of a meaningful history) is always bound up with that of modern democracy; both arise from the duality of postulated *reason* and ascertained *desire*—a duality which democracy cannot sever and only universal reasonable historical action can reconcile. The individual may be able to choose *either* reason (morality) *or* desire (amorality—that of Nietzsche, for instance). He may impose his choice on a group, a people, or a state; but it is significant that, for all theories stemming from such a choice, history either has absolutely, or nearly, run its course, or else has no sense to it; either only a limited number of men (even one only) are reasonable, or else there exists no reason in the world. The ideas of (modern) democracy, progress, and the union of desire and reason in reasonable political action appear and disappear together.

III. *Formal democracy—popular democracy.*—In view of the

13. It would be absurd to consider this *philosophical fact* as a vice peculiar to democracy: there is a postulate at the heart of every polity and it would be illegitimate to ask for more than (*a*) the analysis of an empirically given political constitution; (*b*) the development of the inherent consequences of a given principle.

existence of this postulate, there is an agreement between the two opposing camps which today claim their allegiance to democracy. But this fundamental agreement does not make the actual conflict between them any the less real.

Reference to the fundamental ideas of the Marxist theory may serve to throw light on this discussion. According to these, the majority of the people have no means of expressing their desires, since the political machinery is controlled by the various groups of the minority in power, opposed to one another on points of detail, but united in their opposition to the interests of the masses. Nor have the majority the capacity of expressing their desires, since they have not yet become aware of their particular class interests. But it is these latter interests of the majority that constitute the real interest (the good), firstly of the community, and secondly of humanity as a whole, since it is only through attainment of the (unconscious) aims of the oppressed class that society can be freed of the obstacles placed in the way of scientific, technical, and human progress by the particular interest of the ruling class (this interest being likewise unconscious, especially in as far as it is particular). The world in its present state is not ripe for democracy; man, since he lives in want, is not *reasonable*, but is dominated by his own *particular* interests (desires) and will continue to be so until, through the transformation of social organization and through increase of output, all men are free from want. A compromise between the desire for contentment (traditional) and the public good (defined objectively) cannot be achieved until power is wielded by a group of men who have acquired a thorough understanding of the various ideological systems (i.e., the pseudo-rational expressions of traditional interests), and who, working with all the necessary objective knowledge at their hands, succeed in training the people to accept the freedom inherent in reason.[14]

In other words, democracy is regarded here not as a *means* for attaining good and transforming tradition for greater good but as an *end*, which can be achieved only by a lengthy process of training the masses and transforming conditions. It is not enough to overthrow the old ruling class; we must also change the mentality of

14. Until kings become philosophers—which is impossible from this point of view—or philosophers become kings, to use Plato's words.

the masses, steeped as they are in the propaganda of their former masters.[15]

It would be unjust to regard this as tantamount to a renunciation of the democratic ideal; this ideal is maintained as an ideal, not merely as an ornament or for propaganda purposes, but as the very basis of the theory: the ideal community is the community in which each man acts reasonably and where, consequently, the state as an instrument of constraint becomes superfluous. It would be unjust also from the historical standpoint; progress in its modern form has only come about under the protection of an authoritarian state. Nowhere would the masses have accepted *voluntarily* the change-over from agricultural to urban life, the abolition of their primitive family or patriarchal economy, or the sacrifices required by the rapid accumulation of capital, i.e., the deflection of a large percentage of the national income to investment at the cost of reducing both the output of consumer goods and leisure, involving, often, a superhuman physical strain. For the majority of the population of the world, the position is similar in our day; he who adheres to the objective definition of progress must, in all justice, admit the need for authoritarian governments in all "nondeveloped" regions, that is, in regions where capitalization has not yet reached a sufficiently advanced stage.[16]

In short, the purpose of a dictatorship of this kind will be first to implement the "modern" part of the definition of democracy, and thus to pave the way for the conditions stipulated in the "classical" definition. While adhering, in principle, to the postulate of democracy, this dictatorship asserts that man, *hic et nunc*, is not reasonable but is dominated by desires of a purely traditional and nonreasonable nature, and it aims therefore at the reasonable transformation of the world and of material living conditions so as to enable man to develop reason within himself and to put into practice what is at present only potential in him.

The conflict between democracy, on the one hand, and dictator-

15. Only a short time ago, people (western Europe) still talked openly of the need for a dictatorship of the proletariat; and the Communist Party was described as the brain and executive organ of the proletariat.

16. Since we are not dealing with questions of foreign policy or economics, we shall not touch on the problem of international economic co-operation, i.e., the transfer of capital goods from rich to poor countries; pointing out, however, that we consider this one of the key problems for the democratization of the world.

ship as a method of attaining democracy, on the other, is thus not absolute: the dictatorship to which we refer aims (to vary the famous saying of Woodrow Wilson) at creating not a world *safe* for democracy, but a world *ripe* for it.

There is, I think, in present-day discussions a tendency to forget this very real necessity: while it is not necessary for every citizen of every state to understand all problems, it is nevertheless essential that it should be possible to explain to him the questions on which he has to take a stand, and that there should be a living tradition of discussion forums (local, trade union, religious, ideological, and industrial groups), where individuals can learn to understand and formulate their interests as members of such groups; to look on certain other individuals as their spokesmen and representatives; and to master the technique of discussion, negotiation, and compromise.[17] This assumes social riches sufficiently great to give time for study and the formation of opinions. Those democracies which are most convinced of their democratic character are so keenly aware of the necessity of education that they force their young citizens to devote an ever increasing proportion of their time to training of this kind, without asking either their consent or that of their parents.

But while we may argue that every democratic government trains its citizens, and while we may justify temporary dictatorship on these lines, we must remember that it is, all the same, a dictatorship; and we must ask whether a régime of this type does not tend naturally to perpetuate itself and whether, instead of training its citizens to participate in public affairs and to discuss public interests and the means of fulfilling those interests, it does not end by excluding an ever growing percentage of its citizens from participation in public life. The government, seeing enemies on all hands, and enemies, moreover, who are prepared to use violence, suppresses all discussion with groups outside the (ever narrowing) circle within which it recruits its members and supporters. It has no longer any doubt that it alone possesses the real truth on which the training of the masses must be based. And the importance attached to the improvement of living conditions, for the purpose of which it seized power, diminishes constantly in proportion as ideological factors

17. An essential function of these *"intermediary bodies"*—parties, trade unions, groups founded on common interests—is to clarify "popular aspirations," eliminate plans technically incapable of fulfilment, and permit the proper definition of questions.

gain ground. The critic becomes a traitor. Training is never ended, and it appears impossible to reach a point at which legality of action is sufficient to uphold the state. Loyalty is the sole criterion of the citizen's value. The result is a state which, though based on quite contrary intentions, resolves finally—in so far as there is anything final in history—into a dictatorship, and an ever decreasing proportion of citizens is allowed to take a constantly diminishing part in discussion more and more specialized and less and less universal. Universal suffrage in these conditions becomes practically meaningless, since it is impossible to elect anyone who will criticize the government, while equality before the law no longer constitutes a guaranty of freedom of discussion, as the laws may be couched in terms such that every citizen can be declared a criminal at any moment. This is Terror; but, in modern conditions, it is imposed not necessarily by an arbitrary government, but rather by a law which punishes all discussion not instituted by the government.[18]

Nevertheless, a state of this nature may even be considered, at a certain moment and formally speaking, a democratic state; when all opposition has disappeared as a result of the suppression of all divergent opinion within the country, and the sealing of the frontiers against infiltration of opposing ideas from without, then unanimity can be achieved. But if by "democracy" we understand, as we suggest, a system allowing free discussion for the achievement of progress, then a state of this nature cannot actually be regarded as a democracy notwithstanding its (exclusively fundamental) principles. All modern progress has been based on free discussion—discussion, that is, protected against persecution or penalization on grounds of opinion. In a state of the type we have described, on the other hand, the very idea of discussion will disappear, and there can be no fresh contribution except by the importation of methods (not ideas) from abroad.

IV. *Democracy, tolerance, and treason.*—If, then, we take the word "democracy" to mean the right of all citizens to take part in open discussion, without the use of violence, directed toward the elaboration of decisions calculated to further the common good,

18. In this sense, it may be said that a dictatorship does not respect the *rights of man;* since it attributes prime value to ideological factors, no idea can be "neutralized," i.e., treated as nonpolitical, personal, scientific, etc. On the institutional level, the requirements of propaganda, and the need for protecting the citizens against "harmful influences," lead to constant increase in the strength of the police and a constant (legal) reduction of the guaranties of public trial.

while taking account, as far as possible, both of the wishes of the citizens and of the prevailing social and (external) political conditions, then the central problem of this inquiry, on the political plane, is clearly the problem of tolerance, or, more exactly, the problem of circumscribing the rights of opposition and criticism.

On the basis of the definition we have just reformulated, it is clear that democracy, in principle, permits all manner of opinions, including, therefore, nondemocratic or antidemocratic opinions. This does not imply, however (and it is probable that many discussions at the present time arise from confusion on this point), that the democratic state either should or can countenance *all organizations* and *all forms of action*. It will thus be perfectly lawful to assert that free examination of the profoundest problems of human existence is a sin; and that none but an organization absolutely independent of the choice and criticism of the citizens is in a position to make valid pronouncements on the nature of salvation and the methods of attaining it. Equally, it may be asserted that the executive power should be above group-conflicts, parties, opinions, criticisms, and independent of the "will of the people." But it is illicit, in a democracy, for a group to combine to attain its ideal by force, to make use of terror, to persecute its opponents, to apply organized discrimination, or to form a secret association, stating its views neither in nor for discussion.

To state the same idea in a different way: democracy can and must allow the expression of all *opinions*. It can and must oppose any *organization* preparing to use violence to seize and retain power. It can and must require all minority groups to make an open statement of their fundamental aims.

But what will be the position if a democracy is overthrown by democratic means? To this question there is no *de jure* answer. If the majority of the population is prepared to transform the state into a nondemocratic state, there is but one conclusion: that democracy, for that people, at that time, is impracticable. In this case there is only the choice between two possibilities: either a dictatorship, established for the purpose of training the people for democracy, or the authoritarian government desired by the majority of the nation. It is impossible, after all, to convince people by reasonable argument of the absolute value of reason and progress; and it is difficult, if not impossible, to prove that a particular society or state is ripe for democracy. It is conceivable that certain groups and peoples may prefer spiritual salvation or contemplation or repentance to progress, as we have defined it; while others may think that democracy is inferior to, e.g., an absolutist polity. Provided that the groups or states in question do not practice *coge intrare* and that their refusal to co-operate does not, in the event of war, affect the internal resistance of the state or the peace of a group of states, the formation of such groups either within states or as independent states does not constitute a danger either for the rest of the population or for other countries. It is possible, it will be objected, that groups such as these may gain the support of the majority: admitted; but it should be noted that, in the present-day world, the state would then have but small chance of survival, and the dissenting groups would quickly fall under the domination of a foreign power opposed to their ideals of life under an "eternal," "true" order without discussion and progress and victorious because opposed to these ideals. And it is impossible, it seems, to dissuade an individual or a group or a state from committing suicide or submitting to foreign domination, if such is its wish.

It is thus both the right and the duty of democracy not to leave without defense the freedom of discussion. But, except in cases of clear and present danger, it is in the interests of democracy to interpret this right and duty in the most restricted way; it is probable that the supporters (if not the founders) of dissenting doctrines and the supporters (if not the leaders) of the organizations involved are people with a grudge; and that their membership of such groups is due less to profound and clear conviction than to discontent. The success enjoyed by antidemocratic political doctrines is an indication of the fact that the existing *social* order does not satisfy all the citizens, though they would in most cases be incapable of explaining why. It will be more profitable to define and remedy the causes of their discontent than to persecute the discontented elements because they do not know exactly what it is they want. A democratic government should not intervene except when there is a clear and present threat to the right of discussion without violence; but it is of *vital and permanent interest* to a democratic state (an interest increasing with the growth of antidemocratic doctrines) to insure that the maximum number of its citizens enjoy the intellectual training and the material conditions necessary to qualify them for competent participation in the administration of public affairs.

When democracy is being defended, the nature of the constitutional changes proposed by the opposition need therefore not be taken into consideration, provided that violence is not employed in bringing these changes about. It must be *assumed* that, in a state ripe for democracy, any program involving the establishment of a non-democratic régime will be rejected by the majority; if it is not, then it must be concluded that the social constitution is faulty (from the point of view of democracy) and needs modification.

It is impossible to ascertain a priori whether a state which is at present democratic will remain so; whether, under certain conditions, it will not become a dictatorship; or whether, from the democratic point of view, it is not desirable that it should be transformed into a temporary "training dictatorship"; there is no guaranty that any particular nation will *never* abandon its democratic faith and will not cease to accept the anthropological postulate at the basis of democracy. Likewise is it not possible to affirm that a given state, built up as a dictatorship, will never become a democracy. For the examination of concrete cases, some criteria have been outlined above: observe whether the freedom allowed by the government in question, as regards discussion of public affairs and principles of policy, is being extended or restricted. What is immeasurably more difficult is to judge whether the government in question, in view of the situation both inside and outside the country, could act otherwise than it does without endangering the internal authority of the state (the monopoly of violence) and/or its external security. As long as a state has not rejected the democratic postulate, it must be regarded as *theoretically* democratic (the Soviet system, being *actually* a dictatorship, differs *fundamentally* from the Nazi dictatorship). The *quaestio facti* does not belong to the realm of philosophy. The philosopher can indicate the nature of democracy and the general conditions necessary for its attainment. Practical diagnostics and prognostics are the business of the statesman.

XXXIII

QUINCY WRIGHT

Like all social and political terms which serve at the same time as slogans for movements and as symbols for conceptions, the word "democracy" has in fact varied in meaning according to time, place, and circumstances. This variability is, in fact, a condition of most terms of popular discourse. They are continually acquiring new meanings as can be seen by studying any historical dictionary. While this does not rule out philosophic analysis of the elements which have dominated in the use of the term "democracy," it suggests that such a study has to proceed with continuous awareness of the historical variation.

Democracy has always suggested a wide popular participation in the support, conduct, and benefits of government, but the conception has taken color from the conditions and opinions which advocates of democracy have at particular times and places found in opposition to their aims. Thus, in a struggle against an unpopular rule of a monarch or oligarchy, democracy has referred to government by the many, rather than the few; in a struggle against social privilege, class, or race discrimination, and economic inequality, democracy has referred to equality in social position and economic welfare; in a struggle against government monopoly of economic initiative, public opinion, and political association, democracy has referred to freedom of enterprise, communication, opinion, and association; in a struggle against corrupt and arbitrary manipulations of opinion, democracy has referred to procedures for regulating elections and party action in order to assure freedom of opinion, wide participation, and fair representation; in a struggle against excesses of majorities and oppression of minorities, democracy has referred to the rule of law and protection of fundamental human rights; in a struggle for freedom of dependent or oppressed peoples, democracy has referred to home rule, self-government, and self-determination of distinctive groups; in a struggle for influence of suppressed groups or classes, democracy has referred to consent of the governed, non-discrimination and procedures for consultation among all interested groups in policy formation.

Consideration of this variability of the aims of movements which carry the banner of democracy suggests that the concept of democracy cannot be understood by an analysis of any definition thought to be valid in all times and places, but only by historical examination of the meaning which has been attached to the term by theoretical writers of different countries and periods, and by the practices which have been established and pursued to realize democracy at different times and places. Such a treatment can be found in many studies of democracy, as, for example, Harold J. Laski's discussion of the term in the *Encyclopaedia of the Social Sciences.*

The numerous emphases which have been given to the term, in different historical contexts, seem to permit of four contrasting distinctions.

1. Is democracy primarily a political or primarily a social term? Political democracy has been contrasted with social and economic democracy and opinions have differed as to which is prior. The liberals have tended to regard political democracy or a wide participation in government as the *sine qua non* for advances in economic and social democracy, while the socialists have tended to consider "real" political democracy improbable until a high degree of economic and social democracy has been achieved, some of them even urging an abandonment of political democracy until the "dictatorship of the proletariat" has developed more economic and social democracy.

2. Does democracy describe a goal of social and political action, or does it describe a procedure which should be used for the achievement of any goal? Lincoln recognized government *for* the people as well as government *by* the people as within the concept of democracy, but these two aspects may be in conflict. Under conditions of general ignorance, superstition, and poverty, a benevolent dictator may do more for the people than they can do for themselves. At least this thesis has been urged both by imperialists and communists. On the other hand, experience has shown that the benevolence of autocrats can never be relied upon. Autocracies, oligarchies, and even aristocracies tend to act in their own interests and to forget the welfare of those whom they govern. The history of democracy has therefore usually exhibited more interest in pro-

cedure for assuring fair representation, consultation with all the interests, genuinely popular elections of policy-making officials, legal protection of basic freedoms than in any particular social policy. It has often been assumed that a policy produced by genuinely democratic procedures will be a good policy. The scientific test of evaluating truth by the technique which has been used in demonstrating it has been followed. On the other hand, movements in the name of democracy have not been wanting which have placed substance above procedure, ends above means, and have striven for a certain economic, social, religious, or political goal by whatever means seemed at the moment most available upon the theory that the end justified them. Thus, democratic procedures were abandoned while allegedly democratic goals were being sought by other methods.

3. In so far as democracy is treated as an end, is the end primarily equality or primarily liberty? Both of these objectives have usually figured in democratic doctrine and sometimes their inconsistency, if either is pushed to an extreme, has not been fully appreciated. There can be equality in slavery, and there can be liberty for the strong to oppress the weak. Neither would be recognized as democracy. Liberals generally place liberty first and insist that unless the individual is free under the protection of general law to express himself in the fields of opinion, religion, culture, and economic enterprise, there can be no "genuine public opinion" to serve as a guide to democratic government and policy. Socialists, on the other hand, generally place equality first and insist that freedom, especially in the economic field, will inevitably result in such differentials of power and influence that the successful will make opinion in their own interest and democracy will fail. Clearly, compromise between the demands of equality and of liberty are necessary if there is to be democracy. The term must be broad enough to include both these often conflicting goals, possibly reconciled through the general prevalence of the spirit of the third element of the trilogy, "fraternity."

4. Treated as a procedure, does democracy mean that the will of the majority should rule, or does it mean that the minority must be protected even from the majority? Clearly majorities which once in power take effective measures to prevent present minorities from ever becoming the majority subvert democracy. If democracy

means rule of the majority, it must include the opportunity of new majorities to develop. On the other hand, minorities that utilize the freedoms accorded them by the majority to sabotage by undemocratic methods the policy which the majority has accepted destroy democracy. A compromise between majority rule and minority right is clearly necessary. Such a compromise has developed in the conceptions of "public opinion" and "rule of law" which set limits both to majority tyranny and to minority disobedience. Unless both opinion and law develop a conception of "public interest," superior both to the power of the majority and the freedom of the minority, democracy cannot flourish.

Statement of these contrasts and appreciation of the necessities of compromise suggest that democracy is not a doctrine which can be expressed in absolute terms. It cannot be defined as a hierarchy of values but only as a balance of competing values. Democracy opposes callousness to human suffering, denial of human dignity, unfair or oppressive means to achieve any end, and intolerance of minority opinion, thus allying itself with the general philosophy of humanism, liberalism, pragmatism, and relativism which has characterized modern civilization.[1] Democracy, however, recognizes that antisocial individuals and groups may have to be forcibly suppressed in the general interest, that individual rights must be reconciled with social rights, that the most "democratic" political procedures must always be subject to criticism and change by popular judgment upon the results they have achieved, and that the opportunity of the policy of the majority to prove itself must not be destroyed by a skepticism which holds that all opinions are equally valid or equally invalid. While no opinion is absolutely right, in a given situation one may be better than another.

Democracy is a theory, policy, procedure, and art, emphasizing human welfare, individual freedom, popular participation, and general tolerance. It can adapt itself to many conditions, but it thrives in an atmosphere of education, toleration, peace, and prosperity. Ignorance, dogma, war, and poverty are its enemies. They breed absolute and arbitrary government, uncritical and lethargic people, which are the reverse of democracy.

1. I have discussed the significance of these terms and their importance in modern civilization in my *A Study of War* (Chicago, 1942), pp. 166–217, 615–24.

ANALYTICAL SURVEY OF AGREEMENTS
AND DISAGREEMENTS

A R N E   N A E S S   *and*
S T E I N   R O K K A N

INTRODUCTORY

In its recommendations for the use of the material collected through the UNESCO inquiry into ideological conflicts, the Committee of Experts which met in May, 1949, suggested that *an analytical survey of agreements and disagreements* explicit or implicit in the material be worked out and published along with a selection of the more significant of the contributions received in response to the inquiry. On the following pages an attempt will be made to trace the outlines of such an analysis.

To facilitate assessment of the validity of whatever conclusions are suggested in the following, a few remarks on the character and limitations of the material under scrutiny seem called for.

The inquiry undertaken by UNESCO was from the very outset conceived of as an enterprise in *philosophical analysis:* in analysis of meanings, conceptual differentiations, theoretical implications, and normative foundations. The preparation of the inquiry was guided by the idea that considerable progress toward the clarification of the grounds of current conflicts could be made through the initiation and organization of philosophically detached debates across national and ideological frontiers. Several avenues of approach to the implementation of this idea were discussed. The assembling of general essays on themes like "The Nature of Ideological Conflicts," "Disagreements over Democracy," "The Essence of Democracy," etc., was found to be of little avail. Some device had to be found that would insure a higher degree of comparability between opinions held on the more precise problems involved in the general issue. In an effort to achieve this end a fairly detailed *questionnaire* was worked out. In its final form,[1] this questionnaire did not make any pretensions toward exactness in its formulations but was mainly intended to serve the purpose of provoking scholars and experts into

1. See Appendix I, pp. 513–21.

focusing their discussions on approximately the same range of basic problems and thus make it possible to reach a clearer picture of the location of agreements and disagreements.

The questionnaire thus devised was distributed directly or through National Commissions to almost six hundred philosophers, political scientists, jurists, historians, sociologists, economists, and others who had given evidence of interest in the foundations of ideological conflicts. Of those thus approached, more than one hundred sent in direct contributions to the inquiry. Others confined themselves to referring to or sending books or articles where they thought they had already stated their views on the problems at issue. Others again explained that lack of time and the urgency of other commitments prevented them from taking any part in the inquiry. A few of those approached complained of the abstruseness, or futility, or both, of the undertaking, but on the whole the reactions registered were positive and sympathetic.

The ensuing survey of agreements and disagreements will exclusively be based on the direct contributions received. Following is a list of the scholars and experts who so generously devoted time and energy to the preparation of direct responses:

Professors K. M. Abbott and H. Sperber, United States

Professor Gordon W. Allport, United States

Professor Paul H. Appleby, United States

Mr. H. C. Baldry, South Africa

Professor M. Barzin, Belgium

Dr. Joseph Bernhard, Germany

Dr. Charles Bettelheim, France

Professor George Boas, United States

Professor M. M. Bober, United States

Professor I. M. Bochenski, Switzerland

Professor G. A. Borgese, United States

Mr. John Bowle, United Kingdom

Professor Stuart Gerry Brown, United States

Professor Lyman Bryson, United States

Father J. Cardijn, Belgium

Mr. E. F. Carritt, United Kingdom

Dr. Oliver Cromwell Cox, United States

Professor David van Dantzig, Netherlands

Professor John Dewey, United States

Dr. Doraiswami, India

Professor Curt J. Ducasse, United States

Professor Charles Eisenmann, France

Dr. A. C. Ewing, United Kingdom

Professor Marvin Farber, United States

Professor James K. Feibleman, United States

Professor G. C. Field, United Kingdom

Professor Louis Finkelstein, United States

Professor Risieri Frondizi, Argentina

Professor Morris Ginsberg, United Kingdom

Mr. J. W. Gough, United Kingdom

Professor J. M. Hagopian, Lebanon

Professor Charles Hartshorne, United States

Professor Gunnar Heckscher, Sweden

Professor W. E. Hocking, United States
Mr. Christopher Hollis, M.P., United Kingdom
Professor Barna Horvath, Hungary
Professor Yousuf Hussain, India
International Society for Significs, Netherlands
Professor Jørgen Jørgensen, Denmark
Professor Humayun Kabir, India
Professor Horace M. Kallen, United States
Professor Felix Kaufmann, United States
Professor Hans Kohn, United States
Professor M. C. Konczewski, Poland
Professor Jean Lacroix, France
Professor Georges Langrod, Poland
Professor Jacques Leclercq, Belgium
Mr. Henri Lefebvre, France
Professor C. I. Lewis, United States
Professor Arnold J. Lien, United States
Lord Lindsay of Birker, United Kingdom
Professor Ralph Linton, United States
Professor J. H. A. Logemann, Netherlands
Professor Arthur O. Lovejoy, United States
Mr. J. D. Mabbott, United Kingdom
Professor Richard McKeon, United States
Mr. James Marshall, United States
Mr. Wilson Martins, Brazil
Mr. Emmanuel Mounier, France
Professor Lewis Mumford, United States
Dr. Naidu, India
Mr. Ture Nerman, Sweden
Dr. Max Nomad, United States
Professor Albert Noyes, United States
Professor Stanislaus Ossowski, Poland
Professor Umberto A. Padovani, Italy
Professor Ricardo R. Pascual, Philippines

Mr. Aimé Patri, France
Professor Chaim Perelman, Belgium
Professor Gerald B. Phelan, Canada
Mr. John Petrov Plamenatz, United Kingdom
Professor Ithiel de Sola Pool, United States
Professor H. J. Pos, Netherlands
Mr. G. C. Povel, Netherlands
Professor S. V. Puntambekar, India
Professor Rammurti, India
Professor Svend Ranulf, Denmark
Professor Ladislaus Rieger, Czechoslovakia
Professor Wilhelm Röpke, Switzerland
Professor W. Rollo, South Africa
Professor Alf Ross, Denmark
Professor M. Ruthnaswami, India
Professor G. H. Sabine, United States
Professor D. Santos, Portugal
Mr. W. Scheffer, Netherlands
Dr. Rudolf Schlesinger, United Kingdom
Professor Herbert W. Schneider, United States
Mr. H. J. Simons, South Africa
Professor T. V. Smith, United States
Professor Luigi Stefanini, Italy
Professor Charles L. Stevenson, United States
Dr. Paul M. Sweezy, United States
Father Teilhard de Chardin, France
Professor Marten ten Hoor, United States
Mr. L. M. Thompson, South Africa
Professor N. S. Timasheff, United States
Professor S. N. de Volder, Belgium
Professor Jean Wahl, France
Dr. Emil J. Walter, Switzerland
Mr. Eric Weil, France
Professor Francis G. Wilson, United States
Professor Quincy Wright, United States
Professor A. Wylleman, Belgium
Professor Juan Zaragueta y Bengoechea, Spain

A considerable number of these contributions took the form of letters discussing one or more aspects of the problems at issue. Others were confined to laconic replies to the questions listed or consisted of short notes on a small number of points that had been found particularly important. But a majority of the contributions were fairly thoroughgoing in analysis and argumentation and were undoubtedly based on conscientious rethinking of the problems in terms of the approach adopted by UNESCO. Some of these took the form of general essays on the theme of the inquiry, while a few actually made up monographs on more limited topics like the history of the usage of "democracy," the Marxian conception of "democracy," Soviet definitions of "democracy," etc. Most of the more thoroughgoing contributions, however, kept fairly close to the order of questions in the questionnaire: while very few found it worth while to work out replies to *all* the questions, a great many gave their views on more than half of the questions.

A small number of the contributions were mimeographed and distributed to other contributors for cross-discussion of points of disagreement. Unfortunately, only a small beginning could be made within the framework of the UNESCO inquiry toward systematic organization of such cross-discussion. A few samples of comments and replies to comments have been included in the present volume.

The material made available through the UNESCO inquiry cannot in any way be claimed to be representative of world opinion in any statistical sense. Nevertheless, the material may be said to make up a significant cross-section of enlightened opinion on the foundations of current conflicts concerning democracy. All the major trends of ideological thinking in the world of the postwar era have, in one way or the other, found expression in the material, but unfortunately not always in direct proportion to their world importance, however that may be measured.

In the account of agreements and disagreements that will follow, no attempt have been made at statistical tabulation of the data in the material. Given the relative smallness of the sample and the geographical as well as ideological arbitrariness of the distribution of responses any effort toward quantification would seem futile. Instead, all cases of complete agreement or disagreement have been explicitly noted, while intermediary cases have been described by vague phrases like "the majority," "many," "some," "few." In a number of cases it was found very difficult to work out any definite classification of opinions and far more fruitful to outline analyses of the relationships between individually stated opinions. Adequate surveying was also made difficult by the fact that hardly one of the thirty questions of the questionnaire was given explicit answers by *all* the contributors. For several questions so few answers were found in the material that it was thought advisable to pass them by in the survey.

It should be borne in mind that the analytical survey given in the following sets itself the task of taking into account opinions expressed in *all* the direct contributions received: it will not be confined to those published in this volume. For reasons of space as well as repetition of similar views, all the material could not be printed: a selection had to be made. This survey may serve to remedy to some extent the inevitable shortcomings of a selection of this nature by supplying direct or indirect accounts of the ideological opinions and the philosophical analyses of a number of the scholars and experts whose contributions could not be printed in this volume.

The publication of a volume of this kind will serve the purpose of acquainting a wider public with the complexity and diversity of ideological thinking. In the existing literature on the controversies on "democracy" only rare and unsystematic attempts have been made at comparative analysis of opinions held on the precise issues that the general problem can be broken down into. The UNESCO questionnaire has served to press the argumentations of the opposed parties into common or nearly common thematic channels and thus made a comparative survey possible.

The aim of the ensuing account is to trace the outlines of such an analytical survey of agreements and disagreements explicit or implicit in the material at hand.

The analysis will make it abundantly clear how desperately difficult it is to compare ideological patterns of argumentation in terms of theoretical agreements and disagreements rather than in terms of historical affiliations or concrete political antagonisms. By stating these difficulties in a frank and intellectually honest way, the analysis may serve the purpose of counteracting tendencies toward ideological black-white thinking and toward propagandistic oversimplification of the issues. In this way, painstaking analysis of ideological opposition may serve the purposes of UNESCO by counteracting

tendencies to obscure whatever is common to the doctrines of conflicting groups. An important step toward world understanding
might be achieved through concerted action to thwart the effects of
the kind of ideological thinking and propaganda that tends to exalt
existing antagonisms beyond all possibility of settlement.

The classification of opinions expressed in the material under
scrutiny has proceeded from the tentative assumption that ideologists mean what they say: that when someone expresses an opinion
as his own, he has that opinion. The possibility that he lies—deliberately or unintentionally—is not discarded by this tentative assumption. But the assumption serves the pragmatic purpose of counteracting any tendency to succumb to the temptation of interpreting
and classifying ideologically opposed statements so as to fit into preconceived and stereotyped pictures of the antagonism. The aim is to
analyze controversies, not to continue them. One way to achieve
this end is to classify statements at their face value. This is what has
been attempted in the ensuing survey.

The obvious objection to the adoption of an initial assumption of
this kind is that no understanding of conflicts can be achieved without an analysis of the *motivations* of the statements from the opposed camps, without an analysis of what is *really meant* and *really
wanted* by those who use ideological concepts and appeal to ideological principles and ideals: it is such a trivial truism that people
may really want and mean the very opposite of what they appear
to say.

But nevertheless our tentative assumption can be upheld, and for
three reasons at least:

1. What people say is, after all, one important symptom of what
they "mean": any opinion leader attacking ideological opponents
will easily deceive his audience if for each statement he does not
make it clear whether he is describing what his opponents *say they
believe* or what he indirectly *infers that they "really" believe.*

2. Any one of us who have honestly tried to compare the doctrines of our own group with those of our opponents will have to
admit how much harder it is to apply the brutal tools of motivational analysis to our own rationalizations, hypocritical appeals, and
tacit assumptions than it is to those of our ideological opponents.
Deeper insight into the intricately biased character of current imputations of "real" meanings and motives may result in valuable

attempts to treat ideologically opposed doctrines on an equal footing, either by subjecting both to the same rigors of motivational
analysis, or by taking the more lenient approach of analyzing both
in their surface expressions.

3. Even if we can prove that the opinion leaders of our ideological opponents hold doctrines very different from those they say
they hold, there may well be large masses among their followers
who believe just as sincerely in their expressed doctrines as we believe in our own. Uncritical emphasis on motivational analysis may
therefore serve to strengthen the widespread ideological tendency
to picture opponents as a homogeneous mass manifesting the same
evil traits as have been imputed to its ruling group.

It goes without saying that this argumentation in favor of *a comparison of expressed doctrines* does not imply any depreciation of
efforts to go beyond the verbalized reactions of human beings. But
the comparative analysis of expressed doctrines is an important
initial phase in ideology research. The material under scrutiny does
not allow us to go any further in this analysis: the study of the
behavioral correlates and the social and historical settings of ideological controversies will have to be based on broader foundations
of theoretical inquiries, historical investigations, and experimental
research.

A. THE SEMANTICS OF "DEMOCRACY"

I. *Is "democracy" ambiguous?*—From the very outset of the inquiry nearly every one of those who discussed the matter seemed
to expect universal agreement among the experts consulted on the
first of the questions in the questionnaire: they were all expected to
answer that "democracy" is ambiguous. A survey of the actual answers, however, reveals that they did not. A few of the contributors
expressly deny that "democracy" is an ambiguous term. Several
others attribute to it an unambiguous core of meaning unaltered
throughout its usage in historically and geographically different
contexts. But the majority of the contributors expressly affirm the
ambiguity of "democracy." It is true that the introduction to the
UNESCO document and the very wording of the question may
have led a number of them to adopt this view without critical
scrutiny, but that is a matter that will have to be left to conjecture.

One outstanding reason for the discrepancies in the reactions to the ambiguity question must be sought in the imprecision of current semantic terminology. Only crude beginnings have been made toward critical assessment and theoretical integration of basic concepts in semantics. Current usage of terms like "meaning," "definition," "synonymity," and "ambiguity" is so vague that agreements as well as disagreements of purely verbal character are constantly apt to crop up. There is no semantic highway opened up anywhere to the clarification of ideological disputes: rigorous analysis and codification of the theoretical structure of semantics and the logic of concepts and definitions will have to precede any successful attempt in this direction.

As used in the UNESCO document the word "ambiguity" easily lent itself to divergent interpretations. There is ample evidence that the respondents did not all understand the word in the same way. The disagreement registered between respondents affirming and respondents questioning or denying the ambiguity of "democracy" may not necessarily have reflected ideological or theoretical discord, but simply a difference in interpretation and usage: the disagreement might not have emerged at all if the question had been given a more precise formulation.

Those who deny the ambiguity of the term "democracy" do not therefore deny divergencies in its usage; on the contrary, they all expressly affirm that the term has been used in different ways in different contexts by different groups. *That the word "democracy" is used in different and occasionally incompatible ways is not questioned by anybody.* What is questioned is whether these divergences of usage constitute ambiguity and whether they are at all relevant to the determination of the meaning or meanings of 'democracy."

Several of those who have entered upon an analysis of this problem have taken a stand for strict separation of meaning from usage.

Frondizi[2] takes the view that the word "democracy" is neither ambiguous nor unambiguous in itself, per se; it is only its *usage* that is ambiguous. An almost identical assertion is made by Ducasse,[3] but maybe for very different reasons. Statements by Brown, Eisenmann, and Heckscher seem to go in a similar direction.

But how is the meaning of the word to be determined if its actual usage is not to be taken into account?

2. This volume, p. 89.   3. P. 69.

A number of respondents simply postulate one sense as 'the only legitimate one, as the intrinsic, strict, or correct sense: actual usage may deviate from this sense but cannot alter it.

Thus, Lewis does not think that "democracy" is more ambiguous than most words in "its first, literal, or strict meaning": "All will agree that strictly it applies to any political régime in which the sovereign power is vested in the people at large, and that it applies to no other."[4]

Lefebvre does not think there is any ambiguity in the concept of democracy: "Democracy clearly implies justice, liberty, order, progress, reason, fraternity, and a living community of individuals within the nation."[5]

Horvath identifies democracy with "good self-government": "government by unanimous decisions proved to be good and useful to all." This *general sense* of the term is stated to be perfectly clear and entirely free from ambiguity.[6]

Other respondents are equally bent on finding a central formula for the fundamental meaning of democracy but take greater care to determine the relation of this meaning to the traditions of usage.

Thus, McKeon does not consider "democracy" ambiguous "in the sense that many different formulas have been proposed to define its meaning, but in the sense that many different interpretations have been proposed and elaborated for a formula on which there has been remarkable continuity of agreement." "Very few discussions of democracy, adverse or favorable, would be distorted in interpreting 'democracy' as the rule of the people in their own interest."[7]

Limiting his discussion to the nineteenth and twentieth centuries, Plamenatz feels convinced that implied by practically all serious statements which Communists as well as liberalists have made about "democracy" is a *primary meaning* he thinks can be roughly defined as "government by persons who are freely chosen by and responsible to the governed."[8]

Going all the way back to Greek origins, Field thinks there is "overwhelming evidence" that traditional usage bears out a similar definition: "A state is democratic . . . *in so far as* the whole body of

4. P. 164.
5. P. 147.   7. P. 195.
6. P. 95.   8. P. 303.

citizens . . . exercise an effective influence on the decisions of government."[9]

Jørgensen discerns a far more general core-meaning through the variations of usage and application: to him, democracy should be equated with "a general process of liberation and equalization" in all fields of human life.[10]

All those who have thus tried to formulate what in their opinion is the fundamental meaning of "democracy" have immediately felt themselves confronted by the problem raised by current ideological controversies over this keyword: Why the divergencies in usage despite the unity in meaning? Why the disagreements in interpretation despite the agreement in definition?

Solutions of the kind suggested by McKeon are explicitly or implicitly accepted by a number of respondents; agreement can certainly be reached on a central formula defining a basic concept, but disagreement will arise as soon as the *different elements of the formula* have to be interpreted in and applied to concrete social and political situations.

Perelman amplifies this approach by analyzing the possibilities of establishing a "normal sense" of the term: attempts might be made to arrive by way of inductions from empirical investigations at determining a structure common to all historically known usages of "democracy." An empirical definition of this kind might take the form of a propositional function of one or more variables: agreement might then be possible on the structure of the function while controversies would continue on the value of the variables. It might, for instance, very well be possible to define "democracy" as "government for the equal welfare of all as determined through the free decisions of all": the only advantage, if any, would be to have transferred the focus of controversy from "democracy" to "welfare," "equality" and "freedom."[11]

Several respondents go into further detail in explaining the relationship between the fundamental meaning and the divergencies of usage.

Horvath, Lefebvre, Plamenatz, and Heckscher, however different their approaches may otherwise be, can all be classified as taking the view that the general meaning of "democracy" is as clear and free

9. P. 80.
10. P. 112.   11. P. 297.

of ambiguity as ordinary language permits: it is the expression of an *ideal*, a *standard*, and a *goal*, a reflection of human aspirations. Ideological disputes do not arise from disagreements on this general meaning and the ideal type of human relationship it expresses: the disputes concern the *conditions* that make for progress toward the ideal, the *means* by which it can be reached, the order of *measures* to be taken in developing it. As a consequence, current ideological controversies do not center on the *meaning* of "democracy" but on theories of the conditions of its growth and the means of its accomplishment; what stands opposed are not analytical statements of definitions but synthetic statements of social and political interrelations. Accusations of ambiguity and misuse arise from unconscious confusions of means with goals as well as from deliberate attempts to identify accomplished conditions with the general ideal.[12]

The difficulty inherent in this kind of approach is that in actual practice it is very hard to reach agreements on what is end and what is means, what is ideal and what is accomplishment. Ideological statements constantly oscillate between analyticity and syntheticity, between the expression of the meaning of words and the formulation of empirical relationships between the matters denoted by the words. Statements about what "democracy demands," what "democracy implies," what "democracy means" may be interpreted either way: what one party may question as a possible *condition* of democracy may be taken as an essential element of its *concept* by the other party.

Lewis seems to find the reasons for the ideological disagreements in a process of a similar kind when he states that although the primary meaning of "democracy" is clear and simple, controversies over its meaning will arise "because different parties wish to require *further* characteristics of anything they will allow to be called a democracy, and because they disagree as to *what* further characteristics are to be so required."[18]

A number of the respondents may be inferred to be in disagreement with this view, partly because in actual practice the "strict" definition given by Lewis will turn out to admit of a great variety of interpretations, partly for the reason that a line cannot easily be drawn between a strict primary sense on the one hand and incom-

12. See Horvath, this volume, p. 95; Lefebvre, p. 147; Plamenatz, pp. 303–5.
13. P. 164.

patible ideological uses on the other. The contradiction between the positions taken by Jørgensen[14] and Ross[15] goes to show how mutual charges of ideological exploitation can be leveled even at attempts to formulate strict primary meanings.

In a short letter on this matter Stevenson suggests an approach that ought to inspire further elaboration: it merges into one model most of the elements introduced into the discussion of the ambiguity question by other contributors. To Stevenson, current ideological usage of "democracy" is characterized by *multi-dimensional* ambiguity. However used, the term covers complex concepts analyzable into a number of factors expressive of indices or criteria of "democraticity": the term is never ambiguous or vague in one respect only but in several. The indeterminacy of its reference can be traced down to a number of reasons: (1) there is no agreement on what criteria to include in the concept, (2) there is no agreement on what relative weight to give each criterion, (3) there is no line of demarcation agreed upon between "democratic" and "nondemocratic" on the theoretically possible scales that may be constructed to determine the degree to which each criterion is fulfilled.

The short formulas suggested by a number of contributors may serve to express opinions on the first point: the choice of criteria to take into account. Formulas emphasizing the political core of meaning will imply concepts based on criteria like: percentage of population having access to influence on government decisions, degree of independence of popular opinion formation, directness of popular influence, revocability of mandates and decisions, etc. Other formulas might give further emphasis to less clearly political criteria: equal distribution of economic benefits, equality of social status, degree of legal security, absence of discrimination, etc. Others again may indicate concepts of an exclusively economic, social, or "way of life" character, thus opposed to the predominantly political concepts. Stevenson's main point, however, is that even if agreement were reached on the choice of criteria, "democracy" would still be multi-dimensionally ambiguous because each concrete application of the criteria would be indeterminate and a potential source of violent controversy: What relative weight should be given to each criterion? What scales of measurement or comparison should be chosen

14. Pp. 111–12.   15. Pp. 367–68.

to determine the degree of fulfilment of each criterion? Where on each scale should the line be drawn between "democratic" and "non-democratic"?

Several other contributors have stressed the impossibility of establishing strict lines of demarcation. Thus Field, Horvath,[16] and Ewing all maintain that in concrete cases no clear-cut distinctions between what is "democratic" and what is "not democratic" can be made; it is all a matter of degree, of more or less. Ewing states that "strictly speaking, we should talk, not of democracies, but of a democratic element in states." Statements of this kind must not be construed to imply indifference to democratic ideals. The point has been admirably put by Field: "On the other hand, there is, of course, no reason why we should not continue to speak, roughly, of one state as democratic if it has a considerable degree of democracy, and another as undemocratic if it has very little or hardly any at all, in just the same way as we speak of the weather as warm or cold, though we could not fix an exact point on the thermometer at which one ended and the other began. But we must not fall into the blunder, either with regard to democracy or the weather, of speaking as if a difference of degree was not important. The phrase, 'It's *only* a difference of degree' is nearly always a mark of political illiteracy."[17]

Ross takes an approach closely similar to that of Stevenson: he suggests the construction of a multi-dimensional "ideal type" concept of "democracy" that might serve as the basis for comparative assessments of the degrees of "democraticity" achieved in "real types."[18] But, while Stevenson is mainly interested in mapping out the various modes of indeterminacy, Ross is primarily concerned with the construction of one working concept. Both attempts, however, point to the need for more painstaking analysis of the elements involved and for greater precision in the formulation of theories of their interrelations in ideological argumentation as well as in socio-political reality.

The majority of the respondents, however, do not enter into any detailed analysis of these problems. A great number affirm the existence of incompatible usages of "democracy" and refrain from any attempt to single out any one of them as the "correct" one, the "primary" one or the "strict" one. Among those who take this attitude

16. Pp. 96–99.
17. P. 80.   18. Pp. 365–66.

are Bettelheim,[19] Kabir,[20] Lindsay,[21] Perelman,[22] Pool,[23] Röpke,[24] Sweezy,[25] Boas, Nerman, Ranulf, and Smith. Lovejoy does not hesitate to characterize "democracy" as one of the most ambiguous words in current use.

It should be emphasized that respondents who thus affirm the existence of incompatible usages do not therefore deny the possibility that the usages may have common characteristics; but they do not think that these common traits suffice to make up a useful concept of democracy. Neither does the affirmation of equally valid but incompatible usages exclude the justification of proposals for the discontinuation of some of the usages. It does not even preclude the possibility of characterizing one or more of the usages as misuse in the sense of their being potential tools of deceit.

Complications of this kind have to be faced by any one wishing to obtain clear-cut evidence of ambiguity. The question arises: What practical criteria are used by ideologists to *identify* cases of ambiguity? The second question in the questionnaire was formulated in the hope that respondents might quote different occurrences of the term "democracy" in historically given ideological texts and give their reasons for referring to one occurrence as an instance of one sense of the word, another occurrence as an instance of a second sense, incompatible with or at least divergent from, the first.

II. *Evidence of ambiguity.*—To any analyst interested in the elaboration of reliable procedures for the determination of minute as well as wide differences in usage, answers to the second question must be said to have been disappointing. The majority of respondents did not think it at all necessary to corroborate their affirmations of ambiguity by arguments from historically given occurrences of "democracy": they either stressed the superfluity and futility of searching for evidence for such an obvious fact or they considered the UNESCO inquiry and questionnaire alone sufficient proof of the ambiguity of the word. A small number of contributors took care, however, to list a number of examples of what they considered usages sufficiently divergent to establish ambiguity: thus Jørgensen,[26] McKeon,[27] Ross,[28] Cox, Hagopian, Ranulf. But the

19. Pp. 1–2.
20. Pp. 120–21.   23. P. 330.
21. Pp. 172–73.   24. P. 361.
22. Pp. 295–96.   25. P. 391.
26. In a section not included in this volume.
27. Pp. 196–98.   28. P. 364.

ANALYTICAL SURVEY   461

difficulties involved in establishing rigorous criteria for the identification of cases of ambiguity are not explicitly discussed by anyone
except van Dantzig.[29] In assessing the relevance of the quoted
occurrences to the determination of ambiguities, two points should
be kept in mind:

1. The fact that ideologist A calls "democratic" a state which
ideologist B violently rejects as "undemocratic" does not exclude
the possibility that they both use "democracy" in the same sense;
the disagreement may be due to opposed *descriptions* of the state in
question. If A's description were established as adequate they might
both agree that the state would fulfil the requirements of a democracy; if B's description were established as adequate they might
agree to reject the state as undemocratic. Violent controversies over
"democracy" may consequently be possible without any ambiguity
in the concept.

2. Ideologist A may restrict his use of "democracy" to one kind
of structure or relationship while ideologist B thinks it justified to
use the term to characterize a number of other kinds of structures
or relationships. This disagreement does not necessarily establish
ambiguity since a wider and more diluted sense may be constructed
common to all the structures or relationships thus characterized.

To take an example: Ross seems to believe that sufficient evidence
of ambiguity is implied in these four instances of occurrences of
"democracy" or close derivatives in everyday use: (1) The Danish
state is a democracy. (2) This law, which deprives widows of economic support, is undemocratic. (3) The army ought to be democratized. (4) It is undemocratic not to take one's meals with one's
servants.[30]

Everybody will agree that in these four cases "democracy" is
applied to very different kinds of structures or relationships. Several of the respondents, and particularly Jørgensen,[31] may, however, be inferred to disagree with the implication that this diversity
of application establishes ambiguity; "democracy" may very well
be interpreted to have been used in the same—although highly diluted—sense throughout the four examples.

The fact that practically all respondents leave untouched the
intricate problems involved in establishing reliable distinctions be-

29. Pp. 47 ff.
30. P. 364.   31. P. 112.

tween usages should surprise no one who is familiar with the present predicament of semantics and the linguistics of ideological discourse. As long as no reliable methods have been developed, it is quite understandable that even the most competent experts in ideology research fail to agree on what sense "democracy" has been used in by the great ideologists of the past; it may not at all be necessary to explain their disagreements by assumptions of political bias.

III. *Is "democracy" misused?*—The analysis of the widespread complaints of ambiguity and looseness leads the way to a general discussion of the causes and justifications of the indignant charges of *misuse* that are so frequently hurled in all directions in current ideological conflicts.

This is a problem that seems to have attracted the attention of a greater number of respondents than most of the other questions listed in the questionnaire. A considerable number of contributors try to give explicit formulations of their criteria of misuse. Fairly thorough analyses of concepts of misuse are given by van Dantzig,[32] Ducasse,[33] Jørgensen,[34] Lewis,[35] Bochenski, and Lovejoy. A comparison of the definitions arrived at will set off the terminological difficulties involved in the clarification of ideological controversies.

Ducasse works out a definition of misuse that furnishes a fruitful point of departure: "Misuse of a word is *provable* if either: (*a*) A definition of it is *agreed upon*, but the concrete things to which the word is *then* applied lack some of the characteristics specified in or implied by the agreed definition. This is misuse in the sense of *misapplication*. (*b*) One or more concrete things are *agreed upon* as being ones to which the word shall be applied, but the word is *then* applied to connote one or more characters not in fact possessed by all the concrete things agreed upon as the ones to which the word shall be applied. This is misuse in the sense of *mischaracterization*."[36]

Ducasse is well aware of the difficulties involved in concrete applications of these criteria. The likeliness of agreements on *denotation* is just as small as the likeliness of agreement in *connotation*. An essential part of ideological controversies is focused on disagreements on the characters "in fact possessed" or not by such and such "concrete things." What is the character of the state of affairs in

32. Pp. 48–49.
33. P. 69.   35. P. 165.
34. Pp. 106–10.   36. P. 69.

the United States or in Soviet Russia? Charges of misuse in the Ducasse sense would be justifiable only on the assumption of agreement on descriptions of states of affairs of this kind: a highly unrealistic assumption as far as ideological controversies are concerned.

Bochenski introduces several additional elements in his definition of misuse:

There is misuse if and only if (*a*) the word "democracy" is used in a sense A in addressing a public who understands it in a sense B different from A, (*b*) the public addressed resents the shift in meaning from B to A, and (*c*) the state of affairs referred to by sense A is associated with negative value judgments, while the state of affairs referred to by sense B is associated with positive value judgments by the public addressed.

The important factors in this definition are the difference between sender use and receiver interpretation, the valuational relevance of the shift in meaning and the relativity of misuse to the attitudes and moral dispositions of the public addressed. The definition does not require that the public has been actually *misled* by the shift in meaning: it is enough that there is resentment against it.

The definitions introduced by van Dantzig,[37] Jørgensen,[38] Lewis,[39] and Lovejoy all give particular emphasis to the *deceit* factor: charges of misuse involve moral indignation at attempts to *mislead* audiences to accept opinions or adopt attitudes on false premises.

Lovejoy formulates a definition of this kind in the following way: ". . . I should define the *'misuse'* of a term as its use in such a manner that it is certain, or highly probable, that it will not be understood in the same sense by the readers and hearers as by the writers or speakers, but will nevertheless predispose the former to a favorable attitude toward the ideas favored by the latter, or lead to actual confusion of the two senses of the term."

On this view, the use of value-loaded words with unstable cognitive connotations is a powerful tool of *attitude influencing and control*. The use of words of this character makes up an integral part of ideological *persuasion processes*: the very act of branding some usage "correct" and others "misleading" is a step in the process. Van Dantzig, Jørgensen, Lewis, Marshall,[40] Perelman,[41] Pool,[42] Ross,[43]

37. Pp. 48–49.
38. Pp. 109–10.
39. P. 165.
40. Pp. 221–22.

41. P. 295.
42. P. 330.
43. P. 364.

DEMOCRACY IN A WORLD OF TENSIONS

and the authors of the memorandum submitted by the International Society for Significs have given particular emphasis to this persuasive function of statements on "democracy" and its "misuse."[44]

Some disagreement seems to exist on the question whether charges of misuse should be focused on the *actual act* of using the keyword in a sense different from the one it is apt to be understood in by the audience, or on the *deceitful motive* of misleading the audience by operating a shift in meaning. Bochenski seems to be inclined to the former position. So does ten Hoor who seems to think that misuse can be charged even in cases where the speaker or writer only fails "to realize that there are other meanings of the term than his own." On the other hand, Jørgensen does not think that unconscious or unintentional misleading of this and similar kinds can be charged as misuse: the meanings of ideological keywords being as unstable as they are nobody should be charged with, and thought guilty of, misuse unless *a deliberate motive of deceit* can be established at the basis of the misleading use of the word in question.[45] In a similar vein, Kallen does not think the divergencies of usage can be traced to any kind of "misuse" unless "insincerity or malice is attributable to the user."[46] The difficulties involved in the identification of concrete cases of deceitful or insincere motivation have not, however, been attacked by any of the contributors.

The divergencies of emphasis and scope manifest in the definitions given to the concept of "misuse" are reflected in one way or another in the disagreements registered in concrete exemplification.

Lovejoy concludes that in the sense he has given the word, "there appears to be extensive misuse of the word 'democracy' nowadays, particularly in the propaganda of the Soviet Union." A considerable number of other contributors make statements to the same effect, waiving, however, qualifications and reservations of the kind indicated by Lovejoy.

Lefebvre states that "democracy" is being misused by middle-

44. The general problem of persuasive use of key-terms is discussed in Ch. L. Stevenson, *Ethics and Language* (New Haven, 1944); cf. also Ch. Perelman, *De la justice* (Brussels, 1946). Results of psychological experiments on persuasive use of keywords are found in G. W. Hartmann, "The Contradiction between the Feeling-Tone of Political Party Names and Public Response to Their Platforms," *Jour. Soc. Psychol.*, VII (1936), 336–57; M. Sherif, "The Psychology of Slogans," *Jour. Abn. and Soc. Psychol.*, XXXII (1937), 450–61; Leonard W. Doob, *Public Opinion and Propaganda* (New York, 1948).

45. Pp. 109–10.   46. P. 132.

class politicians who mislead the people by trying to let their bourgeois democracy pass for the ideal democracy—be it from unconscious prejudice or from "a deliberate, cynical determination to bamboozle."[47]

Bochenski stresses the relativity of any justifiable charge of misuse to the language habits and expectations of the group addressed: "Any man using the word 'democracy' in the current Russian sense in addressing a Western audience misuses the word just as much as any one using it in the Western sense in addressing a Russian audience."

A considerable number of respondents find it hardly justifiable, possible, or meaningful to charge anybody with misuse. Thus McKeon,[48] Perelman,[49] Gough, Ranulf, and many others emphasize that in the absence of a *generally accepted* usage taken to define the "correct sense" no misuse can be charged. Others, like Pool,[50] Wright,[51] Boas, and Sabine urge the conventionality of word-meaning relations and tend to imply that charges of misuse cannot be upheld without inconsistency by those who adopt this view.

It seems plausible to infer, however, that the "misuse" notion repudiated by these two groups of contributors has more in common with the Ducasse concept of misuse than with the Lovejoy concept; they do deny the justification of charges of misuse in the sense of deviation from usage agreed upon as "correct," but they may very well affirm the justification of charges of misuse in the sense of deceitful exploitation of the language habits of the groups addressed. The surface disagreement may thus resolve itself into substantial agreement; this is only one of many cases of this kind we shall have occasion to note in this survey.

What, then, are the main trends of answers to the questions on misuse?

The confusion of terminology and the complex entanglement of issues make most of the answers hard to compare. Any conclusions on "main trends" will consequently tend to be vague and airy.

First of all, the material at hand gives evidence that charges or denials of "misuse" may have largely divergent meanings even among experts and that the diversity of meanings is not generally known to them.

47. P. 147.
48. P. 198.
49. P. 295.
50. P. 330.
51. More explicitly so in answers not included in this volume.

Two main meanings of "misuse" vie with each other in the contributions: one "logical," another "ethical." In the first sense, there are charges of misapplication and mischaracterization without any necessary moral relevance. In the second sense, there are charges of deceitful manipulations of meanings in processes of persuasion—charges with just as ethical implications as lies and fraud.

Practically all contributors would agree that "democracy" is being misused in the latter sense. But opinions differ in the concrete attribution of guilt: What ideological groups are most addicted to misleading use of the keyword "democracy"?

On the questions of misapplication and mischaracterization considerable disagreement is evidenced:

Some respondents seem to favor the assumption that a definite sense, a "strict," "correct," "real" meaning of "democracy" can be established and formulated; all use deviating from this meaning is automatically "misuse."

Other respondents deny the possibility of singling out any such "correct" meaning and the existence of any universally accepted meaning; this they take to imply that no "misuse" of "democracy" is possible or chargeable—at least in the "logical" sense of deviation from "correct" use.

Confronted with this complex and confused picture, the analyst can only conclude that mutual charges of misuse cannot contribute to the clarification of ideological disputes—at least as long as in each case the criteria of misuse adopted are not explicitly formulated and empirical evidence proffered to substantiate the assumption that the criteria are fulfilled.

IV. *Aspirations versus achievements.*—Why is so much indignation focused on the *terminology* used in ideological disputes? One of the reasons has been sought in the frustrations experienced through constantly *misleading* use of keywords: this subject has already been dealt with. Another reason may be sought in the frequent *confusion of facts and ideals* manifest in the use of keywords in ideological defense as well as attack: "democracy," for instance, may oscillate between denoting an *established* power structure in a society and connoting the *ideal limits* toward which the society strives to develop. Some of the violence of controversies and some of the indignation at ideological terminology may be traced to the mutual misinterpretations caused by this oscillation:

1. Our own high-pitched proclamations for democracy will tend to be interpreted as out-and-out praise for our *status quo* by our ideological opponents, whereas we—at least upon closer analysis—would reluctantly concede that our enthusiasm was largely directed toward characteristics so far not realized in our country.

2. Inversely, our criticism of the undemocratic character of an ideologically opposed people is by them interpreted as an attack on their cherished democratic ideals, whereas in fact our criticism was limited to the actual degree of achievement of these ideals in the rival country.

One of the questions[52] in the UNESCO document focused on misinterpretations of this kind: it was asked whether the confusion of ideals with actual conditions was apt to increase the violence of discussions.

The majority of the relatively few who discussed the matter gave affirmative answers to the question, thus Ducasse,[53] Horvath,[54] Jørgensen,[55] Gough, Heckscher, Nerman, Puntambekar, Ranulf, Walter.

Lovejoy tries to determine in a more precise way the conditions for an increase in ideological violence. His brief remarks may be construed to indicate the following possibilities: (1) if everybody is confused about the meaning of the term, no increase is likely; (2) if one party is aware of the distinctions but believes that the others are trying to mislead them by their ambiguous use of the term, increase is likely; (3) if both parties are aware of their equal immunity to terminological misleading, a truce may take place or new strategies develop.

McKeon takes the view that "the violence of controversies seldom results from the confusion of ideals with actual conditions": far more active as causal factors are disagreements on the character of the imperfections and the means to remove them.[56]

The problem of the causes making for violence in ideological disputes is an empirical one that will have to be settled by investigations within psychology, sociology, and political science. The suggestions made in the UNESCO document and the answers given by

52. Question 7, see p. 516.
53. P. 71.   54. P. 98.
55. In a section not printed in this volume.
56. P. 199.

contributors largely reflect intuitive opinions on the choice of thera-
peutical procedure in assuaging controversies.

V. *New uses.*—All questions that have been raised in order to
throw light on the terminological tangles around the keyword "democracy" lead up to one that cannot be answered without painstaking research:

What can historical studies of the development of usage contribute to the clarification of the controversies over the "meanings,"
"ambiguities," and "misuses"?

Most of the contributors have not had time to concern themselves with historical questions. Those who have given them more
than passing attention are easily counted: Bober on Marx-Engels
usage, McKeon on the relation between conflicts found in classical
and modern uses, Ossowski on bourgeois versus socialist uses,
Plamenatz on Marxian-Leninist usage, Pool on the development of
the split between Western and Eastern usages, Schlesinger on Soviet
usage, and Sweezy with his remarks on the history of socialist
usage. The conclusions arrived at in these studies cannot be sur-
veyed in this context.[57] Suffice it to say that they reveal deep-
rooted disagreements which can only be settled by patient and detached research on a widely larger scale than any so far undertaken.

The focal point of interest has, as might have been expected, been
the historical relationship between the liberalist-Western usage and
the Communist-Eastern usage. In the UNESCO questionnaire[58] the
question was raised whether any of the current usages—and it was
apparent that the East-West split in usage was what was referred
to—could be considered "new" in relation, e.g., to nineteenth-
century or prewar usages. The question was deliberately left as
vague as that in order that respondents might feel provoked to
develop their views at greater length. But even though only a few
could take time to do so, a considerable number of others expressed
fairly definite opinions on the subject without taking very great
care to document them.

Practically all those who find that "new" usages have emerged in
the twentieth century locate the main innovations in the usage of
revolutionary Marxists and particularly in that of the ideologists of
the Soviet Union and the popular democracies of Eastern Europe:

57. All these longer historical studies are included in this volume.
58. Question 4, p. 515.

thus Ross,[59] Brown, Heckscher, Nerman, Puntambekar, Ranulf. A few also consider usages stressing the social and economic content in general "new" in relation to nineteenth-century use. It is quite apparent that the charges of innovation are closely correlated to general charges of misuse.

On the other hand, a number of respondents of divergent ideological affiliation take the view that both the two major usages current can claim ample historical justification: thus Lindsay,[60] McKeon,[61] Ossowski,[62] Plamenatz,[63] and Sweezy.[64] The position taken by Pool is slightly more sophisticated; both current usages are innovations in relation to the "classical" usage prevalent in Europe and America until around 1848.[65]

The material at hand cannot support any positive conclusions one way or another. Further research is of importance for efforts of clarification and reconciliation because arguments from the history of usage play active parts in controversies over "right use" and "misuse": theories of terminological innovation support claims that usages have been deliberately coined in order to confuse and profit from the confusion. Research may show that the development of the use of "democracy" is *too complex and many-sided to justify any monopoly of the term* in favor of any particular ideological group. It is not, however, the task of the present analysis to conjecture what results further research will yield.

VI. *Common characteristics.*—As a direct sequel to the question on the historical basis of current usages, the UNESCO questionnaire takes up for scrutiny the widespread opinion that the meaning of "democracy" cannot be understood *in abstracto*, but only in its historical relations to concrete social and political structures that have been classed as "kinds" of democracy. The question was asked whether these historical structures have any characteristics in common *that make them democracies.*[66]

Answers to this question present a muddled picture because it is rarely clear exactly which of the many interpretations of the question the respondent has focused on.

Everybody agrees that "democracy" is not a proper name for one unique structure but a term that can be applied to structures that,

59. Pp. 364–65.
60. Pp. 178–81.
61. P. 198.
62. P. 264.

63. Pp. 304–6.
64. Pp. 391–93.
65. Pp. 331–46.
66. Question 6, see p. 516.

although similar in a number of features, may well differ to the point of incompatibility in others. There is disagreement, however, on the range and extent of application of the term; thus, some do not think it is properly used in the phrase "Athenian democracy," others would not class "bourgeois democracy" among democracies, and others again think "Soviet democracy" a misnomer, since in their opinion the Soviet régime is a dictatorship.[67]

The majority of answers, however, express the opinion that all historically given democracies have common characteristics. It is true that these characteristics are not always held to be common to all structures that have ever been called "democratic" but only to those that have "properly" been so called. Thus Lewis states: "In so far as all are truly democracies, they have in common two characteristics: (1) sovereignty is vested in the general will of the people, and all of them equally; (2) the government is such that it is a rule of laws and not of men."[68]

Most of those who affirm the existence of common characteristics do not make any such reservations, however. But their formulations of the characteristics reveal very wide differences of scope and emphasis.

To Feibleman, the different "kinds" of democracy have nothing in common but a common misuse of the term "democracy." To Nomad, the only common characteristic of the various kinds of "democracy" is the fact that they all claim to be representative of the will of the people. Other contributors are more specific in their formulations of common characteristics. Bettelheim takes the view that, although each democracy has to be judged in its historical context, they have at least one characteristic in common: that, at its particular stage in history, each represents an attempt to reduce to a minimum the scope and intensity of social coercion. Kabir finds a common characteristic to "all the different political systems and ideologies which we call democratic" in "the urge to establish an equivalence if not an identity" between duties and rights.[69] Gough finds that there are common exclusions: hereditary privileges, race discriminations, etc. McKeon[70] goes into further detail: "All democracies have in common (1) political institutions designed to

67. Bober, in an answer not included in this volume.
68. P. 166.
69. P. 123.   70. P. 199.

make effective the will of the people in the regulation of the common life, without discrimination, of all the people, and (2) provisions in the organization of these institutions to protect against arbitrary action, by such devices as the protection of human rights and the promulgation of a rule of law."

The problem whether the structures referred to by current Western usages have anything in common with the structures referred to by current Eastern usages is dealt with at greater length than any other.

Ossowski[71] emphasizes the historical community of values that exists between the two conceptions. Similar views are taken by Horvath,[72] Jørgensen,[73] Farber, and Lien. The material does not, however, furnish any detailed analysis of the individual characteristics thus deemed common to the two kinds of structure. There is approximate unanimity that such common traits exist, but the ones on which there is most widespread agreement are hardly such as to affect the opposition of valuational attitudes toward the two kinds of structure.

VII. *Concluding remarks.*—What kind of lessons can we learn from the answers to the terminologically centered first part of the questionnaire?

First of all, that there are deep-rooted disagreements in matters where the common man cannot expect to be able to make up his own opinion: on the technicalities of semantics, in the descriptions of divergencies of usage, on the history of the semantical fluctuations of the term "democracy."

Second, that these disagreements among experts in a large number of cases reflect divergencies of ideological bias. There is a manifest tendency to present one's own views as the only ones worthy of serious consideration, while those of opponents are more often than not found to be due to misrepresentation, distortion, and even deliberate fraud. There is a tendency to picture one's own efforts as serving the purposes of clarification only, while the tenets set forth by ideological opponents are primarily treated as instruments of persuasion adapted to political tactics. There is a tendency to use history as a tool of ideological justification and to affirm the validity of conclusions from historical study in ways more violent and absolute than is warranted by the meager empirical evidence at hand.

71. Pp. 246–51.   72. Pp. 95–98.
73. In answers not included in this volume.

There are notable exceptions to be found in the material, but this is a report on general trends.

The lesson of all this lies in the realization that knowledge of ideological processes is still so little developed that standardized oversimplifications of controversial issues can win widespread acceptance under the shelter of scholarly authority.

The answers to the questions on the semantics of "democracy" furnish excellent illustrations of this predicament: they show how even outstanding experts are apt to treat complex historical, linguistic, and philosophical issues as if there were only a choice between a true account and a definite analysis on the one hand and a heap of crude misrepresentations and deliberate distortions on the other.

Intense analysis and painstaking empirical studies may, if conducted by researchers free of direct ideological entanglements, prove a powerful weapon against oversimplification and black-white thinking and thus make it harder to appeal to violence on false pretensions. The urgency of an expansion and intensification of ideology research is clearly manifested in the material on the first part of the UNESCO questionnaire.

B. POLITICAL AND OTHER DEMOCRACIES

I. *The Lincoln formula.*—Having in its first part focused on the general linguistic problems involved in current ideological use of "democracy," the UNESCO questionnaire in its second and third parts proceeded to detailed analyses of two of the fundamental issues that were assumed to lie at the root of the violent controversies on terminology: (1) the problem of the relationship between political "democratization" and economic and social "democratization," dealt with in Part B of the questionnaire;[74] (2) the problem of the right of opposition and the limits of toleration within states to be classed as "democracies," dealt with in Part C.[75]

None of the respondents have directly criticized this procedure. It is true that there is wide disagreement on the relative emphasis to be given the one and the other cluster of problems, but it seems safe to infer that there is general agreement that both are pivotal issues in the controversies raging in the contemporary world. An extensive survey of current ideological literature seemed to point to the same conclusion.

74. See pp. 516–19.   75. Pp. 519–20.

In its details, however, the UNESCO procedure has occasionally aroused emphatic criticism.

In the second part of the questionnaire, the Gettysburg *of, by, for* formula was chosen as a tentative point of departure for the analysis of current meanings of "democracy": provocative interpretations of the three famous prepositions were given and scholars and experts asked to work out their comments.[76]

A small but vocal number of respondents resent this choice of approach. Thus, Boas does not think anything can be cleared up by starting out from a formula that "had an immense emotional force for Americans," but an emotional force that "was in inverse ratio to the clarity of its meaning." And Hocking: "Lincoln was not professing to define democracy in his 'of ... for ... by' phrase; those who turn it into a definition must bear the blame of wholly superfluous confusion." Lewis: "I should interpret Lincoln's Gettysburg address as a tribute to the dead, and not as a political document."[77]

Schlesinger is convinced that the procedure chosen is a highly misleading one as an approach to the analysis of the differences between the Western and the Soviet conceptions of "democracy": these differences cannot by any artifice of interpretation be reduced to differences of emphasis on the elements of the Lincoln formula.[78]

However all this may be, the Lincoln formula was chosen as a point of departure because it is still the central slogan of all groups professing their allegiance to "democracy"; it has not only preserved its enormous emotional force with Americans and Westerners but is also constantly being used as a formula defining "democracy" by ideologists of the Soviet Union and the eastern European states.[79] In terms of analysis this means that an inquiry need not start out from the mere word "democracy" as a common denominator but can take its departure from the Lincoln formula and proceed to an analysis of the divergencies manifest in interpretations of its elements.

The interpretations suggested in the questionnaire for the *of, by,* and *for* relations have provoked a considerable amount of disagreement. On closer analysis, however, this disagreement may be seen to be more apparent than real. Opinions differ because they

76. Question 8, p. 516.
77. P. 166.   78. P. 379.
79. See e.g., David Zaslavski, *La Démocratie soviétique,* French trans. (Paris, 1947).

are not answers to the same questions. Part of the discord is un-doubtedly due to the vagueness of reference of the question put to the experts: Does it ask for the meaning Lincoln himself may be presumed to have attached to his words? Or does it ask for the general interpretation the American public of his time understood the words in? Or again, does it ask for the meanings they may be con-jectured to have for the different groups appealing to them in the present age? Distinctions along these lines are generally ignored by the respondents; it is apparent that formulations of the "real" meaning of those historical words are sensed to be of vital impor-tance in ideological persuasion.

In the questionnaire, the *of* relation was provocatively interpreted to indicate "the *obedience* of the people to the government."

Surprisingly, the majority of respondents seem to have agreed to this interpretation, although rather few state their view on this point explicitly. It seems safe to infer, however, that the word "obedience" has been taken in a very weak sense by those who have thus agreed to the interpretation suggested: "*of* the people" is simply taken to mean that what is being governed is the people, that the people are the object of government.

Those who thus accept the "obedience" interpretation of the *of* clause do not therefore take it to express any necessary criterion to be fulfilled by régimes that are to be classed as "democracies."[80] Ross is very emphatic on this point: "The preposition *of* would not seem to indicate anything beyond the bare fact that a government exists; any government is a government of the people. Who else should it govern?"[81]

Exactly the same argument is by Bober,[82] Perelman,[83] and Schle-singer[84] used *against* the interpretation suggested in the question-naire: if the *of* relation were only to indicate the fact of obedience, it could not serve to distinguish democratic from nondemocratic régimes. Against the diluted "obedience" interpretation, therefore, are pitted interpretations that make *of* an important index of "de-mocraticity." Perelman—and with him ten Hoor—take the *of* clause to indicate that the people are the source of the power of govern-ment, while Bober—and with him Nomad—take the closely related

80. Question 9, see p. 516.   81. P. 367.
82. In answers not included in this volume.
83. P. 297.   84. P. 579.

view that it means that the government is such that the people desire it and have affection for it. The difficulty with interpretations of this kind is that they tend to make *of* close to indistinguishable from *by;* this point is particularly stressed by Lewis.[85]

The "obedience" interpretation of the *of* relation may, however, be construed in the more positive sense that the decisions of government are regularly conformed to by the people. Patri makes a point of stressing this construction by analyzing the distinction between "democracy" and "anarchy."[86] Sweezy, on the other hand, very emphatically denounces the "obedience" interpretation as an attempt to impute to Lincoln a conservative attitude of admiration for "law and order"; instead, Sweezy maintains that Lincoln by "of the people" must have meant "belonging to the people," emanating from the people, forming an inseparable part of the people.[87] Commenting on this interpretation of Sweezy's, Ducasse expresses serious doubt whether this was what Lincoln meant or his audience understood him to mean.[88] It may be questioned whether any such search for "real meanings" can contribute to the clarification of the issues involved; it is more important to analyze the persuasive function of imputations of meanings to authority loaded statements.

In the cases of *by* and *for* there is little disagreement on the general interpretation of the relations they indicate between people and government; what is violently debated is whether both *for* and *by* should count in the determination of what is and what is not "democratic." Opinions are almost evenly divided in the material: one group of respondents give exclusive emphasis to *by* as the essential criterion while another group stress the equal importance of *by* and *for* in the determination of "democraticity." Attitudes and arguments on this matter are, however, so closely correlated to those registered on the question of "narrow" versus "broad" usage of "democracy" that separate treatment does not seem called for.

II. *The "narrow" versus the "broad" usage.*—However vague, however laden with emotional associations, the Lincoln formula opens the gate to further scrutiny of the role of the keyword "democracy" in current ideological struggles: What is the nature of the disagreements over the relations between the *by* element and

85. P. 166. 86. Pp. 283–84.
87. Pp. 393–94.
88. In a passage not included in this volume.

the *for* element in the formula? What part do these disagreements play in the fundamental political oppositions of our age?

The division of opinion manifest in our material between adherents of exclusive "by the people" criteria and adherents of inclusive "by *and* for the people" criteria of "democraticity" reflects an issue of old standing in the history of political argumentation. A great variety of formulations have been devised to express what is taken to be the crux and essence of this opposition: from terse sloganized catch phrases to complex systems of philosophical reasoning. Formulations have largely varied with political affiliations and ideological proclivities, and rare indeed are the cases where opponents have been able to agree on any joint description of the opposition between them. In the UNESCO inquiry, this presented a dilemma that had to be faced squarely: the choice was between producing a formula so complicated and studded with reservations as to make it unreadable and indifferent and setting forth a cruder one at the risk of accusations of ideological bias. At the end a compromise was devised: the opposition was tentatively described as one between a democracy concept "designating methods of decision-making" only and a democracy concept "designating conditions and methods as well as results of decision-making." The former of these concepts was then labeled a *narrow* political one, the latter a *broad* socio-economic one.

Objections to this formulation of the dichotomy took different forms. To several contributors, thus McKeon;[89] Ross,[90] Hollis, and Walter, the formulation appeared ideologically biased in favor of one camp—the Communist camp. Not only does the term "narrow" have derogatory connotations while "broad" has laudatory ones, but the entire formulation seems calculated to leave the impression that the criteria involved in the one concept are engulfed without impairment in the larger concept—an impression the one camp has a vested interest in spreading, the other in combating and stamping out.

In assessing these accusations it must be borne in mind that the formulation was set forth in an attempt to urge opinions on central divergencies in trends of argumentation and persuasive appeals, not on differences in application and achievement. It might well be questioned—and the material shows that it has been—whether the

89. Pp. 200–202.   90. Pp. 367–68.

opposition thus formulated is the fundamental one in the ideological conflict currently raging between West and East; this, however, is a matter that will be dealt with in a later section.[91] The opposition formulated reflects one of the many aspects of the general disagreement and deserves scrupulous analysis before the inquiry proceeds to further clarification.

A great deal of the debate revolves around the terminological question: Should "democracy" be used to cover the "narrow" or the "broad" concept?[92]

A small number of respondents resent this question very strongly. There is no "should" about it, says Ducasse.[93] The question poses a pseudo-problem, states Sweezy.[94] The same position is taken by Lewis.[95] Bochenski is even more explicit: "All questions asking how a word *ought to be* used are without scientific meaning and cannot be answered. All that can be said is how *in fact* a term is being used by a [logical] class of men *k*."

Nevertheless, the overwhelming majority of respondents do not hesitate to announce how "democracy" *should* be used; a large group is in favor of the "narrow" use, while an almost equally large group comes out for the "broad" use. How are we to explain this striking opposition of reactions to the terminological question? A fuller restatement of the positions taken will show that the opposition is very far from being irreconcilable; the issue seems to turn on the interpretation of "should," the minority taking it in an absolutistic sense close to its use in moral discourse, the majority in the pragmatic sense of recommendation and advice. The two positions can be outlined in the following way:

1. To legislate, moralize, or dictate in matters of terminology is futile and nonsensical. There is no usage such that it *intrinsically* should or should not be followed. There is no court sanctioning the observation of terminological norms. It is futile to press for terminological uniformity if there are groups that have vested interests in the continuation of existing usages, however heterogeneous. The ethos of science and the honesty of communication demand that current usages be carefully kept apart and specifically labeled; there is no justification for terminological *Gleichschaltung*.

91. This survey, Part B, Sec. IV.
92. Question 11, see pp. 516–18.   94. P. 396.
93. P. 71.   95. P. 167.

2. It has a sense to recommend or discourage usages; terminological advice can be based on considerations of economy and efficiency of communication, stabilization of expectations, and avoidance of frustrations, etc., and is just as open to rational argument as most advice on problems of interhuman behavior. And attempts to influence and change the usage of others are very far from futile; they make up a normal element in communication processes.

In the material under scrutiny the arguments used to justify preferences and recommendations in the choice between the two usages of "democracy" can be classified as follows:

2.1. If two usages of the same term are found side by side and the one covers a more precise concept, the other a more confused one, the former usage is to be preferred and recommended for general adoption while the latter is to be rejected and its further application discouraged.

2.2. If the one is already established in technical discourse among scholars and experts and has been found to serve a useful cognitive purpose, whereas the other only prevails in popular parlance and has never been adopted in any field of systematically organized knowledge, the former is to be preferred for general application while the latter is to be eradicated.

2.3. If the one usage defines a concept bringing together closely interdependent elements sharing significant features while the other isolates one or a few of these elements from the others and thus diverts attention from what they have in common, there is reason to adopt the former usage and reject the latter.

2.4. If a usage can claim a representative history judged by the length of time since its emergence and by the authoritative status of its users, its continuation is justified.

2.5. If a term is heavily loaded with positive emotional associations, any attempt to use it in any but its "strict," "original" sense should be banned; the new-coined usage serves as an ideological tool of deceitful persuasion by effecting a transfer of favorable attitudes evoked by the term to objects, conditions, and actions that do not deserve them.

None of these arguments are, of course, very clear-cut: there is not only disagreement over their tenability but even more so over the relevancy of their application in concrete cases. In the answers to the terminology question on "democracy," arguments 2.1 and

2.2 are almost invariably used to justify preference or recommendation of the "narrow" usage, argument 2.3 usually serves the cause
of the "broad" usage, while arguments 2.4 and 2.5 are just as often
used in favor of the one as in favor of the other usage.

Argument 2.5 is naturally the most malleable of them all. To a
number of those who are convinced that the "narrow" use is the
"strict" and "original" one, all "broader" uses stand condemned as
cunning attempts to usurp the traditional goodwill acquired by the
term "democracy." Adherents of the "broader" usages do not hesitate to return the charge; the "narrow" usage serves propagandistic
purposes in so far as it bolsters up attitudes of complacency with
the *status quo* of the political setup and impedes the progress of
reforms in social and economic conditions.

Jørgensen, accordingly, rules out arguments of the 2.5 group as
cutting both ways: "There is no reason why the proponents of the
narrow political concept should have a monopoly on the positive
charge that for a long time already has made 'democracy' a most
valuable tool of persuasion. By reserving the word for the narrow
concept they exploit for their own purposes the traditional good
will it has acquired. Their reproach that the broad use is propagandistic can be countered by the argument that the narrow use
is just as propagandistic in its effects."[96]

On the whole, when debated on a level of philosophical detach-
ment, the opposition between "narrow" users and "broad" users
does not seem so trenchant as is generally assumed. Even the
staunchest protagonist of the strict technical use will admit that
as used to a larger public the word will always tend to evoke associations and expectations far beyond what would be warranted by
its definition as a narrow concept. Inversely, the advocate of the
broad usage will generally concede that within limited contexts the
narrow usage may have its cognitive advantages. Both will admit
that usage preferences will depend on circumstances; factors like
audience expectations, fields of application, purposes of communication will all have to be taken into account. The material at hand
does not give reasons to believe in the existence of irreconcilable
antagonisms on the terminological issues; the majority seem to
attach importance to them less for their own sake than as reflections of the more deep-rooted theoretical and normative conflicts.

96. P. 112.

Mediating efforts are not lacking in the material. A number of respondents think that both usages can claim ample justification: thus Horvath,[97] Logemann,[98] Ossowski,[99] Sweezy,[100] Eisenmann, Farber, Schneider, and several others. They do not think that there is any reason to give the one usage preference over the other as far as cognitive usefulness is concerned. Neither do they think that appeals to history can tilt the scale one way or another. There is no sense in monopolizing the term for one of the established concepts.

This does not mean that they advocate obedient conformity to the terminological *status quo*. But they take the view that the growing public awareness of ambiguities and divergencies in usage will gradually force ideologists and opinion leaders to refine their terminology; the isolated use of "democracy" will decrease and a differentiation of conceptual expressions will take place through specification by adjectives and indices and through explicitation by more complex formulae. "Democracy" will then gradually cease to have a cognitive meaning of its own: it will only serve as an element in longer phrases designating the different concepts it has come to suggest.

This process is already well under way in both of the major ideological camps. Ossowski is particularly emphatic on this point. In his view, "Western democracy" and "popular democracy" are both integrated terms that have meanings independent of what "democracy" used in isolation may mean; the two do not designate species of some genus because the sense of the element "democracy" varies with the adjectives prefixed to it.[99]

A process of this kind will naturally lead to differentiations far more refined than the one suggested in the UNESCO questionnaire between a "narrow" and a "broad" concept. The very formulation given for the "broad" concept invites further differentiation. Concepts of *conditions* of decision-making may be differentiated from concepts of *methods*. Concepts of *methods* of decision-making may again be differentiated from concepts of *contents*.[101] A number of "narrow" concepts may thus be constructed and in their turn combined into "broad" concepts differentiated by the relative weight given to the criteria they engulf. This analytical process

97. P. 102.   99. P. 264.
98. P. 188.   100. P. 396.
    101. In question 11, the word "results" was used; "contents" covers more adequately what was had in mind, see p. 517.

will, however, automatically lead away from considerations of terminological niceties to inquiries into the actual and potential empirical relationships between the factors isolated or combined in the concepts thus elaborated.

III. *Political democracy—social democracy.*—The relations singled out for scrutiny in the UNESCO questionnaire were (1) those between conditions of decision-making and methods of decision-making; (2) those between methods of decision-making and contents of decisions made.

A number of respondents emphasize the practical and theoretical difficulties of keeping apart aspects that are so closely interrelated in one continuous process. But the majority of the contributors seem to agree in the heuristic value of the distinction made between conditions, methods, and contents of decision-making.[102]

All three factors play important parts in current ideological use of "democracy." Schematically their relations may be outlined in this way:

Does "democracy" require the existence of established *methods* for popular control of governmental decision-making; to this question practically all respondents may be inferred to answer *yes*.

Does "democracy" require the existence of *conditions* making for independence of opinion formation affecting the efficiency of these methods of popular control; to this most respondents answer *yes*, but there is violent disagreement on the nature and scope of the conditions thus required.

Does "democracy" require limitations of the *contents* that the popularly controlled decisions may have: on this question there is widespread controversy and no definite conclusions to be drawn from the material.

The *methods* requirement takes the form of a definitional statement: factual disagreements on this point concern institutional devices developed to insure maximal efficiency of control.

The *conditions* requirements more often than not take the form of factual statements; disagreements concern empirical relations between economic, social, educational, communicational conditions on the one hand and the efficiency of popular control on the other.

The *contents* requirements express value statements more than

102. Opinions on the methods-contents distinction were urged in question 16, see pp. 517–18.

anything else; disagreements concern the purposes that popular control ought to serve and opinions vary from the acceptance as "democratic" of any decision the people may make—be it even directly suicidal—to the restriction of "democratically" acceptable decision contents to full conformity with an a priori theory of what the real interests and the real goals of the people are.

How do the terms "political democracy" and "social democracy" stand in relation to the distinctions thus made?

Most of the respondents seem to hold that "political democracy" is the more precise term of the two. It is not held to coincide, however, with the "narrow" *methods* concept outlined in the questionnaire; it is broader because it implies criteria that fall under the *conditions* requirements. Among such criteria the material gives prominence to conditions roughly indicated by phrases like "absence of intimidation," "freedom of expression," "open access to information on public issues," etc. There seems to be practical agreement in the material that régimes not fulfilling criteria of these kinds should not be called "political democracies"; the trouble is that there is little agreement on the interpretations of these criteria in concrete contexts.

"Social democracy" is generally held to be much vaguer in its connotations. Interpretations differ markedly in the material under scrutiny. To some, the term simply signifies an organization of society establishing maximal equality of status in *all* respects: distribution of power, authority, respect, prestige, economic benefits, legal security, education, etc. Others do not include the equal distribution of power in the connotation of the term, thus contrasting it to *political* democracy. Others again do not include the economic element, thus distinguishing "social" from "economic" democracy. A considerable number leave out the emphasis on uniform equality and equate "social democracy" with "the general welfare of the people," "the process of raising the economic and cultural level of the masses," etc. Some explicitly identify it with government *for* the people, *demophilia*, as contrasted to *democratia*, government *by* the people.[103] Another potent source of ambiguity is introduced when the term "social democracy" is not only used to define *goals* to be attained but is focused on sets of *means* advocated for their

103. A distinction particularly elaborated by Zaragueta along traditional Catholic lines.

attainment; thus a considerable number of respondents identify the meaning of the term with measures and policies like socialization of the means of production, abolition of private property, governmental planning and regulation of economic life, etc.[104]

All these divergencies in usage result in a confusion of issues and a mingling of problems that make systematic comparison of expressed opinions a highly difficult task. So complex and varied are the relations of facts at the bottom of ideological controversies that formulations of questions and answers in terms of general catchphrases and stereotypes can only obscure and jumble up the issues. Clarification can only be achieved through a painstaking process of differentiation, specification, and explicitation.

A number of respondents stress this point in their comments on the two questions raised on the mutual relationship between "political democracy" and "social democracy."[105] Thus Lewis finds the questions unanswerable because of the ambiguities of the terms to be related; to him, "social democracy" may mean economic equalitarianism or its very opposite, all depending on the general will of the people and the context it has to act in.[106]

Some respondents have tried to formulate in their own manner what they consider the fundamental problems involved in the vague opposition of "political" and "social" democracy. In this way they have made a more definite contribution to clarification than those who have contented themselves with setting forth their responses without making explicit what interpretation of the questions they are answering. The UNESCO questions were expressly stated to be too vague and too general to admit of straight answers: the experts consulted were therefore urged to reformulate the problems in their own ways and thus further the clarification process by attacking them from different angles.[107]

Explicit reformulations and implicit interpretations have largely revolved around two fundamental questions: (1) the relations of *conditions* to *methods* of decision-making; (2) the relations of *methods* to *contents* of decision-making.

In a first approximation, there may be said to be widespread though implicit agreement that these problems may be expressed

104. A list of meanings is given by Field, p. 84.
105. Questions 12 and 13, see p. 517.   106. P. 167.
107. See final paragraph of the questionnaire, p. 521.

in formulations more or less equipollent with the following: (1) Under what conditions—social, economic, educational, communicational—will methods of popular control of governmental decision-making function efficiently? (2) What methods of control of decision-making are most likely to insure the formation of governmental decision contents aiming at bringing about optimal conditions of demand satisfaction for the people?

Answers to questions along these lines diverge partly because each element in their formulation is differently interpreted in different contexts, partly because different theories are held about the actual empirical relationships between the sets of facts denoted, and partly because different value orientations lead respondents to focus on different aspects of the problem clusters outlined.

Question 1 leads most of the respondents to tackle the problem of the economic foundations of democracy: Can the masses of the people express their will adequately in a social organization based on private ownership of the means of production? Can the masses control governmental decision-making if all economic power is vested in the higher bureaucracy of the state? Can the people get to know what its interests are and find adequate and efficient expression for them if all instruments of large-scale opinion formation are controlled by groups bent on keeping the masses in a state of submissive obedience?

Violent disagreements are evidenced in answers to questions of this category. The discords are partly focused on the definition of what constitutes "adequate control of decision-making," partly on hypotheses on the conditions of independent opinion formation, partly on the criteria to be postulated for the determination of the "real" interests of the people.

Question 2 has absorbed the attention of even more contributors: it raises one of the pivotal problems in current ideological controversies. In more concrete terms it might be formulated as follows: If the entire adult population is given access to control of public decision-making in a society characterized by trenchant inequalities in social and economic status, will the contents of the thus controlled decisions be such that they will make for a leveling out of inequalities and a general increase in the welfare of the people?

It is very difficult to give brief formulations of this problem without running the risk of accusations of ideological bias. It is even more difficult to report objectively on trends in the responses registered. Tentatively, two trends may be distinguished and roughly formulated in this way:

2.1. Popular control of decision-making must be expected to lead to increased and generalized welfare because the people can be assumed to perform the control in the interest of the satisfaction of its own demands; any social reorganization for the improvement of general welfare must meet the test of actual preferences in the people and cannot be based on theoretical and a priori conceptions of what is "really" the optimal state of society and the "only" means to establish it.

2.2. Popular control of decision-making does not necessarily lead to a state of general welfare because in a society characterized by economic inequalities the opinions and attitudes of the people are not developed to the point of conformity with its interests: a social reorganization is necessary to create the conditions that alone can make for efficient and adequate popular control of decision-making.

In their extremes these two trends may be exemplified by the contribution by Field for the first line of argumentation, by Lefebvre for the second line.

Field concludes his analysis of the problem by announcing as his choice for a platform slogan for democracy not the hackneyed Lincolnian formula but the words of William Jennings Bryan: "The people have a right to make their own mistakes."[108]

Lefebvre develops the distinction between form and content to the point where he opposes to the Marxist definition of democracy by *the interests of the people*, a *formal* democracy "based on the body of opinions, more or less transient, more or less variable, and more or less well founded of the individuals constituting the majority."[109]

"It is not impossible that, at a particular time, one man, standing alone or almost alone, may be the true representative of a people or of all the peoples, and the whole of mankind."

"May it not seem that Lenin, in 1914 . . . , stood for the true understanding of the historical situation, in spite of his isolation? That he thus became an active factor in that situation, grasped the content, the real significance and the underlying trend of history and was working *for* the people."[110]

108. P. 415.
109. P. 152.   110. Pp. 150–51.

This deep-rooted opposition in outlook and value orientation has been given thorough attention by a number of contributors. Weil builds up his entire essay around this dichotomy.[111] Bettelheim,[112] Ducasse,[113] Lindsay,[114] McKeon,[115] Patri,[116] Plamenatz,[117] Pool,[118] and Eisenmann all contribute significantly to its clarification.

The opposition is partly due to differences in *expectations* of results from the institution of democratic methods of decision-making. General hypotheses about the relationships—causal or otherwise—between methods and decision contents can scarcely be formulated or made testable: there are such an infinity of factors to take into account, not least such relative intangibles as personality traits and general characteristics of behavior and attitudes in the peoples in question. But the opposition must also be seen in the light of conflicting value orientations resulting, on the one hand, from actual satisfaction with, and support of, the social order in question and, on the other, from actual impatience and discontent with the same social order. Supporters of the existing order may be presumed to be interested in preserving actual methods of decision-making in the hope that popular control will not lead to radical social changes, at least not in aspects important to them. Opponents of the existing order will tend to be impatient with the working of the actual method of decision-making and attribute its failure to the immaturity of public opinion preserved through centralized control of opinion-molding institutions. It is important to emphasize, however, that both sides in the opposition profess unswerving allegiance to democracy as a method of popular control of and participation in governmental decision-making; the central difference lies in their opposed evaluation of the actual conditions under which the method is functioning. The analysis of question 2 thus leads back to renewed scrutiny of question 1: Under what conditions will methods of popular control work efficiently?

This leads us straight up to an inquiry into the crucial differences between the ideological systems that stand in most direct opposition in current controversies: the Eastern and the Western.

IV. *The crucial differences.*—The UNESCO questionnaire was deliberately concentrated on the ideological opposition that makes

111. Pp. 432–40.
112. Pp. 1–12, 16.
113. P. 72.
114. Pp. 173–77.

115. Pp. 201–2.
116. Pp. 287–92.
117. Pp. 315–21.
118. Pp. 345–53.

up the greatest potential threat to world-understanding and enduring peace: the opposition between the social and political views taken in western Europe and the Western Hemisphere, and the social and political views taken in eastern Europe, the Soviet Union, and Communist China. There is no way of making this opposition a simple and clear-cut one; the actual variety of opinions and outlooks is too great in both camps. But there tends to be general agreement that the power conflict between the two groups of peoples stands in direct, if not always clear, correlation to a deeper-rooted opposition of ideological principles, theories, and value systems. A main purpose of the UNESCO inquiry was to encourage ideological experts to formulate their view of this opposition and assess the possibilities of its reconciliation and peaceful solution.

Formulations of the opposition show striking variations. On the level of mutual vilification, both camps have formulated their difference as one between "real" democracy and "mock democratic forms" masking the ruthless dictatorship of one group over the rest of the people. On a more reflective level, the opposition has variously been characterized as one between a "libertarian" and an "authoritarian" democracy, between Girondism and Jacobinism, bourgeois liberty and socialist equality, capitalist exploitation and working-class liberation, individualism and collectivism, open society and closed society, etc. The amassing of slogans and stereotypes of these kinds has not contributed much to clarification. Fortunately, the material collected occasionally penetrates deeper into the analysis of the problems raised by the existence of this opposition.

To tie up the discussion with the distinctions introduced in the analysis of meanings of "democracy," the questionnaire took off from the "majority rule"–"majority interest" formulation coined by Bertrand Russell.[119] This seems to have been a fortunate choice because reactions proved so very varied and threw light on the problem from so many different angles.

Most of the respondents seem to accept the Russell formulation as a first approximation to a description of the central difference; among these respondents are undoubtedly ideologists from both camps. Evidently, the formulation is not taken to have pretended to give more than a rough indication of *where to look for* the de-

119. Question 10, see p. 516.

cisive difference; a one-sentence dictum could scarcely achieve much more. Those, therefore, who set forth accusations of over-simplification and distortion of issues seem to have overlooked the limited pretensions of the formulation.

However, all the attempts at closer scrutiny that are found in our material reveal the need for further differentiation and greater preciseness in the formulation of the opposition of ideologies. It may be that the Western ideology can be said to emphasize the "*by* the people" aspect, but it is important to specify in what sense this is true because there seem to be other senses that make Eastern ideologists just as firm adherents of "government *by* the people." Inversely, it may be plausible to hold that Eastern ideology gives predominant emphasis to the *for* element, but it is highly important to distinguish the sense in which this is true from the sense in which Western ideologists may be said to advocate "government *for* the people."

The need for more elaborate distinctions is particularly urged by Borgese,[120] McKeon,[121] Ossowski,[122] Pool,[123] Schlesinger,[124] and Sweezy.[125]

Sweezy takes violent issue with the identification of Western democracy with "majority rule." Quite to the contrary, it seems to him to mean "the inviolability of the rights and privileges of minorities," *in concreto* the privileges of the propertied classes. Ducasse,[126] Field,[127] and Ewing take him strongly to task for this statement. It seems that he would have made a stronger case for himself if, instead of imputing to his opponents meanings they would scarcely acknowledge as theirs, he had elaborated the hypothesis that under Western conditions of economic equality the majority of the people are unable to make their demands count despite the existence of universal suffrage rights and normal election procedures.

On the other hand, Sweezy accepts the Russellian definition of Russian democracy as rule in the interests of the people and amplifies it by stating as the essence of the Soviet conception "the elevation of the economic and cultural level of the masses." But he

120. P. 43.
121. P. 200.
122. Pp. 258-59.
123. Pp. 340-44.
124. P. 379.
125. Pp. 394-95.
126. In comments not printed in this volume.
127. Pp. 412-13.

adds, very significantly: "and their active involvement in public affairs." In this way, the Soviet conception is made to appear to give emphasis to the "*by* the people element," too. Bettelheim,[128] Lefebvre,[129] and Rieger[130] all concur in this analysis. Schlesinger is particularly concerned with developing the point. In his view, the Russell formulation of the East-West opposition over "democracy" is dangerously misleading.[131] In a lengthy and well-documented analysis of Soviet ideological texts he develops the view that mass participation in the formation and execution of public decision-making and not just the raising of the standard of life of the masses is the essence of Soviet democracy. He expressly rejects the assumption that it is "government *for* the people" in the sense of concentration on *mass consumption;* improvement in economic conditions is not deemed an end in itself, but an indispensable means to the bringing about of the "active involvement" of the masses in public affairs.[132]

Inversely, a number of respondents resent the implication that Western democracy is only *by* the people, not *for* the people; in their view the democracies are so much more *for* the people as the general welfare developed has come about through deliberate action *by* the people. The by-for dichotomy is rejected as unrealistic and invalid by several contributors. Thus Borgese: ". . . it is impossible to conceive 'a rule of the majority' in which that rule is or may be deliberately or consciously at variance with the 'interests of the majority.' Such a democracy should be defined the government of the people by the people against the people."

"If 'democracies' of this kind were extant, there would be a point in Gromyko's definition of his own 'people's democracy.' Our purpose, he said, is the well being of the people, 'whether they like it or not.' "[133]

Argumentation along these lines raises anew the two problems outlined in a previous section: (1) Under what conditions can the people be expected to act politically in open consciousness of its "real interests"? (2) Can the "real interests" of the people be determined theoretically prior to observations of its actual preferences and overt choices?

128. In answers not printed in this volume.
129. Pp. 152–54.
130. Pp. 356–57.   132. P. 388.
131. P. 379.   133. P. 43.

Scrutinizing the philosophical implications of these problems, McKeon arrives at the conclusion that the West-East opposition cannot possibly be formulated in terms of a by-for dichotomy. "The broader opposition is between the use of factions and classes as a safeguard of the common good, and the appeal to wisdom or knowledge for the discrimination of the true good from the common good."[134] "The one conception of democracy . . . would provide for social, economic, and political decisions, and even for the use of science in arriving at these decisions, within a frame that makes possible the resolution of differences, according to the preference of the majority, on the assumption that no one has infallible scientific knowledge in any sphere and that the progress of science no less than the equitable resolution of differences depends on the toleration of diversity. The other would provide for social, economic, and political decisions through the application of the principles of dialectical materialism in resolution of problems in these spheres by the party of the proletariat, on the assumption that the method of dialectical materialism is the true scientific method and that not even all workers (since they have been demoralized by capitalism), much less the capitalists and those who incline toward capitalism, can contribute to the decision."[135]

To McKeon the focus of controversy is thus on the cognitive status of political propositions: Are they invariably fallible expressions of the conflicting or converging interests of the groups that make up the people or can they be made into infallible scientific statements of measures and policy for the attainment of a state of society in true harmony with historical laws of development? Can, in general, political problems be solved by a science of society capable of establishing true statements everybody will have to accept?

The discussion is thus transferred from the realm of socio-political relations dealt with in Part B of the questionnaire to the problems taken up in Part C: Can scientific knowledge of social processes be developed to the point where extermination of opposition to and criticism of the conclusions it leads to can be justified?

This problem is discussed in an illuminating way in the comments made by Ducasse[136] and Field[137] on the position taken by Sweezy:[138] the discussion of "democracy" is clearly seen to open a highway

134. P. 203.
135. P. 201.
138. See also his replies, pp. 410 ff.

136. Pp. 406–7.
137. Pp. 416–17.

toward the clarification of basic issues in contemporary epistemology and methodology.

Marshall and Pool[139] develop views on the East-West opposition closely related to those taken by McKeon, Ducasse, and Field; but, instead of the philosophical, they concentrate on the psychological aspects of the opposition. To them, the opposition is one between appeals to different *personality types* and ideals of *interpersonal relationships;* on the one hand, the emphasis is on the development of self-reliant, independent personalities free to challenge and criticize the authority and the theories of those in power, be they capitalists or bureaucrats; on the other, the emphasis is on the molding of submissive and obedient personalities lastingly conditioned to unquestioning reverence for authority and the ideologies of the power-holders. On the institutional level, this opposition translates itself into one between, on the one hand, devices for efficient expression of a plurality of opinions and the formation of a plurality of parties and pressure groups and, on the other hand, devices for the *Gleichschaltung* of opinions, the extermination of nonconformity, and the establishment of single-party government.

A survey of the opinions registered in the material on the question of the crucial differences between the Western and the Eastern ideological outlook reveals in both camps a marked tendency to mold analytical distinctions on the value orientations already taken for granted. Formulations of the crux of the opposition vary with ideological affiliations: the value attachments of the analysts determine their perspective to a degree that makes agreements on the nature of the problems at issue virtually unattainable. Of particular interest is the widespread tendency to formulate oppositions in terms that set off the lofty aspirations of the one camp against the meager achievements of the other. A basic prerequisite for clarification would seem to be to reach an agreement *either* to stick to aspirations on both sides *or* to concern one's self solely with the dismal realities of actual achievement. In the former case thoroughgoing comparative studies in ideological argumentation might clear up what is as yet a virgin field for dispassionate research. In the latter case empirical investigations of social and political structures in their relation to actual attitudes and wants are urgently called for to set off in a truer light the teeming multitude of ideologically

139. See Marshall, pp. 216 ff.; Pool, pp. 347 ff.

tilted statements that thrive on our general ignorance of the facts involved.

V. *Opinion: influence versus pressure.*—A problem constantly recurring in ideological analyses—outside as well as inside the UNESCO material—is this: How are the "real interests" of an individual or of the people to be determined?[140]

A number of respondents, particularly Ducasse,[141] Plamenatz,[142] Brown, and Ranulf agree in considering this the most fundamental of the issues taken up in the inquiry, but almost none have ventured further into this highly controversial and extremely difficult matter.

The main difficulty lies in the establishment of intersubjective agreement on criteria and conditions of "real-ness": it seems practically hopeless to disentangle what an individual is *wanted to* want from what he may be *predicted to* want under given circumstances.

Ducasse suggests this general formulation of criteria: "The real interests of the individual are those he actually prefers when (*a*) he knows what the possible alternatives are among which a choice is possible, and (*b*) knows both the hidden price and the hidden values, as well as the surface price and values."[141]

The crucial factor in this as well as in a number of less articulate formulations is the amount and reliability of information conditioning the preference. The analysis of the function of this factor leads to a general discussion of the conditions of opinion formation in societies that claim to be "democratically" governed. In the UNESCO questionnaire the question was given this form: "In general, how would you trace a line between "democratically justifiable" and "democratically unjustifiable" processes of opinion-influencing?"[143]

Responses to this question evidence a surprising degree of agreement. It is true that almost none of the respondents try to trace any definite line of demarcation of the kind asked for. But this they consider futile and close to impossible in view of the tremendous differences in concrete situations. There is a large consensus, however, on the general standards that opinion-influencing should ideally conform to within a "democratic" society: these may not be explicitly or fully stated but they may safely be said to be implied

140. Question 19, p. 518.
141. Pp. 73–74.
142. In answers not included in the present volume.
143. Question 20, see pp. 518–19.

by the overwhelming majority of statements made on the subject.

It must be emphasized that the general consensus thus registered only holds on the level of ideals. There is violent disagreement on the conditions making for optimal fulfilment of the ideals: whether a capitalist, social democratic, or Communist organization of society.

The ideals of democratic opinion-influencing implicitly agreed on by the respondents may very tentatively be formulated and classified in the following way:

1. *Full information:* If and when a public is invited to express its opinion on an issue, the whole of the public should be given the means to acquaint themselves with all arguments they would possibly consider relevant to the issue. Descriptions of what is at stake in the issue should be as impartial as feasible. If a small group within the people have informational privileges, e.g., by their position in the governmental bureaucracy or in the direction of a large financial or industrial concern, the public should be granted access to any part of the informational material of the group that would possibly be considered relevant to the issue.

Only if these conditions are fulfilled are individuals and groups justified in making propaganda for a particular solution of the problems involved. As long as the public is deprived of tools with which to resist opinion-influencing, any invitation to take independent part in decision-making is nothing but hypocrisy.

2. *Education and leisure to digest information:* If a group cannot partake in decision-making because it lacks the general education and leisure that are at the disposal of other groups, every available means should be used to remove the disproportion. The more decisions touch the specific interests of the handicapped group, the more urgent is the elimination of these inequalities.

3. *Honest presentation of issues:* Given the inescapable fact that a public cannot effectively partake in all decisions affecting its welfare, the influence expert is forced to make a choice not only of issues for presentation, but also of aspects of the frequently complex problems involved. The temptation is always great to interpret expressions of public opinion and election results to imply positive or negative stands on questions never envisaged by the public. By refined and subtle as well as by crude and obvious bias in the presentation of public problems, the opinion molders can easily use this

process of interpretation and elaboration to falsify the general picture of public opinion to suit their own interests. By clever selection of issues for presentation and by focusing public attention on those thus selected, the opinion leaders can elicit responses easily fitting their preconceived patterns and avoid responses that might be embarassing or clearly opposed to their interests.

On the basis of these considerations, a third ideal may be formulated in the following way: If and when complex problems are brought before the public by groups with information privileges controlling means of mass communication, the selection of issues for public discussion and decision-making should be such that the public is granted an adequate chance to influence decisions on issues vital to its own interests and to influence them in directions that may go counter to those advocated by the groups enjoying influence privileges.

4. *Absence of intimidation:* Voting and opinion declarations of a similar character should not be influenced by threats of reprisals or promises of rewards. No pressure other than that of relevant arguments should be deliberately used in attempts to influence opinion. In particular, unpopular minority opinions should be protected against groups exploiting the prestige of popular majority status as a means to counteract minority influence.

These and other closely related ideals can of course be formulated in very different ways. The ones adopted express only a few of the many possibilities.

The advocacy of these ideals of opinion-influencing does not necessarily imply more than that their realization is viewed as something desirable. Consequently, there is no need to be committed to view their violation as more undesirable than the violation of any other ideal. Ideological controversy creeps in as soon as in concrete situations attempts are made to assign a "proper place" to ideals in a *hierarchy* of interests and norms.

As soon as the discussion shifts from the proclamation of ideals to the concrete confrontation of ideals clashing with ideals and of ideals clashing with what are considered "necessities," the analysis of agreements and disagreements gets vastly more complicated. It is not at all surprising that so many of the respondents have found it impossible to trace any sharp line between "justifiable" and "unjustifiable" procedures of opinion-influencing.

C. TOLERANCE AND TREASON

I. *What should be repressed?*—Answers to the third part of the UNESCO questionnaire include judgments on things, *x*, which *should* be tolerated or not tolerated, or which *can* or cannot be tolerated. The *x*'s are labeled by not too clear designations such as: "antidemocratic propaganda," "attacks on democratic institutions," "propaganda to change the form of government," "groups promoting a régime which would destroy the advantages of democratic procedure," "treason," "proposed changes through violence," "dangerous propaganda," "antidemocratic propaganda presenting a clear and present danger to the constitution," "people who do not support the existing social order," "opinions that make for insurrection," "secret organization with the goal to change the form of government," etc.

To compare the opinions of two ideologists one of whom tells us we should not tolerate *x*, whereas the other tells us we should tolerate *x*, we shall have to make sure that they are speaking of the same *x*'s, the same things—a task that often proves quite difficult. There is a tendency to class an ideologist as more tolerant than another if he *proclaims* tolerance and denounces intolerance in a more violent, pointed, and louder way than another. But close analysis may reveal that the things x_1 which the seemingly very tolerant person tolerates represent a much narrower class of things than the class of things x_2 which the seemingly less tolerant person is willing to let develop undisturbed. Or, analysis may reveal that the designations used to characterize the *x*'s are too crude to warrant any conclusion as to what the ideologists in question wish to tolerate and what they do not. Here as in many other cases, we shall have to analyze the actions of groups in order to be able to judge what they mean by their words. It is important to note, however, that inferences from nonverbal behavior are open to serious pitfalls even if made by neutral observers.

To obtain a survey of some important stands taken in the tolerance discussion we shall work with the following classification of classes of things that should or should not be tolerated:

x_1: Opinions, advocated or not advocated in agitation, which, if held by sufficiently many, are apt to justify acts undermining the democratic form of government, or acts that would make it less democratic. The acts in question may be lawful within a democracy.

x_2: Opinions advocated in agitation, which, if held by sufficiently many, are apt, etc.

The acts in question may be use of force, insurrection, high treason.

x_3: Agitation explicitly justifying acts of incitements to acts undermining the democratic form of government.

x_4: Incitements, direct planning, and organization aiming at forceful overthrow of the democratic form of government.

These, very roughly delimited classes of things, are sufficiently different to make it important to know which, if any, of these classes a given ideologist proposes for repression.

In order not to introduce tremendous complications, we have not differentiated between different concepts of "democratic form of government" and "less democratic." This seemingly uncritical attitude is based on the following opinion: However great the differences are between concepts of democracy, there is practically full agreement that the word should stand for something very valuable, something that it is worth establishing or maintaining. Whatever their particular definitions of "democracy" may be, the answers of ideologists therefore reveal how they conceive of relations between things very valuable and policies of repression.

But there are other distinctions even as important as that between classes of things tolerated. Suppose one respondent advocates repression of a relatively wide class of phenomena but that he adds that he takes as a premise that the times are troubled, that there are enemies of democracy which, if given the opportunity, could profit by the mere existence of opinions of the kind x_1. Thus, the seemingly intolerant ideologist may limit the intended field of application of his principles to a very narrow class of historical situations, whereas a seemingly very tolerant ideologist preaching suppression only of things of class x_3 may choose a very wide field of application for measures of repression. Close analysis may reveal that he means that in times of slight troubles of a rather common type, a much wider class of opinions and acts should be repressed. Thus, to understand the import of views proclaimed it is necessary to try to find out *on which conditions*, historical, social, economic, etc., the recommendations are pretended to apply. If we call these circumstances the y-conditions, we could specify different y-classes such as:

y_1—*all* conditions (i.e., suppression under any conceivable circumstance)

y_2—times of trouble, of economic crises, of internal stress

y_3—times of civil war or of impending or actual international war.

Thirdly, two ideologists both proclaiming that something ought to or must be suppressed may possibly mean rather different things by "suppression." If, for instance the one by "suppression" thinks only of legal prosecution by the authorities of the country, whereas the other by "suppression" means any means whatsoever of putting something to a stop, the seemingly tolerant ideologist saying that antidemocratic propaganda should not be "suppressed" may be in practice less tolerant than one in favor of suppression: the one may advocate very effective measures of social discrimination, economic boycott, etc., whereas the other may reject these measures but recommend "suppression" in the sense of legal prosecution with lenient rules. Mostly, but not invariably, the "suppression" and "nontolerance" spoken of in the answers relates to the question of interference by state authorities. Thus we have a third variable to take care of, when interpreting the ideologies of toleration and suppression; let us call it the z-processes: thos constituting the *kind* of suppression or noninterference contemplated.

Although very few of the respondents have gone into detailed analysis of the difficulties involved in delimiting areas of tolerance from areas of suppression, most of them emphasize the practical impossibility of formulating universally valid and applicable rules in the field.

These difficulties are reflected in the confusing variety of opinions registered in the material. Any attempt to classify opinions on the tolerance problem runs the risk of distorting the significance of the statements made. Almost all formulations of scope and limits of toleration are studded with vague value expressions that make it a venturous task to locate them even approximately along the x-, y-, and z-axes of reference suggested.

The majority of the respondents focus their discussion on the tolerance requirements implicit in their conception of "democracy": their main concern is with the problem whether allegiance to "democracy" implies the duty of tolerating or repressing opinions directly or indirectly aiming at the overthrow and destruction of the institutions and structures they identify with "democracy."

Pool,[144] Ross,[145] and Ranulf advocate the toleration of such opinions, at least in so far as they may be classed under x_1, x_2, and x_3, but probably not under x_4.

Ross distinguishes, however, between opinions and the *means* used to propagate them; just as he does not accept the toleration of physical constraint and violence as means of propagating an opinion, he will not tolerate the use of deceitful agitation and fraudulent distortion as means to gain adherence for it.

A number of other respondents seem willing to defend and advocate the toleration at least of opinions of classes x_1 and x_2: thus Carritt, Ewing, Lovejoy, and others. It is very difficult, however, to map out exactly how opinions are divided. The distinctions between opinions according to the directness of their relations to overt acts of violent subversion are at best very fuzzy. Some respondents, particularly McKeon,[146] Brown, and Kohn seem to find a reliable guide in the famous "clear and present danger" rule coined by Justice Holmes. It seems doubtful, however, whether a rule of this kind can fruitfully be applied under circumstances of such ideological complexity as those prevailing in our days.

A number of respondents discuss the limits of toleration directly in terms of their interpretations of the requirements of "democracy."

Sweezy[147] and Hollis agree that any curtailment in the freedom of opinions is *ipso facto* a move in the direction of "less democracy": this does not exclude, however, that in concrete situations such moves may be perfectly justifiable.

Others emphasize the right and duty of their "democracy" to defend and protect itself from being undermined by opinions that might bring about its destruction. Democracy does not imply an obligation to commit suicide, as Horvath puts it.[148]

Some stress the necessity that opinions directed against democracy as a *method* of decision-making be repressed. Others go further and require that opinions going counter to and endangering "democratic" decision *contents* be repressed: thus Bettelheim,[149] Le-

144. Pp. 350–51.   147. P. 401.
145. Pp. 372–75.   148. P. 104.
146. P. 208.   149. P. 13.

febvre,[150] and Rieger[151] all seem to think that any "democracy," whether bourgeois or Communist, will only tolerate opinions favoring the social order it is based on. They even go further to state that repression of opinions is compatible with "democracy" if it is directed against groups bent on reverting the trend toward greater and broader "democracy."

A similar view is taken by Sweezy but not on any basis of deduction from a definition of "democracy": in his view suppression of opinions is justified if designed to further the progress toward greater democracy, but not justifiable if it paves the way for further infringements of democracy.

A slightly different trend of argumentation is manifest in the Jørgensen contribution: antidemocratic propaganda should not be permitted as long as differences in social, economic, and educational status make parts of the population unable to resist such propaganda.[152]

The less ideologists find themselves content with proclamations in terms of vague value judgments, the more they are forced to penetrate into the realm of concrete complexities of cases and situations. If current ideological doctrines were analyzed from a casuistic angle instead of an idealistic one, their interrelations would be found to be marked by incomparability rather than by incompatibility. Each ideological system bears the marks of its formation under the impact of states of affairs never seriously envisaged in rival systems. Ideologies cannot be understood and clarified unless they are seen against the particular historical setting in which they have developed, and related to the particular state of affairs faced by those who have vindicated them as well as those who have accepted them and believed in them.

It is not the aim of the present analysis to take up causal points, but I hope I am excused for suggesting that part of the ideological controversies is due to the general neglect of explicit statements of past and present conditions limiting the intended validity of "ought-," "should-," and "must"-sentences. That this neglect has its distinct advantage in consolidating ingroups and justifying hostility toward outgroups may to some extent explain why it has not been more seriously combated.

150. Pp. 156–57.
151. Pp. 359–60.   152. Pp. 113–14.

II. *One-party systems.*—On the level of surface expressions the respondents may be divided into four groups: (1) those who find one-party systems incompatible with any democracy; (2) those who find one-party systems compatible under some conditions and for some of the established usages of "democracy"; (3) those who find one-party systems compatible with democracy, without any reservations; (4) those who consider the party question irrelevant to the question whether a régime is democratic or not.

A definite majority of the respondents take the position that one-party systems are incompatible with democracy: thus Lewis,[153] Patri,[154] Plamenatz,[155] Wright,[156] Eisenmann, Hagopian, Martins, Nomad, *et al.*

Horvath,[157] Jørgensen,[158] and Pascual take the view that ideally "democracy" does not require the institution of a party or of parties at all; the only system compatible is a "no-party" system.

A few contributors, particularly McKeon,[159] Pool,[160] Farber, and Simons, find that one-party systems may be compatible with democracy in societies characterized by conditions like homogeneity of attitudes and valuations, absence of public issues, identity of interests, etc. But they all emphasize that these conditions are so rarely found and so unlikely to be realized that one-party systems can be considered incompatible with democracy in all major societies of the present age. Inversely, group 1 may be inferred to agree that under most of the extreme and unlikely conditions listed by group 2 one-party systems would be compatible with democracy. Thus the surface disagreement may be discounted as a verbal one.

Another potent source of verbal disagreement lies in the fact that few of the respondents have made explicitly clear what usage of "democracy" they are referring to in their judgments of compatibility or noncompatibility. Group 3 and to a large extent also group 2 seem to be using "democracy" in a broader sense that respondents in group 1 would quite certainly not recognize as theirs.

Some respondents introduce distinctions according to usages: thus Logemann,[161] Perelman,[162] Bochenski, and others emphasize

153. P. 170.
154. P. 293.
155. Pp. 325–26.
156. Pp. 445–46.
157. Pp. 105–6.

158. P. 114.
159. P. 209.
160. P. 350.
161. P. 193.
162. P. 300.

that, while one-party systems may be incompatible with democracy in the Western sense, there are certainly other plausible senses in which even proletarian dictatorship and Fascist totalitarianism will be found compatible with democracy. It is obvious that if broad usages of these kinds are adopted answers to the one-party question cannot very well be anything but positive.

Group 3 manifest close similarities in their argumentation for compatibility: they all stress the uselessness of pluralities of parties *if* there are no essential differences of opinion among those competent to judge and *if* the doctrines of the one party in power have the status of science and not mere opinion. If such conditions hold, it is argued, deviations are sure symptoms of incompetence or of unsocial, essentially criminal, behavior.

Thus, Bettelheim,[163] Lefebvre,[164] and Rieger[165] all assert that in socialist society—the only society where these conditions are or will be fulfilled—pluralities of parties have no *raison d'être*. Less categorical positions within the same group are argued by Horvath,[166] Jørgensen,[167] and Sweezy.[168]

What is the nature of the disagreement between group 3 and the other groups? It is not necessarily based on terminological deviations. Group 3 may well adopt the same usage of "democracy" as, say, group 1 and yet be able to argue its case. The difference is one of perspective and outlook: conditions of society and developments in social knowledge which the one group consider close to realization are by the other groups held to be very far from realized or even impossible of realization. The real issue is not whether one-party systems are compatible or incompatible with democracy, but whether the conditions of unanimity of opinion, community of interests, and absence of issues that alone are agreed to justify one-party systems are realized or likely to be realized in any of the societies existing in our age. On this issue opinions clash in a real way: they mirror the general opposition evidenced in ideological controversies over the status and potentialities of social science and over the scope of toleration of dissentient opinions and critical attitudes.

III. *Skepticism and democracy.*—The problems of toleration and

163. P. 14.
164. Pp. 156–59.
165. Pp. 358–59.

166. Pp. 105–6.
167. P. 114.
168. Pp. 404, 411.

repression lead directly up to fundamental philosophical questions of the validity of ideologically opposed opinions and the possibility of establishing a science of society capable of commanding universal consensus for its conclusions.

In the UNESCO questionnaire the problem was formulated in terms of the relations between "skepticism" and "democracy."

Philosophical dichotomies like "skepticism" versus "dogmatism," "relativism" versus "absolutism," "fallibilism" versus "infallibilism," "empiricism" versus "rationalism" have come to play pivotal parts in twentieth-century ideological controversies. In the twenties and thirties a significant trend in political argumentation focused on epistemological and axiological skepticism as a basis for theoretical defense of a formal *methods* conception of democracy as against the *contents* conception advocated on the left as well as on the right on the basis of philosophical absolutism and dogmatic rationalism.[169] In later years ideological controversies have even more pointedly been concentrated on basic philosophical issues; the debate has been pushed far beyond questions of political and economic instrumentalities toward ultimate problems of cognition, valuation and normation.

In the questionnaire a suggestive catch phrase coined by the British political scientist, D. W. Brogan, was chosen as a point of departure for the discussion: "Skepticism is part of our faith."[170]

No straight answers to the question could be expected. It was hoped, however, that respondents might feel provoked to answer in terms of *kinds* of skepticism and *kinds* of subject matters to be skeptical about. As a slogan in ideological debates "skepticism" may not indicate more than an attitude of doubt toward things the user wants to focus attention on.

As might have been anticipated, the Brogan formula was interpreted in strikingly different directions. There is accordingly little sense in classifying responses according to surface agreements or disagreements.

It is highly important, however, to note the near-automatic rejection of the Brogan formula by all those who advocate the justification of one-party systems: to them, "skepticism" seems to be a term of strictly dyslogistic connotation only to be applied to waver-

169. Hans Kelsen, *Vom Wesen und Wert der Demokratie* (Tübingen, 1929).
170. Question 26, see p. 520.

ing and uncertain opponents. Taking for granted that a reliable science of society has been developed and that competent and honest people necessarily agree on basic issues, they cannot but find the Brogan formula a highly misleading expression of "democratic" ideology however the formula be interpreted.

Jørgensen[171] interprets the question to ask whether the view that human beings are incapable of deciding whether divergent political proposals and measures are equally good or not can be used as an argument for the establishment of democracy in the sense of majority rule. He rejects the view both as in itself tenable and as a valid argument for political democracy. In this conclusion probably all respondents may be inferred to agree; Jørgensen is the only one, however, who has gone into detailed analysis of the problems involved.

Wright[172] emphasizes in a similar way that if "skepticism" is taken to mean that "all views are equally valid or invalid," it does not have any affinity to requirements of democracy. There is nothing to indicate that any respondent would disagree with him on that point.

Sweezy rejects the Brogan formula on the basis of a similar interpretation of "skepticism": he argues that the existence of a science of society refutes the claim that "all opinions are equally valid" and concludes that there is no longer any justification for raising skepticism to the level of a principle of democratic ideology and for denying "that one political creed may be more compatible with democracy than others."[173]

In their criticism of the position taken by Sweezy, Ducasse,[174] Field,[175] and Pool[176] do not deny that there are political opinions that can reasonably claim a higher degree of validity than others, but they nevertheless defend "skepticism" as an important democratic principle expressing the urgency of constant alertness and critical-mindedness, and the conviction that only the open toleration of widely dissentient opinions can provide a safeguard against the perpetuation of errors backed by power and authority.

Lovejoy introduces a set of very important distinctions into the

171. Pp. 114–18.
172. In answers not included in this volume; cf. p. 446.
173. P. 404.
174. In his comments, pp. 406–7.   175. See his comments, pp. 416–17.
176. In comments not included in this volume.

debate on this issue: "Democracy does not imply the assumption that no political principle or assumption can be known to be true. It does, however, imply three assumptions: (*a*) that any individual's judgment on a political question may possibly be erroneous; (*b*) that no individual, *as* an individual, has a moral right to coerce other sane and adult individuals; (*c*) that—since, in the political state, it is necessary that on some matters joint and collective action be taken, and also that individuals be protected against coercion by other individuals, through the exercise of coercive power by the state—it is essential that some method be found of peaceably determining *what* collective action shall be taken and how far and in what ways the coercive power of the state shall be exercised; and (*d*) that the best and most effective means of settling peaceably such political questions, i.e., questions of state actions, is to permit all citizens of the state to participate in the settlement of them and to accept as the final settlement the decision of the majority. On these propositions democracy does not imply "skepticism": it implies that the propositions are true. It does not, however, imply that the judgment of the majority is inerrant; and it therefore allows freedom to minorities to agitate and vote for the reversal of previous majority decisions."

Most of those who, like Bober,[177] Bowle, Brown, Smith, and ten Hoor, indorse the Brogan dictum without reservations may be inferred to agree to the points made by Lovejoy; the skepticism implied by democracy does not extend to what are considered basic principles of its maintenance and growth. What is basic is, of course, highly controversial and reflects the divergencies in conceptions of "democracy": this, however, is only another way of saying that with the majority of ideologists the principles lie well beyond the reach of any possible "skepticism."

D. VALUE FOUNDATIONS OF THE CONFLICT

In the last part of the UNESCO questionnaire scholars and experts were invited to develop their views of the general philosophical foundations of the conflicts and controversies under scrutiny. A set of very vague and abstract questions and suggestions were given in order to stimulate reflective commentaries in the direction of formulations of the general nature of ideological disagreements

---

177. In answers not included in this volume.

and assessments of the conditions of their possible reconciliation. Classification of opinions registered in this part of the material is practically hopeless and theoretically close to futile. The questions set forth have given rise to responses in highly different directions, but answers are only rarely comparable because different issues and interpretations are focused on.

A number of respondents have taken up for scrutiny the question whether current ideological disagreements are fundamentally terminological, descriptive, or normative in character.[178]

Responses to this question largely reflect attitudes to possibilities and procedures of settlement and reconciliation: Should attention and efforts be primarily concentrated on semantic clarification, empirical and theoretical research, or direct action to bring about changes in basic attitudes? There is no incompatibility between the views taken by "terminologists," "descriptivists," and "normativists": there is a difference in perspective and approach without direct ideological relevance.

The greatest number of those who discuss this problem tend to stress as the focus of discord a difference in the analysis and theoretical conception of structures and relationships in society: views of this kind are taken by Bettelheim,[179] Bober,[180] Horvath,[181] Jørgensen,[182] McKeon,[183] Pascual,[184] Sweezy,[185] Weil,[186] and Lien. In principle, a difference of this kind might be expected to lose in violence with the gradual advance of scientific knowledge of social facts; this is what is anticipated by some of the respondents, but others point to the force of traditional patterns of thinking and the vested interests of privileged groups as obstacles on the road to settlement. Thus Sweezy thinks that what is holding back the development toward general consensus is "that those who have vested interests in the maintenance of capitalism do not want the truth to be taught."[187] Others return similar charges against Communists. In the view of Ducasse[188] and Field,[189] there is no cognitive basis for reducing the current opposition to one between scientific truth in the one camp and tradition-molded prejudices and intellectual dis-

178. Question 30, see p. 521.
179. P. 17.
180. In an answer not included in this volume.
181. P. 105.
182. Pp. 118–19.
183. Pp. 211–12.
184. In an answer not included in this volume.
185. P. 405.
186. Pp. 436–37.
187. P. 405.
188. Pp. 406–7.
189. Pp. 416–17.

honesty in the other; the differences in analyses and interpretations of social relations reflect differences in value perspectives and political motivations.

Similar conclusions are reached from discussions of the relationships between ultimate political goals and means advocated for their fulfilment.

In the questionnaire, one ,of Lenin's formulations of the ultimate aim of political activity was given as an example and opinions on its compatibility with other formulations of ultimate aims were urged.[190] None of the contributors take issue with the ultimate aim formulated by Lenin. There seems to be genuine agreement between all concerned that the ideal end of social development can well be described in terms like those used by Lenin.

But, as has so often been found to be the case in this inquiry, general agreement on ideals is unfortunately of little relevance to the clarification of ideological disagreements.

Perelman is particularly emphatic on this point: to him, the controversies are by no means assuaged by "the consoling thought that all political philosophers proclaim the same ultimate goal."

"The ideological differences relate to real societies and not to utopia. Once conditions allow for the attainment of a utopia, ideological conflicts lose all interest and meaning."[191]

In the same vein ten Hoor comments: "It is possible, of course, to state the aims of government in such general terms that there can be no incompatibility. However, incompatibility becomes a problem when we "descend" to the level of implications, consequences, conceptions of ends, choice of means, etc. . . . It does no good to devise some generalization which seems to serve no function except to conceal this fact."

It might perhaps be objected that descriptions of ultimate goals need not necessarily be given in excessively general terms. Generality and abstraction are harder to avoid in proclamations on the choice of means to arrive there.

Respondents generally concede that agreements on ultimate goals are entirely compatible with violent disagreements on methods to be used in their attainment, on the potentialities of the existing conditions, on the solution of actual differences of evaluation and judgment.

190. Question 29, see p. 521.   191. P. 301.

A number of respondents, however, stress an important qualification: it may well be so that ideological controversies are mainly centered on means and conditions, but the possibility is not thereby excluded that the disagreements embrace a decisive *normative* element. Oppositions over the choice of means to a given end do not take place in a vacuum, but are conditioned by the existence of a number of different intrinsic norms that may preclude the adoption of otherwise effective means. The disagreements are to a large extent concerned with intrinsic norms of this kind: values like the dignity of the human person, intellectual integrity, minority rights, etc., are frequently referred to as crucial in these respects. Neither of the parts in the conflict denies any of these values although they may be very differently interpreted in concrete situations: controversies take the form of mutual charges that they are not respected or lived up to in the opposite camp.

Are the chances of reconciliation better or worse if the conflict turns out to be predominantly descriptive in nature? In the UNESCO questionnaire it was suggested that conflicts turning on ultimate norms might prove irreducible. Several contributors seem to take a similar view and emphasize, with Wright[192] that "so long as opinions are regarded as relative and no values in the field are taken as absolute, there is always a possibility of reconciliation or of temporizing."

Others, however, take the contrary view that disagreements on means may well turn out to be equally deep-seated and intractable. Thus, Sweezy states that "people will cling to traditional or accepted patterns of analysis and interpretation just as tenaciously as they will to what are often regarded as more basic value judgments."[193] He even suggests that the very fact that both camps profess their allegiance to the same ultimate goals and values turn into a source of contention and bitterness; each camp will accuse the other of hypocrisy and deceit.

Among the great variety of reflections made in the material on the general relations of value antagonisms to prospects of diminishing the acuity of the conflict, the following might be singled out as possible points of departure for further mediation:

Conflicting views on ultimates will exclude rational but not other

192. In an answer not included in the present volume.
193. In an answer not included in this volume.

approaches to the peaceful settlement of ideological conflicts. There is, of course, always the possibility that convictions on ultimates may change or simply wither away; this may affect the alignment of agreements and disagreements. The possibility must not be overlooked that ideological clashes are more or less deliberately kept going on semantic confusions and distortions of issues as a means to divert public attention from the nonideological clashes of naked ambitions for economic, strategic, and other kinds of power.

If the ideological conflicts can be traced to different conclusions from analyses of social conditions and to different predictions of how common aims can be achieved, potent rational approaches may be open for the reduction of the more violent consequences of the conflicts. Chances to obtain moral and general ideological sanctions for warlike measures will decrease if the conflict in question is set before the peoples involved as one centered on the choice of effective means for the attainment of compatible if not common goals. The possibility must, however, be taken into account that theories of social conditions and instrumentalities may be stubbornly adhered to in the teeth of otherwise adequate demonstration of their falsity: this emotional and volitional element in social knowledge may prove much harder to cope with and provide an important obstacle to possible progress toward peaceful settlement of conflicts for long times to come.

CONCLUSIONS

An attempt to compare ideological doctrines without prejudging the issues by taking a stand for or against some of the doctrines is perfectly possible, but requires a motivation that is rarely found among people who are engaged actively in political struggle.

Even the possibility of comparison has been implicitly denied, particularly by those (Nietzsche, Spengler, Sorokin, et al.) who believe that a human being cannot arrive at other conclusions than such as are favorable to his interests, basic cultural heritage, biological drives, or other noncognitive factors. One of the reasons not to take the statements of these theorists too seriously is that they implicitly assume that they are exceptions from their own principle. They indulge in vast comparisons and do not seem to doubt the objectivity of their findings.

Stripped from misleading philosophical entanglements, the problem of the objectivity of ideological comparisons seems to boil down to that of getting a sufficient number of researchers of diverse cultural and political backgrounds to work permanently and in a spirit of intellectual integrity on the issues involved.

Today nationalist trends and political servility are fostered in research centers by their dependence on official bureaucracy or economic power. Social pressure is constantly at work on the researchers to make them produce statements agreeable to the dominant political trends. They are even implicitly expected to adapt themselves to the foreign policy of their nation: in times of shifts of alliances or outbreak of war, sudden shifts in theories are expected, accounts of the history of allied powers are to be more sympathetic, accounts of hostile powers are to be altered in the opposite direction. There is scarcely a single country where those resisting such "revisions" have not been subjected to crude attempts at *Gleichschaltung*, instead of being encouraged and applauded as valuable organs of equilibrium in the planetary community of men.

Strong currents of international—or supranational—character can reduce the pressure on the researchers and make international loyalties compete with national ones. But such currents cannot prevail without strengthening trends toward fair play in the struggle between national or subnational groups who compete for prestige and power. If on the subnational level we have ingrown habits of picturing antagonists in black and ourselves in brilliant white, and of looking at our opinions on controversial issues as absolute certainties, while regarding those of our opponents as distorted and biased, we shall have no force to resist prejudged accounts of ideologies. We are easily made victims of "official" versions of the ideological situation.

It should be added that significant progress toward fair presentation of ideological oppositions cannot be expected as long as there is internal strife of such an intensity that a split morality is propagated by all opinion leaders: one when presenting the outgroup platform and another reserved for the ingroup.

These are reflections relevant to any conclusions on findings on ideological differences in our age. The ensuing statements of conclusions must be interpreted on the background of these reflections.

1. The material gathered by UNESCO reveals that even among specialists in ideological research there are great *differences of*

opinion as regards matters of fact of unquestioned relevance to the description of ideological antagonisms.

2. Consequently, a large part of the statements made in the contributions should be viewed as expressive of *working hypotheses* justifiable on the basis of present-day efforts in ideology research, but subject to continuous corrections in the future.

3. It is beyond the powers of present-day research to determine in any exact way the lines of agreement and disagreement between ideological doctrines. If sufficient knowledge were stored in individual minds, it could not easily be conveyed to others. Present-day language habits are not adapted to the immense task of exact comparison of beliefs of groups and nations engaged in struggles for material and spiritual dominance.

4. Attempts at such a comparison encounter the difficulty that the language habits are adapted to agitation and preaching in the field of ideology, not to fair presentation. Basic terms in the vocabulary of ideologies are emotionally loaded slogans, and to make them resistant to analysis is a virtue in the eyes of the indoctrinated.

5. The function of ideologies to stabilize motives of joint action and encourage the fighting spirit of its adherents, makes it of little concern to formulate carefully the particular socio-historical situation which makes joint action possible and purposeful. Thus the researcher who wishes to compare the normative statements of two competing ideological trends must himself, as historian, sociologist, economist, psychologist, etc., find out *which unstated premises of action are common and which are specific* to each competing group. It is not in the interest of ideologists to bring to attention the historical conditions of their normative proclamations. Rather to the contrary, they tend to stress any timeless, universal, or a priori character they can conceive of.

6. It is a peculiar feature of our time that there is one positively loaded slogan which is common to all powerful ideological groups and which does seem to express more than mere positivity: it is more than a synonym for "good." This slogan is the term "democracy" and closely related derivatives.

7. Because of its universality, an inquiry into doctrines which are set forth as expressing democratic ideology is a convenient point of departure for the study of possible common features of all domi-

nant ideological trends of this era. This method of study does not assume a priori that a common slogan implies the existence of a common belief.

8. Any formulation of universal ideological trends must be *prefaced by warnings:* the formulation presupposes successful clarification of linguistic, particularly semantico-terminological, confusion. It presupposes the even more difficult task of finding and *formulating implicit premises* of programs of social action. No individual or group can claim more than to give tentative *ad hoc* conclusions on these matters.

9. The Lincoln formula affords a convenient point of departure for the analysis of ideological agreements on a "democracy." There is a general agreement that to serve the people in the broadest sense of the term, and ultimately the people of the earth, is the sole justification of government. Further, it is generally agreed that the people are served by giving the fullest possible access to the means by which each member can develop personal possibilities without jeopardizing the chances of others.

10. There is general doctrinal agreement that government should be "by the people," that is, that one should develop the most intense and widespread participation of the inhabitants in preparing, reaching, and carrying out decisions of importance to the welfare of the community. But it is also agreed that such participation is only possible if there is a minimum of general education and leisure and energy available for studies of the issues brought before the people. It is further agreed that in times of severe crisis, popular participation must be more or less reduced and opportunities of incitement to violent change of form of government curtailed.

11. From the unanimity on the principle of equal possibility of access to economic, educational, and cultural values flows an agreement that no individual should be allowed, by his particular talents or shrewdness, to reduce others to permanent dependence on him or to reduce permanently their and their offspring's access to economic, educational, and cultural values.

12. From the generally accepted broad interpretations of "people" flows a general rejection of race or color discrimination and a rejection of discriminations on the basis of religion, philosophical inclinations, or nobility of birth.

13. Implicit in the doctrines of government by the people and the appeals to knowledge as the guide to solution of questions of policy, there is a rejection of leadership on the basis of mystical insight of élites, of a *Führer* and *Gefolgschaft* following "the instincts of the pure blood."

14. There is no indication of disagreement on the opinion that there are in all ideological camps people who sincerely accept the foregoing doctrines, try to live up to their severe requirements and deplore the shortcomings of achievements so far realized.

15. The agreements thus listed make it possible to formulate severe criticism without leaving a common ground of accepted doctrines. The basic criticism will be that of inconsistency.

16. Even if the view were accepted, that mere lip service to the *common aspirations and principles* is the rule and sincerity the exception, their codification and the *increasing frequency of appeals to them* the world over by individuals and institutions on the national and international level, give to those who wish to propagate their sincere acceptance *a unique instrument* that should be tentatively perfected by research and worldwide educational drives.

APPENDIX I

THE UNESCO QUESTIONNAIRE ON IDEOLOGICAL CONFLICTS CONCERNING DEMOCRACY

The peoples of the world, laymen no less than experts, have never been more conscious of conflicts of convictions than in the years after World War II.

Ideological conflicts are present everywhere, between nations, within nations, between minds, within minds.

Few words have played a greater role in these conflicts than the word "democracy." What does it mean, connote, imply? Does it cover one and the same meaning to all and everybody, or is it just used to express whatever anybody thinks worth fighting for?

It has been the common watchword in two world wars. The victory of November, 1918, was said to be the victory of democracy. The common aim of the Allied Powers in World War II, as formulated by Roosevelt, Stalin, and Churchill at the Teheran Conference in December, 1943, was the establishment of "a world family of democratic nations." The declarations of Yalta in February and of Potsdam in August, 1945, both stressed the same principle: the Great Powers announced their intention of "meeting the political and economic problems of liberated Europe in accordance with democratic principles"; they made these principles the basis of their joint policy in Germany.

Did they mean the same by "democracy," the same by "democratic," when they used these words in these declarations? Did they only agree on the *words,* or did they agree on substance?

The events that have followed: the disagreements on elections in eastern Europe, the disagreements on the "new type democracies," the "people's democracies" established in these countries, the general disagreement within the United Nations Organization, have given ample evidence that the words did not connote any definite criteria *that could be agreed upon* in cases of concrete application of the principles laid down in the declarations of the Great Powers.

The disagreements have given rise to long series of ideological criticisms and countercriticisms; to give instances of cruder arguments it has, on the one hand, been claimed that "democracy" cannot thrive where free scope is given to racial discrimination and exploitation of toiling masses and colonial peoples, on the other, that "democracy" cannot exist where only one party takes part in elections and opposition is not tolerated.

What was the background of these violent disagreements? How were the divergencies in usage and interpretation of the word "democracy" to be clarified?

The problem is one of vast implications. It is not just a question of terminology. It has its background in contrasts of historical development, of social conditions, of political patterning, of ideological structuration, of public opinion formation, of education. It is deeply entangled in the immense cluster of problems raised by the impact of technology and industrial civilization on the lives of the peoples of the world; it is part of the general problem of world-integration under conditions never before experienced in the history of mankind. It is not only a problem of philosophy, of the normative basis of the relations between the individual and the state, it is a problem of war or peace.

A multitude of articles, pamphlets, and books published in the years since the end of World War II have attacked the problem. Philosophers, humanists, sociologists, political scientists, journalists, and statesmen have tried to analyze the divergencies and discuss the causes and responsibilities for the disagreements experienced in the concrete applications of principles once so heartily agreed upon.

But the problem has not yet been attacked on the international level, within the general framework of organized efforts toward international understanding.

It is the central aim of the inquiry launched by UNESCO to remedy this shortcoming, to organize *philosophically detached debates between nations, between opposed ideological camps:* to elucidate, through international exchanges of views, the divergencies of usage and interpretation, to analyze the normative foundations of those divergencies and to search for potential sources of reconciliation.

At this stage, the inquiry will concentrate on four clusters of problems which have seemed to be among the crucial ones in the controversies so far:

First, the general problem of the ambiguity and slogan-like character of the word "democracy": Are there divergent concepts covered by the word, what are the criteria of misuse, what historical basis is there for adopting one usage as the correct one and rejecting others?

Second, the general problem of the relations between "formal" democracy as an exclusively political concept and "real" democracy as a broad social *and* political concept: Does "democracy" connote universal and equal suffrage rights only, or does it even connote other rights to equality—educational, economic ones?

Third, the problem of tolerance, of the right of opposition: Does "democracy" connote the right of any group of any opinion whatsoever to take part in political life and influence public opinion, or are there limits to such rights, and what are these? Does "democracy" necessarily imply the existence of several parties? Does "democracy" imply the duty to fight any "antidemocratic" group?

Fourth, the problem of the normative bases of the divergencies of usage and interpretation manifest in current controversies: Do the divergencies reflect irreducible conflicts of value, or do they conceal deeper agreements and forces working toward reconciliation?

It is hoped that answers will be formed in such a way as to make exact comparison possible. This implies that *direct* answers to some or all the questions listed are highly preferred to indirect ones, but it does not preclude answers being made part of an essay covering some of all questions.

To avoid duplicating existing literature on the subject, it is expressly emphasized that well-documented answers to a small number of questions are preferred to replies which give conclusive answers to all questions, but omit argumentation.

In the preparation of questions, the ensuing principles have guided the choice of procedure.

    1. While pursuing the supreme aim laid down in its Constitution, UNESCO

cannot manifest a preference for any particular set of controversial views held by representative groups in any member state, but it can invite such groups to take up and co-operate in ideological inquiries under its auspices. UNESCO functions as a clearing-house of ideas, an international forum; it does not act as an umpire.

2. The present invitation rests on the assumption that all possibilities of reconciliation should be discussed in an unbiased manner before a particular disagreement is judged basic and irreducible.

3. The inquiry is conceived of as a philosophical analysis in so far as it is intended to center on the clarification of concepts and the formulation of basic value judgments.

Experts are invited to keep these principles in mind in considering the problems of this inquiry. It is UNESCO's hope that they will, as far as they think feasible, attempt to formulate their views and their judgments without abandoning the standards of preciseness and objectivity that are fostered in their special fields of research.

A. Ambiguity and Misuse

1. AMBIGUITY.—Voices of complaint on the looseness and vagueness of current use of the word "democracy" have been heard at least since the days of the French Revolution. But they did not rise to a storm of indignant protests until two disastrous world wars, solemnly proclaimed to have been fought in the defense and for the victory of DEMOCRACY, but followed by violent disagreements on the meaning and application of that holy word, had opened the eyes of a wider public to the problems involved.

To what extent will you agree that the word "democracy" is ambiguous?

2. EVIDENCE.—Could you quote evidence on this point?

3. MISUSE.—The largest part, however, of the indignation manifest in ideological controversies on the word "democracy" is focused, not on *loose use* but on *misuse*. These complaints may be grouped in four classes:

a) Complaints that the word is used without any *definite meaning* at all, only serving as a catchword, a slogan expected to elicit positive attitudes to the group using it, to its creed, to its policy;

b) complaints that the word is used in *divergent senses*, with the result that people are being misled;

c) complaints that the word is used in *new and illegitimate senses*, wrong and improper senses invented to steal adherents from groups that are using it in proper senses as the justified expression of their creed;

d) complaints that the word, though correctly defined and interpreted, is *improperly applied* to countries, to states that do not satisfy the requirements implied in the definition.

Taking these distinctions into account, would you let us have your opinion on these points:

On what conditions would you find it justified to charge any ideological group with *misuse* of the word "democracy"?

4. NEW USES.—Is the word currently used in significations that you consider *new* in relation, e.g., to nineteenth century and prewar usages?

In general, what *historical* basis is there for recommending some usages, rejecting others?

5. "GENERAL DEMOCRACY."—The opinion has become very widespread that there is no such thing as *"democracy"* in general, but only a long series of *"democracies,"* differing with different historical, social, and psychological conditions: there is Athenian democracy, medieval democracy, bourgeois democracy, proletarian democracy, Soviet democracy, but no "general democracy."

To what extent would you subscribe to this opinion?

6. COMMON CHARACTERISTICS.—Do these various *kinds* of democracy have any common characteristics and, if so, what? What makes them democracies?

7. IDEAL VERSUS FACT.—Definitions and basic characterizations of "democracy" are often formulated in terms of lofty ideals rather than in terms of realized institutional patterns.

Some of the violence of current discussions on "democracy" may stem from the widespread tendency to confuse ideals and actual conditions; the fight for the ideal is confused with the fight for the country or the state that is labeled "democratic."

To what extent would you think that this is a potential source of confusion making for an increase in the violence of controversies?

B. SOCIAL VERSUS POLITICAL DEMOCRACY

8. THE LINCOLN FORMULA.—Abraham Lincoln's famous Gettysburg phrase "government of the people, by the people, for the people," has often been taken as a point of departure for clarifications of the essential criteria of "democracy"; the preposition *of* indicating the obedience of the people to the government, the preposition *by* indicating the active participation of the people in the formation of the decisions taken by the government, and the preposition *for* indicating the value of these decisions for the general welfare of the people.

How far do these formulations correspond to your own interpretation of the Lincoln formula?

9. NECESSARY CRITERIA.—Do *all* the three prepositions state *necessary* criteria for anything to be called "democratic"?

10. WESTERN VERSUS EASTERN DEMOCRACY.—The relations between the prepositions *by* and *for* have furnished the basis for violent discussions.

Thus it is a widespread opinion that the opposition between the Eastern and the Western conceptions of "democracy" is largely due to a difference in emphasis on these prepositions. The British philosopher Bertrand Russell, to take an example, thinks that the contrast boils down to this: "The Anglo-Saxon definition of 'democracy' is that it consists in the rule of the majority; the Russian view is that it consists in the interests of the majority, these interests being determined in accordance with Marxist political philosophy" (*What Is Democracy?* [London, 1946], p. 14).

To what extent do you find this opinion on the nature of the opposition between the two conceptions borne out by the facts?

The problem set by the relation between *by* and *for* can be broken down into a set of subproblems that are not always kept apart in current controversies:

11. THE "NARROW" VERSUS THE "BROAD" SENSE.—There is the terminological problem: Should "democracy" be used to cover a *narrow* concept, a political concept designating methods of decision-making, or should it be used to

cover a *broad* concept, a socio-political concept designating conditions and methods as well as results of decision-making?

12. THE SOCIAL PROBLEM.—There is the psychological and sociological problem: Can a "democracy" in the narrow sense fulfil any of the requirements it involves if nothing is done to make it "democratic" in the broad sense?

13. THE POLITICAL PROBLEM.—There is the political problem, the problem of priorities, of relations between means and ends: Is "political democracy" the best means to achieve the goal of "social democracy"? Is "social democracy" the best means to achieve the goal of "political democracy"? Is "political democracy" a means to any single goal at all? Are the two concepts at all related as means to ends?

14. HISTORICAL DEVELOPMENT OF THE TWO USAGES.—The opposition between a "narrow" political concept and a "broad" social concept of "democracy" became acute for the first time in the 1848 crisis in western Europe. The problems raised might be said to focus on the social and economic implications of the introduction of universal suffrage. Socialists and Communists conceived of "democracy" as logically and necessarily implying the extension of the equality of rights from the political to the social and economic field, i.e., the abolition of privileges, the reduction of class distinctions, and even the socialization of the means of production. The reaction among Liberals and Conservatives was to a large extent a terminological one; they made efforts to prove that the term "democracy" was exclusively a political one with no necessary implications whatever in the social and economic field. In a famous speech in the Assemblée Constituante on September 12, 1848, Alexis de Tocqueville gave vent to this line of opinion in these words: "No, gentlemen, democracy and socialism are not necessarily interconnected. They are not only different, they are opposed. Are you perchance trying to tell me that democracy consists in the creation of a more vexatious, more meddlesome and more restrictive form of government than any other, with the sole difference that you let the people elect it and make it act in the name of the people? But then what would you have done but confer on tyranny an air of legality which it did not possess and ensure for it the force and independence it lacked. Democracy extends the sphere of individual independence, socialism contracts it. Democracy gives to every man his full value, socialism makes of every man an agent, an instrument, a cipher. Democracy and socialism are linked only by the word 'equality'; but note the difference: Democracy wants equality in freedom, socialism wants equality in constraint and enslavement."

Could you contribute to a broader outline of the historical development of those opposed conceptions of "democracy"?

15. DEMOCRACY AND SOCIALISM.—To what extent and in which senses of the words involved would you hold any of de Tocqueville's arguments valid for the situation in our time?

16. METHOD VERSUS CONTENT.—The distinction stressed by de Tocqueville has been vigorously carried through in a long series of Western treatises on political philosophy and political science. In his classical work on *Modern Democracies*, the late Lord Bryce stated his position in the following way: ". . . Democracy—which is merely a form of government, not a consideration of the purposes to which government may be turned—has nothing to do with economic equality, which might exist under any form of government, and

might possibly work more smoothly under some other form. . . . Political equality can exist either along with or apart from equality in property" (*Modern Democracies* [London, 1929], I, 76).

To what extent do you consider the strict distinction between the concept "method of decision-making" and the concept "contents of decision made" a justified and fruitful one?

What arguments would you think valid for supporting the tendency to reserve the word "democracy" for the *method* of decision-making, thus rejecting it as a broader term comprehending the conditions, the methods and the contents of the decision-making?

17. THE CRUCIAL DIFFERENCES.—The *attacks* upon this line of arguing have not lagged behind in violence.

The "formal" concept of democracy has been the subject of caustic analyses by Socialists and Communists, by Anarchists and Syndicalists. One of the most outstanding of these attacks was that launched by Lenin in the *State and Revolution:* "In capitalist society, under the conditions most favourable to its development, we have more or less complete democracy in the democratic republic. But this democracy is always restricted by the narrow framework of capitalist exploitation, and consequently always remains, in reality, a democracy for the minority, only for the possessing classes, only for the rich. Freedom in capitalist society always remains about the same as it was in the ancient Greek republics: freedom for the slave owners. Owing to the conditions of capitalist exploitation, the modern wage-slaves are also so crushed by want and poverty that "they cannot be bothered with politics"; in the ordinary peaceful course of events the majority of the population is debarred from participating in social and political life" (*Essentials of Lenin* [London, 1947], II, 200).

Quite along the same line is Stalin's comparison of bourgeois and Communist democracy in his speech on the Draft Constitution in 1936: "They talk of democracy. But what is democracy? Democracy in capitalist countries, where there are antagonistic classes, is, in the last analysis, democracy for the strong, democracy for the propertied minority. In the U.S.S.R., on the contrary, democracy is democracy for the working people, i.e., democracy for all" (*Leninism* [London, 1946], p. 579).

What are, in your view, the crucial differences between the line of argumentation taken by de Tocqueville and Bryce and the line taken by Lenin and Stalin? Do de Tocqueville and Lenin disagree on the relation between "democracy" and "liberty"; if so, of what nature is their disagreement?

18. REAL AND TERMINOLOGICAL DIFFERENCES.—To what extent would you say that these differences are of a terminological nature?

19. THE EXPRESSION OF "REAL INTERESTS."—It has been maintained that the gist of the matter lies in disagreements on the *measurement of interests:*

What criteria are to be postulated as essential to any method of political decision-making which is to give a "full and equal" expression to the *"real interests"* of each individual within the people?

Are these criteria primarily political, social or economic?

20. OPINION INFLUENCE VERSUS PRESSURE.—Take a fictive example like the following:

Given a people of whom 90 per cent repeatedly vote for the continuation of the capitalist economic system in elections carried through under a mini-

mum of direct opinion pressure, what should the government be called—
"democratic" or not? But what if 80 per cent of these voters were kept in
conditions of minimal intellectual independence and no social and economic
efforts were being made to reduce this percentage? Would their electoral expressions of their interests be on a level of "democratic equality" with those
of the others? In general, how would you trace a line between "democratically justifiable" and "democratically unjustifiable" processes of opinion-influencing?

21. DEMOCRACY AND PLANNING.—Closely related to these problems are those
raised by the impact of the principle of *economic planning* on political life.

Do you think it possible to trace a line of demarcation between "democratic" and "undemocratic" delegation of decision power? If so, would it be
possible for you to give a precise formulation of the criteria of demarcation
you think essential?

C. TOLERANCE AND TREASON

Another crucial point in the controversy on "democracy" is the problem
of the *rights of opposition* to the existing government, of the toleration of
opinions divergent from or contrary to those of the groups that have the decisive influence on policy-making.

22. THE TOLERATION OF DISSENTIENT OPINIONS.—Analyzing the general opposition between the two conceptions of democracy, the English political scientist, Edward Hallett Carr arrives at the following conclusion on this point:
"The question posed by the recent impact of Soviet democracy on the west
is whether that toleration of dissentient opinions which is declared to be the
essence of democracy means toleration of all dissentient opinions, even of
those hostile to democracy, or whether it means toleration of dissentient
opinions on specific issues among those who accept the fundamentals of democracy. This is not an academic question, and it has not yet been answered
by the spokesmen of western democracy. Neither of the alternative answers
is free from difficulty" (*The Soviet Impact on the Western World* [London,
1946], p. 14).

Along what lines would you think it possible to solve this problem?

23. THE REPRESSION OF PROPAGANDA.—Under what peace-time conditions,
if any, would you consider it consistent with democratic government to repress propaganda advocating a change of the form of government? Is the
kind of change advocated relevant to the question of repression?

24. DECISIONS INCOMPATIBLE WITH DEMOCRACY.—If you agree that there are
kinds of political propaganda that ought not to be tolerated within a democracy, according to what criteria of "democratic" decision-making would you
find justification for decisions on the limitation of "democratic" tolerance?
In general, does "democracy," even if conceived of primarily as a method
of decision-making, necessarily imply any restrictions upon the kinds of contents that the decisions, individual or collective, can have? Does "democracy"
presuppose general agreement on fundamental, indisputable principles within
the groups it is applied in; if so, what are these?

25. ONE-PARTY SYSTEMS.—Discussion of the tolerance question has in recent years taken more concrete forms in controversies over one-party versus
many-party systems. The question has a multitude of aspects; what interests
us is the point of principle: In what relation do many-party versus one-party

systems—as they are intended to work—stand to concepts of "democracy"? What kinds, if any, of one-party system do you consider compatible with a democratic form of government?

26. "SKEPTICISM" AND DEMOCRACY.—Some thinkers have tended to defend many-party systems as expressions of the philosophical attitude that no opinion is infallible, that no group has any self-evident right to claim universal allegiance to its political creed: "Skepticism is part of our faith" (D. W. Brogan, in *What is Democracy?* [London, 1946], p. 17).

To what extent would you think this philosophical principle a necessary basis for "democracy" in the sense you would use the term?

27. THE TOLERATION OF THE ANTIDEMOCRATIC.—This view has often been attacked as testifying to a lack of faith in the cause of democracy, a defeatist attitude to movements hostile to democracy.

To what extent, if any, do you think that tolerance of antidemocratic propaganda reflects the presence or absence of firm convictions on the principles of democracy?

D. THE VALUE FOUNDATIONS OF THE CONFLICT

Contemporary ideological argumentation proceeds largely in terms of what democracy is and is not. But if it is held, as is common among experts as well as laymen, that "democracy" is an honorific word, the *assertions* about what democracy *is* may in many cases be translated into *appeals* stating what *ought to be* and assertions about what it is not, into negative value judgments. Thus we are led from the consideration of terminological niceties to questions of what ought to be, questions which presumably are in part responsible for the fierceness of the conflicts.

If this is the case, the problem must be raised—which are the divergencies and how deep are they?

Considering the vast differences in immediate tasks calling for concerted action in different countries and under different historical conditions, and considering that each set of conditions is more or less trivial and consequently unformulated where they prevail, it must be expected that the verbalized ideological patterns, as seen from a planetary point of view, will primarily mirror local cravings and therefore may not be symptoms of basic differences in valuation.

The guiding idea of the following questions is to judge the extent and intensity of those disagreements on values which are implicit in the discussions on democracy. The seriousness of the disagreements might be measured in terms of the rank which the controversial values have within hierarchies of values of disputing groups or nations. To take an example:

28. THE MORALITY OF TOLERATION AND REPRESSION.—Do the disagreements between those advocating repression and those advocating tolerance of Fascist propaganda touch basic moral evaluations of both groups, one group or none of the groups?

Is the disagreement one concerning the *best means* to realize the common goal of stabilizing democratic government? Or is the tolerance or absence of tolerance in this case a matter of principle, independent of its consequences in relation to long-run stability or even in relation to any ulterior purpose? Just where lies the disagreement?

Answers to questions like these are highly relevant to the prospects of assuaging ideological controversies. If a verbal conflict is a symptom of a conflict of basic norms, it must be assumed to be held in a highly stable and tenacious manner. Efforts at reconciliation will in that case be viewed as the betrayal of what is sacred and beyond dispute.

Or the conflict may be a symptom of diverging instrumental values, divergent opinions on the means to reach a common goal—a divergence likely to diminish or disappear in the course of human experience.

Verbal disagreement on values may be due not to contrary, but to complementary evaluations. The disagreement may be due to differences in priorities, in plans of social and political action which all tend towards compatible goals but along different, historically and geographically, determined roads.

To make it more clear what kind of explicit or implicit doctrines we would like to have your opinion on, a quotation from Lenin is taken as an example: "We set ourselves the ultimate aim of abolishing the state, i.e. all organized and systematic violence, all use of violence against man in general. We do not expect the advent of an order of society in which the principle of the subordination of the minority to the majority will not be observed. But in striving for Socialism we are convinced that it will develop into Communism and, hence, that the need for violence against people in general, the need for the *subjection* of one man to another, will vanish, since people will *become accustomed* to observing the elementary conditions of social life *without force* and *without subordination*" ("The State and Revolution," *The Essentials of Lenin* [London, 1946], II, 197).

29. ULTIMATE AIMS.—*Is there any incompatibility between the ultimate political aim described by Lenin and the aims proclaimed by other ideologists to be of ultimate or intrinsic value?*

30. THE NATURE OF THE DISAGREEMENT.—*Of what nature, terminological, factual or normative, is the disagreement between ideologists stressing the priority of "political democracy" as a means to realize "social democracy" and ideologists advocating "social democracy" as a means to realize "political democracy"?*

In general, to what degree are the contemporary ideological controversies concerned with valuations which on closer analysis can be shown to be mainly instrumental or dependent on passing historical conditions, and to what degree with values that prove to be fundamental and intrinsic?

The questions set forth in this document are not in any way meant to be comparable to items in social science questionnaires. The questions are too vague and too comprehensive for any purpose of opinion surveying. They only function to direct the attention of experts to clusters of problems that have appeared to be of crucial importance in current controversies. The questions are intended to serve as a first set of stimuli increasing the likeliness that experts will focus their discussions on *approximately the same* range of topics. It is only too obvious that any man who has not abandoned all standards of intellectual integrity will find it hopeless to give anything comparable to *complete* answers without writing volumes. It is our hope, however, that respondents will not be discouraged by the vastness of the problems suggested, but will try to concentrate their efforts on the topics they find most worth while, that they will try to formulate the issues involved in more precise ways and to give detailed analyses of the difficulties and the possible solutions.

APPENDIX II

This statement is issued by the undersigned group of experts brought together by UNESCO to consider the causes of ambiguity and confusion in the
present use of the term "democracy" and their role in political disputes today.

During the period between the two world wars the use of propaganda in
stimulating and inciting social and political action assumed crucial importance. Improvements in means of mass communication have increasingly
made the widespread discussion of policies and ideas an influential factor, or
at least an element to be considered, in national government and social change
as well as in international negotiations. These changes have been accompanied
by a radical alteration in the manner in which international diplomacy is
conducted. Polemics among nations and criticisms of situations and doctrines
frequently assume a sharpness of tone more appropriate to the hostilities of
war than to the negotiations of peace. Statements of political oppositions on
particular points of policy or action are supported by appeal to opposed
theories of social good and opposed systems of political organization, by
reference to opposed interpretations of fact, and by use of opposed meanings
of words. This meeting of experts, brought together from various countries
to discuss the bases of the ideological conflicts which surround the term "democracy," is merely one of the innumerable indications both of the need
widely felt to study the nature of language in order to clarify communication
and statement, and also of the new interest in re-examining the commitments
and the instruments of democracy. Although we differ in the manner in
which we would develop and implement the statement of fundamental agreement which follows, we are in accord on the possibility of substantial contributions to the solution of practical problems from the analysis of ideological
conflicts.

We agree to the following propositions:

1. In spite of the violence of conflict concerning basic social and political
ideas and concerning means of international co-operation, there are abundant
indications of fundamental agreements. The agreements in statement of purpose and in aspiration appear in a controversial context of contradictory
interpretations of the intentions that motivate the statement or of facts that
seem to belie them. The agreements are themselves involved in the ideological conflict. Yet the unanimity which appears in the statements of aims is an
impressive fact. For the first time in the history of the world, no doctrines
are advanced as antidemocratic. The accusation of antidemocratic action or
attitude is frequently directed against others, but practical politicians and
political theorists agree in stressing the democratic element in the institutions
they defend and the theories they advocate. This acceptance of democracy
as the highest form of political or social organization is the sign of a basic

agreement in the ultimate aims of modern social and political institutions—
an agreement that the participation of the people and the interests of the
people are essential elements in good government and in the social relations
which make good government possible.

2. This common basis in the ultimate aims of all varieties of democracies
is closely connected with the history of their common traditions. Even the
most sharply contrasted forms of democracy share a common tradition of
humanism. The various forms of collectivism as well as the forms of liberal
democratic institutions derive from the Christian tradition and the American
and French Revolutions. They seek justice, equality, liberty, liberation of
man for the development of his faculties, equal access to the advantages of
the progress of civilization, and free participation in public functions. All
peoples who aspire to free and democratic forms of common life have joined
themselves to the same tradition in the ends they profess. No great nation
professes a doctrine of the superior worth of one race or the priority of the
state to the individual.

3. These basic agreements in statement are overlain with a great complexity of disagreements. There are many differences in the interpretation of
democracy, freedom, and justice, some of them so extreme that actions in
accordance with one interpretation must seem to those who do not share
that interpretation to be examples of the contraries of what they profess to be.
There are therefore accusations of antidemocratic action and attitude, even
though there are no defenders of antidemocratic institutions. Both sides in
the mounting political dispute find good reason to suspect cynical bad faith
and misrepresentation in the statements and actions of others. Both sides profess good reasons to believe that the conditions essential to democracy in the
one sense are incompatible with democracy in the other.

4. Power rivalries tend to sharpen the ideological conflict into two opposed
positions and to conceal the great variety of theories and parties. The ideological positions vary in manner of approach as well as in degree within a
single approach and in basic principles as well as in interpretation of common
positions. They include the numerous radical and socialist movements short
of communism as well as the numerous liberal and conservative movements
short of laissez-faire free enterprise. They include partially formulated or
adapted statements of the aspirations of dependent people and inhabitants of
underdeveloped regions of the world. This richness of ideological variety
may contribute to the resolution of power rivalries. If it is not preserved and
understood, the opposition of power will reduce the discussion of issues to
the opposition of two ideologies.

5. The fact that the word "democracy" is used both in a political and also
in a social and economic sense is a fertile source of ideological controversies.
The propriety of one or the other usage may be questioned, or if both meanings are granted the relation of the two sorts of democracy may be disputed.
The dispute is the more acrimonious since, despite ambiguities of terms, the
effects on political institutions of measures directed to securing social and
economic equality and the effects of political actions on social and economic
relations are apparent in the lives of all men.

6. Discussion and clarification of ideas is an important means for promoting
co-operation and common action. On the other hand, discussions of differences which might have been resolved by agreement on a common course,

or on mutually compatible courses, of action may be rendered more difficult when the initial differences are given foundations in opposed sets of principles. The acrimony of theological disputes in the past and the manner in which they eventually ceased to disturb the public peace, usually without having been resolved, afford illustration of the fashion in which the lines of ideological opposition harden and disappear. To point out the danger of such ideological oppositions is not to deprecate the importance of ideas or to ignore the grave differences in practical action to which they lead. On the contrary, analysis of the sources and devices of the ideological conflict may serve to clarify ideas and to open the possibility of common or at least consistent action.

7. Ideological conflicts are based, in part, on devices calculated to render the opposed positions incompatible or incommensurable. One such device, commonly used, is to treat the statement of ideal as description of fact and to present reports of actual situations as if they were the ideal intended. Democrats, who are Communists, will set forth violations of civil liberties and economic and social inequities in contrast to the ideal of socialist democracy. Democrats, who are Liberals, will present the restrictions and controls of opinion, statement, and movement and the continuing economic and social inequalities and problems in contrast to the traditional ideas of liberal democracy. To the Communist, toleration of dissentient opinions inimical to democracy is weakness or latent fascism; to the Liberal, suppression of opinions is the mark of totalitarianism and potential fascism. Understanding is impossible unless alleged facts are treated as facts and contrasted with facts, and unless ideals and theories are treated as aspirations and contrasted with other expressions of purpose and intention.

8. The ideological conflict reflects more than only differences of verbal usage and terminology. It affects the statement of fact, since what is relevant to one conception of democracy is unimportant in another, and the description of the same situation will therefore differ or even be opposed in reports couched in opposed ideologies. It affects the interpretation of intentions and motives, since obstinate adherence to statements which seem contradicted by facts can be accounted for only by negligent indifference or a purpose to deceive. It affects the statement of ideal, since agreement concerning justice, liberty, equality becomes meaningless if different significances are attached to those terms and conflicting means are recommended to achieve them.

9. In the ideological conflict, words, facts, intentions, and theories are all involved in uncertainty and confusion. Clarity cannot be achieved in statement by appeal to facts if the interpretation of facts is affected by the statement. Confidence cannot be felt in expressions of intention if the action which carries out the intention is contrary to what was anticipated. Common purposes cannot be pursued if there is no common understanding of what is in fact the case, of what problems are presented in the situation, and of what solutions are desirable.

10. Clarification of the present-day ideological conflict, and resolution of some of the ambiguities of opposition and debate, while important, is not in itself sufficient to insure peace. It will serve to separate the real issues from the problems which arise from confusions of statement. By isolating those problems it will simplify the total situation and permit the concentration of attention on practical issues and possible actions. Equally important is the

effect that such clarification will have on the climate within which the discussion is carried on. When the opposite sides to a discussion understand each other, mutual confidence is possible. When understanding is absent, uncertainty and fear increase the tensions produced by the opposition. The clarification of ideas and statements will probably not lead to agreement in doctrine and ideal, between the groups of powers at present opposed. Fortunately such doctrinal agreement is not necessary for common action. But clarity of statement will make understanding possible, and understanding is essential not only to such complete agreement, but also to co-operation in common actions agreed upon for different fundamental reasons as well as to the formulation of separate but compatible courses of action.

11. The fact that the ideological conflict is not between two fixed and extreme views, as political conflicts tend to be, affords grounds for the expectation that the conflict of ideologies may be clarified. The effort to clarify the differences is therefore an appeal to world public opinion.

12. The clarification of the issues will attenuate the effect on the general public of propaganda tending to incite to violence. Ideological conflicts, in so far as they present the opposed position as based on bad faith, give those who wish to suppress ideological opposition by force the advantage of doing so with a good conscience. Clarification of issues should show that there may be ideological opposition without bad faith.

13. We need to know more concerning the different ideologies of the world if the conflict which threatens to narrow to an opposition between two ideologies is to be avoided. Ultimately the resolution of ideological conflicts depends on the free interchange of information, of cultural materials, and of persons. The peoples of the world cannot understand each other in all the diversities of their cultural, social, and political lives or in all the varieties of their needs and aspirations, without freer and fuller contact with each other.

SERGIO BUARQUE DE HOLLANDA
EDWARD HALLETT CARR
RICHARD MCKEON
CHAIM PERELMAN
PIERRE RICOEUR
ALF ROSS

APPENDIX III

Report of the Committee on the Philosophical Analysis of Fundamental Concepts

The committee of experts on the Philosophical Analysis of Fundamental Concepts was convened to study and discuss the replies to the questionnaire concerning the variant meanings assigned to democracy in present-day oppositions and statements and, after study and discussion, "to prepare a report synthetizing and interpreting the contributions to this inquiry" (*Resolutions*, 1948, 5.41) and to advise the Secretariat concerning "how the results of the inquiry may be given wide publicity" (5.42).

Professor E. H. Carr was elected chairman, Professor C. Perelman vice-chairman, and Professor R. P. McKeon rapporteur.

In its preliminary discussion of the purposes of the meeting and the means by which they might be accomplished, the committee came to the conclusion that the problems of synthetizing and interpreting the results of the inquiry should be related closely to the problems of using and popularizing them. The committee is convinced that the replies to the questionnaire should be analyzed and tabulated more systematically than the committee was able to. The discussion of the committee was therefore concerned with the broad lines of the relations among the positions taken in the replies, which might be useful to guide such analyses and tabulations, and with the significances of the oppositions and agreements in their bearing on the political and social problems of our times. The report of the committee is divided into two parts: (1) a suggested schematism of problems and of fundamental positions with respect to those problems, in which the use and interpretation of "democracy" is involved, and (2) suggestions concerning ways in which the inquiry may be carried further and in which the materials thus far assembled might be used to advance understanding and peace.

1. PROBLEMS PRESENTED IN THE OPPOSITION OF CONCEPTIONS OF DEMOCRACY

The discussion of the committee fell under four headings suggested by the four parts of the questionnaire. A, The Ambiguity of the Word "Democracy"; B, The Forms of Democracy; C, Tolerance and Treason; and D, Democracy and Value Judgments.

A. Ambiguity of the Word "Democracy"

The answers to the first seven questions of the questionnaire, concerning the ambiguity and misuse of the word "democracy," brought to light a basic ambiguity in the word "ambiguity." Any generalization concerning the answers must therefore involve some interpretation and adjustment of meanings. It must also neglect the differences of the means suggested or advocated to remove the ambiguity. None the less, the committee found general agreement on three important points. In the first place, the idea of democracy was considered ambiguous and even those who thought that it was clear or capable of clarity were obliged to admit a certain ambiguity either in the institutions or devices employed to effect the idea or in the cultural or historical circumstances by which word, idea, and practice are conditioned. In the second place, in spite of, and sometimes because of, the appeal to traditional usage in the definition of the term, the criteria of abuses of the word were, for the most part, moral in character, such as the intention to deceive or the probability that a given meaning would in given circumstances deceive. Finally, the committee was struck by the fact that there were no replies adverse to democracy. Probably for the first time in history, "democracy" is claimed as the proper ideal description of all systems of political and social organization advocated by influential proponents.

The committee is convinced that the agreement on these points indicates important characteristics in the present ideological conflict: (1) that the interests and participation of the people are prominent in all statements of the ideal of social and political relations, (2) that the ambiguities arise from conflicting conceptions of what interests can be achieved by participation of the people and what participation is practicable, (3) that the use and abuse of the term is conceived as a mode of argumentation in supporting or depreciating particular forms of democracy.

B. The Forms of Democracy

In one sense, the agreement on a single term with at least some nucleus of common meaning holds forth some hope for the resolution of the ideological conflict. In another sense, the problem is rendered more acute and elusive by that agreement, since the oppositions in interpretation must be sought in the qualifications or the instrumentations sought for the basic idea of democracy. Forms of political and social organization that were sometimes contrasted to democracy are now conceived as instrumentalities of democracy, and the whole political and social debate now takes place between different forms of democracy. Moreover, that change has affected the manner in which the debate itself is conducted and the significance which is attached to ideological differences. If democracy is conceived primarily in terms of institutions designed to facilitate coming to agreement on a common course of action and carrying such decisions out, the adjustment of ideological differences is a means for the determination of values and itself an important value. If democracy is conceived primarily in terms of institutions designed to achieve the social and economic well-being though not necessarily the immediate preference of the people, the ideological conflict is a historical fact and its resolution must be a consequence of social change.

The replies to questions 8–21, on social versus political democracy, illustrate the complexity of confusions—terminological, factual, and theoretic—involved in discussions of the relation of the social and the political elements of democracy. None the less, three general points of agreement underlie the differences. In the first place, there is agreement that participation of the people is an essential part of the definition of democracy, but there are sharp differences concerning the manner of participation. In the second place, while there is general agreement that the word democracy is used both in a political and a social sense, some contributors hold that the term of democracy is properly political and is applied only by analogy to social and economic conditions, others regard political democracy as prior in time to social democracy; others consider that there is and always has been a mutual relation and dependence between the two concepts. Finally, there is general agreement that democracy entails the real interests of the people, in some sense, and depends on the delegation of power, but the details of the deviations of interpretations are indicated only sketchily in the replies. In the opinion of the committee the most important aspect of the issue of political and social democracy in its present form is the question of the application of the political procedures of democracy to large scale social and economic planning.

C. Tolerance and Treason

The fundamental agreement which underlies the different conceptions of democracy and the different statements of the forms in which it may be realized concretely are reflected in the attitudes taken toward toleration of differences of opinion. There are fundamental differences in the views expressed or implied concerning the relation of expression of opinion to action and concerning the relation of civil liberties to social policy. These differences may be said to reflect the divergences of interpretation of democracy and of the actions essential to its establishment and preservation. In the answers to questions 22–27, on tolerance and treason, general agreement was found on three points. In the first place, there was agreement that opinions as distinct from actions might or should be tolerated, but the differences in interpretation of that principle ranged all the way from answers which held that all expressions of opinion, even antidemocratic opinions, should be tolerated to answers which held that no valid distinction can be drawn between expression of opinion and action, and it is proper, or even imperative, therefore, to suppress any opinion dangerous to democratic institutions. In the second place, there was general agreement that some expressions of opinion must under some circumstances be controlled, but the interpretations ranged from one extreme at which the control of expressions of opinion must be limited to times of crisis or war, whatever the content of the expression, to the other extreme at which statements endangering democracy, in any circumstances, including even statements in the fields of science or art, must be suppressed. Finally, there was agreement, even within these divergent views, that the criterion of tolerance must be found in the possible effect of expressions of opinion on the basic constitution of the state and on the social order, but the conception of basic constitution, at one extreme, limited the conception of democracy to a method and procedure of coming to decisions and executing them, joined to an attitude of skepticism with respect to any doctrine advanced for universal acceptance, while at the other extreme, the conception of democracy was thought to be inseparable from definite moral, social, economic or political ideals.

D. Democracy and Judgments of Value

Such agreements as can be found in conceptions of the bearing of statements and actions on the concrete realization of the ideals of democracy are thus diversified in interpretation by fundamental differences in judgments of value or of practicability. The answers to questions 28–30, concerning the relation of the conflict to value judgments, reflected three different attitudes toward values and the means of their achievement by co-operative action. In the first place, many of the answers were based on a confidence that there is a fundamental agreement concerning ends underlying the most diverse political positions and theories today, but no agreement concerning means. Most of the answers based on this conviction took the position that the agreement on ends, in view of the differences concerning means, was not of much importance in practice. Some, however, considered the agreement concerning ends an important indication of the possibility of agreeing on means to those ends. In the second place, some answers found in the differences of judgments of value an indication of a basic difference of ends which makes discussion of means ambiguous until there is some common understanding of ends. A few of the answers took the position that a fundamental difference of social theories or even of ends is compatible with agreement concerning proximate ends and co-operation in action to achieve them. In the third place, some of the answers denied the validity of the distinction between means and ends and argued that the basic differences were to be found in social theory, philosophy of history, or conception of cultural relations.

2. RECOMMENDATIONS CONCERNING FUTURE DEVELOPMENTS OF THE PROJECT

The recommendations of the committee concerning the further developments of the project have to do:

A—With the use of the materials examined in the first part of this report and the publicity to be given them, and

B—With possible extensions of the project in the continuing program of UNESCO.

A. MEANS BY WHICH THE RESULTS OF THE INQUIRY SHOULD BE GIVEN PUBLICITY

1. The Committee recommends that a volume be prepared similar to the volume on Human Rights recently published by UNESCO. The volume should contain the questionnaire, a selection of important or typical answers, the report of the committee of experts and their declaration, and a more extended analysis of the answers to be prepared by the Secretariat.

2. The Committee recommends that a pamphlet be prepared, for inclusion in the series of pamphlets on Human Rights now in preparation, to contain a popularly expressed statement of the results of the inquiry together with the declaration of the committee of experts.

3. The Committee recommends that the attention of the National Commissions of member states be drawn to the materials and that the national commissions be requested to consider means by which the materials might be used at various levels of the educational systems of the member states. The Committee is convinced that excellent use might be made of them in the general courses of social studies of colleges and in the philosophy years of Lycées as well as on the level of graduate studies for seminars in philosophy, political science, and international affairs, and in other ways suited to different educational structures. Plans have already been put in motion in several universities for the use of the questionnaire and some of the replies to it.

4. The Committee recommends that the materials and problems treated in this inquiry be made the basis for a theme about which UNESCO might present its work during the year 1949–50, much as the "Universal Declaration of Human Rights" and "Food and People" served as centralizing themes during the present year. The Committee suggests that the theme be developed under some such title as "Democracy—World Hope." In the opinion of the Committee such a theme would afford a continuation to the programs developed under both the "Human Rights" program and the "Food and People" program, and it would provide a synthetizing note to be introduced into all the work of UNESCO. The Committee thinks of the program as subject to such implementations as the following:

a) A series of pamphlets or possibly a quarterly devoted to the presentation of the fact, which impressed the Committee, that democracy has in the last few years received universal acceptance as an ideal of human relations, and to the examination of problems faced by men in giving that ideal its concrete realizations. The pamphlets or the quarterly should contain: (1) brief popular statements, by experts in the various fields and by men of affairs, of some of the themes developed in the process of this inquiry, and (2) news of progress in democracy, ideological conflicts that endanger it, and the effect of historical and social change on the fashion in which the problems of democracy must be faced today.

b) A series of weekly releases for radio programs similar to those prepared on the theme "Food and People." They might take the form of commentary drawn from the inquiry of UNESCO on conflicts concerning democracy in the United Nations or in the press of the world. They might take the form of expounding the implications of the common effort of men to present their institutions and social developments as democratic. They might take the form of setting forth the important historical developments since the formation of the democratic constitutions of the eighteenth century, which have now brought economic and social developments to bear on political institutions and have introduced further dimensions to the realizations of democracy.

c) The idea "Democracy—World Hope" might be used to integrate the statement and the presentation of the various parts of the program of UNESCO. Thus, fundamental education is of basic importance to world democracy. The program in international understanding should be conceived of and presented to the world public as a step to the establishment of democratic relations essential to the peace of the world. What UNESCO does in its library program, in its study of tensions, in reconstruction and in extending the advantages of the technological advances of mankind to the underdeveloped portions of the world are all parts of the development of "Democracy—World Hope." In the opinion of the Committee such a use of the theme would have the double effect of making the program of UNESCO more easily comprehensible to the majority of people by presenting them a unifying idea and also the advantage of emphasizing interrelations in the actual development and execution of the program.

B. The Extension of the Project

The Committee recommends that the general project, of which the inquiry into human rights and into democracy were parts, be continued in 1949–50 with an examination of the concept of "liberty." This project should be conceived in close relation with other projects of UNESCO, such as the publicizing of the Declaration of Human Rights and the project concerning the freedom of the artist. The Committee considered the desirability of recommending that the project be referred to the newly formed International Council of Humanistic and Philosophic Studies for development and execution and, after extended discussion, decided unanimously against such a disposition of the project. The Committee is convinced that the project is so directly connected with the purposes of UNESCO as set forth in the preamble to its Constitution, that it depends so much on the co-operation of men in many fields, and that it requires the interplay of theoretic competence and practical insight to such a degree, that UNESCO should undertake a special supervision in its development on an international basis. Such supervision might, moreover, be based on some of the devices which UNESCO is developing in its new experiments in the stimulation of international intellectual and cultural co-operation.

The Committee recommends that the inquiry be conceived in two steps, first, a series of preparatory explorations in the member states, and second, a meeting of experts representing these national preparatory commissions to place the inquiry on an international scale. If this sequence is feasible, UNESCO might recommend to the General Conference in 1949 that the National Commissions be requested to plan and execute, according to the arrangements best suited to the respective countries, an inquiry into ideological conflicts concerning "liberty." A committee of experts drawn from these National Commissions should meet in time to make a recommendation to be considered at the General Conference of 1950. If that recommendation is favorable and is approved the international inquiry should be instituted for the following year.

Paris, May, 1949

EDWARD HALLETT CARR, *Chairman*
CHAIM PERELMAN, *Vice-Chairman*
RICHARD McKEON, *Rapporteur*
SERGIO BARQUE DE HOLLANDA
PIERRE RICOEUR
ALF ROSS

APPENDIX IV

A Selected Bibliography of Texts on Democracy and Its Role in Ideological Conflicts

Acton, J. E. D. *The History of Freedom and Other Essays* (London, 1907), chaps. i–ii.

Adler, Max. *Politische oder soziale Demokratie* (Berlin, 1926).

Adler, Mortimer J., and William Farrell, "The Theory of Democracy," *The Thomist*, III (1941), 397–449, 588–652; IV (1942), 121–81, 286–354, 446–562, 692–761; VII (1944) 80–131.

Alain. *Éléments d'une doctrine radicale* (Paris, 1925).

———. *Le citoyen contre les pouvoirs* (Paris, 1926).

Aleksandrov, G. F. "O sovetskoi demokratii," *Bolshevik* (1946), No. 22, pp. 9–37.

———. *The Pattern of Soviet Democracy*. Transl. by L. Gruliow (Washington, D.C., 1948).

Anshen, Ruth N., ed. *Freedom: Its Meaning* (New York, 1940).

Aristotle. *Politics* iii. 1–3, 6–13.

Arnold, Matthew. "Democracy," *Mixed Essays* (London, 1879).

Ascoli, Max, and Fr. Lehmann, eds. *Political and Economic Democracy* (New York, 1937).

Attlee, Clement. *The Labour Party in Perspective* (London, 1937).

Bagehot, Walter. *Physics and Politics* (London, 1872), chap. v.

Bakunin, Michael. *Dieu et l'état* (Paris, 1882).

Barker, Sir Ernest. *Reflections on Government* (London, 1942).

Beard, Charles A. *The Republic: Conversations on Fundamentals* (New York, 1944).

Becker, Carl L. *Modern Democracy* (New Haven, 1941).

Benda, Julien. *La grande épreuve des démocraties* (New York, 1942).

Beneš, Ed. *Democracy Today and Tomorrow* (New York, 1939).

Bernstein, Ed. *Die Voraussetzungen des Sozialismus und die Aufgaben der Sozialdemokratie* (Stuttgart, 1899). Transl. as *Evolutionary Socialism* (New York, 1909).

Blum, Léon. *A l'échelle humaine* (Paris, 1945).

Brandeis, Louis. *The Curse of Bigness* (New York, 1934).

Bryce, James. *Modern Democracies* (2 vols.; London, 1921).

Calhoun, John C. *A Disquisition on Government* (Charleston, 1851), new ed. New York, 1947.

Carr, E. H. *The Soviet Impact on the Western World* (New York, 1946).

Cole, G. D. H. *The Intelligent Man's Guide to the Post-War World* (London, 1947).

———. *Europe and the Problem of Democracy* (London, 1948).

Commager, Henry S. *Majority Rule and Minority Rights* (New York, 1943).

Constitution (Fundamental Law) of the U.S.S.R., December 5, 1936, with later amendments.

CRIPPS, SIR STAFFORD. *Towards Christian Democracy* (London, 1945).
CROCE, BENEDETTO. *Politics and Morals* (London, 1946).
DAWSON, CHRISTOPHER, and MALCOLM SPENCER. *Democracy and Peace* (London, 1947).
DEWEY, JOHN. "The Democratic State," *The Public and Its Problems* (New York, 1927), chap. iii.
———. *Freedom and Culture* (New York, 1939).
DICEY, A. V. *Law and Public Opinion in England during the Nineteenth Century* (London, 1914).
DUGUIT, LÉON. *Les transformations du droit public* (Paris, 1913). Transl. as *Law in the Modern State* (New York, 1919).
DURBIN, E. F. M. *The Politics of Democratic Socialism* (London, 1940).
ENGELS, FRIEDRICH. *Herrn Eugen Dührings Umwälzung der Wissenschaft* (Leipzig, 1872). Engl. transl. New York, 1935.
———. *Der Ursprung der Familie, des Privateigentums und des Staats* (Zurich, 1884). Engl. transl. New York, 1942.
The Federalist. A Collection of Papers by Hamilton, Jay, and Madison (New York, 1787-88).
FRANKFURTER, FELIX. *The Public and Its Government* (New Haven, 1930).
GOMULKA, WL. "People's Democracy: The Way to the Peaceful Development of Poland," *Political Affairs* (April, 1947).
GRABOWSKI, ADOLF. *Demokratie und Diktatur* (Zurich, 1949).
GREEN, THOMAS HILL. *Lectures on the Principles of Political Obligation* (London, 1890).
GROETHUYSEN, BERNHARD. *Dialektik der Demokratie* (Vienna, 1931).
GUIZOT, FR. *De la démocratie en France* (Paris, 1849).
HALÉVY, ÉLIE. *L'ère des tyrannies* (Paris, 1938).
HAYEK,.F. A. *The Road to Serfdom* (London, 1944).
HOBHOUSE, L. T. *Liberalism* (London, 1911).
HOBSON, J. A. *Imperialism* (London, 1912).
HOLMES, OLIVER WENDELL. *The Dissenting Opinions of Mr. Justice Holmes.* Ed. A. Lief (New York, 1929).
Human Rights: A Symposium Edited by UNESCO (New York, 1949).
HUMBOLDT, WILH. v. *Ideen zu einem Versuch, die Grenzen der Wirksamkeit des Staates zu bestimmen* (Breslau, 1851), new ed. Nuremberg, 1946.
JAURÈS, JEAN. *Études socialistes* (Paris, 1902).
JEFFERSON, THOMAS. *Democracy.* Texts selected and arranged by Saul K. Padover (New York, 1939).
JOUVENEL, BERTRAND DE. *On Power: Its Nature and the History of Its Growth* (New York, 1949).
JØRGENSEN, JØRGEN. *Det demokratiske Samfund* (Copenhagen, 1947).
KAUTSKY, KARL. *Diktatur des Proletariats* (Vienna, 1918). Engl. transl. Manchester, 1920.
———. *Terrorismus und Kommunismus* (Berlin, 1921).
———. *Social Democracy vs. Communism* (New York, 1946).
KELSEN, HANS. *Vom Wesen und Wert der Demokratie* (Tübingen, 1929).
———. *The Political Theory of Bolshevism* (Berkeley and Los Angeles, 1948).
KOCH, HAL, and ALF ROSS, eds. *Nordisk Demokrati* (Copenhagen, 1949).
LAIRD, JOHN. *The Device of Government* (Cambridge, 1945).

LASKI, HAROLD J. *Liberty in the Modern State* (London, 1930).
——. *Democracy in Crisis* (London, 1933).
——. "Democracy," *Encyclopaedia of the Social Sciences* (New York, 1934).
——. *Reflections on the Revolution of Our Times* (London, 1943).
LAURAT, LUCIEN. *Le marxisme en faillite?* (Paris, 1939). Transl. as *Marxism and Democracy* (London, 1940).
LECKY, W. E. H. *Democracy and Liberty* (New York, 1896).
LENIN, VLADIMIR ILYITCH. "What Is To Be Done?" 1902; "One Step Forward, Two Steps Back," 1904; "The Two Tactics of Social-Democracy," 1905; "The State and Revolution," 1917; "The Proletarian Revolution and the Renegade Kautsky," 1918; " 'Democracy' and Dictatorship," January 3, 1919; "Theses and Report on Democracy and the Dictatorship of the Proletariat," March 4, 1919; "The State, a Lecture," July 11, 1919; "A Contribution to the History of the Question of Dictatorship," November, 1920; "Left-Wing Communism: An Infantile Disorder," 1920—all in *Selected Works*, ed. J. Fineberg (New York, 1937, and later eds.).
LEO XIII, "Immortale dei," 1885; "Libertas praestantissimum," 1888; "Rerum novarum," 1891; "Graves de communi," 1901—all translated in *The Great Encyclical Letters of Pope Leo XIII* (New York, 1903).
LERNER, MAX. *It Is Later than You Think: The Need for a Militant Democracy* (New York, 1938).
LEWIS, GEORGE CORNEWALL. *The Use and Abuse of Political Terms* (London, 1832).
LIEBER, FRANCIS. *On Civil Liberty and Self-Government* (Philadelphia, 1853).
LINCOLN, ABRAHAM. Speech at Peoria, October 16, 1854; speeches at Springfield, June 26, 1857, and June 16, 1858; address at Gettysburg, November 19, 1863; Second Inaugural Address, March 4, 1865.
LINDSAY, A. D., SALVADOR DE MADARIAGA, H. J. LASKI, BERTRAND RUSSELL, D. W. BROGAN. *What Is Democracy?* (London, 1946).
LINDSAY, LORD A. D. *Essentials of Democracy* (London, 1929).
——. *The Modern Democratic State* (London, 1943).
LIPPMANN, WALTER. *The Phantom Public* (New York, 1927).
——. *The Good Society* (London, 1938).
LUXEMBURG, ROSA. *Sozialreform oder Revolution* (Leipzig, 1899).
——. *Die russische Revolution* (Berlin, 1922).
MACIVER, R. M. *Leviathan and the People* (University, Louisiana, 1939).
——. *The Ramparts We Guard* (New York, 1950).
MADARIAGA, SALVADOR DE. *Anarchy or hierarchy* (London, 1937).
——. *Victors, Beware* (London, 1946).
MAINE, SIR HENRY SUMNER. *Popular Government* (London, 1885).
MANNHEIM, KARL. *Man and Society in an Age of Reconstruction* (London, 1940).
MARITAIN, JACQUES. *Freedom in the Modern World* (New York, 1936).
——. *Christianity and Democracy* (New York, 1943).
MARX, KARL. "Zur Judenfrage," *Deutsch-französiche Jahrbücher* (1844), Engl. transl. in *Selected Essays* (London, 1926).
——. *La misère de la philosophie* (Brussels, 1847), transl. as *The Poverty of Philosophy* (Chicago, 1910).
——. *Die Klassenkämpfe in Frankreich* (1850), transl. as *The Class Struggles in France, 1848-50* (New York, 1934).

APPENDIX 535

——. *Der achtzehnte Brumaire des Louis Bonaparte* (1852), transl. as *The Eighteenth Brumaire of Louis Bonaparte* (London, 1926).
——. *Zur Kritik der politischen Oekonomie* (Hamburg, 1859), Engl. transl. Chicago, 1911.
——. *Das Kapital I* (Hamburg, 1867), numerous English translations.
——. *Der Bürgerkrieg in Frankreich* (1871), transl. as *The Civil War in France* (New York, 1933).
——. *Letters to Kugelmann* (1862–74) (New York, 1934).
—— and FRIEDRICH ENGELS. *Die heilige Familie* (Frankfurt, 1845).
——. "Die deutsche Ideologie," 1845–46, printed in *Marx-Engels Gesamtausgabe*, ed. D. Rjazanov, Vol. I, 5 (Moscow); Parts I and III translated New York, 1939.
——. *Manifest der kommunistischen Partei* (London, 1848). Ed. and transl. D. Ryazanoff, London, 1930.
——. *Critique of the Gotha Program*. Ed. C. P. Dutt (New York, 1938).
——. *Correspondence* (New York, 1942).
MASARYK, T. G. *Die philosophischen und soziologischen Grundlagen des Marxismus* (Vienna, 1899).
——. *Les problèmes de la democratie* (Paris, 1924).
MCKEON, RICHARD. "Discussion and Resolution in Political Conflicts," *Ethics,* LIV (1944), 235–62.
——. "Democracy, Scientific Method, and Action," *Ethics,* LV (1945), 235–86.
MERRIAM, C. E. *What Is Democracy?* (Chicago, 1942).
MICHELS, ROBERTO. *Zur Soziologie des Parteiwesens* (Leipzig, 1913), transl. as *Political Parties* (Glencoe, Ill., 1949).
MILL, JOHN STUART. *On Liberty* (London, 1859).
——. *Considerations on Representative Government* (London, 1861).
MITIN, M. "Sovetskaja demokratija i demokratija burzhuasnaja," *Bolshevik* (1947), No. 6.
MOLOTOV, V. Speech on the Seventh Union Congress, February 7, 1935.
——. Speech on the New Constitution, November 1936.
MOSCA, GAETANO. *The Ruling Class* (New York, 1939).
MYRDAL, GUNNAR. *An American Dilemma: The Negro Problem and Democracy* (2 vols.; New York, 1944).
NORTHROP, F. S. C. *The Meeting of East and West* (New York, 1947).
——., ed. *Ideological Differences and World Order* (New Haven, 1949).
PASCHUKANIS, E. B. *Allgemeine Rechtslehre und Marxismus* (Vienna, 1929).
PIUS XI, *Quadragesimo anno* (Encyclical letter, May 15, 1931).
PLAMENATZ, JOHN P. *Consent, Freedom and Political Obligation* (Oxford, 1938).
PLEKHANOV, G. C. *Fundamental Problems of Marxism* (London, 1929).
POPPER, KARL R. *The Open Society and Its Enemies* (2 vols.; London, 1945). *Probleme der Demokratie*, Vols. I–II (Berlin, 1929–31).
PROUDHON, P.-J. *Idée générale de la révolution au XIXe siècle* (Paris, 1857).
——. *Solution du problèm social* (Paris, 1868), chap. ii.
RENNER, KARL. *Demokratie und Bureaukratie* (Zurich, 1946).
REVAI, JOSEF. "On the Character of Our People's Democracy," transl. from the Hungarian, *Foreign Affairs* (October, 1949), pp. 143–52.
ROHDEN, P. R., ed. *Demokratie und Partei* (Vienna, 1932).

ROOSEVELT, FRANKLIN D. "Four Freedoms" speech (January 6, 1941).
RÖPKE, WILHELM. *Die Gesellschaftskrisis der Gegenwart* (Zurich, 1942). Engl. transl., *The Social Crisis of Our Time* (Chicago, 1950).
ROSENBERG, ARTHUR. *Demokratie und Sozialismus* (Amsterdam, 1938), Engl. transl. New York, 1939.
ROSS, ALF. *Hvorfor Demokrati?* (Copenhagen, 1946).
ROUSSEAU, JEAN-JACQUES, *Du contrat social* (Amsterdam, 1762).
ROUSSET, DAVID, and JEAN-PAUL SARTRE, *Entretiens sur la politique* (Paris, 1949).
RUSSELL, BERTRAND. *Authority and the Individual* (London, 1949).
SCHMITT, CARL. *Die geistesgeschichtliche Lage des heutigen Parlementarismus* (Munich, 1926).
———. *Staat, Bewegung, Volk* (Berlin, 1933).
SCHUMPETER, JOSEPH A. *Capitalism, Socialism, and Democracy* (New York, 1942).
STALIN, JOSEPH. "Foundations of Leninism," 1924; "On the Problems of Leninism," 1926; "On the Draft Constitution of the U.S.S.R.," November 25, 1936; "Some questions of theory," in Report to the 18th Congress of the C.P. S.U.(B.), March 10, 1939–all in *Leninism* (London, 1940).
———. *War Speeches* (New York, 1946).
STEPHEN, JAMES FITZJAMES. *Liberty, Equality, Fraternity* (London, 1873).
STRACHEY, JOHN. *The Theory and Practice of Socialism* (London, 1936).
SWEEZY, PAUL M. *Socialism* (New York, 1949).
TAWNEY, R. H. *Equality* (London, 1931).
THUCYDIDES, "The Funeral Oration of Pericles," *History*. ii. 37.
TINGSTEN, HERBERT. *Demokratiens problem* (Stockholm, 1945).
TOCQUEVILLE, ALEXIS DE. *De la démocratie en Amérique* (Paris, 1835), Engl. ed. by Henty Reeve, New York, 1838; new ed., 1945.
———. "Discours à l'Assemblée Constituante sur la question du Droit au Travail, September 12, 1848," *Œuvres*, IX (Paris, 1866), 536–52.
TRAININ, J. P., "O demokratii," *Sovietskoe Gosudarstve i Pravo* (1946), No. 1, pp. 11–22.
———. "Demokratija osobova tipa," *ibid.* (1947), No. 1, pp. 1–15; No. 3, pp. 1–14.
TROTSKY, LEON. *The Defense of Terrorism* (London, 1921).
———. *Dictatorship vs. Democracy* (New York, 1922).
VARGA, E. "Demokratija nivoga tipa," *Mirovoje Khosaistvo* (Moscow, March, 1947).
VISHINSKY, ANDREI. *The Law of the Soviet State* (New York, 1949).
WALLACE, HENRY A. *Democracy Reborn* (New York, 1944).
WEBB, SIDNEY and BEATRICE. *The Decay of Capitalist Civilization* (London, 1922).
———. *Soviet Communism: A New Civilization* (New ed., London, 1942).
WEBER, MAX. *Wirtschaft und Gesellschaft* (Tübingen, 1922), transl. as *The Theory of Social and Economic Organization* (New York, 1947).
WELDON, T. D. *States and Morals: A Study in Political Conflicts* (London, 1946).
WILSON, WOODROW. *The New Freedom* (New York, 1913).
WOOTON, BARBARA. *Freedom under Planning* (Chapel Hill, 1945).
ZASLAVSKI, D. *La démocratie soviétique* (Paris, 1947).

INDEX OF TOPICS TREATED IN THE CONTRIBUTIONS

The Index is arranged according to the thirty questions of the UNESCO questionnaire and gives references to relevant comments as well as to direct replies.